THE DEPORTATION REGIME

NICHOLAS DE GENOVA *and*
NATHALIE PEUTZ,
editors

The Deportation Regime

SOVEREIGNTY, SPACE, *and the* FREEDOM *of* MOVEMENT

Duke University Press   Durham & London   2010

Printed in the United States of America on acid-free paper ∞
Designed by C. H. Westmoreland
Typeset in Warnock with Magma Compact display by Achorn International, Inc.
Library of Congress Cataloging-in-Publication Data and republication
acknowledgments appear on the last printed pages of this book.

Contents

—⟐—

Acknowledgments

This project, devoted to the critical study of deportation and its global ramifications, arose from shared interests that were already well established in our respective intellectual and research itineraries. It is animated by a deep and growing concern, shared not only between us but also by all the contributors to this volume, that both scholarly and public discourse about deportation has been terribly disabled. Deportation has jealously been protected as a precious arena where state power's more despotic proclivities may be exercised without inhibition while largely shielded from robust critical scrutiny. On the one hand, deportation has been obscured by the complete or partial segregation imposed by the multiple boundaries of the legal, administrative, and enforcement regimes of nation-states. On the other, it has been parochialized by the relative myopia and mutual inscrutability that characterize the insularity of academic disciplines.

In an effort to surpass these impediments to greater analytical rigor, theoretical clarity, and political imagination, it has been our extraordinary privilege to bring together scholars and activists from a variety of intellectual fields, social contexts, and political geographies. Although this anthology, like most scholarly publications, has ultimately been a few years in the making, our contributors have been consistently enthusiastic, energetic, responsive, patient, and, above all, intellectually inspiring. Thus our greatest gratitude extends primarily to each and all of our contributors and to the felicitous circumstances that enabled this exciting collaboration.

We also thank Ken Wissoker, our editor at Duke University Press, for the keen interest and friendly encouragement he exuded from very early on, and then for ushering the project through to fruition. In addition, Ken's editorial assistant, Mandy Earley, guided us steadily during the final stages of the book's production. Two anonymous reviewers for Duke University Press gave much of their time to read carefully through the lengthy manuscript. Their invaluable suggestions and thoughtful critiques have made this a better book, and we only regret that we cannot thank them by name.

Additionally, we would like to acknowledge the institutions that supported us as we worked on this volume. During the most crucial period in the genesis of the book and the preparation of his own contributions to it, Nicholas De Genova enjoyed a generous Marie Curie international fellowship from the European Research Commission, sponsored by the Centre for Research in Ethnic Relations at the University of Warwick in England. Nathalie Peutz is thankful to the Princeton Graduate School for extended support during the early phases of the project. The Council on Middle East Studies at the Whitney and Betty MacMillan Center for International and Area Studies at Yale University provided generous support and an engaging intellectual environment during the year that she was contributing most directly to the shaping of the book. Nathalie is especially grateful to Ellen Lust-Okar for the opportunity to be part of the council and thanks Lindsay Benstead, Daphna Canetti-Nasim, and Greta Scharnweber for stimulating and sustaining conversations throughout this period.

Nicholas De Genova would like to acknowledge that the impetus and catalytic ingenuity behind the project may be attributed fully to Nathalie Peutz, who suggested the idea of this volume in a rather casual e-mail exchange at the beginning of 2006. We had never met in person, but I had previously had occasion to read and comment on an early draft of Nathalie's fascinating and insightful article (published shortly thereafter) about a prospective anthropology of deportation, which, in somewhat revised form, appears as her chapter in this book. Truly inspired by her work, I initiated a collegial exchange. Encouraged by my enthusiasm, Nathalie provisionally suggested the concept of something remarkably close to what has taken shape as the present volume. Confronted with an idea that was too compelling to discount or disregard, I was quite effortlessly convinced of the value and necessity of such a volume and readily embarked with Nathalie on this editorial project. This book is the fruit of the collaboration that ensued. Nathalie's original vision and subsequently her creative intelligence and critical acumen, her admirably meticulous editorial care, and her sheer energy have been deeply rewarding. My greatest debt of gratitude and appreciation is due to her.

Nicholas De Genova would also like to express his deep appreciation for the inspiration afforded by the courageous example of Elvira Arellano, whose struggle he discusses in part 1 of this book. Although I have never met her, Elvira's bold defiance of the deportation regime has been a resounding source of hope and has attracted my abiding admiration. I also owe a special note of appreciation to Ken Wissoker in his capacity as the chief editor at Duke for our enduring professional relationship. In addition, I had the benefit of presenting various ideas developed in relation to this work to colleagues and students in Britain at the Birkbeck Institute for Social Research (University of London), Cardiff University (Wales), the American Studies Seminar at the University of Manchester, and Oxford University; in the United States at the University of Texas, Austin, and Wellesley College; and in Switzerland at a special thematic doctoral seminar on mobility and migration, sponsored by the Swiss Ethnological Society. I am thankful in particular to Anastasia Karakasidou, Martha Menchaca, Dimitris Papadopulous, Eithne Quinn, Sasha Roseneil, Nina Glick Schiller, Brian Ward, and Hans-Rudolf Wicker for their gracious invitations and intellectual engagement on these occasions. Finally, as always, Magdalena Rodríguez—my partner in all that matters in life—has my most enduring gratitude for her loving persistence in challenging me to pursue the sorts of intellectual projects that aspire toward a way of life in which human freedom is paramount. I have learned much about both mobility and freedom from her.

Nathalie Peutz's initial involvement in this project owes much to the guidance from, and interactions with, much of the faculty and several graduate cohorts of Princeton University's Department of Anthropology. Specifically, I wish to recognize Carolyn Rouse, James Boon, Carol Greenhouse, Abdellah Hammoudi, Liz Hough, Kavita Misra, Rachel Newcomb, and Carol Zanca. My ethnographic research on deportation in Somalia and in Yemen was supported by the Social Science Research Council, the American Institute for Yemeni Studies, the Princeton Council on Regional Studies, and the Princeton Graduate School. Steve Caton and David Buchman gave me useful advice and necessary encouragement at a pivotal juncture. My husband, Justin Stearns, devotedly accompanied me on my first, admittedly unnerving boat trip from Yemen to Somalia, a passage across the aptly named Bab al-Mandab (the Strait of Tears), where, to this day, so many migrants perish. I have been very fortunate that ours was a safe crossing and that his loving companionship has been keeping me afloat ever since.

Most importantly, Nathalie Peutz is exceedingly grateful to Nicholas De Genova for diving with no reservations into a joint project with a then graduate student whom he barely knew. Nick's engaged scholarship, enthusiastic collaboration, generous advice, and, in the process of our work together, genuine acts of friendship have been and are exemplary; in addition to the larger message of this book, it is his fine example that I strive to take away from this endeavor.

Finally, together and in collaboration with all the contributors to this volume, we have learned much and sharpened the acuity of our critical skills as scholars through this project. We remain hopeful that this work may serve to refine the precision of the intellectual tools with which we and you, our readers, might aspire together to enhance the power of struggles to subvert and ultimately dismantle the deportation regime.

NATHALIE PEUTZ

AND NICHOLAS DE GENOVA

—〰—

Introduction

Undocumented migration and allegedly "bogus" asylum seeking have widely become the central and often constitutive preoccupation of immigration politics and policy debates in migrant-receiving states during recent decades, on a global scale. The practical effect of such immigration lawmaking has not only meant that so-called "illegal aliens" are more or less explicitly deemed unsuitable for citizenship and increasingly criminalized but also that the specific deployments of immigration law *enforcement* have rendered ever greater numbers and ever more diverse categories of migrants subject to arrest, detention, and deportation. But *deportation*—the compulsory removal of "aliens" from the physical, juridical, and social space of the state—is seldom recognized to be a distinct policy option with its own sociopolitical logic, as well as far-reaching effects. Whereas deportation should reasonably be considered merely one conceivable response to "unauthorized" or "irregular" migration, it has come to stand in as the apparently singular and presumably natural or proper retribution on the part of state powers to this apparent "problem." Yet persons found to be either traversing state borders (and thereby transgressing a state's territorial jurisdiction) or simply living and most commonly working (earning a living) without "permission" never present a state with such a severe crisis or pose such a dire threat that sudden and summary expulsion should appear to be the only logical response. How precisely does deportation come to be so ubiquitously regarded as a self-evident recourse of statecraft and law enforcement? How, indeed, has undocumented migration become effectively defined, enforced, and lived as a more or less categorical susceptibility for deportation?

If deportation has been fashioned as a paramount means of defending, enacting, and thus verifying state sovereignty against those who have allegedly violated the material and symbolic boundaries of "the nation," then it cannot be apprehensible as merely the unfortunate but predictable consequence of an "illegal" migration gone awry or a "failed" petition for refugee asylum. A deportation tends to be profoundly disruptive and plainly debasing for all who are immediately affected. Yet there is indubitably something greater at stake in such practices of "removal"—notably, the formulation and emphatic reaffirmation of state sovereignty itself. Concomitantly, deportation entails the production and reconfiguration of political subjectivities for "natural" and "naturalized" citizens, all manner of "immigrant" and "foreign" denizens, and, of course, the deportees themselves. Likewise the wider communities from which deportable members are abruptly and forcibly commandeered, as well as those to which the deported are more or less coercively "returned," become sites (distributed across the planet) where the expansive and punitive ramifications of deportation insinuate the inequalities and excesses of state power and sovereignty into the everyday production of social space and the disciplining of mundane social relations.

This book explores the contentious relationship between sovereignty, space, and the freedom of movement through a critical analysis of deportation. As its point of departure, it addresses three primary intellectual and ethical concerns. First, although conventionally considered a "natural" or inevitable response on the part of sovereign states exercising their prerogative, if not obligation, to control their borders and regulate entry based on membership, deportation is in fact the expression of a complex sociopolitical *regime* that manifests and engenders dominant notions of sovereignty, citizenship, public health, national identity, cultural homogeneity, racial purity, and class privilege. Second, the practice of deportation and the sociolegal production of deportable populations are not limited to bilateral transactions between "host" and "sending" states but rather must be comprehended as an increasingly unified, effectively *global* response to a world that is being actively remade by transnational human mobility, in which state power can only perceive the freedom of movement as the index of a planetary social order that is ever more woefully "out of control" and "insecure." Within this global arena, territorially defined ("national") states compete to reassert and extend their spectral sovereignty vis-à-vis a volatile world of restless bodies whose human impulses, needs, desires, and capabilities seem to ever increasingly surpass and defy the capacities of nation-states to define their subjectivities, command their loyalties, and contain their energies.

Branding this human mobility as "illegal" is merely part of the larger strategy of these states and the incipient planetary regime constituted by their concerted efforts to regulate the freedom of movement. Therefore, critical scholars cannot abide by the commonplace notion that these migrants or their movements may be understood in any simple sense to be "illegal." For this reason, throughout this book, we consistently deploy quotes wherever the terms "legal," "illegal," or "illegality" refer to migrants or migration in a persistent effort to emphatically de-naturalize the reification of this invidious distinction.

The "security" of the privileges and prerogatives of the planet's relatively affluent zones—exceeding the territorial borders of any single nation-state, while also always rather more restricted and exclusive than any given "national" space—comes to appear ever more besieged and thus contingent upon the regulation of human mobility and concomitant illegalization of particular migrant movements. Finally, therefore, as the third preoccupation of this collective inquiry, it is necessary to recognize this global deportation regime, as policy and problematic, to be as much about the freedom of movement as it is about border control and the ostensible exclusion of "undesirable" foreigners. The deportation regime, then, requires scholars, advocates, and activists—citizens, denizens, and deportees alike—to engage politically and theoretically in renewed ways with questions of *freedom*, in one of its most basic and meaningful senses: the freedom to traverse space and to make a place for oneself in the world.

This anthology addresses these concerns by staging a broadly interdisciplinary and international dialogue across boundaries of academic disciplines, nation-states, and global regions. It marshals the diverse critical insights, theoretical perspectives, and research methods of scholars variously situated in anthropology, history, political science, sociology, and legal studies. Moreover, it examines its subject through the empirical investigations and critical energies of researchers working on deportation and deportability in a range of national, regional, and international contexts: the U.S.-Mexico border; the European Union; Bahrain; Canada; Israel; Switzerland; Nigeria; Germany; Italy, Libya, and the broader trans-Mediterranean space; El Salvador; Somalia; and the United States. The contributions to this unique collection together represent a remarkable conjuncture of research from multiple fields of intellectual inquiry, directed toward the legal, sociopolitical, and historical specificities of numerous immigration and asylum regimes. What emerges from this diverse array of distinct case studies, nonetheless, is an empirically robust and heterogeneous evidence for the ascendancy of deportation as an ever more pervasive and increasingly standardized instrument of statecraft. As a routinized and entrenched state practice, forced removals (and also the anti-deportation struggles that they increasingly provoke) therefore provide an instructive occasion and vital impetus for the critical reexamination of dominant conceptions and conceits regarding the privileges and practices of citizenship, and the constitution of state sovereignty itself through the universal distinction between "alien" and "citizen."

A DEPORTATION REGIME?

With the advent of the post-September 11, 2001, global preoccupation with border "security," deportation has achieved a remarkable and renewed prominence as a paramount technique for refortifying political, racial, and class-based boundaries and purportedly allaying (while in fact further inciting) socioeconomic *in*securities "at home," within the "domestic" spaces of nation-states. This is the case not only in the United States, where antiterrorism has become a veritable creed, but also (owing largely to the singular political and military power of the United States) increasingly on a global scale. In the United States, any and all matters of immigration law enforcement, as well as all procedures regarding migrant eligibility for legal residence or citizenship, have been explicitly and practically subordinated to the imperatives of counterterrorism and Homeland Security. Consequently U.S. immigration authorities have declared a ten-year strategic enforcement plan (2003–12), whose stated mission is to promote "national security by ensuring the departure from the United States of *all* removable aliens" (USDHS-ICE 2003, ii; italics added).[1] This severe and, frankly, unattainable aspiration toward mass deportation on an unprecedented scale is performatively framed as a matter of "national security." However, there ensued a rather steady campaign of targeted enforcement (especially since the likewise unprecedented upsurge of "immigrants' rights" protests in the spring of 2006), characterized above all by large-scale workplace raids against innocuous undocumented workers. Predictably, these targeted enforcement operations generate a massmediated spectacle of enforcement "results." In Europe, where asylum petitions have decreased since the levels of the early and then the late 1990s (when claims rose owing to the wars in Yugoslavia and Kosovo, respectively), state officials have nevertheless been pressured to meet predetermined record-high targets for the detention and deportation of "failed" asylum seekers, including families and even unaccompanied children (Fekete 2007b). Concurrently, the European Commission has been coordinating joint expulsions between two or more member states while also seeking to prevent asylum seekers and refugees from crossing into the Eu-

ropean Union in the first place—by warehousing them in Transit Processing Centres (detention camps) located in the regions of origin or transit
of these migratory movements (Fekete 2005; Andrijasevic, this volume;
Karakayali and Rigo, this volume).[2]

Efforts have also been on the rise to extend the spaces of interception
and expulsion. EU member states are now routinely collaborating with
neighboring "transfer" or "sending" countries to expand the purview of
their detention and deportation powers. For example, Italy has financed
the construction of camps for "irregular migrants" entering Libya from
Egypt and Sudan and has paid for the repatriation of these migrants from
Libya to sub-Saharan Africa (Andrijasevic 2006, this volume; Cornelisse,
this volume). The Moroccan government, furthermore, has been deporting sub-Saharan Africans to the Algerian frontier, keeping its "foreigners"
from migrating to Europe, even as its own citizens depend heavily on the
remittances of those who migrate (de Haas 2005). Similarly, in the early
summer of 2001, through Mexico's Plan Sur (the Southern Plan) and Guatemala's Venceremos 2001 ("We Shall Overcome") initiatives, both sides
of the border shared by those countries became the stage for large-scale
militarized police actions aimed at stemming the flow of "illegal" migration from Central America headed for the United States. These actions
were part of a regional program, sponsored and financed by U.S. authorities, coordinating efforts by Mexico and the countries of Central America
and the Caribbean Basin, which resulted in the deportation of more than
6,000 Guatemalans, Hondurans, and Salvadorans from Mexico, as well as
another 3,666 people (predominantly Hondurans and Salvadorans) from
Guatemala.[3] The overall intent of such internationally coordinated mass
deportation schemes, plainly, is not only to remove "illegal" migrants,
"suspect" refugees, and "bogus" asylum seekers from the borders of the
United States or Europe but to remove them even from the borders of
their borders, through the creation of an expanded buffer zone of graduated securitization.

Although deportations have attracted an increasing scrutiny from
activists, a greater but nevertheless always ephemeral incidence of mass-
media coverage—as with the dramatic case of Elvira Arellano in the
United States (see De Genova, this volume)—and also some noteworthy
scholarly attention, it is evident all the same that the social and political
ramifications of deportation and the attendant condition of deportability
remain very much underexamined and insufficiently explored. In recent
years, social scientists, cultural critics, and historians (notably including
many of the scholars who have contributed to this volume) have indeed

begun to direct sustained critical energy toward deportation as something more than a prosaic or inevitable conclusion to various ostensibly "failed" migrant or refugee aspirations. Many of these provocative advances have considered deportation as a *disciplinary* practice while also an instrument of state sovereignty that renders certain populations "deportable," regardless of their practical connections or affective ties to the "host" society (cf. Bhabha 1998; Coutin 2003a, 2003b; De Genova 2002, 2005; Goldring, Berinstein, and Bernhard 2007; Hindess 2000; Nijhawan 2005; Zilberg 2004). Others have demonstrated that the current increasingly punitive deployment of deportation is long foreshadowed by comparably draconian (and equally global) histories of labor subordination, ideological suppression, and ethnic and racial discrimination (cf. Caestecker 2003; Cole 2003; Davies 2001; De Genova 2005; Kanstroom 2007; Kingston 2005; Ngai 2004). And several have situated deportation in relation to other kinds of coercive movement, such as forced dispersal or displacement, extradition, and rendition, as well as forced sedentarization, involving detention or encampment (Bloch and Schuster 2005; Cunningham and Heyman 2004; De Genova 2007; Dow 2004; Schuster 2005; Simon 1998; Walters 2002a; Welch 2002). Additionally, a number of scholars have interrogated the "paradox" that deportation apparently poses for the liberal-democratic state (Gibney and Hansen 2003; see also Fekete 2005, 2007b; Hing 2006a; Khosravi 2009), while others have focused on its enduring effects on deportees, their families, and the communities from which and to which they are "repatriated" (Burman 2006; Coutin 2007; Human Rights Watch 2007, 2009; Núñez and Heyman 2007; Peutz 2006, 2007; Willen 2007d; Zilberg 2007a, 2007c). And yet deportation—as an exceedingly normalized and standardized technique of state power and thus as an effectively global regime—continues, through its routinized practice, to obscure the historically particular political and administrative processes by which deportability, or the very possibility of being deported, is produced and imposed. This book builds on and consolidates many of the important contributions of this recent scholarship on deportation and deportability while emphatically situating the question of deportation in direct relation to the problem of a more elementary human freedom of movement.

DEPORTATION, CITIZENSHIP, AND THE FREEDOM OF MOVEMENT

Writing in the United States just a decade after the infamous Palmer raids (which had targeted thousands of noncitizens as alleged "subversives" for summary deportation from the United States in the wake of the extraordinary labor insurgency and strike wave of 1919), and during a period of renewed hostility toward "foreigners" (triggered, in part, by the avalanching economic depression that began in 1929), the legal scholar Jane Clark interrogated what she called the "increasingly prominent deportation scene" (1931/1969, 16), wherein deportation had become "emphasized in the press and in Congress as a cure for the ills of the country" (28). She lamented: "We are still in a day . . . when the socially inadequate are passed from country to country as they formerly were from town to town. The day may arrive when the individual will be regarded internationally and will be thought of as the product of more than the country where he happens to have his legal citizenship and nationality. But then, it seems, millennium may have come" (491). Eighty years later, the lessons of the World War II internment camps and postwar *making* of refugees and stateless persons notwithstanding, Clark's doleful vision of an improbable future in which the individual might amount to something more than a mere product of the largely incidental vagaries of her legal citizenship and nationality appears to remain immeasurably remote indeed. In recent years, numerous configurations of "postnational" (Soysal 1994), "flexible" (Ong 1999), "cosmopolitan" (Linklater 1998a), or "global" citizenship (Dower 2003; Falk 1993) have been variously identified, theorized, or cheerfully promoted by academics and activists alike. Nevertheless the continuing significance and ever-intensifying magnitude of deportation as a presumptively legitimate and merely "administrative" state practice seriously challenge any theoretical advances and undercut even empirical evidence toward an alternative world, or way of life, in which membership, entitlement, and virtue would *not* be always already inscribed in one's relationship to the spaces of (nation-)states, their borders, and their appalling inequalities of wealth and power.

Deportation, then as now, is premised on a normative division of the world into territorially defined, "sovereign" (nation-)states, and within these states, the ubiquitous division enacted between more or less "rightful" members (citizens) and relatively rightless nonmembers (aliens). This regime of nation-state sovereignty and citizenship has become the conventional determinant of an individual's liberty to move into, out of, or across various national, international, and sometimes even subnational spaces. This point is so evident as to seem banal, and yet it invites more than just casual or momentary reflection. Much of the world's political, economic, and geographical landscapes have been dramatically transformed and even integrated in recent decades—consider only the end of the polarizing Cold War and subsequently the "unipolar" military dominance of the United States, which has culminated in the proclamation of a so-called *Global* War on Terror; or the calamitous demise of protectionist welfare states and the feverish spread of the neoliberal order. In both examples, the formerly supposed sanctity of national sovereignty, the presumed inviolability of nation-state borders, and the ostensible insulation of "national" economies afforded by such boundaries and barriers—or at least, the highly charged geopolitical stakes of their transgression—have all been radically destabilized. Yet the now effectively global deportation regime continues to meticulously allocate individuals to their designated spatial locations in accord with what would appear to be a stubbornly anachronistic perception of their decisively if not definitively "national" places in the world. Simultaneously, the inequalities of citizenship modulate individuals' differential access to national and transnational labor markets through the regulation of migratory movements (Anderson 1994). Critically, this heavily restricted and thoroughly regulated access to global space tends to be enforced by the same capricious limitations that the sovereign "protection rackets" of national states pretend to provide and ensure for their citizens (Tilly 1985). In fact, the inscription and embodiment of human liberties within the inescapably nationalist mantle of citizenship serve precisely to *confine* human freedom.

In part 1 of this volume, Nicholas De Genova frames the wider theoretical project of the book as a whole. Revisiting Hannah Arendt's suggestion (1959/1968, 9) that the freedom of movement is truly prototypical for any further consideration of liberty, De Genova contends that adequate theoretical reflection upon this freedom has nevertheless been sorely neglected, while its formulation as a practical problem for politics, predictably, has likewise been disregarded. At the same time, the relentless and suffocating regulation of human mobility has become an ever-greater obsession of states in their quests to fortify their spectral control over space and territory as the supposed manifestation of their "national" sovereignty. In this regard, De Genova poses a fundamental question: "What, in the end, is *movement*—and therefore, the freedom of movement—if not a figure par excellence of life, indeed, life in its barest essential condition?" In his effort to elaborate the problem, De Genova insists on the analytical and political necessity of distinguishing between the *freedom* of movement—as an ontological condition of human life, as such—and anything that might be glossed as a *right* to move. "Rights," he argues, assume their meaning and substance only insofar as they have been stipulated within one or another normative or juridical framework. Rights are therefore inseparable from some form of political regime.

In this regard, the freedom of movement may best be understood, precisely, *not* as a right. The freedom of movement must be radically distinguished from any of the ways that such a liberty may have been granted, circumscribed, and domesticated within the orbit of state power. Instead De Genova stresses that human life, in its socially undifferentiated or unqualified (animal) sense, is inseparable from the uninhibited capacity for movement which is a necessary premise for the free and purposeful exercise of creative and productive powers. The exercise of these vital powers is, after all, the foundation for all properly social life. Thus, he argues, the freedom of movement is inseparable from that still more basic human power which is generative of the very possibility of social life, namely, *labor*—the capacity to creatively transform our objective circumstances.

By critically engaging the concept of "bare life," as elaborated by Giorgio Agamben in his work on sovereign power, De Genova resituates bare life in relation to living labor and examines the indispensable disposability of ever deportable migrant labor not in terms of exclusion but in terms of its *incorporation* within the mutually constituted regimes of global capitalism and territorially defined and delimited ("national") state sovereignty. From the critical vantage point of deportation and deportability, he reflects, moreover, on the state's productions of space, citizenship, nativism, and national identity. With recourse to a consideration of the constitutive role of labor in the genesis of both capital and state power, and the centrality of formally *free* labor in the global social formation of capital accumulation, he elaborates the significance of the enigmatic *freedom of movement* for further theoretical inquiry and empirical research into migrant deportability and deportation as crucial sites for the constitution and preservation of state power, sovereignty, and space.

SOVEREIGNTY AND SPACE

Migratory movements across space are central to inquiries into the problem of sovereign (state) power. Beginning from this insight, the three chapters that make up part 2 of this collection are devoted to historicizing and theorizing the theme of sovereignty and space. While each of these essays (as well as a number of the volume's subsequent chapters) points to ways in which the contemporary deportation and detention of noncitizens are being transformed, their authors focus primarily on subjecting the deportation regime and its components—expulsion, detention, and mobility control, respectively—to historical-genealogical analyses. In so doing, they reveal the underlying and abiding violence of a spatial-political order that most states today, in spite of an abundance of evidence to the contrary, accept and defend as immanent and immutable.

In his previously published landmark essay "Deportation, Expulsion, and the International Police of Aliens," the political theorist William Walters argues that modern deportation is "a legalized form of expulsion" that must count among its genealogical antecedents the classical Athenian and Roman practices of political banishment and exile, the expulsion within and from Europe of the poor and of variously constituted corporate groups (based on religion, for instance) during the Middle Ages, the mass transportation of convicts up through the early modern period, and the population transfers of "minorities" that plagued Europe throughout the first half of the twentieth century and peaked—but did not end with—the forcible resettlement and ultimately genocidal policies of Nazi Germany. Although today's deportation of so-called "illegal" or "criminal" *aliens* would strike many as more benign (if not absolutely necessary and categorically legitimate), deportation law remains founded on a series of legalized discriminations, variously based on class, race, or belief, that are no less disturbing than were those that animated these earlier episodes of enforced exclusion.[4]

Modern deportation law—whereby immigration enforcement became a matter of *national* sovereignty—emerged from the particular confluence in the late nineteenth century and the early twentieth of sovereign nation-states monopolizing the legitimate means of movement (Torpey 1999); the post–World War I enactment of the *citizen*, not the individual person, as the only formal bearer of inalienable rights (Arendt 1951/1966); and the concomitant production of "illegal" migration as a threat to, while also the result of, sovereign power (Ngai 2004). Significantly, Walters argues, it was during this period that deportation was not only nationalized but also socialized. In other words, states increasingly used deportation as a way of governing the welfare of their populations, both by excluding the socially "undesirable" (paupers, prostitutes, anarchists, criminals, the insane, excludable races, etc.) and by removing foreign labor (as a market-regulating mechanism) during periods of economic recession. By the end of World War II, however, the categorical and legal emergence of "the refugee" and "the stateless" had revealed the disjunction of the ostensibly seamless union of state sovereignty, territoriality, and the nation (or people) (Arendt 1951/1966; see also Kerber 2007; Macklin 2007; Malkki 1995). Those who could no longer be repatriated or deported to a state of ostensible origin or presumably proper belonging were relegated to internment camps, detention centers, or third countries—an unsavory "solution," at best, which remains without remedy today.

Indeed, it has widely been recognized that both internment and deportation pose a fundamental challenge to the liberal self-image of Western democratic regimes. Walters addresses this problematic by showing deportation—and, by implication, the camp—to be part of an older regime of *policing* that operates as a form of governmentality, both on the national scale and globally, effectively allocating all populations to their respective sovereign powers and territories. More recently, starting with the heightened anxieties regarding the perceived influx of potentially "bogus" asylum seekers and "illegal" migrants produced by the end of the Cold War and the subsequent ongoing restructuring of the global economy since the 1990s, further aggravated by the renewed emphasis on securitization after the events of September 11, 2001, states in the West have become even more preoccupied with the regulation of migratory movements. And yet deportation is not only a technique by which governments exert their sovereign power over bodies, space, and "the nation"; it has become a mechanism by which governments measure and signal their own effectiveness.[5] Most importantly, Walters emphasizes that deportation not only is a consequence of a world partitioned into territorial nation-states but is "actively involved in *making* this world."

The legal scholar Galina Cornelisse builds on Walters's insights by examining the historical development, steady entrenchment, and critical consequences of *territoriality*—the articulation of sovereign power and the framing of individual rights by territory—as an organizing system. Cornelisse reveals the detention and deportation of migrants to be the inevitable outcome of this system, which continues to curse the application of any semblance of a truly universal human rights regime. Deportation and detention therefore constitute the "litmus test," Cornelisse argues, for the way in which territoriality "shapes the world and the life of its inhabitants."

Although both deportation and immigration detention are technologies used to preserve and tidy the division of the world into separate, sovereign, territorially based national states, detention in particular enacts and affirms this territorial ideal in at least two distinctive ways. First, this spatial confinement and sedentarization within the state's domain provide what Cornelisse calls "a territorial solution" to the so-called problem of migrant movements that are seen to transgress, and thus to resist and challenge, the territorial order. Second, immigration detention camps, as brutal and "exceptional" as they are, have remained immune to any of the presumably corrective mandates of international law and human rights discourses, both of which are founded on and uphold the territorial sovereignty of the modern state. Cornelisse's treatment of territoriality leads her, finally and necessarily, to consider the detention camps currently set up beyond the political borders of the European Union, which many have held up as examples of the "externalization" or "deterritorialization" of the EU's frontiers. And yet, here again, the logic of territoriality and the consequent impotence of contemporary human rights imperatives serve only to legitimate the routine imprisonment of untold thousands of migrants, "not on account of what they have done, but merely on account of what they are."

It is not, however, these externalized or deterritorialized borders that constitute the legal and political space of "Europe," contend the anthropologist Serhat Karakayali and the political and legal scholar Enrica Rigo, as much as the *movements* of the people who cross them. Moreover, they argue, the European space exists only to the extent that it is thus circulated. With this as their theoretical starting point, Karakayali and Rigo reject any strict separation between "citizens" and "aliens" in Europe and look instead to the government of human mobility, both inside and outside the European Union's geographic borders, and the discursive construction of the various migrant figures that have animated European migration regimes since World War II: the "labor migrant" (whose mobility was mediated through short-term rotations and his exclusion from the welfare state); the "refugee" or "asylum seeker" (which emerged after the end of formal labor recruitment programs in 1973 as the only administratively recognized and thus the exclusive legal means of migration); and, since the turn of the millennium, the "undocumented migrant." This current, illegalized figure of migration gained prominence, on the one hand, through the lack of any comprehensive migration policy, which thereby produces these movements as clandestine, and on the other, through the externalization of the EU frontier, which predefines a migrant as "illegal" even before she or he has crossed a border of the European Union. And yet, rather than aiming to keep migrants on the supposed outside, the authors demonstrate, the European authorities *expect* migrants to circulate through the European political and legal space and thus dedicate their regulatory energies to governing these circulations accordingly. Indeed, controlled circular migration has been promoted as a successful model in that it, like the detention camps at Europe's borders, regulates the (continued) *temporality*—and thus the ultimate disposability—of migrant labor. Moreover, although the European Union's external borders have been extended or made virtual and its internal borders have been lifted, the "real" borders of Europe now exist anywhere migrants may come to experience their crossing and hence, at least potentially, everywhere they move.

The sovereign power to regulate and restrict human movement through space is thus never simply a matter of "administration" or "belonging." It is the imposition of a power over life itself. If this claim seems exaggerated, one needs only to confront the excessive and utterly avertable fatalities that occur routinely as migrant bodies wash up on shores or perish in desert crossings. Furthermore, inasmuch as migratory movements expose the limits of the discourses (such as citizenship, international law, and human rights) which have variously sought to constrain the violence inherent in the exercise of sovereign power, as Cornelisse demonstrates, they compel a reconsideration of the very meanings which have, over time, ensnared human freedom within the constrictions of state power and its regimes of territoriality. And yet new spaces and practices are emerging through which the sovereign power of the state is being challenged. Karakayali and Rigo argue that circulation itself is an act of citizenship, much as Walters looks to the sanctuary movement as a social formation for the articulation of new political claims (see also Nyers, this volume). In these and other practices of migration, therefore, we may identify and theorize potential spaces of freedom. Much as these migratory movements may be constituted within the diverse spaces of deportability, which, after all, are never merely physical sites of confinement or geographic zones of obstruction, they nonetheless remain persistent reminders that freedom is never given its substance as a right, but only as a practice.

SPACES OF DEPORTABILITY

If, for over a century, the deportation of "illegal" or "undesirable" aliens has consistently been deployed by modern states as a prosaic technique for controlling the putative integrity of their spatial domains and memberships, then its continuing *ineffectiveness*, as practice and policy, must be accounted for and made sense of. In the early 1990s, worldwide, the number of national laws and regulations concerning migration grew exponentially—as did the number of countries that became host to foreign labor (United Nations 2002). Despite the increasing restrictiveness of migration policies everywhere and, in conjunction, the staggering numbers of individuals deported each year from both traditional and new labor-importing countries, deportation enforcement, as scholars as well as anti-immigration pundits never tire of insisting, remains "ineffectual." Indeed, deportation is in most cases time-consuming and expensive, and sometimes politically controversial. It hinges on the proper identification (with documentary evidence) of the individual to be deported, as well as the agreement and cooperation of the individual's country of origin;

moreover, it is almost always hampered by lack of funds and personnel, implausible goals, and generally the simple incapacity to actually stop or even control the flow of migratory movements (Gibney and Hansen 2003; Schuster 2005, 612; Hing 2006a, 148–52; in this volume, see also Castañeda; Cornelisse; Wicker).

Departing from the literal-mindedness of such observations, however, and interested instead in the veritable *effectiveness* of regimes of immigration lawmaking and border enforcement, Nicholas De Genova has argued that "it is deportability, and not deportation per se, that has historically rendered undocumented migrant labor a distinctly disposable commodity" (2002, 438; 2005, 242–49). It is *deportability*, then, or the protracted possibility of being deported—along with the multiple vulnerabilities that this susceptibility for deportation engenders—that is the real effect of these policies and practices. *Deportation regimes are profoundly effective*, and quite efficiently so, exactly insofar as the grim spectacle of the deportation of even just a few, coupled with the enduring everyday deportability of countless others (millions, in the case of the United States), produces and maintains migrant "illegality" as not merely an anomalous juridical status but also a practical, materially consequential, and deeply interiorized mode of being—and of being put in place.

The recent critical literature on migration (including the work of many contributors to this volume) has been ever more attentive to the ways in which "illegality" and deportability are produced through law and border enforcement, both within the geopolitical space of the nation-state and also "external" to it. Much of this scholarly work elucidates ways in which deportable migrants serve capital accumulation through their flexibility and tractability as an often docile labor force and similarly serve the sovereign state through their embodiment of the elementary distinction between citizens and others, "insiders" and "outsiders." In some of these analyses, especially those that draw on Giorgio Agamben's theorization (1995/1998) of the camp as a space of sovereign exception, deportable or detained populations are conceptualized as the "bare life" that is excluded from the juridical-political order of citizenship, only through its inclusion within it (see De Genova, this volume). As such, today's migrant detainees and deportees emerge as the figurative progeny of the post–World War II "stateless," who, having been stripped of their citizenship, effectively came to lose, as Hannah Arendt famously proclaimed, the very "right to have rights" (1951/1966, 296). As Linda Kerber elaborates, the stateless, cast as the "citizen's other," in fact become constitutive of the state: "The stateless serve the state by embodying its absence, by providing frightening models of the vulnerability of those who lack the sufficient awe of the state. The stateless serve the state by signaling who will not be entitled to its protection, and throwing fear into the rest of us" (2007, 31). Inasmuch as citizens in most nation-states today cannot legally be deported, the deportable are similarly pressed to "serve the state" as "the citizen's other," marking an apparently absolute and durable separation between the security of one condition, aligned with the state, and the other, indefinitely if not permanently expelled from its grace.

In contrast with the stateless, however, deportable populations do not embody the supposed absence of the state but rather become the object of its sovereign power to exclude, even while it incorporates them. After all, the deportable may only become such to the extent that they are already counted *within* the purview of a state's power, as an effect of their inclusion in the space of the state as an abject population, usually as eminently disposable labor. Indeed, it is important to recall that even "legal" migrants, despite other comparative advantages, substantive entitlements, and ostensible protections, remain ultimately deportable.[6] Additionally, the deported are (as a rule) "returned" only to the jurisdiction of a state that will claim or accept them, meaning that many "stateless" individuals are in fact indefinitely detained rather than deported, while others may be handed over directly to the punitive indiscretions of an illiberal state (cf. Bach 2001; Fekete 2005). Thus deportation and deportability are thoroughly saturated by the presence of the state and infused with state power (see De Genova, this volume; see also De Genova 2002).[7] It is precisely this ambivalent and, in fact, intimate relation between deportability, citizenship, and the state that the chapters of part 3 explore. As each author explores the historical and regional particularities of his or her respective case study, these contributions respectively illuminate the significant recent developments in each of the states examined, specifically over the past decade.

With the end of the Cold War and the subsequent opening of the borders of the former Soviet bloc, the reconfiguration of the internal and external borders of the European Union in the wake of its expansion, and the occurrence of several high-profile civil wars and ensuing humanitarian crises that produced large numbers of refugees and asylum seekers from sub-Saharan Africa and southeastern Europe (most notably Rwanda and what was formerly Yugoslavia), states became increasingly anxious about controlling migratory flows across their borders. In Germany, soon after its transformative reunification in 1990, a xenophobic reaction to the surge in migrants and asylum seekers convulsed the newly reconstituted nation, and by 1993 the right to asylum was severely restricted (Castañeda, this volume). Switzerland, too, had had a relatively tolerant history toward guest workers and other migrants that was surely grounded, at least in part, by its unique role as a politically neutral advocate of international human rights; and yet, following the practices of its EU neighbors, Switzerland introduced stringent and exclusionary measures toward "illegal aliens" in the early to mid-1990s (Wicker, this volume). Especially as northern European countries imposed more severe restrictions on migration, Italy underwent a remarkable shift over just the last two decades from its historical status as a migrant-sending country to a significant destination for migrants in its own right, which is pivotally situated nonetheless as a gateway to Europe more generally (Andrijasevic, this volume).[8] In Bahrain, as in other petroleum-rich Gulf States, the recruitment of guest workers that had skyrocketed in the 1970s—in contrast to the states of northern and western Europe, where this form of labor migration was brought officially to an end with the global recession provoked by the 1973 oil embargo—flourished until the early 1990s. It was then rendered increasingly precarious by the outbreak of the Gulf War (1990–91) and the subsequent concerted efforts throughout the region to nationalize (in this case, "Bahrainize") the labor force (Gardner, this volume). Meanwhile, the mounting allegations that "illegal" migration threatened to incapacitate the welfare system of the liberal democratic state were given voice nowhere more clearly than in the United States with the concurrent passage in 1996, within only weeks of each other, of two major laws (one concerning immigration and the other dramatically restructuring public assistance to the poor) which stigmatized welfare recipients and undocumented migrants alike—imposing severe restrictions and penalties on both, and on "immigrants" generally, regardless of legal status (Talavera, Núñez, and Heyman, this volume; Maira, this volume).

It is Israel that provides the instructive counterexample to this rough chronology, for it was there, in the early 1990s, in response to the political and social crisis instigated by the Palestinian insurgency against occupation (1987–93), that a guest worker program was instated as a (temporary) "solution" to the ever more aggressive expulsion of Palestinian workers from the Israeli labor market and body politic. In recent years, countries such as Germany and the United States have debated various legalization schemes, guest worker programs, and other means to ease some of the restrictions that in fact have exacerbated the "problem" of "illegal" migration. In contrast, Israel abruptly reversed its relatively liberal policy from the mid-1990s of enthusiastically recruiting transnational labor migrants and, in 2002, initiated a criminalizing mass deportation campaign targeting both "legal" and "illegal" migrants, whom it now blamed for the stagnation of the Israeli economy and the escalation in unemployment

(Willen, this volume). As Sarah Willen's essay helps to demonstrate, the legal regimes of national states are always preconditioned by the historically specific and uneven tempos of various forms of social struggle and in fact institutionalize the political strategies designed to intervene in and ultimately contain those disruptive forces. Indeed, Israel's violent criminalization of the migrants whom it formerly recruited for their labor ultimately bears a striking resemblance to the fiercely anti-immigrant climate which has accompanied and facilitated the increasing prominence and political viability of guest worker schemes in the United States. Thus, far from merely focusing narrowly on their respective national contexts, the chapters brought together in part 3 achieve still greater critical force in concert and add comparative depth to the everyday practices and embodied experiences within these various spaces of deportability.

The comparative perspective facilitated by these chapters into the production of deportability across these diverse "national" spaces of state power and their distinct immigration regimes sharpens our understanding of the deeper political interconnections of various states' attempts to control and structure global migrant flows. Notably, six of these seven cases are distinguished as "receiving" countries exhibiting either exceptionally high levels of migration (in absolute numbers) or a preponderant and decisive dependency on foreign labor. While the United States and Germany are among the three countries with the largest absolute number of migrants or foreign-born residents according to the most recent UN International Migration Report, Israel and Switzerland are among the ten countries with the highest proportion of foreign migrants relative to their total populations (United Nations 2002). Bahrain, although not included in the UN report owing to its considerably smaller population, follows the pattern of the other oil-producing countries of the Persian Gulf region (and even exceeds much larger countries like Saudi Arabia) in that, as of 2005, at least 40 percent of its population comprised foreign labor migrants.[9] In this respect, Italy provides the instructive counterexample as a country with a history of relatively recent (and therefore lesser) migration, where migration has rapidly been increasing, and situated at one of the more critical ostensible frontiers of the larger European sociopolitical formation. In addition, four of these six countries—Italy, Bahrain, Germany, and Israel—have sociopolitical regimes deeply informed by an overtly "ethnonational" model of belonging, for which the "naturalization" (nationalization) of "foreign" migrants (or their children) is distinctly impeded by perceived divergences from the presumed "ethnic" (and religious) character of the nation. Even where there are relatively less restrictive requirements regarding eligibility for or access to citizenship, however, as in the cases of Switzerland and the United States, there is ample evidence that the logic of deportation remains similarly undergirded by a more diffuse but no less racialized or "ethno-national" biopolitics through which the state's deportation regime fashions its citizenry only by sorting and ranking the greater or lesser "foreignness" of various migrant others.

Despite the preponderance of these extensive and overlapping migration restrictions, each of these chapters also emphasizes the ways in which deportability, as lived experience, is both suffered and also surmounted. Indeed, the women's studies scholar Rutvica Andrijasevic challenges the prevailing theorization of the detention camp as a zone of migrant *immobilization* and exclusion. Considering the example of the Lampedusa camp (off the coast of Italy), Andrijasevic demonstrates how detention camps at the European Union's external borders play a pivotal role in directing and differentiating migratory movements both within the territorial boundaries of the European Union and in the transnational spaces that exceed it. Instead of depicting detention camps as *spaces* of exception, Andrijasevic points to their *temporal* function in the deceleration of migrants' admission into the Italian and broader European labor markets (see also Karakayali and Rigo, this volume). Migration may be interrupted temporarily at Lampedusa or be diverted through deportation to Libya, which collaborates with the Italian government in its detention and deportation efforts. The camp thus serves to mediate and modulate migratory movements as they continue in multiple directions, at various tempos, and at alternating speeds. Building upon the insights of Enrica Rigo (2007) and others, Andrijasevic argues that the detention camp, like deportation, is therefore not primarily a manifestation or reassertion of state sovereignty but rather an example of the deterritorialization of European space, the delocalization of border control and the "sharing" of sovereignty, and the reorganization of European citizenship. By considering the temporal dimensions of detention and deportation, Andrijasevic effectively casts off the rigid dichotomization of movement "inside" and "outside" EU territory and instead draws attention to migrants as integral actors in the transformation of the European polity and space.

Turning to another border region, the U.S. anthropologists Victor Talavera, Guillermina Gina Núñez, and Josiah Heyman discuss how deportability reconfigures and reconstitutes various spaces over time. Based on ethnographic fieldwork in two areas (one urban, one rural) in El Paso County, Texas, their chapter demonstrates how the collusion of federal and local agencies in the enforcement of U.S. immigration laws through "processes of entrapment" engenders a pervasive and acute sense of deportability among individual migrants and within their broader communities. Although these deportable populations are internally varied and are not all equally subject to the palpable risk and visceral fear of deportation, their anticipatory anxieties and painful memories of deportation—of their own, or of their family members' or other acquaintances'—are widely shared, internalized, and accumulated. Deportability is thus a distinctive presence in the everyday lives and maneuvered spaces of all undocumented migrants, enduring even into legal residency (which, after all, remains subject to revocation and deportation). And yet the entrapment of deportability itself does not render its target population passive or docile. While the authors constructively focus on deportation as a persistent presence, they nonetheless demonstrate that their informants' narratives are additionally replete with a ghostly absence that haunts households, networks, communities, and their larger sociopolitical landscape—yet also mobilizes individuals toward collective action.

In the following chapter, the anthropologist Andrew M. Gardner draws from ethnography on both skilled and unskilled foreign labor in Bahrain to demonstrate how, as in other national contexts, "illegality" is in fact produced by the very system responsible for the management of foreign labor. Through the *kafala* system, however, every foreign laborer is sponsored by, and thus also beholden to, a private citizen or corporate entity that maintains complete (and effectively despotic) control over laborers' working conditions and legal status. Deportability, in this context, is thus produced and sustained not primarily by the state—although the state is, of course, complicit in its support of this system—but by the individual citizen and his or her whims. Consequently deportability is experienced equally by documented and undocumented migrants alike, all of whom can ill afford to lose the job for which they have indebted themselves (through the costs of visas, travel, and intermediaries) to acquire. Gardner's recognition that the structural violence of the kafala system extends to *all* noncitizens challenges the common assumption that deportability is inherently tied to "illegality" or to the unlawful actions of individual migrants. It also provides an instructive example of how the deportation regime extends into spaces (both geographic and political) beyond the putative sovereignty of the state.

The anthropologist Hans-Rudolf Wicker considers the deep and contradictory ethical ambivalence surrounding deportation for Switzerland as a self-consciously democratic and constitutional state with a pronouncedly liberal self-image. And yet, especially with the development of legal frameworks for the regulation of migration, which have increasingly legitimized deportation practices, what has emerged is a whole range of distinct categories of persons who are or might be subject to expulsion. Although their common denominator is predictably their status as noncitizens, this group is not at all homogeneous, resulting from a panoply of parallel regulatory regimes regarding sojourn, work, and residence permits, as well as criminal law. Through this proliferation of legalities, the Swiss state is able to assert its firm stance against "illegal" migration while also remaining distinctly unconcerned with its actual enforcement. For example, many of these various types of "illegal" migrants are "tolerated" by the various Swiss authorities, but only insofar as they remain inconspicuous. In delineating the various constructions of "illegality" in Switzerland, Wicker exposes the ambivalences of the dominant notion of "tolerance" and the ambiguities of social and political visibility and invisibility.

The themes of "tolerance" and visibility are revisited by the anthropologist Heide Castañeda, who focuses on the temporary suspension of German deportation orders and the complex ambivalence—toward state coercion, but also "illegality"—which they reveal. Castañeda examines how these "exceptions" are framed as examples of benevolence on the part of the host society, even as they highlight the intolerant and arbitrary nature of deportation practices. Ironically, those who receive a suspension during the maternity protection period or due to illness are in fact subject to even greater restrictions and come to "inhabit a state of hypervisibility" until they are ultimately deported or, in rare cases, granted residency on humanitarian grounds. Although Germany is home to a number of prominent anti-deportation campaigns, its policies rest on its citizens' ultimate complicity (and even outright participation) in producing this protracted state of exception that generates and sustains migrant "illegality." Castañeda argues that the suspension of deportation (or *Duldung*) thus becomes merely another mechanism for ordering migrants, in the combined sense of both disciplining them and differentiating between them.

As the anthropologist Sarah Willen demonstrates, the biopolitical production of otherness is historically situated and locally configured in ways that simple binary oppositions tend to obscure. Examining an aggressive deportation campaign organized in Israel in 2002, Willen analyzes how the state relied on a (tacit) governmental template of biosocial profiling and threats of physical violence to cast its undocumented transnational migrants as criminal, threatening others—analogous, in many ways, to its indigenous and constitutive others: the Palestinians. Notably, both groups (the Palestinians and the undocumented migrants) had come to be racialized, targeted, and expelled in a strikingly similar manner, albeit profoundly informed by their disparate positions and particular histories vis-à-vis the Israeli state. Willen argues that we cannot adequately comprehend the exclusion of one group without relating it to exclusion of the other; whereas the deportation campaign against migrants had been promoted as a "solution" to Israeli unemployment, it was in fact clearly part of a broader project to secure the demographic contours of the Israeli state as a Jewish "nation."

The anthropologist and Asian American studies scholar Sunaina Maira further analyzes deportation as a form of biopolitical regulation framed and legitimated by a concern for protecting national "security" against both internal and external threats. Maira emphasizes the convergence between the neoliberal deployment of deportation as an economic strategy that disciplines transnational labor and the imperial use of deportation as a political instrument for repressing ideologies or movements that oppose U.S. policies "at home" and abroad. By focusing on the impact of post-September 11, 2001, acts of surveillance, detention, and deportation targeting South Asian (Muslim and non-Muslim) and other migrants in the greater San Francisco Bay Area, Maira demonstrates how these particular forms of intimidation have affected entire migrant communities. Through its surprisingly intimate reach, the state is implicated in redrawing the boundaries between public and private spaces and aspiring to constrict the possibilities for any form of shared dissent. Nevertheless, as Maira and many of the other authors here demonstrate, it is precisely from within these spaces of deportability that disparate migrant individuals and collectivities have begun to form alliances to contest the deportation regime.

FORCED MOVEMENT

> Anne Hutchinson: "I desire to know wherefore I am banished."
> John Winthrop: "Say no more, the Court knows wherefore and is satisfied."
> —General Court of Massachusetts, 1637 (quoted in Morgan 1999, 136)[10]

The "nationalization" of deportation policy and enforcement, the formulation and codification of deportation law, and the strict differentiation between the legal status of citizen and alien, in the United States as elsewhere, were only fully established and institutionalized toward the end of the nineteenth century. Thus when the Puritan theologian, protofeminist, and dissident Anne Hutchinson was brought to trial by the General Court of Massachusetts, declared a heretic, and banished from the Massachusetts Bay Colony under the governorship of John Winthrop in 1637, this early colonial incident of distinctly premodern expulsion was not simply notable for its naked display of arbitrary and despotic power but also is quite striking, from the perspective of deportation law and practice today, for other reasons. This episode, like countless others of its era, is remarkable for having been carried out under the jurisdiction of an entity other than a comprehensive English colonial authority, which might have been analogous to the subsequent federal government of the U.S. nation-state. Thus this case is likewise noteworthy for the absence of any clear and all-encompassing deportation or immigration law to which Hutchinson could appeal. Furthermore, it is a stunning reminder of a person's vulnerability, historically, to banishment despite having been a long-established legal resident and ostensible "citizen."

In his recent history of deportation in the United States, Daniel Kanstroom emphasizes an additional and significant dimension of deportation practice during the period of its initial nationalization: the mounting use of deportation law as a form not only of "extended border control" but also of "post-entry social control" (2007, 92). This utility of deportation for social control was not entirely new, of course; Anne Hutchinson, for instance, was banished precisely on the grounds of her unorthodox beliefs and unauthorized conduct. Nevertheless, at the beginning of the twentieth century, U.S. deportation law was rapidly expanded and transformed to determine not only what categories of "foreigner" would be permitted to enter and reside in U.S. territory but also what practices, predicaments, and predilections constituted grounds for removal. Specifically, the increasing implementation and regularization of deportation policies were accompanied by a proliferation of stipulations about which juridical statuses (such as various early formulations of migrant "illegality" or "criminality") or subsequent types of conduct (as in the vague catchall category of crimes involving "moral turpitude" or retroactive evidences of the likelihood to become a "public charge") would count as susceptible for deportation. If, by the 1990s, various long-standing ideological or behavioral bases for exclusion or removal (such as the espousal of communism or homosexuality) had officially been relegated to the same rubbish bin as earlier racial or national-origin exclusions and prohibitions against anarchists, new and still more amorphous ones (such as "terrorism") arose in their stead.

By the beginning of the twenty-first century, we can point to three further trends in immigration and border control, both in the United States and globally: the increasing securitization of borders and with it the increasing restrictiveness of immigration and deportation law, as already discussed; the proliferation and expansion of deportable offenses based on various sorts of (mis)conduct; and consequently the escalating "individualization" of deportation procedure (De Genova, this volume; Walters, this volume). That is—despite the continued collective targeting of groups based on their racialized national identities or "inassimilable" religious or political beliefs—deportation, at its point of application, tends to operate as a radically individualizing and thus also atomizing and isolating event, through which the full force of the sovereign power of the state is wielded against an individual life and deployed to circumscribe it. And yet, as the chapters of part 4 reveal, regardless of the many administrative and bureaucratic developments that have rigidified the deportation regime since the days of Hutchinson's banishment from Massachusetts, the enduring arbitrariness and sheer despotism of this distinctly undemocratic operation of the Rule of Law continue to be experienced by individuals deported today—as absurd.

The three chapters of part 4 tackle the actuality of deportation, head-on, in a variety of ethnographic efforts to capture the lived consequences of "removal" as *forced movement*. Whereas many of the previous chapters have primarily concentrated on the material and discursive productions of alienage and "illegality" through the diverse spatial configurations, metaphors, and controls surrounding deportability, the chapters here focus primarily on the ways in which the law and its execution—through the event of deportation—have rendered individual lives enduringly "illegal" and truly "inviable" (Coutin, this volume). The majority of the individuals whose cases are analyzed in this part were "legal" residents of the United States until the acute convergence of criminal justice and immigration policies in 1996 made them subject to retroactive policies of mandatory detention and removal. Generally faced with criminal convictions or charges and thus divested of their "right" to remain in the United States, these individuals were forcibly removed to their (supposed) countries of origin—"returned," in many cases, not to their homes but to sustained violence, the threat of torture, or the very conflicts which they (or their parents) had originally sought to escape. As Susan Coutin points out in her chapter, and as reiterated by some of the interlocutors in Nathalie Peutz's, many individuals experience deportation "not as a *return* but as a *departure*" from the country they consider their home. In other cases, such as the ordered removal of a previously authorized foreign student who has committed no offense, discussed by Aashti Bhartia, the forced movement of deportation is experienced as a banishment from "justice" itself.

Bhartia, an activist-scholar and journalist, traces the remarkable documentary record of a single deportation. In March 2003, Sulaiman Oladokun, a native of Burkina Faso but a long-term citizen and resident of Nigeria, was arrested by the U.S. Joint Terrorism Task Force on charges that soon thereafter were revealed to be fraudulent. And yet during a trial that eerily evokes Kafka's fictional account of an "empty law" or the suspension of law, Oladokun's visa was revoked, and he was removed to Nigeria. Indeed, it was the immigration proceedings themselves that had rendered Oladokun "guilty" and thus potentially subject to torture upon his arrival in Nigeria. Bhartia demonstrates that the juridical extension of state power over migrant bodies not only incriminates migrants but also elides the state's role in producing the conditions of their migration, as well as the very circumstances of their need for state "protection." Paradoxically, it was the threat of torture and Oladokun's subsequent plea for protection from torture that became his last and only (but ultimately failed) recourse for remaining in the United States.

In the following chapter, the anthropologist Susan Bibler Coutin narrates the story of Alex Sanchez, a former street-gang member and the director of a gang violence prevention program in Los Angeles who in 1994 had been deported to his native country of El Salvador for gang-related activities, after which he reentered the United States. Coutin draws attention to the ways in which deportation is a transformative event for individuals whose "belonging" is far more complex than their actual citizenship may reflect. Once deported to El Salvador, "criminal alien" deportees such as Sanchez find themselves in an environment that is largely unfamiliar and even hostile, making their unauthorized and now-criminalized return to the United States one of their only viable options. Moreover, such so-called "criminal aliens" deported to El Salvador are subject to the same sorts of zero-tolerance antigang policies that they faced in Los Angeles, "security" policies that El Salvador has adopted from the United States (see Zilberg 2007c). Deportees with criminal convictions are thus stigmatized and rendered "illegal" in both states, and their deportations serve to exacerbate the very lawlessness that deportation was purportedly designed to remedy.

Nathalie Peutz examines a parallel situation of "criminal aliens" who have been deported to a postwar environment in which they similarly encounter great suspicion and stigmatization because of their forced "return."

Peutz recounts the experiences of a group of thirty-one Somalis deported from the United States and Canada to war-torn Mogadishu. Significantly, many had been ordered removed years before their deportation in 2002 but had been detained indefinitely owing to Somalia's lack of a functioning state. After the events of September 11, 2001, however—with the renewed emphasis on "national security" and consequently the newfound priority placed on removing Arabs and other Muslims with outstanding deportation orders, and also in the context of an official fear that stateless Somalia could become a harbor for terrorist operatives—these Somalis experienced their sudden, summary deportation as an exceptional event, which endowed their personal suffering with seemingly global significance. Yet, as both Bhartia and Coutin also argue, instead of reconciling them to their presumably "natural home" and their apparently proper juridical identities, their deportations dramatically unsettled them, effectively denied them any recourse to the law itself, and seemed to render them the irredeemably abject refuse of a global deportation regime.

FREEDOM

Finally, part 5, comprising just one quite poignant chapter, theorizes social and political movements against deportation in a concluding attempt to resume the volume's focus on an agonistic but profoundly meaningful configuration of the problem of *freedom*. In his important (previously published) chapter, "Abject Cosmopolitanism: The Politics of Protection in the Anti-Deportation Movement," the political scientist Peter Nyers considers the radical political act (radical because this kind of agency is conventionally consigned exclusively to citizens) of abject migrants engaged in an audible and visible challenge to the sovereign state's claim to monopolize the parameters and possibilities of their protection. The politics of "protection"—regarding who will or will not be protected and thereby included (through asylum), or conversely who may be denied such protection (through deportation), as well as who may authorize the protection, and who will execute it—are normally governed by the state as a critical, if not constitutive, component of its sovereign power. Anti-detention and anti-deportation campaigns around the world have increasingly come to contest these national and transnational deportation regimes, struggling to assert or even re-*take* the right to unrestricted movement and migration. By analyzing a significant anti-deportation campaign in Canada through which nonstatus Algerians in Montreal contested the government's reversal of its policy regarding deportations to Algeria, Nyers demonstrates how these refugees risked making claims and taking rights by demanding their political recognition and regularization of their status.

The abject diaspora of deportable or deported asylum seekers, refugees, undocumented migrants, "criminal aliens," and others constitutes a veritable *deportspora* that encircles the planet. That same global deportspora, which Nyers theorizes, tragically informs all the chapters of this volume. But, as Nyers contends, the deportable of the planet must be considered not only in relation to the figure of a cosmopolitan political subject (whether as its inverse, or its constitutive other) but also *as* properly cosmopolitan, rights-taking subjects in and of themselves. Nevertheless, this reinvigoration of political speech and space—indeed, of freedom—is precisely *unprotected* and ever vulnerable to being (re)captured by the sovereign power of the state. Very much in accord with the freedom of movement itself, as elaborated by De Genova in part 1, the rights-taking modes of being political, which Nyers identifies as the abject cosmopolitanism of the deported and the deportable, even as they remain distinctly circumscribed and utterly unprotected, are crucially *practices* of freedom.

DEPORTATION: FROM MARGIN TO CENTER

The essays in this collection address some of the most vital questions that have challenged recent scholarship in migration and citizenship studies, and embody an audacious but still emergent research agenda. By foregrounding the historical and contemporary significances of deportation, this volume seeks to open new avenues of intellectual inquiry and to map new directions for future scholarly research. These essays are empirically rich, analytically rigorous, and theoretically ambitious contributions to the elaboration of a sociopolitical problematic that has scarcely begun to receive the kind of serious intellectual and ethical scrutiny that it commands. The central concerns of this anthology, then, have profound ramifications for advanced research—across several interdisciplinary fields, in multiple academic contexts, and around the world—on the fundamental relation between deportation (and migration more generally) and the complex intersection of state sovereignty, citizenship, national identity, and the social productions of (nation-)state spaces. Precisely as deportation might appear to be a relatively marginal matter—ostensibly a trivial business of human refuse disposal, involving only "disposable" and seemingly inconsequential people who have presumably transgressed the outer borders of states or otherwise violated the law—the contributions to this collection demonstrate and theorize the veritable centrality of deportation and deportability to any further critical inquiry into the urgent questions and struggles surrounding the constitution of state power and sovereignty, the global sociopolitical production of space, and the freedom of movement that remains to inspire and provoke us as one of the very foundations for any conception of human freedom.

NOTES

1. In the United States, "removable aliens" include, among others, undocumented migrants who have been laboring in the country for years ("illegal aliens"); lawful permanent residents who have committed a crime of "moral turpitude," including minor offenses such as shoplifting or the possession of marijuana ("criminal aliens"); lawful permanent residents who have, for instance, made charitable contributions or donations in support of the legal and public activities of organizations which have been designated unilaterally by U.S. authorities as "terrorist," and therefore have been charged, even if only retroactively, with "providing material support" to a terrorist organization (de facto "enemy aliens," who in fact tend not to be deported but rather may be subjected to indefinite detention); and any noncitizen found to be in violation of numerous technicalities of immigration law, namely, administrative procedures, such as failing to submit a change of address to the immigration authorities. Under the USA PATRIOT Act, the Immigration and Nationality Act of 1952 was amended to expand the power of the federal government to detain and deport aliens. For example, under title IV ("Protecting the Border"), section 411, a noncitizen may now be deported as a *terrorist* for merely committing a crime using a "weapon or dangerous device" or for having provided support to an organization even before it was officially alleged to be a terrorist organization. Section 412 permits the attorney general to detain or deport individuals solely on his word that he has "reasonable grounds to believe" that a person is engaged in terrorist activity (Abele 2005; see also Cole 2003; De Genova 2007). These retroactive charges are not new. In 1996 the U.S. Congress enacted two laws—the Antiterrorism and Effective Death Penalty Act (AEDPA) and the Illegal Immigration Reform and Immigrant Responsibility Act (IIRIRA)—that had already instated mandatory deportation and detention, even for legal permanent residents, who had been convicted of "aggravated felonies" (now defined as any conviction with a sentence of one year), whether or not the conviction and sentencing had occurred before the passing of these laws (Morawetz 1998, 2000; J. Hafetz 1998).

2. In 2004 the European Commission established the European Agency for

the Management of Operational Cooperation at the External Borders (Frontex), which, among other border control provisions, coordinates multistate expulsions from Europe. Notably, the United States has similarly been collaborating with the Canadian government to conduct and share the costs of joint U.S.-Canadian deportations from the North American continent.

3. Of the 6,000 deported by Mexico, 50 percent were Guatemalan, 28 percent Honduran, and 22 percent Salvadoran. Guatemala deported more than 1,600 Hondurans, 1,500 Salvadorans, 100 Nicaraguans, and 400 from other countries, including Ecuador, Peru, Pakistan, India, and Iran. Similar operations were conducted in Honduras and El Salvador, where approximately 1,000 additional "illegal aliens" were apprehended (Jaramillo 2001). U.S. supplemental financing of Mexico's deportations is reported to have been discontinued with the creation of the Department of Homeland Security in 2003. On October 22, 2007, however, George W. Bush announced his request to fund the Mérida Initiative, a new "security cooperation initiative" with Mexico and the countries of Central America, principally directed toward more militarized border enforcement, to "combat the threats of drug trafficking, transnational crime, and terrorism in the Western Hemisphere. See U.S. Department of State, Bureau of Public Affairs press statement, available at http://www.state.gov/r/pa/prs/ps/2007/oct/93800.htm.

4. Walters (this volume) and others have demonstrated that deportation law can be traced at least as far back as the 1662 Law of Settlement and Removal mandating the forced relocation of the poor to their "settlement" (in many cases, their place of birth) and consequent laws against vagrancy and transients who were to be exported to the colonies along with other "criminals." As much as these early forms of forced movement and exclusion targeted the poor and the socially undesirable, they also explicitly targeted slaves and free people of color. In the United States, for example, it was only with the Alien and Sedition Acts of 1798 that the distinction between citizen and alien was sharpened, and aliens, as such, became specifically susceptible to deportation. Notably, from its inception, U.S. deportation law has been animated by race-based policies, its doctrines honed through the successive efforts to remove or exclude indigenous populations (the 1830 Indian Removal Act), freed slaves (the 1850 Fugitive Slave Act), Chinese laborers (the 1882 Chinese Exclusion Act), and other "racially ineligible" groups (the 1924 Johnson-Reed Immigration Act) from the U.S. body politic (Kanstroom 2007; see also Calavita 1984; Ngai 2004).

5. Fekete argues that deportation from the European Union "is designed more for global consumption than anything else" (2005, 10); that is, it is meant to discourage potential refugees from even attempting to seek asylum in Europe. This use of deportation to send a signal—to a nation-state's citizens as well as its "outsiders"—has become blatantly evident, both in words and in practice. For example, a former managing director of the Dutch Immigration and Naturalization Service claimed, "Charter [deportation] flights are important for the public image. The image in the Netherlands should be that people living here illegally are really going back" (quoted in Fekete 2005, 10). Fekete provides a

similar example of the UK government "explaining that a film crew videoed the forced deportation of approximately two dozen Afghans from Gatwick airport so that the film could subsequently be broadcast in Afghanistan as part of a programme warning against refugee flight" (2005, 20).

6. In the United States, for example, 20 percent of the 897,099 noncitizens deported between 1997 (when stringent new deportation laws went into effect) and 2007 had been "legally" present in the country and were deported for having committed nonviolent offenses (Human Rights Watch 2009, 2).

7. Deportability, in this sense, represents what Kerber, referring to the cosmopolitan existence of multiple citizenships, in contrast to statelessness, calls a "state*full*ness" (2007, 7)—but, in this case, it is a negative image of state*full*ness, an abject state*full*ness with devastating effects on already vulnerable migrants (see also Nyers, this volume).

8. Indeed, of the approximately four million migrants "legalized" and granted residency documents in Europe over the last twenty-five years, roughly two-thirds of the total have been accounted for by Italy and Spain alone (DeParle 2008).

9. This estimate is taken from the United Nations Population Division database on "world migrant stock," available at http://esa.un.org/migration/p2kodata.asp (accessed June 10, 2008). According to the CIA World Fact book's July 2009 estimate "nonnationals" currently make up 44 percent of Bahrain's population in the fifteen-to-sixty-four-year age group (see https://www.cia.gov/library/publications/the-world-factbook/geos/ba.html). Because the 2005 UN report concerns itself specifically with migrants and refugees, as opposed to the more ambiguous term "nonnationals," we employ the UN figures.

10. We are indebted to the work of Daniel Kanstroom (2007, 30), from which this exchange was drawn to our attention.

PART ONE —w— *Theoretical Overview*

NICHOLAS DE GENOVA

—⅏—

The Deportation Regime

Sovereignty, Space, and the Freedom of Movement

> Of all the specific liberties which may come into our minds when we hear the word "freedom," freedom of movement is historically the oldest and also the most elementary. Being able to depart for where we will is the prototypical gesture of being free, as limitation of freedom of movement has from time immemorial been the precondition for enslavement. Freedom of movement is also the indispensable precondition for action, and it is in action that men primarily experience freedom in the world.—Hannah Arendt, "On Humanity in Dark Times"

> To be a human being in the true sense of the word, one has to be unsettled. —Vilém Flusser, "To Be Unsettled, One First Has to Be Settled"

If the freedom of movement is truly "elementary" and "prototypical"— and, furthermore, if it is fundamental—for any serious reflection on or practice of liberty, it is revealing that such a basic freedom has been relegated to an ominous political neglect as well as an astounding theoretical silence. Indeed, various formulations of such a freedom have been intermittently institutionalized since ancient times and then, after the founding of the United Nations in 1948, enshrined in article 13 of its Universal Declaration of Human Rights. Yet one can scarcely encounter a reference to the freedom of movement that is not immediately encumbered with the pertinent qualifications, limitations, and restrictions. Notably, the ineffable fault line in modern times for the positing of such a freedom has been the primacy, prerogative, and presumptive sovereignty of territorially defined ("national") states. If the freedom of movement has remained utterly beleaguered, its persistent and pernicious regulation has nevertheless become an ever-greater preoccupation of these states in the reentrenchment of their spatial jurisdictions. This ever-increasing attempt to control human mobility tends to be promoted, in fact, as nothing less than a putative manifestation of these states' ("national") sovereign power.

Amid proliferating spectacles of increasingly militarized border policing and the expanding purview of securitization in all aspects of travel and transit, globally, deportation has thus recently achieved an unprecedented prominence (see, e.g., Bloch and Schuster 2005; De Genova 2002; Fekete 2005; Hing 2006a; Kanstroom 2007; in this volume, see also Peutz; Walters). Associated with the ascendancy of an effectively global, neoimperial sovereignty (and a more general rescaling of various state functions and capabilities), a decidedly inverse relation may be detected between the distinctly waning fortunes and diminishing returns of nation-state sovereignty, as such, and the exuberant attention to ever more comprehensive and draconian controls that states seek to impose upon the most humble cross-border comings and goings—and settlings—of migrants (cf. Bosniak 1998, 2006; Dauvergne 2007; Nyers 2006a). At the beginning of the twentieth century, it was commonly considered to be frankly unconscionable, even by some immigration judges, to inflict the plainly punitive, "barbarous and cruel" hardship of expulsion on unauthorized but otherwise lawful long-term migrants and their families (see Ngai 2005, A21). By century's end, deportation had become utterly banal.[1] Indeed, despite the inevitable and irreducible historical specificities of particular states' legal bulwarks concerning the regulation of immigration (De Genova 2002), the practice of deportation has nonetheless emerged as a definite and increasingly pervasive convention of routine statecraft. Deportation seems to have become a virtually global *regime*.

DEPORTABILITY AND STATE SOVEREIGNTY

A paramount task of social criticism, according to Giorgio Agamben, concerns identifying "where, in the body of power, is the zone of indistinction (or, at least, the point of intersection) at which techniques of individualization and totalizing procedures converge" (1995/1998, 6).[2] Plainly, deportation is precisely such a point of intersection. In deportation, the whole totalizing regime of citizenship and alienage, belonging and deportability, entitlement and rightlessness, is deployed against particular persons in a manner that is, in the immediate practical application, irreducibly if not irreversibly individualizing (see Walters, this volume; for further examples in this volume, see especially the essays by Bhartia; Castañeda; Coutin; Gardner; Maira; Peutz; Talavera, Núñez, and Heyman; and Willen).

The extravagant and truly unforgiving individualization that comes with deportation may nowhere more tellingly be illustrated, however, than in the breach. Here it is instructive to consider the case of Elvira Arellano. Previously deported in 1997 and then arrested during an immigration raid in 2002 at Chicago's O'Hare International Airport, where she worked "illegally" cleaning the passenger cabins of commercial airliners, Arellano would appear an improbable candidate for *Time* magazine's list of "People Who Mattered" in 2006, where she was counted alongside George W. Bush (as well as Dick Cheney, Donald Rumsfeld, and Condoleezza Rice), Hugo Chávez, Pope Benedict XVI, and Kim Jong-il, among others. Thus Arellano was aptly depicted in 2007 as "perhaps the most famous undocumented immigrant" in the United States (Terry 2007). Yet even her tireless anti-deportation activism seems unlikely to have ever garnered such renown. On August 15, 2006, however, in defiance of a final order to report to the U.S. Department of Homeland Security for deportation to Mexico, Arellano (with her eight-year-old son, a U.S. citizen) publicly took refuge in Chicago's Adalberto United Methodist Church, where it was proclaimed that she and her child would be provided "sanctuary." Arellano's humble but courageous act of civil disobedience forcefully challenged immigration authorities to storm the premises and apprehend her.

Arellano remained confined to the storefront church and a small apartment above, as well as its modest enclosed parking lot and garden, for the year that followed. Her captive deportability arose amid a spectacular escalation of workplace and community immigration raids (initiated in April 2006 in response to the mass protests in defense of "immigrants' rights" and unabated during the subsequent year). Moreover, Arellano's public act of defiance flagrantly spited the U.S. immigration authorities' bombastic declaration of an avowed but absurdly implausible mission "to remove all removable aliens" (USDHS-ICE 2003, ii). Much as it may seem paradoxical, the deportation regime in which Arellano was embroiled nonetheless reserved its sovereign prerogative, during the year that ensued, to look the other way and bide its time. Confronted with an audacious affront to its juridical order, the sovereign power of the U.S. state was pressed to decide on the remarkable quandary presented by one Elvira Arellano. In response, the U.S. state tacitly instituted a peculiar state of exception whereby the law was suspended rather than enforced (Agamben 2003/2005). What appeared, however tentatively, to be Arellano's de facto immunity from deportation was indubitably a testament and a tribute to the vitality and potential volatility of the mass social movement from which her bold but desperate act of insubordination arose. It was likewise a measure of the state's prudent assessment of the movement's demonstrable success at garnering significant public sympathy.[3] Undoubtedly the state's reluctance signaled a palpable gain for the movement and also a definite victory (albeit only in the strictest and most narrow sense) for a person prepared to make extraordinary sacrifices *not* to be deported. Nonetheless Arellano incurred not merely a dramatically more excruciating kind of deportability but also a radical *immobilization*—a veritable encirclement, an asphyxiating abrogation of her freedom of movement.[4]

If the law regarding Arellano's actionable deportation was at least temporarily set aside, therefore, the norm of her *deportability* remained rigorously in-force. Thus the "state of emergency" that long defined her more mundane condition as an undocumented migrant worker remained not the exception but rather, precisely, the rule (see Benjamin 1940/1968, 257). For if the state's seeming *indecision* may yet have been apprehensible as a kind of decision, might we not detect that the efficiency of Arellano's deportability was exorbitantly enhanced, under these exceptional circumstances, by the deferral of her actual deportation?[5] It is precisely in deliberations over the exception, Agamben (1995/1998, 2003/2005) would contend, that the sovereign power of the state is constituted. Thus, in the face of imminent deportation, Arellano effectively exchanged the life of an undocumented migrant worker (for whom onerous exploitation was the quotidian price of her routinized legal vulnerability as an "illegal alien") for one of self-selected captivity and a heightened and unrelenting exposure to the unfathomable caprices of the state (albeit accompanied by an improbable sort of individual celebrity). Upon the one-year anniversary of her defiant custody, Arellano announced in a press conference that she would soon abandon her church sanctuary in Chicago by traveling to Washington, D.C., to participate in an immigrants' rights protest as an anti-deportation activist. She then momentarily returned to public life by surreptitiously traveling to Los Angeles, where she addressed a similar rally and then was swiftly apprehended (now as a "high-profile criminal fugitive alien") and summarily deported. Arellano's deportation came, notably, only once she had violated the tacit terms of her voluntary internment.

SOVEREIGN POWER AND BARE LIFE

What, we might ask, do examples such as Elvira Arellano's besieged condition of deportability serve to illuminate, if not the outright and agonistic *politicization* of her (bare) life? The concept of *bare life*, elaborated by Agamben (1995/1998),[6] in its barest distillation, is only apprehensible in contrast to the plenitude of ways in which human beings really live, namely, within and through one or another ensemble of *social relations*. Bare life is thus a conceptual foil for all the historically specific and socially particular forms in which human (biological) life is qualified by its inscription within one or another sociopolitical order. That is to say, "bare" or "naked" life may be understood to be *what remains* when human existence, while yet alive, is nonetheless stripped of all the encumbrances of social location, and thus bereft of all the qualifications for properly political inclusion and belonging (cf. Agamben 1999/2002).[7] Agamben's poignant formulation of bare life has enjoyed a rapid and increasing prominence in critical scholarly discourse, but as is often the case with currency, its accelerated circulation has also entailed a certain inflation and consequent devaluation. That is to say, the concept of bare life has been rather too presumptively reduced to a figure of mere "exclusion." Agamben's formulation is rather more subtle, however, as it revolves around "the zone of indistinction between outside and inside, exclusion and inclusion," whereby bare life is *produced* by sovereign (state) power.[8] Bare life, then, presents itself as the "originary political element." As a "threshold of articulation between [human life as] nature and [human life as] culture," it must be perennially and incessantly *banned* from the political and legal order which is enacted and orchestrated through the state (Agamben 1995/1998, 181). Nevertheless this banishment or abandonment of bare life by sovereign (state) power, which excludes it from all political life and denies it any juridical validity, implicates it in "a continuous relationship" (183). Indeed, inasmuch as it is precisely the regimentation of our social relations and identities by state power that radically separates the phantom of our naked (animal) life from the real (social) lives we lead, bare life perfectly "expresses our subjection to political power" (182).

Surely the politicization of Elvira Arellano's combined condition of deportability and containment did not evoke the iconic figure of bare life that Agamben identifies in the space of the Nazi concentration camps (1995/1998, 166–80), which many (rather too hastily) presume to be virtually dispositive of the concept. Nor did her insubordination resemble at all that of those unfortunates "abandoned . . . to the most extreme misfortunes" (159), such as the "brain-dead" medical patient sustained by an artificial life-support system and rendered the prospective object of euthanasia (136–43, 160–65, 186). Much less may we discern any correspondence between her quite outspoken and passionate condition and that of the "living dead"—the so-called *Muselmänner*—whose utter loss of sensitivity and personality itself literally embodied the ultimate unspeakability of the Nazi extermination camps (1999/2002, 41–86; cf. 1995/1998, 184–85).[9] Nevertheless, here, in this Mexican undocumented-migrant worker/mother's life, was indeed a life in its barest rudimentary outline, reduced to the most elementary facets with which human existence (as we presently know it) must, under ordinary circumstances, *sustain it-self*—which is to say, by its *labor*. And here likewise was the unrelenting and unforgiving politicization of that life. What was at stake, after all, was whether Arellano would be allowed to simply live her life, mother her child, and earn her livelihood without exceptional obstructions and intrusions by the state—whether she would be left alone to eke out her subsistence within the wider (global) regime of the market, that is—or whether this individual migrant, whose real infraction was simply her free (transnational) movement and her "unauthorized" labor, would be coercively removed from the space of the U.S. nation-state.[10] That *space* operates simultaneously as both the setting and the stakes of such struggles, as Henri Lefebvre notes (1974/1991, 386; cf. Isin 2002, 283–84), is a crucial point to which I shall return. As Linda Bosniak notes, "it is . . . the very fact of their *hereness*"—which is to say, their *presence*, their being in space—"that renders [the undocumented] deportable" (2006, 139; italics in original). Relying on a palpably spatial metaphor, Agamben has characterized such a politicization of bare life as the defining "threshold" where the relation between the living (human) being and the sociopolitical order is substantiated, and where sovereign state power therefore presumes to decide upon and inscribe the humanity of living men and women within its normative order (1995/1998, 8). If Agamben therefore posits as his most elementary conclusion the proposition "that the inclusion of bare life in the political realm constitutes the original—if concealed—nucleus of sovereign power" (6), then such an inscription is fundamentally an *incorporation* while nonetheless a negation. Surely, *illegalized* migrant labor—and therefore also deportation—enacts exactly such a constitutive contradiction.

It is precisely their distinctive legal vulnerability, their putative "illegality" and official "exclusion," that inflames the irrepressible desire and demand for undocumented migrants as a highly exploitable workforce—and thus ensures their enthusiastic importation and subordinate incorporation. And this is above all true because of the discipline imposed by their ultimate susceptibility to deportation, their deportability (De Genova 2002; 2005, 8). And yet the sheer autonomy of migration (Mezzadra 2004), especially that of "unauthorized" migration, remains a permanent and incorrigible affront to state sovereignty and the power of the state to manage its social space through law and the violence of law enforcement. Thus deportation in particular must emerge as a premier locus for the further theoretical elaboration of the co-constituted problems of the state and its putative sovereignty, on the one hand, and that elementary precondition of human freedom which is the freedom of movement.

What, in the end, is movement—and therefore the freedom of movement—if not a figure par excellence of life, indeed, life in its barest essential condition? Here, of course, we must emphatically distinguish between freedom—as an ontological condition—and anything on the order of a "right" that has been so ordained within one or another normative or juridical framework. In this regard, the freedom of movement may best be understood, precisely, *not* as a "right"—and neither as something so juridical (and decidedly modern) as a "human right," nor anything so metaphysical as a putative "natural right." Likewise, the freedom of movement must therefore be radically distinguished from any of the ways that such a liberty may have been stipulated, circumscribed, and domesticated within the orbit of state power ("national," imperial, or otherwise).[11] Instead I am underscoring the fact that human life, in its most apparently "biological" and socially undifferentiated or unqualified (animal) sense, is inseparable from the uninhibited capacity for movement which is a necessary premise for the free and purposeful exercise of creative and productive powers. The exercise of these vital powers is, plainly, the foundation for all properly social praxis. (And social praxis is what makes the life of the human species truly human, after all.)[12] Thus the freedom of movement is inseparable from that still more basic human power which is generative of the very possibility of social life, namely, our capacity to creatively transform our objective circumstances.

This intersection of the freedom of movement with the capacity for work, simply put, does indeed mark a "zone of indistinction" (in Agamben's phrase) between naked (unformed, generic) human life and each historically particular configuration of social relations, or "way of life," in which its distinct humanity is realized. That is to say, it marks the necessary and inescapable point of convergence between bare ("natural") human existence and any viable social formation as such. If this is so, I hasten to emphasize, then that freedom (to move in the world) and also that power (to transform the world) are grounded in a process whereby human life purposefully mediates its own embeddedness within nature:

> Man, through his own actions, mediates, regulates, and controls the metabolism between himself and nature ... *as a force of nature.* ... Through this movement, he acts upon external nature and changes it, and in this way simultaneously changes his own nature. He develops the potentialities slumbering within nature, and subjects the play of its forces to *his own sovereign power.* (Marx 1867/1976, 283; italics mine)

Hence Marx long ago identified the capacity of human beings (collectively) to purposefully transform our objective circumstances as the elementary and constitutive condition of specifically human life, as such, and he designated this power, precisely, as labor.[13]

Bare (human) life, then, can be qualified as "exclusively human" only by its intrinsically social and distinctively purposeful productive characteristics as open-ended creativity, as pure potentiality. If this sort of "purposeful activity" (284) is inseparable from the ontological (natural) necessity of tenaciously mediating our metabolic predicament in relation to external nature, it is also true that this "natural" (or "animal") life of the human species is intrinsically and necessarily *social* life. It is inherently interdependent and collaborative. In this regard, the recuperation of Marx's more expansive sense of the meaning of (living) labor as life-activity—as a creative vocation, which is itself an existential condition—has an enduringly political significance. Its affirmation, as Michael Hardt and Antonio Negri rightly contend, "is the affirmation of life itself" (1994, xiii). Notably, Marx repeatedly glosses this life-*activity* as "energy" (1867/1976, 982), "unrest" (287, 296), "motion" (296)—indeed, as "movement" (982). Furthermore, the productive power and creative capacity that are thus defining—and, in effect, definitive—of the species particularity of the human, as such, likewise are posited by Marx explicitly (and emphatically) as "sovereign power." Thus this restless, energetic, purposeful, free movement (namely, labor) ought to instructively assume a foundational significance for any theoretically viable concept of sovereign power.

Discourse about "power" and "sovereignty" has proliferated among scholars in recent years, but in a manner that seldom if ever does more than recapitulate the one-sided reification of power as synonymous with domination and sovereignty as an exclusive preserve of the state. Thus these discourses tend to fetishize the fetish of "power" (Holloway 1994, 52–53). The fetishism of the state (or power) recalls the fetishism of the commodity. Power is very much like the seemingly ineffable, eminently social substance of "value" that Marx discerned in the commodity, which assumes the thinglike status of an alien power looming above the human beings who have produced it (1867/1976, 163–77). Similarly, the reified power of the state is nothing if not yet another congealed manifestation of the objectified, estranged productive power and creative capacity of "bare" laboring human life, as that sheer vitality has come to be ensnared in distinctly capitalist social relations (Pashukanis 1929; cf. Holloway 1994). From this standpoint, it is instructive to recall Marx's terse but poignant remarks in his otherwise vexed essay "On the Jewish Question" (1843) about the expressly "imaginary sovereignty" that is "the *sophistry of the political state* itself" (1978, 34; italics in original). What begins as precisely the sovereign power of human life itself—once it becomes ensconced within one or another regime of estrangement and expropriation—necessarily presents itself as the apparently independent and durable but fundamentally illusory sovereignty of the state. However, like the value of the commodity itself—"abounding in metaphysical subtleties and theological niceties" (163)—the power of the state is in fact the fetishized expression of a *social relation* of alienation while yet one also of active, unresolved struggle (Holloway 1994, 52–53). In Marx's account, centuries of outright and extravagant violence devoted to the subordination of labor to capital—for which the state-form is instrumental, and through which it becomes rigidified and institutionalized—eventually secure what comes to appear as merely "the silent compulsion of economic relations," and thus normalize "the requirements of [the capitalist] mode of production as self-evident natural laws." Only thereafter may the sorts of "direct extra-economic force" that distinguish the repressive apparatuses of state coercion come to be reserved for "*exceptional* cases" (1867/1976, 899; cf. 915–16; italics mine).[14] Thus only thereafter, historically, does it become substantially tenable for one such as Agamben (in spite of his otherwise brilliant exegetical recourse to ancient textual sources) to elaborate a theory of (state) sovereignty as crucially involved in the decision concerning "the state of exception" (1995; 1996; 2003).[15]

Power is therefore an elementary facet of human possibility and productive capability that is ontologically prior to, and ultimately autonomous of, the reified power of the sovereign state which captures and cannibalizes it. With recourse to such a critical perspective, it may be possible to retrieve and reclaim power from its ordinarily preconceived, always already a priori, (pre)theoretical status as abject domination. Such an alternative conception may thus provide a much-needed corrective to what may be called the Foucauldian "iron cage" of power. Perhaps nowhere is Foucault's formulation of power more forcefully and persuasively articulated than in his methodological commentary in the first volume of *The History of Sexuality* (1976/1978). On the one hand, Foucault supplies a refreshing departure from more stultified renditions of power and notably insists on its plurality, proliferation, and productivity:

> The omnipresence of power: not because it has the privilege of consolidating everything under its invincible unity, but because it is produced from one moment to the next, at every point, or rather in every relation from one point to another. Power is everywhere; not because it embraces everything, but because it comes from everywhere. And "Power" [as a group of institutions and mechanisms that ensure the subservience of the citizens of a given state], insofar as it is permanent, repetitious, inert, and self-reproducing, is simply the over-all effect that emerges from all these mobilities, the concatenation that rests on each of them and seeks in turn to arrest their movement. (1976/1978, 93)

Thus Foucault usefully identifies the sovereign power of the state or the normative order of law as merely endpoint "crystallizations" (ibid.).[16] He emphasizes as well the instability of power that is implicated by precisely what we might call the freedom of movement, and consequently the state's dire and constant need to subjugate and suspend that movement. Furthermore, Foucault disavows the reification of power in favor of its immanence within social relations:

> Power is not something that is acquired, seized, or shared, something that one holds on to or allows to slip away; power is exercised. ... Relations of power ... have a directly productive role, wherever they come into play. Power comes from below. ... (94)

> Where there is power, there is resistance ... consequently, this resistance is never in a position of exteriority in relation to power. Should it be said that one is always "inside" power, there is no "escaping" it ... because one is always subject to the law in any case? Or that, history being the ruse of reason, power is the ruse of history, always emerging the winner? This would be to misunderstand the strictly relational character of power relationships. (95)

All of this is compellingly subtle and unquestionably supple. And yet:

> Power's condition of possibility ... is the moving substrate of force relations which, by virtue of their inequality, *constantly engender states of power*. (93; italics mine)

> There is a plurality of resistances, each of them a special case. . . . By defini-
> tion, they can only exist in the strategic field of power relations. . . . They are
> the odd term in relations of power; they are inscribed in the latter as an ir-
> reducible opposite (96).

Incessantly and ineluctably, then, inequalities of power operate strategically in Foucault's analysis in tandem with their rightful resistances, here
and there converging transversally and getting systematized into a more
enduring and overarching hegemony, occasionally trading places as one
subverts the other.[17] "Power," Foucault remarks elsewhere, is "something
that circulates . . . that functions only when it is part of a chain . . . exercised thorough networks," in which individuals "both submit to and exercise this power" (1976/2003, 29). Thus the play of power finally seems
relentless—in effect, one damned thing after another. And the admirable
methodological emphasis on the multiplicity, relationality, and restless-
ness of power with which Foucault begins ultimately turns out to be
tantamount to its (re)essentialization. "We have to analyze [power]," he
remarks concisely, "by beginning with the techniques and tactics of domination" (34; cf. 1982, 788). His polemical emphasis is on the plurality of
techniques and tactics; domination is nonetheless the constant. What at
first appeared to be chiefly distinguished by its "strictly relational" nega-
tivity, therefore tends to end up, fetishized yet again, as an elusive but
ubiquitous positivity.

With these considerations of the limitations of Foucault's formulation of
power in mind, we may better appreciate the reelaboration of his notion
of *bio-power*, through which Agamben (1995/1998) postulates his conception of the relation between sovereign power and bare life. For Foucault,
the eclipse of premodern (monarchical) sovereignty was deeply entangled
with the demise of an authoritarian sovereign's prerogative to kill with impunity. It was accompanied by the concomitant ascendancy of a more impersonal political power that "had assigned itself the task of administering
life," one "whose highest function was perhaps no longer to kill, but to
invest life through and through" (1976/1978, 139), by means of "the administration of bodies and the calculated management of life" culminating
in "the control of populations" (140).[18] Biopower refers, therefore, to "the
set of mechanisms through which the basic biological features of the human species became the object of a political strategy," and through which
"modern Western societies took on board the fundamental biological
fact that human beings are a species" (Foucault 1978/2007, 1). Agamben
unreservedly credits Foucault's analysis with having restored "the natural

['bare' or 'naked'] life of human beings ... to the center of the polis" (1996/2000, ix), and plainly reaffirms that "politics in our age [have] been entirely transformed into biopolitics" (1995/1998, 120). However, in his various treatments of "disciplinary power" or biopower, Foucault tends to be judicious about avoiding any thematic focus on sovereignty (which retains for him the odor of the *pre*-modern; see 1976/2003, 35–38), in favor of a more dispersed and multifarious notion of power.[19] Agamben often appears to recapitulate precisely what, for present purposes, may be considered to be the weaknesses of Foucault's formulation of power, while yet reinstating it as the specifically *sovereign* power of the biopolitical state.[20]

In contrast to Foucault, nonetheless, Agamben posits a frankly predatory relation between sovereign (state) power and bare or naked (human) life, which is founded always upon their mutually constitutive *separation* (1996/2000, 4; cf. 2003/2005, 87). Nonetheless bare life—as the reification of a notion of human life that could somehow be merely "biological"—is, for Agamben, precisely *not* a biological given that ontologically precedes sovereign power, as if in a state of nature. Rather, bare life is precisely a "product of the [biopolitical] machine" (2003/2005, 87–88). Bare life, in other words, is for Agamben the debasement of the human specificity of human life. Thus his analysis of this constitutive separation between bare life and the sociopolitical order of sovereign power aspires always to problematize and effectively repudiate that same distinction.[21] Indeed, politically, Agamben instead seeks nothing less than a life "in which it is never possible to isolate something such as naked [or 'bare'] life," "a life for which what is at stake in its way of living is living itself . . . in which the single ways, acts, and processes of living are never simply *facts* but always and above all *possibilities* of life, always and above all power" (1996/2000, 4; italics in original). Thus Agamben's propositions gesture toward "a *life of power*" predicated upon an emancipation from the very division of sovereign (state) power and naked ("biological") life and an "irrevocable exodus from any sovereignty" (8–9; italics in original).[22]

The supersession of the sovereign power of the state, therefore, would emphatically not be some kind of romantic return to bare life as an ostensible state of grace. Rather, it would be a concomitant transcendence of the condition of bare life itself—a condition to which, according to Agamben (1996/2000, 5), virtually all human existence has by now been reduced. Hence, in contrast to the quite constant juxtaposition that Foucault finally sustains between (bio-)"power" and "life" (thereby upholding their seemingly immutable analytical opposition), Agamben invokes a notion (not unlike Marx's) of a restitution of human life to its own intrinsic power (the originary power that Marx characterizes as "sovereign"). The "life of power" that Agamben proposes would *inhabit* precisely the zone of indistinction where the opposition between "life" and "power" collapses, and would thereby effectively suspend and transcend the very distinction. In this sense, Agamben revisits what in Marx (1843/1978) was in fact a radical disarticulation of "*human* emancipation" from all notions of citizenship, rights, the state, and even politics, as such (cf. De Genova 2007).[23] If Agamben confronts us with the abjection of bare life as paradigmatic of our universal condition, therefore, that critical move is not an end but rather, in his words, a *threshold*—one which we must venture to cross. "Criticism has torn up the imaginary flowers from the chain," Marx once admonished, "not so that man shall wear the unadorned, bleak chain but so that he will shake off the chain and pluck the living flower" (1844b/1975, 176).

Indeed, it is *citizenship* that remains for us the imaginary and purely deceptive flower dissimulating our subjection and adorning our abjection. In the effort to demonstrate that "biological life and its needs [have] become the *politically* decisive fact," Agamben deftly elucidates how citizenship in particular comes to entail "the primary inscription of life in the state order" (1995/1998, 122, 129; italics in original). Citizenship, in the modern (bourgeois-democratic) era, he argues, "does not simply identify a generic subjugation to royal authority or a determinative system of laws" but rather "names the new status of life as origin and ground of sovereignty, and therefore, literally identifies . . . 'the members of the sovereign'" (129). Such, at least, is what we may consider to be the game of modern sovereignty. The allure of "membership" within (state) power serves precisely as the device for entrapment that is otherwise named citizenship and consecrated as a virtually natural (birth-)"right."[24] "The very natural life . . . placed at the foundation of the order" (127) is figured—in its very humanity and by dint of nothing so much as its mere birth (or nativity)—as the foundation and the source of the purportedly democratic state's sovereignty (as "nation"). And yet, through its capture by the state (precisely in the form of citizenship and its putatively inalienable and indefeasible "rights"), this elemental and naked life is thereby expelled from view. "Rights are attributed to man (or originate in him)," Agamben concludes, "solely to the extent that man is the immediately vanishing ground (who must never come to light as such) of the citizen" (128; cf. 1996/2000, 20).

Thereafter ensues, however, a persistent task of regulating and revising the definition of *which* particular human lives could qualify as "natural" citizens of the nation-state—the task of determining, in other words, ex-actly whose *nativity* may serve to verify *national* belonging. This is nothing less than an incessant (re)politicization of that same bare life, tantamount to a "constant need to redefine the threshold in life that distinguishes and separates what is inside from what is outside" (131). But the presumptive inside and outside become irredeemably confounded, and their indistinc-tion becomes the site of a cascade of exceptions through which state power aims to ban and expel the bare life that otherwise supplies its very foun-dation (cf. Nyers 2006a; in this volume, see also Castañeda; Wicker; and Willen). Indeed, Agamben concludes (again echoing Marx) that "every attempt to found political liberties in the rights of the citizen is . . . in vain" (181).[25] Following Hannah Arendt (1951/1966, 267–302), Agamben then elaborates the figure of the refugee as "a limit concept that radically calls into question the fundamental categories of the nation-state" (1995/1998, 134; cf. 1996/2000, 22). For it is the refugee "who has become now the decisive factor of the modern nation-state by breaking the nexus between human being and citizen" (1996/2000, x; cf. p. 20). This irruption of the refugee, which confronts the sovereign power of the state with a bare life that cannot readily be subsumed within the normative juridical order of citizenship, therefore has ample implications for our consideration of the figure of the "deportable alien."[26]

THE INDISPENSABLE DISPOSABILITY OF DEPORTABLE LABOR

For the "deportable alien," there is an ever-tenuous frontier between her abject subjection to the state and the imminent peril of her descent into the utter statelessness that signals the refugee as precisely a figure of bar-est life, naked humanness, humanity shorn of any juridical personhood.[27] That frontier is distinguished by the spectral vestiges of some previous (and, in any case, *exterior*) citizenship, a "proper" belonging elsewhere, within the orbit of some other state power. If the refugee may be invoked as an icon of statelessness and therefore also of bare life, then deport-ability perfectly and precisely marks the zone of indistinction between a condition that is (virtually) stateless and one that is positively saturated with the state. Deportation, moreover, enacts the gambit where this un-decidable condition must be decided (for examples in this volume, see Bhartia; Coutin; Peutz). Deportation is, indeed, a premier means for per-petrating, embellishing, and reinstating a "threshold . . . that distinguishes and separates what is inside from what is outside." It is no mere contrivance or exaggeration, therefore, to say of the "deportable alien" that—like the exiles and bandits to whom Agamben analogizes the figure of bare life (1995/1998, 183–84), excluded from all political life, disqualified from any juridically valid act, and yet in a continuous relationship with the power that banishes it—no life is more "political" than hers.

Indeed, it is precisely in the "illegal" migrant's deportability that we may encounter anew the centrality and constitutive role of *labor*. Her ever-vexed placement within the juridical order of citizenship, while always by definition outside it, precisely as its most abject "alien," is no mere logical conundrum or normative inconsistency (in this volume, see Cornelisse; Gardner; Karakayali and Rigo; Nyers). Rather, this peculiar sociopolitical relation of juridical nonrelationality is the material and practical precondition for her thoroughgoing incorporation within a wider capitalist social formation, in which an effectively global market is fractured systemically into a political order of territorially delimited nation-states (Holloway 1994; cf. Hindess 2000; see also Walters, this volume). The "illegal" migrant is conscripted, after all, for the raw productive capacity of her human life as living labor (commodifiable, in Marx's telling formulation, as labor-*power*). This sheer productive and generative capacity of human life (the power to transform itself, as well as its always already *social* configuration, by transforming its objective/external circumstances), becomes *politically* apprehensible, in Agamben's terms, as bare life. And as bare life, it must thus be subsumed to (and mediated by) the constituted sovereign power of the state. If this is so, this raw life-force is nonetheless *immediately* apprehensible, *economically*, as a constituent and constitutive power—(living) labor—which must assiduously be subordinated to the everyday mandates of capital accumulation.[28] The exquisitely refined legal vulnerability of undocumented migrant labor—above all, materialized in its deportability—plainly serves to radically enhance the preconditions for its routinized subordination within the inherently despotic regime of the workplace (De Genova 2002; cf. Calavita 2003; Fekete 1997; see, for example, Gardner, this volume).[29] But this deportability likewise emerges as a telltale site where the totalizing procedures of otherwise partitioned "politics" and "economy" enter a zone of indistinction. Likewise, the susceptibility to deportation signals the exact point where these totalizing systems converge upon the irreducible singularities of individual lives.

If bare life is the vanishing ground of the citizen in the state's disappearing act of sovereignty, it is no less the foundational element of sovereign power that obstinately *resurfaces* in the figure of the noncitizen (in this volume, see Andrijasevic; Karakayali and Rigo). As Elvira Arellano remarked on the eve of her arrest, "I'm not challenging anyone. I'm just bringing to light what those who are in power don't want to see" (Olivio 2007). Yet unlike the refugee, whose naked humanness elusively tends to be figured as statelessness (Arendt 1951/1966, 297–300), the deportable alien makes her obtrusive appearance almost always fully clad, in her work clothes.[30]

STATE SPACE AND THE FRONTIERS OF NATIONHOOD

> Man will ultimately be known for a mere polity of multifarious, incongruous, and independent denizens. —Robert Louis Stevenson,
> *The Strange Case of Dr. Jekyll and Mr. Hyde*

If, indeed, it is labor—that eminently social and inherently purposeful creative capacity and productive power—which truly distinguishes and is finally constitutive of *human* life in its barest elementary form, of naked humanity as such, then the very existence of "the" state (and likewise of each and every particular one) is revealed for its instrumental role in usurping, for itself on behalf of capital, the sovereign power of living labor for itself. Whereas life-*force* manifests itself diminutively as an infinite plenitude of particular instances of labor-power in the marketplace, it acquires a rarefied yet spurious unity—as "Power," so seemingly pure and simple—only when it is gathered and reified in the state. "What on the side of the worker appeared in the form of unrest," Marx demonstrates with regard to the commodity, "now appears, on the side of the product, in the form of being, as a fixed, immobile characteristic" (1867/1976, 287). Likewise, state power institutes its putative sovereignty and may appear as "power" in general only by gathering together and objectifying the innumerable and diverse potentialities of living labor's restless subjectivity.[31]

What is at stake here is nothing less than the common ground of the citizen and the deportable noncitizen. That common ground, of course, is not some vague, mystified, and ultimately vacuous universality entailed in their "shared humanity" but instead the positive content of bare life. The positive content of the bare life lurking behind the juridical forms of both citizen and alien is, then, a humanity that is precisely material and *practical*—namely, labor—"*life activity, productive life* itself . . . species-life . . . life-producing life" (Marx 1844a/1975, 276; italics in original). If this vitality, this "form-giving fire" (Marx 1858/1973, 361), is posited always in a negative relation to the sovereign power of the state, as mere (bare) life, this is because the state (like the commodity) may assume the fetishized form of an alien power, a thinglike positivity, only to the extent that it evacuates living labor of its own originary (life) force.

This process of constituting the singular power of the state from the heterogeneous powers of living labor simultaneously requires a variegated and diffuse fragmentation of laboring humanity as a whole. One such process of fragmentation—one that splinters and segments laboring humanity into two generic categories defined in terms of their differential relations to the reified unity of the state—supplies the very basis for the spurious distinction that thereafter divides the *citizen* from the *noncitizen*. Indeed, the differentiation and regimentation of such a palpably practical humanity into the (nation-)state-mediated status abstractions of citizen and alien decompose genuinely human universality and recompose it into two mutually exclusive yet co-constituted, homogenized "identity" camps (cf. Hindess 2000; Isin 2002; see also Karakayali and Rigo, this volume).[32] Indeed, every territorially defined state formation ("national," imperial, or otherwise) does this in turn, repeatedly fragmenting laboring humanity in the course of assisting its subordination as labor-for-capital. And as a consequence of these decisively unequal relations to the state, the everyday life of the citizen and noncitizen tends likewise to be chiefly distinguished by an unequal social organization of the particularities of their respective labors.

This same process has likewise conventionally decomposed each respective camp into a multitude of interchangeable, atomized individuals.[33] In this manner, nationalism—the self-referential theology of every nation-state—aspires to produce its signature treachery, the elusive promise of what Benedict Anderson has memorably depicted as a "deep horizontal comradeship" (1983/1991, 7), juxtaposed always and inevitably to an amorphous but vaguely menacing mass of humanity that huddles just beyond the frontiers of nationhood. By implication, this consignment to existentially opposed camps of citizens and aliens is thus a pronouncedly *spatialized* one. Thus the pervasive assumption of a polity of citizen-comrades who inhabit a "domestic" space, always starkly demarcated from an amorphous "foreign" exterior, is symptomatic of what John Agnew (1994) has depicted as "the geographical unconscious" and stands as one of the enduring effects of "the territorial trap" of contemporary political thought. As Neil Brenner and his collaborators note, "this establishes the national scale as the ontologically necessary foundation of modern political life" (2003, 2). These separations of state space are ideally partitioned by durable and "secure" borders (rather than the "porous" sort that seems to proliferate everywhere) and are sanitized by the stringent reassignments perpetrated by one or another regime of deportation. Yet, as Anderson has noted, even the most durable "truth-claims" of belonging or attachment to particular states have in fact become "less attestations of citizenship, let alone loyalty to a protective nation-state, than of claims to participation in labor markets" and transnationally "figure differential tariffs on human labor" (1994, 323–24). All of life is thus assigned to a "proper" location within one or another of the vast labor camps that are nation-states, ostensibly endowed with the rights of citizens, while the vital mobility and autonomy of labor simultaneously ensure a more or less reliable and precisely fluid reserve of "dislocated" life which may be relegated to the relative disenfranchisement sanctimoniously allotted to noncitizens.

If *labor* supplies the crucial theoretical key that opens up the practical linkage between the apparently antithetical poles of bare life and sovereign (state) power, the literal and also conceptual terrain that necessarily conjoins them, therefore, is *space*. Here I have in mind the physical territories (nation-state jurisdictions) across which migratory movement—along with deportation, as its coercive reversal—is enacted (in this volume, see Nyers; Peutz; Walters). Simultaneously, it is necessary to attend to the unforeseen transnational spaces produced by those movements (e.g., De Genova 2005, 95–143; cf. Burman 2006; Zilberg 2004; in this volume, see also Coutin; Nyers). Mediating both state space and the transnational spatial conjunctures that exceed them, furthermore, are the pronouncedly "national" or, in other instances, supranational spaces of border patrols, detention, and incarceration through which deportation regimes are enforced (in this volume, see Andrijasevic; Karakayali and Rigo; Nyers; Talavera, Núñez, and Heyman; Wicker; Willen; cf. Andreas and Snyder 2000; Dow 2004; Fekete 2005, 2007a; Heyman 2004; Schuster 2005; Simon 1998; Wacquant 1999; Welch 2002). "The establishing of frontiers," Walter Benjamin memorably observes, "is the primal phenomenon of all law-making violence" (1921/1979, 149). The spaces of frontier policing, through which the law of borders is enforced and preserved, are therefore the various "thresholds" (to revisit Agamben's phrase) or "mezzanine spaces" (Nyers, this volume) at which, or across which, the regulation and disciplining of human mobility (and thereby the subordination of labor) supply some of the crucial foundations of state power. They do so by supporting an intricate and spectacular scaffolding which presents itself always in terms of the ostensible "inside" and "outside" of the space of (state) sovereignty. If these spaces figure here in ways inextricable from the state's abjection of noncitizens in the performance of its putative sovereignty,

however, these same spatial practices are therefore intrinsically also formative practices of citizenship itself (Bosniak 2006; Isin 2002; McNevin
2006). Moreover, insofar as deportation is truly a "technology of citizenship," as William Walters has argued in this volume, its constitutive
dimension as a spatial practice at the international level implicates it in
a veritably *global* governmentality. The successive governmental management of citizenship and alienage by territorially defined states, then,
may best be understood in terms of the global *politics* of the capital-labor
relation.

CITIZENSHIP, IDENTITY, AND NATIVISM

> Somewhere I remember
> these clothes are not my clothes.
> These bones are not my bones.
> —Khaled Mattawa, "Echo and Elixir I"

Rather than a secure and stable entitlement accruing "naturally" or inexorably to co-"nationals," citizenship has instead been a site of struggle
(cf. Balibar 2001/2004; Hall and Held 1989; Isin 2002; McNevin 2006;
Nyers 2004; Stasiulis and Bakan 1997; Walters 2004; see also Nyers, this
volume). Citizenship struggles garner and tentatively institutionalize an
ever-beleaguered (and by no means assuredly expanding) circle of protections for the presumed "rights" or "entitlements" of those who come to
be counted as "properly" belonging "inside" the space of the state. Those
who claim the status of citizens assume their "rightful" place at the point
where the citizenry of a state is equated with "the nation" that is figured
as the ostensibly natural source of its sovereignty. But in this way, citizenship struggles ultimately become ensnared in the state's foundational but
incessant project of producing a "people" in its own image (De Genova
2005, 215–16). Importantly, one of the principal outcomes of such struggles over the presumed "rights" of citizens has commonly been to demand
(at least by implication) and, to varying extents, effectively ensure that the
arbitrariness of state violence be largely expelled to the far side of nation-
state borders, where "foreigners" may supply a proper target for its callous
power (Hindess 2000; Nyers 2004; in this volume, see also Cornelisse;
Walters).

There is then a deep complicity between this vision of citizenship with
the related notion that the Schmittian friend-enemy distinction becomes

reducible to a distinction between *citizen* and *enemy* (Schmitt 1927/1996, 26). Through a logic of warfare that effectively militarizes nation-state borders (and thereby insulates citizens from the state's violence while also implicating them in its perpetration), this alignment of citizenship on the side of state violence likewise has palpable implications for theorizing the relation of citizen and deportable noncitizen (or resident "alien") (cf. Balibar 2004; Mezzadra, in Bojadžijev and Saint-Saëns 2006, 21). But despite their flamboyant rhetoric, such otherwise bloodless structuralist conceptions may contribute nevertheless to the ultimately misleading sense that the state necessarily and consistently *succeeds* in its mission to deploy citizenship toward the efficient subjection of the "population" captive within its bounded space, thus galvanizing citizens' unquestioning loyalty. (And this remains pertinent even if that captive population is understood to include, albeit only in a graduated and unequal manner, noncitizen resident "aliens.") In other words, such a position might too readily concede and consign us to the "sovereign" power of the state, without even a fight. In any case, it would be a naive liberalism indeed that could so credulously imagine that the "enemies of the state" should always and everywhere be (external) "foreigners" or, in other words, that the state, whose defining mission and existential vocation are purportedly to secure the interests of "the nation," could not possibly unleash its most concentrated powers against its own ostensibly rightful citizens and lawfully resident subjects.

It is obvious that any bright lines between the inside and outside of nation-state space are always inevitably sullied. Indeed, there is hardly a more apt exemplar of this tendency than the anti-immigrant politics of nativism and hostility to "foreign"-ness that commonly imbue regimes of deportability and deportation. Notably, these regimes seek always to exorcise the "foreign"-ness that is most reprehensible precisely because one encounters it *within* the space of the nation-state (in this volume, see especially Bhartia; Castañeda; Maira; Wicker; Willen). Thus they effectively transform the entirety of the interior of any territorial space of "national" community into an unrelenting regulatory sphere for migrants, a "border" that is implosive, infinitely elastic, and, in effect, truly everywhere *within* the space of the nation-state (Balibar 2002, 84; 2004, 109; Bosniak 2007, 397; De Genova 1998, 106; 2005; Mezzadra, in Bojadžijev and Saint-Saëns 2006, 22–23, 24; in this volume, see also Talavera, Núñez, and Heyman; cf. Ngai 2003, 70). Against such nativist campaigns of exclusion—and, moreover, also against the systemic inequalities and forms of disenfranchisement, more generally, that are tantamount to outright "tyranny" for all noncitizens (Walzer 1983, 59)—some liberals advocate an ethics of shared "territoriality." The palpable social fact of migrants' presence and habitation within the same territorial space as citizens, in these accounts, ought to serve as normative grounds for more expansive communitarian impulses devoted to a capacious notion of "national" membership—one that could include migrant residents within the more substantive purview of citizenship.[34] But such "cosmopolitan" democratic conceptions of more or less communitarian cohabitation (Bosniak 2000; Honig 2001; Isin 2002; cf. Nyers, this volume) remain irremediably anathema (indeed, virtually incomprehensible) to the legal fetishism and "status" obsessions of more restrictive notions of entitlement (Bosniak 2007, 403n35).[35] Moreover, in spite of these apparent discrepancies, Linda Bosniak notes, such notions of territorial inclusivity almost invariably rest upon the presupposition of durable borders to reliably and consistently define the very territory within which inclusion is to be upheld (see also Cornelisse, this volume). Such territorialist commitments to the enhanced "inclusion" of the "foreigners" who already reside *within* the space of a "national community" tend therefore to merely *intensify* the constitutive separation of the "aliens" on the far side of the frontier. Indeed, the detention and deportation authorities of states increasingly tend to swell the spatial scope of their regulatory powers, spilling border enforcement *beyond* the residual semblances of "national" frontiers (Mezzadra and Neilson 2003; Walters 2004, 251–53; in this volume, see Andrijasevic; Karakayali and Rigo; Walters).

The politics of "immigrant" inclusion and nation-state enclosure thus inexorably share a deeper nationalist conceit. Indeed, nationalism is deeply entangled with the premises of social contract theories, wherein the (modern, democratic) state is largely figured as a dutiful yet impersonal servant, protecting its "people" (however broadly or narrowly construed) and provisioning them with the Rule of Law in return for entrusting the state with the sovereignty that is otherwise supposed to be the people's by birthright. Any simplistic liberal faith in these most magnanimous gestures of nationalism finally rests, however, on the most profound sort of *nativism*. This indeed is what supplies the bedrock for what Agamben identifies as the crucial biopolitical affiliation of "the nation with nativity itself.[36] As I have argued in greater detail elsewhere (De Genova 2005, 56–94), nativism is best apprehended precisely as *native*-ism—a promotion of the priority of "natives," on no other grounds than their *being* such—and thus operates inextricably as a politics of *identity* animating all nationalisms. And with or without all the associated assumptions (however fictive or spectral) of common ancestry, mutual kinship, and shared substance, any such notion of "native" identity at the base of nationhood is inextricably bound up with an assumption of *natal* entitlement. Thus the purported "inclusion" of "immigrants" into the more elemental and fundamental "national community" inevitably sustains and upholds the primacy and priority of "natives" that is the submerged identitarian commitment of nationalism itself.

What bears further consideration here is the fundamentally *spatial* character of nativism as a particular metaphysics of identity. Étienne Balibar has depicted an image of "two humanities," historically constituted by the global racism of capitalist (colonial) modernity as sub- and superhuman categories, respectively associated with abject destitution and gross overdevelopment. The members of this bifurcated humanity of "tendentially incompatible masses" confront one another, however, on an unprecedented scale and, ever more ubiquitously, *within the same spaces* of practical everyday life (1991c, 44; see also 1991a, 14; cf. Anderson 1994, 321). Without ever ceasing to be excruciatingly unequal and significantly segregated, these two human camps become ensnared anew amid the unforeseen physical proximities and incidental intimacies that arise with shared spaces of cohabitation, work and production, and, to a lesser but not negligible extent, also consumption. This transnational and decidedly postcolonial reconfiguration of global class inequalities marks an unfinished decolonization indeed (Balibar 1991a, 12; 2001/2004, 7; 2003, 42). It is emblazoned as before by bluntly racialized differences, in a peculiar but predictable "recolonization" of "immigrants" and "immigration" (Balibar 2004, 38–42; see also De Genova 2006; Mezzadra 2006, 39; Bojadžijev and Saint-Saëns 2006, 15–18; Mezzadra and Rahola 2006). Now, however, these global inequalities tend to operate without the conventional luxury of fixed or overriding spatial separations of the sort that distinguished the incarceration of whole populations within the militarized borders of colonies, which served to *immobilize* human energies within the confines of vast de facto prison labor camps. Now, in a proliferation of postcolonial metropolitan spaces, regimented under the fastidious juridical constellations of citizen and (ever-deportable) alien, migrant labor is mobilized transnationally, and these inequalities come as never before to operate under the banners of the native and its inimical but ineffable other—as mere differences of "identity." Hence, historically, it was more or less viable to juxtapose an ostensibly exclusionary "xenophobia" (which mobilized hostility to "foreign"-ness against migrant "outsiders") to the varieties of racism that took as their primary target precisely those "insiders" who could be marked as constitutionally different (e.g., Native Americans, New World blacks, European Jews and gypsies, Palestinians, etc.).

Now as never before, however, these sorts of seemingly definitive distinctions—much as they certainly endure and retain their salience to varying extents—become ever increasingly confounded, if not anachronistic (see, e.g., Willen, this volume).[37] Indeed, new dynamics of racialization and new formations of racism become inextricable from the social production of migrants' "differences" in ways that, as often as not (or rather, more often than not), dissimulate their racisms and disarticulate "race" and "immigration" through a politics of nativism.

With recourse to this pronouncedly spatialized politics of identitarian difference, race need not always speak its name. The exorbitantly more convoluted and heterogeneous dimensions of race in its contemporary manifestations, in any event, render the seductive but illusory coherences of "biological" categories distinctly less useful. Instead the apparently race-neutral and presumptively "legitimate" politics of *citizenship* may serve to achieve the elision of race with the full panoply of nativist conceits entailed by the ever elusive and evasive phantom called "national identity." Likewise the promotion of the priorities of natives may even masquerade as an avowedly "antiracist" politics of redress for "native" (racial) "minorities"—a nativism, so to speak, "from the left" (De Genova 2005, 68–79; cf. Balibar 1991a, 15).

Within regimes where citizenship's liberal halo of putatively sacrosanct rights, protections, and entitlements retains its devious allure, then, the deportation of noncitizens may finally be apprehensible as the premier instrumentality for enforcing an absolutist ethics of "native" entitlement. Recall, however, the exceedingly judicious and, indeed, juridical denationalization of European Jews and myriad other so-called undesirables by German fascism (Agamben 1995/1998, 126–35, 166–80), which culminated in the meticulous mass deportation of abject or enemy *citizens*. In this lurid historical light, the deportation regime must finally be situated alongside other prospective resources of state power and sovereignty, including mass incarceration and even extermination.[38] Deportability would therefore have to be seen in a continuum with "detainability" (De Genova 2007). And the freedom of movement would necessarily have to be apprehensible, simultaneously, in opposition not only to deportation and other forms of forced movement but also to coercive immobilization and the full range of diverse forms of "dislocating localization" (Agamben 1995/1998, 175), captivity, and confinement (cf. Walters 2004, 248). In these ways, however, as Sandro Mezzadra has argued, "the problematic of *exclusion*" resurfaces and insinuates itself yet again "within the formal space of citizenship," such that "the condition of migrants can be defined [now] as *paradigmatic*" (2004, 273; italics in original).

THE FREEDOM OF MOVEMENT

> The question of freedom is no longer one of coming and going but one of remaining foreign, of remaining different from others. . . . It is the freedom to change oneself and others.—Vilém Flusser, "Exile and Creativity"

> We, the countless millions of migrants . . . recognize ourselves not as outsiders but as vanguards of the future.—Vilém Flusser, "The Challenge of the Migrant"

At the outset of his intellectual itinerary, Marx famously discerned in the incipient proletariat "a class with *radical chains*"—a class bereft of property, with no standing in civil society, no historical entitlements, and no particular claims, which embodied not a one-sided and self-interested antithesis to modern conditions but rather a complete antithesis to the very premises of capitalism and the modern state. Thus here was a class that was not an estate with a positive station within the social order but rather one that was constituted only negatively, as an abject and "foreign" but inextricable presence, inherently corrosive and always potentially subversive. This class alone revealed "a universal character" and could thus invoke "only a *human* title" (1844b/1975, 186; italics in original). Its very existence as a class was both a symptom and a harbinger of "the *dissolution of the existing world order*," and therefore its own abolition would be its existential vocation (187). Many years later, Marx identified "the basis of the whole process" of the formation of the capitalist class to be those "epoch-making" historical moments "when great masses of men [and women] are suddenly and forcibly torn from their means of subsistence, and hurled onto the labor-market as free, unprotected, and rightless proletarians" (1867/1976, 876). Free. Unprotected. Rightless.

Radical chains were forged, therefore, of a treacherous sort of freedom. The freedom of movement is inseparable in practice from the movement of "free" people, the mobility of free labor, which is, within the global regime of capital accumulation, a freedom that is distinctly circumscribed. This is the freedom to dispose of one's own labor-power as a commodity, as if one were the owner of a commodity like any other. At the same time, this is also the peculiar freedom of being unencumbered by any other means of production with which that elemental capacity for productive labor might be set in motion (272–74). *Vogelfrei*—literally, free as a bird, expelled from any proper human community, entirely exposed and legally unprotected (896n). The capital-labor relation is mediated by money as an exactingly temporary and apparently voluntary contract, a "free" market

relation (strictly juridical in form) between one who buys the virtual commodity that is labor-power and another who is compelled to sell her vital
energies to earn the money necessary for her survival. In Marx's phrase,
those in the latter position are compelled to sell the whole of their active lives in return for the price of their customary means of subsistence,
"to sell [their] birthright for a mess of pottage" (382), "like someone who
has brought his own hide to market and now has nothing else to expect
but—a tanning" (280).

Capitalism commands the great mass of humanity to "willingly" deliver
themselves to one or another contractually delimited employer (likewise
free of any permanent obligations), to work in exchange for money, without which they would face certain destitution and likely starve. In contrast, other (historically prior) forms of exploitation largely relied on unfree labor, bound to a definite spatial location in an enduring condition of
servitude and indefinitely or permanently beholden to a particular master.
For as long as chattel slavery could be sustained in the United States, for
instance, African American homelessness was always already apprehensible as the anomaly of masterlessness, equated with fugitive status and
thus "criminality." Similarly, postemancipation African American mobility always signaled for the propertied classes a dangerously inadequate reconstruction of black servitude, such that their freedom of movement had
likewise to be reconstructed as willful "vagrancy," shadowing literal bond-
age with the ostensible crime of vagabondage (Hopper and Milburn 1996,
124).[39] Such histories, which could abundantly be multiplied (cf. Marx
1867/1976, 896–904), are simply the most brazen and thus revealing examples whereby migration itself has been persistently figured precisely as
desertion from specific regimes of labor subordination (Mezzadra 2004).
As such legacies remind us, and as suggested earlier, there is a long and
complex array of quite bloody histories that have supplied the preconditions for this generalized disenfranchisement and expropriation of the
mass of humanity from any and all alternative means of production, and
consequently, an effectively universal dependency on money—the "silent
compulsion of economic relations" (Marx 1867/1976, 899). And surely
these epochal calamities and upheavals which distinguished what Marx
derisively called "the so-called primitive accumulation" (871–940) have
never ceased to convulsively deliver an ever-widening circle of humanity
into the global market for labor in the abstract. Sheer productive capacity,
creative potential power. Free and unprotected.

A recurrent feature in the larger struggle to subordinate labor to the requirements of capital accumulation, predictably, has nonetheless been its
intermittent mobilization (as in the event of labor shortages) in the form

of migration. And yet, more generally, in order to maintain a captive and tractable workforce, labor subordination tends to require its more or less enduring immobilization—an effective suppression of working people's freedom to "escape" (Mezzadra 2004) their particular predicaments and seek better prospects elsewhere. These immobilizations of labor tend to be enforced through the always contingent and historically specific "territorial definition of coercion" enacted most commonly by national states (Holloway 1994, 31). The unbounded (effectively global) mobility of capital, then, demands that the parallel freedom of movement of laboring humanity—once emancipated from various forms of subjection to precapitalist authority and spatial containment—thereafter be more or less regulated, when not inhibited altogether. Whether mobilized or captive, however, the mobility of labor tends in either case to be more or less stringently encircled and disciplined by the tactics of state power. Deportation reminds us that the radical chains forged of a freedom without rights or protections may serve not simply to confine and fetter us in place but also to drag us mercilessly to the ends of the earth and back again.

The tumultuous, permanent fluidity of the global market in human labor-power, which renders migration a defining feature in the intricate global choreography of capital accumulation, also then renders the ever-widening prospect of deportability a planetary condition. All those who may be conscripted across vast distances into the laborious service of capital may likewise come to be subjected to the caprices of the global deportation regime's Rule of Law and its endless interstate matrix of barbed-wire borders. It is not so much that the plight of migrants is a hideous symptom inherent in the existing universal order, such that the "deportable alien" may be figured as the only point of genuine universality, however (cf. Žižek 1997, 50–51). Rather, if wage labor and its defining mobility indeed signal universal abjection within a global social order premised on private aggrandizement, then deportation looms, ever more ubiquitously, as an abject horizon.

And yet the freedom of movement remains the freedom of life itself, not merely the mundane necessity to make a living but the freedom to truly live. Deportation, as a more or less juridical, more or less arbitrary, exercise of state power, is therefore an exquisitely concentrated abnegation of that freedom, one more usurpation by the state of the sovereign power of humanity itself. The freedom of movement, as an inherently unpredictable and definitively open-ended precondition for human self-determination, can only ever be a perpetual and troublesome affront to the self-anointed sovereignty of state power. It manifests a restless and inassimilable alterity busily working both within and against state power's most cherished ideal: social order. Thus the freedom of movement supplies a defiant reminder that the creative powers of human life, and the sheer vitality of its productive potential, must always exceed every political regime. The deportation regime, then, reveals itself to be a feckless and frenetic machinery, its rigid and convulsive movements doomed to always present but a tawdry caricature of the human freedom that always precedes it and ever surpasses it.

NOTES

The composition of this theoretical overview has benefited greatly from the insightful criticisms and commentary of my coeditor, Nathalie Peutz, as well as the intellectual generosity of Nahum Chandler, Sandro Mezzadra, Magdalena Rodríguez, and Hans-Rudolf Wicker, who each read an earlier draft with exemplary care. This essay has likewise been literally provoked and enriched by the fine work of all the scholars who have contributed chapters to this volume.

1. In his recent study of the history of deportation in the United States, Daniel Kanstroom writes: "We are in the midst of a large-scale, decade-long deportation experiment. The fact that this episode has received rather little public attention renders it no less significant" (2007, ix–x). Seventy-six years earlier, however, already in 1931, Jane Perry Clark had struck a remarkably similar chord: "In the decade from 1920 to 1930 a nostrum often advocated for the ills of the United States was the removal of aliens from the country. The numbers sent forth crept up from 2,762 in 1920 to 16,631 ten years later. Nor is the matter finished, for the Commissioner General of Immigration tells us 'the task of house-cleaning has practically only just begun. To continue the work and do it thoroughly is the big job ahead.' Considering the importance of the problems involved in sending aliens from the country and the increasing emphasis upon them, it is somewhat surprising that the deportation law and its administration have been so little examined. So far as can be ascertained, no study has been made of the law as it appears on the statute books and in actual administration, nor has the problem been approached in the light of the social and international questions involved" (1931/1969, 9). I am grateful to Nathalie Peutz for bringing these references to my attention and suggesting their striking juxtaposition.

2. Here Agamben is responding critically to Foucault, whom he faults for having never resolved an ambiguity in his own work regarding the intersection or convergence of "these two faces of power" (1995/1998, 5). Foucault refers to these "political structures of individualization techniques and of totalization procedures" within modern state power as "a tricky combination," unforeseen in human history (1982, 782).

3. Indeed, Arellano's act of defiance provided new direction and inspiration to the movement for "immigrants' rights." Following the Arellano sanctuary, members of seven denominational and interdenominational organizations,

including representatives of twelve religious traditions from eighteen cities, convened in Washington, D.C., on January 29, 2007, to establish a "new sanctuary movement" for migrants seeking refuge from "unjust deportations." See http://www.newsanctuarymovement.org; see also Abramsky 2008; Shahani 2008. For an extended ethnographic study of the sanctuary movement that arose during the 1980s in defense of Central American asylum seekers in the United States, see Coutin 1993. For related discussions of sanctuary as a tactic in the struggles of deportable migrants, also see the chapters by Nyers and Walters in this volume. Beyond the immigrants' rights movement, moreover, Arellano became an important symbol for Latino political movements more broadly. In Chicago, in a truly extraordinary gesture of inter-Latino political unity, the Twenty-ninth Annual Puerto Rican People's Parade (2007) nominated Arellano and her son as honorary grand marshals, and the procession mobilized thousands of predominantly Puerto Rican marchers (all U.S. citizens by colonial birthright) to celebrate her resistance and salute her through a window at the site of her sanctuary, where she waved a Puerto Rican national flag.

4. While Arellano's case is extraordinary, it is important to note the analogies here with the theme of entrapment of undocumented migrants more generally, as elaborated in this volume with specific regard to the U.S.-Mexico border region by Talavera, Núñez, and Heyman; see also the essays in this volume by Castañeda; Willen; cf. Coutin 2000, 27–47; Gehrig 2004; Nijhawan 2005; Rouse 1992.

5. Indeed, the U.S. Bureau of Immigration and Customs Enforcement concludes its press statement announcing Arellano's deportation with a smug triumphalism scarcely veiled by its understatement: "In the first 10 months of this fiscal year, the agency carried out more than 220,000 alien removals" (USDHS-ICE 2007).

6. It is important to note that Agamben's conception of bare life is substantially an elaboration of Walter Benjamin's discussion of "mere life" in his "Critique of Violence" (1921/1979, 151–53), wherein mere life signals the point where "the rule of law over the living ceases" because lawmaking violence is a "bloody power over mere life" for the sake of nothing but that same violence (151). I am grateful to Nahum Chandler for pressing me on this point. Agamben acknowledges this genealogy in a brief passage (1995/1998, 65).

7. Here again it is instructive to compare Agamben's sense with that of Benjamin, who elaborates a sense of mere life as analogous to the notion of mere "existence" in contradistinction to "life" as "the irreducible, total condition that is 'man' " and insists, "Man cannot, at any price, be said to coincide with the mere life in him" (1921/1979, 152, 153). Similarly, Agamben treats bare life as "that naked supposedly common element that is always possible to isolate in each of the numerous forms of life," in juxtaposition with "a life that can never be separated from its form" (1996/2000, 3), "in which the single ways, acts, and processes of living are never simply *facts* but always and above all *possibilities* of life," such that "no matter how customary, repeated, and socially compulsory . . .

it always puts at stake living itself," making human beings "the only beings for whom happiness is always at stake in their living" (4), "beings that cannot be defined by any proper operation—that is, beings of pure potentiality that no identity or vocation can possibly exhaust" (141).

8. For merely one rather high-profile example of this oversimplified misreading of Agamben, see Judith Butler's emphatic repudiation of the pertinence of the concept of bare life with regard to the condition of those whom the state expels or banishes through acts and formations of coercion "designed to produce and maintain the condition . . . of the dispossessed" (Butler and Spivak 2007, 5); Butler here equates "bare life" with being "outside of politics" (5) and juxtaposes this with the situation of those who are "without legal recourse" but "still under the control of state power," whose predicament she describes as "a life steeped in power" (9). Yet for Agamben, this is precisely what "bare life" is intended to name, as the ensuing discussion will demonstrate.

9. Notably, Agamben is prudent about not reifying bare life: "For bare life is certainly as indeterminate and impenetrable as [pure Being], and one could say that reason cannot think bare life except . . . in stupor and astonishment." Instead bare life remains an "empty" concept (1995/1998, 182).

10. Arellano was charged with and convicted for a federal felony; not only had she secured employment on the basis of a fraudulent Social Security number, which is a commonplace practice among undocumented migrants working in the United States, but she had done so specifically at a major airport, which was targeted by a highly publicized national enforcement sweep, called Operation Tarmac, directed against "security breaches" at airports in the year after the events of September 11, 2001. Because she had previously been deported, her reentry into the United States was also classifiable as a felony.

11. The freedom of movement for subjects *within* the parameters of a (nation-) state has been one significant historical achievement of citizenship, after all (see Walters, this volume). Furthermore, it has been a hallmark of both modern colonial empires and contemporary neoliberal reconfigurations of "globalized" citizenship that restricted mobility or outright immobilization for some is paralleled by enhanced freedom of movement for others (Hindess 2004, 311; cf. Bigo 2002, 2006; Hindess 2002; Kapur 2007; Stasiulis and Ross 2006; Walters 2004).

12. As Agamben notes emphatically, however, even the juxtaposition of something like "biological" (human) life in contradistinction to (human) life as it comes to be specifically inscribed socially or politically is ultimately untenable and merely signals a "secularization" of the figure of bare or naked life, which is an irreducibly *political* concept in the first place. Thus such juxtapositions thereby recapitulate the *separation* of the figure of bare life from the sociopolitical order whose putative sovereignty is premised on its subordination (1996/2000, 6, 7).

13. For heuristic purposes here, Marx analyzes labor transhistorically—"independently of any specific social formation" (1867/1976, 283), and "in a form

in which it is an exclusively human characteristic," which is to say, with an emphatic distinction between the consciously premeditated and purposeful characteristics of human labor and the instinctual work of some other species, such as bees constructing a hive or beavers building dams (283–84). Notably, the analytic distinction between "labor" and "work" underscored by Hannah Arendt (1958/1998, 79–135) in her critique of Marx originates precisely from what begins ontologically as a zone of indistinction in Marx's own elaboration (which Arendt depicts as equivocation and a "fundamental and flagrant" contradiction [104]). For Marx, this sense of the inextricability of human life from labor only thereafter is further specified in terms of the decisive analytical difference between the labor process in general (i.e., "independently of any specific social formation" [1867/1976, 283], "in its simple and abstract elements . . . [as] a universal condition for the metabolic interaction of man and nature, the everlasting nature-imposed condition of human existence . . . common to all forms of society" [290]) and the labor process as one of alienation and exploitation, "by which the capitalist consumes labor-power" (291).

14. Evgeny Pashukanis provides the classic if underappreciated elaboration of Marx's insights regarding "the precipitation of a political authority as a separate power, functioning alongside the purely economic power of money" (1929/1989, 40), accompanying "direct, unmediated class rule" with "indirect, reflected rule in the shape of official state power as a distinct authority, detached from society" (138), taking on the form of "an impersonal apparatus of public power" (139).

15. Agamben's formulation of sovereignty (as the decision regarding the state of exception) is deeply shaped by Carl Schmitt's avowedly fascist "political theology" (Schmitt 1922/1985). Anticipating the explicitly "theological" apotheosis of the state elaborated by Schmitt's propositions regarding "the metaphysical kernel of all politics" (51), Marx notably remarks: "The political state, in relation to civil society, is just as spiritual as is heaven in relation to earth. It stands in the same opposition to civil society, and overcomes it in the same manner as religion overcomes the narrowness of the profane world; i.e., it has to acknowledge it again, re-establish it, and allow itself to be dominated by it" (1843/1978, 34). Thus "the *criticism of religion* [turns] into the *criticism of law* and the *criticism of theology* into the *criticism of politics*" (1844a/1975, 176; italics in original). Pashukanis similarly cites Friedrich Engels as having characterized "the juridical way of looking at things [as] the classical world view of the bourgeoisie" and moreover as "a kind of 'secularization of the theological,' in which . . . the state takes the place of the church" (1929/1989, 33).

16. "The analysis, made in terms of power," Foucault likewise contends, "must not assume that the sovereignty of the state, the form of the law, or the over-all unity of domination are given at the outset; rather these are only the terminal forms power takes" (1976/1978, 92).

17. Foucault makes his position still more explicit: "There is no binary and all-encompassing opposition between rulers and ruled at the root of power re-

lations, and serving as a general matrix" (1976/1978, 94). Étienne Balibar has characterized this "ideal type of pure politics . . . neither caught in ideology nor in economy"—approvingly, but nonetheless suggestively—as Foucault's "utopia" (Bojadžijev and Saint-Saëns 2006, 25).

18. Notably, Foucault's discussion of what he calls "the anatomo-politics of the human body," as evinced through disciplinary power in the more strict sense, "centered on the body as a machine: its disciplining, the optimization of its forces" (1976/1978, 139). "It was a mechanism of power," he elaborates elsewhere in a related discussion, "that made it possible to extract time and labor . . . from bodies" (1976/2003, 35–36). In spite of this emphasis on the "forces" of human bodies, associated above all with labor, Foucault nonetheless seems to be either impervious or averse to the idea that power might in fact derive therefrom.

19. Foucault depicts the emergence of "a new mechanism of power" in the seventeenth and eighteenth centuries, " 'disciplinary' power," which is "absolutely incompatible with relations of sovereignty" (1976/2003, 35), its "exact, point-for-point opposite," which "can therefore no longer be transcribed in terms of sovereignty" and "should logically have led to the complete disappearance of the great juridical edifice of the theory of sovereignty" (36).

20. Jacques Rancière, for instance, critiques Agamben's position as one in which "sovereign power is the same as biopower," whereby "politics is equated with power, a power that is increasingly taken as an overwhelming historico-ontological destiny from which only a God is likely to save us" (Rancière 2004, 300, 302).

21. This is a point which tends to be lost in more depoliticized readings of Agamben, usually restricted to the more esoteric *Homo Sacer* (1995), which likewise lends itself to a more narrowly Foucauldian interpretation.

22. Here one might detect significant resonances between Agamben's position and Hannah Arendt's pronounced aversion to sovereignty in her essay "What Is Freedom?": "The famous sovereignty of political bodies has always been an illusion, which, moreover, can be maintained only by means of violence, that is, with essentially non-political means. Under human conditions, which are determined by the fact that not man but men live on earth, freedom and sovereignty are so little identical that they cannot even exist simultaneously. Where men wish to be sovereign, as individuals or as organized groups, they must submit to the oppression of the will, be this, the individual will with which I force myself, or the 'general will' of an organized group. If men wish to be free, it is precisely sovereignty they must renounce" (1954/1968, 164–65; cf. 1958/1998, 234–35). Notably, however, Arendt's position retains a stubbornly liberal commitment to a notion of the genuinely "political" as analytically opposed to violence and somehow innocent of all oppression. We might venture to call this Arendt's utopia (see Balibar's remark in note 17), an "ideal type of pure politics" if ever there was one.

23. Agamben explicitly notes that this "Marxian scission between man and citizen is thus superseded by the division between naked life (ultimate and

opaque bearer of sovereignty) and the multifarious forms of life abstractly re-codified as social-juridical identities" (1996/2000, 5), but he suggests that the classic (bourgeois-democratic) distinction of man and citizen is itself nonetheless the necessary precondition for the inscription of naked or bare life, as such, and therefore proposes his concept of "form-of-life" as an alternative that could facilitate the abandonment of the very notion of bare life (11; cf. 1995/1998, 188).

24. Here Foucault concurs with Marx and Agamben. Foucault accounts for the survival of the theory of sovereignty through its "democratization," which "made it possible to superimpose on the mechanism of discipline a system of right that concealed its mechanisms and erased the element of domination and the techniques of domination involved in discipline," establishing "a public right articulated with collective sovereignty . . . heavily ballasted by the mechanisms of disciplinary coercion" (1976/2003, 37).

25. Agamben likewise calls into question "every attempt to ground political communities on something like a 'belonging,' whether it be founded on popular, national, religious, or any other identity" (1995/1998, 181).

26. Agamben himself cites the phenomenon of "illegal immigration" as evidence and justification of his perspective and explicitly notes the analogy of this "de facto statelessness" of the undocumented with that of refugees (1996/2000, 22).

27. For a thoughtful critique of the elision of the figure of the refugee, alternately, with "statelessness" or "rightlessness," however, see Macklin 2007.

28. For an instructive discussion of Paolo Virno's analogous critique of Agamben's uncritical appropriation of the Foucauldian concept of biopolitics, elaborated in terms of labor-power, see Neilson 2004. Virno (translated from the Italian by Neilson) remarks: "The living body, stripped of any quality that is not pure vitality, becomes the *substratum* of the productive capacity, the tangible *sign* of potential, or the objective *simulacrum* of non-objectified work. If money is the universal equivalent for exchange-values, life is the extrinsic equivalent of the only use-value 'not materialised in the product.' . . . The non-mythological origin of . . . *biopolitics* can be traced back to *labor-power*" (76; italics in original). See also the English translation of an interview with Virno, first published in Spanish: "The problem is, I believe, that the biopolitical is only an effect derived from the concept of labor-power" (Virno 2002).

29. For an elaboration of the proposition that the capitalist labor process is characterized by a "despotic" form, see Marx 1867/1976, 44–50.

30. It is noteworthy that in contexts such as that which prevails in the United States, where workplace immigration raids provide a major impetus for the deportation machinery, deportees also tend to always make their (re)appearance (in their countries of origin), likewise, clad in their work clothes (see Peutz, this volume; cf. De Genova 2005, 243–44).

31. If the multiplicity of specific forms of concrete laboring activities only achieve a semblance of universality—as "abstract labor"—through their gener-

alized commodification and the materialization of their value-form as money (Marx 1867/1976, 125–63), then the state, I am arguing (following Holloway 1994, following Pashukanis 1929/1989), acquires its own illusory universality only as a similarly alienated and fetishized reification of precisely the real universality of the abstraction of human labor once it has been subsumed within the effectively global regime of capital accumulation.

32. Notably, colonial state formations often complemented this binary division with a third term—the (noncitizen) *subject*—which produced an analogous bifurcation internally (Hindess 2004, 309–10; see also Mamdani 1996; Mezzadra 2006).

33. The requirements of a neoliberal global order may increasingly be altering this dynamic, however. Hindess (2002), Muller (2004), Ong (1999, 2006), Stasiulis (2004), and Stasiulis and Ross (2006) variously argue for evidence of an increasingly differentiated denationalization of citizenship, "flexibilized" or "hybridized" in distinctly transnational terms.

34. "Territorialism embodies an ethic of inclusiveness and equality," notes Linda Bosniak. "It is the ground (both literally and figuratively) of national community belonging" (2007, 395; cf. 2006, 122–40).

35. Some of these impulses toward immigration restriction or exclusion notably may nonetheless retain comparably liberal commitments to "democratic" notions of majoritarian social contract and consent (e.g., Schuck and Smith 1985; cf. Bosniak 1998; Hindess 2004).

36. It is instructive, for instance, that the U.S. Constitution includes a provision stipulating that no U.S. president may be a (merely) naturalized citizen but rather must have been born in the country (cf. Anderson 1994).

37. Indeed, as I have considered elsewhere for the example of contemporary Latino and Asian racial formations in the United States (De Genova 2006), such apparent anachronisms may themselves animate precisely what is new about these formations that Balibar has called "neo-racisms" (1991b; cf. 1991c).

38. Indeed, it is instructive to recall that the Nazi concentration and extermination camps were significantly slave labor camps, devoted to the concentration of living labor, instrumentally organizing a sinister process of selection that culminated in the slow "annihilation through work" of the most able-bodied Jewish inmates (Black 2001, 491), rather than death camps, pure and simple.

39. I am grateful to Lynn Lewis, whose research as an activist and scholar concerned with race and homelessness in the United States clarified for me this particular reference and the convergence of these themes.

PART TWO ⟿ *Sovereignty and Space*

—⟋⟍—

CHAPTER 1

Deportation, Expulsion, and the International Police of Aliens

> See the world through different eyes! Travel in exotic style with Lufthansa's Deportation Class service. Don't miss out—act now to take advantage of our specially priced low fares from North America or Europe to destinations all over the world. We are constantly expanding and improving our Deportation Class service, which remains the most economical way to travel the globe. With Lufthansa Deportation Class you can now reach dozens of exciting destinations worldwide—Tunis, Damascus, Jakarta, Alma Ata, Harare, Lima, Quito . . .—http://www.deportation-class.com (accessed October 13, 2006)

This little piece of political satire comes from the website deportation-class.com.[1] Anti-deportation activism has for some time been one of the more prominent and visible aspects of political campaigns against exclusion and restrictionist immigration policies in western Europe. Among the most notable of these have been the sanctuary movements, including the occupation of churches by people threatened with deportation,[2] and protests at airports targeting airlines that regularly transport deportees. But recently some activists have shifted their emphasis away from a focus on individual anti-deportation actions to the targeting of major national airline companies. Just as clean-clothes campaigns have engaged in "image-polluting" campaigns against high-profile brands like Nike and the Gap, these groups and networks subvert the typical images, colors, logos, and themes of airlines and holiday imagery, revealing their connection to deportation. The aim is to strike at the system's commercial vulnerability. One of the more imaginative of these is the Deportation Class project affiliated with the German antiracist network Kein Mensch Ist Illegal,[3] from which this chapter's epigraph comes.

What is so significant about these tactics is how they unsettle our view of deportation. From seeing it as merely the unpleasant branch of a refugee and immigration system, we apprehend deportation in a different light: as an industry. Instead of seeing it as an administrative procedure, we are provoked into seeing it as a system that implicates all manner of agents—not just police and immigration officials but airline executives, pilots, stewards, and other passengers. Most pointedly, we are reminded that private companies profit from this form of suffering. Deportation is business. Immediately one makes connections with other moments in the history of the mass-orchestrated and forced movement of people. The history of transportation, for instance, is replete with stories of greedy shipping companies that were contracted to ship England's "criminal class" to New South Wales. But we are also struck by the fact that deportation is political and open to contestation. Deportation Class displaces the practice of deportation. It enables us to recognize it in terms of other lineages of practices. In this way, it unsettles our present.

The aim of this chapter is to contribute to this process of rethinking and expanding what we understand by deportation, not at the level of its popular representation but by subjecting the practice of deportation to historical and genealogical analysis. Deportation has been studied in terms of international law (Goodwin-Gill 1978; Henckaerts 1995; Pelonpää 1984). It is also increasingly the subject of policy sciences that seek to make it more efficient and humane (Koser 2000). But with a couple of notable exceptions,[4] deportation has not been studied as a political or historical practice, as a disciplinary tactic and an instrument of population regulation. Frank Caestecker is therefore correct to observe that "whereas immigration and refugee policy have already been closely scrutinized, the historical analysis of expulsion policy is still in its infancy" (1998, 96). This is somewhat surprising, since other forms of expulsion and forced migration—such as ethnic cleansing (Bell-Fialkoff 1993; Jackson Preece 1998; McGarry 1998), religious expulsion (Kedar 1996), the transportation of criminals (Hughes 1986), political exile, and population transfer (de Zayas 1985, 1988; Rieber 2000)—have indeed been subjected to such critical scrutiny. Perhaps it is the case that these other forms appear so draconian. Deportation, because it remains embedded within the contemporary administrative practice of Western states, strikes us as less remarkable.

The genealogical study of deportation as a practice of power is valid and timely not just as a means to enhance our understanding of a relatively ignored but highly pertinent aspect of public policy. More broadly, this chapter makes a contribution to the genealogical investigation of modern citizenship. Citizenship studies is now a vast field. This chapter concerns itself with but one area within this larger domain, namely, the growing subfield of research exploring citizenship in terms of the citizen-alien relationship (Bauböck 1994a, 1994b; Benhabib 1999; Carens 1995; Soysal 1994), as well as the relationship between the citizen and other figures of alterity (Isin 2002). Following Benhabib (1999), we can note that these investigations of the alien-citizen complex can be grouped into normative, political philosophy, and sociological approaches. The sociological perspectives, she suggests, view citizenship in terms of key *social practices* such as "collective identity" and "social rights and benefits." This chapter is situated closer to the sociological pole. However, it will assume a somewhat different conception of social practice from this. In highlighting deportation, I am engaging with practices that are *constitutive* of citizenship. Put differently, I will be treating deportation as a "technology of citizenship" (Cruikshank 1999). What I have in mind here are the spatial practices that Engin Isin suggests are the central but often ignored factors in the formation of group identities and relations. As he puts it: "Groups cannot materialize themselves as real without realizing themselves in space, without creating configurations of buildings, patterns, and arrangements, and symbolic representations of these arrangements" (Isin 2002, 43). To this end, he reminds us that buildings like the guildhall, configurations like the forum, and arrangements like the assembly play an irreducible role in the constitution of citizenship.

Many of the technologies that Isin discusses involve the constitution of citizenship at the level of the city. I want to push the concept in a different direction, toward the space(s) of international and global relations. In studying deportation, I will be tackling one of the constitutive practices by which citizenship is implicated in what Barry Hindess terms "the international management of population." Western discussions of citizenship have largely considered citizenship as "an aspect of life within a state" (Hindess 2000, 1495). However, Hindess argues that "to properly understand the modern, international culture of citizenship we have to look at the role of citizenship in the overall government of the population covered by the modern state system" (1495). He suggests that we need to see citizenship not only in terms of rights, responsibilities, and identities *within* a polity but also "as a marker of identification, advising state and nonstate agencies of the particular state to which an individual belongs." In this view, the remarkable thing about citizenship is that it represents a regime that regulates the "division of humanity into distinct national populations" and operates "as a dispersed regime of governance of the larger human population." We will see that while the ends and the functions of expulsion have been historically variable, the modern practice of deportation is central to the allocation of populations to states.

This chapter pursues a twofold strategy to historicize and problematize deportation as a political practice. In the first section, I situate it within a wider field of historical practices. Here I develop the theme that we can understand deportation as a particular form of expulsion. We should not take for granted its location within contemporary immigration policy or its connection with the government of aliens. By considering some of the various ways in which people have been expelled, cast out, or banished, the reasons given and the methods chosen, we can grasp something of the particularity of deportation. In the second section, I set the practice of deportation within a different analytical field—forms of power. This links deportation to wider questions concerning the government of population. Far from being merely an unchanging administrative routine or a procedure subject to gradual and humane evolution, deportation might be seen in terms of certain governmental practices. Here I argue that deportation has affinities to the international police of population. In the final section, I consider the detention centers and other carceral spaces that are today a part of the deportation game, and relate them to Giorgio Agamben's (1995/1998) thematization of "the camp." Though the practice of deportation might seem to imply abstract, international spaces rather than the more intimate, lived spaces of the city, we will see that it can be theoretically and empirically grounded in the figure of the camp.

FORMS OF EXPULSION

What is deportation, and what might we learn about it by seeing it as a particular form of expulsion? Immediately we need to confront a terminological question. Goodwin-Gill begins one of the more extended treatments of the subject in international law with the following observation: "The word 'expulsion' is commonly used to describe that exercise of State power which secures the removal, either 'voluntarily,' under threat of forcible removal, or forcibly, of an alien from the territory of a State" (1978, 201). Goodwin-Gill notes that terminologies vary from state to state. For instance, at certain times in its history, the United States reserved the term "deportation" to refer strictly to proceedings initiated at a port of entry designed to send aliens on their way after refusal of admission. Henckaerts (1995, 5) notes that "expulsion" is more generally used in international law, whereas "deportation" is more common in municipal law. In what follows, I take "deportation" to refer generally to the removal of aliens by state power from the territory of that state, either "voluntarily," under threat of force, or forcibly. This is how the term is commonly used in many countries today. By using "deportation" in this way, I am able to retain "expulsion" as a term to refer to a much broader field of practices. This field encompasses the forced or mandated removal of individuals and groups from territories under the authority of political, and some-times quasi-legal and private, authorities. In this way, we will be able to specify deportation as one particular type of expulsion, albeit one that now occupies a central place in modern immigration policy.

In the following section, I compare deportation with other forms of ex-pulsion. I make no claim as to the exhaustiveness of my list.[5] Nor do I want to imply these are in any way watertight or mutually exclusive categories. The point is simply to capture something of the historical specificity of deportation, in terms of its subjects, its characteristic forms of reason and purpose, its social and political assumptions, and its methods.

Exile

"Exile is the most ancient custom of all nations." These were the words chosen by Bernardo Tanucci, minister to the king of Naples, to justify the expulsion of the Jesuits from the Kingdom of Naples (Delle Donne 1970, 142; Kedar 1996, 172). While Tanucci may have been exaggerating for ef-fect, we can nevertheless concede that exile is indeed an ancient practice. Exile is used against the individual who is understood to be a member of the political community or nation. It is used as a form of punishment, but also security. Typical encyclopedia entries reveal that in ancient Greece, exile was often the penalty for homicide, while ostracism was reserved for those guilty of political crimes.[6] Athenian law on ostracism gave the Popular Assembly the opportunity once a year to vote whether to banish for ten years the citizen considered most dangerous to the establishment (Thomsen 1972). In early Rome the citizen under sentence of death had the choice between exile and death. The Romans used the word *deporta-tio* to mean banishment to some outlying place within the empire, often an island (Kedar 1996, 166). Exile was also a common form of punishment in the late Middle Ages, when, again, it had a strong class component. Exile for the poor could often result in banishment from their town only to find the gallows waiting where they sought refuge. For the rich it could be a less severe form of punishment, allowing for travel, business, and the prospect of an early and glorious return (Rusche and Kirchheimer 1939, 20). Generally exile seems to have had the function of transmuting or lessening the punishment for serious crimes. The Italian jurist Beccaria recommended banishment in cases where individuals were guilty of disturbing the public peace, but also in cases where they were accused of some great crime but there was no certainty of guilt. It left the accused "the sacred right" of proving his innocence. Banishment was a practice that "nullifies all ties between society and the delinquent citizen." In such cases, "the citizen dies and the man remains. With respect to the body politic, [civil death] should produce the same effect as natural death" (Beccaria 1963, 53; brackets in the original). It is perhaps this type of political reason that Foucault has in mind when he equates expulsion with a form of "political death."[7]

This idea that with banishment and exile the citizen is liquidated, leaving only some kind of bare human, is one that is echoed powerfully in more contemporary reflections on the practice of deportation and the experience of the refugee. For Hannah Arendt, the political condition of the stateless did not even approximate that of a prison inmate, who, though deprived of various freedoms, was nevertheless still within the political and legal order. The experience of the stateless was altogether more dangerous and unprecedented. They represented "a new kind of human being—the kind that are put in concentration camps by their foes and in internment camps by their friends" (Arendt 1994, 111). They had lost the "right to have rights" (Arendt 1951/1966, 296).

For Arendt the fate of the refugee was to endure "the abstract nakedness of being human and nothing but human" (297). More recently Giorgio Agamben has developed this insight, arguing for the political significance of liminal experiences like banishment and the contemporary condition of statelessness. These phenomena reveal how Western politics are founded on a particular relationship to, and politicization of, "bare life." "In Western politics, bare life has the peculiar privilege of being that whose exclusion founds the city of men" (Agamben 1995/1998, 7). Whereas Foucault (1976/1978) places the entry of biological life into politics on the threshold of modernity, for Agamben it is much more ancient. Modern declarations of the rights of man further inscribed bare life within the political order. However, it took the Holocaust, in particular the terrible space of the Nazi concentration camp, to reveal how bare life can become exposed. Within the camps, bare life inhabits an indeterminate zone both within and beyond the political order, where it is placed at the mercy of sovereign power. According to Agamben, today's global refugee crisis, coupled with the vast numbers of people involved in clandestine work and migration, points to a growing disjunction between a politics organized in terms of nation-states and bare life. The camp is both a symptom and a response to this crisis.

The Expulsion of the Poor

The second kind of expulsion I want to consider is associated with poor policy in early modern Europe. In his magisterial account of the rise of a capitalist market order in England, Karl Polanyi draws our attention to the fact that land and money were liberalized and mobilized before, and therefore in contradiction with, labor. For our purposes, the salient feature of Polanyi's account is the Act of Settlement and Removal of 1662. This established the principles of "parish serfdom" and was not loosened until 1795. The act cemented parish responsibility for the poor and sought at the same time to protect the "better" parishes from an influx of paupers. "Only with the good will of the local magistrate could a man stay in any other but his home parish; everywhere else he was liable to expulsion even though in good standing and employed" (Polanyi 1957, 88). These provisions were considered harsh and were later amended so that only those who were likely to become recipients of poor relief were subject to removal (Clark 1931/1969, 34).

Since the early poor law was notoriously fragmented and uneven in its operation, the act no doubt proved difficult to enforce. Nevertheless the determination to restrict relief to the local poor, as well as the denial of such rights to foreigners, was a general feature of western Europe in the sixteenth and seventeenth centuries. Here we find an important source of modern deportation practice. The policing of the foreign poor becomes, by the late nineteenth century, a major preoccupation of deportation policy. The vital qualification, of course, is that in the sixteenth and seventeenth centuries, the foreigner is not defined in national terms. As John Torpey notes in his historical sociology of the regulation of movement: "Historical evidence indicates clearly that, well into the nineteenth century, people routinely regarded as 'foreign' those from the next province every bit as much as those who came from other 'countries'" (1999, 9). As modern aliens policy takes shape in the nineteenth century, with deportation as an important weapon in its armory, it will reproduce this poor law logic, but increasingly in a context where the salient distinction is not local versus foreigner but national versus foreigner.[8] Hence we can agree with Leo Lucassen, who notes that in earlier centuries "the restriction of the poor relief by the cities formed a prelude to the national aliens policy of later days" (1997, 249).

Corporate Expulsion

If expulsion on the basis of nationality and state membership is a relatively recent phenomenon, expulsion on the basis of group membership is not. This is a kind of expulsion that Kedar (1996) distinguishes from exile on the grounds that it involves the banishment of an entire category of subjects beyond the physical boundaries of a political entity—whether principality, town, city-state, or absolutist state. Whereas exile is typically targeted at specific individuals, here we encounter the expulsion of collective subjects. Without doubt, the basis that recurs most frequently for corporate expulsion is religion. From the end of the Middle Ages, expulsion serves as "a radical and important tool of governance" situated along a continuum between massacre and conversion, aiming to police the religious beliefs and practices of populations (Kedar 1996, 174). While the religious persecution of Christians was certainly a feature of political life in Rome, or of non-Zoroastrians in Persia, during the Middle Ages such persecution was institutionalized for substantial periods (Bell-Fialkoff 1993, 112). Jews were a frequent target for such expulsions—for instance, from England (1290), France (1306), Spain (1492), Cracow (1494), and Portugal (1497). Similarly, in this category we should note the expulsion from Spain of Muslims in 1526 and Moriscos (converted Muslims) in 1609–14.

That questions of religion and political loyalty are intertwined is clear by the sixteenth century. Corporate expulsion can be seen as a tool of state formation, occurring against the backdrop of the breakup of the universal church. Indeed, for some observers, its frequency and concentration in the western part of Europe are related to the fact that it goes hand in hand with the emergence of the modern state system there (Kedar 1996, 175). The expulsion of Irish Catholics from Ulster in 1688, making land available for settlement by English and Scottish Protestants, fits this pattern. The strategic motive was to deny Catholic France and Spain a base for operations against England. Similarly, the revocation of the Edict of Nantes in 1685, which prompted the flight of thousands of Protestant Huguenots from France, reveals a certain connection between expulsion and confessional conflict.

Transportation

As far as western Europe is concerned, by the eighteenth century, Alfred Rieber argues that "expulsion as an official policy of dealing with 'the other,' however perceived, gave way to various forms of internal control and integration into a state system shaped by the consolidation of the secular power of the national monarch around a centralized bureaucracy and professional army" (2000, 5). He gives the impression that expulsion was a sort of convulsion accompanying the birth of the modern state system, but as states matured, political authorities soon found other means to regulate their populations. This argument is attractive because it moves us away from seeing expulsion in singular or exceptional terms and regards it as belonging instead to a repertoire of techniques of social regulation and, in this case, state building.

However, the argument that expulsion waned with the consolidation of modern state power in western Europe works only when confined to the government of religious dissidents.[9] The advantage of framing our inquiry in terms of *forms* of expulsion is that we identify other practices of expulsion that operate in relation to different historical trajectories. There is no singular expulsion. This is clear if we take the case of the transportation of convicts and political exiles. If the emergence of a more or less settled system of states in western Europe saw the withering of the corporate expulsion of religious dissidents and "minorities," the external practices of colonization beyond Europe and internal practices of social repression underpinning these states saw the opening of a political context for this different type of expulsion.

With transportation we encounter a form of expulsion with certain resemblances to exile. These include its use as a form of punishment for political as well as civil crimes, its deployment to commute a death sentence, and in some cases its holding out the possibility of return. But it differs in several key respects. First, it has a strong utilitarian underpinning. Transportation combines the tactics of exile and forced removal with projects of territorial colonization and economic exploitation. Spain and Portugal had attempted this as early as the fifteenth century, but England was the first country to employ the transportation of criminals in a systematic way. George Rusche and Otto Kirchheimer argue that the Vagrancy Act of 1597 legalized deportation for the first time. The act stated that "such rogues as shall be thought fitt not to be delivered shall be banyshed out of this Realme and all the domynions thereof and shall be conveied to such parttes beyond the seas as shall be at any tyme hereafter for that purpose assigned by the Private Counsell" (Rusche and Kirchheimer 1939, 59). Colonies like Virginia and Maryland were among the first to receive England's poor and undesirable. But this was not to last. With the availability of an alternative supply of forced labor in the form of slaves transported from Africa, and with the liberation of the colonies from the monarchy after the American Revolution, the transportation of convicts to North America was soon brought to an end. Rather, it was Australia, and especially New South Wales, where this experiment in recycling convicts would be taken to its furthest point (Hughes 1986). Between 1787 and 1868, when agitation by settled free laborers brought an end to the policy, over eighty thousand convicts and political prisoners were shipped to Australia. Yet Britain was by no means alone in pursuing this practice, even if it did undertake it on an unparalleled scale. Until 1898 France used its colonies in New Caledonia for transportation purposes, including its exiles from the Paris Commune, and French transportation of convicts to Guiana was only finally abolished in 1937. Interesting also are the cases of countries like Germany that, without appreciable colonies in the nineteenth century, sought arrangements with other colonial powers for the transportation of their criminals or simply sold them as slaves. For instance, Prussia had an agreement with Russia to accept Prussian convicts in Siberia (Rusche and Kirchheimer 1939, 123–25). In such international relations of coerced migration, we hear echoes of contemporary practices like the "safe third country" agreement.

This connection with colonization explains aspects of transportation's genesis, but also, by the end of the nineteenth century, its increasing political impossibility. Yet transportation differs in other ways from the practice of exile or corporate expulsion. We should also note at this point that transportation is a mass phenomenon carried out on a routine, almost bureaucratic basis. Exile was less often a mass phenomenon. More typically it targeted the influential or those with political prestige. It is perhaps a compromise between the subject and the sovereign. Transportation is a mass exercise. Spurred on by the overcrowding of gaols and colonialism's thirst for unfree labor, and targeting the nameless and the faceless, transportation democratizes the practice of exile.

Population Transfer

The final form of expulsion that I want to highlight in this genealogy of deportation is "population transfer." If corporate expulsion is a form of expulsion that reflected the Treaty of Augsburg's principle of *cujus regio ejus religio*—the religion of the state is that of the prince—then population transfer belongs to a more recent time, an age of biopolitics when principles of ethnic, racial, and national homogeneity have displaced or reinscribed religion as the marker for political order.

Population transfer is the neutral, technical name that national and international experts gave to more or less planned mass movements ("voluntary" and "forced") of people that convulsed Europe throughout the first half of the twentieth century. Population transfer was a policy to address what Europe understood as its "problem of minorities." This "problem" was in turn the expression of, and the obstacle to, the application of the principle of nationalities to the political map of Europe, especially its central and southeastern areas (Jackson Preece 1998). As new national states emerged with the breakup of the old Kingdom of Prussia and the Ottoman and Austro-Hungarian empires, the phenomenon of national "minorities" located within the territory of other national states became acute. The perception, especially under the circumstances of the world wars, was that the separatist and irredentist practices of these groups would undermine national and international security. If the political norm was one of self-determination for national peoples, and the idea that each state should be a "home" for its people, and conversely that each people should be represented by a state, then population transfer was one technique fashioned to meet this end. In this respect, population transfer belongs to a series of methods for governing the problem of minorities including minority treaties, the redrawing of borders, the staging of plebiscites, and the most dreadful measure of all—genocide.

An early instance of population transfer was the "exchange" of thousands of minorities between Greece and Turkey, under the supervision of the League of Nations and the terms of the Treaty of Lausanne (1923). Other exchanges involved Bulgaria (de Zayas 1988, 1989). But World War II saw increasing use of population transfer, with Nazi Germany as one of its leading and most murderous practitioners. Ethnic Germans were repatriated from Romania, Estonia, Yugoslavia, Bulgaria, and many other states. At the same time, through a combination of resettlement and genocide, Nazi Germany sought to "cleanse" itself of Jews, Slavs, and other groups that it regarded as antisocial or subhuman. In the Nazi state, then, population transfer, understood as a program of Germanification, was taken to its apocalyptic extreme.

Yet it would be wrong to see population transfer and other forms of forced "racial adjustment" as confined to the policy of the Nazi state. While today it might be associated with ethnic cleansing, for statespersons at the middle of the twentieth century, population transfer was legitimated as an unpleasant but expedient and technical means of effecting national and international order. Hence population transfer did not end with the defeat of the Nazi regime. Under the Potsdam Protocol, the Allies sanctioned a wave of transfers that would culminate in the removal of more than fourteen million ethnic Germans from countries such as

Poland, Hungary, and Czechoslovakia. "I am not alarmed by the prospect of the disentanglement of populations," Churchill famously commented on the Potsdam proposals, "not even by these large transferences, which are more possible in modern conditions than they were ever before" (de Zayas 1989, 11). Academic commentators could be equally sanguine, viewing transfer as "an instrument of the greatest importance in eliminating the most explosive danger spots in Europe and securing the future peace of the Continent and the welfare of its peoples" (Schechtman 1946, 24).

To take the trajectory of population transfer further would be to follow its use in contexts such as postcolonial nation-state formation and Soviet communism, but also, as a number of researchers have done, to find its contemporary application in the form of "ethnic cleansing" (Jackson Preece 1998). As useful as this exercise might be, it would deviate from my concern here, which is the study of the deportation of aliens. But population transfer is mentioned here to demonstrate how expulsion, by the twentieth century, has become, in Foucault's sense, "governmental." I expand on the subject of governmentality later, but here we can note that expulsion becomes governmental with population transfer because it is now targeted at and rationalized in terms of knowledges of population. It is perhaps worth noting that in the early modern period, expulsion was frequently used as a threat. It could be avoided if the subject agreed to accept baptism or conversion or to forswear the practice of usury. Expulsion as population transfer operates on a biopolitical territory where difference is marked indelibly. Expulsion is no longer aimed at the holders of particular beliefs or practices. Or rather, inasmuch as these are relevant considerations, they become so now because they are markers of a deeper racial-ethnic essence. There is no question of conversion or assimilation, since one's race is now fixed, immutable, interior. The persecution of refugees and others happened, as Arendt observed, "not because of what they had done or thought, but because of what they unchangeably were—born into the wrong kind of race or the wrong kind of class" (1951/1966, 294).

Preliminary Observations on Deportation

Having surveyed certain key aspects of expulsion in history, at this point we can make several macrohistorical observations about deportation as a form of expulsion. First there is the question of its political spatiality and scale. As long as deportation is studied in a purely contemporary setting, or within the terms of international law, we fail to appreciate that for many centuries the expulsion of people has been played out not across a space of states but rather within empires, out of parishes and cities, from estates and commons. Modern deportation is both a product of the state system and, as I argue in the second section, one of a number of techniques for the ongoing management of a world population that is divided into states. Much the same can be said of population transfer. In this respect, the practice of deportation is like the category of the refugee: not natural but, as recent work has argued, an effect of the division of the world into territorial states (Soguk 1999). In a postcolonial era in which the sovereign state norm and form have been more or less globalized, expulsion cannot avoid raising the question of the destination of the expelled. International law generally recognizes the principle that states have an obligation to admit "their" nationals. The rise of deportation as a form of expulsion is therefore marked from the latter half of the nineteenth century onward by the proliferation of international treaties and laws, alongside diplomacy and informal agreements, which seek to institutionalize this norm. As Caestecker astutely observes in the case of continental Europe, where contiguity encouraged national cooperation in matters of expulsion, if the practice had previously been a unilateral affair, an act where the state casts out the unwanted, deportation would tend to be bilateral (1998, 91).[10] The international character of deportation means that it is always susceptible to politicization not just on a domestic level, where protests may be mounted in the name of the rights of the expellee; it will also be contestable at an international level, where states may bridle at the prospect of (re)admitting the undesirable.

Deportation is more complex, however, than repatriation to a national state. In countless instances, expulsion, especially when preceded by denaturalization or denationalization, will condemn the subject to a condition of statelessness. In the war-torn chaos of mid-twentieth-century Europe, Hannah Arendt clearly saw the implications of a world organized into territorial states, and its concomitant, the national organization of citizenship. "Only with a completely organized humanity could the loss of home and political status become identical with expulsion from humanity altogether" (Arendt 1951/1966, 297). Expulsion in the twentieth century will go hand in hand with the camps. These became "the only practical substitute for a nonexistent homeland" and "the only 'country' the world had to offer the stateless" (284).

The second point to make at this stage is that deportation concerns aliens, who, unless they are stateless, are at the same time legally citizennationals of other countries. Again, this might seem so obvious that it does not need to be said. Indeed, international law's treatment of the subject presents the link between deportation and aliens as axiomatic and implied. However, seen in terms of the long history of expulsion, the gradual restriction of expulsion to aliens, and its corollary, the delegitimation of ethnic transfer, need to be remarked upon and explained. As we have noted, practices of exile, corporate expulsion, transportation, and population transfer took the expulsion of indigenous or long-settled populations to be normal. (For ethnic cleansing, it still is.) The right to reside in a given territory, or its corollary, the removal of the threat of expulsion, is an aspect of the genealogy of modern citizenship that remains underexplored. It is beyond the scope of my work here to suggest explanations as to how citizens come to be more or less inexpulsable by their own governments. But when that story is told, it will no doubt reveal that the path of progress was not linear but prone to reversal—no more so than with the mass denaturalization and denationalization of German Jews in Nazi Germany, but also of "naturalized citizens of enemy origin" in many other European countries (Arendt 1951/1966, 279n25). Perhaps we will find that the gradual strengthening of the citizen-territory link had less to do with any positive right of the citizen to inhabit a particular land, and more to do with the acquisition by states of a technical capacity (border controls, etc.) to refuse entry to noncitizens and undesirables. In the broader sense, it is also a consequence of former colonies and dominions (e.g., the United States and Australia) gaining independence and state sovereignty and thereafter refusing the status of dumping grounds for the undesirables of the old imperial metropoles.

My final preliminary point concerns the symbolic field on which deportation borders. Deportation represents a legalized form of expulsion, and its legitimacy rests on its administrative nature and the observance of national and international norms and laws. However, because of its proximity to the wider field of expulsions that I have sketched here, deportation is always susceptible to, and associable with, these other practices. These other forms of expulsion lurk in its shadows; their invocation always threatens to destabilize its legitimacy. They are historical memories, like slavery with regard to the contemporary politics of race, which can always be summoned by political action. Doesn't a plane full of deportees resemble transportation? Don't the shackling and chemical pacification of deportees invoke the galley slaves? Doesn't the clandestine way in which immigration authorities cooperate with public and private airlines to prosecute certain deportations resemble human trafficking in reverse—trafficking by states and big businesses? Don't politically orchestrated campaigns to deport Kurdish or Vietnamese refugees recall the many other groups historically expelled within Europe? Perhaps the contemporary deportation of aliens is invested with former practices and historical memories in such a way that it can never be *merely* the deportation of aliens.

DEPORTATION AND FORMS OF POWER

If the first half of the chapter has situated deportation within a historical grid of forms of expulsion, the second will locate it within a different analytics—of forms of power and government (Burchell, Gordon, and Miller 1991; Barry, Osborne, and Rose 1996). This is a second axis on which we can enhance deportation's intelligibility. Here we will try to see deportation in terms of wider logics of power—of sovereignty, governmentality, and police. This exercise allows us to grasp something of the history of the rationalization of deportation. It enables us to avoid the position that sees in expulsion only the remorseless and monotonous persecution of the other (R. Cohen 1997). Expulsion has certainly been imbricated with all manner of fears of the other, but the question posed here is: how have the conception and treatment of the other been bound up historically with specific forms of power?

Deportation and Sovereignty

Deportation is clearly implicated in the exercise of sovereignty. Its intelligibility with respect to sovereignty has mostly been secured through the discourse of international law. I will only touch on this discourse here, since it is the dominant discourse about deportation, and this chapter is devoted more to examining other dimensions of deportation and expulsion.

Within the discourse of international law, the practice of deportation can be derived from the sovereign right of states to control their territories and the discretion they have regarding the admittance and residence of aliens. "The right of a State to expel, at will, aliens, whose presence is regarded as undesirable, is, like the right to refuse admission of aliens, considered as an attribute of sovereignty of the State. . . . The grounds for expulsion of an alien may be determined by each State by its own criteria. Yet the right of expulsion must not be abused."[11] The treatment that international law accords to deportation and expulsion revolves largely around this question. International law examines deportation as a question of right. At the risk of oversimplifying, we can observe that until the middle of the twentieth century, this was a discourse almost exclusively about the rights, obligations, and duties of states to one another with regard to the treatment of their subjects. It concerned the terms under which expulsion might be considered arbitrary and the legal and administrative processes involved in enacting deportations. This legalistic discourse has been transformed in the postwar era by the rise of the human rights agenda. As with other areas of international relations, this has meant that states no longer monopolize the space of international relations in quite the same way. While states remain the agents with responsibility for interpreting and enforcing human rights, this shift nevertheless does mean that individuals and peoples have acquired a certain level of legal personhood and status within the international sphere. As far as deportation is concerned, this is reflected in various treaties and conventions that prohibit mass expulsion and call for some kind of due process to be followed (Henckaerts 1995). At the level of administrative and legal practice, therefore, we might observe there has been a certain *individualization* of expulsion.

Deportation and Governmentality

While deportation will be legitimated in terms of the right of the state—and countered often in terms of alternative principles of right—such a juridical perspective misses another dimension of power. This is its governmental character. Modern deportation lies at the intersection of these logics of sovereignty and government. What is governmental power in contrast to sovereign power? Here I follow Foucault (1991) and others who have advanced the notion of governmentality. Foucault uses governmentality in a number of overlapping but distinguishable ways (Dean 1999, chap. 1). Governmentality is used generally to refer to governmental mentalities, the link between power and knowledge. However, it is a second, more historically specific use that interests me here. Foucault uses governmentality to identify the emergence of a distinctly novel form of reflection on, and exercise of power in, modern societies. It is connected with the discovery of a new reality, the economy, and a new object, the population. Foucault dates this moment to the early modern period in western European societies. Governmentality marks the point at which political power comes to be concerned with the wealth, health, welfare, and prosperity of the population. Sovereign power involves the exercise of authority over the subjects of a state—the deduction of taxes, the meting out of punishments, and the taking of life. Government, on the other hand, is marked by its concern to optimize the forces of the population. Government does not replace other forms of power but rearticulates them. Hence taxation, law, and punishment are directed not primarily toward augmenting the power and glory of the sovereign but to promoting the ends of population. Conversely, the promotion of population will be used to advance the sovereign power of the state, where the state is understood as inserted in a field of perpetual geopolitical conflict.

The deportation of aliens needs to be situated within this field of governmentality, and not just sovereignty. My argument is that in the course of the nineteenth century, we can speak of a *governmentalization* of deportation. While I cannot undertake here a full account of this process, I can sketch some of the significant ways it is evident in the latter part of that century. First, it is well illustrated in the cases of Britain and the United States by the shift that occurred at the level of the law in terms of what kinds of subjects and problems were identified as grounds for expulsion. At the end of the eighteenth century, the practice of deportation was still concentrated around the pole of sovereign power. Its principal targets were political enemies of the state—agitators, subversives, revolutionaries—who undermined its authority. Britain's Aliens Act of 1793 was a direct response to fears of revolution unleashed by the French Revolution. For the first time, Parliament sanctioned the expulsion of aliens. While this act fell into disuse after the Napoleonic Wars, the revolutionary wave of 1848 saw the passage of further legislation, this time the Removal of Aliens Act (R. Cohen 1997, 357–58). Similar in character were the U.S. Alien and Sedition Acts of 1798, which empowered the president to remove any aliens suspected of "treasonable or secret machinations against the government" (Clark 1931/1969, 37).

To this day, deportation remains an instrument to be used against those who can be defined as political enemies of the state. It will target foreign trade unionists and dissidents during times of crisis, especially during wars. However, we can observe that by the end of the nineteenth century, its targets expand to embrace not just political but also social enemies in the form of various categories of socially undesirable persons. The enemies of the state henceforth include various categories of persons who are deemed to pose a threat to its population, which is increasingly understood in racial and biopolitical terms, or to its economy or system of welfare provision. Hence there is Britain's Aliens Act of 1903, a response to fears regarding an "alien menace" associated with the influx of Russian and eastern European Jews. While this act sought to maintain a general policy of openness in immigration, it defined as socially undesirable, expulsable, and excludable the mad, the destitute, fugitive offenders, and previous deportees (R. Cohen 1997, 358). In the United States there has been a gradual expansion of the classes of person who warranted exclusion and deportation. The initial targets had been Chinese immigrants under the Chinese Exclusion Act, but by 1891 "the number of excludable classes had been greatly enlarged by the addition of paupers, persons suffering from loathsome or dangerous contagious diseases, polygamists," and so on (Clark 1931/1969, 44). In the twentieth century the practice of expulsion is not only nationalized—as we saw with population transfer. Simultaneously, it is socialized.

Another way we can trace this governmentalization of deportation is around the question of foreign or alien workers. As states became involved in the regulation of labor markets and the management of economies in the twentieth century, deportation found economic uses that paralleled its social purposes. Here deportation was to function as the corollary of immigration policy and the supplement to voluntary emigration. If immigration policy was often driven by the need to recruit so-called "migrant" labor from abroad, deportation was used to regulate and enforce the return of these "temporary" hands during times of economic downturn. This use of deportation first became clearly evident during the interwar depression when France, a state that had traditionally relied on immigration to meet labor shortages, and to a lesser extent Belgium used deportation as a means of "exporting their unemployment" (Strikwerda 1997, 63; Cohen and Hanagan 1996; Arendt 1951/1966, 286).

In key respects, then, the practice of deportation mirrors the rise of welfarist policies and programs. In the cases just given, it is an instrument to defend and promote the welfare of a nationally defined population—a fact reflected in the title of anti-immigration legislation such as France's Law for the Protection of National Labor (1932). But it is shaped by and reflects the rise of welfarist rationalities and mentalities at a more technical, administrative level as well. If deportation was coming to be used as a de facto employment policy in countries like France between the wars, then certain "social" principles pertaining to employment would be extended to it. If responsibility for the origins and relief of unemployment is socialized under the welfare state (Walters 2000), and ceases to be the sole responsibility of the worker, then it is possible to observe something similar with deportation. Like industrial disability, unemployment, and old age, the view was that employers, and more generally "society," since they utilize and benefit from foreign hands, should also be responsible for a share of the cost of repatriating such labor when it becomes "surplus" to requirements. Hence in France in the 1930s we find mining companies, and later the French government, financing the journey "home" of their deportees (Caestecker 1998, 93–94).

But deportation and welfarism are connected in other ways. As the governmentality literature has emphasized, political programs and projects only become governmental when they find certain technologies capable of making them implementable (Rose 1999). It is fruitful to analyze citizenship at the level of its technologies. If deportation becomes a technique concentrated on the noncitizen, as I argued earlier, this presumes the availability or the invention of means to identify who is a citizen and who is a foreigner. It also presumes the administrative capability to police borders. Scholars of the history of regulation and documentation tend to confirm that World War I is a watershed in this respect, a time when borders were systematically patrolled and passports checked (Caestecker 1998; Sassen 1999; Strikwerda 1997; Torpey 1999). From 1914 onward we see a proliferation of schemes to document and identify the alien, including identity cards, registrations with police, employer and residence permits, and passports. The nonrenewal of these various permits by officials could henceforth operate as a means to initiate deportation. Of course, in many cases the national identity of a person was unclear. In this case the act of deportation also entails a practice of identification, as it may with the asylum process today, a site where the identity of, and the proper responsibility for, the subject must be fixed.

While I lack the space to trace other mutations within this trajectory of the governmentalization of deportation, there is one development pertaining to the present that bears noting. In many Western countries today, we see a concern with deportation less as a mechanism for shaping the substantive identity or profile of a population or for intervening directly in the labor market. Instead there is a concern with the governmental mechanism itself. Governments are presently obsessed with the need to "tighten up" their deportation and repatriation policies. One of the main reasons they give is the need to maintain the "integrity" of their immigration and asylum systems. The problem identified is one where lax administration of deportation—the failure to execute deportation orders and actually remove the subject—marks a particular state as a "soft touch." The fear is that asylum "shoppers" will then flock to that state to profit from its generous terms of admission. Strictly enforced deportation policies supposedly send "signals" to asylum seekers and "illegal" migrants. What is being governed is not the population in a direct manner, as it was with population transfer or the deportation of the socially undesirable, but the governmental system. The parallel is with the neoliberal critique of "the welfare system," where the governmental system is identified not as a solution but as a contributing factor in problems of poverty and exclusion. The call is then for welfare reform, a term that becomes synonymous with poverty policy. This seems to fit the trend that Mitchell Dean calls the "governmentalization of government," whereby "the mechanisms of government themselves are subject to problematization, scrutiny and reformation" (1999, 193). When deportation rates become "targets" to be met by immigration and other departments, when national and international agencies seek to compare levels and techniques of deportation across nations and exchange information for "best practices," then it seems we have the governmentalization of government.

Deportation as International Police

Thus far I have argued that we can historicize deportation in terms of a process of governmentalization. Governmentalization is a development in which states become actively involved in the protection and promotion of the welfare of their populations. But we can go beyond merely identifying deportation in terms of governmentality and ask what *kinds* of governmentality invest and rationalize this practice. The literature on governmentality has been concerned mostly with liberal forms of government. Among the most important characteristics of liberal government is indirect rule, a reliance on the positive knowledges of the social and human sciences to delimit certain fields and objects of intervention, and an ethical concern that government should be limited. Liberal rule is haunted by the constant fear of governing too much. It seeks to govern not in totalizing ways but with the grain of spheres of existence that are always "beyond" the formal institutions of power. The government of economic policy exemplifies liberal government, as does much welfare and social policy with its will to empower individuals and families. However, I want to suggest that deportation does not properly belong to this regime of liberal practices of rule but belongs to an older lineage—that of police. Research on governmentality is beginning to recognize the various ways in which older forms of nonliberal and illiberal rule continue to structure the present or are reactivated in modern settings (Dean 2002). Deportation is consistent with this observation.

What is police as a form of governmentality, and in what ways is deportation rationalized by it? While today police refers to a body of officials charged with preventing crime and maintaining the peace, in early modern Europe, *polizei* referred to something broader—an art of government.

Unlike liberal forms of rule, which define themselves in part through their political critique of police, police sees order not as spontaneous or natural but as the effect of regulation. Police sits alongside other totalizing arts of government such as cameralism and mercantilism. Security is attained through detailed administration and ordering. As Gerhard Oestreich observes, police is characterized by its "regulation mania" (Dean 1999, 91). Its original setting is local or municipal government, where police regulation extends to a vast and, from a contemporary perspective, heterogeneous array of issues, including sanitation, religious practice, the treatment of the poor, sumptuary codes, civic manners, and public morality.

There are at least two ways in which deportation can be understood in relation to police. First, at a national level, it is a form of policing territory and population. We have already noted how deportation was anticipated by the local police of the poor in sixteenth- and seventeenth-century Europe. But in the latter part of the nineteenth century, as administrators came to reflect on the problem of aliens and to rationalize the use of deportation, they understood it in its modern sense as a form of national police. "L'expulsion n'est pas une peine; c'est une mesure de police" (Martini 1909, 3). In its review of Europe's policies on aliens, Britain's Royal Commission on Alien Immigration (1903) observed: "On the Continent the question of the admission and still more of the expulsion of undesirable Aliens is a matter of police regulation" (30). Although the twentieth century witnessed the juridification of deportation within national and international law, in its inception it was an administrative, not a juridical, measure. It was an instrument to protect and sustain public order and tranquillity, akin to the removal of a nuisance. Consider the following summary of reasons for deportation, which was produced by the Institute of International Law in 1892, at a time when legal experts and administrators were formulating the modern powers of deportation. Here we find the overlay of deportation as an instrument of police, of routine administration with expulsion as an instrument to perpetuate sovereign power:

(1) fraudulent entry into the territory, unless followed by a sojourn there during a period of six months; (2) establishment of domicile or residence in violation of a formal prohibition; (3) illness dangerous to public health; (4) mendicancy, vagabondage, pauperism; (5) conviction in the country for offences of a certain gravity; (6) conviction or prosecution abroad for grave extraditable offences; (7) incitement to the perpetration of grave offences against public safety; (8) attacks in the press or otherwise against the institutions of a foreign State or sovereign or against the institutions of a foreign State; (9) attacks or outrages in a foreign press against the country of sojourn

or its sovereign; (10) conduct in time of war or impending war threatening the country's security. (Pelonpää 1984, 52)

Here is a form of power, then, that does not envisage a spontaneous order. Unlike the classical image of immigration, where actors "voluntarily" move in response to "push" and "pull" factors, and more broadly various forms of liberal government, where the welfare of the population and social order are to be optimized by harnessing the freedoms and desires of individuals, and the self-regulating mechanisms of market and population, deportation belongs to a different rationality of rule. It employs a similar tactic to the poor law, drawing a categorical distinction between those who should be granted the benefits of citizenship, however meager, and those who must be managed authoritatively, even despotically.

But deportation is more than just a form of police that operates on a national population. Here I want to argue for a second and potentially more significant dimension to the police character of deportation. It is that *we should see the deportation of aliens as a form of the international police of population.*[12] Seen from a national or purely internal perspective, deportation appears as the exclusion and expulsion of aliens and "the uninvited"; it stands as an expression of the hierarchical relationship between citizens on the one hand with full rights, and aliens or denizens on the other, or the ways in which states discriminate against noncitizens and outsiders. But seen from an international perspective, deportation represents the compulsory allocation of subjects to their proper sovereigns or, in many instances of statelessness, to other surrogate sovereigns (e.g., the current practice of returning certain asylum seekers to "safe third countries"). In the face of patterns of international migration, deportation serves to sustain the image of a world divided into "national" populations and territories, domiciled in terms of state membership. It operates in relation to a wider regime of practices including resettlement, voluntary return, political asylum, temporary protection, and so on, which together can be said to comprise a global police of population. Extradition belongs to this series as well, though extradition is in certain respects the inverse of deportation—a recognition of the sovereign's claim to have its subjects returned for the application of justice. Following Hindess, we can see citizenship in a different light, less "the rights and responsibilities accruing to individuals by virtue of their membership of an appropriate polity" than "a marker of identification, advising state and nonstate agencies of the particular state to which an individual belongs" (2000, 1487).

By discussing deportation as a practice within the international police of population, I want to highlight its affinities with poor law practice. Despite their significant differences, both operate with a logic of dividing and allocating populations to the territorial authorities deemed properly responsible for them. The poor law does this between localities; with deportation it is international. One consequence of this observation is that we need to further revise conventional understandings of the welfare state and the Marshallian narrative of social citizenship. The Marshallian narrative is an account where universalism triumphs over particularism, and where the advent of social rights spells the victory of an ameliorist and social rather than a penal approach to poverty. For some time now, welfare state and citizenship theory has challenged this rather Whiggish account on a number of scores, not least for its Anglocentrism and its gender blindness. But we can add a further challenge here. It is that the evolutionary account is sustainable only if one ignores the international dimension of the welfare state and, by corollary, the national particularity of social rights. The evolutionary account of social citizenship makes sense only if we ignore the treatment of groups like aliens who were often present alongside these social citizens but did not enjoy the same level of social rights. From the perspective of the alien, the advent of the welfare state does not represent the full liquidation or transcendence of the poor law. Rather, it involves a certain reconstitution of its logic on a regional, and today a global, scale. Seen from a global perspective, the world comprises a patchwork of welfare states. Many of them are extremely rudimentary, but the vast majority are organized in terms of norms of residency. The age of the welfare state does not fully escape the logic of the poor law. As the history of aliens policy reveals, at the same time that social policy was being nationalized, deportation was a regular instrument in the export of the "foreign" unemployed and other undesirable groups. Or put differently, at the same time that technologies like social insurance and child care were serving to constitute socially integrated societies, deportation, along with other legislation on mobility rights, was operating to manage the disciplinary division and distribution of social responsibilities across states.

There have been notable and positive changes in the status of aliens, as theorists of postnational citizenship and membership suggest (Soysal 1994). Foreign workers in most Western states are not generally exposed to the same level of arbitrariness of expulsion as before. In terms of social and civil rights, and to a limited extent political rights, there has been a notable convergence between aliens, residents, and citizens in the post–World War II period. This has been taken furthest with the project of European Union citizenship, which, according to one reading, embodies the goal of diminishing and even eliminating "the disabilities of alienage in other States."[13] But aside from the situation of EU citizens, Rogers Brubaker points out that many European countries did not dare expel guest work-ers despite terms in their contracts that allowed the workers' expulsion, because it was actually felt that they were a part of the societies in which they lived (Brubaker 1989, 19; quoted in Schnapper 1997, 206). However, as much as the social and legal situation of many categories of nonnationals may have improved in many European states, it is important to recall that new projects and new subjects of expulsion and exclusion have been con-stituted in the past twenty years or so, representing a countertendency to the process of dealienage. Amid public and political anxieties over "bo-gus asylum seekers" and "illegal immigrants" (Huysmans 1995), there are new targets for expulsion and deportation. What is notable here is the way that deportation is itself becoming regionalized. Multilateral agree-ments under the Schengen and Dublin agreements, and now under the EU's Amsterdam Treaty, point to tendencies for deportation and exclusion to take place not just from national territories but from the EU's emerging regional "area of freedom, security and justice." One of the main aims of the Dublin Convention was to prevent "multiple applications" for asylum in member countries and to put an end to "asylum shopping." In effect, member states operate as proxy European authorities, deciding on and in many cases deporting asylum seekers from the European space. In sum, in the future, we might expect this international police to work not only between nations but also between regions and nations.

The Camp: Spaces within and beyond Modern Citizenship

I have discussed deportation as a form of international police that seeks to divide and distribute population on a global basis and presupposes the idea of citizenship as a marker of belonging within the state system. As it stands, however, this account of deportation as international police and, more generally, in terms of sovereign and governmental power is seri-ously incomplete. For the most controversial and troubling forms of de-portation are not usually the return of nationals to their "home" states. Rather, they have involved the stateless, the refugee, the German Jew or Russian denationalized and stripped of citizenship, the refugees who, in desperate circumstances, have destroyed their own citizenship papers, and today the rejected asylum seeker. The fact is that when deportation has featured in these cases it goes hand in hand with the camp. Practices of deportation need to be seen in relation to a wider carceral archipelago of detention centers, refugee camps and *zones d'attente*.

I want now to examine the camp. This is not just for reasons of consistency or out of some desire for completeness but because it offers important insights about contemporary citizenship, sovereignty, and forms of power. Foucault is well known for his observation that "a whole history remains to be written of *spaces*—which would at the same time be a history of *powers* . . . from the great strategies of geo-politics to the little tactics of the habitat" (1980, 149). What might the study of the camp contribute to such a history? Here we can return to Arendt and Agamben—two figures who have explored the implications and consequences of the refugee for modern political thought. A key insight that I take from Arendt is her observation of the pervasiveness of the camp in twentieth-century Europe. While the concentration camp was the specific outcome of the Nazis' genocidal dream of racial purity, its horrors should not obscure the fact that camps of one kind or another became "the routine solution for the problem of the domicile of the 'displaced persons'" by the time of World War II in a large number of European countries (Arendt 1951/1966, 279). When she notes that the internment camp became "the only practical substitute for a nonexistent homeland" and the "only 'country' the world had to offer the stateless" (284), she reminds us that, like deportation, the camp is not merely a dreadful anomaly or the expression of discrimination on the part of this or that government. Rather, it is a logical consequence and an almost necessary correlate of a world fully divided into territorial nation-states. The great spaces of geopolitics and their biopolitical assumptions crystallize, and find their supports, in the camp.

However, it is with Agamben that we encounter the attempt to thematize the camp as a diagram of power.[14] For Agamben the camp holds the key to understanding the complex place of bare life inside and outside the polity. Foucault proposed the panoptical prison as one (though not necessarily the only) diagram for understanding certain critical features of the political and social logic of modernity, its deployment of power and subjectivity. Agamben attributes a similar significance to the figure of the camp. The camp is a frightening zone of indistinction where we encounter sovereignty as *nomos*—"the point of indistinction between violence and law, the threshold on which violence passes over into law and law passes over into violence" (1995/1998, 32). If sovereignty operates through its capacity to define situations as "exceptional," therefore requiring and justifying actions and procedures outside the normal juridical order, then the camp is "the materialization of [this] state of exception" (174). But the camp is not a finite or particular institutional complex. Rather, it is a system of relations that is actualized in diverse settings. We find ourselves "virtually in the presence" of the camp every time "exceptional" measures are taken to institute a space in which "bare life and the juridical rule enter into a threshold of indistinction" (174). Hence the camp is materialized with the internment and concentration camps of the 1930s and 1940s, but also in other forms. It appears momentarily in the form of the stadium in Bari where Italian police in 1991 herded Albanian immigrants before returning them. It is also actualized with the "international zone" (*zone d'attente*) of Roissy–Charles de Gaulle airport, which has converted a hotel for the detention of asylum seekers and which the French authorities define as outside the territory of France.[15] Within the international zone, the airport is configured as the "high seas" from the point of view of the immigrant: French obligations and commitments to the refugee under international treaties are suspended. Meanwhile the camp proliferates in the form of detention centers, the front line of the Western states' response to the global refugee crisis. The more notorious examples include Campsfield in the UK and Woomera in Australia, but more than a hundred such centers now exist across Europe (Hayter 2000, 113). The camp is often a matter of expedience—a detention area under the Palais de Justice in Paris, or the British authorities' use of a converted ferry (with its echoes of the prison hulks) to detain mostly Sri Lankan Tamils in the port of Harwich (121). These are all spaces where the exception becomes the norm, where those without the "right to have rights" are exposed to indeterminate waiting times, the risk of arbitrary treatment, and the threat of physical and psychological abuse.

In addition to defining a space of emergency in which particular exceptional modes of treatment become normal, the camp represents a crisis of Western politics and citizenship. It signals a sort of surplus of bare life that can no longer be contained within the political order of nation-states: "What we call *camp* is this disjunction" (175). In the absence of a working cosmopolitan model of citizenship or other ways of organizing and distributing rights, belongings, and identities, and with the menacing growth of a politics of xenophobia and racism that encourages publics to see the presence of refugees and aliens as threats to their freedom, culture, and security, we have the camps—we have border zones, detention centers, holding areas, a panoply of partitions, segregations, and striations. The figure of the refugee reveals that the rights of man that become ours "naturally" through birth are in fact partial, provisional, and inadequate. The camps stand as a sign of the rupture of the state-people-territory complex, but also the permanently temporary attempt to suture it.

The dream of the perfect prison, the school, and other disciplinary spaces was the production of a docile, useful body and a self-regulating, interiorized citizen. However, the diagram of the camp does not presuppose a comparable, positive kind of subjectivity. Rather, its logic is one of expedience and exemption. It is not interested in projects of reform so much as countering the putatively dangerous "illegal" global flows of impoverished humanity. If, following Giovanna Procacci (1991, 161), the eighteenth century and the early nineteenth were transfixed by a fear of pauperism, with its dangerous, "fluid, elusive sociality, impossible either to control or to utilise," and if the governmental response included the great strategies of "territorial sedentarization" to produce "fixed concentrations of population" (e.g., anti-vagabondage laws, the poor law, and later public housing), then camps and deportations represent components of a contemporary sedentarization campaign that operates in relation to a local-global space. The camp delivers surplus humanity into a zone of indistinction, invoking a near-permanent state of emergency to place its subjects indefinitely "on hold" at the edge of the juridical order—all so that the sovereign system of states and its division of citizens to states can be reestablished. Here surplus humanity is caught in the crosscurrents between the police and immigration authorities and their moves to extrajudicial and arbitrary treatment, and the countermovements of the human-rights and immigrants-rights groups who protest such forms of treatment. The camp is extraterritorial, in the sense that it can stand outside the legal and juridical order, but also intensely territorial to the point where the territorial regime of citizenship becomes dependent on these exceptions if it is to sustain the principle that all the world's population can be ascribed a "country." Yet if the camp is quite different from the disciplinary spaces that Foucault and others associate with modernity, it has at least one thing in common. Like the workhouse or the prison, the camp is to be highly symbolic; its harshness stands as a "semio-technique" of deterrence (Dean 1991, 184–85; Foucault 1975/1977, 93–103), a signal that "our" immigration systems are not a "soft touch."

Despite the importance of Agamben's contribution in linking questions of refugees, migration, and expulsion to broader questions of citizenship and power, his account is not without its problems. Above all, it is rather one-sided and crushingly dismal. In this respect it might be useful to consider some of the various ways in which camps have been contested, both by antiracist activists and by potential deportees themselves. Perhaps one could develop a counterconcept alongside the camp—call it *the sanctuary*. Just as the camp has been made to materialize in airports, hotels, and even in the ships that transport refugees once they are held at sea, then the sanctuary has been made by popular struggles to materialize in a countermovement, most particularly within churches. Take the case of the occupation of Saint Ambroise Church in Paris in 1996 by 324 Africans. This is an event that is now regarded as the founding of the sans-papiers movement, a campaign that has sought to move beyond opposition to particular deportations to the demand for the legalization of so-called "illegal immigrants." One reason for the significance of this movement is that through it undocumented workers and "illegals," especially the women within these communities, have sought to become autonomous political subjects, rather than merely the causes for which external groups struggle. As the movement's manifesto declares: "We the Sans-Papiers of France, in signing this appeal, have decided to come out of the shadows. From now on, in spite of the dangers, it is not only our faces but also our names which will be known" (*Liberation*, February 25, 1997; cited in Hayter 2000, 143). The sanctuary involves a strategic reinscription of the sacred space of the church as a defense against the sovereign power of the state. Like anti-deportation activities at airports, it dramatizes the practice of deportation. Whatever else it may or may not accomplish, the sanctuary ensures that deportation will not operate as a silent, routine administrative process. Rather, it guarantees that deportation will be performed as a site of sovereignty—either the state negotiating with the subjects of deportation (and thereby recognizing them *as* subjects), or the state as armed bodies of men smashing down church doors, seizing, arresting, pacifying, terrifying, removing bodies in full display of the public.

In short, with the sanctuary—but also the various other campaigns to close detention centers, the border shacks and camps that demonstrate the fortification of European and North American border controls (see http://www.noborder.org), the activities of the Collectif Anti-Expulsion and deportation-class.com to mobilize passengers against deportation in airports,[16] and the mobile human-rights "caravans"—one sees a politicization of the permanent-exceptional order of the camp. A pessimistic reading would see the sanctuary as an extension of the camp—self-internment? And doubtless many occupations of churches and other spaces are little more than a last, desperate bid to avoid deportation that it would be wrong to romanticize or conscript as a grand political gesture. But a more hopeful and arguably more nuanced reading of such events and movements is that they are inventing ways to contest the expulsion of people from humanity. In the process, they are posing profound questions about our politics and practice of citizenship. The question that the very name of the antiracist network Kein Mensch Ist Illegal poses is precisely: within what kind of politics can a human be "illegal"? Arendt wrote of freedom as a practice rather than a fixed value or set of institutions, a practice

in which participants call "something into being which did not exist before, which was not given, not even as an object of cognition or imagination, and which therefore, strictly speaking, could not be known" (Arendt
1954/1968, 151; Tully 1999, 179). As counterintuitive as it seems, perhaps
we can see camps and sanctuaries not just as spaces of nomos but as the
invention of new practices of freedom and subjecthood.

CONCLUSION

What is the relevance of this study of deportation for our understanding of citizenship? First, it has observed that deportation is more than an
unpleasant, coercive aspect of immigration policy. Deportation is less a
contingent feature and more a logical and necessary consequence of the
international order. It is actually quite fundamental and immanent to the
modern regime of citizenship. If citizenship, following Hindess, can be
seen not just as rights and responsibilities exercised within a polity but
as a "marker of identification, advising state and nonstate agencies of the
particular state to which an individual belongs," then deportation (along
with extradition and other forms of repatriation) represents a means by
which this principle can be operationalized.

Deportation is certainly legitimated and authorized by the modern regime of citizenship—though we have seen in the course of this study that
it is only one of a number of ways in which expulsion has historically been
rationalized. But deportation is more than just a logical consequence of
this regime of citizenship. To call it a constitutive practice, a technology
of citizenship—as I did at the outset—is to say something else. It is to
argue that deportation is actively involved in *making* this world. The modern order of citizenship—in which population is divided and distributed
between territories and sovereigns, and in which rights depend mostly
on national membership within territorial polities—does not reproduce
itself naturally. In other words, we can see deportation, like diplomacy,
economic policy, border controls, or schooling, as a practice that is constitutive and regulative of its subjects and objects. Nothing illustrates
more powerfully, and more tragically, this sense of deportation as constitutive than the practice of "population transfer" during the middle of
the twentieth century, when the state was brutally harnessed to the goal
of creating ethnically homogeneous nations. If this vision of the nation
authorized mid-twentieth-century deportation practices (and still does
with ethnic cleansing), a question that I have not resolved but begs further

research is: what kind of image of political community is presupposed by deportation today?

But there is also a methodological point to be made here about how we might study the changing *content* of modern citizenship. A key analytical assumption of this chapter is that it is useful to select a particular practice and follow it over a relatively long historical period. In this way we avoid some of the pitfalls of more presentist perspectives. By comparing different forms of expulsion, it has been possible to trace significant shifts in the package of rights, duties, and expectations that attend citizenship. For example, we have seen that a history of deportation offers certain insights regarding the relations between citizenship, population, and territory. A distinguishing feature of the contemporary practice of deportation—at least in most Western states—is that of a form of treatment reserved for aliens. As long as we study deportation in a presentist light, we are likely to take this fact for granted. Yet it is something that actually needs to be explained rather than assumed. We saw that exile and banishment, understood as practices that strip away a person's rights and sunder the ties to their community, have at various times been considered appropriate forms of punishment for citizens.

The question of how and why citizenship comes to imply a right to remain in one's own country, and deportation a practice suited only to noncitizens, commands further scrutiny. However, I suspect that a convincing answer will require this process to be set within a framework that more fully considers the international relations of citizenship (e.g., Mann 1987). The trend away from deporting one's own citizens is strongly conditioned by international factors—not only the pressure of international norms and conventions but also, more significantly, the long-term process of territorial organization. It is only when the world becomes more or less fully divided into territorial states that deportation begins to confront its subjects with the fate that was consciously intended by the much older practice of banishment—namely, expulsion from humanity.

NOTES

This is a slightly amended version of a paper first published in *Citizenship Studies* 6, no. 3 (2002). I am grateful to Taylor and Francis for their permission to reprint the piece, and to Christina Gabriel, Barry Hindess, and Robyn Lui, as well as three anonymous reviewers, whose insights and comments helped me write the original. Part of the impetus for the original publication came from what I perceived to be the dearth of what one might call a critical and theoretically informed literature on practices of expulsion, deportation, and removal. Perhaps catalyzed in part by the way in which the U.S.-orchestrated War on Terror has thrust deportation, rendition, and other forms of seizure and removal into the public spotlight, this situation has recently changed. There is now a significant, interdisciplinary body of work that engages issues of deportation in both its historical and contemporary forms and examines its relationship to changing social experiences of migration under conditions of heightened securitization, new configurations of power and resistance, and novel experiments in the making and unmaking of citizens. See, among others, Nyers 2003; De Genova 2002; Peutz 2006; Kingston 2005; Ngai 2004; and Caestecker 2003.

1. What originally appeared as http://deportation-class.com has been relocated at the noborder.org site, http://www.noborder.org/archive/www.deportation-class.com.

2. Among the most notable of these has been the occupation of churches in Paris by mostly African sans-papiers. See Hayter 2000.

3. "Aviation Campaigns," http://www.noborder.org/avia/index.html, accessed October 13, 2006.

4. See, for instance, Robin Cohen (1997), who examines deportation policy in the UK. Another exception is the important literature on sanctuary movements operating in solidarity with refugees in the United States. See, for example, Coutin 1993. Frank Weber (1996) offers a particularly sophisticated theorization of expulsion that examines this practice in terms of a Foucauldian *dispositif* and traces the variable ways in which this system of laws, practices, and spaces has been articulated with the regulation of population. Weber concentrates on Germany, whereas I have tried to study deportation in a slightly broader, European context.

5. Consider that the U.S.-organized War on Terror has brought to light a relatively new form of removal, namely, "rendition." This extralegal measure would surely need to be included in a more comprehensive inventory of forms of expulsion. Amnesty International (2006) equates rendition with "a variety of practices by the U.S. authorities involving transfers of individuals from one country to another, without any form of judicial or administrative process such as extradition."

6. "Exile," http://www.encyclopedia.com.

7. Foucault 1992, cited in and translated by Higgins and Leps 1998.

8. Concomitant with the rise of the state system is therefore the *nationalization* of immigration policy. This becomes a policy dealing with the inside and outside of states and the crossing of state borders. It intertwines with the nationalization of the border, a matter I have addressed elsewhere (Walters 2002b).

9. I am grateful to Barry Hindess for pointing this out.

10. The contemporary use of readmission treaties might be located within this trajectory; see Noll 1999; King 1997. Such treaties are often between wealthier

and poorer countries and have marked power effects. One way of reading the readmission agreement is as a form of international discipline whereby poor states are coaxed into assuming new governmental responsibilities for their nationals. On the other hand, with "safe-third-country agreements," states are obliged to accept certain persons who are not their nationals but have passed through their territories in the process of claiming asylum in other countries. At present EU states employ such agreements to oblige postcommunist states to shoulder responsibilities for providing asylum. See Lavenex 1999.

11. Oda 1968, 469, 482; cited in Goodwin-Gill 1978.

12. A possible objection to my adaptation of police as an art of *international* government might be the following: how can there be an international police in the absence of a centralized, global policing authority? Yet as Dean and Hindess helpfully point out, although centralizing tendencies developed in seventeenth- and eighteenth-century Europe, the enterprise of police was not synonymous with centralized power. Police "was expected to be taken up locally and by a variety of non-state agencies" (Dean and Hindess 1998, 3). Similarly, it seems reasonable to consider the international police of aliens and others as an activity undertaken on a dispersed, only loosely coordinated basis—certainly by states, but by other agencies (e.g., UN agencies) as well. Further analysis could usefully examine the place of the international policing of aliens within wider arrangements of globalization, understood less as a determinate process and more as an instance of global liberal police (Dean 2002, 53–54).

13. See Preuss (1998, 146), who explains that this principle was first articulated in nineteenth-century American constitutional debates.

14. But compare Agamben with Gilroy (1999), who uses the concept of camp and "camp mentality" to problematize formations of race and nation. Gilroy advocates diasporic culture as an alternative to that of the camp and calls for a politics situated "between camps."

15. See the critical discussion of such international zones in Council of Europe 2000.

16. See *A Practical Guide to Intervening in Airports*, published by the Ile de France section of the Collectif, at http://www.bok.net/pajol/ouv/cae/intervention.e.html.

—ᴡᴡ—

CHAPTER 2

Immigration Detention and
the Territoriality of Universal Rights

Deportation and detention are often merely regarded as simple instances of immigration law enforcement. In official political discourse, they are presented as the proper and natural response of the sovereign state to those who have violated its territorial sovereignty. With specific regard to detention, such perceived naturalness is reflected in the fact that the immigration prison as an organizational structure to administer the entry and deportation of foreigners increasingly prevails over other forms of such administration in contemporary European societies (Challenge 2006). Criticism, be it political, academic, or activist, revolves mainly around the conditions under which growing numbers of individuals are deprived of their liberty in European democracies, but the actual detention of those who have transgressed the modern state's territorial boundaries is portrayed merely as the unfortunate but predictable consequence of unwanted immigration.[1]

However, as stated so evocatively by Nicholas De Genova and Nathalie Peutz, there must inevitably be something greater at stake in practices of detention and removal, including "the formulation and emphatic reaffirmation of state sovereignty itself," and also the concomitant "production and reconfiguration of political subjectivities for 'natural' and 'naturalized' citizens, all manner of 'immigrant' and 'foreign' denizens, and, of course, the deportees themselves" (Peutz and De Genova, this volume). Their words accurately express my claim that deportation and detention constitute the litmus test for the way in which *territoriality*—a concept that links political power with clearly demarcated territory—shapes the world and the life of its inhabitants. Furthermore, deportation and detention of unwanted foreigners make clear what sovereignty is about, both with regard to its aspect of monopolist violence and with regard to its claim to determine the "inside" from the "outside." Ultimately the indiscriminate detention of unwanted foreigners, under conditions that seem to flagrantly violate some of the very values that supposedly underpin liberal Western democracies, makes painfully clear that the modern discourse of human rights has not been able to live up to its universal aspirations.

The aim of this chapter is twofold. On the one hand, I elucidate the relationship between territoriality, sovereignty, and immigration detention. Put differently, what does the immigration prison tell us about the contemporary organization of the global political system and present forms of state power? On the other hand, I seek to explain the related issue of the impotency of the international human rights discourse when it comes to the imprisonment of thousands of people under exceptional conditions, not on account of what they have done but on account of what they are. Hannah Arendt's observations on the "perplexities of the rights of man" (1951/1966, 290–302) have retained their validity, exemplified as they are in the contemporary immigration prison, and as such they will prove particularly valuable to contextualize the two specific concerns of this chapter.

This chapter consists of two parts. Its first part deals with the conceptual and normative framework in which the contemporary practice of immigration detention takes place. As immigration detention is at once both the expression of modern state sovereignty *and* part of a whole array of mechanisms that aim at keeping in check perceived threats to the territorial state and the system that it forms a part of, it is necessary to first present a concise overview of the development of the modern state based on clearly demarcated territory and its concomitant notion of state sovereignty. Furthermore, immigration detention in liberal democracies is an instance of state violence unchecked, which is why I will subsequently address the discourses that have over time attempted to impose constraints upon the violence inherent in the exercise of sovereign power, such as citizenship, international law, and the human rights regime. We will see that as a result of territoriality, a political particularist reality has triumphed over the universalistic ideals underpinning both citizenship and classic international law. And although the human rights discourse explicitly intends to overcome this particularism, its universal aspirations remain mere aspirations, the inevitable result of an enduring perception of territoriality as a self-evident, natural, and innocent concept for the organization of the global political system.

In the chapter's second part, it will become obvious why I have chosen to commence with a detailed discussion of the way in which territoriality implicates the global political order and the rights of the individual, in order to contextualize my claim that immigration detention is at once the inevitable outcome of contemporary territoriality, and the ultimate illustration of the immunization of territorial sovereignty against conventional forces of legal correction. Here I examine the current practice of immigration detention in light of sovereignty's territorial logic. We will see that immigration detention and territoriality are related in three ways. First, I argue that deportation—the alleged aim of immigration detention—emerges as a *technology* by which the sovereign state attempts to preserve the status quo of the global state system and the ensuing territoriality of the Rule of Law.[2] In this respect, detention is comparable to, and inseparable from, deportation. However, detention in particular is unique among other tools of a restrictive immigration policy. It is not merely a technology by which states violently seek to reproduce the territorial ideal according to which distinct populations belong to distinct states (Walters 2002a). Second, I propose that through spatial confinement, immigration detention provides an immediate (territorial) solution for those who do not fit within this very ideal. Finally, I show that by resorting to immigration detention, states do not only seek to perpetuate a territorial image of the world but in doing so simultaneously make ultimate use of territoriality's logic: only a discourse in which territorial demarcations drawn in the past determine which kinds of violence are prone to legal correction can make possible the very existence of the immigration prison. Indeed, the untamed existence of a practice as violent as immigration detention is only possible because international human rights are incapable of fully addressing the human interests that are affected whenever the national state bases the exercise of power on its territorial sovereignty. This is so because the very language that the international legal discourse reserves for issues bearing on territorial sovereignty is the language of the sovereign state alone and thus leaves the individual interests that are implicated in these issues invisible and inarticulable.

Finally, this chapter identifies the real dangers of "extraterritorial" detention centers that are currently set up at the instigation of the European Union member states in third countries (non-member states of the EU). By exporting detention in this manner, the contemporary reconfiguration of "Europe" is distinguished by a serious and deplorable instance of unaccountability for violations of human dignity.

SETTING THE STAGE: TERRITORIAL SOVEREIGNTY
AND INDIVIDUAL RIGHTS

International movement across borders has produced a growing feeling of crisis in many countries because of its association with the loss of control and sovereignty in a globalizing world (Mills 1996, 81). National states employ increasingly restrictive tools of migration management such as deportation and detention in order to demonstrate their continuing control over territorial boundaries. However, it seems that these tools, "in promising more than they can deliver, . . . only exacerbate the feeling of crisis, so that these extraordinary measures seem normal and justifiable" (Bloch and Schuster 2005, 509). Inefficacious immigration law enforcement thus fuels the perception in which migration forms a threat to a territorial ideal that must be maintained at any cost, a mechanism that is in fact indispensable for, and arguably even orchestrated by, governments that want to sustain the perceived naturalness of the "nation-state space" (De Genova 2002, 436–39).

The Territorial Logic of Immigration Law Enforcement

Contemporary illustrations of the impact of border-enforcement mechanisms on the real lives of individuals are numerous and diverse. Their similarity lies in their testimony to human suffering. Accounts of how many persons died at Europe's frontiers over recent years differ, but in any case they reach into the thousands. Every week newspapers recount new occurrences of shipwrecked migrants, drowned in their attempts to reach the coasts of European states. Because of their desire for a better life and future in another place, countless women from poor countries fall victim to trafficking networks and are sexually exploited in European democracies.[3] Undocumented migrants are exposed to inhuman working conditions in states that apply sophisticated social legislation to those who are officially acknowledged to be "present." The debasing living conditions that sub-Saharan immigrants endure in the Moroccan forests around the Spanish enclaves of Ceuta and Melilla destroy any belief in political commitment to the universality of human rights.[4] The human dramas that unfold every day are a result of the common perception in which migration poses a problem to the global system based on territory and the social system of the nation-state, which therefore needs to be prevented and contained by the use of particularly violent dissuasive measures (Düvell 2004, 9; Médecins sans Frontières 2005, 4), of which detention is one of the more conspicuous, not least because it is (also) taking place within the territorial borders of Western democratic states.

Indeed, although immigration detention is seldom a transparent practice, because information concerning detention facilities is often not made public and many of these facilities are located in isolated places, the public media nonetheless regularly bring to light evidence of unacceptable conditions in "closed centers" for immigrants. In addition, numerous reports by NGOs in European countries describe multiple instances of abuse in immigration detention, lack of structures of adequate accommodation, illegal detention beyond the foreseen time limits and other serious legal gaps, and the detrimental effects of detention on the mental health of immigration detainees. More often than not, these reports are confirmed by the findings of the European Committee for the Prevention of Torture and Inhuman or Degrading Treatment or Punishment (CPT) during its visits to places where immigrants are deprived of their liberty (CPT 2007, 2008a, 2008b).

Under these circumstances, the detention of thousands of people in Europe, merely because they allegedly breach the state's territorial sovereignty, may easily be labeled as an anomaly for Western liberal democracies, especially when seen in the context and development of citizenship discourse, constitutionalism, and human rights. However, it would be too easy to portray immigration detention solely as an incongruity for otherwise liberal regimes. Instead I believe that the practice of depriving unwanted foreigners of their liberty is a consequence of the territorial foundations of the modern state and the global political system, and their impact on constitutional discourse. More specifically, I argue that immigration detention is a form of state violence that has become so deeply embedded within the dominant understanding of the sovereign state and the global territorial structure of states that it has remained insulated against the usual forms of legal correction and political control.

However, before addressing the particular logic that governs immigration detention, it is imperative to understand the logic that governs immigration law enforcement in general. To do this, we need to delve a little deeper into the way in which territory and notions of political power have become so intricately linked that political territoriality—the result of historical contingencies—has acquired a halo of naturalness and necessity in the contemporary global order.

The Modern State and Territorial Sovereignty

The sovereign state as the dominant form of political organization is a relatively recent phenomenon. Before 1648, the year in which the Peace of Westphalia ended the Thirty Years' War, political power in Europe was not linked to clearly demarcated territory but was largely based on personal relations. These relations were manifold, and medieval Europe consisted of a patchwork of overlapping political loyalties and shifting hierarchies of authority. However, by the end of the fifteenth century, monarchical power had grown enormously in almost all of Europe at the expense of medieval institutions, such as feudalism, free city-states, and the church. The state surpassed other forms of political organization in the late Middle Ages, as it was large enough to withstand military attacks but small enough for effective central administration (Linklater 1998b, 27). Furthermore, the balance struck by the emerging territorial state between possession of the means of violence and capital accumulation made it more successful in vindicating its claims to power in comparison to other political entities that concentrated mainly on only one of the two means of power (Tilly 1992, 30–31).

Thus other claims to political power gradually diminished in significance, and the medieval patchwork was slowly transformed into a more rigid system of independent territorial states in which political power was exercised over people, no longer on account of their specific position in the body politic, but because they lived in a certain, clearly demarcated territory. *Territoriality* is the term that is used to denote the founding of political authority on demarcated territory. This still-current way of organizing global political life is founded on the modern concept of sovereignty.

For the notion of sovereignty to reemerge from Roman law and acquire its fundamental place in political thought, the gradual consolidation of power and territory under a single and supreme ruler in fifteenth-century Europe was crucial. The political turmoil and religious wars of the subsequent two centuries likewise played an essential role. Before the Reformation, the political order of Europe was perceived as a single community, even if only in theory: the Res Publica Christiana. Formal theories on political order were inevitably influenced by the breakdown of the medieval religious order.

In addition to considerations of theoretical coherence, early theorists who developed the modern notion of sovereignty, having witnessed the violence that ravaged Europe in the medieval era, were also in a very real sense preoccupied with political stability and the unity of the body politic. They thought that such unity and stability could be achieved only by strengthening the power of the ruler, internally as well as externally. Sovereignty, "the perpetual and absolute power of a republic,"[5] was to provide the answer. Sovereignty became a notion that was necessary for the very existence of the body politic, thus conceptually detached from God, pope, emperor, or king (Allen 1926/1967, 59).

These changes were reflected in what we would now call international relations: when the Peace of Westphalia in 1648 anchored the principle of territorial sovereignty in international law, it meant that the sovereign exercised exclusive and ultimate power over people because of their presence in a certain territory. Although sovereign power initially continued to reside in the king, in due time the perception that relations of political authority were personal would change under the influence of theories of popular sovereignty. Indeed, the very abstraction of the concept of sovereignty, through which it distinguished itself from earlier theories by which men had attempted to legitimize political power, made possible the dispute between monarchical and popular sovereignty.

For our purposes, it is important to grasp that the territorial system of mutually independent states does not only constitute states or merely regulate their conduct. Territoriality also brings about what Barry Hindess calls a "dispersed regime of governance covering the overall population of the states concerned" (1998, 65). Indeed, sovereignty in international law does not only entail exclusive authority over clearly demarcated territory but in practice assigns each and every state with the responsibility over a distinct, territorially defined population. This external construction of state sovereignty corresponds with its internal claim of distinguishing the inside from the outside, a distinction that, in later times, would evolve to the distinction between "us" and "them." The contemporary portrayal of immigration as a phenomenon that upsets the existing order is the result of the perceived naturalness of the way in which the modern notion of sovereignty has linked people, territory, and authority and its particular construction of an inside and an outside.

However, territoriality's role is more insidious than its contribution to the "false necessity" of immigration law enforcement in our societies, to which I will return later. Territoriality has decisively influenced the discourses that, over time, sought to restrain the exercise of absolute sovereign power. By focusing on the particular historical institutionalization of these discourses within either the territorial state itself or, alternately, a global system of territorial states, we find the key to understanding the immigration prison.

Citizenship as Inconsistent Universalism

The development of territoriality has consistently obstructed the realiza-tion of universalistic ideals that also underlie the idea of the modern state. Despite the universalistic ambitions of modern citizenship and the human rights discourse—as the most recent form of modern constitutionalism—these discourses have in some senses contributed to a strengthening of the sovereign territorial ideal: in our world, access to national territory is determinative for the extent of rights to be enjoyed. As such, states benefit from keeping people out of their territories. What is more, the assumed necessity of territory as an organizing device for the global po-litical system has led to an immunization of territorial sovereignty against the conventional forces of legal correction. Immigration detention is the ultimate example of how national states can freely resort to their hitherto unrestrained territorial powers in order to validate sovereignty's claim to distinguish the inside from the outside.

At no point in history has sovereignty meant absolute rule without ac-countability, and arbitrary use of power by the sovereign has never gone unchallenged. The rise of territorial concentrations of power in the West-phalian era in particular has been checked by developments in two dif-ferent areas. Internally, the growth of state power led to the demand for citizenship rights, offering protection to the people against the arbitrary use of power by the state. Externally, the state was to undergo constraints formulated by international law (Linklater 1998b, 213).

Within the body politic, material limits to the power of the ruler—be it emperor, king, or the modern state itself—have always been entailed by individual liberties. At the time that relations of political authority were perceived as personal ties, these liberties were of a contractual character (Shafir 2004, 13; Burkens 1989, 3). The modern notion of individual rights, as opposed to the medieval privileges, emerged during the seventeenth century, finding its origins in the Christian tradition. It developed further in the eighteenth century under the influence of Enlightenment thinking with its emphasis on the notions of liberty and equality. The fundamental difference with the medieval era was that in theory, rights were accorded to people because of their membership in humankind and not any lon-ger on account of their specific position in the body politic. Fundamental rights were deemed to exist independently and antecedently of any kind of political power (van der Pot and Donner 1995, 24; Sabine 1941, 525), an idea that found its most famous expression in the French Declaration of the Rights of Man and Citizen of 1789.[6]

However, the same rights that the French Revolution had declared inalienable and inherent in man because of his membership of the human race soon became inextricably linked to national citizenship. In practice, people enjoyed protection of their fundamental rights on account of their membership in the territorial state instead of by reason of their "humanity." Such novel political particularism could be witnessed in the whole of western Europe: whereas the revolution had at least been inspired by the ideal of universal mankind, the spreading of revolutionary ideals over Europe led to demands for national rights of peoples, not to claims concerning the universality of mankind (Kristeva 1991, 151). To understand this apparent paradox, we need to distinguish between the formation of the territorial state and the building of the nation as different, even if converging, processes (Habermas 1996, 283).

Already before the eighteenth century, monarchs had attempted to homogenize their populations through, *inter alia*, the expulsion of religious minorities and the encouragement of language standardization. However, these attempts had little to do with nationalism in the modern sense. Instead they were a result of the wish to create strong territorial entities inhabited with individuals of whose allegiance one could be certain. In the medieval order, with its emphasis on difference, there was little awareness of the people as more than a collection of individuals (Melzer 2000). Nationalism, a relationship between individuals that goes deeper than their common allegiance to the ruler (Fitzsimmons 1993, 29; Habermas 1996, 285), entered the political arena only when the modern ideals of equality acquired political significance. This can partly be explained by the fact that territoriality was an established fact at the moment that the modern reformers wished to revolutionize the former foundations of political power. Thus the universalist ideals of the eighteenth century came to be executed within the existing framework of the territorial state system, each accorded with responsibility over a territorially defined group of people.

In addition, and this is a structural shortcoming of liberal thought in general, social contract theories fail to define what is meant with a concept as intangible as "the people." They do not explain why the free and equal individual from the state of nature does not commit himself to the whole of humanity. By lacking an adequate justification for the fact that in reality the social contract is territorially limited, these theories open the door to the "nationalization of political communities" and the "political-ization of national communities" (Yack 2001).

The Declaration of the Rights of Man, which holds that sovereignty rests with the nation, provides an ultimate illustration of the identification of the notion of the people with the concept of the nation. The struggle for control of state power was surely no longer a matter of divine right, but it had not become solely an issue of natural rights for the people. Instead it had shifted to the area of national identity (Xenos 1996, 238). In the same way, the declaration creates a duality between man and citizen: "The man supposedly independent of all government turns out to be the citizen of a nation" (Kristeva 1991, 150). The Italian philosopher Giorgio Agamben claims that "declarations of rights must therefore be viewed as the place in which the passage from divinely authorized royal sovereignty to national sovereignty is accomplished. This passage assures the *exceptio* of life in the new state order that will succeed the collapse of the *ancien régime*" (1998, 128). Only the "bare life" of the individual who is also a national can thus be transformed into citizenship. In Agamben's view, it was inevitable that the condition for access to inalienable rights changed from the abstract notion of a common humanity to the exclusive and particular concept of national citizenship.

Hannah Arendt writes that the disastrous consequences of the identification of the rights of man with the rights of the citizen in the European nation-state system became clear only in the twentieth century (1951/1966, 291). Nationalism had by then long lost its original function of integrating diverse social strata and peoples in one nation, but under the influence of romanticism, it had led to an exclusive ideal of the nation-state, purport-edly constituted by a people whose bonds to each other and to its territory were prepolitical. The plight of refugees and the stateless, and the suffer-ings of the victims of totalitarian governments, showed that "the Rights of Man, supposedly inalienable, proved to be unenforceable—even in coun-tries whose constitutions were based upon them—whenever people ap-peared who were no longer citizens of any sovereign state" (293).

For those not belonging to the territorial nation-state, rights had be-come illusionary: the loss of national rights in practice meant the loss of human rights. The terminology that was adopted to address forced mi-grations after World War II gives a clear example of the process by which identity and space had become incontestably linked and by which space is inscribed with strong political meaning. Massive population transfers based on ethnicity were tellingly called "repatriation," and people without a nationality were termed "displaced."

Classic International Law, Contemporary Human Rights,
and Their Territorial Bias

After 1945, the international community recognized the dangers of a system in which the sovereign state was the ultimate arbiter with regard to the question of who was entitled to the enjoyment of fundamental rights. International human rights were supposed to close the gap between the universal aspirations of the discourse of fundamental rights and an everyday reality that was to a high degree characterized by political particularism. However, before I turn to international human rights, I will briefly address classic international law and the way in which it has articulated legal norms with regard to state violence in the past. We can properly assess the alleged novelty of international human rights law only after we appreciate territoriality's influence on what was before 1945 solely the law for and between sovereign states. We will see that in classic international law, violence and territorial boundaries are connected by a comparable logic as that which binds people, territory, and authority together within the nation-state.

International law emerged at a time when the state was not the decisive political entity that it was later to become. Early theorists of international law fully included the individual as a subject of international law (Nijman 2004, 46–47). However, the process of territorialization doubly diminished the position of the individual in international law. In the first place, through that process, the state became gradually perceived as a unified force, with supreme and exclusive authority within a certain territory (Plender 1972, 10). The reification of the national state by the use of constructed concepts such as territoriality and nationality led to a perception of international law as the law for and by sovereign states alone, the cornerstone of which became the exclusion of external authority from the state's territory.

Second, the inside-outside distinction that was brought about by territorialization had the insidious effect of drawing a corresponding distinction between internal and external violence. Violence perpetrated on the individual within the territorial state's boundaries was a matter for the sovereign state alone, and classic international law has largely ignored the question of violence by the state within the state (Mansbach and Wilmer 2001, 63; Donnelly 1994, 8; Henkin 1999, 4). Violence between states, on the other hand, was regulated by the articulation of norms through the laws of war, which were based on strong territorial assumptions (Mansbach and Wilmer 2001, 60; J. Fitzpatrick 2002). Classic international law's main aim was to protect the territorial sovereignty of the modern state, thereby guaranteeing the continued existence of the Westphalian state system, in which each state was accorded the exclusive responsibility over a well-defined population. Thus classic international law rarely took into account the interests of individuals as such, neither with regard to the exercise of a state's jurisdiction over persons within a certain territory, nor with regard to the deployment of its spatial powers.

The separateness of the discourses regulating internal and external restraints on state power led to a gap between national and international law. When, between the two world wars, sovereignty's exclusive link between territory, identity, and rights was at its firmest, the existence of that very gap resulted in the absence of any enforceable rights for large groups of individuals. The terrible consequences thereof became clear during World War II, exemplified as they were in spaces of rightlessness, such as the concentration and extermination camps and, to a lesser degree, the internment camps for displaced people and refugees.

After 1945, the welfare and dignity of the individual, irrespective of nationality, were increasingly considered a matter of international concern by the international community (Oda 1968, 495). The Nuremberg war crimes trials prosecuted individuals on the novel charge of crimes against humanity. Crimes committed against a state's own population, irrespective of nationality or other status, became a general matter of concern for international law. The emerging human rights regime captured in various legal documents carried this process further. Although international law is largely silent with regard to the national state's discretion to admit or refuse aliens, once they are present within the territory of the national state, international human rights norms impose important obligations upon the state with regard to noncitizens (Dummet and Nicol 1990). In this sense, international law has significantly restrained the state's jurisdictional sovereignty.

However, the discourse of international human rights has not been able to live up to its devotees' claim that it brought about a "new model of membership, anchored in deterritorialized notions of individual rights" (Soysal 1994, 3). We can distinguish two separate causes behind human rights' inability to become truly universal. In the first place, human rights and their realization depend on the state system (Henkin 1999, 7; Shafir 2004, 23), a structure in which, as we saw, governance is undertaken on a territorial basis that disperses authority for the human community as a whole into the mutually exclusive jurisdictions of territorial states. Celebrations of so-called postnational citizenship tend to overlook the territoriality of the global political system and thus fail to appreciate its pivotal role in the practice of fundamental rights protection. Thus the impact of human rights is solely investigated as a process taking place within the Western modern state as a closed container. Only from that inherently limited perspective does it make sense to claim that nationality may no longer be decisive for the extent of access to rights.

Yet a great part of the world's population lives in states where even the rights that accrue to them by virtue of their citizenship status do not live up to the standards set by the modern human rights discourse, while they are at the same time prevented from entering Western liberal democracies that accord the full range of human rights only to those whose presence the state has authorized. Apparently, then, the discourse of human rights has not learned a lesson from citizenship's past: just as in 1789, so today the territorial borders of the Western nation-state determine the exact limits of the universality of fundamental rights. The reason for this failure of the human rights discourse has to be sought in the very concept of the territorial state and the system of which it is part (cf. Agamben 1993/2000, 20).

Furthermore, international human rights have not departed from classic international law's canonization of the integrity of national territory. The result is that even though they have put limits to the modern state's jurisdiction within a given territory, they have not constrained the exercise of power when based on sovereignty's territorial form. The safeguarding of its territorial boundaries remains the exclusive prerogative of the sovereign state. Regarding territorial sovereignty, contemporary international law is still the law for and by sovereign states alone, solely serving the narrow interest of the stability of the global territorial order (McCorquodale 2001, 138), in which the individual as such has no role to play and his interests do not need to be accounted for.

I have argued here that the territoriality of the global system impedes the realization of human rights' universal aspirations, as the question of access to rights is still largely determined by a global regime of governance that decrees where one belongs. Furthermore, human rights have not made any significant inroads in the state's assertion of its territorial sovereignty. International law has not developed a language that is able to address the personal interests that are affected whenever the state bases its claims on sovereignty's territorial form. As a result, whenever the state presents an issue—such as immigration—as an urgent threat to its territorial sovereignty, international law falls back on the classic legal discourse designed to address interstate violence, which merely emphasizes the integrity of territorial boundaries, and in which personal interests remain inarticulable. As I will argue hereafter, in our contemporary societies, the territorial biases of the modern version of the Rule of Law are nowhere more visible than in the practice of immigration detention.

IMMIGRATION DETENTION AND TERRITORIALITY

Before turning to immigration detention in particular as both an inevitable outcome of the territoriality of the global political system and the result of the territorial bias in modern constitutional discourse, I will analyze deportation—the alleged aim of immigration detention. Deportation constitutes a means by which the national state attempts to keep the Westphalian ideal intact, therewith anxiously guarding the territoriality of the Rule of Law. Indeed, a practice such as deportation is not simply a "functional by-product of some presumed (and thus teleological) structural logic" (De Genova 2002, 424); rather, it actively contributes to reproducing the territorial order (Walters 2002a, 288).

Immigration Law Enforcement as a Technology to Maintain the Territorial Ideal

Deportation is not the singular response of states to one singular situation. On the contrary, various forms of deportation have been used at different times as a tool to facilitate state building and to regulate wealth, and as a means of social regulation and a way in which to realize national ideology. Modern deportation practice, which, in principle, solely targets nonnationals, can be understood only in the context of the territorial state system, in which distinct populations are ascribed to distinct territorial entities. The practice of deportation is constitutive of the contemporary territorial order, a situation reflected in modern international law that has delegitimized historical forms of expulsion while simultaneously it naturalized the link between deportation and foreign nationals (Walters 2002a, 288). Once again it is possible to discern international law's opposing tendencies: it couples concern with, and limitations on, the state's exercise of jurisdiction over those who "belong" with acquiescence to the state's exercise of power whenever it is based on sovereignty's territorial form. Immigration law enforcement is portrayed as solely engaging territorial sovereignty, frequently even in a language that explicitly refers to the sanctity of territorial boundaries in the context of armed conflict.[7] As a result of the resonating force of that language, the personal interests that are indisputably involved in a practice such as deportation remain inarticulable. Thus we will understand contemporary international law's differentiation between the transportation of the socially undesirable, religious minorities, or citizens in general and the deportation of the "foreigner" only if we take into account the "sacred" territorial basis of the sovereign claim to regulate immigration.

Moreover, deportation does not only function as a concrete way in which to govern populations. In light of the ineffectiveness of many expulsion measures in the majority of Western states (Nascimbene 2001; Schuster 2005, 612), deportation's significance is perhaps also of a symbolic and indirect character. Matthew Gibney and Randall Hansen argue that although deportation measures are often ineffectual, they are a necessity for governments who need to appear in control of migration and borders, because deportation "assuages public opinion which would not view the state's incapacity in this area with equanimity" and because it acts as an "(unquantifiable) disincentive" to other potential migrants (2003, 15). In addition, what Nicholas De Genova calls "the spectacle of 'enforcement' " makes the sovereign claim to determine a certain "inside" from a certain "outside" seem natural, necessary, and urgent (2002, 436).

Hence the practice of deportation elucidates two features of contemporary state power. In the first place, by appreciating that deportation is central to the allocation of populations to states (Walters 2002a, 267), we are presented with a view of state power that aims to keep intact the territorial system of sovereign states in which the Rule of Law remains territorially limited. This is the structural role of each state's territorial sovereignty. In the second place, the practice of deportation also presents an internal image of state power. Deportation is necessary to prove that a state takes control of its borders, and it epitomizes *and* justifies sovereignty's claim to distinguish between the inside and the outside.

The structural and internal manifestations of state power thus revealed by contemporary deportation practices are complementary and mutually reinforcing, as is illustrated by the continuity between the externalization of border control such as visa requirements and readmission agreements and its internalization resulting precisely from practices such as deportation and detention (Rigo 2003, 11). Similarly, the criminalization of "illegal" stay in a national territory also shows how both features of state power complement each other: territorial governance of populations has reached a peak when merely administrative sanctions no longer seem to suffice and the tendency to criminalize migrants internally gives a powerful incentive to the inside-outside distinction. Likewise, the widespread use of the word "illegal" in conjunction with migration and migrants when discussing preventive and international approaches to migration—though logically "a migrant can only be illegal once he finds himself within a state whose laws define his presence as illegal" (Guild 2005, 27)—has the same effect of both emphasizing each individual state's territorial sovereignty and calling attention to an international structure of territorial governance of the larger human population in which certain kinds of movement are taken for granted while other forms are undesir-able and thus penalized.

The Immigration Prison as a Site of Sedentarization

The foregoing observations on state power and deportation hold equally true for administrative practices of immigration detention: if their aim is to facilitate removal and prevent illegal stay, they perpetuate a territorial image of the world. And even if the majority of those held in detention centers are eventually released (Schuster 2005, 612–13), detention—like deportation—is a necessity for states that want to be seen by their own populations to be in control of their borders. Furthermore, the symbolic function of immigration detention lies also in its deterrent effect to the outside world (Walters 2002a, 286) and the way in which it makes vis-ible migrant "illegality" (De Genova 2002, 438). However, immigration detention is special among the other venues through which states try to stem unwanted immigration. It is this practice that, even more so than deportation, exemplifies in the clearest possible way the consequences of a world fully divided into territorial nation-states. In order to place the contemporary regulation of human mobility by the immigration prison in a broader perspective, it is instructive to take a brief look at various forms of imprisonment in the history of the modern state.

In *Madness and Civilization*, Michel Foucault traces the origins of, and rationale behind, the great confinement of the seventeenth century, which ascribed "the same homeland to the poor, to the unemployed, to pris-oners and to the insane" (1967, 39). The poor laws of medieval Europe were in the seventeenth and eighteenth centuries replaced by regulations that provided for the "territorial sedentarization" (Walters 2002a, 286) of those who would previously have been expelled (Foucault 1967, 48). Thus, instead of being simply excluded, the poor and those without a fixed abode were now governed, albeit still by a logic that was driven by the "fear of pauperism, with its dangerous 'fluid, elusive sociality, impossible to control or utilise' " (Walters 2002a, 286).

The emergence of imprisonment as an instituted response to serious crime dates from the eighteenth century and was linked in important ways with the development of the modern state (Foucault 1975/1977). In the first place, practices of imprisonment had for centuries been linked with the worst abuses of royal power, a despotism of which the infamous *lettres de cachet* offer the best example (Foucault 1975/1977; 1967, 38). Yet, in modernity, prisons became a site where the very power to punish was made accountable and measurable, and as such, imprisonment can be seen as an "enabling technology of what we would now call the rule of law" (Simon 1998, 597). Second, the imprisonment of criminals, just as the confinement of the poor, had important reforming functions. These two elements in particular ensure that the "rise of the penitentiary . . . is in a very real sense a story of rights and liberties as much as it is a story of prejudice and oppression" (597).

Such a story of rights and liberties is conspicuously absent in Hannah Arendt's account of the internment camps that were set up for the stateless and refugees of totalitarian regimes during the 1930s in Europe. Toward the end of World War II, millions of refugees and displaced people were kept in these camps, scattered all over Europe: many of the former work and concentration camps in Germany were used as "assembly centers" for these people after the war had ended (Malkki 1995, 499). The very existence of the internment camps before, during, and after the war made it painfully clear that by then everybody was supposed to "belong" somewhere. As the national state did not know what to do with those foreigners who had lost the protection of their national governments, they were forced to live outside the jurisdiction of the law, interned in camps, which became "the only practical substitute for a nonexistent homeland" (Arendt 1951/1966, 284). In other words, the very construction of a world made up of territorial nation-states with their rigid link between identity, territory, and rights caused the internment camp to become "the only 'country' the world had to offer the stateless" (284).

The detention of the unwanted foreigner in contemporary Europe can be seen as a similar technique of territorial control of persons in order to deal with perceived threats, not merely to the nation-state but also to the international territorial system as a whole. The changing character of the logic currently used to designate those imagined dangers should not distract us from the fact that the specter of the contemporary "illegal immigrant" and "bogus asylum seeker" represents *and* evokes the same fear of losing territorial control as did the stateless and displaced people of more than half a century ago.

Hence immigration detention is not solely a technology that aims at preserving the territorial state system and its concomitant link between territory and rights. Immigration detention is an explicit exception to the assumption that all the world's populations belong to a country, but at the same time that very assumption depends on the existence of immigration detention (Walters 2002a, 286). The immigration detention center provides an immediate place for those who do not fit within the territorial ideal of the world. Thus the asylum seeker and the "illegal" immigrant "represent the nomadic excess that the state seeks to capture and normalize through panoptic confinement" in detention centers (Diken and Laustsen 2003, 3).

Immigration Detention as a Tale of Exceptionalism

We have seen that immigration detention is a tool by which states violently reproduce the territoriality of the global state system. Furthermore, detention serves as a validation of sovereignty as the power to distinguish the inside from the outside. In addition, it has become clear that the immigration prison provides a territorial solution for something that is perceived as a problem in our contemporary world precisely because it resists the conventional territorial solution. Yet even more is at stake in practices of detention.

Perhaps most important of all, by employing detention, states resort to the sharpest technique to achieve the related goals of imaginary unity, maintenance of the territorial order, and sedentarization. Personal liberty and sovereignty are conceptually intertwined: the protection of personal liberty is the reason for the existence of sovereignty. The intimate relationship between the two warrants the utmost scrutiny when assessing the detention of the individual in light of traditional safeguards against sovereign power. Nevertheless, these traditional safeguards are conspicuously absent when it comes to the indiscriminate detention of thousands of noncitizens in liberal democracies.

Indeed, their very exceptionalism makes complete the parallel between the postwar internment camps and the contemporary immigration prison. In Hannah Arendt's portrayal of the internment camps, elements of reform, as can be discerned in the historic confinement of the poor, were absent. Nor did Arendt's account resemble a partial story of rights and liberties, as may be perceived in the development of the prison as an answer to crime. Rather, she presents us with a pure image of exceptionalism: sovereign power that is reduced to violence, a situation in which the Rule of Law has reached its limits. Innocent people were placed outside the normal legal order, and it seemed easier to deprive them of their right to have rights than to similarly deprive those who had committed a crime: a situation that Arendt calls one of the perplexities of the rights of man.

Contemporary immigration policies that result in the indiscriminate detention of thousands of people, frequently for periods that are not bound to a maximum by law, under special security administration, special laws, and wide administrative powers in places that are difficult to access and control, are without doubt a practice that is outside the usual legal framework of the *Rechtsstaat*. Bülent Diken and Carsten Laustsen recount the outbreak from the Australian Woomera detention camp in 2002, where fifty people managed to escape. Most of them were captured afterward but "are unlikely to be prosecuted or jailed—if they were, they would have visiting rights and a definite length of imprisonment, luxuries denied them as asylum seekers inside Woomera" (Diken and Laustsen 2003, 5). The inability of the Rule of Law to address the human interests that are affected whenever the state bases its claims on territorial sovereignty results in spaces of near rightlessness, such as the immigration prison. Its twofold logic of sedentarization and exceptionalism leads to what Agamben (1998) has called "exclusionary inclusion." Although detention puts those who belong elsewhere outside the normal legal framework of the liberal state on account of the perceived threat they pose to the global territorial system, their life inside the immigration detention center is strictly ruled and restricted by the law, and they are thus in a real sense included in the state's domain of sovereign power (Diken and Laustsen 2003, 2–3; Foucault 1975/1977, 301).

THE TERRITORIAL LIMITS OF THE RULE OF LAW IN AN IDEAL WORLD

I have argued that territoriality as a social construction is crucial in understanding the contemporary regulation of human mobility. Territoriality has turned the instruments that intend to protect against the violence of the state into political particularist discourses. With specific regard to the discourse of human rights, I have argued that questions of access to, and enjoyment of, human rights remain territorially determined. In addition, the human rights discourse has not developed a way to address violations of human dignity that occur as a result of the state's exercise of its territorial sovereignty. Western states are only too eager to protect the territoriality of fundamental rights protection, as is shown by the practice of deportation. Moreover, by using detention to keep the territorial ideal intact and reduce the visibility of disruptions to that very ideal, states avail themselves of the fact that with regard to territorial sovereignty, international law is still the law by and for sovereign states alone, in spite of the advent of human rights norms. Thus the very particularity of immigration detention lies in the cynical use that governments make of a system in which territory and rights remain firmly linked, despite celebrations of universal rights and assertions of postnational citizenship. Immigrants who are deprived of their liberty inside or at the borders of liberal Western democracies are in essence outside the pale of the law: even in the case that they are actually within the territory of a national state, the absence of initial state authorization for their presence on national territory leads to the usual safeguards embodied in international legal norms not applying to them. Even an international constitutional court such as the European Court of Human Rights in Strasbourg does not deem it within its powers to reverse this situation (cf. Cornelisse 2004).

Camps for "illegal" immigrants are also set up in countries such as Algeria, Tunisia, Mauritius, Morocco, and Libya, if not under formal supervision of European Union member states, then certainly at their instigation (Helmut 2005; Andrijasevic 2006, this volume). Italy finances the construction of various detention camps in Libya (European Commission 2005, 59), and Spain has agreed to pay for the construction of several detention centers for "illegal" immigrants in Mauritania (Reuters, March 17, 2006). The European Commission recently adopted measures to help Mauritania contain the flow of "illegal" immigrants to the Canary Islands. Resources for detention form part of the package, a €2.45 million program, which furthermore includes capacity building for detection and apprehension, the revision of existing legislation, and institutional support (European Commission 2006). The background of such initiatives is a growing unwillingness on the part of the EU to deal with the effects of migration on its own soil, but to contain the problem in non-member states, who are enticed to cooperate with political and financial advantages. By exporting the immigration prison in particular, Western states have perfected their strategy of unaccountability for violations of human dignity in the field of migration.[8] That a real danger exists that this will cause the international legal regime to be "perceived by the rest of the world as a . . . tool that primarily serves to perpetuate the advantages held by the West" is the least of its evils (Tamanaha 2004, 135).

The postwar internment camps made painfully clear that the Rights of Man depended entirely on citizenship. Evidently the rationale for their exceptionalism was the assumed threat of the stateless and refugees to the unity of the state and the overall order of the state system. In this respect, not much has changed over the last sixty years. Although those sixty years saw the emergence of yet another discourse that is supposed to be based on the universal dignity of the individual, the camp is still the only place that we have to offer those people who do not fit in our particular image of the world.

NOTES

I would like to thank my colleagues at Utrecht University and Dr. Victor Igreja for helpful comments on an earlier draft. I am also grateful to the editors of this volume for their valuable suggestions, from which the chapter has greatly benefited. The usual disclaimer applies. The research for this work was made possible in the framework of the Challenge project (the Changing Landscape of European Liberty and Security), a research program funded by the European Commission's Directorate-General for Research under the Sixth EU Framework Programme.

1. In an interview with the *Corriere Della Sera* on July 3, 2006, the Italian president Giorgio Napolitano said, "There isn't any alternative to the immigration detention center. One can perhaps discuss the way in which these centers function, but it is an entirely different thing to require their closure. If problems of overpopulation exist—instead of thinking of closing the centers—we need to open new ones."

2. The perceived naturalness of the link between detention and deportation is emphasized by official communications such as the following by the British Home Office when it announced plans to substantially increase immigration detention capacity: "The extra spaces, which will total between 1,300 and 1,500 detention places, will help the government continue to increase the number of deportations of illegal immigrants. Already one illegal immigrant is deported from the country every eight minutes." UK Home Office, May 19, 2008, http:// www.homeoffice.gov.uk.

3. For a critical appraisal of the legal responses in Europe to this phenomenon, see Askola 2007.

4. See documentation and witness accounts reported by Médecins sans Frontières (2005).

5. Jean Bodin, in *Les six livres de la république* (1576), a work written in, and clearly influenced by, the disorder of a secularizing France in the late sixteenth century.

6. At this point, it is important to note that the universal values of Enlightenment ideology were never as universal as might retrospectively be inferred.

The discourse was exclusively European, equating humankind with so-called "civilized society." In addition, it would take centuries until women and those without property were even nominally included in the discourse of rights and equality. Arguably, some of those "groups" are still not fully included, in that the concept of rights even within the well-defined borders of the territorial nation-state cannot wholly be separated from social relations that assume a contractual form of appearance.

7. See, for example, the U.S. Supreme Court ruling *Chae Chan Ping v. United States*: "To preserve its independence, and give security against foreign aggression and encroachment, is the highest duty of every nation, and to attain these ends nearly all other considerations are to be subordinated. It matters not in what form such aggression and encroachment come, whether from the foreign nation acting in its national character or from vast hordes of its people crowding in upon us" (130 U.S. [1889] 581, at 606).

8. European states' policies are clearly inspired by Australia's "Pacific solution," its asylum policy consisting of "patrolling a naval barrier created around Australia's territorial waters in order to prevent unauthorized vessels carrying asylum seekers from entering. Intercepted vessels are diverted to offshore processing centers in countries to host [them] in return for financial incentives. . . . If granted refugee status, the refugees are then resettled in third countries" (Lynskey 2006, 242).

—w—

CHAPTER 3

Mapping the European Space
of Circulation

This chapter addresses the illegalization of people's movement in terms that are different than those of mainstream sociological and migration theory by describing the increasing "externalization" of mechanisms of migration control in Europe and exploring the way in which policies against clandestine migration are discursively justified. Current scholarly and political debates about migration tend to be framed by functionalist misconceptions of clandestinity. In contrast, we call into question the very possibility of identifying any objective category of analysis such as "illegal migration" by shedding light on the continuity between the externalization of border control regimes and the internal migration policies of the European Union. Rather than keeping trespassers on the outside, this continuity appears to define the European legal and political space as a space specifically dedicated to governing mobility, both inside and across the EU's official borders.

This particular condition of migration today has its origins in the history of struggles around migration in Europe. This chapter provides an overview of the different figures of migration that have been central to public discourse during the various stages of mobility control since World War II. As in the case of guest workers or asylum seekers, clandestine migration needs to be placed in a wider framework of analysis that fully considers the dialectical relationship between national and supernational policies and the subjective drive that is inherent to any form of human mobility.

In adopting this approach, we analyze the economic system in which clandestine migration takes place, refuting the functionalist interpretations and conspiracy theories that often shape public debate. Instead we attempt to understand how the legal framework regulating recruitment, flexibility, and rotation has shifted, with a particular focus on the changes to the contemporary European legal and political space.

Finally, we discuss the kinds of subjectivities that are produced through the illegalization of people's movements and the ways in which these reconstitute the distinction between aliens and citizens. By conceptualizing mobility as a specific form of political articulation that is not simply induced by economic factors and regulated by rules imposed by institutional actors, we reclaim the active role of global migration practices in undermining the foundations of "border sovereignty" and in reshaping the political and legal space of Europe.

DEFINING THE BORDERS OF EUROPE

In November 2003 the European Council adopted the concept of "the virtual maritime border" in order "to reinforce the legal borders of Member States by means of joint operations and specific measures in the places where illegal migratory flows originate or transit."[1] One of the main purposes of the council's decisions has been to overcome the limitations imposed by the Montego Bay Convention,[2] which did not allow for the shipping authorities of a state other than the flag state to intercept and inspect a ship at high sea on the suspicion of "illegal" immigration. The general principle of freedom at high sea meant that the sea was a common and free space, which belonged to—and could be used by—everybody. Today, however, every vessel suspected of transporting "illegal" migrants is considered a virtual border when its nationality is unknown or uncertain. As a consequence, it is excluded from cases of "innocent passage" in territorial waters (section 3 of the Montego Bay Convention) and is subject to joint controls by member states irrespective of the geographic distance between the patrolled waters and the coastlines of member states. Such controls are conducted with the most advanced military equipment.[3]

The virtual maritime border is only one example of the recent process of "externalization" of the European Union's frontiers, which has sought to tackle so-called "illegal migration."[4] This process comprises various sets of migration and asylum policies such as the safe-third-country policy whereby asylum seekers are readmitted to non-EU countries through which they pass,[5] the capacity-building policies that use development aid to create the conditions so that the EU may conclude agreements for the readmission of "illegal" migrants with third countries' governments,[6] and—more recently—the proposal of "outsourcing" policies,[7] under which all or most asylum seekers who arrive or apply in member states would be sent to transit processing centers located outside the EU for the processing of their application by EU-appointed officials. According to the proposal presented by the British government in 2003, the intended function of such centers is to deter "those who enter the EU illegally and make unfounded asylum applications," while it remains under consideration "whether the centre would also receive illegal migrants intercepted en route to the EU before they had lodged an asylum claim but where they had a clear intention of doing so."[8]

The use of the term "externalization" has become increasingly common both in European public debates and in the literature on migration and asylum. For example, the Hague program of November 2004—which sets out the strategies for European asylum and migration policies over the next five years—summarizes the rationale of its approach under the label "external dimension of asylum and migration" and states that "asylum and migration are by their very nature international issues."[9] However, while the literature is increasingly emphasizing the threat connected to these policies with respect to humanitarian concerns (cf. Schuster 2006; Byrne, Noll, and Vedsted-Hansen 2002), less attention has been given to a number of issues that externalization processes raise in relation to the functioning of European borders and the discursive construction of people's mobility as the target for new sets of governing strategies. On the one hand, the fight against "illegal migration" is frequently supported—or alternatively criticized—on the basis of its greater or lesser effectiveness, the degree to which it meets human-rights standards of protection, its consistency with economic paradigms rather than with constraints on freedom, and other such arguments. On the other hand, "illegal migration" itself as a specific object of policies or as a distinct category of analysis is rarely questioned.

In contrast to this approach, which is widespread among both official discourse and its critiques, the example of the "virtual" border, as well as the example of "transit processing" centers located outside the EU, raises doubts over whether people's movements can be considered "illegal" when they have yet to reach one of the EU's official frontiers. As far as legal definitions are concerned, EU official documents on externalization policies do not actually use the term "illegal migration" in a technical manner: they do not directly affect or modify the legal *status* of migrants but rather identify sets of operational policies and nonbinding practices or establish common lines according to which national and international rules should be interpreted (as in the case of the "programme of measures to combat illegal immigration across the maritime borders"). That said, "illegal migration" is undoubtedly considered as an objectified target of these same practices and policies, thus implying an already established normative categorization of people's movements.

The performative (and not merely prescriptive) nature of legal discourses, as well as their ability to reverse commonsensical understandings of the relationship between rules and their objects, is not new.[10] Authors critical of mainstream migration theory have highlighted the extent to which legal rules and discursive practices construct and redefine the dichotomy between citizens and foreigners, as well as that between "legal" and "illegal" aliens (cf. Andrijasevic 2004; P. Fitzpatrick 1995; Ong 2003). The examples of border externalization mentioned earlier raise further theoretical issues, as they shed light on a spatial dimension of Europe that can be discussed only by taking into account the dialectical role that people's movements play in defining and activating the EU's borders. As a matter of fact, virtual borders do not exist *unless they are crossed*. At the same time, the very possibility for them to be crossed by "illegal" migrants implies that a boundary of difference between "legal" and "illegal" movements has already been traced. Thus "illegal migration" as an object of policies seems ultimately to be defined by the very possibility of detaining and deporting women and men who migrate, rather than by rigorous legal definitions, and regardless of the fact that these different forms of deportation and detention may take place within or outside the EU's official frontiers. Indeed, it is the very possibility that a migrant can be deported from European space, repatriated to or "received" by (and detained in) a third transit or origin country, that constitutes the difference according to which the vessel that carries him or her is considered a virtual border and is discouraged from entering European space.

Another term that has become common in public debates about Europe as well as in theoretical debates is "deterritorialization": of citizenship and rights (cf. Soysal 1994), of sovereignty (Panagiotidis and Tsianos 2007), of communities' borders (Papastergiadis 2000), and so on. Referring to the deterritorialization of European borders, we assume not that they have lost any relationship with a spatial dimension but rather that they no longer delimit given portions of geographical territories. As has been underlined by other scholars, from this perspective the European Union lacks an essential quality of stateness: "The Union's geography is derived from and mediated through the member states; unlike in federal states, it is not co-original with the member states' territoriality, and even less does it exist prior to it" (Preuss et al. 2003, 4). However, while we agree that the geographical extension of Europe may be defined through the territoriality of the member states, the spatial dimension of its political authority does not coincide with the perimeters of the member states or with the sum of their territories.

Even in the modern state, the notion of legal and political space has not always overlapped with the geographical extension of the territory (for a comprehensive discussion, see Donati 1924; Rigo 2007, 2008). Nevertheless, in classical legal theory state territoriality was based on the assumption (probably never verified) that the people of states are "sedentary," and that this characteristic of sedentariness therefore extends to the state itself (Jellinek 1900/1949, 12). In contrast to this assumption, we argue that the deterritorialization of the EU's external and internal borders defines the European legal and political space as a space that is dedicated not to a sedentary community but to the government of mobility, both inside and outside official member states' perimeters. In adopting this view, we also suggest that the unity and continuity of the European legal and political space may only be reconstructed through migrants' experience of its borders, which therefore contests and (re)constitutes any given distinction between the "alien" and the "citizen" in Europe.

Our aim here is not to empirically describe such experiences but rather to question the figures of migration that have been used in public discourses during the transformation of mobility control in Europe. Drawing on categories recently used by Saskia Sassen (2006), such an analysis reveals a new "assemblage of territory, authority and rights" that rejects a strict separation between the *status* of insider and outsider with regard to European legal and political space. In other words, we will argue that migrants, even when formally (i.e., legally) excluded from citizenship, are politically included in its domain to the extent that they contest the existing territorial distribution of membership and compel the legal and political space to reorganize itself around human mobility.

FIGURES OF MIGRATION: A GENEALOGY OF MOBILITY CONTROL

The European space has always been a space of mobility. When today migrant mobility is represented as opposed to sedentary citizenship and when this opposition takes the form of a "natural" dichotomy, it becomes necessary to examine the making of both mobility and the mechanisms of taming mobility. From the Middle Ages to industrialization, mobility of the subaltern classes remained a central problem for authorities all over Europe. Mobility was mainly handled by repression, because it was regarded as a threat to the feudal order that tied workers to their lords and masters and respectively to a piece of territory. The early mobile workers were called vagabonds, vagrants, or beggars, because they represented an anomaly within the social order. But neither workhouses nor cruel penalties could solve the problem. Only with the beginning of industrial capitalism did a fundamental solution begin to emerge. In the nineteenth century, control over mobility was accelerated and transformed across Europe such that internal mobility was facilitated, and in return, external, "international" mobility was hampered. This transformation resulted in a systematic separation of the legal forms of citizen and foreigner.

The emergence of national borders was connected with the increasing representation of social interests within state apparatuses. Around 1850 in France, for example, hospitals were obliged to treat patients regardless of their citizen status. But by the Third Republic in 1871, almost all laws concerning social benefits contained a privilege for natives (Noiriel 1996). Crossing the border increasingly ceased to represent solely a symbolic and practical challenge for the ruling classes. Labor organizations such as trade unions referred to the boundaries of the labor market in order to define the boundaries of a "given" working class. Part of the effort of the local workers' organizations to limit the number of competitors on the labor market was to ban women and children from industrial labor. Étienne Balibar (1998) speaks thus of the *état national social* to refer to the embeddedness of social rights and citizenship. Migration thus becomes a specific field of struggles, in which conflicts over mobility, social rights, and segmentation of labor markets shift into a language of "penetration" of the social body.

Societies and states have developed tools to deal with the contradictions and frictions related to transborder mobility. It is crucial to understand that in contrast to the common notion that these instruments initiate and control migration, they represent reactions to already existing forms of mobility. The recruitment program (similar to the Bracero Program in the United States) was and still is widely regarded as a starting point of migration, which in the terminology of the mainstream sociology of migration is a "pull factor." But these migration regimes have often been erected in response to the self-organized mobility of migrants. This has been demonstrated in the case of the German recruitment program after World War II, where each agreement between Germany and the countries of emigration was preceded by irregular and clandestine migrations (Bojadžijev 2008; Jamin 1998; Karakayali 2008; Yano 1998). Migration programs thus represent regularizations of formerly irregular migration, which they intend to "channel" and govern. To do so, more than a set of rules or a juridical framework is needed. To govern migration is to create a social consensus and a specific rationality allowing individual and collective subjects in a society to articulate the specific conflict around migration.

When we speak here of "figures of migration," it is not our aim to deduce certain prototypes from empirical evidence. Rather, figures such as the "guest worker" or the "refugee" represent categories of governance. They allow state authorities, public discourses, and collective agents to relate to and govern migration in a specific way, according to the given social and political compromise of migration. Individual motives for migration are irrelevant for the construction of these categories or figures. In postwar Europe, migrants from countries ruled by dictatorships such as Spain, Greece, and Portugal fled to France, Belgium, or Germany as "economic" guest workers. Subsequently, when the only legal means of immigration remaining after 1973 was the asylum system, labor migrants in the 1970s and 1980s had to invent stories of their "political" persecution.

We want to examine the traces of migration policy in these figures and conceptualize labor and its mobility without reproducing the common dualism of migration theory that presumes that mobility must be explained economically and that its control is a matter of the state. Instead of developing models out of empirical data, we turn the perspective around: we identify figures of migration that correlate to certain constellations of migration policy. In the analysis of these figures, we point out trajectories and impasses produced by them. Hence figures do not represent social groups but instead conceptually reflect *relations* of migration.

In Europe after World War II, the figure of the "guest worker" represented the matrix of migration policy, resulting from a compromise between trade unions and employers. Organized labor agreed to hire migrant workers on the condition that contracts were limited ("guest") and that local workers were promoted, while migrant workers mostly had to perform unskilled tasks ("worker").[11] Slowly, with the end of this period, the figure of the "refugee" or "asylum seeker" emerged. Eventually there were almost no other "legal gates of entry" left, at least not for those who could not avail themselves of family reunification. The "refugee" then took center stage until the early 1990s. Since then we have been observing the transformation of the paradigmatic figure of the migrant. The figure of the "illegal migrant" has taken the place of the "guest worker" and the "asylum seeker"—but this does not mean that undocumented migrants did not exist during the era of guest-worker migration.[12] Rather, it points to the fact that all these figures organize the epistemological and political terrain of migration. Administrative categories materially construct human behavior when migrants try to fulfill the "needs" of governmental procedures. Nonetheless we should be careful not to assume that if, for example, Sweden does not provide a legal system for labor migration, every migrant in Sweden must be a refugee.

Labor migration took the form of refugee migration, giving rise to an increasing propaganda against asylum-migrants who were accused of being "fake" refugees. Clearly, migrating for economic reasons after recruitment ended had become politically unacceptable. Consequently promigrant groups and organizations were also constrained in their discursive strategies and therefore insisted on the refugee character of any migration under the label of asylum, which in turn undermined any representational space for migrant agency. The struggles around migration were now dominated by two different discursive strategies. One claimed that migrants were no longer welcome as guest workers, because the underlying economic framework—extensive accumulation on the basis of the deployment of unskilled labor—ceased to be the basis for the social compromise of migration. Instead of contributing to economic growth, migrants were considered "parasitic" consumers of social welfare. The other strategy was based on a human rights paradigm and simply disregarded any economic argument.

What we want to suggest is that regimes of migration entail epistemological structures, which often result in representational barriers. Migrant agency in both regimes has been constrained in a specific way—in one model, the figure of the guest worker was reduced to a *homo oeconomicus*; in the other model, the migrant had to meet the legal requirements of the respective asylum system. Shortly after the countries of the former Warsaw Pact repealed their measures for immobilizing their populations, asylum laws in western Europe were radically restricted. Around the end of the twentieth century, only a small minority of migrants entered Europe as asylum seekers. Instead a growing number of migrants were crossing the borders "illegally." The current dominance of the figure of the "undocumented migrant" can be traced back to the emergence of a pan-European migration policy. Although European politicians proclaimed their intention to establish a common regime of immigration, this declaration remained empty for over a decade. What has been strengthened instead since the first agreements of the core countries of migration control in 1985 in Schengen was the common administrative body of "combating" migration.

ECONOMY OF CLANDESTINITY

It is evident that the juridical status of migrants and their position within the labor market are related to each other. From this point of view, clandestine migration fits into the picture of neoliberalism, privatization, and the proliferation of insecure jobs. Authors like Emmanuel Terray (2002) or Alain Morice (1997) refer to the fact that the outcast position of migrants fits perfectly into the neoliberal principles of the ongoing restructuring of labor relations: "Foreigners are being turned down by juridical means but recruited at the same time for economical reasons" (Morice 1997). In addition to commentators who are critical of neoliberalism, there are the neoliberal thinkers of migration themselves. For them, labor migration is the effect of a market mechanism distributing productive factors: countries with a surplus of labor power have low wages, and countries with a shortage of workers have high wages. Scholars who share this perspective can be divided into those who oppose open borders, though they recognize their alleged economic advantages, and those who advocate open borders (cf. Veenkamp, Bentley, and Buonfino 2003). To the latter camp belongs Nigel Harris (2003), who argues that irregular migration is simply the effect of a certain type of demand for labor that can never be regulated effectively by the state, neither through recruitment programs nor through any requalification measures for citizens.

The dualism between political and ethical arguments on the one hand and economic rationales on the other is characteristic of the international debate on "illegal migration." For neoliberals, migration can only be explained by the demand for labor that cannot be satisfied on the national level, but its illegalization, through the closure of borders, seems unrelated to this very demand. Conversely, critics of neoliberalism assume that there is a hidden agenda behind the closure of borders that secretly turns Fortress Europe into a permeable filter for the selection and recruitment of laborers (cf. N. Bell 2002; Kasimis, Papadopoulos, and Zacopoulou 2003). Unlike the situation during the guest worker regime, however, the current mode of employment does not result directly from a social compromise.

Temporal restriction models such as "rotation" or limited residence status were the core elements of the social compromise of migration. The central function of the guest worker regime was the implementation and assertion of temporary residence. Thus national labor could be privileged without changing the legal and structural framework of the welfare state by discriminatorily excluding labor migrants. This model of flexibility has led many scholars to the hypothesis of an "industrial reserve army," according to which migrants were a kind of cyclical shock absorber on the labor market (cf. Castles and Kosack 1972). But with the new clandestinity of migration, this model becomes invalid. Control of migrant mobility is not mediated through the welfare state but seems to take place in an unregulated manner—exposed to border controls and raids. This is why we suggest replacing the state theory of migration, where bargaining and compromise result in juridical structures such as the recruitment system, with a *regime theory of migration*. The notion of a migration regime helps both to stress the interdependence of knowledge, discourses, and practices of migration and to conceptualize migration politics as structured by gaps and ambiguities. Without such a change of perspectives, it would seem as if a sort of rotation today is rooted in the seasonal cycle of production in many of these sectors (agriculture, construction, and tourism). Yet what we need to understand is how the legal framework that organizes recruitment, flexibility, and rotation has shifted. If we do not want to succumb to conspiracy theories of migration, we must take into account both the history of migration struggles and the autonomy of its social practices.

Irrespective of the regime, migrant workers occupy predominantly low-income jobs—a characteristic of migrant labor in general (cf. Boutang et al. 1986; Piore 1980). Also, undocumented migrants do not represent a static social group. Rather, being undocumented is a passage, because transition between "legal" and "illegal" work and residence is often smooth; whether migrants are regularized collectively (as in Spain, Italy, or France) or manage to obtain "legal" status individually, only a small minority remains without any documents for a long period of time. What counts is disposability: for example, seasonal workers often have a regular work permit for only a short period of time and then turn systematically "illegal" again (cf. Diminescu 2000). Thus flexibility has roots both in a transitory moment between residential status and statuslessness and in a collective transnational movement of migration, however corrupted, providing labor markets permanently with new manpower.[13]

The present European regime of combating "illegal migration" is characterized not simply by the absence of regulation but by the effect of historically accumulated and institutionalized experiences. This is how we can explain why, regardless of a massive demand for migrant labor, there is almost no legal framework for recruitment. (Even more significant is that in the media and political discourse not even a "language" of labor migration exists—instead, migrants are represented primarily as refugees, asylum seekers, or sans-papiers.) But is it satisfactory to suggest, as a number of critical scholars and politically engaged people do, that the "old" democratic model of migration control has been replaced by an authoritarian police regime without any public control? The increasing role of the European executive authorities, operational agencies, and so-called experts seems to support this hypothesis.[14] However, there is no functionalist explanation for the proliferation of undocumented labor migration—neither police raids and deportations nor the "toleration" of undocumented migrants is structured by the logic of supply and demand.[15] Employers in these industries may form pressure groups to facilitate access to cheap migrant labor, but the techniques of entering a territory that is allegedly sealed off rely on what Saskia Sassen (2002) has called the "human rights regime." For instance, migrants crossing the Aegean Sea know that if they are detected by the Greek coast guard, they have to jump into the sea because, as the coast guard is obliged to rescue anyone in danger, this is the only way the migrants can avoid being returned to Turkey (Transit Migration Forschungsgruppe 2007).

The nonfunctionalist way in which we want to analyze the economy of clandestinity can be made clear if we consider the proliferation of (detention) camps at the borders of Europe. Rather than stopping the circulation of mobility, detention camps for migrants reinsert a socially commensurable time in the migrants' movements. They bring "illegal" and clandestine migration back into society by making it visible and compatible with a broad regime of temporal control.

The Schengen camps are less panoptical disciplinary prison institutions than, for instance, the "speed boxes" that Paul Virilio sees as regulating the "speed" of movement (Virilio 1986). Camps for the detention of migrants are *also* communication and information centers and rest houses. Against the background of Foucault's *Discipline and Punish* (1975/1977), it would also seem important to examine the figure of decelerated circulation in light of how it alters the relation of time, body, and productivity. The centrality of temporal over spatial regulation for understanding migration today is also clear when we consider how the time regime of the camp is distinguished by the disassociation of the body from its direct economic utilization. Previously, mobility was rendered productive by territorializing movements and inserting them into a spatial regulation of bodies. Consider, for example, the workhouse or the situation of the first foreign worker hostels of the *Gastarbeiter* era, which territorialized mobility to create a productive workforce. However, with the current configuration of camps, this seems to have changed.

Camps do not attempt to make migration economically useful by making migrants productive in a spatial order; rather, they make migrants productive by inserting them into a global temporal regime of labor. This regime is not based on disciplining bodies and regulating whole populations. The temporal regime of global labor follows the movements of people and invests where it finds a productive workforce in a state of flux. This allows global capital to thrive on labor and life conditions that are in a state of transition and, most importantly, are primarily unregulated and informal. With this global temporal regime of labor, the moving and changing workforce is rapidly embedded into capital's productive structure. However, global capital also quickly abandons those recently and opportunistically embedded workforces as soon as new possibilities for exploitation emerge elsewhere. What is significant for us here is that this is a temporal regime, rather than a spatial regime: the spaces where global capital invests do not exist as they did previously; rather, they constantly emerge and vanish as people move, migrate, and change their lives.

THE BORDERS OF THE "EUROPEAN ORDER"

Today tackling "illegal" migration at the European level has not replaced the previous figures of migration that have been the object of national policies—instead, it overlaps with them. In fact, it is important to underline that the role played by national borders and migration policies has not lost importance but is included in the processes of transforming EU borders.[16] This can also be exemplified through the concept of *public order*, which identifies the legal restrictions imposed on the access to the common European space of circulation: in other words, through the features that territorial borders assume when translated into legal discourse. According to article 5 of the convention that applies the Schengen Agreement, to be admitted into the territory, an alien must not be considered dangerous to the national security, the public policy, and the international relations of *any one* of the member states. Due to the overlapping of the different conditions of entry into Schengen territory, the concepts of "security" and public "order" (or "policy") applicable in the area of "freedom, security, and justice" are not the result of an autonomous elaboration but the sum of restrictions established in each country.[17] Far from being removed, national frontiers have thus been relocated to the perimeter of the Schengen area.

In view of identifying a notion of public order peculiar to the migration regime implemented in the European space, we should attend not to the documents and legal measures that define foreigners' residential *status* or entry conditions (which are left to the member states' competences) but rather to those which establish procedural conditions for the *circulation* of migrants, both "legal" and "illegal" ones. It is in this specific field that the EU has adopted a wide range of binding legislation, as well as other nonbinding documents.[18] Only a few of these documents concern migrants *"legally"* residing in the territory of the member states, while all the others relate to the "illegal stay" of migrants, which the official terminology defines as "the presence on the territory of a Member State, of a third-country national who does not fulfil, or no longer fulfils the conditions for stay or residence in that Member State" (art. 3[b] COM [2005] 391 final).

In other words, EU legislation does not define the entry conditions and the residential status of third-country nationals, nor does it specify the statutory preconditions according to which expulsion decisions are issued. Nonetheless it assumes that the circulation of migrants—even "illegal" migrants—is a matter that needs to be governed at the European level. The scope of documents such as the *Directive on the Mutual Recognition of Decisions on the Expulsion of Third-Country Nationals*, adopted in May 2001 (2001/40/EC), allows for an expulsion decision issued by one member state to be enforced in another member state without the second state having to issue a new expulsion decision. Hence it actually presumes that a migrant—although "illegal"—circulates and moves through European legal and political space. In addition, the council's decision concerning joint flights for the repatriation of aliens is part of this European common framework of circulation management as it relates to the transit of migrants across the EU's internal and external frontiers during the return process. The government of circulation is a priority not only with regard to the expulsion and repatriation of aliens but also when the EU legislation focuses on migrants' right of establishment and work in European space. The *Council Directive concerning the Status of Third-Country Nationals Who Are Long-Term Residents* (which took effect in January 2006) provides, for the first time, "legally" residing migrants the right to circulate and establish their residence in other member states, including for the purpose of work.[19] Although the directive specifies the length of the residential period required (five years) and other conditions for acquiring the status of "long-term residents," it recognizes the right of member states to refuse this status on grounds of "public policy or public security" (article 6), thus implementing once again the limit of the *national* "public order" in defining the status of *European* "long-term residents." In fact, the only right genuinely defined at a transnational level is not the long-term residential status itself but "the right to reside in the territory of Member States other than the one which granted him/her the long-term residence status, for a period exceeding three months" (article 14): a right that relates to the management of people's circulation and the mobility of workers.

It would be possible to list other examples that constitute a merely "procedural order" of the European migration regime. These include the whole set of measures that deal with standards of migrants' expulsion, detention, removal, and repatriation.[20] As pointed out already, the shift to a regime theory of migration rather than a state theory of migration intends to underline the apparently paradoxical outcomes of migration policies. On the one hand, the externalization of borders targets (or "tackles," according to EU terminology) "illegal migration" long before the presence of aliens on member states' territory can legally be defined as "illegal stay," thus dramatically increasing the illegalization of people's movements. On the other hand, "illegal migration" seems to take place in a rather uncontrolled manner—to the extent that the lack of comprehensive migration policies diminishes migrants' expectations of acquiring citizenship status or even a stable residential status. One could even say that what had been the rotation organized by guest worker contracts has today been replaced by rather informal procedures that lead to the precarization and clandestinization of migrants' lives.

This understanding of the European space is consistent with a recent communication of the European Commission where the concept of "circular migration" is presented as a successful model for the management of human flows. According to EU institutions, "Circular migration can be defined as a form of migration that is managed in a way allowing some degree of legal mobility back and forth between two countries."[21] Although this definition does not refer to a limit on the length of stay, as others have noted (Cremona 2008), temporariness is nevertheless considered one of the crucial characteristics of circular migration. The commission indicates two main forms of circular migration: third-country nationals settled in the EU—mainly business people and highly qualified professionals—who should be given the opportunity to engage in activities in their country of origin while retaining their main residence in one of the member states; and persons residing in a third country who come to the EU "temporarily for work, study, training or a combination of these, on the condition that, at the end of the period for which they were granted entry, they must re-establish their main residence and their main activity in their country of origin."[22] It should be noted that while the communication often uses the terms "sending" and "receiving" countries, migrants are rarely "sent from" or "received by" any country on the basis, for example, of a migration program. They are more likely to choose to leave on their own accord. EU institutions do not actually propose a comprehensive framework of migration policies to implement or encourage circular migration, and the communication does not propose radical changes to the legal framework of member states as it affirms that national legislation "already contain[s] rules that promote some circularity."[23] Rather than an innovative model, circular migration, on the contrary, appears to be a way of managing migration *as it is*.

Nonetheless two elements of the official discourse on circular migration require further attention: first, the way in which circular migration and the fight against "illegal" migration are seen as complementary to each other, and second, the temporal character of circular migration. With regard to the first issue, the communication proposes the implementation of "packages" called "mobility partnerships" whereby the mobility agreements can be negotiated with third countries under the condition of their cooperation in the management of migration flows and in particular the fight against "illegal" migration. With regard to the second issue, we have already underlined the present centrality of the temporal regulation of migration and how this allows for the mobility of people and the shifting of investment to wherever capital finds a productive workforce. At the same time, temporariness is one of the main factors that *produces* clandestine migration because it diminishes the possibility of acquiring stable legal status. However, these two aspects of the official discourse on circular migration are only apparently contradictory because, as we have already pointed out, the increasing illegalization of people, both through the "tackling" of uncontrolled movement and the loss of legal residential status, ultimately produces an informal rotation of migration. In other words, and despite official rhetoric, the illegalization of migrant movements is a de facto way of managing circular migration.

Besides referring to the government of migration movements, the notion of a regime theory of migration also indicates a peculiar way of governing the political space that becomes particularly important when analyzing the transformation of citizenship in the European polity. In modern states, the monopoly over the legitimate means of human mobility (Torpey 1999) has been granted through the establishment of solid and fixed borders, which have delimited a homogeneous space of internal circulation. As exemplified by the successful history of the passport, this mechanism has played on the fact that it has represented not an instrument of mobility constraint but one of freedom: citizens have the right to circulate freely within the homogeneous territorial space because the passport allows them to identify themselves—and be identified—as *citizens*, a "quality" that would otherwise be difficult to determine.

In contrast, in contemporary Europe, borders become normative devices that can continuously be reproduced. They do not trace the limits of any given space but reproduce a *territorial* authority every time that human conduct is differentiated according to the "quality" of the individuals who circulate across the same physical space, or, in other words, every time that migrants' rights remain anchored to their authorized or unauthorized movements. The "European order"—although concerned with the management of the circulation of migrants—does not provide the statutory preconditions for the residential *status* of foreigners within the European space. This in turn reflects the fact that the European polity is deficient in one of the essential characteristics of stateness: namely, the territory. From the perspective of legal theory, as a nonterritorial polity, Europe is unable to grant to migrants any *territorialization* of rights independently of the authority of the member states. As a consequence, the procedural order briefly described earlier appears to be more than a transitory phase within a teleological process oriented toward the creation of a homogeneous legal and political space. Rather, it becomes an internal method of governing human circulation.[24]

MOVEMENTS OF MIGRATION AND THE NEW ORDER OF EUROPEAN CITIZENSHIP

European citizenship has been described in theoretical debates as a "post-national" model of membership, where rights are held by individuals on the basis of personhood rather than nationality (Soysal 1994). That a number of civil and social rights can be enforced without any regard to an individual's nationality has led scholars to consider the European Union as "really a new animal species in the Hobbesian jungle of the global state system" (Bauböck 2003). However, while much attention has been paid to the development of rights granted to "legally" residing migrants, the concomitant *illegalization* of people's movement has often been ignored.[25] Europe appears to be a fortress not only because of its physical, legal, and administrative borders but also in light of a theoretical debate that tends to consider measures of detention, deportation, and "discouragement" of migrants from entering the EU space as mere "side effects" of otherwise sustainable and virtuous migration policies. Those who are addressed as the "new citizens" of Europe are generally only the migrants who are already somehow included in the renegotiation of the framework of rights, thus confirming that almost no consideration is paid to the government of the circulation of people as a factor for the (re)constitution of the citizen-alien distinction. In contrast to this approach, we argue that the spatial dimension of the European authority can be scrutinized and comprehensively discussed only by considering how migrants themselves—both "legal" and "illegal"—subjectively experience its borders, whether these borders are inside or outside the official perimeters of the European Union.

In the modern state, territory has represented the "physical basis" of the unity of states that occupy only a limited portion of space (Jellinek 1892/1949, 29). However, space itself can be unified only through the "psychical processes" of individuals who live in the same space and "pursue common, permanent, unitarian and connected goals which can only be achieved by stable institutions" (29).[26] Borders in modern states as well as in the European space are part of these institutions. Nonetheless, their unity—the fact that they are ascribed to the same political authority or that they encircle the same legal and political space—cannot be seen only through an institutional prism. The unity of European borders has at least two components: an institutional one, and the one perceived as unitarian by individuals who encounter them while approaching the European space or while they are living in the territories of member states. Regardless of their legal or institutional definitions, borders established by "externalization" or "outsourcing" policies—such as detention centers for migrants built in third, origin, or transit countries—are European borders to the extent that they are perceived as such by the migrants who cross them. As a consequence, the very fact of crossing these borders is a *practice* of citizenship that reconstitutes the distinction between citizens and aliens despite any institutional or legal definition of the political space.

Describing the transformations of European citizenship through what we have defined as a *regime theory of migration* inscribes the constitutive role of borders within the making of the concept of citizenship itself. In the ideal model of modern-state citizenship, the citizen-alien and the citizen-subject distinction overlap to the extent that everyone is a citizen of some state. It is due to this representation that the concept of citizenship has been described as a "universal" one, despite its exclusiveness. In a similar way, "aliens" find their place only as the alterity of citizens (and

thus as a negation of citizenship) although they share the same political and daily-life space with citizens. However, when one focuses on the
spatial dimension of the European governance of circulation, this representation becomes more complex. The inner difference between the assemblage of territory, authority, and rights in the state system of mobility
control, on the one hand, and in the European space, on the other, is that
Europe does not exist as a space that can be identified by the establishment of fixed and solid borders. Europe exists as a legal and political space
(i.e., a space autonomous from the sum of the member states' territories)
only to the extent that it is circulated, whether this means the circulation
of *goods, people,* or *rights.* This is also reflected in the "procedural" order
of the European migration regime, which does not aim to stabilize migrants' movements into a sedentary juridical community, neither through
their integration nor through the definitive removal of those who resist
integration. Rather, its aim is to govern human mobility. Thus migrants
are—here and now—the citizens of the European political space.

Adopting such a perspective does not mean ignoring the harsh conditions that migrants face by being excluded from formal citizenship rights,
nor does it mean considering the European assemblage of territory, authority, and rights to be a "softer" system of governance than the state
territorial system. Rather, we have sought to disclose a series of inner
characteristics of the European space and to lift the veil of incongruence
from a mainstream discourse on migration that normatively represents
the integration of migrants into citizenship as a linear and homogeneous
path. If we instead regard citizenship and borders as battlegrounds, some
pressing questions need to be asked. What are the weapons in this struggle
over citizenship and movement, and what strategies are employed? What
kind of subject is inherent in this precarious migratory citizenship? In
the recent history of struggles of migration in Europe, migrants and their
migratory projects are often situated within a dispositive of victimhood
(cf. Karakayali 2008). The representation of migrants' agency within this
dispositive is constrained by a specific dichotomy: they are either villains,
committing crimes such as smuggling and trafficking, or they are victims
of poverty in their countries of origin or at Fortress Europe's borders. This
is a way of taming the migration beast that does not permit us to understand migration itself as a social movement. Moreover, it overshadows the
fact that the crisis of citizenship not only reconstitutes the citizen-alien
dichotomy but is constitutively affecting the very concept of *citizen* itself.
The European migration regime and its procedural order are not only the
outcome of institutional engineering but also the result of a dialectical

struggle between migrants' subjective instance of freely moving across borders and the control of human mobility. This is the means by which migrants *practice* and experience citizenship.[27] This could paradoxically be defined as the practice of "illegal citizenship,"[28] which nevertheless prevents us from identifying the cognitive boundaries of the political domain with the institutional borders of mobility control.

NOTES

1. General Secretariat, Programme of Measures to Combat Illegal Immigration across the Maritime Borders of the Member States of the European Union, 15236/03 FRONT 170 COMIX 717, November 28, 2003, p. 2.

2. United Nations, Convention on the Law of the Sea, Montego Bay, December 10, 1982.

3. For further details, see Statewatch's analysis at http://www.statewatch.org/news/2003/nov/10euborders.htm.

4. The use of the term "illegal migration" is problematic to the extent that it is not a sociological category, and as we argue throughout this text, its common use in political and public discourse does not correspond to any fixed legal definition.

5. Council Regulation Establishing the Criteria and Mechanisms for Determining the Member State Responsible for Examining an Asylum Application Lodge in One of the Member States by a Third-Country National, EC no. 343/2003, February 18, 2003.

6. European Commission, Communication from the Commission to the Council and the European Parliament, Integrating Migration Issues in the European Union's Relations with Third Countries, COM (2002) 703 final, December 3, 2002.

7. The term "outsourcing" is used also in the report of Human Rights Watch, Stemming the Flow: Abuses against Migrants, Asylum Seekers, and Refugees 18, no. 5 (September 2006).

8. General Secretariat, *New International Approaches to Asylum Processing and Protection*, DG H I, 13206/01, attachment to a letter from Tony Blair to Costas Simitis, March 10, 2003.

9. European Council and Commission, Action Plan Implementing the Hague Programme on Strengthening Freedom, Security, and Justice in the European Union, Official Journal C 198, August 12, 2005, p. 10.

10. Directly addressing Kelsen's (1925, 1945) conceptualization of normativity, Foucault observes that every law refers to a "normal" relation. This implies that the rule according to which the object of the law is identified is predominant with respect to the "normality" or "abnormality" of the relation (Foucault 1978/2007, 56–57; see also 1973/1994).

11. Indeed, a central instrument of this institutionalized compromise between labor and capital was the temporal limitation of migrant work ("rotation"), combined with "underclassing." Rotation agreements were supposed to prevent migrants from settlement and reduce the social "costs" of a temporary working class, since migrant workers came without their families and lived in residential establishments (in Germany they were sometimes placed in former displaced-persons camps). Underclassing meant that migrant workers were largely given poorly paid jobs at the bottom of the labor hierarchy, enabling domestic workers to be promoted to foremen or to white-collar jobs. Their income could thus be secured in the short and long term. During the guest worker regime, an "economic" governmentality had been dominant. Recruitment was seen as an economic procedure, similar to the import of any other commodity necessary from the standpoint of the national economy. The collapse of the recruitment system in the 1970s revealed the impasses of the guest worker model, which was largely related to its economic reductionism, ignoring the autonomous character and cumulative effects of migration movements. Between 1973 and 1974, every country in Europe running a recruitment program proclaimed an end to recruitment, stating the oil crises as its reason. In fact, instead of circulating, migrants increasingly became residents and thereby undermined the compromise based on the concept of rotation. Instead of ending migration, however, these measures only led to its metamorphosis.

12. The figure of the asylum seeker dominated debates on migration in the "old" immigrant-receiving Europe (Germany, France, Belgium, etc.) from the late 1970s onward, representing the effects of the failure of migration governance. In the "new" countries of immigration, such as Italy and Spain, all figures have appeared simultaneously: labor migrants, asylum seekers, and now "illegal" migrants.

13. To some degree, state regulation of migrant mobility in Europe learned its lesson from the history of recruitment programs and their "failure." A statement from the early 1960s by the novelist Max Frisch, "We called for manpower, people came," is often quoted in countries of "old immigration" to point at the impasses of any migration policy that reduces migrant workers to mere containers of manpower. In the 1960s, governments thought of migration as a water tap that they could turn on and off (Boutang 2007).

14. The European agency for border management (Frontex) is one of the main examples of these operational bodies.

15. Surprisingly this seemed to be the case during the 1960s in Germany, when authorities delivered work permits with no legal basis to migrants who entered Germany as tourists (Karakayali 2008).

16. The signing of the Schengen Agreement, its incorporation into the Amsterdam Treaty, and the repositioning of national borders at the external frontiers of the European Union determined structural changes in border control regimes. At a superficial level, the lifting of internal borders created a common space of circulation that widened the range of subjects able to enjoy a transnational freedom of movement. At a deeper level, the reciprocal respon-

sibility implied by a communitarized concept of borders and the establishment of an area of "freedom, security, and justice" transformed every internal and external frontier into a frontier belonging to each member state.

17. The criteria of data on "undesirable aliens" registered in the pan-European information system (SIS) are defined at national levels and range from criminal offenses to simple breaches of administrative rules. In reality, the most common condition that defines a migrant as an "undesirable alien" is that he or she has been issued with a deportation order.

18. See, for example, the Council Directive concerning the Status of Third-Country Nationals Who Are Long-Term Residents (2003/109/EC of November 25, 2003); Council Decision on the Organization of Joint Flights for Removals from the Territory of Two or More Member States, of Third-Country Nationals Who Are Subject of Individual Removal Orders (2004/573/EC of April 29, 2004); Council Directive on the Mutual Recognition of Decisions on the Expulsion of Third-Country Nationals (2001/40/EC of May 28, 2001); Green Paper on a Community Return Policy on Illegal Residents (COM [2002] 175 final).

19. The convention applying the Schengen Agreement grants to third-country nationals legally residing in member states the right to circulate in the Schengen space only for ninety days per year and for reasons other than work-related ones.

20. The Directive of the European Parliament and of the Council on Common Standards and Procedures in Member States for Returning Illegally Staying Third-Country Nationals (COM [2005] 391 final) was approved on June 18, 2008. By establishing "minimum standards" of rights protection, the directive extends the detention of "illegal" migrants to a maximum of eighteen months, a limit far longer than had previously been implemented in most member states. As a result, the document implicitly legitimates an increase in the severity of current measures; this is precisely what has happened in Italy, where one of the first proposals of the right-wing Berlusconi government elected in April 2008 was to increase the length of migrants' detention to eighteen months. This so-called "return directive" also imposes a penalty of banishment from EU territory for five years on those detained and deported.

21. Commission Communication on Circular Migration and Mobility Partnerships between the European Union and Third Countries (COM [2007] 248 final), 8.

22. Ibid.

23. Ibid.

24. For a further discussion of this argument, see Rigo 2007, 2008.

25. For the case of the EU eastern enlargement, see Rigo 2005.

26. On the properties of space for human communities and on the spatial organization of societies, see also Simmel 1908.

27. Étienne Balibar (1998) has argued, for instance, that the sans-papiers movement in France claims political rights by already performing these rights. According to this view, citizenship is not an asset but a concrete practice. In a radical version of this argument, the philosopher Jacques Rancière (1995)

suggests that there is a fundamental difference between police and politics. While police holds that in the political order all sections of the community have been assigned their proper place, it is those who are yet "uncounted"—in our case, migrants—who perform politics. They do so by claiming a new "place" in the social and political order.

28. On the concept of "illegal citizenship," see Rigo 2007; Balibar 2007.

PART THREE —⚓— *Spaces of Deportability*

—∿—

CHAPTER 4

From Exception to Excess

Detention and Deportations across

the Mediterranean Space

It is the last day of August 2005 on Lampedusa, a small Italian island situated south of Sicily. On the airport runway, two airplanes are parked approximately twenty meters away from each other and are waiting for passengers. A group of tourists pour out of the airport building and stroll toward the Air One plane, an Italian tourist carrier. The adjacent Air Adriatic plane, a private Croatian air company, is boarded by a group of passengers walking in fixed formation. Seven groups of ten men are escorted to the plane by four police officers wearing civilian clothing and heavy black protective gloves. The detention camp, separated from the runway by barbed wire, is situated only fifteen meters or so away from the Air Adriatic plane. Behind the barbed wire, several hundred migrants sit in small groups on the ground. When the plane takes off, most of them rise to their feet, waving.

The detention camp for irregular migrants in Lampedusa came for the first time to a larger public attention in the fall of 2004 when Italian authorities expelled more than a thousand undocumented migrants to Libya on military and civil airplanes. Since then, the Lampedusa detention center has been denounced repeatedly for instances of procedural irregularities and human rights violations. European NGOs, the European Parliament, the European Court of Human Rights, and the United Nations' Human Rights Committee have called on Italy to stop the degrading treatment of migrants in detention, to respect asylum seekers' right to international protection, and to refrain from the collective expulsion of asylum seekers and irregular migrants to Libya.

A number of factors led scholars to identify the situation in the detention camp in Lampedusa in terms of the "state of exception": Italian authorities' disregard of these demands and their denial that any human rights violations are taking place in the camp; their unwillingness to suspend the deportations to Libya; and the difficulty faced by Italian MPs, the UNHCR, and NGOs in both accessing the camp and implementing any form of monitoring mechanism. The "state of exception" is a Schmittian notion reformulated by the Italian philosopher Giorgio Agamben (1995/1998) to signify a decision, enforced by the sovereign, to place (or "abandon," in Agamben's terms) certain subjects outside the boundaries of the polis and hence beyond the protection of, or recourse to, the law. The camp stands for a material spatial manifestation of the abstract juridical dimension that is the state of exception in which, through the suspension of the normal Rule of Law, the category of citizen is no longer operative and in which the individual is divested of all rights and placed in the state of "bare life." Agamben takes the figure of the refugee as paradigmatic of the condition in which the rights of an individual are derogated and in which she or he is made vulnerable to acts of extreme violence and ill-treatment with impunity.

Scholarly analysis of detention camps for irregular migrants draws on Agamben's conceptualization of the camp and the state of exception. The growing body of literature on the workings of the camp explores detention camps and the practices enacted within them as manifestations of nation-states' sovereign power to suspend the normal or national Rule of Law through the state of exception and to abandon those detained in a juridical void (Papastergiadis 2006; Perera 2002). Detention is identified as a means by which the state immobilizes the "outside" within its borders (Diken and Laustsen 2006). Through subsequent deportation, the state expunges the "foreign" from the borders of its polity. This strategy, identified by Nicholas Mirzoeff (2005) in terms of the "detain-and-deport" model of jurisprudence, is arguably geared toward preventing the free movement of people, which undermines the operation of cheap labor markets.

These scholarly conceptualizations of the detention camps for irregular migrants offer important insights into the working of the camps and shed light on the abuses that migrants undergo while in detention. Yet the overwhelming emphasis of this literature on migrants' displacement from the Rule of Law and camps as devices of immobilization supports the analysis of detention camps as a mechanism of exclusion *in extremis*, in which this exclusion is enforced by nation-states in an attempt to police their borders and stem unwanted migratory flows. Using the example of the Lampedusa camp, I will show, however, that an understanding of the detention of irregular migrants as principally a manifestation of state sovereignty is inadequate to account for the workings of camps in contemporary Europe. In this context, the case of Lampedusa is of particular importance, as its position at the external border of the European Union exemplifies the function that camps perform with regard to transforming European space, the constitution of its citizenship, and the organization of its labor markets. Such an understanding of camps requires that camps are not viewed as abstract and dematerialized spaces of exception; rather, detention must be examined in relation to deportation. This is necessary not simply because, according to the official rationale, detention and deportation are complementary, since detention is considered indispensable for the operation of effective removal policies throughout Europe, but, more importantly, because an approach that examines detention and deportation together points to the limits of the state-centric model of sovereignty and enlarges the analytic framework to a transnational space that exceeds the boundaries of the European polity.

Accordingly, I focus here on the notion of the deterritorialization of European borders and consider camps as modes of temporal regulation of transit migration. My discussion brings to the fore both the importance of the continuity of European space as it expands beyond its geopolitical borders and the movements of migration that incessantly traverse that space. By considering both the transformation of European space and the temporal dimension of internment, I analyze detention and deportation in relation to larger movements of migration and reinterpret them as instances of migration control that intersect migrants' transnational trajectories. To consider detention and deportation from the perspective of the movement of migration opens the space for the analysis of agency and resistance that, as some critics have underscored, is absent from the scholarship on camps grounded in the notion of the state of exception (Papastergiadis 2006). Most importantly, this approach permits a shift of perspective away from the analysis that views detention camps as sites where the category of citizen is no longer operative (Perera 2002, 3), and toward detention as a mechanism that plays a pivotal role in the formation and organization of European citizenship through the principle of differentiated inclusion. Detention and deportation, as I suggest in my conclusion, are privileged sites where we may observe the tensions and contestations that accompany the reorganization of Europe's spaces and its citizenship.

THE STATE OF EXCEPTION

Positioned some two hundred kilometers south of Sicily and three hundred kilometers north of Libya, the Lampedusa detention camp is one of eleven so-called "holding" centers,[1] most of which are located in the south of Italy. These centers were established by the Italian state for the purpose of the administrative detention of third-country nationals pending deportation from Italy with the rationale that they would ensure the effective functioning of expulsion procedures.[2]

In January 2005, ten European NGOs[3] took legal action against the Italian government with regard to the Lampedusa detention camp and filed a complaint with the European Commission, calling on it to sanction Italy for (1) violation of the right to asylum, (2) violation of the prohibition of torture and inhuman or degrading treatment, (3) violation of the prohibition of collective expulsions, and (4) violation of the non-*refoulement* principle.[4] These NGOs gathered evidence of degrading treatment, arbitrary detention, and lack of access to the asylum procedure in the Lampedusa detention center and denounced the authorities for allowing overcrowding, poor hygienic conditions, the use of coercive and violent police methods, the use of improvised identification procedures,[5] and the failure of the center's authorities to provide migrants with information about the possibility of claiming asylum and to guarantee individual examination of asylum through individual interviews.[6]

Given the seriousness of the allegations raised by the NGOs, a delegation of twelve Members of the European Parliament from the Committee on Citizens' Freedoms and Rights, Justice, and Home Affairs (LIBE) of the European Parliament went to Lampedusa to assess the identification and removal procedures, the treatment of detainees, and the running of the detention center.[7] Particular concern was expressed regarding the collective expulsions of irregular migrants and asylum seekers to Libya, because Libya has no asylum system and has not signed the 1951 Convention on the Status of Refugees.[8]

Between October 2004 and March 2005, Italian authorities expelled more than 1,500 irregular migrants and asylum seekers from Lampedusa to Libya. The biggest operation took place between October 1 and 7, 2004, when 1,153 migrants were deported. Although Human Rights Watch believes that the majority of them were detained in Libyan detention camps, no information is available concerning the whereabouts of the migrants who were expelled. The Libyan detention centers are in fact almost inaccessible to international organizations or human rights groups, and UNHCR is unable to access people returned from Lampedusa to Libya, since it cannot operate its protection mandate in Libya.

These allegations of degrading treatment of third-country nationals in detention, the difficulties faced by asylum seekers in gaining access to the asylum determination process, and the large-scale expulsions to Libya had prompted the European Parliament (EP),[9] European Court of Human Rights (ECHR), and United Nations' Human Rights Committee (UNHRC)[10] to call on Italy to grant UNHCR free access to the Lampedusa camp, to respect the rights of asylum seekers and refugees to international protection, and to refrain from further collective expulsions. Notwithstanding this, however, collective deportations from Lampedusa to Libya continued throughout the spring and summer of 2005. In August 2005 they took place on a nearly weekly basis following the signing of an agreement between the International Organization for Migration (IOM) and the Libyan government that aimed to deter irregular migration both from and into Libya.[11]

The Italian government agreed on the charge of camp overcrowding but rejected the other allegations advanced by the NGOs and European institutions.[12] It claimed that deportations from Lampedusa did not amount to collective expulsions but rather were refusals of entry made on an individual basis,[13] and that as the majority of migrants reaching Lampedusa are economic migrants rather than asylum seekers, Italy had not violated the *refoulement* principle or breached any of the Geneva Conventions.[14]

The circumvention of international human rights conventions, the persistence of unlawful treatment of migrants, the extreme difficulty faced by Italian MPs and NGOs in gaining access to the camp, and Italy's continuation of the deportations in the face of EP, UNHCR, and ECHR calls to refrain from collective expulsions to Libya all point to the state of exception as a most appropriate conceptual framework within which to understand the space of the detention camp in the Lampedusa context. This interpretation is reinforced by applying the notion of *emergency* by means of which the sovereign avails itself of the power to institute a temporary state of exception (Agamben 2003/2005). The Italian government has described the situation at the island of Lampedusa, in recent times the main arrival point for boats carrying migrants from Libya to Italy, in terms of "emergency" and has spoken of a "million illegal migrants" waiting on Libyan shores to cross over to Italy.[15] In this light, it can be argued that the Italian government views the detentions in the Lampedusa camp and the successive deportations to Libya as indispensable measures for countering the supposed emergency caused by the mass influx from Libya.

At first glance, the image of a "million illegal migrants" might suggest Italy's difficulty in managing large-scale migration from the south. However, as I have argued elsewhere, the expression merits a more serious consideration because it brings together a number of misconceptions that inform Italy's migration policies: it inflates the numbers so as to produce the imagery of invasion, assumes that the entries via Italy's southern border constitute the majority of the country's undocumented migrants, and conveys the image that most migratory flows in and through Libya are of a clandestine nature and specifically geared toward Europe (Andrijasevic 2006). As for the migration from eastern Europe during the 1990s—which scholars now refer to as "the invasion that never took place" (Simoncini 2000)—so for the current migration to Italy via Libya: the reference to the magnitude of migratory flows invokes the fantasy of invasion from the south. However, the existing data offer a different image of migratory flows toward Italy. A recent report by the Italian Ministry of Internal Affairs indicates that the majority of third-country nationals residing "illegally" in the country have reached Italy neither via sea nor by crossing its borders without documentation. They have, on the contrary, entered the country at its land borders with valid entry clearance and have become undocumented either once their visas expired or after they overstayed their residence permits. According to the same source, only 10 percent of undocumented migrants currently residing in Italy entered the country "illegally" via its sea borders.[16]

Scholars have suggested that these contradictions play a crucial role with regard to the representation and regulation of irregular migration or, as Nicholas De Genova puts it, with regard to examining the visibility of "illegal immigrants" and the invisibility of the law (2002, 431). I take this discussion a step further and argue that these contradictions have an additional theoretical bearing, as they allow us to interrogate the conceptualization of the camp in terms of a space of exception. Starting from the discussion of the geopolitical transformation of European borders, I suggest other possible analytic paths that question the binary logic "inside" and "outside" on which rests the conventional understanding of sovereignty and of camps as spaces of its manifestation and reaffirmation.

DETERRITORIALIZATION OF BORDERS

The classical conception of a geopolitical border rests on a strict connection between state and territory.[17] Imagined as a continuous linear structure, borders are seen as enclosing a political territory and demarcating a sovereign state's external edges. This notion of the border, resting on the distinction between inside and outside, determined the definition and the organization of the modern state in Europe (Mezzadra 2006; Walters 2002b).

Recent debates on the borders in contemporary Europe have drawn attention to the transformations that are reshaping the notion and the institution of the border. The processes of European integration and enlargement have brought significant changes to the spatiality and the rationale of the border (Walters 2002b). As part of the integration process and following the Schengen Agreement, internal borders between member states were lifted to allow for a free circulation of goods, services, and citizens. This lifting of the internal borders of the EU also meant a simultaneous relocation of control to the EU's external borders toward the east and south. While much emphasis has been placed on the high level of policing and control taking place at the EU's external borders, scholars have also underscored the fact that the EU's external borders are not impenetrable barriers, as the expression "Fortress Europe" implies, but rather are characterized by their viability and mobility (Beck and Grande 2004, cited in Rigo 2007, 89).

To convey the specificity of the EU's borders, scholars speak of the "deterritorialization" of borders and "delocalization of control" (Bigo and Guild 2003; Rigo 2005). The term "deterritorialization" implies that Europe's external borders do not match a fixed geographical demarcation but rather can be traced both within and beyond EU space. Readmission agreements with third countries, the Schengen system of visa regulation, and the diversification of legal status are all instances of border deterritorialization.[18] Such a displacement of borders creates new loci of control. The control, once located at the borders, is now exercised by a variety of means and in a variety of locations, so much so that scholars talk of a "virtual border" (Freudenstein 2000) and "indeterminate zones" (Bigo 2003).

The case of the EU's external border between Italy and Libya illustrates this point well. Since 2000, Italy and Libya have developed a close collaboration on issues of irregular migration. Beginning in 2000 with a general agreement to fight terrorism, organized crime, and "illegal migration," the collaboration extended in 2003 and 2004 to include a readmission agreement, border-guard-training programs, the construction of detention centers, and the funding of deportation schemes. In 2003 and 2004, Italy financed the construction of three detention centers for irregular migrants in Libya, as well as a program of charter flights for the repatriation of irregular migrants from Libya to West Africa.[19] Future detention and deportation schemes are being developed under a EC-funded program and implemented in collaboration with the IOM, who were called on to develop a so-called assisted voluntary return (AVR) and reinsertion program geared toward returning irregular migrants from Libya to their countries of origin and strengthening cooperation on irregular migration between countries of origin and destination.[20]

The matter of the Italian-Libyan partnership on deterring irregular migration, deportations of irregular migrants and asylum seekers from Lampedusa to Libya, their further removal from Libya to countries of West Africa, and Italy-funded construction of detention centers in Libya has so far been mainly addressed in the literature in terms of the "externalization" of asylum (Hamood 2006; Cuttitta 2006). Externalization signals the tendency, which is gaining currency in the EU, toward dislocating asylum-seeker reception facilities and the assessment of asylum application to the EU's neighboring countries. Deportations from Lampedusa to Libya occurred, in fact, in a highly charged political atmosphere surrounding the proposal to set up refugee processing centers in North Africa. The proposal, advanced initially by the Blair government, included "Regional Processing Areas" (RPAs) and "Transit Processing Centers" (TPCs); the RPAs were to be located in the zones of origin of refugees with the aim of strengthening reception capacities close to areas of crisis, and the TPCs, positioned closer to EU borders, were envisioned as centers where asylum seekers could submit their asylum claims (Noll 2003). Although the proposal was rejected by several EU member states, concerns about externalization to Libya remained strong, as when, in October 2004, the informal EU Justice and Home Affairs Council debated the implementation of five pilot projects in Libya and several other countries in northwestern Africa with the aim of upgrading existing detention facilities and developing asylum systems.[21]

The following factors point to the increasing tendency toward the externalization of asylum: a Europe-wide decrease in asylum numbers, the introduction of the "safe-third-country" rule, the construction of detention centers, and the collective deportations to countries neighboring the EU. This is even clearer if we consider the case of Lampedusa, where migrants were first precluded from presenting asylum claims and then deported to Libya, most probably to the detention camps financed by the Italian government. However, there are two major problems in relating deportation to, and detention in, Libya too closely with the externalization of asylum. First, since the external processing centers do not officially exist as yet, and since Libya in practice has no refugee policy, it is better argued that Italy's deportations to Libya constitute a retraction of the right to asylum rather than its "externalization" (Andrijasevic 2006). Second, and an aspect that is of particular interest for this discussion, is that the idea of externalization rests on a neat distinction between the "inside" and the "outside" with regard to the EU territory and its external borders.[22]

However, the debates on the deterritorialization of EU borders and the delocalization of control introduced earlier point to the inadequacy of an analytical model organized around the inside-outside dichotomy. The Italian-Libyan patrolling of the Libyan coastline, the deportations of irregular migrants to and from Libya, and the construction of Italy-funded detention camps on Libyan territory are all instances that delocalize the EU's external border from southern Italy into and, following the itinerary of subsequent deportation, beyond Libyan territory. Consequently they all challenge the idea of the EU's external border as a firm border between Italy and Libya and show that the southern EU border, rather than being a linear and stable geographic demarcation, is a discontinuous and porous space encompassing the area between southern Italy and sub-Saharan Africa.[23]

A close reading of the EU's southern border of Italy and Libya indicates, then, that the EU's external border is not confined to the territorial limit of the EU as political entity and, as argued by Enrica Rigo in her groundbreaking recent work, cannot be seen as the "threshold" to EU's territory (2007; also see Karakayali and Rigo, this volume). Hence Italy-funded construction of detention camps in Libya, the proposal to set up centers in northern Africa for processing claims for asylum in the EU, and European Commission–funded and IOM-implemented deportation programs from Libya to western Africa point not to a separation (i.e., an outside) but to a continuity in relation to the EU's space and its juridical order.

Moreover, the deterritorialization of the EU's internal and external borders and the delocalization of control are bringing about significant transformations to territorial sovereignty. The principle of territorial sovereignty, understood in classical legal theory as resting on the inseparability between sovereignty and the law, has been ruptured through the processes of deterritorialization and delocalization (Rigo 2007). This rupture produces a "discontinuity" in the EU juridical space and results in what Rigo calls "shared sovereignty." It is certainly possible, as some scholars have suggested, to view Italy's permission to the UNHCR and IOM to establish their offices on Lampedusa and its removals of irregular migrants and asylum seekers to Libya as indicators of a weak state's failure to control its borders or of Italy's contracting out its responsibilities on asylum.[24] However, such a reading fails to observe that instead of being an exclusive matter of nation-states' competence, as it traditionally was, at present the authority over entry and stay in state territory is shared among different state and nonstate actors. Hence, rather than simply viewing detention and deportation as mechanisms through which a state's sovereignty is re-affirmed and its geographic and symbolic borders reasserted, it is more fruitful, in my opinion, to consider them as privileged sites in which we may observe the transformations of sovereignty in Europe arising from the "management" of migratory movements.

CONSTITUTIVE TENSIONS

The "spectacle of militarized border enforcement" that regularly takes place in the open sea or along Italian, Spanish, and Greek coasts shines a spotlight on the acts of policing EU external borders (De Genova 2002, 436; see also De Genova 2005, 242–49). Such representation fixes the location of the EU's external border, reduces its denotation to that of a threshold, and reaffirms nation-states as its custodians.[25] As well as overlooking the changed nature and workings of the EU's external border, such a reading oversimplifies migratory movements, as it reduces them to the space of the border and to the act of traversing it. Migrants are thereby represented as being located at Europe's "outside," pushing against its external borders. This kind of account fosters a misrepresentation of northern African migrations in terms that highlight massive "illegal" economic migration directed toward Europe. The Italian authorities' treatment of migratory movements between Libya and Italy exemplifies this quite well.

Libya's migratory reality is that it is far from being either a country of massive emigration or exclusively a transit route for clandestine migrants from sub-Saharan Africa to Italy. On the contrary, Libya is first a destination country and the major country of immigration in the Maghreb. Foreign nationals constitute approximately 25 to 30 percent of Libya's total population. Large-scale economic and social development schemes in the 1970s, launched from the revenues of the petroleum industry, relied in the first instance on migrant laborers from Egypt. Egyptian nationals, employed mainly in the agricultural industry and in education, constitute today the largest migrant group in Libya (Hamood 2006). Libya is home also to a large Maghrebi community (Moroccan, Tunisian, Algerian), and the country's economic development relies on "cheap" seasonal labor from the neighboring countries of Niger, Chad, and Sudan (Boubakri 2004; Pliez 2005). Since the 1990s, the presence of migrant workers from sub-Saharan states has been prompted by Libya's reorientation from a pan-Arab to a pan-African policy and its active role in the foundation of the Community of Sahel-Saharan States (CEN-SAD), which, as an economic project grounded in the free circulation of people and goods between its member states, is oriented toward regional cooperation and integration. Migrant workers from Sudan, Chad, and Niger are generally present in the Libyan Saharan border areas, where they work in sectors such as agriculture, tourism, and local trade. These labor migrations, facilitated by an open-border policy toward sub-Saharan Africa, are of seasonal and pendular character rather than, as commonly assumed, the source of irregular migratory movements to Europe.

Moreover, as recent scholarship on migration has emphasized, global migrations display a "turbulent" nature (Papastergiadis 2000) that exceeds the systemic "push/pull" market logic (Mezzadra 2004).[26] Emphasizing poverty and underemployment on the one hand and demand for migrant labor in particular segments of the economy on the other does not suffice to convey the multitude of arrangements, movements, and subjective claims that inform men's, women's, and children's migratory projects. Migrants and asylum seekers, as Federico Rahola (2007) suggests in his innovative and thought-provoking genealogy of today's "camp-form," share a condition of displacement that can be identified with a form of "exit" from those political categories that consign the individual to only one location. While functioning to circumvent international conventions and to carry out deportations to Libya, authorities' inclusion of all migrants arriving from Libya to Lampedusa under the category of "economic migrants" and their classification to a large extent as "Egyptian" nationals[27] signal the state's attempt to manage the multiplicity of movements, belongings, and histories that characterize contemporary migrations in the Mediterranean region by symbolically reducing this heterogeneity to a single typology (Van Aken 2007).

To fully comprehend the migratory movements across the Mediterranean space, it is therefore necessary to broaden the scope of analysis away from the site of the external EU border and into the broader geographical space marked by delocalized control posts.[28] It is within this space, traversed by turbulent migratory movements, that Dimitris Papadopoulos, Niamh Stephenson, and Vassilis Tsianos propose to rethink the camp from "below" (2008). In their analysis of migration in the Aegean zone, these authors break the progressive linearity by which migrants' journeys are commonly portrayed (i.e., a movement from A/origin to B/destination), and instead draw attention to interruptions and discontinuities such as waiting, hiding, unexpected diversions, settlements, stopovers, escapes, and returns. Careful to show that this does not imply that Schengen camps are not sites of confinement, the authors nonetheless contend that camps represent less a paradigmatic incarceration locale or a present-day social model that is "the equivalent of the panopticon" (Mirzoeff 2005, 119) than a spatialized attempt to temporarily control mobility. Using Paul Virilio's work, the authors challenge the functionalist view of camps as political-disciplinary devices of exclusion and shift the terms of analysis with regard to Schengen camps from space and immobilization to time and mobility. By doing so, they suggest that we rethink camps as "speed boxes" that regulate the time of migration by "decelerating" the speed of migratory flows. Viewed within this dynamic framework of migration, camps acquire a temporary nature and are conceptualized as provisional stations along multiple migratory routes.

The work of Papadopoulos, Stephenson, and Tsianos on Schengen camps is extremely useful in accounting for the ambiguities that emerge from the Lampedusa case that are commonly overlooked by scholars. So far, most attention has been paid to the difficulty faced by refugees in accessing the asylum determination procedure and to the implications of collective removals to Libya. Yet little attention has been paid to the fact that the majority of the irregular migrants and asylum seekers, after being detained in Lampedusa, are transferred to other Italian detention centers for irregular migrants, mainly in southern Italy. While this continuous detention follows the logic intrinsic to the detention centers' constitution, namely, that detention is indispensable to ensure an effective removal policy, a report from Italy's Audit Court shows that in 2004, out of nearly twelve thousand irregular migrants detained in Italian detention centers, fewer than half were deported. Most were released after the expiration of the maximum detention period, and the rest escaped.[29]

Thus, as the case of Lampedusa shows, detention centers represent neither the endpoint of migrational projects nor the place where migrants are "abandoned in the [juridical] void" (Papastergiadis 2006). Rather, as noted by Papadopoulos, Stephenson, and Tsianos, they act as "stopover points" incorporated into broad and multiple migratory movements: migrants are detained, released, and move on. This interpretative framework also allows for a different reading of deportations. Rather than being simply a disciplinary practice that follows an unauthorized entry into a state's territory, it is possible to read deportation from Lampedusa to Libya in terms of attempts to *decelerate* the movement of migration into Italy. As for the case of Greece and Turkey addressed in the work of Papadopoulos, Stephenson, and Tsianos (2008), so for Italy and Libya: the camps in the EU's southern neighboring countries do not prevent or stop migratory movements but instead regulate the time and speed of migrations by "temporarily diverting their directionality." Detention and deportation are thus means of regulating migrants' mobility and circulation both within and beyond the territorial limit of the EU.

The regulation of (migrants') circulation is, Rigo contends, a key device through which Europe governs spaces no longer enclosed by its external border (2007). The organization of these spaces of circulation is the key tenet underlying a "hierarchical order of relationships" in an enlarged Europe (Rigo 2005). The term indicates a regime of differentiated degrees of mobility among the "core" EU states, the "new" member states, and the nonmember states. Yet becoming EU members does not entitle the nationals of the "new" EU member states to the same labor privileges enjoyed by the citizens of "core" EU countries. In fact, the freedom of nationals of the "new" member states to take up employment anywhere in the EU is being delayed for a period between two to seven years after accession. This type of selective citizenship has been described in terms of "partial-citizenship" (Mezzadra and Rigo 2003) and constitutes an example of "deceleration," as it temporarily excludes large numbers of new EU citizens from labor participation and supplies the conditions of possibility for their *inclusion* as "illegal" labor (De Genova 2005).

The EU's government of spaces of circulation extends also to its southern neighbors. The European Neighborhood Policy (ENP), which is oriented toward the countries of eastern Europe and the Mediterranean that have no prospects of imminent EU membership, offers these countries increased political, security, economic, and cultural cooperation. The ENP avails itself of "action plans," namely, a set of common priorities to be agreed with each partner country. The not-yet-finalized action plan with Libya shows that EU policymakers are particularly keen on including so-called "migration management" cooperation schemes in the EU's relations with its North African neighbors. Developed under the framework of the external dimension of the common European asylum and immigration policy laid out by the Hague program with the aim of integrating asylum into the EU's external relations with third countries, the cooperation between the EU and Libya is geared toward defining operational measures to counter "illegal" migration including *inter alia* the enhancement of border control at Libya's sea, southern land, and air borders and the establishment of dialogue on controlling immigration with the main countries of origin.[30]

The areas adjacent to the EU are therefore being organized into spaces that are hierarchically differentiated through a set of devices and measures aimed at governing people's mobility (Rigo 2007). Together with the EU's external borders, detention camps and deportation policies are instruments that produce and establish difference by regulating circulation and mobility across European space. This difference is engendered on the one hand through the "possibility" of deportability (Rahola 2007)[31] and on the other through the temporality of rights enjoyed by third-country nationals (Guild 2007).[32] In other words, the differentiation of juridical status achieved via the deterritorialization as well as the proliferation of internal borders in the metropolis is a method of government through which the EU institutionalizes mobility, thereby regulating the contemporary movements of migration and hierarchically organizing the access to its citizenship.[33] The enforcement of differentiated modalities of mobility, which is a key tenet underlying the constitution of European citizenship, clashes against the movements of migration already present or traversing the hierarchically organized areas of circulation. Rather than being simply an object of institutional regulatory frameworks, migration therefore emerges as a constituent force of the European polity inasmuch as it challenges the concept of citizenship as being formalistically defined from above, and shows that European citizenship is a terrain of struggle constituted through a continuous interaction between migrants' practices of citizenship and its institutional codification.

CONCLUSIONS

Detention and deportation are not metaphors. They are physical spaces and material measures that affect the lives of thousands of men and women throughout Europe. While in detention and during deportations, migrants are kept in degrading conditions and suffer humiliation, physical violence, and even death (Amnesty International 2005; Fekete 2005; FIDH 2005). The abuses of migrants' rights are commonly explained as arising from a state of exception enforced through the condition of "abandonment" in which migrants, subjected to the Rule of Law, are at the same time deprived of recourse to the law or its protection. This process of "inclusive-exclusion," however, does not entail migrants' straightforward excision from the body of the state. Rather, it indicates a technology by means of which the "outside" is captured within the national juridical order (i.e., the field of the political), which seeks coherence and ascertains the boundaries of its political community through the lines of exception. These in turn define the boundaries of citizenship and preserve the state's sovereignty in relation to which migrants are located as its constitutive outside.

Using the case of the Lampedusa detention camp as a starting point for my analysis of detention and deportation, I have investigated the deep transformations affecting the institution of the border and the notion of state sovereignty in contemporary Europe. Rather than seeing the proposal to set up transit processing centers in northern Africa, the EU-Libya joint action plan, and the European Commission's cofinancing and IOM implementation of removal schemes for irregular migrants in Libya as instances of externalizing to the EU's "outside" matters regarding asylum or as a case of contracting out state's responsibilities on migration, I suggest that we interpret these as examples of the deterritorialization of the EU's external border and of shared sovereignty. This is not to claim that space and territory do not play a role in the functioning of the border or that the state has no decision-making power over entry or exit from its territory but rather to highlight the fact that the EU's external border no longer marks the edge of the territorial validity of the European legal system and that the authority over entry and stay in state territory today is shared among state and nonstate actors. This approach challenges the institutional regulatory perspective and the dialectics of inside and outside and puts forward an analytic framework that, by focusing on the continuities in relation to the EU's space and its juridical order, attempts to account for the ways in which the emergence of complex "assemblages" (Sassen 2006) of postnational configuration and the turbulence of migratory movements transform the boundaries of European citizenship.

To view migrants as actors and agents of the construction of the European community rather than its constituent outside challenges the demarcation that defines the realm of the political and produces an interruption in the logic of "omnivorous" sovereignty (Rahola 2007), which reinforces itself and its coherence by incorporating migrants within its boundaries. This is not simply a matter of acknowledging the agency of migrants as they circumvent or struggle against devices of mobility control. What is at stake is a theoretical and political challenge to recognize migration as a constituent force in the production of the European polity and citizenship, thereby redrawing "the borders of the political" (Neilson and Mitropoulos 2007) and rethinking the modernist dichotomies that still structure the definition and concept of state sovereignty as well as the political forms of belonging (Papadopoulos and Tsianos 2007). These considerations, often considered appropriate for the academy rather than for practitioners and activists, need to be kept in mind, as in this changed political landscape the achievement of effective rights-based policies or radical political interventions will depend on the development of frameworks and tactics that are able to adequately grasp the current transformations of sovereign power and citizenship in Europe.

NOTES

The ideas developed in this chapter are not mine alone. My work builds on the collective effort by activists and scholars from the Frassanito Network to develop a radical political analysis of contemporary migrations in Europe. Bridget Anderson and Simon Addison at the University of Oxford offered insightful and provocative comments on earlier versions of this chapter. I want to thank the Open Society Institute/International Policy Fellowship for funding my initial study of detentions and deportations on Lampedusa. Further research and writing were financially supported by the European Commission under the Sixth Framework Programme/Marie Curie Research Grant agreement, MEIF-CT-2006–025775.

1. The official designation of detention centers is "temporary stay and assistance centers" (CPT).

2. The maximum period of detention for both undocumented migrants and asylum seekers is sixty days. While detention of asylum seekers cannot be carried out with the sole purpose of examining their application, it is nevertheless mandatory in cases when asylum seekers present their application after being arrested for entering or attempting to enter the country "illegally," or residing in Italy in an irregular situation (see Andrijasevic 2006).

3. ANAFE, Association nationale d'assistance aux frontières pour les étrangers (France); Asociación "Andalucía Acoge" (Spain); APDHA, Asociación Pro Derechos Humanos de Andalucía (Spain); ARCI, Associazione Ricreativa e Cultura Italiana (Italy); Asociaciòn "Sevilla Acoge" (Spain); ASGI, Associazione per gli Studi Giuridici sull'Immigrazione (Italy); Cimade (France); Federación des Asociaciones SOS Racismo del Estado Español (Spain); Gisti, Groupe d'information et de soutien des immigrés (France); and ICS, Consorzio italiano solidarietà.

4. The non-*refoulement* principle has been reaffirmed by the EU as the cornerstone of refugee protection. It prohibits the forcible return of anyone to a territory where they would be at risk of persecution: "No contracting state shall expel or return (*refouler*), a refugee in any manner to the frontiers of territories

where his life or freedom would be threatened on account of his race, religion, nationality, membership of a particular social group, or political opinion." This principle refers to the lack of individual assessments and to the removal of persons to countries where there exists a serious risk to the physical integrity of those concerned (mentioned in article 19§2 of the European Charter).

5. Migrants and asylum seekers, the NGOs remark, have no effective access to an interpreter and are often identified by staff not qualified as interpreters and through improvised identification procedures in which nationality is determined on the basis of one's skin color and facial characteristics. "Complaint against the Italian Government for Violation of European Community Law," January 20, 2005. The complaint and the accompanying dossier are available at http://www.gisti.org/doc/actions/2005/italie/complaint20–01–2005.pdf.

6. Ibid.

7. European Parliament, Report from the LIBE Committee Delegation on the Visit to the Temporary Holding Centre in Lampedusa, EP/LIBE PV/581203EN.

8. According to the European Court of Human Rights, collective expulsions are defined as "any measure by which foreigners are forced, due to their membership of a group, to leave a country, apart from cases in which this measure is adopted following and based on a reasonable and objective assessment of the specific situation of each of the individuals composing the group."

9. European Parliament, European Parliament Resolution on Lampedusa, April 14, 2005, P6-TA(2005)0138.

10. CCPR/C/ITA/CO/5, October 28, 2005.

11. The International Organization for Migration (IOM), commonly mistaken for a branch of the United Nations or a humanitarian organization, has recently come under attack by NGOs including Amnesty International and Human Rights Watch for managing detention centers, running return programs for irregular migrants and asylum seekers, and implementing EU border regimes. For a more detailed reading of IOM's role in Libya, see Andrijasevic 2006.

12. See the Italian Ministry for Foreign Affairs' written reply prepared for the eighty-fifth session of the UN Human Rights Committee. Ministry for Foreign Affairs, Interministerial Committee of Human Rights, *Reply to List of Issues (CCPR/C/84/L/ITA) (Relating to CCPR/C/ITA/2004–5)*, UN Human Rights Committee, 85th Session, Geneva, October 17–November 3, 2005.

13. Refusal of entry does not equal expulsion and is an administrative measure that does not ban the migrant from entering the Italian territory in the future.

14. Ministry for Foreign Affairs, Interministerial Committee of Human Rights, *Reply to List of Issues (CCPR/C/84/L/ITA) (Relating to CCPR/C/ITA/2004–5)*, UN Human Rights Committee, 85th Session, Geneva, October 17–November 3, 2005.

15. This number was given by the Italian Ministry of Interior G. Pisanu. See *Il manifesto*, April 22, 2005, 9. http://www.ilmanifesto.it/Quotidiano-archivio/22-Aprile-2005/art74.html (accessed April 25, 2005).

16. See Caritas/Migrantes, *Immigrazione: Dossier Statistico 2005* (Roma: Edizioni IDOS, 2005).

17. For a detailed discussion on the classical conception of borders see Rigo 2007.

18. Others include the Schengen Information System, consulates' computerization, common EU visa and asylum policies, bilateral "readmission" agreements between the EU and third countries for return of migrants, the safe-third-country rule, and penalties on airline companies' so-called carriers' sanctions.

19. A total of 5,688 migrants were repatriated on forty-seven charter flights to Egypt, Ghana, and Nigeria as main destinations. European Commission (EC), *Report on the Technical Mission to Libya on Illegal Immigration* (2005).

20. *Programme for the Enhancement of Transit and Irregular Migration Management (TRIM)*, in European Commission, *Report on the Technical Mission to Libya on Illegal Immigration* (2005), 15.

21. The commission denied that these pilot projects are directly linked to plans to create EU reception centers in North Africa. Justice and Home Affairs Commissioner Antonio Vitorino declared, however, that "in the short term the Commission could envisage the possibility of setting up humanitarian reception centres in the countries bordering the Mediterranean." *EUobserver*, October 4, 2004, http://euobserver.com.

22. A third point needs to be made here: not all the migrants expelled to Libya are actually asylum seekers, and therefore it is inadequate to examine the deportations to Libya primarily from the perspective of externalization.

23. A similar argument has been advanced also for the eastern border of the EU. For an excellent and innovative analysis of the deterritorialization of EU borders to the east and its relevance for the issue of European citizenship, see Rigo 2005.

24. After the signing of the asylum agreement between the Italian ministry and the UNHRC, which came into effect on March 1, 2006, the UNHRC was able to set up its office on Lampedusa together with the IOM and the Italian Red Cross.

25. For a gendered reading of the border spectacle, see my work on borders and sex trafficking in Europe (Andrijasevic 2003) and on representation with regard to gender and migration in counter-trafficking campaigns (Andrijasevic 2007).

26. The emphasis, in what has become known as the concept of the "autonomy of migration," is placed on the autonomous, constitutive, and subjective force of the movements of migration rather than on migration as capital driven. For an application of autonomy of migration as a research method, see Transit Migration Forschungsgruppe 2007.

27. See European Parliament, *Report from the LIBE Committee Delegation on the Visit to the Temporary Holding Centre in Lampedusa*, EP/LIBE PV/ 581203EN, p. 3.

28. For a radically different representation of this space that does not follow the traditional cartography, see the project *MigMap—Governing Migration: A Virtual Cartography of European Migration Policies*, http://www .transitmigration.org/migmap/index.html.

29. The 2005 report by Corte dei Conti, http://www.corteconti.it/Ricerca-e-1/Gli-Atti-d/Controllo-/Documenti/Sezione-ce1/Anno-2005/Adunanza-c/allegati-d3/Relazione.doc.

30. The Joint Action Plan is still in draft form. Nevertheless the combined information for the Action Plan (draft of September 2005) and the Draft Council Conclusions on initiating dialogue and cooperation with Libya on migration issues (9413/1/05 REV 1) offer an outline of the main points and suggest the priorities likely to be included in the final Action Plan.

31. The concepts of "illegality" and deportability become clearer when examined in relation to a concrete situation. To use Lampedusa one more time as an example, after being moved to another detention camp, migrants are usually released after they have been served the order to leave Italy. Hence, once released, migrants become "deportable": if they overstay the period within which they must leave the country, they are susceptible to another incarceration for failing to observe the expulsion order.

32. On the topic of time or temporality and the regulation of mobility, see also Rigo 2007; and Neilson and Mitropoulos 2007.

33. While the structure of this chapter does not allow me to develop this point further, the institutionalization of mobility needs to be examined and understood in relation to the transformation of the capitalist mode of production and the capturing of living labor. Among the most innovative and provocative studies in this area are Nicholas De Genova's investigation of the link between the production of illegality and the structuring of the U.S. labor market (2002, 2005; also see De Genova, this volume); the work of Papadopoulos, Stephenson, and Tsianos (2008) on the ways in which the institutionalization of mobility incorporates the movements of migration into capital's productive structure; and Sandro Mezzadra's analysis of the detention camp as a type of decompression chamber that disperses the tensions accumulated on the labor market (Mezzadra and Neilson 2003; Mezzadra 2004).

VICTOR TALAVERA, GUILLERMINA GINA NÚÑEZ-MCHIRI,

AND JOSIAH HEYMAN

—ɯ—

CHAPTER 5

Deportation in the U.S.-Mexico Borderlands

Anticipation, Experience, and Memory

The immigration policy of the United States emphasizes the interdiction of undocumented people and smuggled drugs in the proximity of the international border between the United States and Mexico, before they move north (Heyman 1999). Undocumented people living near the U.S.-Mexico border thus face constant immigration law enforcement in streets, roads, and other open, public spaces. Their deportability is a powerful presence in their everyday lives. We aim to describe and analyze this presence of deportability, beyond the immediate moments of arrest, detention, and removal. How do people who have never been deported experience their deportability? How are actual experiences of deportation, or even its possibility, remembered in retrospect? How does vulnerability to arrest and expulsion shape social organization, from the individual to the community? Does it draw people together or split them apart—or both? How do risk and anxiety impede spatial movement in the borderlands, and how are such barriers avoided and defied? These questions, which we address in this chapter, form part of a larger inquiry we are developing into entrapment processes and experiences caused by intensive border policing.

The literature on deportability offers useful guideposts for our inquiry. Undocumented people face a broad condition of "illegality" in both material and discursive senses (De Genova 2002, 2005; see also Heyman 2001). Attendant to this condition, deportability is the specific vulnerability to arrest and spatial removal, as well as linked legal penalties, such as the loss of rights to future "legal" migration. Thus, in contrast to the study of the deportation process itself (e.g., Coutin 2003b) or postdeportation experiences outside the deporting nation (e.g., Peutz 2006), we focus on deportability as *a presence*: a constant possibility for people precariously living inside the United States. However, because we address the memory traces of past deportations among people who either came back to the United States or had family and friends torn away from them, we do, to some extent, close the loop between past acts of deportation and the conditional state of possible deportation.

Leo Chavez (1992/1998) pioneered the ethnographic study of deportable existence in his important work *Shadowed Lives*. As his title indicates, he focused on the condition of covertness as a response to risk. His descriptive ethnography combines practical coping tactics and experiences with related states of mind, such as anxiety and relief. Roger Rouse (1992), in turn, showed that several different sources of discipline (the capitalist routines of work and consumption, the threat of policing and deportation, the power-laden spatial structure of the United States) combined to "overdetermine" for undocumented Mexican men a sense of vulnerability and caution. Sarah Willen (2007a, 2007b) has recently deepened the analysis of deportability as an embodied experience, an unusually uncertain and vulnerable form of "being-in-the-world." Josiah Heyman (1998) took a different but compatible approach when he focused on the practicalities of crossing the U.S.-Mexico border (whether to enter in the first place or to return from removal), insofar as they affect experience and agency far from the border and into the interior. He discussed the effects of payments to smugglers, borrowed money, personal obligations, and conspiracies to avoid and defeat the law. We are thus mindful of both the experiential and practical dimensions of deportability.

These accounts concentrated on the negative aspects of deportable life, which is in large part justified. However, as Chavez (1992/1998) illustrated, deportability is not all-encompassing, and people find various niches in which to survive and thrive. In this regard, we find useful two analytical moves of Christian Zlolniski (2006). Zlolniski isolates the units of social organization of undocumented life, such as households and communities, and asks how they are divided or pulled together. He also studies collective mobilization by the undocumented in both workplaces and communities and the experience of claiming rights and material goods, as well as coping and avoidance behavior and the experiences of being vulnerable and anxious. We draw from and elaborate on these points, particularly in our final ethnographic section.

We begin by describing our context: the geography and recent history of the U.S.-Mexico borderlands. Here we introduce a key concept, *entrapment processes*, and describe the methods and locations of the study. Beginning our ethnography in humanistic terms, we delineate the main themes in people's narratives about deportability: fear, invisibility, hiding, stigma, loss, grief, depression, anxiety, and bravado. We then step back from the more experiential rendering of the ethnography to organize what people told us about deportability as falling into three temporal moments: *anticipation* of possible deportation and concern about its practical and emotional consequences; *experience* of the moment of arrest itself and the tactics and practices designed to avoid it; and *memory*, both personal and collective, of past or near deportation. These rubrics help characterize the presence of deportability for people who are not immediately in the clutches of the immigration law enforcement system. Next we look at how the deportable population is socially organized and internally varied, examining individual, household, network, and community levels of cooperation and cleavage. We conclude by looking at the human cost of deportability as a public issue in a time of immigration and border debates and by reconsidering the theme of entrapment in the borderlands.

ENTRAPMENT IN THE BORDERLANDS: THE CONTEXT OF DEPORTABILITY

In 2006 we carried out a mixed-methods (survey and ethnographic) study of barriers and access to health care for uninsured "legal" and undocumented immigrants in El Paso County, Texas.[1] The project addressed the health impacts of immigration status, among other topics, and we asked our informants about that status, with strict protections for confidentiality. A few respondents refused, and others may not have been truthful, but many spoke openly about their current or past undocumented status. We worked in two field areas, central El Paso city and the small rural community of Tornillo, in the far southeast of the county. Our study coincided with a program of de facto immigration law enforcement by the El Paso County sheriff that affected Tornillo, and there was federal immigration law enforcement presence in both areas. Because of this, we collected a rich set of observations and narratives on deportability.[2] In this chapter, we report this important case material during a time when immigration law enforcement has become increasingly controversial and intense both in the United States and throughout immigrant-receiving nations of the world. (We will discuss the health dimensions of our study in other publications.)

The analysis and interpretation of culturally and historically significant events in the U.S.-Mexico border region provide crucial context for our study.[3] The border region has much heavier immigration policing than any other part of the country (for example, at the time of this research, approximately 11,000 of the 12,000 Border Patrol officers nationwide operated along this border). Whether in the city of El Paso or near the farms and trailers of Tornillo, immigration law enforcers are an everyday presence. Moreover, the geographic distribution of border policing traps undocumented residents within the long strip of the expanded border. There are major checkpoints on highways some distance from the border and also regular patrols on roads leading away from the area, such that people find themselves pinned between the heavily patrolled and risky international boundary itself and the police stops that interdict travel into the U.S. interior. Guillermina Gina Núñez and Josiah Heyman (2007) refer to this pattern of policing and its results as "processes of entrapment," in which local and state agencies impose constant and significant risk to the movement of undocumented populations. Because people themselves exercise various forms of agency, both by limiting themselves and by covertly defying movement controls, the processual concept of entrapment views people not so much as nailed to the ground as shaped by an unusually harsh geography of risk in movement (Núñez and Heyman 2007).

Historically, in Texas and throughout the U.S.-Mexico borderlands, Mexican populations have often been treated as unwelcome guests, aliens, and illegitimate occupiers (Acuña 1988). State law enforcement organizations, such as the Texas Rangers, have been known for their Mexican "roundups" since the 1800s. Mexican *corridos* (border ballads) have denounced the racism and discrimination that has long existed in Texas law enforcement (Paredes 1958). Deportation and repatriation of Mexicans in the 1930s and during Operation Wetback in the 1950s further illustrate the historical trajectory of antipathy against Mexicans in the United States, and in Texas in particular.

In the El Paso area, such raids are known in Spanish as *redadas*, or "roundups." Today they involve both Anglo and Tejano (Hispanic Texan) law enforcement officers who, acting like cowboys and Rangers, round up Mexican immigrants like cattle. In late 2005 a new series of redadas occurred when the El Paso County Sheriff's Department, under the direction of Sheriff Leo Samaniego, began using routine traffic stops as a pretext for turning over undocumented residents to Immigration and Customs Enforcement (ICE) agents.[4] Sheriff Samaniego conducted these roundups in the context of the recent national immigration panic, in a move to garner law enforcement budget grants from the state of Texas that are designed to encourage these operations. The Sheriff's Department covers areas outside the incorporated city limits of El Paso. These areas include many tiny incorporated towns and unincorporated settlements, partly centered on farm labor in irrigated agriculture. These settlements are served by a spiderweb of farm-to-market roads and small feeder streets and back roads. On these passageways, checkpoints came and went, adding an element of uncertainty and peril. The sheriff especially targeted key choke points leading in and out of heavily Mexicano settlements. In our study, this affected the tiny rural town of Tornillo, whereas it did not affect the central city of El Paso. For this reason, we encountered significantly greater fear and caution in Tornillo than we did in El Paso.

In the summer of 2006, the sheriff's office was publicly scrutinized for using the checkpoints to target suspected undocumented immigrants, thus diverting its energies and resources from county and state law enforcement to federal *immigration* law. These outcries led to a brief suspension of the stationary vehicle checkpoints in June 2006. Throughout this period, Sheriff Samaniego noted his duty and obligation to "enforce the law." After some minor adjustments to his policies, he announced on October 10, 2006, that he would bring back the checkpoints to enforce *traffic* laws. Human rights advocates argue that the practice of singling out Hispanic drivers and occupants—ostensibly to check for compliance with driver's license and insurance requirements, in a quest to identify undocumented immigrants—had racist overtones and that these efforts eroded the public's trust in law enforcement generally (Fonce-Olivas 2006). Notably, such enforcement was effected not only through the interventions of the county sheriff but also, predictably, through the Border Patrol and other ICE authorities, both of which are a persistent presence on the city streets of El Paso and also in the more remote village of Tornillo, where their impact may in fact be greater.

EXPRESSIONS OF DEPORTABILITY

Among the most significant contributions of ethnography is its usefulness in giving voice to people pushed to the margins of society with few means of access to representation in public arenas (Ragin 1994, 83–85). The ethnographic component of our study contributed to this goal, as we amassed voluminous narratives on how it feels to be deportable and what people think about law and the larger society. We offer these brief observations to give a sense of people's expressions before we situate them within our own analytical framework.

The Sense of Being a Target

The El Paso County sheriff's use of checkpoints to examine people's documents triggered many narratives of fear and insecurity. Carlos (a pseudonym, as are all names of immigrants throughout this chapter) noted an incident in which he had to hide on his way to his deceased mother's memorial mass in early May 2006. "I went to El Paso's lower valley for a memorial mass for my deceased mother, but my wife was unable to go because of the sheriff's checkpoints. The sheriffs use the excuse of checking for license and insurance, but they are also checking for papers. There's fear, a lot of fear. It's like in the old days, when they would just stop someone in the street for being Mexican by saying, 'Do you have your papers?'" (All quotations are translated from the original Spanish.) Carlos connected this current practice to a past era of explicit racialization of public space in the borderlands, which—although no longer the pervasive pattern—remains a presence in this region.[5]

One interviewee also discussed fear of the Border Patrol, in this case of raids on various workplaces in El Paso. "My husband's work site has been raided a couple of times already. The Border Patrol shows up without announcing themselves, asking workers for their legal documentation. To stop this, my husband's boss installed doors to the shop which he now keeps locked under padlock during regular business hours to keep the Border Patrol from entering whenever they please."[6] As the woman noted, she and her spouse were quite alarmed at the recent Border Patrol raids taking place throughout the city. They rarely left their home and moved around in a constant rush. The couple also had a habit of calling each other every few hours to make sure all was well.

Public Space as Dangerous and Private Space as Safe

Undocumented populations often feel frighteningly visible and attempt to become invisible in response. Because they are aware that they are deportable, they sense a perceptual "branding" even if there is nothing extraordinary about their actual appearance. Bearing such a stigma, they often feel that they are unable to move freely in open public spaces such as parks, front yards, picnic areas, and busy streets. Enclosed public spaces, such as schools, hospitals, and clinics, are ambiguous sites; valued for their services and hidden from the police outside, they could also be a place where an undocumented person or family might be turned over to immigration authorities when asking for services. Schools are generally more trusted, because by Supreme Court decision (*Plyler v. Doe*, 1982) undocumented children have unimpeded access to them. Health service sites, however, are feared because of federal, state, and organizational policies requiring identification (except in emergencies) and penalizing use of welfare benefits; many informants hesitated to access public health services except in emergencies. Hence undocumented populations often sequester themselves in private, enclosed spaces such as homes, apartment buildings, and some workplaces, living in tightly watched, almost claustrophobic communities.

Several research participants hid in domestic spaces and seldom interacted with neighbors. Elisa noted, "I don't leave my home if I don't have to. I don't even know my neighbors. I'm afraid that if I were to ever have problems with my neighbors, they would go so far as turning me in by reporting me to the immigration officials." Another woman, Anita, mentioned that there were a number of methods used by local law enforcement to catch people. "There are traps and pitfalls used to deport people. I am afraid of going out. You can get deported for even taking care of a simple traffic ticket." She reported not wanting to walk outside her home and leaving it only when it was absolutely necessary. She stated also that she would always continue to be afraid.

In another example, Karina, a fifteen-year-old teenager living in a *colonia* in El Paso County, reported staying at home with her mother as much as possible, venturing outside only when necessary. As she said, "The major difference between me and my brother is that he is much younger than I and he does not fully recognize the possibility of being caught and deported, so he tends to roam around as he pleases." Interacting with outsiders, including neighbors, was also a perceived risk. Staying home and under the "social radar" was one of the many strategies used to avoid bringing attention to an individual's or family's undocumented predicament.

The fear of being seen publicly and possibly turned in to, or picked up by, immigration officials was a recurrent motif throughout our study. It seemed to be stronger among the heavily policed residents of Tornillo than the residents of the city of El Paso, who were somewhat disguised by the city masses (though even they expressed serious worries about public space, such as reluctance to walk in the park). Undocumented residents often discussed the importance of learning how to travel to various places (work, school, relatives' homes), recognizing that some streets, public spaces, and strategic arteries were heavily monitored by local and federal law enforcement officers and that others were less watched, or so they surmised.

However, in the case of medical emergencies and other similar situations, some heavily monitored public spaces were difficult to avoid, and undocumented immigrants had to weigh the benefits of seeking desperately needed assistance versus possibly facing deportation. This induced feelings of intense dilemma and internal conflict. A thirty-two-year-old woman, after telling us that her husband had been deported once already, commented, "If he is picked up by the border patrol one more time, he will go to jail. He is afraid of going to jail. Now he is careful with how he moves around town." She then told us that her husband would not accompany her to seek medical care because they had seen Border Patrol agents at the local public hospital. The woman reported seeing pregnant women with handcuffs being taken away by Border Patrol agents.

Sentiments of Loneliness, Despair, Anxiety, and Depression, and Fear of Severing Relationships

Deportability often leads to isolation and alienation, and many undocumented immigrants expressed sentiments of loneliness, despair, anxiety, and depression. One way this was often reported was disruption of personal contact with family in Mexico because of not traveling there for fear of not being able to return. Another, inverse effect was anxiety and despair at being removed from the United States, both in terms of feeling at home in Texas rather than in Mexico and in terms of the severing of personal relationships with loved ones in the United States. Deportation can result in permanent banishment from the United States or punishment in the form of a ten-year period during which the apprehended is ineligible to petition to adjust her legal status. If one is apprehended a second time before the ten-year period expires, the result is a punishment of a year or more in jail. The case of Maria and her husband showed how the possibility of severe punishment for a "repeat offender" resulted in feelings of anxiety and depression.

Maria reported that her husband had already been deported once but was eventually able to return to the United States after a short time in Ciudad Juárez, Mexico. Immigration authorities warned him that if he was picked up again, he would go directly to prison. Maria said that their greatest fear was that he would be apprehended a second time and that he would be forced to do an indefinite amount of prison time. Her husband now lives his life with a sense of entrapment and is reluctant to travel outside his immediate surroundings, doing so only when necessary and with extreme caution.

Separation through deportation affects not only the individual deported but the family that remains in the United States as well. Luz and her family provide an example of separation through deportation. After several years of living in the United States without documents, Luz reported that she could no longer cope with the stress and anxiety she experienced while living in hiding and decided nearly two years ago to legalize her immigrant status. She went to the INS office near downtown El Paso to begin the process of legalizing her status. Unfortunately, she was too honest and disclosed to immigration authorities that she had already been living within the United States for several years. Much to her surprise, "They refused my petition because I had already been living in the United States." She was then deported without a hearing to Ciudad Juárez and was forced to leave her husband and three sons behind. She was warned by the authorities that she was not eligible to petition for "legal" status for a ten-year period and that if she was apprehended in U.S. territory during this period, she would be imprisoned. Luz's naive surprise at having been denied a visa—apparently in spite of, but in fact because of, her undocumented residence—needs to be understood in terms of the current, rigid law, which prevents most legalization of undocumented people living within the United States even with valid petitions, as opposed to the legalization of those who apply from outside the country.

Luz's forced separation from her family left her extremely depressed, and the fear of trying to cross the border again in an effort to rejoin them, risking arrest and a jail sentence, made her seriously contemplate the possibility of remaining in Ciudad Juárez. Her husband had expressed concerns about Luz living alone in Ciudad Juárez, and their two youngest sons wept daily during her absence. Her husband proposed moving the family altogether to Ciudad Juárez to join his wife, but she insisted that her family remain in the United States.

Luz was initially resigned to her fate and even went as far as finding a job and a place to live, but after two months the emotional strain of being separated from her loved ones forced her to decide to cross into the United States alone, through an isolated area of the border, and she was reunited with her family. Because of her experience, she said she would never again attempt to legalize her status or the status of her three sons for fear of losing them through deportation. She remains hidden in her home, counting the days until her ten-year "sentence" will expire, although she will remain a "prisoner," in the sense of being deportable, for as long as she resides in the United States without documents.

Evading La Migra: A Game That Never Ends and Nobody Wins

Evading immigration and local police officers forces undocumented residents in El Paso to calculate their movements throughout the region. Some identify their movements as stop-and-go, like playing red light/green light, or as a cat-and-mouse game, hiding and reappearing whenever it is considered safe to come out and move around. One woman said, "We move around the city, like rats, quickly, hoping not to be caught." Another woman, also living in the city of El Paso, noted, "I'm always cautious when I'm out in the streets. I only know the streets around my apartment complex, but I worry about getting lost anywhere else. So I don't go to the other side of the [named] large intersection and stay close to my home. One day, I wanted to go to a [named] major street in El Paso, and ended up on the bridge to go back into Mexico. Luckily I was able to turn back in time." Lack of geographic knowledge contributes to feelings of entrapment and fears of deportation. In this case, not knowing her way around the city almost led her to voluntarily deport herself by driving right into Mexico; luckily she was able to catch the error before crossing the border.

How people cope with the stress and anxiety caused by the fear of deportation differs among individuals and households. By contrast with most of the people quoted earlier, some informants expressed their views on the dangers of apprehension with humor, defiance, and an insistence on their "legality," although even then their individual behaviors did not mirror their statements. Yasmin, Lucía, and Berta provided three such examples.

Asked if she was afraid of deportation, Yasmin laughed before stating with a wide smile, "I am not afraid that they will deport me. If they deport me it is because it was my turn." Lucía responded by laughing and slapping her thigh. "It does not make me afraid," she told us. "They would do me a favor. That way I could travel and rest for a little bit in Mexico." Why this bravado? A look at Berta's case helps us understand the implications hidden within these apparently fearless comments.

Berta answered with great hesitation when asked about her legal status, stating meekly that she was indeed a legal resident. When asked if the constant presence of the Border Patrol in Tornillo caused her to be afraid, she answered with some defiance, "Well no, why? If I see illegals near my home, I would call the immigration authorities myself." She may have been defiant in her response, but our observation indicated that she was anything but confident and that her immigrant status could well have been undocumented, though she did not indicate this on our questionnaire.

When we asked her a question about her perception of the Border Patrol's presence in her community, she seemed suddenly paranoid and anxious to end the interview. She later admitted to living a life that called the least amount of attention to itself. She reported that she never left her home even though she knew how to drive and had access to a vehicle, and that she always stayed indoors. She confessed at the close of our interview that she was constantly depressed and spent most of her life locked up in her home. Often she was so depressed that she had little motivation to get out of bed in the mornings, where she remained most days, getting up only to prepare meals for herself and her family.

While we cannot be certain of "legal" or undocumented status outside the explicit statements of the informants, we suspect that Berta insisted on her legality precisely because she was trying to hide her vulnerability to deportation. It is plausible that, when she claimed that she would re-port "illegals" to the immigration authorities, she was trying to tell the researchers what she believed she was supposed to say, based either on a distrust of us as potential spies who might report or arrest her or, more simply, on the basis of her presumptions about the researchers' biases as legal residents or citizens.

The other two women were not really that different from Berta, de-spite their humorous bravado. Yasmin admitted at the conclusion of our interview that she stayed indoors and rarely if ever ventured outside her home. Although she knew how to drive, and transportation was available, she refused to drive because she had no driver's license and was afraid of the sheriff's frequent roadblocks. Lucía's situation was similar. She told us that she never left her home and that her husband, a legal resident, did any driving that was needed for the household.

In our interpretation, bravado was a coping mechanism that enabled Berta and Lucía to deny the fears associated with deportation. Their at-tempt to deal with the daily threat of deportation through humor and a seemingly nonchalant attitude can be understood as the use of expressive language and self-presentation to manage stress and anxiety, maintain mental health, and cope with structural constraints that exerted tremen-dous power over their economic opportunities and life trajectories.

PATTERNS OF EXPERIENCE: ANTICIPATION, EVENT, MEMORY

We find it useful to step back from the humanistic, experiential view by organizing informants' experiences around three analytic moments in their accounts of deportability: anticipation, event, and memory. We understand these three moments in terms of their effects not only on single individuals but also on interrelated and intercommunicating groups of people. Deportation could be understood narrowly as an outcome for specific people, yet we found that it serves also as a catalyst for significant consequences that affect not only deported individuals but their families who remain undetected. Often deportation creates heartache for children and other family members who are left behind and results in hardship and impoverishment for families whose economic situation was already precarious to begin with. The anticipation and memory of deportation are not just matters of self-concern but issues thought about and shared among families and other networks of people.

Anticipatory anxiety concerning family separation, loss of income consequent to deportation, and difficulties faced when crossing back into the United States in the face of heightened border vigilance proved to be a predominant narrative theme. As we know, key information for the inexperienced undocumented migrants concerning their destination, the ways in which to make a successful trip, work opportunities, and shelter possibilities are usually obtained from networks comprising family and friends with past migration experience (Chavez 1992/1998). However, these same networks communicate the first stage of fear and anxiety and fix it in place as an expectation of danger, especially where fear-induced stress is introduced through the sharing of past apprehension experiences. Alongside this anticipation are the practical preparations for possible deportation, which likewise take advantage of household and network connections.

This social learning to anticipate danger is illustrated by Lupe's arrival in the United States. At that time, a friend "who works downtown" discouraged her from shopping in downtown El Paso because of the risk of being apprehended by the Border Patrol. According to this source, Border Patrol agents were concentrated in the downtown area and were stopping shoppers and asking them for identification. Individuals who could not present legal documentation were apprehended and deported. Lupe admitted to never having witnessed this herself; indeed, her fear had prevented her from going downtown since her arrival in the United States five years earlier.

We collected few stories relating directly to the actual deportation of interviewees or their family members, but the cases that had happened and the fears related to this issue were echoed many times over among the undocumented families. To relieve some of the stress and constant fear of apprehension and deportation, many undocumented immigrants find solace and a sense of security within a network of friends and relatives (Chavez 1992/1998). Ironically, association within these social networks also indirectly contributed to, and heightened fears involving the possibilities of, apprehension and subsequent deportation. Although this was an unintentional consequence, it was within these very networks that other people's stories were shared with newcomers, which in turn affected their own individual behaviors and impacted not only their mental health but also their economic situation, as in the story told by Graciela.

Graciela had only recently resumed her work cleaning other people's homes after a break of nearly two months owing to her fear of riding the bus after several sources within her social circle had told her that immigration officials had stopped buses and were seizing undocumented passengers and deporting them immediately. Graciela has no other source of transportation and must rely on a bus that she catches downtown. Her fear drove her to isolate herself in her home while she waited the situation out. As she told us, "We hardly ever leave our home for anything. I tried to stay away from downtown as much as possible. A couple of months have already passed since, but I am still afraid."

Graciela ended up losing a lot of work and has not recuperated it since. The homeowners for whom she worked simply replaced her by hiring other undocumented women to clean their homes. She reported that before she was seized by this fear, she was employed by several homeowners, providing her with a full week's worth of work. On the day of our interview, she was left with only one home to clean, less than one full day of work. Fear involving the much larger consequences of deportation produces effects that often redirect daily social behaviors for each individual immigrant.

One of the frequently expressed fears was the ever-present danger that a family member might suddenly and unexpectedly be apprehended. When a spouse or child was late in coming home, the family's fear quickly mounted, and they immediately assumed that the missing family member had been apprehended and deported by the authorities. Mothers and wives strongly expressed worries of losing a family member to deportation, as illustrated by Susanna, Lupe, and Sonia.

Susanna spoke with great conviction about her fears of deportation. "Clearly yes, that more than anything," she said, "I fear for my husband and my children when they are outside the home. I never let them go anywhere alone. I am always worried about him and my children." Lupe stated that she has tried to come to terms with the consequences of being caught and deported, but readily admitted, "Yes, I am afraid, especially when I have to drive past Fabens [a neighboring town five miles from her home], because if I am stopped by police, they will call the immigration authorities and have me deported. Then my children are left without a mother. I do go out on occasion, but for this reason I do not work."

Sonia was visibly fearful when discussing the danger presented by the constant presence of the Border Patrol in her community of Tornillo. "This is what worries me the most about living here," she said. Sonia recalled how she and her family used to love to spend time outdoors and take long walks for exercise when they lived in Mexico, but that has changed since their immigration to the United States. Now she fears that her husband, after leaving home for work—or her children when they go outside to play—may someday unexpectedly disappear. "I do worry about my husband when he leaves to go to work, but I am more worried about my children, who are undocumented. Now that they are out of school for the summer, they stay locked indoors all summer long. . . . Because of my fear, I do not let them go outdoors."

In addition to the possibility that a family member would one day disappear without notice, another common concern was the stress of dealing with the potential emotional loss and the ensuing anxiety and uncertainty of not knowing what had actually happened to the family member who never returned home. To inquire with authorities about a loved one involves the risk of detection, potentially resulting in the loss of an additional family member or, in extreme cases, the deportation of the entire family. Several families described the fear of "not knowing" what happened to a loved one as an emotional and mental trial they would never want to endure.[7] This fear was only heightened when stories of other undocumented families who experienced such a situation filtered down through their social networks. A case involving friends of Luz offered one such example.

Luz was well aware that the Border Patrol is active in her community, which is why she expressed a deep fear of being separated from her children or of leaving them alone to walk home from school. She said her fear grew when she learned what had happened to another family of undocumented Mexican immigrants who lived nearby. The mother of this household, along with her two daughters, drove off one day to a local store not more than two miles away from their home to purchase some everyday items. Her husband and her two sons remained at home, but she and their two daughters never returned. Luz, who had visited the husband, remarked, "Those poor people did not know what had happened to them. The husband was very worried, and his sons grew extremely sad."

Luz frequently visited the father and his two sons to offer some comfort and to ask if there was anything she could do for them. She described the father as depressed and frustrated that he could not contact the authorities to verify that his wife and daughters had indeed been apprehended and deported for fear that he would be caught and his two sons would be left alone. According to Luz's account, nearly two weeks had passed before he received a communication from his wife in Mexico confirming that she and their daughters had been deported and their car impounded. (Immigration authorities often seize vehicles as "assets" involved in the transportation of undocumented immigrants, and the county sheriff or city police may impound abandoned vehicles or vehicles without proper insurance, registration, or license.) When this story was told, it had been three months since the incident, and the family still remained separated.

This account represents not only the separation anxieties and emotional loss experienced by a family when one of its members was deported, but also the loss of much-needed resources for a marginalized population who are economically challenged. Through a single action, the family was forcibly separated for an indefinite period of time; they lost their only source of transportation, which diminished their mobility; and as a result, the father lost his job. Since the father had no other means of transport to his job as a construction laborer (which required a round-trip commute of sixty miles a day), he was now supporting himself and his two sons through odd jobs that he could obtain locally and through the charity provided by other families who were in a similar situation.

Several families reported that they were particularly concerned about the genuine potential of losing the only wage earner of the household to deportation. When the primary wage earner is deported, an already delicate financial situation turns into a complete economic crisis for the remaining family. Each of the undocumented respondents we interviewed described their families as living in or near poverty. For example, Andrea described her husband as being the only wage earner in the household. After he was returned to Mexico by immigration authorities, she was left without a car and without an income with which to support herself and her three children:

> I did not have a job and we were left without any money. There was no money to buy groceries. We did not eat for three days. There was no money to buy food to eat . . . there was no money for anything. I had to find work in the farm fields nearby. I walked everyday to work in the fields picking onions, but after eight months of working in the fields physically my body could no longer take it. I am too old to do this kind of work. Finally I was able to find a job in a factory, and I now have almost two years working there.

Andrea said that she still does not have a vehicle and depends on a daily ride to work from a friend who works in the same factory. To this day, her husband has not returned, and she has not heard directly from him. In this case, we cannot readily distinguish deportation and abandonment; indeed, they sometimes combine to form wider patterns of separation in the U.S.-Mexico migration process.

Andrea never sought to retrieve their car from the impound lot for the same reason she has not purchased another vehicle to date: lack of financial resources. The $880 she earns each month is not nearly sufficient to pay her rent and utilities and to feed and clothe her family of six, which includes a younger sister and her daughter. Andrea also pointed out, as did other respondents, that at the time the vehicle was impounded, she could ill afford to pay the initial wrecker fee to have the vehicle released to her, and each day that the car remained in the impound lot only escalated the cost of having it released. Within a matter of weeks, the opportunity to have the car released from the impound yard quickly grows outside the realm of economic possibility.

Aside from the financial challenges involved in having their vehicles released, a driver's license, to which no undocumented immigrant in Texas has legal access, was also required. Driving without a license increased their vulnerability to being arrested in the streets and roads near their residences, especially during the commute to and from work. A simple traffic stop or a roadblock set up by local police to check for licenses and automobile insurance could result in arrest and deportation. Furthermore, many had purchased used cars with no legal title, which hindered the release of the vehicle to remaining family members. But the largest barrier that kept undocumented immigrants from inquiring about their lost vehicle was their own legal status and the unsubstantiated fear that simply showing up to inquire about the status of their seized vehicle would result in their own arrest and deportation.

Andrea's story was an example of the impact that separation can have on the economic situation of a single undocumented family, in conjunction with the constraints and risks imposed by poverty and casual labor markets. The majority of the households reported having only one wage earner, which they attributed to a lack of dual transportation, a spouse not knowing how to drive, no one to care for the children at home, fear of apprehension, and lack of local informal or formal job opportunities. One reason for a single wage earner in the family was described as an avoidance of unnecessary risk by both parents commuting to and from work, or what could be described as "double jeopardy." The question posed in return many times during our interviews was, "Why endanger both of us at the same time and risk leaving our children without their parents?"

Many in the U.S. public perceive that the southern borders are wide open and easy to cross surreptitiously. This, of course, is far from the truth, which is in large part why deportation is a major problem anticipated by undocumented Mexican immigrants. Crossing into the United States carries a set of burdens that Mexican immigrants would hope to rarely experience. The U.S. response to the rise in undocumented immigration in the last decade has been to increase the concentration of law enforcement on the southern border, which has made crossing the border a daunting challenge on many levels (see Andreas 2001; Dunn 1996; Eschbach, Hagan, and Rodríguez 2003; Heyman 1999; Nevins 2002). There is not only the horrific threat of death and injury when crossing the border but also—with the renewed focus from government law enforcement agencies on stemming the flow of "illegal" migration—the burden of repeated arrests before successful entry is made. Frequent failed attempts to cross the border may eventually result in a prison sentence of a year or more for repeat offenders.

Because U.S. law enforcement has increased the probability of apprehension for migrants who cross the border on their own, they are more likely to use a *coyote* (labeled by authorities as "alien smugglers") to guide them across the border in the belief that by doing so they increase their chances of escaping detection. As the potential for apprehension increases, so do the fees charged by coyotes (Orrenius 2001). The following case of Norma and her children highlights just how costly these services can be. Norma returned to the United States with her children by hiring a coyote who was referred to her by a friend in Ciudad Juárez with whom she and her children were staying. The coyote's fee for assisting their entry into the United States was $350 for her and $250 for each of her children: a total of $850 for this single endeavor.

Although Norma's reentry with her two children succeeded, the use of a coyote by no means guarantees successful entry into the United States. Some coyote arrangements involve promises to assist crossings until success is achieved, or at least a certain number of attempted crossings, but the loss of the fee remains a significant risk and worry. Saving the money to pay the required fees was no easy task given the migrants' financial situation. It may take months or even years to accumulate the monetary resources required for reentry. The memories of the hardships experienced during their initial entry into the United States, coupled with the real potential for deportation thereafter—and possibly having to endure the process and all its consequences multiple times—only compound un-documented migrants' stress and anxiety.

Memory is a key factor that underlies all the fear of arrest and deporta-tion experienced by the undocumented immigrant population. It involves not only what people remember themselves but also the transmittal of fear from the individual to the family and the rest of the community. Memory outlines the landmarks of their past. These shared recollections between individuals and groups are invoked and then rationally adopted to the present. To put it simply, undocumented immigrants live with one foot in the past and one foot placed firmly in the present. What they think and believe of the future relies on the collective traditions and recollec-tions assembled together with knowledge derived from the present.

How long these memories last and continue to produce effects in daily behaviors and perceptions varies from one individual to the next. It might be assumed that the fears, stress, and anxieties born of the threat of de-portation and its related effects end with the legalizing of their status. For some, however, the fear, or at least the memory of it, remains long after they have legalized their status. The words of Juanita, Leticia, and Gloria illustrate how, for them, the effects of deportability were enduringly inter-nalized. We should note that deportability does in fact continue into legal residency status if a person is arrested for certain crimes or combinations of them, or a variety of other administrative violations. These informants did hold such concerns, such as reluctance to use health benefits for fear of having legal residency removed for being "a public charge."[8] However, the narratives went well beyond a rational view of legal perils to expose a searing memory trace of fear of removal from the United States.

Juanita, for example, told us that it was her continued fear of immi-gration officials that kept her from traveling where she pleased and con-strained her from inquiring about much-needed resources. She expressed a firm belief that she was in danger of being deported for any miniscule reason during the five-year period before eligibility to apply for natural-ization, and admitted that she continued to live her life as if she were "illegal." She firmly believed that she would not be relieved of her anxi-eties regarding deportation until her five-year waiting period expires. "I am waiting for that time to arrive. I am counting the days."

Leticia admitted that during her legalization process she was extremely fearful of the immigration authorities. She would never spend time out-doors or travel much outside her home. "I would not go out into the streets," she said. "I would not even go to the doctor when needed." She has been a legal resident since 2002 but continues to avoid traveling to

Mexico at all costs. Indeed, the thought of even going near the border or into Mexico frightened her, despite her legal status.

When we talked to Gloria, she admitted to being severely depressed and said that her mental state was fragile:

> It has been twelve years since I have not been in Mexico. I lived many years in the United States as an illegal. Today I am a legal resident, but I feel the same. My mind-set has not changed; I continue living in fear. I do not feel important. I continue to live my life in hiding. I still do not go out in public much. I have no self-confidence, and I continue to live my life as though I was still illegal. I want to live my life differently, but I just can't.

Gloria recognizes that her reaction to being deportable lives on in her behavior and feelings, even though she understands intellectually that she no longer needs to be frightened and cautious.

What these undocumented immigrants have experienced and remember marks how they continue to perceive themselves into the future. The constant, long-standing fear and anxiety attributed to the continuous presence of law enforcement and the possibility of deportation and its consequences scar the psyches of undocumented immigrants long after they have legalized their status. The felt and narrated experience of deportability involves a continuous series of interactions between three moments of deportation—the event itself, the anticipation of it, and memories, constantly reworked. Importantly, memories of past moments of fear and actual arrests and deportations loop back to shape present consciousness and anticipation of further possible dangers. Additionally, these experience-framing processes are both internal to the individual and communicated with others, families and friends in particular. It is this social organization of deportability to which we now turn.

UNDERSTANDING COMPLEXITY WITHIN DEPORTABILITY: VARIABILITY, CLEAVAGE, AND COLLECTIVE ACTION

The experiences and effects of deportability vary considerably. There are two dimensions to comprehending this variation. First, deportability can be described and analyzed at various levels or scales of generalization. It is important to carefully delineate the units of which we speak, so as not to erase important dimensions of variability. In our study, there was variation between the two geographic settlements we studied, so that the deportable population was not unitary per se; there was variation within each settlement area, so that we need to generalize about "communities" cautiously; and there was variation among individuals within households, so again we are careful about even the smallest units of generalization.

Second, undocumented people organize themselves for social and political action at different scales, from individuals through households and networks to settlement areas (thus forming communities in the strict sense). Clusters form around communication of ideas and coordination of action, and conversely cleavages form barriers of information flow and divisions of perception and action. For example, not all members of the same household were subject equally to deportability or equally vulnerable to its effects. This was sometimes expressed in cleavages within the household over group interests. In turn, such divisions either were negotiated toward unified action or remained a source of tension and division. Various social differences, including age, gender, and legal status, help account for these potential divisions, but some are also idiosyncratic. The point is not to emphasize variation and conflict only. Rather, following Zlolniski (2006), our emphasis is that deportable people are not simply recipients of oppression but engage in social organization and carry out various kinds of collective action. We thus bring into view communication, negotiation, trust making, and community mobilization, their perils and possibilities, in settings with significant numbers of deportable people.

Households were probably the most common unit of solidarity and collective action. Stand-alone houses and lots with several dwelling structures provided cover and a space safe from immigration officers and sheriffs. We did not record any narratives of law enforcement knocking on doors and entering, although local human rights activists told us that such entrances do occur. But we did observe and also heard about Border Patrol vehicles parking directly outside housing lots while families clustered nervously inside. We also visited apartment buildings that were locked and carefully monitored from the inside by their undocumented residents. In addition to the practical value of huddling together for mutual protection, families and friends also provided emotional support in this stressful situation. The whole mix could be (but was not always) glued together by the ideology of mutual family obligation. The result was that households tended to act collectively vis-à-vis the deportability of their members, but this nonetheless remained fraught with potential divisions. Alternative basic units of action included isolated individuals or groups of unrelated individuals.[9]

A fruitful approach to variability, collectivity, and cleavage is to examine "mixed-status households," which contain both undocumented people and citizens or legal residents. They were common in our study as well as among the national undocumented population.[10] Mixed statuses create differences between household members in terms of access to social programs and vulnerability to deportation and also threaten to tear apart parents and children or even siblings in the event of detection and deportation, as in the case of Guillermo's family. Guillermo, as well as his mother, was undocumented, while his father is a U.S. legal resident and his two younger brothers are U.S. citizens by birth. Because of Guillermo's undocumented status, he does not qualify for public health insurance, for which his brothers do qualify, nor can he be taken to Mexico for relatively inexpensive private medical care without the risk of being detained when reentering the United States. The situation was beginning to prove confusing for Guillermo. His father says, "The child suffers a lot—he asks me, 'Why don't I have Medicaid, why am I different?' " His family sought to maintain unity, which in this case meant limiting itself, even the authorized members, to doing only things that were relatively safe for the unauthorized members. They did not take road trips outside their small settlement, for example, so as not to cross Border Patrol checkpoints and county sheriff roadblocks on the main highways. The legal-resident father explicitly commented on this as a family sacrifice. Although they functioned as a unified household, there were pressures toward division of which they were acutely aware, and it took an active effort to create and maintain solidarity in the face of unequal deportability.

Although Guillermo's family sought to maintain its unity, mutuality did not always accompany deportability. Indeed, cleavages were found not only in mixed households but also among equally deportable individuals who differed in their life circumstances and personal responses to risks. Luis was an undocumented working man in his late teens. He and another brother provided the main income for their family. His mother, Maria Antonia, was also undocumented, but her focus was caring for an adoptive daughter, who had profound and lifelong health problems; this daughter was in the United States without documents in order to take advantage of generous charitable care (this case was unusual, since no other interviewees had migrated to access health care). Luis moved around the city with relatively little fear, or so he reported, and his main concern with deportability was the loss of income. He envisioned himself as being able to cope with removal by returning relatively quickly from Mexico. His mother, on the other hand, was trapped in her home by her and her daughter's deportability and also worried more about their "illegality" and its effects on the daughter's access to health care. This household, bearing a divisive double burden of deportability and illness, was tense during the interview, and the line of cleavage was evident.

Cleavages become more apparent as we step up a level of aggregation, from households to neighbors in settlement areas. Individuals and households in both study areas varied substantially in their legal status and in the tone of their relationships with each other. Thus we cannot assume that settlement areas automatically formed communities of mutual self-interest and protection against the state. The question instead is how community was or was not formed. That, in turn, involves discussing tensions and barriers that impeded collective identity and action. For example, we often heard suspicions expressed that neighbors would turn in undocumented neighbors to the Border Patrol or Immigration and Customs Enforcement. Whether or not this was true in any given case, it made people reluctant to communicate with their neighbors and to be physically seen by or with them, and thus reduced avenues for the creation and maintenance of solidarity. The incompleteness of information and the risk involved in others having such information impelled speculation, rumor, and fear of the others' knowledge—significant sources of division in settlement areas.

Berta (discussed in the first ethnographic section earlier) and her neighbor, Lupe, were mutually suspicious of each other, in part because Lupe thinks that Berta is undocumented, and Berta denies it. It was impossible for us to know the actual situation, but significantly, we encountered an atmosphere of uncertainty, denial, and risk, and the consequent anxiety in their relationship. In addition to telling us that she thought Berta was undocumented, Lupe noted that "that lady [Berta] never leaves her house; she does not open the door for anyone. She's a little illegal [*mojadita*, implying condescension]." Although we had a referral to do a health interview with her, Berta initially refused to open the door for us, claiming later that she had not been home. When we did speak to her, Berta claimed to have no fear of immigration officials because she was a legal resident. However, Berta admitted that she will not venture outside and refuses to drive though she has a car and knows how to drive. (Notably, Berta was constantly depressed, which may provide an alternative explanation for this behavior but may nonetheless also be an effect of the entrapments of deportability.) In any case, these two neighbors were divided by mutual suspicion, one believing the other to be undocumented, the other apparently afraid of her neighbor being a snitch.

Within a settlement area, whether in Tornillo or central El Paso, households have varied legal statuses. This means that we cannot assume solidarity built around a universally or even widely shared condition of deportability. If solidarity does emerge, it may take either the form of solidarity among people and households who share the same legal vulnerability and begin to coordinate as a network (often with other bases as well) or spring from a sense of identification of legal residents and citizens with the undocumented, partly because of their own past experience and partly because of other interpersonal bonds. Both types of solidarity appeared in our research; it is crucial to ask how they were forged.

Social scientists have long known that networks are important tools for the poor and powerless to cope with their vulnerabilities (Lomnitz 1977), and have known in particular that migrants often rely heavily on hometown and kinship networks (e.g., Massey et al. 1987). It was thus unsurprising that we found extensive networks of mutual assistance in both El Paso and Tornillo, and that among their roles were warning about the presence and coping with the effects of immigration law enforcement. Before we turn to these cases, however, we want to emphasize that networks did not always operate productively and were sometimes fractured by the pressure of mutual suspicion.

Mutual suspicion seemed to have had more impact on the outlying rural settlement of Tornillo, which had been under siege by both the Border Patrol and county sheriffs shortly before our study, than in the central city, where immigration law enforcement was not as intense, though certainly present. This generalization can be substantiated by reviewing how we contacted informants within a research design based on a combination of contacts with formal institutions (e.g., health clinics) and network connections (so-called snowball sampling). In both sites, we were outsiders researching hidden populations. In central El Paso, most interviewees were made known to us through networks, and only a few people were reluctant to refer us to others (we also drew a small number of informants from a free, no-questions-asked religious health clinic). In Tornillo, it was initially more difficult to obtain other references from our interviewees, which we think derives from the high level of fear in the community in the aftermath of the sheriff's checkpoints and frequent Border Patrol presence. We obtained most of our interviews through a community health social worker who had excellent knowledge of, and relationships in, the community. As our fieldworkers became better known, we were able to use some interpersonal network connections. People were hesitant to meet with us, however, and often expressed fear of their neighbors. We do not know if this was an enduring characteristic of the rural settlement or contingent on the time when we did fieldwork.

A striking illustration of a network in central El Paso springing into action involved an incident when Immigration and Customs Enforcement (ICE) officers carried out an apprehension in front of Sara, an undocumented person (what follows is summarized from a much longer interview narrative). She had left her apartment for her mother's house, about a block away, to borrow some beans. There, on the street, she witnessed two plainclothes ICE agents questioning a man working on his car in front of his elementary-school-age son. As Sara recounted the story, she thought, "Damn it, I had better act really serious [implying undisturbed]." She locked herself behind the gate that served as the entryway to the second story of her mother's building, and rushed up the stairs to tell her mother that La Migra (immigration law enforcement) was outside. She locked herself in her mother's apartment and continued to spy on the scene below through the window.

The neighborhood was essentially frozen as the ICE agents, and later Border Patrol officers, questioned the man for over two hours. People remained trapped in other people's homes until the agents left the scene. What worried Sara most was that her children were alone in the home. She had expected to be gone only for a couple of minutes; now it was turning into a couple of hours. She was frightened for her children, most of whom were also undocumented. While trapped in her mother's apartment, she made several phone calls to her husband, family, and friends to apprise them of the situation and to find someone who could rush over to her house and keep an eye on her children. She effectively started a "chain call" that alerted the neighborhood to what was going on. Sara's husband left work a little earlier than usual and rushed to her aid. When he arrived, he did not get out of his car but simply honked the horn, which was the signal for Sara to come down. She exited in a place that could not be seen from the street and quickly got into the car. They avoided the scene by driving through the adjacent streets and reached home safely.

When Sara arrived, she found that her children were all right, and that several of the neighborhood women were sitting in her living room, waiting for the agents to disperse. As soon as they had witnessed the apprehension, they had rushed inside her home to seek shelter. Our impression was that the circle of women in the neighborhood formed a strong network and supported one another in crisis. Anyone's home could be an accessible safe house for those caught outside in such a situation. In response to the incident, Sara stated, "For a few beans, I was at the point of being hauled off by the immigration authorities, but they did get the father and the kid. Poor guy, they didn't allow him to fix his car. He was a good friend of my husband. He left the rest of his family over here."

As we can see from her closing remark, the network can cope with and to an extent defend individuals and households from arrest and removal, but it does not push back against immigration law enforcement. Such resistance did happen, however, through the Border Network for Human Rights, an organization that focuses on grassroots human rights education, documentation, and policy advocacy in El Paso and southern New Mexico. A main focus of the Border Network's activities during the time of our fieldwork was the sheriff's checkpoints. The Border Network worked on several levels, including advocating policy change to the county commissioners, but they also drew information from, and organized through, community hearings in the small settlements scattered throughout the county.

At such events, witnesses (both solicited and volunteered) criticized the sheriff's operations in terms that unified the concerns of documented and undocumented people. Key arguments were that the atmosphere of fear and the presumption of "illegality" were stigmatizing everyone in these communities ("legal" or not) and that immigrants' fear of the sheriffs impeded law enforcement from addressing criminal activities such as domestic violence. Specific settlements were identified as "communities" by those offering public testimony to the county commissioners. Through these processes emerged a sense of belonging to a named community with a collective will and mutual interests, overcoming the divisions described earlier, notably those of "legal" versus "illegal."

These organized communities, which had developed a sense of efficacy and unity in local struggles over deportability, were central to the mobilization of three marches or demonstrations during the immigration rights protests of 2006 in El Paso and southern New Mexico. Between five hundred and a thousand people participated in each event. While this may not be an impressively large number, it is significant that the core participants were organized members of these low-income immigrant communities rather than middle-class, cause-driven activists, and that the organizations have continued to function in immigrant communities well after the demonstration fervor ceased (see Gilot 2007). In turn, of course, these events in El Paso were linked to national-level political mobilizations against immigration repression and for immigration reform.

In a less dramatic fashion, named community institutions such as schools—while arms of the same state as the immigration police—also provided elements of safety, unity, and mutual identification in the face of deportability. The elementary school in Tornillo provided a space where we interviewed a number of undocumented people. This was reassuring to our interviewees, who, during a period of heightened law enforcement, regarded the school as a safe place where they could talk freely, without revealing where they lived, to a pair of previously unknown interviewers. Indeed, a small group of women observed our work at the school and then cautiously approached us there, asking if they too could be interviewed (we paid twenty dollars for a completed interview, and yet people also seemed generally interested in the topics we discussed and appreciative of our study). Eventually we visited some of these people at home. The school also hosted the local children's health clinic and was seen as an enclosed space, safe from the sheriffs and the Border Patrol—just like the interior of a house, and unlike the risky open streets and fields between them.

A careful climbing of the scales of social action, from individual through household and network to self-identifying community, has served to help tease out the complex experience of deportability. It enables us to delineate the differences and divisions among people, but also to understand how they construct ideas and practices of mutual solidarity, both among the undocumented themselves and between the documented (including citizens) and the undocumented. It helps us recognize that bonds of mutual trust do not occur automatically but are built gradually in the face of the profound fear and distrust that comes from the condition of being "illegal" (Vélez-Ibáñez 1983).

CONCLUSIONS AND PUBLIC IMPLICATIONS

Scholars and advocates of immigrants' rights have persistently argued that more border enforcement will not deter undocumented immigration (e.g., Massey, Durand, and Malone 2002). Nevertheless, on October 4, 2006, in an effort to appease his anti-immigrant constituents, President Bush signed a homeland security bill that funds $1.2 billion for hundreds of miles of fencing along the U.S.-Mexico border to stem "illegal" immigration. This funding was intended to "modernize" and secure the border, as some of these resources were destined for the acquisition of lighting, infrared cameras, and other tools to enforce and barricade the border. As he signed this bill into law, Bush conceded that border enforcement alone would not stop the flow of undocumented immigration (Riechmann 2006). The immigration policy debate at the time of writing includes possibilities such as legalization of undocumented people who have lived in the United States for extended periods (e.g., more than two years), guest worker programs for above-board temporary labor migration, and also a larger Border Patrol and greater electronic surveillance of the boundary.

The immigrant communities of El Paso, both rural and urban, have begun to have a voice in this process, particularly through the Border Network for Human Rights, which has sent delegations to meet with congressional and White House staff and Washington policy advocacy groups and has suggested specific legislative language. Voices and findings from our study of deportability were included in these efforts; among the key emphases is setting limits on involvement of state and local agencies in federal immigration law enforcement.[11] The situation of the deportable people of the borderlands is becoming more and more difficult as they remain among us in hidden suffering, but on a few occasions they rise in collective solidarity. Not just their painful experiences and feelings but also their will to persevere and create a better life become ever more important.

As applied social scientists, our goal is not only to provide scholarly documentation and analysis but also to share the voices of undocumented people as they face the daily stress of isolation and entrapment, and to join the public debates that affect their lives and ours. We found patterns of loneliness, anxiety, depression, avoidance of public spaces, significant family conflict and distrust among neighbors (but likewise patterns of trust and solidarity), severe impacts on household economies, and reluctance to travel to and use health care services, including preventative services. Key concerns centered on the increased risk and expense in returning from Mexico after removal, including the fear of disconnection from family and the fear of serious material suffering owing to loss of income while deported. All these worries are worsened by massive increases in immigration law enforcement in the border region in recent years.

Several ideas used in this study—including anticipation, event, and memory, and the multiscalar approach to social cleavage and coalescence—may prove useful in future work with deportable people in situations of intensive immigration law enforcement and control of movement. Stress and anxiety, for example, were closely associated with anticipation of family separation, loss of income, and the difficulty of crossing back into the United States because of heightened border security. This was exacerbated by individually held and interpersonally communicated memories of arrests and deportations. However, the social organization of deportable people and their households, networks, and communities results in complex outcomes—interpersonal tensions and shared fear among people, but also collective forms of coping and active social movements for immigrant rights. By documenting and analyzing these layers of experience and organization, we contribute to the study of entrapment processes and the responses to them, and more generally to the topics of mobility and enclosure (Cunningham and Heyman 2004; Núñez and Heyman 2007).

Spatial mobility and its social and cultural implications have become an important focus in the social sciences (e.g., Appadurai 1996). Hilary Cunningham and Josiah Heyman (2004) argue that when we study mobility, we should attend to processes of enclosure that bind people to specific spatial, social, and cultural locations, including the kinds of power involved in such processes. Núñez and Heyman (2007), in turn, focus on the specific situation of immigrants living within the U.S.-Mexico borderlands, where concentrated immigration law enforcement results in a tricky geography of risks and countermoves identified as "entrapment processes." This study of deportability has furthered our understanding of enclosure and entrapment. On the one hand, the framework of anticipation, experience, and memory has clarified how, above and beyond the specific sites and practical considerations of immigration policing, vulnerability to immigration law enforcement penetrates and traps people in their thoughts, feelings, and personal behaviors. Nonetheless, on the other hand, attention to the varied lines of cooperation and cleavage within entrapped communities clarifies the active role of undocumented people rather than their passive victimhood and thus strengthens the understanding of entrapment as a complex interplay of moves and countermoves, leading to similarly complex outcomes.

NOTES

1. The study, "Health Behaviors and Access Barriers to Uninsured, Undocumented Immigrants in El Paso County: An Ethnographic Study," was funded by the Paso del Norte Health Foundation. The principal investigator was Nuria Homedes, and other members of the research team were Carla Alvarado, Victor Talavera, Guillermina Gina Núñez, and Josiah Heyman. We thank the foundation for its support; errors and misinterpretations in the present paper are the sole responsibility of the authors and not of the foundation or other research team members.

2. One peculiarity of our study was the disproportionately female composition of our informants. We sought to have a roughly gender-balanced set of interviewees, but despite considerable efforts, we did not accomplish this. We have a number of speculative ideas about why this was the case, but we cannot explain it with any certainty. Later in the paper, we discuss two other methodological aspects of our study, how we contacted informants and where we interviewed people, because the research process itself provided valuable ethnographic insights.

3. Although small numbers of undocumented non-Mexicans live near the border, we dealt with an undocumented population that was entirely of Mexican origin. Hence we do not consider national origin as a dimension of variation, or differences between border and nonborder geographies, although they deserve attention in other settings.

4. The county's policy under Sheriff Samaniego differed from the City of El Paso Police Department's policy under Chief Richard Wiles. The city police department has not participated in organized immigration law enforcement, though people arrested under other charges by city police may have their immigration status checked with ICE. Chief Wiles has been a public critic of involving local law enforcement in immigration matters. However, the Border Patrol and ICE (two federal immigration police agencies) do operate in the city, including in the central El Paso neighborhoods we studied.

5. The immigration issue at a national level continues to be framed in racial terms, at least partly, equating Mexicans with "illegal aliens" and vice versa. This in turn shapes the concentration of federal immigration policing along the border. However, in borderlands communities, the vast majority of the population (over 80 percent in El Paso County) is of Mexican origin, as is a majority of police forces, local and federal. Without claiming that El Paso is a postracial paradise, which it plainly is not, it is nonetheless the case that casual, phenotypically based racial targeting of Mexicans as Mexicans on streets and highways no longer works. Our informant was therefore referring to an earlier period when people would be stopped and questioned just for appearing to be Mexican. There are covert remnant elements of racialization, however. People of Mexican appearance are possibly stopped for immigration questioning, usually with additional clues besides phenotype, whereas Anglo-Americans and African Americans are rarely stopped. Mandatory stops, such as checkpoints, followed by mandatory inspection of identification documents, accomplish similar immigration policing effects but appear to be racially blind because everyone is stopped, though phenotypically "Anglo" people may pass through more quickly than phenotypically "Mexican" people. There is little scrutiny of Anglo attestations of U.S. citizenship, whereas people of Mexican origin are sometimes scrutinized more thoroughly. See Heyman 2001; more work needs to be done on this topic.

6. Locking a business site might keep immigration officials out temporarily but also increases the risk of trapping employees inside in the case of a fire or emergency. In addition there is a peculiar double edge to this sort of "protective" behavior—on the one hand, it shelters undocumented workers from immigration authorities, but on the other, it creates a potential for physical coercion and hierarchical social obligations (protector-protectee) between employer and employee (see Heyman 1998). Immigration workplace raids, which often originate with called-in tips, can be used by employers against employees or by one faction against another among employees.

7. The heaviest emotional burden is not simply not hearing from loved ones after deportation to Mexico; to this silence is added the anticipatory fear of vio-

lence in Mexican cities, including border cities. Ciudad Juárez is infamous for the unexplained disappearances and killings of more than four hundred women since 1990, and disappearances and killings of men are even more common there.

8. The "public charge" fear stems from the following: U.S. law allows deportation (including removal of legal-resident status) for people who use public health and welfare services of many kinds, during five years after immigration to the United States, and also allows the denial of entry to people newly applying for admission to the country on the basis of past use of such services. Our informants were generally aware and frightened of this, even to the point of not using services that would not carry such a penalty.

9. Our study addressed family health issues, so we did not conduct interviews at workplaces (including workplaces with employee housing) or in households formed by unrelated individuals. Clearly, both of those formations also occur as forms of solidarity in response to deportability.

10. At the time of writing, the quantitative analysis of our material has not been completed, but visual inspection of the interview notes supports this statement. Nationally, 3.1 million children are U.S. citizens living in families with unauthorized immigrant members; 67 percent of children in those families are citizens (Passel 2005).

11. In a Border Network policy delegation to Washington, El Paso County Attorney José Rodríguez admirably took the lead in advocating limitations on state and local involvement in immigration law enforcement. One of the present authors (Heyman) was part of this delegation and presented some of the material from this study. Immigrant community members have testified on a number of occasions in public forums organized by the Border Network, material that formed part of the Washington delegation's presentations to policymakers.

ANDREW M. GARDNER

—w—

CHAPTER 6

Engulfed

Indian Guest Workers, Bahraini Citizens, and

the Structural Violence of the *Kafala* System

In the early months of 2006, newspaper headlines in the Kingdom of Bahrain reported that Bramco, a marble and granite company that employs well over nine hundred South Asian transnational laborers, had narrowly averted a labor strike. Paresh Dholakia, a draftsman at the company, was accused of copying a set of compact discs containing company secrets and had supposedly admitted to company officials his intention to steal and sell these industry secrets on the open market. A Bramco vice-president, contributing to the public indictment of the guest worker, indicated that Mr. Dholakia "was also sending his resume to other companies to try and get a better job" (Bew 2006). The company itself took the burden of punishing the wayward transnational employee: he was "jailed" in his quarters for five days before being deported. The company vice-president noted that Mr. Dholakia was confined to a room with "a refrigerator, bathroom, television and air-conditioning, and [he] was given three meals a day" (Bew 2006).

While the company spokesman stressed the magnanimity of this treatment in the context of the social relations of production predominant in Bahrain, the event nonetheless sparked the South Asian community on the island. One of the few human rights activists in Bahrain stated, "Nobody should be kept against their will. . . . Employers are not the law!" (Bew 2006). Meanwhile, Indian workers at Bramco, enraged that one of their fellow employees and countrymen was being "treated like a dog," threatened to strike but eventually backed down in fear of retaliation from management. Although the event then dropped from the headlines, it reverberated through the "Letters to the Editor" section of the primary English-language newspaper that serves the island. Altogether the event constitutes a microcosm for an analysis of the transnational relations of production that predominate in the petroleum-rich states of the Arabian Gulf (as it is called by those on its immediate western side). I am tempted to begin unpacking the intricacies of the scenario immediately—to describe why Mr. Dholakia's alleged penchant for sending his résumé to other companies was perceived as a form of near treason, why his confinement was a normal sort of response in the context of Bahrain, why he certainly feared deportation, and why his compatriots at Bramco eventually yielded to an implacable management. But as news of the event percolated through the Indian community in Bahrain, a second story with even more lurid details nearly eclipsed the first. This second event is perhaps even more illustrative of the structural violence that characterizes the guest worker system in Bahrain and, for that matter, all the petroleum-rich nations of the Arabian littoral.

The second event took place in Hamad Town, a rough quarter in the Manama suburbs where significant numbers of the citizenry's lower middle class make their home.[1] Police, officials from the Indian Embassy, and human rights activists converged on a scrap yard after receiving a tip from an undisclosed source. The citizen-owner of the garage and scrap yard, it seems, had sold a work visa to an Indian man by the name of Karunanidhi for BD 1,200 (approximately $3,000).[2] While the details remain unclear, indications suggest that Karunanidhi then paid another individual to replace him as a manual laborer, a move that angered the owner of the scrap yard and the issuer of the work visa. This Bahraini citizen-sponsor took Karunanidhi—in other words, moved him by force—and put him under a bathtub in the scrap yard. He then parked his jeep over the bathtub, locked the vehicle, and departed for Manama, the central and singular urban center on the small island kingdom. The scrap yard owner found his way to Karunanidhi's home in central Manama and somehow kidnapped six of the Indian laborer's roommates. Returning to the scrap yard with the men, he locked them in a large freezer, where they remained until the loose amalgamation of help—the aforementioned police force, officials, and activists—came to their rescue. All the men were freed, although their fate in the agencies and courts that govern the island's guest worker population remained in limbo. The scrap yard owner was briefly jailed, then released.

In the Gulf newspapers that carried these stories, both cases were framed as atypical scenarios of citizen-sponsors "gone bad" or, at best,

as anecdotal evidence of the worst-case scenarios that the large transnational labor force at work on the island might face in seeking a better
life through a sojourn in the Arabian Gulf. In 2002 and 2003, however, I
spent a year in Bahrain collecting ethnographic data for my doctoral dissertation, and as part of my aim to explore the matrix of relations between
Indian guest workers and their citizen-hosts, I spent countless hours in
the labor camps and decrepit urban flats in which the poorest of the transnational Indian laborers dwell.[3] The stories I have just described—both
from February 2006—fit seamlessly in the tapestry woven by the many
migration narratives I collected. These narratives, and the newspaper
clippings I diligently filed for 2003, abound with stories of stabbings, murders, rape, deportation, confinement, physical abuse, confidence games,
outright cheating, suicides, suicides under suspicious circumstances, un-
safe working conditions, illness, and more. Moreover, while there are religious, gender, and class aspects to this violence, the most reliable pattern
underpinning these events pits citizens against guest workers.[4] Although
reliable data concerning the scope of this violence are not available,[5] in
the hallway outside my university office I have a large tackboard, perhaps four feet by six feet, on which I maintain a testament to the comprehensive violence levied against Indian guest workers in Bahrain. The
board, comprising a subset of the newspaper clippings I collected during
my year in Bahrain, documents the comprehensive nature of the almost
daily violence that plagues the Indian population of some 140,000 that
make their home, however temporary, on the island. In light of this small
edifice to the Indian experience in the Gulf, the two cases with which I
began this chapter—recent examples that neatly coincide with the push
in the United States toward a guest worker program—are in my mind far
from anecdotal; rather, they are symptomatic of the structural violence
endemic to the system by which the large transnational labor forces that
work in the Gulf are managed and controlled.

In this chapter, I seek to demonstrate how deportation—and the threat
of deportation—becomes a principal fulcrum in the systemic abuse and
exploitation of guest workers in Bahrain. As Nicholas De Genova suggests,
the everyday lives of "illegal" or undocumented workers are shaped more
by *deportability* than deportation per se (2002, 438), an idea that helped
spur an interest in a more comprehensive anthropological investigation
of deportation and removal (Zilberg 2004; Peutz 2006; Willen 2007d).
I draw primarily on the ethnographic data I gathered in 2002 and 2003,
most of which focuses specifically on the Indian community in Bahrain,
the largest and, arguably, most historically significant of the guest worker
communities on the island. My analysis of deportability and deportation

becomes one component of an explication of the *kafala*, the system by which the large guest worker populations in Bahrain and the other Gulf States are managed and controlled. An analysis of the kafala, in turn, helps explain the mechanics of the structural violence that characterizes the experience of the transnational proletariat in all the Gulf States. Like the progenitors of the concept of structural violence (Galtung 1969; Farmer 2003, 2004; Green 1999; Scheper-Hughes 2004), I do not intend to imply that we ignore the agency exerted in the scenarios described at the outset of this chapter—that these scenarios involve humans choosing to abuse, exploit, maim, and dominate other humans. Rather, I seek to couple that basic fact with an analysis of the structural forces that permit, cause, encourage, or in some other way produce the violence between citizen and foreign laborer in Bahrain. Those structural forces, I argue, are essential in understanding the context and nature of the episodic violence levied against guest workers in the Gulf States.

Although the wealthy nations of the Arabian Peninsula, to some degree, provide a fairly unique and understudied way point in the global movement of labor, my analysis of this particular node in the transnational flows of the Indian Ocean world provides two principal contributions to the ongoing articulation of an anthropology of removal. First, in the scenarios described to me by the Indian men and women on the small island, their deportability, or the lived experience of the constant threat of removal, has little to do with their status as either documented or undocumented workers. In fact, my analysis points to systemic qualities of the kafala system that actively encourage the production of a large pool of "illegal" workers. Second, my analysis of the contemporary manifestation of the kafala in Bahrain (and, by proxy, in the other Gulf States) suggests that any ongoing elaboration of an anthropology of removal must accommodate alternative configurations of the state. In Bahrain, the responsibility for managing, controlling, and monitoring the foreign labor force is largely distributed to the citizenry: the citizen-sponsor profits from the transnational labor that he (or occasionally she) controls, but in that citizen-sponsor we can also see a manifestation of the responsibilities that, in other places, are reserved for state bureaucracies and the police force.

AN OVERVIEW OF TRANSNATIONAL LABOR IN BAHRAIN

The Middle East is a major destination in the global migration of labor. The principal receptors of these migration flows are the Gulf Cooperation Council (GCC) States—Kuwait, Saudi Arabia, Bahrain, Qatar, United

Arab Emirates, and Oman. Together these states host a guest worker population of well over ten million men and women, a figure that must be gauged in comparison with a total population, including guest workers and citizens, of nearly twenty-eight million (Kapiszewski 2001, 39). As these figures suggest, the GCC States of the Arabian Peninsula are an important juncture in the transnational migration of labor, a node in the transmigratory network that, looking outward from South Asia, certainly belongs in the same constellation as western Europe and North America. These figures also suggest a noteworthy and unique aspect about the migratory way points on the Arabian Peninsula, for the proportion of guest workers to citizens is astoundingly high. In all the GCC States, foreign labor makes up a majority of the workforce, and in several states (Kuwait, United Arab Emirates, Qatar) guest workers form an absolute majority of the population. As James Clifford noted over a decade ago, diasporic culture and its language are beginning to challenge "the binary relation of *minority* communities with *majority* societies" (1994, 311). In the cities of the Arabian littoral, that challenge is both discursive and demographic: guest workers predominate in many of the public spaces of the cities; they work behind the counters of the businesses and shops beneath the glass skyscrapers reaching into the hazy blue skies; they crowd the narrow streets of the central souk on Friday afternoon. The sheer scope of these guest worker populations has fundamentally altered the social fabric of the urban agglomerations that dot the shores of the Gulf waters, while also playing a central role in shaping the political structures of all the Gulf States (Longva 1997, 2000, 2005; Louër 2005).

While the sources of these migration flows, and hence the demography of foreign labor in the Gulf States, have varied significantly over time, since the 1970s South Asian transmigrants have come to dominate these Indian Ocean conduits. In general terms, the history of the South Asian presence in the Gulf can be divided into three overlapping periods. For much of known history, merchants from the Indian subcontinent maintained a strong presence in the Gulf, moving cloth, rice and other foodstuffs, spices, and a variety of other materials westward to the Gulf and sending pearls—the region's primary export for many centuries—back along that same route (Palgrave 1865/1982; Al Muraikhi 1991, 106; Slot 1993, 498; Buckingham 1829/1971, 454). Powerful South Asian merchant families, the vestiges of which still maintain a presence in the cities of the contemporary Gulf, often served as bankers and bureaucrats to the ruling families or strongest tribes in the region, and those merchant families' long-standing presence in the region comprised the basic framework for the migratory conduits that today connect the Arabian Peninsula with the ports of the Indian subcontinent.

The British colonial presence in the region forged a larger and more sustained connection to the Indian subcontinent and hence constitutes the second of these three periods. After devastating several Gulf ports with its navy, Britain brokered the General Treaty of Peace of 1820, an event that both marked the genesis of the Gulf States and legitimized Sunni leadership and control in Bahrain and many of the other fledgling states of the Arabian littoral. The region was administered through British India, first via the Persian port of Bushire, and later from Bahrain (Khuri 1980, 86; Zahlan 1989, 49). In time, the British crown extended its grasp on the region, forming customs bureaucracies, municipalities, courts, and a variety of other administrative forms of control, all of which drew increasing numbers of low-level Indian bureaucrats from the subcontinent to the cities of the Gulf. The colonial administration also fostered the transmigration of private entrepreneurs to serve the burgeoning population of colonial bureaucrats and to contribute to the ongoing construction of a western-style private sector. In essence, then, the second wave of South Asian migrants arrived on the coattails of the British crown. Many of the established families I came to know during my fieldwork on the island—members of the diasporic elite in Bahrain—arrived as part of this second migration flow: their fathers or grandfathers crossed the Indian Ocean to work for the burgeoning British colonial administration or, equally likely, to engage in various entrepreneurial activities in service of the growing foreign population in the region.

The latest chapter in the history of migration from South Asia to the Arabian Peninsula began in the 1960s, gathered speed in the 1970s, and in many ways continues to this day. The development of the oil industry throughout the region, in conjunction with vast increases in the global demand for that oil, filled government coffers and led the Gulf States to establish a variety of modernization plans, including both infrastructural projects (new highways, bridges, buildings, museums, universities, mosques, and so forth), as well as new bureaucracies, expanded state apparatuses, and comprehensive welfare systems. While the impetus for these projects was already in place at the end of the 1960s, the oil embargo of the 1970s, by increasing state wealth manyfold, fueled a dramatic increase in the number and scope of these projects. At this historic juncture, South Asian migration to the Gulf grew rapidly. The type of migrant typically passing through these migratory conduits also shifted. In the past, transmigrants were typically skilled workers or entrepreneurs.

While the flow of these transmigrants continued, the new arrivals were predominantly unskilled laborers. These men filled new positions generated by the increasing number of infrastructural projects on the island. At the same time, they also replaced unskilled citizen-laborers who increasingly sought positions in the public sector, positions that themselves form a keystone in the redistribution of state wealth and, according to many analyses, in the tenuous legitimacy of the ruling families of the respective states (Champion 1999; Kapiszewski 2001, 9; Longva 1997).

While these historical factors explain the increasing flow of transmigrants to the island, scholars have provided a number of explanations for why South Asia in particular came to play a predominant role in providing labor to the Gulf. South Asia certainly contained a comparatively inexpensive supply of educated and trained clerks, supervisors, and assistants (Holden 1966; Kapiszewski 2001, 4, 62; Azhar 1999, 101; Weiner 1986), and many of them spoke, read, and wrote English, the language of the growing transnational private sector. In addition, and in comparison with established inter-Arab migratory patterns, South Asian laborers were usually unaccompanied by families, and hence the costs of reproduction were largely borne by the sending states. As other scholars have noted, the fact that South Asian transmigrants were neither Arab nor Muslim also made for a more pliable and docile workforce (Nakhleh 1976, 77; Weiner 1986, 53–54; Seccombe and Lawless 1986, 94–98) or, from another angle, a population that the citizenry was more willing to exploit. Through this confluence of forces, and building on long-established connections generated through both mercantile and colonial relations, the South Asian presence in the GCC States grew rapidly over the last decades of the twentieth century. While components of all three of these processes remain in place, it is this last component—a transnational proletariat—that has come to numerically dominate the South Asian populations in the cities of the Gulf.

My own ethnographic work, combined with the ethnographic work of the handful of other scholars with experience investigating one or both ends of the migratory conduits that connect the Gulf States to the Indian Ocean littoral and points farther abroad, suggests a series of patterns that characterize the transmigrant experience in the GCC States (Longva 1997, 2000, 2005; Nagy 1998; Leonard 2002, 2003; Khalaf and Alkobaisi 1999; Gamburd 2000). Foremost, these are *guest worker* populations. While a few notable exceptions exist, naturalization is neither encouraged nor possible for South Asians.[6] Both discursively and practically, Gulf States and Gulf citizens alike reinforce the temporary nature of these transmigrants' tenure in the GCC States, though many guest workers stay for years, for a lifetime, or, in the case of some families, for generations. In spite of both the size and long tenure of many guest worker populations in the Gulf States, South Asian foreigners forge lives largely separate from the host society: in Bahrain, for example, the transnational proletariat dwell in decrepit apartment buildings in the central urban slums now largely abandoned by the citizenry, or bunk in labor camps in the semi-industrial periphery of the city. Families of the diasporic elite send their children to separate schools (e.g., the Indian School, the New Indian School, the Pakistani School) and join social clubs specific to their home nations or regions (e.g., the Young Goans Club, the Pakistani Club). Intermarriage between citizens and noncitizens is extremely uncommon, and many of the elite Indian families I spoke with—families that, in some cases, have been in Bahrain for several generations—had never been invited to a Bahraini house. As Anh Longva (1997) noted in her acute analysis of relations in Kuwait, interaction in these plural societies is largely confined to the arena of work.

Another pattern that characterizes the transmigrant experience pertains to the kafala. Excepting those who arrive "illegally"—a point to which I'll return—all South Asian guest workers arrive through the kafala, or the framework by which transnational migration in the GCC States is organized and controlled.[7] The kafala links individual guest workers to a particular job and, more importantly, to a particular citizen-sponsor or corporate entity (a *kafeel*). This relationship has a contractual facet, in the sense that the men and women who cross the Indian Ocean to work in the Gulf sign contracts that oblige them to work, typically, for two years at a set level of pay. These contracts also oblige the sponsors to pay a certain rate, to cover travel costs, to provide a vacation period, and so forth. As I will argue, by binding guest workers to individual citizens, the kafala represents a keystone in the systemic and structural violence levied against guest workers in the Gulf. At the current juncture, it will suffice to say that the kafala represents a central concern in the lifeworlds of most of the guest workers I interviewed, and as such it plays a predominant role in patterning their experience abroad.

There are also gender, ethnic, national, regional, linguistic, and religious patterns to the migratory conduits between South Asia and the Gulf. The vast majority of transmigrants in the Gulf States are men. Indeed, on a Friday afternoon, when many guest workers have at least some portion of the day free, the central streets of Manama are overtaken by South Asian men. Female transmigrants, both fewer in number and less visible, are also present in the Gulf. The largest contingent serves as domestic workers, a vocation generally seen as one of the poorest-paid and most vulnerable components of the guest worker population (Longva 1997, 70; Kapiszewski 2001, 181–82).[8] At the other end of the socioeconomic spectrum, many professional women do arrive from Asia to work in various capacities for the transnational corporations that serve the region; other women arrive on a family visa reserved for guest workers who meet the minimum income threshold.[9]

It is also notable that the various national and ethnic groups that migrate to the island find their way—or are slotted—into particular types of work: Indians, Pakistanis, and Bangladeshis work in construction and the service sector, Filipinos work as concierges and run beauty parlors, and Indonesian and Sri Lankan women work as housemaids. In part, the association of particular national and ethnic groups with particular sorts of work can be explained by chain migration and the labor brokerage system: brokers serving one portion of the workforce use connections they have established in particular regions of South Asia. At the same time, chain migration—the process by which one transmigrant from one particular place uses his or her knowledge and contacts to pave the way for additional transmigrants—also structures the workforce in this manner. Finally, perhaps as a result of these processes, employers in the region come to believe that particular sorts of people—specific ethnicities or nationalities—are naturally better for certain sorts of positions, and hire accordingly. Together these interlocked processes have forged a workforce deeply patterned by ethnicity and nationality. These patterns and the processes undergirding them characterize all the states of the GCC.[10]

To bring this overview to a close, I must draw a line on the Gulf side of these transnational conduits. What I have omitted, then, are the historical factors and socioeconomic processes generating this abundant and willing labor force in South Asia. In comparison to the ethnographic literature concerned with guest workers *in* the Gulf, this literature is relatively large (Gamburd 2000; Osella and Osella 2000a, 2000b; Kurien 2002; Silvey 2004; Pertierra 1994; Sekhar 1996; Nair 1999; Nambiar 1995; Brochmann 1993; Eelens, Schampers, and Speckman 1992). I also omit the growing literature that traces the complicity, if not compulsion, of the United States and western Europe in maintaining these Gulf regimes and hence in maintaining the particular order that shapes the lives of guest workers and citizens alike. John Holloway (1994) clearly argues that to comprehend the very nature of the contemporary state, we must understand its particular place in global capitalist relations. While these factors are certainly essential in providing a complete map of the structural forces that produce the episodic violence that guest workers face in Bahrain, they are nonetheless beyond the scope of the analysis I provide here.

"ILLEGALITY" AND DEPORTATION IN BAHRAIN

Recent anthropological studies have challenged the static relationship between "illegal" migrants and a rational, bureaucratic state. As Sarah Willen notes, rather than reify the status of "illegality" through ethnographic work, new ethnographic work seeks to portray "illegality" as both "a juridical status and a sociopolitical condition" (Willen 2007d; see also De Genova 2002; Heyman 2001). To this revision, Willen adds a third dimension of inquiry: she argues that the condition of "illegality" also includes a realm of experience and consciousness that merits our attention and analysis (2007d; see also Chavez 1992/1998; Rouse 1992). I too see this experiential realm as essential to understanding the role of "illegality" in the lives of the Indian laborers in Bahrain, and hence I build on Willen's "critical phenomenology of 'illegality'" in explicating the terrain of structural violence that shapes their lives. I focus now on the process by which "illegal" workers are produced, with particular attention to the juridical, sociopolitical, and experiential dimensions of their path to "illegality."

The portrait of an "illegal" worker perceptible in public discourse in Bahrain is strikingly similar to that purveyed in the United States: an individual somehow finds his or her way across the discrete borders of the nation and now works in the country, avoiding the visa fees and the purview of the state. In Bahrain, this portrait of the "illegal" worker meshes with the sectarian imbalance of power on the island, for these workers also take jobs from the underemployed Bahrainis—typically Shiite—and confound the government's attempts to persuade or compel citizens to enter the private workforce (a suite of policies and directives collectively referred to as Bahrainization). Moreover, as individuals outside the systemic controls of the kafala, the "illegal" laborer is also seen as a cultural threat, for he (or she) is outside the purview of the citizen-sponsor. While the purported threat of the large population of guest workers to the cultural integrity of the Bahraini nation is of much interest and debate on the island, the former issue—the presumed path that transmigrants follow to "illegal" status—is largely inaccurate for Bahrain. In part, it certainly represents a projection of the European and American norms on

the Gulf migration discourse. It also reflects the situation in neighboring
Saudi Arabia, where an unknown number of individuals arrive on a hajj
visa (for religious pilgrimage to Mecca) and "illegally" stay to work. Both
of these explanations—sneaking across the border or arriving under false
pretenses—elide the circumstances that broadly produce "illegal" workers
in the GCC States. For most transmigrant laborers in Bahrain, the path
to "illegality" is a strategic response to the systemic abuse enabled, if not
codified, by the kafala. Furthermore, the production of "illegal" workers is
largely contingent on the passivity of the state in enforcing existing labor
laws.

In Bahrain, all the "illegal" Indian laborers I encountered described an
almost identical set of circumstances. Through a contact at one of the
diasporic social clubs, I arranged an interview with a group of struggling
Indian laborers, several of whom were "illegal." We sat in their living quarters, an unfinished cinder-block garage belonging to the men's sponsor.
The men lived six to a room. Rats scurried across the rafters overhead,
and a sick Indian laborer—now unable to work—coughed in the back
bunkroom. One of the men described to me his path to "illegality":

> I came here as a mason, but the company that took my visa, they didn't pay
> me. The other workers approached the labor department . . . and they [the
> workers] complained about the company, but by that point they hadn't re-
> ceived any salary for five months. Me and him [pointing to another man]
> didn't wait that long—we left the company and found work here. The other
> workers never did get their money. Since we left early, we were illegal, and
> now we're afraid to approach the Labor Ministry.

Several weeks later I journeyed to the back of the souk with a friend
who served as a translator in situations where the men spoke neither English nor Arabic. Behind the dense maze of streets of the souk, crowds
of South Asian men move through the streets, in and out of doorways
and small alleys that lead to apartments out of view. The neighborhood,
now largely abandoned by the Bahrainis who once lived here, is widely
known as an urban locus for "illegal" transmigrants. We found our way to
the apartment we sought, and there I heard another version of the same
story:

> I came to Bahrain as a welder in a car carriage repair shop. For four and
> a half months, I received no salary, so I filed a case. Then I finally left the
> company. My case is now in the courts—I filed a case against my sponsor.
> The case states that he did not pay me four and a half months' salary. I filed

the case in the beginning of 1998, and there has been no progress [as of July 2003]. . . .

As an illegal worker, I do have worries. I have a paper that I received from the court, and now I am afraid to go to the police about this paper. I don't want to have to go to jail for being an illegal worker, and that is why I can't go to the courts anymore or ask the police for help. I will wait for amnesty. If amnesty came tomorrow, I would go.

Over the years, some of the standard companies would employ me regularly for some period of time. With those standard companies, there was no problem with the payment—they never withheld my salary. Some companies hired me for a week; some hired me for six months. Others hired me for two months. The standard companies hire for the longest period, and they pay regularly. Some of the other companies pay during the early stages, but then they stop. They pay for the first four months or so, then for the last two months they stop. They cheat us. Of all twenty companies, only five were good to the workers the entire time. The other fifteen cheated me, cheated us.

Building on his long stay on the island, this particular transmigrant is able to put his most recent experiences in context. His description points directly to the process by which "illegality" is produced—most commonly, by a sponsor simply refusing to pay the wages contractually specified, and the subsequent departure of the transmigrant from the sole job at which he may "legally" work. His experience also suggests the systemic character of this abuse. Over and over again, this transmigrant faced the same dilemma. He now awaits "amnesty," one of the periods in which monetary penalties and jail time associated with "illegality" are temporarily suspended in the hopes that "illegal" workers will voluntarily return home.[11]

These vignettes concentrate on the relationship between guest workers and their kafeel in the production of "illegal" workers. In terms of structural violence, their experiences reveal the systemic pressures at work on the island—an interconnected set of factors that overdetermine the violence and abuse I identified at the beginning of the chapter. These men also speak to the ever-present fear and vulnerability caused by their "illegal" status, a lived experience of vulnerability connected to the everyday surveillance of public spaces by citizen-sponsors (De Genova 2002, 438). The next narrative helps us move beyond the complex relationship between guest worker and sponsor and begin to look at the complicity of the state, the arrangement of labor, and other contextual factors that shape the experience of guest workers in Bahrain.

I met Vijay near the end of my fieldwork in Bahrain.[12] My associate in the field—Santosh, who arranged many of my interviews at the labor camps and also translated when necessary—served as the outreach coordinator for one of the prominent social clubs on the island and had been assisting Vijay in working through his relations with the Bahraini court system and the immigration office, as well as with the other related problems described here. The three of us sat in a squalid, cramped room in a central neighborhood that, over the previous decades, had been abandoned by the Bahrainis to the legion of foreign laborers who daily arrive to work on the island. My notes from the interview capture the central thread of Vijay's experience abroad:

> Vijay told me that he had been a tailor in Pondicherry, India. Actually, he was a master tailor, he clarified—the supervisor of the showroom. It was a good job. But then some of his friends left for the Persian Gulf, for places like Dubai, Bahrain, Kuwait, and Jeddah. Then some of them came back. They had lots of money. More than that, they were respected. People on the street, people at the teashop—they looked upon these return-migrants in a particular way. Vijay wanted that respect.
>
> His friends suggested he call a labor broker in Madras, and he did. After some discussion, he agreed to pay 45,000 rupees—that's about $1,000 U.S. dollars—for a visa and a job at a garment factory. He was going to Bahrain. It was a two-year contract, and he'd earn 45 dinars a month, about $120 U.S. dollars. He noted that he didn't really know what a dinar was worth when he made the deal, but the figure was close to what his friends had reported from their own experiences. He would be out of debt in a year [considering the size of the debt he had just incurred and the monthly wages promised by the contract he had just signed], and then he could start to make some real money.
>
> Coming up with the 45,000 rupees wasn't easy. He had a little bit saved. He borrowed some with interest from a moneylender. He got a little bit from his father. To make up for what was left, the family hawked his mother's jewelry. Then he got on a plane—his first ever.
>
> He realized something was wrong right away. He arrived at the airport in Bahrain at two in the afternoon, but no one was there to pick him up. So he just sat and waited. The airport was air-conditioned, and he was cold. He had no food, no money. Someone from the company finally came for him at midnight, and they took Vijay straight to the garment factory. The rest of the workers were just getting off their shift, so he rode to the camp with them. He had a cot in a small bedroom, and there were six other men in the room. They gathered around him and asked why he came. They told him that

the company was very bad, that they had to work until midnight, that the company didn't always pay their wages, and that they certainly didn't receive overtime pay.

He called his father, and his father told him to weather the difficulties. It wasn't a lifetime, he said—just two years. He couldn't understand a lot of what was going on around him, because he only spoke two South Indian languages. He tried to learn some Arabic and Hindi at night at the camp. He began to meet others in the camp, and he discovered the other men faced a similar set of dilemmas [in that they were trapped in these circumstances with a debt held by a job broker in their home country]. When the plant manager would come around, they'd argue with him. The manager was also an Indian—a Gujarati, Vijay noted. None of the workers were allowed to talk directly to the boss, the Bahraini sponsor, and their arguments with the manager went nowhere.

So they decided to wait until they had paid off their debts. They worked long hours, well into the night, and they received no additional pay. A year went by, and most of the workers had paid off their visa-related debts. They began to slow down production on the floor. As a result, the Bahraini boss fired the Indian manager. On the day he was dismissed, the manager gathered all the workers together and told them that if they went on strike they might be able to get their overtime money and back pay. They walked out at midnight the next day, pooled their money, and rented a bus. There were 180 of them. The group from Andrah Pradesh decided to back out. Then there were 110. The next morning they went to the Ministry of Labor and stood outside.[13]

A man finally came out and gave them a piece of paper. The writing was in Arabic, and none of the men could read it, but the man told them to bring it back to the company and they would get their salary and overtime. They showed it to the company man the next day, but he called the police. Although frightened by the arrival of the police, the men were told that the officers only wanted to arrest the manager. The manager escaped by flying back to India the next day. The company gave the men their back salary, but not their overtime, and they worked for five more months. Three weeks before the Ramadan holidays, the company man told them that there wouldn't be any holiday for them. He said they would have to work every day.

They struck again, and went back to the Ministry of Labor. The Ministry officials were upset, and they made them return to the camp. They waited at the camp for two days—then the company closed the canteen. They had no food. The company turned off the electricity, so they had no air conditioning.

Then the company turned off the water. A Ministry official came on the fourth day, and he told the men that this was a matter for the courts. Then a Bahraini lawyer came. She took 1,200 dinars from them—that's $3,000, or ten dinars from each man.

The men were only allowed to go to the court in small groups. The judge asked them if they wanted to go on with the case. If they did, they had to keep working for the company. If they dropped the case, they could get papers to find another job. The company owner returned the passports to the men that dropped the case.

Vijay decided not to drop the case. The factory closed. He no longer had a job. He became an "illegal" worker. He has no ticket home, but he found a job installing air-conditioning ducts. It's under the table, as we say in the United States. If he crosses paths with the police, however, he'll have to go to jail and pay a fine of 10 BD per month—that's about $25 U.S. dollars. He's stuck. He heard rumors that a government-sponsored amnesty period might be granted next year. If he's able to save enough money, he'll buy a ticket home then.

With Vijay's narrative, we have an abundance of detail that allows us to better explicate the forces at work in the production of "illegality" in Bahrain. At the same time, these forces constitute the structural violence levied against guest workers on the island, a structural violence in which the production of "illegality" is but one facet. In addition to the fundamental fact that Vijay was exploited and underpaid, consider the multiple other issues with which he struggled: before his sojourn in the Gulf, Vijay had no clear idea about the exchange rate; the debt he incurred for travel to the Gulf was borne by his family as a whole, and the pressure to stay in place came, in part, from his own family ("His father told him to weather the difficulties"). Note that Vijay was unable to communicate with many of the other workers in the camp, and he does not speak Arabic. He is unable to parse the documents and court orders and unable to understand the court proceedings. He has no direct access to his sponsor, and dissent is channeled through a foreign manager. The court system and police force do little to resolve the situation, and in the final accounting, the state is seemingly complicit in the production of his circumstances. By the end of the narrative, Vijay is an "illegal" worker. While his relationship with his sponsor is central to this condition, numerous other forces conspire to produce these circumstances. In the next section, I provide a rough categorization of those other forces, both as a means of mapping the structure of this violence and also as part of the process of locating the role of deportability and removal in the calculus of citizen–guest worker relations in Bahrain.

MAPPING THE STRUCTURE OF VIOLENCE

To recapitulate, the kafala is the Gulf-wide sponsorship system by which the large transnational populations at work in the Gulf States are organized, managed, and controlled. The kafala is the sponsorship system itself, while kafeel is the Arabic singular noun for the individual sponsor with whom each arriving guest worker is associated. I argue that the kafala itself is key to understanding the structural violence levied against guest workers in Bahrain. I begin with three general observations concerning the kafala: its connection to the larger global political economy, the practical and instrumental aspects of the kafala, and its position as a cultural practice rather than a legal arrangement. Turning to the experiences of the guest workers I encountered in Bahrain, I then describe the four facets of this system of exploitation and control that surfaced time and time again in my interviews with Indian men and women on the island: the transnational character of the contracts and debt incurred in their sojourn to the Gulf, the control of the guest worker's passport by the kafeel, the linguistic and cultural barriers that limit their strategic responses to the dilemmas they face, and the spatial aspects of this system of dominance. As a comprehensive system for controlling guest workers on the island, the kafala clearly resembles what Bales has called "contract slavery" (Bales 2004, 2005). In the section's final paragraphs, I sketch the connections between the kafala and the new slavery that Bales has ably described.

First, in calling the systemic control levied against guest workers in Bahrain a form of structural violence, I point to the global political and economic forces and, more specifically, the poverty and environmental degradation that push men (and women) from India to the Gulf. The stories from my ethnographic data—of farmland drying up, of the inability of poor Indian families to pay for the education or marriage of sons and daughters—certainly form one significant component of the structural violence poor laborers and their families endure. Moreover, in seeking a remedy through employment abroad, Indian laborers and their families typically pay thousands of dollars for the right to work in the Gulf, and the first two or three years of labor are often devoted simply to paying back the debts they and their families incurred. While the bulk of these payments move across the transnational divide to the sponsor, the debt itself remains in India and, typically, with the transmigrant's family. The transnational character of this debt becomes a fulcrum for abuse: a labor strike or individual resistance to the conditions of employment in Bahrain puts distant Indian families and key, oftentimes mortgaged resources at great risk.

Second, I want to point to a variety of practical and instrumental aspects that enable this structural violence against guest workers. The vast majority of the transnational manual laborers I spoke with had yielded their passport to their sponsor, or kafeel, upon arrival. Hence their ability to physically leave the island, as one potential response to violence and exploitation, is controlled by the kafeel, who is, at the same time, the individual or entity positioned to profit from the workers' presence. Moreover, under the terms of a series of recent edicts, only sponsors or their citizen-proxies can deal with critical paperwork at the variety of government offices that contribute to the management and regulation of the large guest worker populations. And while English is the language of the booming private sector on the island, all government agencies, including the court system, operate in Arabic. Combined with the fact that most laborers reside in labor camps located in the distant urban periphery and thus are far from the government offices and embassies to which they might appeal in times of difficulty, Indian transmigrants are systemically unable to mount a defense against the structural violence they encounter.

Finally, the kafala is a system only partly codified in law. As the anthropologist Ahn Longva has noted, in the Gulf nations the kafala emerged in the twentieth century as an outgrowth of a cultural practice used to organize labor on the pearling dhows that plied the waters of the Persian Gulf (Longva 1997, 106–7). Enmeshed in this notion of the kafala as a cultural practice, citizens often balance the systemic abuse levied against guest workers with notions of the kafeel's responsibility for potential moral and cultural transgressions of foreigners in Bahraini society, a notion that posits guest workers as a polluting presence (Peutz 2006, 223, 231; Douglas 1966/2002). These vague interconnections also suggest a link between deportation, "illegality," and the welfare state, for citizens are not just protecting their cultural traditions, or even a certain set of political rights (Isin 2002); they are also protecting a citizenship that confers an abundance of material benefits (Walters 2002a, 279). While the underlying moral discourse is frequently cited by citizen-sponsors as a balancing factor in their relationships with foreigners, I join Longva in noting that no cases I know of portray detrimental results to sponsors for the cultural or moral infractions of sponsored guest workers. In the final accounting, the labor market in the Gulf is not a free labor market, and the fate of the guest worker remains in the hands of the individual who might most profit from his abuse. To return to the example with which I began the chapter, this basic fact explains why Paresh Dholakia's search for another job so affronted his sponsor and eventually led to the draftsman's confinement and deportation.

Power and Transnational Debt

The foundations for the imbalance of power between citizen-sponsor and guest worker are constructed well before the guest worker sets foot in the Gulf States. Over the last twenty to thirty years, the work visa that allows the foreigner to work in the petroleum-rich nations of the Arabian littoral has evolved from a minor aspect of the bureaucratic system—what one of my informants called a "mere formality" upon his arrival in the 1970s—to a valued commodity on the global market. While the men and women who arrived before the 1980s reported paying little or nothing for these visas, the men I interviewed in 2002 and 2003 often paid well over $2,000 for the right to come to Bahrain and work. Moreover, the dramatic rise in the market price of these visas coincided with a steady decline in the monthly wages paid to foreign unskilled laborers. Near the end of my time on the island, I began to encounter new arrivals at the labor camps who had paid thousands of dollars for a two-year work visa permitting them to work for thirty to forty dinars a month (approximately one hundred dollars)—well below the sixty to ninety dinars considered standard for manual laborers upon my arrival in 2002. Excluding calculations for the interest charged by moneylenders, by minimizing expenditures on food, phone calls home, and other incidentals, these men cannot turn a profit until the end of their second year abroad. The risk, of course, is that the contract will not be honored—or that the laborers will not be paid at all, as the men in the previous sections described. The sliver of potential profit that rests in the back end of these calculations depends on the goodwill and honor of the kafeel.

In gauging the structural forces that shape and condition the guest worker experience in the Gulf States, my interests are twofold. First, the sums of money needed to acquire these work visas are large. Vijay, the laborer whose story I recounted at length in my field notes, described a combination of sources for the sum he paid: he drew on his personal savings and borrowed some from moneylenders. His family—more spe-cifically, his mother—pawned her gold jewelry, and he borrowed the re-mainder from family and friends. Nearly all members of the transnational proletariat described similar scenarios, sometimes with additional facets. Households may decide, for strategically financial reasons, to end one child's education so that they might enter the workforce and help with the burden of debt incurred by another's trip to the Gulf. Farmland and other productive resources are put up as collateral for the loans. The overall portrait emerging from my interviews suggests that the indi-vidual laborer is deeply enmeshed in a complex web of household rela-tions and dependencies: his or her success or failure in the calculus of transmigration puts his or her extended family at great risk. Together, these aspects typical of Gulf migration forge unequal relations between guest workers and their sponsors, for in their actions workers risk not only their own lives, well-being, and future, but also those of their families in India.

Second, not only is the balance of power between guest worker and kafeel tipped by the simple fact that the laborer enters the relation-ship with a large and family-held debt, but it is also tipped by the trans-national character of that debt. The details of the system for moving both money and people west to the Gulf States have been well described by other scholars (Gamburd 2000; Fuglerud 1999; Kurien 2002). The $2,000 or $3,000 paid for the right to work in the Gulf is most commonly paid to a labor broker or agent in the sending country. That agent is entitled to some small portion of the funds, but the bulk makes its way across the transnational divide to the citizen-sponsor. The citizen-sponsor pays the various fees to regularize the work visa, typically approximating $800, and the remainder is profit. While the money has, for the most part, moved to the Gulf, the debt itself remains in place in South Asia. Should a problem arise between the kafeel and guest worker, that money remains off the bargaining table: productive land and familial savings re-main at risk, and the laborer is thousands of miles away from the agent with which he or she originally negotiated the contract to work in the Gulf.

The basic premises of the relationship help explain why the threat of removal is so effective. For Vijay and the other men who described their experiences to me, returning home is a poor solution to their problems: they return home to families stripped of key productive resources and burdened by the additional debt incurred to send them to the Gulf in the first place. These forces compel the guest worker to stay in place, to endure the suffering at the hands of exploitative and abusive sponsors, or to flee those scenarios in search of work as an "illegal" laborer.

Controlling the Passport

While the debt accrued in exchange for the right to work abroad builds the unequal basis for the relationship between guest worker–laborers and their citizen-sponsors, the widespread practice of confiscating the guest worker's passport plays a predominant and instrumental role in shaping the outcome of many conflicts. Bahraini law explicitly forbids confiscating guest workers' passports. Nonetheless it is widely practiced: all the laborers I encountered had relinquished their passport to their sponsor upon arrival. And, as Vijay's narrative makes clear, this illegal practice is indirectly supported by the state. Consider again this portion of Vijay's story:

> The men were only allowed to go to the court in small groups. The judge asked them if they wanted to go on with the case. If they did, they had to keep working for the company. If they dropped the case, they could get papers to find another job. The company owner returned the passports to the men that dropped the case.

In the most practical sense, the sponsor's possession of the passport prevents the laborer from departing the island: no matter how difficult the working conditions, no matter how focused the abuse, the laborer is beholden to his or her original sponsor. And while it is expressly forbidden by law, note that in Vijay's case, the court ordered that the men who dropped the case against the citizen-sponsor would have their passports returned, this being evidence, if not of the state's complicity in establishing the parameters of this structural violence, then at least of what Josiah Heyman and Alan Smart describe as "some variety of symbiosis" between the state and illegal practices (1999, 1).

More than merely a mechanism for preventing labor from fleeing, control of the guest worker's passport becomes a key mechanism for deriving additional profit from the transnational proletariat. In times of difficulty or in legal imbroglios, guest workers are often forced to buy back their passports from their original sponsors. For example, for several weeks I attended the meetings of the Ecumenical Council on Charity, one of the many diasporic voluntary associations that informally assist guest workers in crisis. In January 2003 the group made contact with a Sri Lankan housemaid, recently diagnosed with breast cancer, who was languishing in the hospital. The woman hoped to return to Sri Lanka for treatment, but her kafeel refused to release her passport until she paid him BD 300 ($800). These sorts of scenarios recur in the interviews I conducted on the island, and while some, like Vijay, bring their case before the court, most transmigrants end up relying on their savings, personal networks, and the charity of these informal organizations to pay off sponsors and regain their passports in time of distress. More commonly—and as was the case with Vijay's compatriots—guest workers receive the passports only after forfeiting any claims against their original sponsor.

Linguistic and Cultural Barriers

Linguistic and cultural barriers impose another set of limits to the agency of guest workers and hence structure inequities in their relations with sponsors. Consider Vijay's description of the many nights he spent trying to learn Arabic and Hindi as part of his attempt to increase his ability to understand and interrogate the system in which he was enmeshed. While large transmigrant workforces may be made up entirely of South Asians, this is no guarantee that the men can speak with one another. Bahrain and the other Gulf States draw heavily from the South Indian States, from regions and classes where Hindi is not widely spoken. As one construction manager noted, most companies are careful to draw labor from a variety of regions, for the linguistic, national, cultural, and ethnic differences help build a more docile workforce—a workforce with less of an ability to organize and strike. Language plays a predominant role in these arrangements.

The relative powerlessness of the transmigrant laborer is further reinforced by the policies and procedures that situate the sponsor as "mediator between the state and individual migrant" (Longva 1997, 103). As Vijay described, transmigrants often lack direct access to their official sponsor and must instead deal with proxies—often other expatriate laborers in managerial positions—in contesting their working conditions, pay, and hours. The power of the kafeel is buttressed by the inability of Indian laborers to directly interface with the state and its multiple bureaucracies: renewing a visa or switching sponsors requires the intervention and approval of the original kafeel, an arrangement that opens the transmigrant to other arenas of exploitation. Beyond the fact that most of these government ministries operate in Arabic, my informants noted that many of the immigration bureaucracies in the government by policy now only serve Bahrainis, and that expatriates can no longer bring their issues directly to the various ministries but must instead rely on intermediaries.[14] As one laborer described:

> Twice over my ten years here my sponsor got 550 dinars [$1,460] from me for visa renewal. Both times he didn't even regularize my visa. So I paid 1,300 dinars [$3,450] to come to Bahrain, I paid 1,100 [$2,920] and then 450 [$1,195] recently. So that's . . . 2,950 . . . nearly 3,000 dinars [$7,960] for six years. Did I even earn this much? I don't know!

Unable to read contracts and court orders in a language they do not know, and unable to map the complex bureaucracies of the state, workers are forced to channel their dissent through the kafeel, the same person who most profits from their exploitation.

Geographies and Temporalities of Dominance

The interstices of the migration narratives I gathered in 2002 and 2003 pointed to the spatial and chronological aspects of dominance in Bahrain. In the simplest sense, the movement and time of the transnational proletariat are tightly managed. Most of the men I encountered in the labor camps worked six or six and a half days a week. Time off of work usually occurred on Friday afternoon—the weekend in the Middle East, and a time when all government agencies are closed. In addition to the many hurdles I have already described, the guest workers' daily and weekly schedules prevent active engagement with the legal and bureaucratic apparatuses of the state, as well as with the embassies that purportedly represent their interests on the island.

Along with workers' having little free time, many of the labor camps in which members of the transnational proletariat dwell are located at the periphery of the city, in a semi-industrial no man's land distant from the services of Manama and poorly served by public transportation. On workdays, trucks or buses transport the men to and from camp, but the men are typically left to their own devices during the weekends. Other transmigrants—particularly housemaids—are literally locked inside for most or all their stay in the Gulf (see Gamburd 2000). The spatial facet of this structure of dominance slows or altogether prevents communication between guest workers, mitigates their ability to cope with conflicts with their sponsors, and generally constrains what limited agency they deploy in the difficult circumstances of work in the Gulf.

In his seminal work, Kevin Bales argues that in the modern world, labor contracts often mask contemporary forms of slavery. "Contracts are offered that guarantee employment, perhaps in a workshop or factory, but when the workers are taken to their place of work they find themselves enslaved. The contract is used as an enticement to trick an individual into slavery, as well as a way of making the slavery look legitimate" (2004, 20). This contract slavery, he argues, is one facet of *a new slavery*, a contemporary form of slavery where legal ownership is avoided, purchase costs are low, profits are high, there is a glut of potential slaves, relationships between owner and slave are typically short, the slaves are disposable, and ethnic differences are less important than in traditional slavery (15). To some degree or another, all these descriptors resonate with the experiences of the transnational proletariat in the Gulf. Bales's definition of slavery hinges on control: "It is not about owning people in the traditional sense of old slavery, but about controlling them completely" (4).

Like Bales's explication of new slavery, the relationship between Bahraini citizens and the guest workers they sponsor is about control. Thinking about this control in structural terms—and in terms of structural violence—has pushed me to increase the scope of inquiry: What are the arrangements, both local and transnational, that foster these forms of dominance? On what aspects of the complex arrangements of transmigration to the Gulf is this dominance contingent? Unpacking the complexities of control has been my principal task here, but that task should not eclipse the fact that this structure of dominance, and the violence it encourages, has a purpose. That purpose is, of course, profit. When a poor Indian family mortgages its productive assets, pulls children from school, and pawns the mother's jewelry to come up with the thousands of dollars it takes to send a son to the Gulf, only to have him face month after month of no pay and finally be relegated to scrounging for "illegal" work, it may seem a tragic story for that family. When viewed systemically, however, this scenario suggests we move beyond simply thinking about what services these transmigrants supply to citizens, as De Genova suggests (2002, 422). Rather, we can see the outline of what William Walters calls a "deportation industry" (2002a, 266). Walters uses this concept to suggest that deportation, viewed holistically, is a "system that implicates all manner of agents—not just police and immigration officials, but airline executives, pilots, stewards, and other passengers" (Walters 2002a, 266). In Bahrain, and through the mechanism of the kafala, the list of agents must also include the multitude of individual citizen-sponsors on the island, all of whom operate under the tragic logic of the kafala: while there is profit for sponsors who *do* regularly pay their guest workers (after all, they are capturing the surplus labor of these transmigrants), there is also profit for those sponsors who do not pay the men and women they bring to Bahrain. We can then envision this system as a vast transfer of wealth, one whereby thousands of families in South Asia are separated from what little wealth they have accrued, through equity or debt, which is then transferred to sponsors in the Gulf—sponsors who, in conjunction with the state, perpetuate and maintain the deportability of the laborers they bring to the island.[15]

CONCLUSION: CONTEXTUALIZING REMOVAL AND DEPORTATION IN THE GULF TRANSMIGRANT EXPERIENCE

With no path to assimilation, the Indian guest worker community in Bahrain is the largest component of a foreign workforce configured and controlled to buoy Bahrain's place in the booming transnational economy of the contemporary Gulf. As a system, the kafala has emerged as a fulcrum of abuse to which racial, cultural, gender, and religious bigotry cling. By vesting power in individual citizens via the kafala, the Bahraini state enables these vectors of abuse. Right now a variety of informal church organizations, voluntary associations, and other informal institutions are the primary means by which the foreign communities address this abuse: informal and ephemeral diasporic institutions pay for the plane tickets to send the bodies of deceased workers home, help individuals with payoffs to sponsors for releasing them to return to India, and help publicize the most dramatic confrontations between sponsors and guest workers. The Bahraini state has recently announced plans to substantially alter the legal arrangements underpinning the sponsorship system on the island.

Turning, then, to the role of deportation in the lives of these Indian transmigrants, what can we conclude? It is certainly true that Bahrain and its GCC neighbors are atypical migratory way points, particularly when compared with the European and North American migratory conduits that predominate in the literature on transnationalism and migration. The patterns that characterize transmigrants' experiences in the Gulf, significantly different from those of immigrants to North America and western Europe, reinforce De Genova's emphatic call for research that avoids any claims of an overarching, generic immigrant experience (De Genova 2002, 424). Nonetheless, as Peutz and De Genova would suggest, removal, deportation, and the threat of deportation remain integral aspects in the Gulf migrant's experience abroad. However, viewing the many facets of the transmigrants' experiences through the lens of structural violence demonstrates, in theoretical terms, the importance of contextualizing removal, deportation, and the threat of deportation in the larger arena of power relations that shape the migrant and transmigrant experience. This is in line with Andre Gingrich and Gudrun Kroner's suggestion that "neither biographies nor systemic processes allow the separation of the topics of migration and refugees from those of deportation and removal" (2006, 234). Removal, deportation, and the threat of deportation provide a fine starting point for an analysis of the complex and interrelated factors that produce vulnerability among the Indian guest worker community in Bahrain, but in a final accounting, they represent one facet in a complex structure of dominance that shapes the experiences and systematizes the exploitation of guest workers in the Gulf.

What is unique in the case of the Gulf is the distribution of the power in the machinery configured to manage Gulf migration. While the state certainly plays a central role, the kafala nonetheless distributes much of the power traditionally seen as belonging to the state and its various apparatuses to individual citizens, to what Walters calls "private authorities" (2002a, 268). The production of "illegality," the threat of deportation, and removal are powers and processes generated in the relations between individual sponsors and the guest workers they bring to the island, processes disembedded from the "contemporary administrative practice of Western states" (266). It is this arrangement—vesting citizens with the power and responsibility to manage and control the guest worker population—that encourages the sort of violence described at the beginning of the chapter: one Indian guest worker locked in a room for five days before being deported, another confined under a bathtub in a scrap yard. This suggests that further articulation of an anthropology of removal needs to accommodate alternative forms of state power and other distributive grids of power, grids in which the state may make up only part of the calculus.

As should be clear, the cases of violence with which I began this chapter are, in my estimation, far from anecdotal, and while the discursive scope of the international human rights movement has certainly reached the shores of Bahrain, the power of the guest worker to secure basic human rights is, ironically, increasingly attenuated. Sadly, throughout the Gulf, the violence and abuse I have described have become increasingly normalized. As Nancy Scheper-Hughes argues, this normalization is a key aspect of structural violence (2004, 14). Her attention, and that of other scholars interested in identifying and describing structural violence, frequently draws on the discursive terrain that produces this normalization—

on the ideas and beliefs that guide, permit, and condone individual acts of violence (Scheper-Hughes 2004; Holmes 2006). Although that analytic path would certainly complement the analysis I have presented here, I have tried to focus primarily on the machinery of inequality—on the arrangement of relations between citizen and guest worker that produces these beliefs and ideas, and produces the violence I have described. These arrangements, I argue, are essential to understanding the lived experience of the hundreds of thousands of men and women who depart for the Gulf in search of a better life for themselves and their families.

NOTES

1. This story was reported in a sequence of articles in the *Gulf Daily News* (Baby 2006a; Hameed 2006a, 2006b).

2. I have converted all the monetary amounts using the exchange rate at time of writing (1 Bahraini dinar equals 2.6525 U.S. dollars).

3. The research described here was conducted with support of the Wenner-Gren Foundation and the Fulbright Program. I also benefited from the support of the Bahrain Training Institute while on the island.

4. For a description of the conditions of fieldwork and an early attempt at comprehending this scenario, see Gardner 2006.

5. Nor are accurate data available concerning the size or nationalities of these transmigrant populations, or even of the national populations (Kapiszewski 2001, 63). Scholars working in the Gulf point to several overlapping factors to explain this dearth of contextual data. Many of the sending countries lack the bureaucratic infrastructure to accurately gather data about the number of people departing for the Gulf (Nair 1999; Demery 1986, 19). Similarly, the coexistence of formal and informal migration conduits between South Asia and the Gulf would confound any simple calculations based on migration through formal channels even if such capacities did exist. Conversely, because undocumented migration is rare in most of the Gulf States—a point to which I return later—one suspects that at least basic demographic data describing the national components of the guest worker populations must exist. All the guest workers I encountered in Bahrain, for example, had at one point been "properly" registered with the Population Registration Ministry and received an identity card listing their nationality and other data. However, Bahrain and most of its neighbors release only aggregate demographic data concerning the guest worker populations: we know, for example, that the Bahraini government counted 205,626 Asians in the 2001 census, but we have no idea how many of that 205,626 are from Bangladesh, India, and so forth. It's often suggested that this obfuscation reflects the tenuous political and cultural climate of countries where these foreign populations often outnumber the citizenry (Kapiszewski

2001, 27; Leonard 2002, 215; 2003, 133). Compounded by the fact that only a handful of social scientists have had the opportunity and desire to explore these truly massive migratory conduits, the guest worker populations in the Gulf States are uncharted territory in the larger ethnography of transnational migration, and the violence levied against these men and women is a reason for—and a product of—the silence concerning the lives of foreigners in the Gulf. It is also emblematic of what Peutz calls "the difficulty of gaining access to and being present at the various sites of the deportation grid" (2006, 219).

6. While this is generally true, this statement does need some qualification. In Bahrain, Oman, and several other GCC States, wealthy and established South Asian transmigrants, albeit in extremely limited numbers, have received GCC passports. Naturalization has occurred more widely, if sporadically, among Arab and Middle Eastern transmigrant populations in the GCC States. In Bahrain, the racist policies of naturalization are explicit rather than implicit: the law mandates a period of fifteen years for Arab applicants, and twenty-five for non-Arab applicants.

7. Bahrain's crown prince and the Bahrain Defense Force's commander in chief recently declared that a new labor law, now in its final stages, will eventually lead to the scrapping of the sponsorship system (Baby 2006b).

8. As Longva notes, "Lack of legal protection, the predominance of women [in the domestic sector], and low educational background combined to make domestic workers the most vulnerable to exploitation and abuse, a situation of which the labor-sending countries were acutely aware" (1997, 70).

9. In Bahrain, that threshold is BD 250 ($663) a month. Guest workers seeking visas for family members must also secure permission from their sponsor.

10. While there is certainly some uniformity to the transmigrant experience in all the Gulf States, the unique social, cultural, historical, economic, and demographic facets of the individual states connote that neither Bahrain nor any of the other GCC States can serve as an unadulterated proxy for its neighbors. This suggests that the experience of foreigners in each of these respective states, while certainly similar, is not the same. For example, the petroleum wealth in Qatar, Kuwait, and portions of the UAE far outpaces that of Bahrain and Oman—a fact that, in these wealthier states, results in more housemaids per house, different attitudes concerning the work appropriate for the citizenry, and an expanded welfare system. The ethnic patterns of both citizenry and guest worker communities also differ: Oman, both through its proximity to the African continent and through its historical relations with Zanzibar, Saudi and its long tradition of Yemeni transmigration, Bahrain and its long-standing connections to Iran are all factors in shaping the variable ethnic relations in these respective states. So in spite of the commonalities between the Gulf States—all comprise a predominately Arab citizenry, all discourage assimilation, all provide roughly the same sort of work for transmigrants, all are engaged in the process of trying to compel or persuade their burgeoning young population to take the sort of jobs now held by guest workers—there is nonetheless significant variation between the GCC States. The experiences of the Indian trans-

migrants in Bahrain can only serve as a rough proxy for the experience of guest workers in the Gulf as a whole. At the same time, I see much more intercountry continuity with the kafala than Longva, who fails to see the kafala itself as a profit-generating industry (see Longva 1999).

11. In Bahrain, these amnesty periods (the last of which occurred in 2002) are rarely accompanied by any state-organized roundup of undocumented workers. While the state does maintain the ability to conduct such roundups, it has certainly been reticent to do so in recent years.

12. All names, save those that appeared in the newspaper articles described at the outset of the chapter, have been changed to protect the identity of the men and women who participated in this project.

13. This scene is roughly reminiscent of the protest in rural India described by Akhil Gupta—an encirclement of those in power that is, in Gupta's words, "a common form of civil disobedience in India" (2006, 220).

14. Several of the "illegal" laborers I interviewed noted that lawyers, manpower agency representatives, and other citizens had exploited their status by promising to regularize their visas for various fees. Many of these simply disappeared, while others returned regularly with reports of incremental progress and demands for more money. None of the men I spoke with had successfully resolved their status situation through these means.

15. This description closely resembles Kearney's analysis of the U.S.-Mexico border, where "bordering policies and practices result in a net transfer of value from the immigrant-migrant community into the greater U.S. economy" (2004, 143).

HANS-RUDOLF WICKER

—ɯ—

CHAPTER 7

Deportation at the Limits of "Tolerance"

The Juridical, Institutional, and Social Construction

of "Illegality" in Switzerland

Since the 1970s, Swiss migration policies have undergone a profound change following the entry of "illegal" migrants into public discourse. The guest worker (*Gastarbeiter*) policies introduced shortly after World War II that had enabled the booming Swiss economy to recruit cheap labor from southern Europe were checked in the mid-1970s and, by the end of the following decade, had been definitively abolished. At the same time that the numbers of guest workers began to fall, the number of refugees and asylum seekers started to increase. It is no coincidence that public concern over "illegal" migrants is associated not with the image of the Gastarbeiter but with that of the refugee or asylum seeker. Furthermore, as Switzerland's guest workers originated predominantly from southern Europe, whereas refugees and asylum seekers were generally of non-European origin, "illegality" has been associated with migrants from non-EU regions such as the Balkans, eastern Europe, Latin America, Africa, and the Middle East.[1] Hence, as shown by police statistics on "suspicious" groups, today sub-Saharan Africans aimlessly wandering the streets of Zurich, as well as female Thais spotted in the vicinity of a prostitution area, are quickly suspected of residing "illegally" in Switzerland and of conducting unlawful business. In contrast, neither Portuguese construction workers nor domestically employed Slovak nurses taking care of pensioners, both from EU member states, need to fear being accosted by the foreigners' police (*Fremdenpolizei*) although they may not possess Swiss permits and could be working "illegally." Indeed, the probability of being expelled from Switzerland is considerably higher for sub-Saharan Africans or female Thais than for Portuguese or Slovak individuals.

Significantly, a migration regime has steadily been developed in Switzerland over the last thirty years that ascribes great importance to the notion of "illegality" and the deportation of migrants. This shift is contingent on, and an expression of, changes in patterns of transnational mobility (and therefore also in economics-oriented globalization) and must be seen in this context. Simultaneously, the juridical context circumscribing nation-states' actions has undergone a profound modification: individual states have been deprived of their autonomy by a growing international interconnectivity and have been increasingly subjected to international and supranational conventions. In regard to deportation, this interconnectivity shows itself in the fact that only migrants whose place of origin and state citizenship are reliably known, and whose states of origin are furthermore prepared to recognize them as citizens and agree to repatriate them, can actually be deported. In cases where this cannot be ascertained, host states are not permitted to deport individuals, as this would constitute a breach of international law.

Although Switzerland is not unique with regard to its recent migration policies, it is nevertheless instructive to take a closer look at the state's development in these matters for two reasons: first, since World War II, Switzerland has witnessed one of the highest immigration rates in the world, far exceeding the rates seen in traditional receiving states such as Canada, Australia, and the United States, and clearly visible in the fact that, as of April 2008, 22.3 percent of residents in Switzerland were non-Swiss citizens.[2] Second, Switzerland is a small state with little international influence, which sees its role as the depositary state of the international convention on human rights as being its single most prestigious asset. It follows that Switzerland cannot afford to violate international law pertaining to migration matters, nor can it, in regard to its national legislation, afford to act independently from the migration policies of its neighbors and the European Union, even though Switzerland does not belong to the EU.[3]

In this chapter, I analyze notions of "illegality" and deportation from several different perspectives. First, I show how, historically, the Swiss context has politically and legislatively constructed "the noncitizen" as a counterpart to "the citizen." It becomes clear that although the phenomenon of the undocumented migrant has only recently entered the public's awareness, the juridical means and state institutions to deal with this phenomenon are considerably older. In the chapter's second part, I focus on undocumented migrants and their social and societal environment. I show that sans-papiers cannot be regarded as a self-contained "illegal" group but instead display a great degree of differentiation and diverge considerably in their relationship to Swiss legal institutions.[4] In the third part, I turn to deportation and show that the legal mechanisms and police competencies at the state's disposal work together harmoniously enough to deal with "differentiated" groups of undocumented migrants in a "differentiated" way. In this mixture of tolerance and intolerance, the state's access to sans-papiers proves to be ambivalent. The chapter's final part focuses on tolerance and the limits thereof vis-à-vis undocumented migrants. The rather more implicitly than explicitly formulated overarching political and economic discourses—that is, those stating that in a global era "illegal" persons can sometimes be better citizens than "legal" persons—control the distinction between "good illegals" (those allowed to stay despite their lack of legal permits) and "bad illegals" (those to be deported).

THE CONSTRUCTION OF CITIZENS AND NONCITIZENS

In recent years historians have researched extensively how and in which political context the European states of the nineteenth century created what the Germans term *Staatsbürgerschaft*, the French know as *citoyenneté*, and in English is described as *citizenship* (Brubaker 1992; Schnapper 1994). Scholars agree that with the creation of modern constitutional states, diverse concepts of state citizenship were developed. Furthermore, the consensus is that this process was by no means as straightforward and uncontested as is often claimed in retrospect, in particular because a central question at the time dealt with who was to be granted rights within the state entity and who was to be refused, in part or completely, citizens' rights (Noiriel 1988). However, historians have paid relatively little attention to the way in which "illegality" was constructed alongside the articulation and legalization of citizens' liberties. In the case of Switzerland, it becomes clear that the *illegalization* process developed gradually, step by step.

As opposed to, for example, the United States, which by introducing the Chinese Exclusion Act of 1882 inserted a mode of selection into its immigration policy, Switzerland before World War I had an immigration system that could at best be termed liberal: border controls were negligible, and transnational mobility was hardly regulated; foreigners were legally free to settle in Switzerland and subject to control solely by local communities. This open system resulted in the fact that, by 1915, 15 percent of those residing in Switzerland were foreigners, and cities like Geneva, Basel, Schaffhausen, and Zurich were home to a population in which over 30 percent of the inhabitants were foreigners. The demand for the integration of foreigners by the federal state remained weak and was manifest mainly in the call for foreigners to naturalize themselves—something that was possible after just two years' residency. Under these circumstances, the notion of undocumented migrants could not develop.

The situation changed radically in 1918 with the creation of the foreigners' police on both the cantonal and federal levels. It was the duty of the police to control both immigration and resident foreigners. With the passing of the Foreigners' Law (Ausländergesetz) by the Swiss parliament in the early 1930s, it became obligatory for foreigners to possess a residency permit to be able to remain in the country, as well as a work permit to be simultaneously employed. The obligation to register with the communal authorities was expanded to include not only Swiss citizens (as had hitherto been the case) but also foreign residents. The juridical statute of the residency permit from this time on has served as a powerful administrative tool in dividing the foreign population into those "legally" residing in Switzerland and those residing "illegally." Henceforth the state was to have the power to grant permits to welcome foreigners and to reject those deemed to be undesirable. Furthermore, legal temporary residents could be converted into "illegal migrants" by withdrawing or simply not extending their residency permits. Additionally, the extension of the obligation to register with the community led to the recording (*erfassen*) of noncitizens and citizens alike.[5] The data generated by the foreigners' police concerning the granting of residency permits are stored in the central foreigners' register (*zentrales Ausländerregister*), a database under administration of the Federal Department for Migration (Bundesamt für Migration), which contains all information regarding Switzerland's foreign population. It is noteworthy that this register is kept separately from the data on the Swiss population. The symbolism inherent in these separate registries must be interpreted as portraying foreigners resident in Switzerland as aliens (*Fremde*) who are a priori suspected of lacking any loyalty whatsoever and are thus to be placed under police administration. In contrast, the Swiss are under the administration of a civilian authority owing to their automatically assumed loyalties.

With the passing of foreigners' laws in the 1930s and the subsequent introduction and strengthening of the authorities in charge of foreigners at both the federal and cantonal levels, Switzerland has adopted what

Michael Mann describes as "an infrastructural strength quite uncommon to modern states" in regard to both the legal foundations and the administrative *erfassen* of foreigners (1993, 60). Following jurisdiction on the granting and revoking of residency permits, the foreigners' police forces (recently renamed Migration Services) decide on who is permitted to enter Switzerland, who is obliged to leave the country, whether a criminally convicted foreign national is to be expelled after his or her prison term, and whether a rejected asylum seeker is to be immediately compelled to leave or not. Furthermore, it is the migration authorities who can decide to convert a short-term permit into a residency permit and who, by way of their administrative powers, arbitrate on the naturalization of foreigners.

Naturally the legislation regarding foreigners and naturalization has been modified several times over the years, as have the regulations pertaining to asylum seekers that, since the late 1970s, have complemented the foreigners' laws. While considerations of space here do not permit an analysis of these processes, it is my belief that they have nearly always resulted in an intensification of the migration authorities' powers (Wicker 2004).

In light of the state's regulatory aim to control foreigners, it is important to note that both the context and the perception of undocumented migrants have undergone a profound metamorphosis over time. Despite the creation of nationalist laws that, developed between the two world wars, specifically targeted foreigners, undocumented migrants were not a matter for public discussion until the late 1960s. The reason for this lies in the fact that foreigners seeking work found it easy to obtain work permits (and therefore also temporary residency permits) in the economic boom of the postwar years. With the worsening of the economy in the latter half of the 1970s, this was to change, and a temporary freeze was introduced regarding the hiring of guest workers. This was certainly not unrelated to the increase in refugees and asylum seekers taking place at the time, and "illegality" has been a matter for concern ever since.

POLICE MONITORING OF "ILLEGAL" AND ILLEGALIZED PERSONS

Over the past twenty-five years, Switzerland has witnessed an increasing public presence of undocumented migrants that has aroused public and media interest. It is safe to assume that even before this there were people in Switzerland who lacked residency papers, just as there were in other

European countries, but these individuals remained inconspicuous: they neither came to the attention of the foreigners' police nor aroused much scientific interest. The cause for this disregard for "illegality" may lie in the fact that there existed at that time no separate terminology capable of semantically delineating the group of "illegal" residents. Even during much of the 1980s, discourse in Switzerland focused on "foreigners" (*Ausländer* in the German-speaking part of Switzerland, *étrangers* in the French-speaking part, and *stranieri* in the Italian-speaking part), concentrating on these individuals' subjection to the foreigners' laws, and on "refugees," subject to the law on asylum (*Asylgesetz*). Both terms at that time referred to "aliens": those not really welcome, but by no means automatically associated with "illegality." It was not until the introduction in the 1980s of the term "migrant," a semantic figure of speech long neglected in Swiss national languages, that the domains of immigration and "illegality" were connected to each other (Wicker 2002b). Today the term "migrant" is used uncritically by the public to denote those immigrants originating from "third," or non-EU, countries and lacking resources.[6] A set of ascribed negative attitudes (poor, unqualified, culturally distant) serves to make these individuals appear as liminal beings existing between the "legal" and "illegal" spheres.

The discourse about these undocumented migrants is largely speculative because, unlike Swiss citizens and foreigners who possess residency permits, they are not *erfasst* and thus are nonexistent in the registers and cannot be assessed quantitatively from a sociological point of view. Hence the Federal Department of Statistics can give precise data on the Swiss population and its demographic development, the Central Foreigners' Registry has data on the number of short- and long-term foreign residents as well as cross-border commuters (*Grenzgänger*) and naturalized persons, but the undocumented remain in statistical limbo. Trade unions believe there are 300,000 sans-papiers in Switzerland; the government claims there are only 80,000. The reason for this discrepancy lies in the two bodies' diverging interests: the unions, also defending the interests of their foreign members, find within their ranks not just comrades possessing residency permits but also those whose permits have not been extended, and therefore see themselves obliged to claim that there are large numbers of individuals lacking documents. On the other hand, political parties and the administration fear that the public, in particular the right-wing parties, may see in the presence of sans-papiers a defeat of state surveillance and the puissance of the foreigners' police, so they strive to keep the number of undocumented migrants as low as possible. The only credibly conducted scientific study on the phenomenon of "illegal" residents and their impact on the Swiss employment sector concludes that there are roughly 180,000 undocumented migrants in Switzerland (Piguet and Losa 2001). Assuming that this figure is realistic, it would mean that if we account for these undocumented individuals, the foreign population of Switzerland (officially 21.4 percent) would rise by a further 2.6 percent.

Because these migrants are regarded as being "illegal" by the foreigners' police and would thus be obliged to leave the country, these individuals are under constant threat of being deported. Crucially, this is the only element that this group of "illegal" migrants has in common. Closer analysis quickly shows that "illegal" migrants are a fragmented group due at least in part to legal norms and state administration and the way in which they are involved in constructing "illegality," as a closer look at the respective "illegal" groups will show.

Illegalized Persons

This group consists of migrants who "legally" entered Switzerland and therefore once possessed residency and work permits. Frequently these individuals worked for years or even decades for low salaries, only then to lose their jobs and subsequently their work permits. Instead of returning to their countries of origin (as dictated by Swiss law), they remained in Switzerland and have been working under even worse conditions as "illegal" employees. The scant data available attest that these illegalized persons predominantly originate from the Balkans, in particular from the former Yugoslavia. After the independent economic development and growth of local job opportunities in the 1980s, Italy ceased to be a labor-exporting country, and the recruitment of cheap labor for Switzerland shifted to Portugal and Yugoslavia. However, with the economic crisis of the early 1990s, the Swiss authorities definitively prohibited the recruitment of labor from "third countries," and in addition to this, the beginning of the civil war in the former Yugoslavia contributed to the refusal of Bosnians, Kosovars, and Serbs to return home.

Overstayers

The term "overstayers" describes migrants who originally entered the country on a tourist visa, subsequently worked in Switzerland without the necessary work permit, and then remained in the country after their visa's expiry. This has applied far more frequently to women in search of access to the Swiss employment sector than to men, and these women predominantly originate from Latin America and, less frequently, from Asian or east European states. The economic niches that have attracted women have mainly been in private homes and the sex industry, both service-oriented jobs that have grown massively in recent years.

"Illegals"

The category of "illegals" describes migrants who enter Switzerland without any permits whatsoever and either work "illegally" or become criminals. Citizens of the European Union who reside "illegally" in Switzerland (in particular French nationals in the French part of Switzerland and Italians in Ticino) are rarely persecuted, as opposed to "illegals" from third countries (especially from Russia, Romania, Ukraine, and the Balkan states). Although third-country "illegals" seem to be far less numerous, it is they who in public opinion are regarded as the prototype of undocumented migrants: doubly "illegal" because they violate both the foreigners' laws and criminal law. This image stems mainly from broad media coverage of scandalous criminal activities occasionally involving "illegals."

Convicted Foreigners

As far as deportation is concerned, a further group of "illegals" concerns us here: those who have committed crimes in Switzerland and have subsequently been convicted. Because these individuals are automatically assumed by the courts to be highly likely to flee the country, they are generally jailed in closed prisons.[7] As a consequence, 85 percent of prisoners in closed male institutions and 60 percent in closed female institutions are foreign nationals. Prisoners who have never resided "legally" in Switzerland are moved to an expulsion prison (*Ausschaffungsgefängnis*) after their regular prison terms and are deported from there.[8] Individuals who possessed a residency permit before their crime in most cases find this permit revoked over the course of their imprisonment, thereby transforming them into "illegals" and incurring their subsequent deportation after their sentences are up. The reason for this deportation procedure is found in the collusion of the foreigners' law and criminal law: the foreigners' law states that migrants lose their right to a residency permit the moment they violate a criminal law. This legal configuration is significant precisely because it represents a Foucauldian disciplinary instrument that forces foreign resident populations, from a juridical point of view, to be "legal." The case that such a high percentage of prisoners in closed penal institutions are foreigners should not obscure the fact that, statistically, the foreign population permanently resident in Switzerland possesses less criminal energy than does the Swiss population.[9]

If we compile a list of the diverse undocumented migrant population in Switzerland, it becomes evident how much heterogeneity exists within this group. Differentiating characteristics are manifest along two sets of criteria: first, in regard to how "illegality" is constructed along residency law guidelines and, second, in regard to national origin of the undocumented migrants. Although there are roughly 180,000 people without Swiss residency permits (some from "old" EU states like France, Spain, and Portugal; some from "new" EU states such as Poland, the Czech Republic, and Slovakia; and some from Latin American, African, Asian, and eastern and southeastern European states), there can be found practically no ethnic concentrations of "illegals." This is in contrast to countries like Italy and France where undocumented migrants are occasionally "visible" as ethnic groupings because they congregate in specific neighborhoods or housing estates.

Thus invisibility is a common characteristic of undocumented migrants in Switzerland, and this is constituted both actively and passively, as limited ethnographic studies have shown. Passive invisibility is evident in the way that sans-papiers decline to make demands or insist on their rights vis-à-vis both employers and the state. Such actions would subject them rather rapidly to the public eye and could provoke their deportation. This structured and passive subjection to the dictates of the police and the foreigners' law leads sans-papiers to accept minimal wages on the black market in collusion with employers and to accept their exploitation. Active invisibility, on the other hand, becomes evident in the way sans-papiers develop and employ evasion strategies so as not to attract attention either in the neighborhood or from the police. There is a plethora of such evasion strategies, including the decision not to drive cars or use public transport, the correct use of pedestrian crossings, limiting circles of friends to a select few trustworthy individuals, not renting apartments under their own names, and not having bank accounts, and resorting to informal channels in dealing with money, in particular sending remittances back home exclusively through friends and work colleagues.

A further element of invisibility is the attempt by these individuals to integrate as much as possible into the host society, even to the point of assimilation. Sans-papiers in Switzerland often communicate quite well in the official Swiss languages and thereby create an impression of belonging. Inclusion strategies are often supported further by the rejection of physical symbols and public manifestations that hint at their cultures of origin or religious beliefs.

Despite attempts to lead invisible lives either through self-isolation or through as much assimilation as possible, there are in fact some ways in which undocumented migrants can interact with state institutions in a legal manner. For instance, cantonal jurisdiction on compulsory schooling also pertains to the children of "illegal" resident parents. In neighborhoods with a high proportion of foreigners, a number of schools enroll children and adolescents from sans-papiers families. Because school boards refuse to categorize pupils by residency status, no quantifiable numbers exist for this group of "illegals." Furthermore, schools are not obliged to inform the police of the presence of such pupils in their classrooms. However, an institutional conflict nevertheless exists owing to the migration authorities' frequent efforts to gain access to school registers.[10]

The health care system is another example of the interaction between undocumented migrants and Swiss institutions. Those summarized earlier under the category of illegalized persons, mostly former guest workers who have had their work and residency permits revoked, had (in accordance with the law) health care insurance (Achermann 2003). A large proportion of individuals who remain employed despite lacking the relevant permits simply continue to pay their installments regularly and thereby retain their insurance. Undocumented migrants who possess insurance policies thus have the same access to the health care system as foreigners with residency permits and Swiss citizens. Like public schools, health care institutions and health insurance companies do not have registers documenting the residency status of patients, and at present they still refuse to cooperate with the cantonal police authorities. Yet possessing legal health insurance will not prevent (the threat of) deportation. Moreover, there is also contact between health care services and undocumented migrants who do not have health insurance, for example, in emergency and maternity medical services as well as in special clinics offering HIV/AIDS treatment. However, because in such cases health care services request financial support from the cantonal authorities, there do in fact exist ways by which to compare data between the police and health care authorities. This can lead to the uncovering of individuals' "illegal" status, and hence such information interfaces represent potentially dangerous interstices for sans-papiers.

DEPORTATION

In regard to migration, the Swiss state has for a long time had the juridical means to fight "illegality" and implement deportations. It is therefore all the more remarkable to observe how the number of undocumented migrants has risen so drastically over the last twenty years. The cause for this lies mainly in the deregulated employment sectors that attract people from the Third World and newly industrializing countries. Specific economic sectors like agriculture, construction, and gastronomy, as well as certain service sectors such as the sex industry, geriatric care, and domestic assistance, are particularly prone to incorporating "illegal" labor. It follows, then, that "illegal" immigration develops alongside "legal" immigration. In this constellation lies the contradiction inherent in the fight against "illegal" immigration: while the liberal economy is quite willing and able to coexist with the concept of free movement of labor, the social welfare state cannot (Freeman 1986). In practice this discrepancy manifests itself in the development of ever-new niches in the national employment sector that are then saturated with "illegal" workers while the state tries (and invariably fails) to close these niches. A closer look at the legal structures legitimizing deportations in a constitutional state as well as at the implementation of this practice by the police will serve to display these difficulties.

First, it is important to note that "illegal" residence in Switzerland does not violate the criminal code; rather, it runs up solely against the foreigners' law. Specifically this means that when detained by the police, an individual residing "illegally" in Switzerland is not prosecuted as a criminal but instead given an eviction order (*Wegweisung*): a written order to leave the country immediately. The police are generally not able to ascertain whether evicted individuals actually leave or instead elect to remain in the country. The next tool at the state's disposal is an expulsion order (*Ausweisung*), issued by judges and directed at individuals who have ignored an eviction order and at those who have been convicted as criminals. Expulsion orders are usually issued in conjunction with a temporary (or in some cases permanent) prohibition against reentering Switzerland. The last and most powerful tool is deportation (*Ausschaffung*). This entails the jailing of those affected and their administrative preparation and subsequent deportation by police escort. Deportations can be enacted only after determining an individual's nationality and obtaining that state's agreement to recognize the deportee as a citizen and to permit his or her entry. In cases where an individual's nationality cannot be determined or when there are humanitarian reasons preventing deportation to a given state, the deportee must be released into freedom after the maximum detention period prescribed by law has expired. These individuals then find themselves continuing their lives within Swiss society as undocumented migrants.[11]

The multilayered juridical procedure allowing the state to deal with the subnational sphere of "illegality" points to both stringency and uninterest. Stringency is to be discovered in the laws passed, police competencies, and public rhetoric, all of which suggest a zero-tolerance ideology toward irregular migrants. Uninterest, on the other hand, is manifest in the lack of awareness regarding "illegal" migrants and deportations. The state is just as indifferent to statistically detailing sans-papiers as it is to knowing how many individuals are evicted, expelled, and deported annually. While this information is contained within the archives of the cantonal police authorities, no central registry exists for the regulation of undocumented migrants as there does for the Swiss and foreign resident population.

One single study can be mentioned here that succeeds in at least partially shedding light on the repression of undocumented migrants by the state and portrays recorded sans-papiers, describing their origins and the economic niches they have come to occupy (Chimienti, Efionay-Mäder, Farquet 2003). This study, conducted in the canton of Geneva, shows that within just two years, 888 interventions were directed against undocumented migrants and their suspected employers—a high number, pointing toward a high repression density, considering the relatively small resident population of this city-canton (440,000, of which 38.6 percent are non-Swiss). Forty-four percent of those checked by the police were directly deported, meaning that 195 individuals are deported annually from the canton of Geneva alone. A further 46 percent of the checked sans-papiers (thus 204 individuals per year) were given an eviction order. While the following extrapolation is, of course, problematic, it may be instructive (given the absence of other data) to take as a baseline the numbers of actually deported individuals from the canton of Geneva and apply them to the whole of Switzerland, by which we would then arrive at a figure of 3,500 undocumented migrants being forcibly deported from Switzerland annually, or thirteen people per workday.

A profile of the victims' origins is intriguing: of the individuals checked by the police in Geneva, 57 percent are from Latin America, 20 percent are from Europe, 13 percent are from Asia or the Middle East, and 10 percent are from Africa. These numbers in no way reflect the scenario represented by the media or that which is so heavily present in public discourse. According to the media, European countries are most threatened by immigration from Africa, followed by east and southeast Europe, the Middle East, and Asia—with Latin America not even appearing on this scale. Of the migrants checked by the Geneva police, 44 percent were employed in private homes, 17 percent in hotel businesses and eating establishments, 9 percent in the sex industry, 7 percent in heavy industry and construction, and 6 percent in cleaning firms. This distribution most likely comes close to a pan-Swiss profile of irregular migrants' economic activities, especially considering that this would reflect the restructuring of a Swiss society increasingly generating demand for minimum-wage labor in precisely the aforementioned niches.

One final element of this study remains to be mentioned: the statistical imbalance regarding the high ratio of women to men checked and sanctioned (62 percent and 38 percent, respectively) is grounded in specifically local factors. That is, owing to the presence of a multitude of large international institutions, Geneva has disproportionately high growth in the formal and informal service sectors. The informal service sector, characterized mainly by domestic labor and prostitution, attracts female labor in particular. In contrast, the sectors in the canton of Geneva that attract irregular male work (such as industry, construction, and agriculture) have lower growth rates. It follows that female irregular migrants appear in police statistics far more frequently than male irregular migrants do.

IRREGULAR MIGRANTS AND THE SPHERES OF TOLERANCE

Godfried Engbersen's differentiation of the treatment of irregular migrants into three phases, while originally described for the Netherlands, can also be applied in the case of Switzerland (2001, 241). In the first phase, lasting until the end of the 1960s, "spontaneous migrants" were welcomed and integrated into the employment sector. In the second phase, which ended in the early 1990s, "illegal" workers were still being silently tolerated. This was to change in the third phase, beginning in the early 1990s, with the exclusion of "illegal aliens" and their persecution and deportation by the police. This most recent phase has also seen the development of the institutional and physical infrastructure enabling the management of "illegal" and illegalized migrants and their preparation for deportation. Since then, detention centers designed to prepare undocumented migrants for their deportation have sprouted throughout the European Union and the non-

EU states of Norway and Switzerland. To date there are several hundred of these on European territory.

With the increasingly restrictive migration policies of European states, which include strengthened border patrols directed outward and panoptically designed surveillance and repression directed inward to deal with irregular migration, expulsion and deportation have become commonplace instruments employed by the police in dealing with "illegality." These instruments are hardly discussed by the public because of the general populace's acquiescence with them. They are understood as being part of the security policies that accompany renationalization processes and fight against the negative impact of globalization and transnational mobility. As the problem of undocumented migrants can seemingly be solved neither by stronger insulation nor by more repressive methods (if not a single sans-papiers were to enter Switzerland anymore, and thirteen of them were deported per workday, it would take fifty years for Switzerland to no longer contain sans-papiers), and because periodically introduced regularizations as conducted in Italy (Finotelli 2005), Spain (Arango and Jachimowicz 2005), and Portugal (Marques and Góis 2005) do not actually serve to diminish the problem of "illegals," two basic questions arise. First, which strategies and adaptations do the newer sans-papiers develop to attain their goal of staying in the country and being able to generate resources despite increasing repression and the threat of deportation? Second, and more important, which conclusions must we draw from the observation that nearly all modern states have been threatening undocumented migrants with ever more draconian methods of repression and subsequently employing such methods despite knowing full well that they in no way help to solve the problem?

Regarding the first point, it must be noted that the shift from a tolerant to an exclusionary and repressive migration policy has produced a new type of migrant whom I term the "informed migrant." This refers to individuals who, thanks to the education they received in an urban environment in their states of origin, are able to accumulate both the information and the means to, on the one hand, overcome the rising symbolic and material walls of defense meant to block entry into Europe and, on the other, find those vital niches guaranteeing their continued residence, survival, and evasion of deportation by exploiting both legal and illegal opportunities. It goes without saying that knowledge generation specific to migration is routed through formal and informal networks and is significantly enhanced by the use of modern information pools (the Internet) and telecommunications. The informed migrant (a new phenomenon in

Europe) knows the gateways into Europe, the prices to be paid to human traffickers, and how restrictive the different immigration and asylum laws of European states are (Efionay-Mäder et al. 2001). If necessary, informed migrants juggle identities and citizenships to prevent or at least delay extradition. Migrants not permitted to stay know that marrying a citizen of the host country can give them this permission or possibly even citizenship, and accordingly the number of what the literature terms "transnational marriages" has risen dramatically over the past ten years. Quite in keeping with the new and more repressive migration policies is the fact that "spontaneous" migration has lost its predominance, and family reunions have instead become more important. In states such as Sweden and the United States, migrants gaining access through such family reunions already far outnumber all other types of migration. In Switzerland and other European countries, this motive for migration has, supported by international law, also gained ascendancy. Thus informed migrants find themselves at the interface between "legal" and "illegal" immigration, and through their active and precarious ways of life, they thereby differ significantly from "older" migrants (including refugees and guest workers) who had to overcome comparatively few material, symbolic, and juridical obstacles to reach a host country and remain there.

The second point refers to the regulatory system of "illegality," which, at least in the public opinion, constitutes itself as the interplay of panoptic control, police intervention, expulsion, and deportation. As far as Switzerland is concerned, however, it is safe to state that the police in the cantons and political communities do not even attempt to enforce the political zero-tolerance policy: employers who hire "illegal" workers are rarely punished; young women working "illegally" as domestic servants are (usually after being discovered because of neighbors' complaints) merely asked by the police to leave the country; and the naturalized Thai brothel mistress "illegally" employing young Thai women will protect her colleagues from the police by referring to tourist visas and assuring them that the women were only visiting her and not actually working in the establishment. This soft handling commonly (but certainly not always) employed by the police vis-à-vis irregular migrants is supported by both national and international law. However, the juridical context does not tell the entire story: deportations do, of course, occur, even if they are not as numerous as the general public and right-wing politicians would like.

The ambivalence so frequently expressed by the state's attitude toward irregular migrants is obviously systemic and in a certain way reflects undocumented migrants' liminal situation. Liminality means that sans-papiers are structurally integrated but symbolically and socially excluded to such an extent that they become invisible. Structural integration includes the incorporation of sans-papiers into the shadow economies so vital for the survival of Swiss society.

Thus there emerges the question of which situations must arise for the police to intervene in the undocumented migrant scene and order evictions and deportations, and in which situations they do not do this. A closer look at police practices of intervention shows that the security forces employ a tactic of selective monitoring. It is practically only those sans-papiers who, for whatever reasons, no longer remain invisible who become the object of police intervention: namely, undocumented migrants who have committed criminal offenses or are suspected of doing so; those who have been denounced by Swiss neighbors, landlords, or employers; those who draw undue attention to themselves in public and are unfortunate enough to get caught up in a police check; and finally those who, by design or by chance, become a burden to public institutions such as the welfare system.

Selective monitoring means that police intervention takes place according to a classification model that divides sans-papiers into "good" and "bad" migrants. "Bad illegal aliens" are individuals who become visible, become criminal, or become uncomfortable and provoke neighbors or Swiss institutions. "Good" migrants, on the other hand, are diligent and inconspicuous, submit humbly to their exploitation, do not make unreasonable demands, and refuse to claim their rights. It seems as if a functional exploitation model forms the basis of this division. Sans-papiers, along with asylum seekers and temporarily accepted refugees, fill the employment niches at the minimum-wage end of the scale that were formerly filled by guest workers and therefore today experience a dearth of labor supply. This lowest of all employment-sector spheres has grown and become more differentiated owing to increasing transnational economic interconnectivity and burgeoning tertiarization. The neoliberal economy's demand for more flexibility can, through this disassociation with the rules of a deregulated job market, be ideally implemented. Depending on demand, irregular migrants can be hired or fired at will, and they become more attractive to employers because the undocumented do not warrant social benefits.

The Swiss state's ambivalent attitude to irregular migrants evident in the mixed modes of police practice (ranging from tolerant disregard to strict intervention) can obviously not be understood without considering deregulated employment-sector models. The interaction of a societal and economic demand for minimum-wage workers who can be treated as the economic cycle dictates requires the migration police to control and discipline this new caste of invisibles and also to keep them readily available. The incessantly communicated threat of possible deportation that, along with the quest for employment, structures the lives of undocumented migrants represents a first-class disciplinary instrument that serves perfectly to keep the lowest echelon of an increasingly split society both in line and at arm's length.

CONCLUSIONS

Following Emile Durkheim, we can state that irregular migrants are a social fact in a globalized world where societies have become increasingly atomized. Their existence is the result of the dynamics propelling societies forward, evident in the progressive technical development and penetration of market economies and in the successive weakening of the state's regulatory powers. In this context, undocumented migrants mutate to become a new class of people within modern states that, as is common to all classes, adopts its own *habitus*. Part of this habitus is that they populate their own subnational field and survive there only because of their relationship to, and dependency on, legal state and societal spheres. Furthermore, they find themselves obliged to be as socially and culturally invisible as possible for reasons of self-protection. Unlike "legal" migrants, they do not have basic rights and cannot claim freedom of either speech or assembly. Any attempt to claim such rights attracts the public's attention and can provoke police intervention. The social and cultural adaptations made by sans-papiers to withstand the threat of deportation far exceed the compromises that "legal" migrants are willing to make to be integrated into society. Unlike their "legal" counterparts, "illegal" immigrants do not congregate in new social movements aiming at the recognition of minority rights; they do not have a voice to demand the recognition of their own languages or religions; and they do not petition for political participation. From the point of view of their disposition, irregular migrants are reduced to being providers of cheap labor ideally suited to the supply and demand structure of a flexible employment sector.

What is more, modern states employ the threat of deportation as prescribed by migration and foreigners' laws as an effective disciplinary instrument to make unpopular foreign populations more malleable and force them into humility. By means of expulsion and deportation through mechanisms of selective monitoring, individuals who resist the unwritten rules of the irregular migrant's way of life are shut out, while those who willingly subject themselves to the process of invisibility are permitted to remain. The threat of deportation, however, weighs heavily on regular migrants as well, at least until they become naturalized and come to enjoy (as citizens of the host state) the state's protection and the knowledge that they can no longer be evicted. Seen from this angle, the state's right to evict and expel is a hierarchical form of discipline ordered by degrees of the right to remain in the country. Logically this threat is most effective when directed at irregular migrants, who cannot claim any right whatsoever to remain. Short-term residents and those who have settled in Switzerland, on the other hand, risk deportation only if they engage in political agitation or commit a crime.

Modern states today find themselves dealing with deindustrialization, sinking state income, and new social unrest and are increasingly under pressure to generate societal integration, thus finding themselves forced to appeal more and more to sentiments of national cohesion. A valid question, therefore, is whether modern states are not in fact testing new forms of civil obedience in relation to irregular migrants. This is especially pertinent in light of the present tendency to dismantle civil rights, fine-tune surveillance technologies, and (as a zero-tolerance ideology would imply) increasingly introduce sanctions on those who violate state regulations—all measures that in the present moment go far beyond the ones we know from classical state power management. The core feature of this new kind of civil virtue would consist in tolerating the structural integration of individuals into a society without allowing them to demand the rights to protection that should be fundamental to citizens living in a constitutional state. The legal instrument to enforce these rules (which in practice stems from an interplay of forces moving on a continuum ranging from tolerance to intolerance) is the threat of deportation. What is more, if we consider that there are known cases in which even naturalized citizens have had their citizenship revoked to be deported, it becomes clear that the threat of deportation as the ultimate instrument in forcing civil obedience in an era of ever-tougher economic competition, growing transnational mobility, and the dissolution of generally binding values is likely to become even more important.

NOTES

A special thanks to Steven Parham for his initial comments and for translating this chapter into English.

1. While the European Union possesses clearly defined contours owing to its political dimensions, things or persons "European" do not. Since the dissolution

of the Soviet Union, the limits of what is considered to be European or not have successively been shifting eastward. In this chapter, the term "EU-origin" refers to people from EU member states, and "non-European origin" refers to migrants from the Middle East, the Far East, Africa, and the Americas. I do not employ the term "European origin" because of its contested meaning.

2. Bundesamt für Migration 2008, Ausländerstatistik, http://www.bfm .admin.ch/etc/medialib/data/migration/statistik/auslaenderstatistik/2008 .Par.0006.File.tmp/1C-2008_04_d.pdf. Measured in absolute terms, immigration is strongest to the United States, followed by the Russian Federation and Germany. However, if immigration is measured as a percentage of the total national population, a different picture emerges, with the United Arab Emirates ranked first, followed by Kuwait, Jordan, and Israel; Switzerland comes tenth on this scale, followed by Australia, New Zealand, and Canada. The United States, the Russian Federation, and Germany do not figure among the first twenty states (United Nations 2002). According to 2004 statistics, Germany's foreign population amounts to 8.9 percent of its total population, that of the United Kingdom to 4.9 percent, and that of Sweden to 5.1 percent. OECD countries measuring the percentage of their foreign-born population (and thus including naturalized migrants) present the following numbers: Australia, 23.6 percent; Canada, 16.6 percent; the United States, 12.8 percent. OECD, International Migration Statistics 2008, http://titania.sourceoecd.org.

3. This is most obviously shown by the fact that Switzerland signed up to both the EU's Dublin Agreement (regulation of asylum matters) and the Schengen Agreement (exchange of information as well as shared standards in the fields of security and prevention of criminality).

4. The term *sans-papiers* (without papers) is a commonly accepted term in the French-speaking part of Switzerland, as well as in France, for undocumented migrants. In the German-speaking part of Switzerland, civil society and the media today favor this term over the official terms "illegal foreigner" (*illegaler Ausländer*) and "illegal migrants" (*illegale Migranten*) by stating that sans-papiers implies no prejudiced notion of "illegality."

5. Lacking a precise translation into English, administrative *erfassen* has a polysemantic structure: *erfassen* incorporates, on the one hand, the administrative penetration of, and control over, a population and, on the other hand, the bureaucratic organization of state protection and state welfare (Torpey 1999).

6. "Third country" and "third state" are used in Swiss political discourse to denote states not belonging to the EU. Switzerland has signed a treaty with the EU facilitating transfrontier mobility and access to the employment sector; the benefits contained therein do not apply to individuals from so-called third countries.

7. There are three types of prisons in Switzerland for convicted adults: high-security jails and closed and open penal institutions. High-security jails contain almost exclusively Swiss citizens, closed penal institutions almost exclusively foreign nationals, and open penal institutions mostly Swiss convicts. "Open"

institutions strive to resocialize inmates because most of them will return to civilian life sooner or later. "Closed" means that only limited resocialization programs exist and that there is no leniency concerning prison sentences because the authorities consider there to be a high chance of prisoners absconding (Wicker 2002a). Closed institutions contain such a high percentage of foreigners because these inmates will generally not return to Swiss civilian life and instead will be deported.

8. Since the early 1990s, Switzerland has instituted so-called expulsion prisons (*Ausschaffungsgefängnisse*), one of which is situated right at the Zurich airport and another annexed to the state prison of Witzwil. These special prisons serve to detain individuals destined to be deported by court ruling or police decree and to administratively prepare them for their departure.

9. While this may seem contradictory at first glance, the reason for this is found in the observation that the criminality ratio correlates more with residency status than with national origin or ethnicity. Research has shown that foreigners who possess a permanent resident permit in Switzerland (*Niederlassungsausweis*) are slightly less likely to commit crimes than the national population, in contrast to groups lacking such permits or possessing only limited residency rights—both of which, according to police statistics, have an above-average criminality ratio (Tonry 1997; Killias 2001, 147–90).

10. Recently the police in the canton of Zurich definitively demanded that school authorities disclose the names and addresses of all pupils so that they could be compared with data from the foreigners' police's registry, thus exposing sans-papiers children and their parents. Citing the general human rights agreement, school authorities refused to comply with the police order. Similar friction exists between police and school authorities in other cantons. A common police strategy to deal with this resistance (and one that school authorities have tried in vain to prevent) is, for example, to whisk children of families resisting an expulsion order out of their classrooms and deport them along with their parents. Furthermore, sans-papiers children are protected from police intervention only while in compulsory schooling: as soon as schooling ends and they enter vocational training, they are obliged to disclose their nationality and residency status, and as soon as they do so, they risk being persecuted by the police and ultimately deported along with their parents.

11. While to date there have been no systematic studies conducted on the forms of sans-papiers generated by the interventions of the foreigners' police, several individual cases have been well documented. Thus every year hundreds of individuals (in particular, asylum seekers whose cases have been rejected) are let loose with eviction and expulsion orders, and the police are unable to provide information on the whereabouts or activities of these people. The police record only individuals who "legally" leave the country and contact the border control authorities; all others (the vast majority, that is) either remain in Switzerland or "illegally" enter an EU state. It is known that certain evicted individuals (especially those from EU-member states or Latin America) often leave

Switzerland only to reenter "legally" again at some later date as tourists. There are known cases in which foreigners could not be deported owing to a lack of documents and hence had to be released from expulsion prisons after their maximum sentence was over—even if they had not been sans-papiers before-hand, freedom from prison now made them so. Furthermore, there have been cases in which, due to a lack of papers, it was not possible to deport criminals who had served their sentences and had to be released in compliance with the law; one such individual was eventually discovered right back at the prison gate, pleading for admittance after weeks of aimless wandering.

—ᘛ—

CHAPTER 8

Deportation Deferred

"Illegality," Visibility, and Recognition

in Contemporary Germany

In Germany, "illegality" is an exceptionally fluid and often transitory category, produced by shifting practices of inclusion and exclusion. The construct of "illegal" immigration is relatively new, coinciding with the end
of the guest worker programs in the early 1970s. Political pressures after
German reunification and the resulting 1993 changes in asylum law, along
with border militarization in the wake of European Union expansion, have
resulted in increased "illegal" migration. Debates over all forms of migration continue to focus on the mechanism of political asylum; meanwhile
the extremely low rate of approval following the asylum reform has brought
issues of deportation to the forefront. As in most of Europe, deportation
is expensive, often appealed, and has little public support, making it a
seemingly inefficient tool for controlling immigration. In addition, the
historical legacy of the twentieth century has produced a complex ambivalence toward the use of state power and coercion in contemporary
German society. While restrictive immigration policies are generally well
received, there is occasional public resistance to their implementation.
Impending deportations, especially of individuals and families considered
"deserving" of national membership, are often met with organized protest
and media attention. The state has developed specific tactics to exercise its
authority in the face of such protests, resulting in unique and sometimes
contradictory practices related to deportation. However, at the same
time, denunciation practices are prevalent, and most apprehensions are

the result of civilian collaboration. In addition to voluntary reporting, mandates to inform authorities of undocumented persons are codified into law.

Drawing on ethnographic research, this chapter discusses state responses to "illegality" in contemporary Germany by examining suspensions of deportation.[1] By observing the exceptions in deportation practice—namely, moments where there is some agreement that removal should be *postponed*—I highlight the ambivalences inherent in the exercise of state power. Three examples are discussed. First, I describe the failures associated with the practice of issuing the *Duldung*, or temporary suspension of deportation, which has resulted in individuals with indefinitely uncertain legal status (in some cases, for over a decade). The purported discontinuation of this practice has led to even more confusion, the establishment of Hardship Committees to review particularly deserving cases, and a policy dictating that individuals who can sustain themselves and are willing to "integrate" can receive permanent residency permits. Second, I discuss the period before and after childbirth, called the *Mutterschutz*, or maternity protection period, which highlights the tensions between social welfare and law enforcement concerns. During this time, women and their newborns are temporarily not deportable. Finally, illness can provide grounds for a suspension of deportation or even a residency permit for humanitarian reasons.[2]

Suspensions of deportation are based on "benevolence" on the part of the host society and notions of "deservingness" of individuals or families. Saskia Sassen (2002) considers such individuals to be "unauthorized yet recognized," a form of incipient repositioned membership in the nation-state. In the United States, for example, many undocumented migrants were eligible for suspensions of deportation before the 1996 immigration law reform if they could demonstrate seven years of continuous presence, good moral character, and evidence of impending extreme hardship upon return to the home country. Sassen argues that by meeting certain criteria of membership in their communities of residence through daily practices (such as employment, child rearing, and civic participation), undocumented migrants can earn a form of citizenship, even without formal status. However, this membership is based on concepts of the ideal "proto-citizen" of the host society, which includes certain normative lifestyles and behaviors while excluding others (Coutin 2003b). In Germany, which embraces a primarily ethnonational model of citizenship, true membership is more diffuse and difficult to obtain than in many other settings. Instead, ideas of state benevolence based on ideas of humanitarianism, along with migrants' deservingness, dictate which individuals are allowed to stay. While those awarded with suspensions of deportation are "unauthorized yet recognized," it would be exceedingly optimistic to consider this recognition a form of incipient membership.

HISTORY AND PRODUCTION OF "ILLEGAL" MIGRATION TO GERMANY

Political and economic processes in Europe, especially since the second half of the twentieth century, are crucial for understanding the trajectory of German migration policy. It was not until 2001 that the government officially reversed its long-held stance that Germany was "not a country of immigration." This new reality reflected increased migration since the 1990s, along with second- and third-generation guest worker communities demanding increased political participation. Both of these processes provoked debates over whether or not Germany was becoming a multicultural society. In fact, Germany currently ranks as the world's third-largest migrant-receiving nation. The country has seen migration across its national boundaries since its founding, with an especially dramatic series of shifts since World War II. During the postwar years, West Germany experienced a period of rapid growth, during which immigrant labor was brought in through a series of recruitment programs. Guest workers from primarily southern Europe (especially Turkey, Spain, Italy, Portugal, and Greece) constituted the largest source of immigration, peaking at 2.6 million by 1973, or about 6.7 percent of Germany's total population at the time (Castles and Miller 2003). In the German Democratic Republic, a similar demand for labor prompted the recruitment of "contract workers" from socialist brother nations, such as Poland, Hungary, Vietnam, Mongolia, Mozambique, Angola, and Cuba. Throughout this period, West German authorities tolerated "illegal" migration. During the 1950s and 1960s, "illegal" migration was considered the "third way" to immigrate—the first being via guest worker programs and the second via individual work visas. In this framework, many people entered the country under tourist visas, found work, and were eventually given official residency and work permits—a form of de facto legalization.

German reunification in 1990 set additional population shifts in motion, challenging the boundaries of the newly integrated nation. Increased freedom of movement for citizens of former socialist countries, combined with civil conflict in many regions of the world (particularly the former

Yugoslavia), led to a surge in immigration. Between 1988 and 1993, some 1.4 million people applied for political asylum. The asylum mechanism was also used because other channels (such as labor migration) had become too restrictive or closed entirely. Asylum seekers, under Germany's dispersal system, are relocated to various, often underdeveloped parts of the country. This tactic is intended to spread the expenses of receiving refugees, especially for housing. However, local municipalities began to argue that they could no longer shoulder the costs of supporting the increasing number of refugees. By the early 1990s, a concern with *Überfremdung* (overforeignization) became a dominant discourse in public debates, and a wave of xenophobic violence gripped the nation. Brutal attacks and arson strikes led to the deaths of refugees and their families in several cities, especially in the former East. While revealing significant racist attitudes in some sectors of German society, these events also provoked profound responses on the left, including massive demonstrations and the establishment of antiracist networks.

Despite these mass expressions of protest and solidarity with refugees, the state's response was to severely limit the constitutional right to asylum in 1993. This marked a turning point in migration policy and effectively institutionalized the position of an extremist minority. The new law dictated that refugees entering via a third "safe" country could not apply for asylum in Germany. It simultaneously reworked definitions of safe countries of origin and made appealing a rejected claim more difficult. As a result of the new policy, approval rates for refugees plunged to about 4 percent, and applications for asylum dropped dramatically. The right to asylum had previously held a special place in West German political life and in the consciousness of postwar society, and it is the only nation in the world to have enshrined this right in its constitution. This was part of the postwar reaction to the horrors experienced by minorities under the Nazi regime, along with recognition that German dissenters had been granted asylum in other nations. Throughout the 1980s, asylum was considered an ideological tool to combat socialism, since refugees from communist countries were the primary recipients. This changed, however, with the increase of applications by poor people (often of color) from countries of the South owing to intensifying violence in those nations.

German migration policy must be understood with the European Union agenda in mind. The process of European integration is intimately intertwined with the concept of "illegal migration," and free movement within the EU rests on the creation of what has been called "Fortress Europe," with strong controls at the outer boundaries. The EU has concerned itself with issues of border control, refugees, and migration since the 1980s. The 1985 Schengen Agreement set forth a common policy on the temporary entrance of persons, removing border controls between signatory countries and allowing travel between these nations under a single "Schengen visa." This necessitated increased border patrol and law enforcement cooperation. Since then, a number of conventions and agreements have sought to harmonize immigration policies. Beginning in 1999 with the Amsterdam Treaty, EU member states have adopted common measures against "illegal" immigration, leading to an increasingly restrictive policy environment. In more recent years, EU policy has focused on carrier sanctions and harmonizing asylum policy. Rather than seeking a genuine solution to the "asylum problem," the new restrictive harmonized regulations have merely channeled the problem elsewhere, as evidenced by the 300,000 to 500,000 migrants attempting to cross into Europe via the Strait of Gibraltar every year. The European project also entails continually shifting notions of inclusion and exclusion. With the expansion in 2004 of the European Union to include primary countries of origin for Germany's migrant workers (e.g., Poland), another de facto amnesty was declared for many undocumented migrants. However, concerns regarding the potential influx of low-wage workers led Germany to champion protectionist measures to restrict free movement of labor from the new EU nations until 2009. This reflected anxieties regarding job competition and concerns about added stress on western European social welfare systems. It also underscores how migrants from eastern European nations have historically functioned as a reserve labor force, driven by the fluctuating demands of the German agricultural and service sectors.

With the calculated removal of "legal" entry options, especially asylum opportunities, undocumented or "illegal" migration has increased since the mid-1990s. This period was characterized by increased surveillance and border militarization as a means to combat "illegal" immigration. In less than a decade, the German Border Patrol (Bundesgrenzschutz) dedicated three times more personnel to its eastern borders and today has one of the largest staffs in Europe. These repressive systems of control have in turn led to increases in criminal activity, more risky attempts at crossing, and humanitarian predicaments. Indeed, with increased militarization of the borders in Germany, migrants have been choosing more costly and dangerous ways of entering the country. In addition, as borders have become less porous, migrants have decreased seasonal visits and stayed for longer periods of time, often encouraged to bring family members to live with them. The fatalities associated with border crossing have received comparatively little public attention in Germany. This is likely because the majority of deaths occur at the outer EU border (e.g., between Poland and the Ukraine, or in the Mediterranean) and not directly in the heart of Europe.

In addition, new technology has allowed various governmental agencies to better share information about foreigners living in Germany. It should be noted that showing personal identification is normative for many processes and is generally acceptable to the population. Thus people who lack proper identification quickly become objects of suspicion. In recent years, stricter employer sanctions were put into place. Both of these factors have led to a flourishing industry in fraudulent documents. Additionally, since 1998 the Border Patrol has the authority to stop and check the papers of anyone within the country's interior. This has led, perhaps not surprisingly, to a number of discrimination charges and an increase in ethnic profiling.

An overhauled immigration law, the *Zuwanderungsgesetz*, was put into place on January 1, 2005. The new law confirmed Germany's commitment to restricting immigration, although it made some forms of "legal" immigration easier (for the few who might qualify), simplified some asylum procedures, and included new grounds for asylum (most significantly, gender-specific persecution). However, at the same time, it sought to further penalize so-called economic migrants who have "illegitimately" filed asylum claims and remain in Germany "illegally." In fact, debates over all forms of migration continue to be strongly linked to the topic of asylum. Today a large number of Germany's estimated one million undocumented migrants are either (1) people who would have qualified as refugees before the 1993 change in immigration law severely restricted asylum opportunities, (2) rejected asylum seekers who decide to remain in the country, or (3) people who likely qualify as refugees but, discouraged by the low approval rate, do not bother applying. Thus increasing numbers of individuals from diverse backgrounds and with varying reasons for migrating have become subject to arrest, detention, and deportation.

AMBIVALENCE TOWARD COERCION: MOBILIZATION AGAINST DEPORTATIONS AND STATE RESPONSES

In contemporary Germany, there is an apparent ambivalence toward the state's exercise of power. On one hand, anti-immigrant legislation retains public support, and denunciation practices play an important role in enforcing law. Authorities rely on and promote civilian collaboration to enforce immigration regulations. For example, the Border Patrol elicits citizen reports using posters with a hotline number. Some 70 percent of all border apprehensions, and the vast majority of workplace raids, are the result of following up on such "suspicious persons" reports. While some analysts consider these voluntary reports to be popular "cultural practices" in Germany (Stöbbe 2000), they are clearly encouraged by the authorities. Many workplace raids are the result of disgruntled regular employees or competitors. In addition to such voluntary "snitching," other forms of denunciation are written into law. Article 87 of the Residence Act, which is often referred to as the "Denunciation Law," mandates that persons residing in Germany "illegally" be reported to the appropriate authorities if they seek services at public facilities.[3] Article 96 states that "assisting" such persons is a crime punishable with a fine or imprisonment for up to five years. This is generally referred to as the "Trafficking Law," since various forms of assistance can be pursued as a human trafficking charge. Some civilians have been charged with these crimes, including clergy and landlords. German taxi drivers operating near the Polish border have been fined for (even unknowingly) transporting "illegal" border crossers. As a result, taxi drivers have, in some areas, reportedly stopped accepting "foreign-looking" passengers. Needless to say, these incidences have led to allegations of discrimination, especially potent because this dynamic entails surveillance both by public servants and the private sector.[4] Despite protests by civil and human rights groups against these laws, they remain in effect.

However, at the same time, "the historical legacy of the Holocaust has given rise to a political culture shaped by a particularly profound ambivalence about the state's use of coercion" (Ellermann 2006, 299). While restrictive immigration policies are generally valued, there is occasional large-scale public resistance to their implementation, invoking humanitarian and familial values in the case of particularly "deserving" or well-"integrated" individuals and families. Impending deportations, especially of "deserving" families with children, are often met with grassroots resistance and media attention. For example, the activist group Kein Mensch Ist Illegal (No One Is Illegal) regularly stages demonstrations against deportations. Such protests have been effective in many cases and evoked a moratorium on deportation in the state of Berlin during 2006. Numerous "Transnational Days of Action," in conjunction with activist groups across Europe, have been staged to pressure European Union leaders to close detention camps and end deportation proceedings. In addition, a number of faith-based groups provide support to undocumented migrants and refugees in the church asylum (*Kirchenasyl*) movement.

Church asylum encourages parishes to harbor individuals facing deportation if there is reasonable doubt of their safety upon return. Seeking (legal or physical) asylum in the church has deep historical roots, reaching back to the fifth century, and rests on theological foundations. In Germany the first church asylum campaigns emerged in 1983 in Berlin and Gelsenkirchen; by 1990 there were fifty participating parishes in twenty cities nationwide. The Ecumenical Network for Church Asylum (Ökumenische Bundesarbeitsgemeinschaft Asyl in der Kirche) reported assisting some 2,500 cases between 1983 and 2000, 70 percent of which had favorable legal outcomes for refugees. The role of traditional church asylum has waned over the years, but new initiatives have sprung up, such as a "rotating" church asylum system (*Wanderkirchenasyl*) established in 1998. This allows several parishes to share the burden of harboring groups of deportable persons. These types of activist and faith-based initiatives continue to shape public opinion on immigration policy.

Yet public resistance to deportations has resulted in specific practices that allow the state to exercise its authority nonetheless. Ellermann (2006) discusses three strategies used by German immigration officers in response to public opposition to the use of physical force. First, officials attempt to preempt negative attention by rendering the exercise of coercion as invisible as possible. In the past, deportations were fulfilled using commercial airliners. In some cases, other passengers (tourists and business travelers) protested the use of force against detainees. As a result, immigration officials now hire private charter flights. Escorting tasks are also contracted out to foreign security personnel. This enables the physical act of deportation to be hidden from public view, as well as removing liability from German officials. A second tactic is to contain conflict by insulating immigration officials from the influence of locally elected politicians. In the past, grassroots mobilization often targeted the decision-making ability of local mayors and others at the municipal level. By moving the implementation of, and logistics for, deportations to the *regional* level, elected officials in these municipalities could no longer be pressured. Finally, a third strategy has been to resolve conflicts before they can be made public, primarily by encouraging voluntary return through financial incentives. Because deportation involves physical, sometimes violent removal, it is often the source of considerable contestation between the state and its citizens. By deploying strategies to hide the practice of removal, the state has achieved an even more unrestrained ability to exercise power.

Another result of this tension is the availability of suspensions of deportation, moments of exception to a heavy-handed immigration policy. The remainder of the chapter focuses on three variations of suspensions of deportation.

HARDSHIP CASES AND THE FAILURES OF THE *DULDUNG* PRACTICE

One important feature of "illegality" as a juridical construct is its ability to render certain populations deportable despite existing social networks, personal achievements, and emotional ties to the host society. In Germany, deportability is both defined through and tied to its opposing condition, the Duldung. The Duldung is a temporary suspension of deportation, which can be issued based on Article 60a of the Residence Act. It is a liminal status that can be assigned to undocumented migrants but is not identical to a residency permit. The term "Duldung" literally means "toleration"; in other words, their presence is "tolerated," a rather undignified condition. It marks individuals as neither fully "legal" nor fully "illegal" and does not alter the fact that the person is obligated to leave the country. This status is most typically issued to asylum seekers whose claims have been denied but who cannot be returned to their respective countries of origin, for example, because of political strife. Thus the Duldung is the badge of deportability. Since the 1993 change in the asylum law, increasing numbers of individuals have held the status of Duldung, and some have found themselves in this in-between situation for over a decade. The Duldung has generally been issued to groups of individuals with specific characteristics, such as migrants who are considered well integrated or traumatized refugees. Most long-term holders of the Duldung come from Afghanistan and the nations of the former Yugoslavia.

Individuals with a Duldung are registered with the government, distinguishing them from other deportable populations, such as undocumented labor migrants. This makes them, to rephrase Sassen's language, "recognized" yet (not fully) "authorized." In fact, they inhabit a state of hypervisibility, since they must continually notify officials of their location and activities. In contrast to all other EU countries, asylum seekers with a Duldung in Germany must remain in the district to which they are assigned under the dispersal system (this is called the *Residenzpflicht*). Critics charge that this is an unjust practice, since it means they cannot participate in social or cultural events, visit friends, or seek more competent legal counsel elsewhere than may be available where they happen to live. This requirement to remain in a specified area is regularly breached, creating opportunities for authorities to threaten individuals. The Duldung status also restricts the holder's rights in other ways; for example, only emergency medical care is covered, and employment is effectively prohibited.[5] Individuals are expected to sustain themselves through meager allowances provided by the state (allowances that are set at a lower rate than regular welfare benefits), and the state prosecutes "illegal" employment as a criminal activity.

In the past, the Duldung holder was required to reappear at the Immigration Office (Ausländerbehörde) at regular intervals, at which time this status was reevaluated and possibly extended (e.g., for three months). Notably, members of the same family are often approved for different lengths of time. This practice of successive suspensions of deportation was supposed to be eliminated with the new immigration law implemented in January 2005. In principle, people who have held the Duldung status for six months, and certainly by eighteen months, are eligible to receive a residency permit. Instead, in the two years after the law went into effect, thousands of individuals continued to hold temporary suspensions of deportation that had been extended more than eighteen months—clear evidence that the government has not seriously followed through with the implementation of the promised regularization. In November 2006 the state interior ministers decided on a new policy for the 190,000 long-term holders of the Duldung who have lived in Germany at least eight years (six if they have school-age children). According to this policy, only individuals who have established employment are eligible to receive a permanent residency permit. Critics have charged that these conditions are unfair, since employment was severely restricted for holders of the Duldung.

MUTTERSCHUTZ: MATERNITY PROTECTION PERIOD

Another means by which deportation can be suspended is through the circumstances created by pregnancy, based on the idea that travel presents special risks. Under the 1968 Maternity Protection Act, all women in Germany are protected from risks and eligible for maternity leave six weeks before and eight weeks after the birth of a child.[6] This delineated time is called the Mutterschutz. During this period, women and their newborns are not legally deportable. To formally take advantage of the Mutterschutz, a pregnant woman must register at the local courthouse and then apply for a Duldung, which also authorizes access to prenatal care and covers delivery. If the woman does not register, her child is born into "illegality," and obtaining a birth certificate becomes difficult. Even without the registration and formal Duldung, pregnant women are entitled to the protection period, though the formal paperwork makes compensation for costs related to prenatal care and delivery possible. For this reason, many hospitals and organizations working with migrants encourage women to complete this step and seek this semilegal status.

However, by making themselves known to officials, women draw attention to themselves and face immediate deportation once the protection period is over. This fear is reinforced by instances where the Mutterschutz was not honored by immigration authorities. From the mother's perspective, the benefits of applying for a Duldung are limited and short-term, while the cost is total visibility (and with it, greater susceptibility to deportation). Staying hidden provides considerably greater freedom of movement and more long-term protection. This, combined with a generalized distrust of German authorities, led many women to refuse to complete this process. Let me provide an example:

> Fayola, a young woman from Nigeria, came to the migrant clinic where I conducted fieldwork. Eight months pregnant, she had received no prior prenatal care. She had heard that the clinic was able to help undocumented women arrange a delivery spot at a local Catholic hospital, where she would not have to fear drawing the attention of the authorities or raise the suspicions of overzealous nurses wanting to call the police. She was accompanied by the father of the child and their first son, who was three years old.
>
> When the doctor suggested applying for the Duldung in order to cover the costs of hospital delivery, the couple reacted strongly. "No, no, no, we don't want to do that," the father said. "You don't know how they treat us Africans. Yes, it says one thing in the law, but there is a different law in reality. The law I see is different. There are two laws, the official law and then the law when you go to that Office." Fayola then related a story circulating among her friends. "I have heard about a woman who was arrested and put into *Haft* (detainment) when she was nine months pregnant. It was very dirty in there, they did not care that she was pregnant, and she could not see the doctor. When she was giving birth, right then they put her onto a plane to get her out!" (field notes, Berlin, July 2006)

Nongovernmental organization and hospital staff told similar tales of bureaucratic injustice. For example, some complained that women were not given the proper paperwork when they went to the Immigration Office.

One hospital social worker told me about a woman she sent to apply for the Duldung, who returned the next morning screaming mad because of the ill treatment she received there, including a condescending interview and fingerprinting. After this, the social worker said she was more sympathetic toward patients' unwillingness. All these experiences coalesce in preventing applications for the Duldung, which would provide temporary legalization and access to resources. Women's expectations of state bureaucracy were based on a combination of rumors and prior experience and were confirmed by doctors and hospital staff with whom I spoke. Rather than engage with the state, which they perceived as discriminatory and often brutal, they preferred to pay money they could ill afford for private-pay deliveries and, later, lawyers' fees to appeal deportation proceedings. This reinforces the erasure of "legal" personhood that many undocumented persons experience, which has also been characterized as a process of "civil death" (Gibney 2000).

SUSPENSIONS OF DEPORTATION DUE TO ILLNESS

Finally, deportation may be suspended in the case of illness, through the application for either a Duldung or temporary residency permit for humanitarian reasons. Ironically, as asylum opportunities for victims of political violence were being restricted all across Europe during the 1990s, new criteria based on humanitarian principles have opened doors for migrants with severe illnesses. In this way, "the suffering body" became the primary resource and bargaining chip for undocumented migrants seeking legalization (see, e.g., Fassin 2005; Ticktin 2002, 2006). Humanitarian residency permits have been issued to the very (physically or mentally) ill, victims of torture, unaccompanied minors, women facing gender-specific persecution, elderly people without ties to their homeland, those who care for a relative with special needs, and stateless persons. Applying for asylum for humanitarian purposes is a lengthy and complicated procedure, requiring medical opinions, specialized lawyers, and research on services available in the home country. These cases typically go to a Hardship Committee for review. These committees were established in response to demands made by charitable organizations, churches, and refugee associations to recommend deserving individuals and families for residency permits on humanitarian bases. Cases are reviewed by Hardship Committees in the state of residency, which then make recommendations to the Ministry of the Interior, which can choose to provide the individual or family with a residency permit. However, there is no obligation for individual states within Germany to convene such committees, so that some (e.g., Bavaria) do not have one. Public opinion generally favors appeals on behalf of these hardship cases, perhaps because they are rare.

As noted, a temporary suspension of deportation can also be granted during illness. Arguing for a Duldung because of an illness involves one of two approaches. First, it can be assigned to an extremely sick person who is unable to travel, which applies only as long as the illness persists (article 60a, section 2, of the AufenthG). Importantly, the "risk" is associated with the travel itself—for example, on an aircraft—not with the conditions faced once the patient lands. A second possibility is the delay of deportation for reasons of "mortal danger" (article 60, section 7, of the AufenthG). This is employed when the patient is technically able to travel, but the illness would not be treatable in his or her home country (including if it is too expensive).

One man was caught in such an indeterminate state for years because of his illness. Grigor had lived and worked in Germany for almost thirty years as an undocumented migrant before he became seriously ill. In 2001 he sought out the aid of a migrant organization, which sent him to a specialist based on his symptoms. There he was diagnosed with cancer. The organization helped finance his treatment—surgery and chemotherapy—even though the oncologist had pronounced it to be terminal, with a life expectancy of less than a year. Because of this grim prognosis, the organization encouraged Grigor to notify the Immigration Office of his presence and apply for a Duldung. They hoped this would allow him to relax and help his chances of receiving some palliative care as the end drew near. But Grigor lived. Every few months for five years, he went in for a battery of tests to confirm the cancer was still in remission. And every few months, he went to the Immigration Office to renew his Duldung. He described the latter process to me as "living like a rat, or a pig, in a cage. Like a pig that goes before the butcher, standing there with a knife to decide your fate." As he spoke, he made a motion as if whetting a knife. Eventually his luck ran out. No, the cancer did not return, but because of his (good) health, the Duldung was no longer approved, and he was notified of his deportation date. Although cancer treatments are possible in his home country of Macedonia, the medications he was taking, along with the method of delivery (via implant), were virtually unheard of. Moreover, after thirty years, Grigor had few ties to his home country, and no exact plans for housing or income. His doctors urged him to take his case to

Berlin's Hardship Committee to ask for a residency permit on humanitarian grounds. Grigor refused to take his case to them, arguing that he was sick of living "like a pig" and wanted to return home to die.

> "What will you do when you are returned to Macedonia?" I asked him, wondering about his plans for medical care.
>   "What will I do?" he smiled, "I will dance!"
>   "Dance?" I repeated, puzzled by his response.
>   "Yes, I will dance, dance with all the ladies, I will dance and wait for the end. What else can I do?"

Since the implementation of the new immigration law in 2005, the practice of issuing the Duldung sequentially was supposed to be phased out and replaced with a (temporary) residence permit for humanitarian reasons (Article 23a of the AufenthG). It should be noted that Grigor's Duldung was still being renewed well over a year and a half after the new law was in place. Officials should have provided him with the residency permit, since the successive issuance of his Duldung lasted well over eighteen months. Like so many others, for years he had been held in a legal limbo that had excluded both a permanent residency permit and deportation. He finally chose expulsion—and ultimately, perhaps, a death sentence—over the never-ending indeterminate state of suspension and indignity.

REFLECTIONS ON SUSPENSIONS OF DEPORTATION

The criteria for "deservingness" vary depending on particular ideas about who is included in the body politic. The German case I have presented here has its own unique characteristics, anchored in historically produced notions of moral identity. Importantly, there has been a shift in ideas of deservingness in recent years, moving away from a response to political oppression and increasingly toward policies of compassion in the face of suffering. Today deservingness is defined chiefly by humanitarian considerations (such as illness or pregnancy), and the state is compelled by notions of compassion and justice. This is particularly evident when tracing the trajectory of asylum law as the moral compass of the state: once the most liberal in the world, it became overwhelmed and then abruptly and severely restricted. Asylum policy has become the machinery for the generation of attenuated gradations of "illegality" under conditions of intense visibility and thus of protracted deportability through the various forms of temporary suspensions of deportation discussed here.

Susan Coutin (2003b) has examined suspension of deportation hearings in the United States, noting that favorable outcomes were linked to how well migrants lived up to constructions of the ideal citizen. Deservingness in the United States, she notes, was measured by factors such as length of residency, lack of a criminal record, church membership, tax payments, family ties, and language skills. In Germany, however, the idea of "social citizens"—that is, individuals who for all intents and purposes participate in a community through long-term residence, employment, and raising family—does not resonate powerfully. For example, it is impossible to argue that one has worked and paid taxes, since those with a Duldung face severe work restrictions, and crackdowns on "illegal" employment have been prominent in the media. Civic participation is also rewarded less. Nonetheless the ability to "integrate properly" is an important measure of deservingness. Length of residence in the country is frequently mentioned as an important criterion for suspending deportation, and advocates often emphasize the percentage of those who have lived in Germany for more than five, even ten years with a Duldung. The 2006 policy that allows the 190,000 long-term holders of the Duldung to apply for a permanent residency permit (provided they can sustain themselves financially) also requires individuals to demonstrate a "desire to integrate," for example, by proving their German-language ability. This overlaps to some degree with what Coutin describes as demands for ostensible evidence of migrant "acculturation" into "mainstream" U.S. society, as measured by language facility, celebrating mainstream holidays, enjoying "typical" leisure activities, and education in the country's schools (2003b). She notes that in this framework, gendered, racialized, class-based, and heteronormative models of the proto-citizen prevail.

In Germany, strict notions of national belonging mean that the path to citizenship is arduous. Until very recently the ethnonational model has dominated (i.e., based on an exclusive ideology of ethnic descent rather than residency). This is similar to the situation in Israel, as Sarah Willen (2006) notes, where rigid ethnonational conceptions of belonging mean that criteria such as compliance with the law or affective ties rarely influence ideas of deservingness to citizenship. Similar to the German context, there are specific notions of the national body politic and migrant incorporation. Even today it would be unheard of to talk about a migrant's "Germanness" in the way Coutin describes various measures of putative

"Americanness." Quite the contrary: a unique vocabulary has emerged in Germany to emphasize the distinction between naturalized citizens, other ("legally" residing) foreigners, and genuine incorporation to the national body. Thus permanent residents and even foreign-born, naturalized German citizens are referred to as *ausländische Mitbürger* (foreign co-citizens), *Menschen mit Migrationshintergrund* (persons of migrant background), or *Deutsche ausländischer Herkunft* (Germans of foreign descent). While persons with a Duldung may in fact be "unauthorized yet recognized" (Sassen 2002), it would be optimistic to call it a form of incipient membership, as this remains out of reach even for the most "legal" and most welcome of migrants. As noted earlier, the Duldung status restricts individuals more markedly than it provides them with rights, so that truly "illegal" (yet unrecognized) individuals are actually able to move about more freely. Thus it is never a matter of how "German" migrants have become, but only how well they have been effectively subjected to a German regime of "legality," surveillance, and sustained deportability.

Finally, suspensions of deportation—as moments of exception in an otherwise restrictive migration regime—highlight the ambivalences and contradictions inherent in the exercise of state power. Denunciation practices are encouraged and often lead to deportation. At the same time, anti-deportation movements by citizens challenge the state's ability to exercise authority through physical removal. By developing practices that render the use of force invisible during deportations, the state is allowed even more unrestrained power. Exceptions are also built into the system, not by accident, to relieve some of the tensions between law enforcement and humanitarian concerns. Here I have discussed some instances where deportation is suspended, including in times of pregnancy, illness, and other forms of hardship. While this appears to invoke a more participatory model (with input from Hardship Committees, NGOs, and citizens), the state is not obligated to follow these recommendations. Similarly there has been no straightforward implementation of current laws ostensibly providing residency permits for all long-term holders of the Duldung. Despite short-term exceptions that provide a veneer of equity and justice in extremely small allocations, these practices ultimately serve the long-term interests of restrictive policy. As this case illustrates, state policies and their implementation are sites of contestation, where positions of moral obligation are squared with notions of suitability for citizenship. Suspensions of deportation emerge as one facet of deportability as a disciplinary practice, providing a mechanism for differentiating between various categories of migrants.

NOTES

The author is grateful to Karin Friederic and Namino Glantz for insightful comments during the preparation of this chapter.

1. I collected ethnographic data in Berlin from 2004 to 2006 as part of a dissertation study on medical aid for undocumented migrants.

2. Based on the updated Immigration Act, implemented in January 2005, this refers to a temporary residence permit for humanitarian purposes and not a (permanent) "settlement permit."

3. The Aufenthaltsgesetz (Residence Act) is one of the components of the 2005 Immigration Act. Hereafter cited in the text as the AufenthG.

4. See, for example, Coutin's discussions on capillary forms of power in the U.S. migration regime (2000).

5. After one year with a Duldung, individuals may apply for a work permit. However, they may apply for jobs only if it does not "negatively affect" the job market, and cannot be hired if a German or "legally" residing foreigner has applied for the same position. While a new law (2006) allows long-term holders of the Duldung to apply for a residency permit, they must first provide proof of employment—a Catch-22 that is often difficult to resolve.

6. This is the law enacted by the Federal Republic of Germany (West Germany, at the time), which remained in effect after reunification. The German Democratic Republic had passed various laws guaranteeing women's rights since 1950; however, these are not relevant to the undocumented women discussed here.

SARAH S. WILLEN

—ᘟᘡ—

CHAPTER 9

Citizens, "Real" Others, and "Other" Others

The Biopolitics of Otherness and the Deportation of

Unauthorized Migrant Workers from Tel Aviv, Israel

Seventeen days he was in prison, seventeen long days. When he was arrested, the police officer hit him in the neck. I have no idea why. This is how criminals are treated. In our country it's horrible to be a criminal. Criminals murder, things like this. Is he a criminal? How is he a criminal? He just doesn't have a visa.—Marina, "illegal" migrant from the Philippines, on the arrest of her common-law husband, Raymond

In the past, everyone said if they try to catch you, make an attempt to run and they will not follow you. Now, you can run how many miles and they will follow you. If you go crawl in a hole they will wait for ten hours for you to come out. I can't continue like this forever. I can't continue like this forever. I can't continue like this forever. I can't continue like this forever. I can't continue like this forever.—Kofi, "illegal" migrant from Ghana and father, with his Nigerian wife, of two Israeli-born sons

I'm not for the [suicide] bombings. I think they're wrong. But if this is what the Israelis do in the center, where everyone can see, just think of what they must be doing to the Palestinians in the bush, where no one can see what's happening.—Supi, "illegal" migrant from Ghana, whose daughter attends a public elementary school in Tel Aviv

In 2002 the Israeli government responded to an escalation in unemployment by initiating a mass deportation campaign targeting the estimated one hundred thousand unauthorized transnational migrant workers who had joined the country's labor force, along with a roughly equal number of authorized migrants, over the course of the preceding decade. At considerable state expense, a new Immigration Authority and Immigration Police force were quickly created, four hundred new police officers were hired, and three new detention centers were established. In the months and years that followed this intensification of governmental power, unauthorized migrants' everyday lives in Israel—and, moreover the condition of migrant "illegality" itself[1]—were radically reconfigured (Willen 2006, 2007d). Before the campaign, migrant workers figured in Israeli public and government discourse as benign if excluded others and, as in many other host-society settings, were relegated to the margins of the Israeli social body and body politic. Indeed, it was these forms of social and political exclusion that facilitated transnational migrant workers' inclusion as a subordinated class of workers within the Israeli labor market in the first place. As long as they made no efforts to gain formal membership or even to organize and demand rights, they were regarded as a politically palatable alternative to the Palestinian workers who had been driven out of the Israeli labor market in the wake of the first intifada, or Palestinian popular uprising, in the late 1980s. With the initiation of the deportation campaign, however, migrant workers in general—and unauthorized workers in particular—were thrust into the center of public and political discourse. The campaign heralded a dramatic shift in governmental policy and practice from the pre-2002 stance of willful ignorance of migrants' living and working conditions in Israel to a much harsher stance of aggressive criminalization and systematic expulsion. As a result of these concerted and costly government efforts, more than fifty thousand unauthorized migrant workers from West Africa, South America, eastern Europe, the former Soviet Union, and Southeast Asia were arrested, detained, and deported between 2002 and 2005.[2] In the same period, tens of thousands of others were "encouraged"—in other words, regularly and systematically intimidated—into leaving "voluntarily." While the media blitz and accompanying political discourse framed the campaign primarily as a response to the country's skyrocketing unemployment, its parallel and concomitant objective—to patrol and regulate the boundaries of the Jewish-Israeli body politic—was barely concealed beneath the surface.

I contend that we cannot make sense of the Israeli government's swift conversion to an aggressive deportation agenda without situating it within the broader biopolitical framework via which otherness is articulated and given expression in Israel. My argument hinges on two claims, one historical, the other theoretical. First, I argue that to make sense of Israel's recent mass deportation campaign, it is necessary to consider how the Israeli state imagines and treats not only this new population of foreign others but also another group of noncitizens who are typically constructed within the Israeli public imagination as its indigenous, "real others": Palestinians. Indeed, even this rough dichotomy is imprecise, for Palestinians are themselves divided among two groups who are cast into substantially different positions within the local biopolitical framework: first, Israel's minority population of Palestinian citizens—often described by the Israeli state as the "Arabs of Israel" and by Palestinians as " '48 Palestinians" or "Palestinians on the inside"—and second, noncitizen Palestinians in the Occupied Territories of the West Bank and Gaza.[3]

More specifically, I contend that the transformation of unauthorized transnational migrant workers into a deportable population dovetails with a broader shift that has taken place in Israeli state policy and practice since the Oslo "peace process" of the mid-1990s. For the most part, Israel's interest in negotiations has stemmed not from moral compunction regarding the occupation of Palestinian people and territories but from a widespread conclusion that the country's continued existence as a "Jewish state"—implicitly conceived as a state with a Jewish voting majority—would require separation between the Israeli and Palestinian populations.[4] In the mid-1990s, the expulsion of Palestinian workers from the Israeli labor market emerged as one strategic element of this geopolitical strategy, and the recruitment of transnational migrant workers to replace them constituted another. In that decade, however, the number of "legal" migrant workers increased exponentially; many of them remained in Israel and became illegalized; a separate population of unauthorized migrants arrived at more or less the same time; and Israeli unemployment rates rose dramatically (Willen 2007c). By 2002, therefore, these new groups of noncitizens—collectively described in Israeli public discourse as "foreign workers"—were no longer construed as part of the solution to Israel's economic and demographic woes; instead they were redefined as part of the problem. The deportation campaign thus was not the result of a grassroots xenophobic upsurge; rather, it represents a single governmental move within a much more complex, ongoing strategic game of biopolitical regulation and statecraft. As I will elaborate shortly, the interconnections between Israel's treatment of these groups of "real" and "other" others—one indigenous, the other foreign; one constitutive, the other disposable and hence deportable—can best be unpacked by considering two dominant themes shaping contemporary patterns of state governance in Israel and elsewhere: first, the theme of security, which takes on a specific meaning and significance in the ethnographic context of Israel-Palestine; and second, the theme of biopolitics, including, in particular, the "biopolitics of Otherness" (cf. Fassin 2001).[5]

According to the political theorist Giorgio Agamben, all politics in the modern era are biopolitics, and "one of the essential characteristics of modern biopolitics . . . is its constant need to redefine the threshold in life that distinguishes and separates what is inside from what is outside" (1995/1998, 131). This ongoing negotiation results in the exclusion of certain groups and individuals who are abandoned by the sovereign to the abject, depoliticized, vulnerable status of "bare life," or *zoë*, in contrast with citizens' "politicized life," or *bios*. For Agamben, bare life is symbolized by the figure of *homo sacer*, a concept from ancient Roman law that originally referred to an individual who could be killed with impunity and whose death held no sacrificial value. Tapping into the term's etymological origins, Agamben takes "sacred" to mean both holy and accursed, or ritually set apart "both from the sphere of the profane and from that of the religious" (82). In a juridico-political sense, homo sacer represents the paradoxical space in which "sovereign violence opens a zone of indistinction between law and nature, outside and inside, violence and law" (64).

Popular and compelling as Agamben's formulation has become, it is not without problems. Indeed, my second, theoretical goal here is to offer a critique of the manner in which Agamben's concept of homo sacer has come to be applied in analyzing locally specific biopolitical regimes. An example is illustrative. In an important article analyzing the labor migrant system in Israel, Adriana Kemp (2004) remarks—briefly, in passing—that transnational migrants in Israel, by virtue of their regulation, racialization, and construction as unproblematically deportable, constitute the "ultimate *homo sacer* of the Israeli state and society" (271). While appreciative of Kemp's careful and nuanced analysis—which, indeed, is consistent with my own ethnographic findings (as elaborated later in the chapter; see also Willen 2007a, 2007b)—I aim to complicate her comment, and others like it, by eschewing its implicit logic of superlative suffering in favor of an ethnographically grounded analysis of how different patterns of social and political otherness and strategic exclusion, and different logics of removal, are intertwined.[6]

While my critique focuses on applications of Agamben (rather than on his theory itself), it is noteworthy that the danger of oversimplification is, in a certain sense, embedded within the very logic of his concept of homo sacer. As Didier Fassin has pointed out, Agamben's analysis is "a philosophical thesis and not a historical narrative," and his theorizations "cannot be discussed as a desocialized space or in an ahistorical time" (Fassin 2005, 377). Beyond Agamben's compelling theory, there thus lies a powerful impetus for in-depth, extended ethnography of local configurations of biopolitics. Such investigations can help unpack the ideological, sociocultural, and bureaucratic foundations of particular biopolitical frameworks. When conducted with sensitivity to historical process, ethnography can also open windows on to the evolution of biopolitical regimes over time (see Walters 2002a). So, too, can ethnography help elucidate the impact of such regimes within the everyday realms of social interaction, political life, and, as I have argued elsewhere, embodied, lived experience (Willen 2007b, 2007c). Overall, then, ethnographic approaches can help us sort through the growing confusion generated by the freewheeling application of Agamben's concept of homo sacer to an increasingly long list of groups whose particular relation to the states they inhabit, or whose peripheries they inhabit, varies widely.

Overall I contend that while there are substantial differences in how these groups are imagined and treated by the Israeli state, the existence of a sharp distinction between who does and does not, can and cannot, belong to the Israeli nation—a sense of Jewish Israelis as authentic citizens and Palestinians, whether citizens or subjects of military occupation, as others—has influenced the state's discursive and pragmatic responses to the presence of a heterogeneous new population of noncitizen residents. I aim to show that a new category—the category of the foreign worker—initially existed in an ambiguous discursive space within the Israeli biopolitical framework, which the state, via its newly created Immigration Authority, actively sought to reshape and redefine at a particular historical moment to advance its objective of expelling some of these new foreign, disposable others en masse with public support.

In other words, in throwing its weight behind a mass deportation campaign after nearly a decade of turning a blind eye to transnational migrant workers' growing presence, the Israeli state made its first major move toward filling the protean discursive category of foreign workers with politicized content. In so doing, the Immigration Authority has drawn, albeit implicitly, on discursive tropes and governmental practices that were already being deployed by the state in relation to Palestinian citizens and Palestinians in the Occupied Territories. Like Palestinians before them, transnational migrant workers in Israel have thus come to both represent and inhabit a discursively labile "zone of indistinction" in which sovereign power perpetuates itself by distinguishing between forms of "detritus humanity" (i.e., Palestinians and unauthorized migrant workers) and "interiorized humanity" (i.e., ratified Jewish-Israeli citizens) (Rajaram and Grundy-Warr 2004; interpreting Agamben 1995/1998).

Put differently, after 2000, the Israeli state began to paint a portrait of transnational migrants that hinged on the impossibility of their inclusion within the Israeli national body,[7] thereby implying their closer proximity to Palestinians (including both citizens and noncitizens)—who are popularly and politically constructed as the nation's "real others"—than to its fully ratified Jewish citizens. Against this ideological backdrop, I thus examine a transitional moment in which a new kind of otherness was given shape, definition, locally specific meaning, and powerful governmental form in keeping with an evolving biopolitical agenda. This agenda includes an unacknowledged element of racialization; in effect, Jewishness is racialized in Israel to the benefit of citizens with Jewish heritage and to the detriment of all other citizens and residents.

Before proceeding, it is important to state clearly what this chapter does and does not aim to achieve. First, I am not proposing a direct analogy between Israel's systematic and institutionalized discrimination against its Palestinian citizens and its recent treatment of the more recently arrived multinational population of transnational migrant workers. Nor do I mean to suggest a direct analogy between the protracted and often brutal occupation of Palestinian people and lands, on the one hand, and the recent campaign to criminalize and expel transnational economic migrants from Israel proper, on the other. My more modest aim is to explore one moment in the evolution of a dynamic, multidimensional biopolitical framework within which different groups are relegated to different forms of status that evoke, but do not uniformly recapitulate, Agamben's notion of homo sacer. In other words, my goal is to identify points of resonance among Israel's treatment of these different groups to shed light on how ideology, discourse, and power converge in the state project of defining and monitoring the boundaries of the national body and body politic and, by the same token, of protecting the security of the Israeli state and society, broadly construed.

My analysis draws on several sources of data. Discussion of Israel's treatment of Palestinian citizens and Palestinian residents of the Occupied Territories relies on research by social scientists (especially Bornstein 2002; Kanaaneh 2002; Rabinowitz 1997; Rabinowitz and Abu-Baker 2005; Torstrick 2000), as well as reports and analyses published by Israeli and international human rights organizations and the Israeli media. Discussion of unauthorized migrant workers draws on twenty-seven nonconsecutive months of ethnographic fieldwork conducted between 2000 and 2007 within the flourishing, institutionally well-developed Nigerian,

Ghanaian, and Filipino communities that emerged in South Tel Aviv in the late 1990s and almost completely disappeared in the wake of the mass deportation campaign.

The chapter's first section provides a brief overview of recent patterns of non-Jewish, non-Arab transnational labor migration to Israel and their relationship to the expulsion of Palestinian workers from the Israeli labor market after the first intifada in the late 1980s. The second section shifts from these historical considerations to a discussion of Israel's perpetual focus on, and anxiety about, matters of security, multiply defined, which find ideological and pragmatic expression in its local biopolitics of otherness. I then examine how Israeli concerns about security and techniques of governmentality are translated into regulatory practices that shape and constrain the lives not only of Israel's constitutive Palestinian others but also of its new, diverse population of disposable foreign others. Put differently, the final sections consider how the Israeli state's ways of interpellating and treating Palestinians, both in Israel and in the Occupied Territories, have provided elements of an unwritten governmental template for the deportation campaign that targets unauthorized migrant workers but also, as we will see, catches other non-Jewish, non-Palestinian residents in its dragnet. Drawing on the ethnographic research I conducted in South Tel Aviv both before and during the deportation campaign, I aim to illustrate how elements of this implicit ideological and pragmatic template have imprinted themselves on the lives of individual migrants and migrant communities. The quotations from Marina, Kofi, and Supi at the beginning of the chapter anticipate these ethnographic findings.

TRANSNATIONAL MIGRATION TO ISRAEL

In discussing Israel's recent move to systematically expel transnational migrant workers, it is crucial to recognize that their initial arrival in the country was directly related to the expulsion of Palestinian workers from the Israeli labor market, and from Israeli space, after the first intifada.[8] Widespread recruitment of transnational workers on an authorized ("legal") basis began in the early 1990s, when key sectors of Israeli industry, most notably agriculture and construction, experienced severe labor shortages after Israel imposed sustained, hermetic closures on the West Bank and the Gaza Strip (Bartram 1998). Despite initial government resistance, the state-authorized recruitment of transnational laborers quickly became a politically desirable solution to the needs of Israeli industry.

Reasons for this rapid change of heart stemmed from the ample supply of recruitable overseas workers, their presumed docility (in contrast to Israeli workers, but comparable to Palestinians), and their putative disinterest in the simmering Palestinian-Israeli conflict. Furthermore, some government officials explicitly described the recruitment of migrant workers as an expedient form of collective punishment against Palestinians (Raijman and Kemp 2007). Like the Palestinian workers they were recruited to replace, transnational migrant workers were (and are) unequivocally undesirable as potential citizens, yet highly desirable for their labor power, docility, and exploitability. It is important to note that from the state's perspective, the importation of foreign labor was intended and promoted as a temporary solution to a temporary problem, not as a permanent solution to the needs of the labor market (Kemp 2004; Rosenhek 1999, 2000).[9] Nonetheless, a high proportion of authorized workers remained in the country and, through various pathways, became illegalized.

In addition to the recruited, "legal" workers who were imported to replace Palestinians, growing streams of unauthorized migrants also began arriving in Israel at approximately the same time via the "tourist loophole" in the country's otherwise rigid migration regime (Willen 2003)—in other words, as tourists or Christian religious pilgrims—and finding employment in the informal labor market, primarily as cleaners of homes and offices or as menial workers in other labor sectors in metropolitan Tel Aviv. Although both authorized and unauthorized transnational migrant workers began arriving in Israel en masse only in the early 1990s, by 2002 they numbered approximately 240,000 and constituted 11 percent of the labor force, ranking Israel among the industrialized countries most heavily dependent on migrant labor (Kemp 2004).[10]

Like other countries in other world regions, Israel has been eager to employ both legally recruited transnational migrant workers and their unauthorized counterparts in multiple labor sectors but has been conspicuously uninterested in drawing any of these migrant groups into the social body or the body politic. In addition to typical anxieties about growing influxes of Third World migrants, which have become especially prominent in Europe and North America of late, Israel's reluctance is further intensified by its ethnonationally defined "migration regime" (Freeman 1992; Rosenhek 2000),[11] which is governed by a basic principle of "explicit and formal demarcation between Jews and non-Jews" (Rosenhek 2000, 53). Briefly, formal, ratified migration to Israel is governed by the Law of Return, according to which citizenship is allocated on the basis of (1) proven Jewish descent, (2) close familial relationship to someone Jewish, or (3) conversion to the Jewish religion via state-approved channels. Given the preeminence of Jewishness as a criterion for citizenship eligibility, it is virtually impossible for non-Jews or their Israeli-born offspring to become Israeli citizens.[12] In this manner, Jewishness—which was racialized in nineteenth- and twentieth-century Europe in discriminatory ways to Jews' great detriment—has in a certain sense been reracialized by the Israeli state in the inverse, this time as a means of privileging Jewishness, linking it with full citizenship and membership and ascribing lesser forms of social and political status (or denying recognition and status altogether) to all other citizens and residents.

Despite the rigidity of Israel's exclusionary migration regime, it is important to note that successive Israeli governments refrained from developing consistent or long-term policies regarding either authorized or unauthorized labor migrants for nearly a decade. Because migrant workers were desirable for their labor power but undesirable on biopolitical grounds, the state effectively abandoned them in a manner that gave employment contractors and individual employers considerable, and in some cases complete, control over migrants' living and working conditions. One key feature of this pattern of government neglect has been a considerable degree of administrative and bureaucratic heterogeneity both among the policies of different government agencies and between agencies at the national and municipal levels of authority (Alexander 2007; Filc and Davidovitch 2005; Kemp and Raijman 2000, 2004; Rosenhek 1999). A second result was the emergence of large, institutionally developed (mostly unauthorized) migrant communities in the southern neighborhoods of Tel Aviv in the latter half of the 1990s, including the West African and Filipino communities in which I conducted field research (Kemp et al. 2000; Sabar 2007; Willen 2003).

After nearly a decade of overlooking the country's growing migrant communities, the atmosphere changed dramatically in mid-2002, when former prime minister Ariel Sharon initiated the mass deportation campaign that was framed as a solution to skyrocketing unemployment and related economic woes. At that point, politicians and policymakers acknowledged that simply assuming transnational migrants' presence was temporary would not make it so. In the context of the campaign, government officials began paying attention to the increasing numbers of unauthorized worker-residents and reframing their growing numbers and increasing rootedness as a burgeoning threat to the state and, more specifically, as a major economic and social "problem" in need of a concerted, systematic solution. In place of previous governments' occasional, haphazard efforts, the Sharon administration thus affirmed the gravity of the problem and developed a coordinated response involving several government ministries, the creation of a new government office (the country's first Immigration Authority), and, most significantly, massive investment of state funds. As noted earlier, this resource- and personnel-intensive campaign, which reached its peak in 2003 and 2004, proved highly successful in achieving its aims. Even as tens of thousands of "formerly legal" and "illegal" workers were rounded up and deported, however, thousands more "legal" workers have continued to be recruited and integrated into the labor force, primarily in the construction and agricultural sectors.[13]

An overview of the campaign's central techniques is helpful in illustrating, first, the scope and impact of the supporting regime of governmentality and, second, the multiple levels—discursive, psychological, and material—on which it operates. These techniques include (1) "biosocial profiling" (Shamir 2005); (2) a propaganda campaign designed to mobilize public support and cooperation by disseminating powerful anti-immigrant messages; (3) an information hotline that some citizens have used to "snitch" on unauthorized migrants; (4) police informers, including migrants as well as Israelis; (5) systematic arrest and deportation of known community leaders; (6) a "voluntary departure" campaign that provided subsidized plane tickets to departing migrant families; (7) police surveillance of public and private areas; (8) the marking of apartment doors in preparation for late-night arrests; (9) arrests and deportations, some of which involve humiliation and psychological violence; (10) use of physical violence and brutality in the course of arrest; and (11) a generalized failure to investigate or punish police brutality (for more on these techniques and their impact on migrants' lived experience, see Willen 2007b).

ON MEMBERSHIP AND EXCLUSION: ETHNONATIONAL IDEOLOGY, FLEXIBLE DEMOGRAPHY, AND THE MULTIPLE MEANINGS OF "SECURITY"

The mass deportation campaign thus elaborated on an existing, deeply entrenched ideology of membership and exclusion that shapes multiple forms of everyday interaction within Israeli social and political space. This ideology relies on a naturalized, common-sense distinction between "brothers and sisters" (Jews, Israelis) and "others" (non-Jews, non-Israelis) (Rapoport and Lomsky-Feder 2001). This unwritten system for differentiating between insiders and outsiders is reproduced and reinforced not only through messages disseminated by the state and other mainstream social institutions (Rabinowitz 1997; Rabinowitz and Abu-Baker 2005; Reiss 1991; Rouhana 1997; Torstrick 2000) but also by the perpetual public discussion surrounding issues of demography (Kahn 2000; Kanaaneh 2002; Willen 2005)[14] and by the unwritten and implicit racialized hierarchy into which Israeli citizens are socialized over the course of a lifetime (Bar-Tal and Teichman 2005).

It is important to point out that Palestinian citizens, Palestinians in the Occupied Territories, and migrant workers occupy substantially different places within this implicit hierarchy. As a result of the enduring and evolving conflict, Palestinians are consistently portrayed both individually and collectively, and in subtle and not-so-subtle ways, as enemy others (Bornstein 2002; Kanaaneh 2002; Rabinowitz and Abu-Baker 2005; Rouhana 1997; Slyomovics 1998; Torstrick 1993). Palestinian citizens of Israel—who began explicitly identifying themselves in Israeli public discourse as "Palestinian" only relatively recently[15]—are habitually treated in accordance with a prevailing "paradigm of suspicion" (Shamir 2005); in other words, they have been widely viewed as a possible " 'fifth column' inside the Jewish state [whose] relationships with their brethren across the border would bring about undermining activities" (Harel 1989, 440; cited in Rouhana 1997, 56). Palestinians in the Occupied Territories, cast as even more deeply suspect, are consistently and categorically presumed to pose a physical threat to Israeli individual and collective security; in particular, they are collectively regarded as potential initiators of violent resistance and uprising. Despite the different threats these two groups are constructed as posing, Palestinians in Israel and Palestinians in the Occupied Territories are nonetheless linked within the Israeli imaginary as the nation's indigenous, constitutive others in explicit contrast to the recently arrived population of foreign, disposable others discussed here.[16]

The Limits of Flexible Demography

While transnational migrant workers have come to inhabit a new kind of other slot in the brother-other binary, this did not necessarily have to be the case. Another possibility meriting mention emerges from the work of Ian Lustick (1999), who contends that the modern-day Israeli state project, in effect, is less about ensuring that Israel remains a Jewish state than about keeping it a non-Arab state. In empirical terms, Lustick's argument hinges on a major demographic shift that took place in Israel in the 1990s: the arrival of approximately nine hundred thousand actively recruited, formally welcomed new immigrants (*olim chadashim*) from the former Soviet Union (Central Bureau of Statistics, Israel, 2002). A substantial proportion of these ratified immigrants neither claim to be Jewish nor are recognized as such by the state; instead, their pathways to residence and citizenship hinge on their proven genealogical connection to someone who is recognized by the state as a Jew. Lustick shows how the problem of so many former Soviet immigrants' non-Jewishness has been consistently swept under the rug by statisticians, bureaucrats, and government officials, who have engaged in an ongoing game of classificatory and statistical smoke and mirrors in their efforts to confirm the continued existence of a Jewish demographic majority. Lustick interprets these practices as evidence that the state's primary interest lies not in preserving the country's Jewish majority but in maintaining a majority voting populace of non-Arabs.

Following Lustick's logic, it might have been possible—at least in theory—for the country's population of approximately one-quarter million non-Jewish, non-Arab migrant workers to be folded into the Israeli national body precisely on the grounds of their non-Arabness. Yet this has not taken place, nor did it ever emerge in political or public discourse as a thinkable option. Instead of embracing transnational migrants as a boon to the "demographically challenged" state, the government's preferred path of action has instead hinged on discursively transforming these non-Jewish others from a relatively innocuous if growing "nuisance" population into a metastasizing population of "criminal" interlopers.

The overwhelming success of the deportation campaign has thus stemmed from the government's reasonably convincing portrayal of non-Jewish, unauthorized migrants as something *other than* either a curiosity or a nuisance—that is, as a threat to the security and integrity of the Israeli state and society. To understand this rhetorical and practical transformation—which cannot fully be explained by the government's justification of the deportation campaign as a response to high unemployment among Israeli citizens—it is necessary to consider the multiple meanings of "security" in contemporary Israel.

"Security" in Israel, Multiply Defined

In his elaboration of Foucault's thinking, Colin Gordon contends that "contemporary society, according to Foucault, has become preeminently a 'society of security' including a circuit of interdependence between political and social security" (1991, 35). Nowhere, one might argue, is this observation more relevant than in Israel, where an official state of emergency has been in effect since the state's establishment in 1948 and where questions of state security are perpetually at the center of political, policy, and public discourse. The majority of Jewish Israeli leaders and citizens are persistently anxious not only about the country's political, physical, and economic security but also about its ethnonational, or demographic, security (Rouhana 1997, 57–58). The notion of "ethnonational security" has less to do with the material conditions necessary for the continued physical and economic viability of the state than with preserving its status as a Jewish homeland in accordance with the founding vision of the Zionist movement: as a safe haven for Jews worldwide. This vision, which might be described in its original sense as more deliberately preservationist than exclusivist, was forged in the crucible of nineteenth-century European nationalist fervor and, subsequently, of the Shoah, or the Nazi attempt at Jewish annihilation during World War II.

Although the basic tenets of Zionism have become objects of considerable critical reevaluation within Israel in recent decades, mainstream Israeli society and the vast majority of actors on the Israeli political scene nonetheless remain deeply committed to preserving the "Jewish character of the state," which implies a nationalist program with two distinct dimensions. One dimension involves the public's commitment to keeping Israel's doors open to all potential Jewish immigrants (via the Law of Return) and retaining the public symbols and ceremonies that mark the country as socioculturally Jewish, including the state flag, the national anthem, and the schedule of the workweek (with Saturday as the national day of rest) and of the calendar year (within which Jewish holidays are observed). The second dimension is entwined with Israel's self-characterization as a "Jewish and a democratic state." In other words, maintaining the Jewish character of the state is a common euphemism for the deeply entrenched national goal of preserving a Jewish (or non-Arab) voting majority within the state's borders to prevent the possibility that the "Jewish and democratic state" might be voted out of existence.[17] Ultimately, as Nadim Rouhana points out, "The framework of a Jewish state, democracy, and security illustrates the three pillars of state ideology. All three are based on the concerns of the Jewish population, but the implications of these guidelines for the Arab population are of great consequence" (1997, 42).

Against the backdrop of these three key concerns, virtually any state measure taken in the name of security—physical, economic, or ethnonational—tends to garner a strong and reflexive measure of mainstream public support; as one scholar proposes, "the Israeli public will accept in the name of security afflictions that had they been applied in other domains . . . would cause a revolt to erupt" (Pinkas 1993, 67; cited in Rouhana 1997, 42). To think productively about the abandonment of certain groups in the service of maintaining state boundaries, it is thus necessary to look at the *range* of the Israeli state's anxieties about security and the different ways in which such anxieties have been translated into governmental practice. Put differently, and as the discussion thus far would suggest, any binary interpretation of the distinction between citizen and homo sacer fails to capture the complexity of the Israeli biopolitical framework.

TEMPLATES OF OTHERNESS: ISRAELI STATE TREATMENT OF PALESTINIAN CITIZENS AND PALESTINIANS IN THE OCCUPIED TERRITORIES

To illustrate the complexity of this multilayered model of othering and sociopolitical exclusion, I now explore some of the specific ways in which a single state has sought to maintain its sovereign power, anchored in a state of exception, by manufacturing multiple, shifting configurations of "bare life." The present section briefly describes Israel's treatment of both Palestinian citizens and Palestinians in the Occupied Territories and highlights two key modalities of governmental power: biosocial profiling and the perpetual threat of violence. As shall become evident in the section that follows, these and other forms of Israeli state treatment of Palestinians have become part of an unwritten governmental template for the treatment—or, more precisely, for the criminalization and expulsion—of non-Jewish, non-Arab transnational migrant workers.

Palestinian Citizens

Approximately one-fifth of Israel's citizens are either Palestinians who managed to remain in what became the state of Israel after the 1948 war or their descendants. Although formally granted citizenship at the time of the state's establishment, Palestinian citizens of Israel nonetheless lived under military rule until 1967. Since then, and despite their ostensibly equal status, they have faced numerous forms of institutionalized, systematic, and conjugated discrimination (see, for instance, Kanaaneh 2002; Rabinowitz and Abu-Baker 2005; Reiss 1991; Yiftachel 1995, 1997). These include mass expropriation of private land for the creation of Jewish

Israeli towns, agricultural settlements, and industrial areas, as well as government restrictions on construction that impede the natural growth of Palestinian communities. Such communities also consistently receive fewer government resources for basic social needs such as health and education than do Jewish communities. Schools for Palestinian children (where instruction is in Arabic) and Jewish children (in Hebrew) are largely separate, and curricula in Arab schools are defined by representatives of the Jewish majority. As Dan Rabinowitz and Khawla Abu-Baker note in their recent book about generational transformations in Palestinian identity within Israel (a book that, it is worth noting, was published in Arabic, Hebrew, and English):

> Economic stagnation, underdevelopment, unemployment, and poverty in the Palestinian community are inextricably linked to long-standing government policies of neglect and discrimination. All Israeli administrations, with the sole exception of Rabin's government in the early 1990s, left Palestinian towns and villages outside the loop when assigning subsidies and development incentives. Palestinians are excluded from a variety of welfare benefits and state-subsidized mortgages reserved for army veterans and new immigrants. The exclusion of Palestinians from essential economic spheres such as banking, import and export franchises, and advanced technology further contributes to economic marginalization. (2005, 7)

Overall, the authors continue, "Palestinian citizens have remained unwanted guests in the Israeli economy, members of a community whose needs and claims are deemed irrelevant to what mainstream Israel defines as its worthy national goals" (7). According to the political scientist Yoav Peled, there are thus two forms of citizenship in Israel: liberal citizenship for Palestinians (based on passive possession of a bundle of rights) and republican citizenship for Jews (i.e., active participation in the determination, protection, and promotion of the common good) (Peled 1992, 433; see also Shafir and Peled 1998).

Aggravating the impact of Palestinian citizens' second-class citizenship are two forms of governmental power that have a powerful impact on the fabric of everyday individual and communal life: first, routine patterns and mechanisms of racialized "biosocial profiling," and second, the latent but real threat of state-sponsored violence. According to Ronen Shamir, biosocial profiling constitutes "an emergent technology of social intervention that objectifies whole strata of people by assigning them into suspect categories, thereby enabling the paradigm of suspicion to be translated into elaborated practices of containment. . . . Profiling [also] predicts behavior and regulates mobility by situating subjects in categories of risk" (2005, 210). Although racialization can, and in this case does, involve more than just the ascription of social meaning to phenotypic character- istics, biosocial profiling does tend to operate via what Fassin describes as a "reduction of the social to the biological" that effectively "challenges the notion of a common humanity by differentiating among people at the deepest level of their being, looking for the marks of their origins. Racial discrimination is founded on an insurmountable difference, because it is inscribed in the body, indeed even in the genes" (2001, 5; citing Simpson 2000). In the moment an individual is profiled in this manner, she is in- terpellated, or "hailed" (Althusser 1971), in a manner that gives palpable social form and subjective content to the prevailing paradigm of suspicion and "hermeneutic of distrust" (Seeman 1997).[18]

Palestinian citizens are targets of racialized bioprofiling at multiple loci within Israeli space. Rebecca Torstrick, for instance, notes that despite Jews' and Arabs' common "Semitic" roots, "physical appearance is com- monly used to mark significant others," and "distinguishing Arabs from Jews and Ashkenazim [Jews of European descent] from Mizrahim [Jews of Middle Eastern descent] becomes a matter of amateur biology and com- mon sense" (2000, 34). Moreover, as Rabinowitz and Abu-Baker point out, "Despite appearances as bustling, liberal, and open areas, Israeli cities remain, in essence, spaces designed for Israeli Jews" (2005, 131). Guards stationed at the entrance to restaurants, malls, movie theaters, and other public spaces are trained to be suspicious of individuals with Arab bio- profiles, who are often subject to additional surveillance measures and sometimes to outright harassment. Both at Israel's international airport and at airports abroad, Palestinian passengers on Israel's national airline, El Al, are often subjected to lengthy and humiliating security screenings (Rabinowitz and Abu-Baker 2005, 146; Cohen-Eliya 2004).[19] Like African Americans in the United States, Palestinian citizens of Israel are consis- tently subject to harsher treatment at all levels of law enforcement—in- cluding the police, state prosecutors, and the courts—than Jewish Israelis (Rabinowitz and Abu-Baker 2005; citing Gurr 1993; Green 1994).

Beyond these everyday modes of formal and informal racialization and discrimination, Palestinian citizens have also become the targets of state-sponsored violence at several defining moments in recent decades (Al-Haj 2005; Bishara 2001; Or 2006).[20] First, six Palestinian demonstrators were shot and killed at mass demonstrations held on March 30, 1976, in the Galilee to protest the government expropriation of land for purposes of "security and settlement." The annual Yawm al-Ard (Land Day) events held to commemorate these instances of police brutality have proved central to the politicization and mobilization of Palestinian citizen activists in subsequent years. More recently, the violence that erupted in October 2000 at a number of peaceful political demonstrations in northern Israel has further solidified Palestinian citizens' sense of exclusion from, and abandonment by, the state. In the first half of that month, the Israeli police killed thirteen Palestinians, of whom twelve were citizens, all but one were under thirty, and two were in their late teens. While state-sponsored violence against Palestinian citizens is by no means a common occurrence in Israel, these two unforgettable moments, although separated by a quarter of a century, are indelibly imprinted within many Palestinian citizens' consciousness as indications of their second-class status.

Palestinians in the Occupied Territories

The two modes of othering described here—biosocial profiling and the persistent threat of violence—are even more prominent features of Israel's treatment of Palestinians in the Occupied Territories, where a wide array of policies and practices are deployed by the Israeli state, primarily via the military, to regulate and control the Palestinian population in the name of Israeli security.

Since first gaining military control over the West Bank and Gaza after the 1967 war between Israel and neighboring Arab states, Israel has deployed a sophisticated, multidimensional, and constantly evolving regime of governmentality in ruling over the noncitizen Palestinian population in the Occupied Territories. Especially since the late 1980s, Palestinians in the West Bank and Gaza live their lives within a tight grid of Israeli military regulation and control that is neither consistent nor predictable (Bornstein 2002). From Palestinians' perspectives, this constellation of military, administrative, legal, and other measures is perhaps most clearly and concretely embodied in the military checkpoints, the newly constructed "separation wall," and other tangible barriers situated along the border with Israel and at numerous points within the territories themselves. As the local human rights organization MachsomWatch (Checkpoint Watch) reports, "The regime practiced at the checkpoints is arbitrary and random. The rules change frequently, often to suit the whims of the soldier on duty at the moment." Moreover, the group contends, "The policy of suppression and dehumanization that pervades the nature of control over another nation necessarily seeps into the awareness and behavioral patterns of the soldiers who serve at the checkpoints and in the territories."[21] Overall, as MachsomWatch and other human rights organizations have demonstrated in their many reports and press releases, the techniques, policies, and practices comprised by the occupation—all deployed in the name of safeguarding Israeli security—constrict and constrain Palestinians' everyday lives and severely impair the everyday functioning of the Palestinian economy and Palestinian society.[22]

At the checkpoints and in virtually all other zones of Israeli-Palestinian interaction within the Occupied Territories, racialized biosocial profiling is a fundamental feature of everyday life; those who appear Jewish are typically granted freedom of movement, and those who appear Palestinian are typically trapped within a tight, militarized gridlock. At the checkpoints dividing the West Bank from Israel proper and scattered throughout the West Bank itself, an "appropriate" biosocial profile is generally sufficient to propel an Israeli Jew through. The particular characteristics signaling such a profile include a convincingly innocuous Hebrew accent (i.e., an accent not tinged with Arabic), a Jewish name listed on a blue identity card (as opposed to the orange identity cards Palestinians carry), yarmulkes (*kipot*) or women's head coverings (distinguishing religious Jews), and yellow license plates (in contrast to green Palestinian plates). While many Israelis of Middle Eastern and North African descent (Mizrahim) are phenotypically similar to Palestinians, soldiers stationed at checkpoints—many of them Mizrahim themselves—learn to read difference in accordance with the ideologically motivated hermeneutic of suspicion and the racialized biopolitical regime they are charged with enforcing.

In contrast to Jewish Israelis' smooth bidirectional crossings, individuals with Palestinian biosocial profiles, including men, women, and children, must queue up either in cars or on foot in an effort to cross. At some checkpoints, Palestinians wait for hours, often in the beating sun or driving rain, for an opportunity to plead their case. When they finally do arrive at the front of the line, they must provide adequate proof of their need to cross. Such negotiations often take the form of strained, linguistically constrained dialogues with young soldiers in their late teens or early twenties with weapons slung over their shoulders, who address Palestinian petitioners either in Arabic (often broken Arabic) or in Hebrew, which many Palestinians, especially women from rural communities, do not speak or understand.[23] When Palestinians do manage to cross the militarized border into Israeli space, they are subject to routine biosocial profiling within Israel as well.

Overall, the impact of the occupation on Palestinian life epitomizes what Arthur Kleinman, Veena Das, and Margaret Lock have characterized as the "soft knife" of state policies through which experiences of racism, violence, violation, and social suffering become naturalized and woven into the fabric of everyday life (1997, x). Significantly, this soft knife of everyday oppression is further sharpened by the perpetual threat of direct physical violence, which armed Israeli soldiers occasionally use against Palestinian men, women, and sometimes even children in public spaces, in private homes (e.g., during house searches), and behind the locked doors of prisons and detention centers. While soldiers are formally authorized to use violence in some instances, Israeli and international human rights organizations have accumulated extensive documentation of occasions in which violence is deployed without formal authorization, in violation of basic human rights, and often with impunity.[24] Even when periods of time pass during which no physical violence is deployed, it is always present *in potentia*, indexed by the barbed wire, concrete barricades, tanks, armed soldiers, and occasional sounds of gunfire that form the persistent backdrop of Palestinians' everyday lives. As Avram Bornstein notes in his ethnography of Palestinian life in the West Bank, "The lingering effects of violence continued to work even when it was not actually happening because it created permanent scars, both physical and psychological. It weighed in the air with imminence" (2002, 8). In other words, the ever-present *threat* of violence is a cornerstone of the occupation, and it advances the governmental goals of material, social, and psychological domination and control.

A NEW KIND OF OTHER

In light of these circumstances, it seems less helpful to search for an "ultimate homo sacer" within the Israeli state system (as Kemp does) than to acknowledge the existence of a complex biopolitics of otherness within which an overarching racialized ideology of national inclusion and exclusion is translated into techniques of governmental power that are differently deployed at different moments in time, in different configurations, and in relation to different groups defined as others. I aim now to show how the criminalization of unauthorized transnational migrant workers in Israel and their reconfiguration as a disposable, and legitimately deportable, population have been implemented through techniques and practices already regularly employed by the Israeli state in relation to both groups of Palestinian "real others" described earlier.

Xenophobia from Above

First, however, it is important to recognize that the government did not assume that the Israeli public would automatically accept its argument that unauthorized migrant workers were the cause of high Israeli unemployment or, more importantly, support its campaign of criminalization and deportation. Indeed, the government had to confront the fact that many of the occasional media reports about migrant workers published before the initiation of the deportation campaign were actually sympathetic to their cause.[25] The state, via its newly created Immigration Authority, thus embarked on a widespread media campaign to convince Israelis that unauthorized migrants constituted a substantive threat to the security of the state and society and, as such, that these forms of treatment were deserved. In other words, the state sought to reconstitute unauthorized migrants in the public imaginary by imbuing their presence—like that of the Palestinians who preceded them as a form of banned or abandoned "detritus humanity"—with powerful negative connotations.

The core tactic in this discursive battle involved a series of inflammatory anti-immigrant "public service announcements" disseminated within the mainstream print and broadcast media. At the peak of the campaign, such radio announcements were broadcast frequently enough and regularly enough (i.e., just before the hourly news, several times a day) to record them off the air. While their content varied, the announcements, all narrated in an authoritative, low-pitched male voice over a background of haunting music, uniformly characterized the euphemistically labeled "foreign worker problem" as a grave social issue requiring a nationwide—and, indeed, a personal—response. The following, rather typical announcement, for example, was broadcast in November 2002, just a few months into the deportation campaign:

> One in fourteen workers in the state of Israel is an illegal worker. In other words, there are 160,000 illegal foreign workers. No taxes are paid on their earnings, but their residence here is very costly to the state. This doesn't make economic sense. It's an impossible situation for the Israeli economy. We created it; it's our obligation to fix it. So with all due respect to whoever comes to work for you, this doesn't work.[26]

Not only does this Immigration Authority announcement attempt to impress on listeners the scope of the country's "foreign worker problem" in both (inflated) numerical and statistical terms, but it also identifies the "problem" as a source of serious financial strain for the beleaguered Israeli economy. Moreover, it insists that (microeconomic) arguments in favor of unauthorized migrant workers' continued employment are trumped by (macroeconomic) arguments in favor of their expulsion.

Other announcements, including the following, went one step further. In addition to arguing that unauthorized migrants' presence yields negative *economic* consequences, these announcements also implied that their presence entails a vague form of insidious—albeit unidentified—*social* harm:

> Right now, a national campaign is being conducted to end the phenomenon that is causing the state tremendous economic and social damage. Every day, hundreds of businesses and private homes are being investigated. Violators are subject to fines as high as 80,000 shekels [US$18,000], criminal convictions, and/or two years imprisonment. Employing a worker without a permit is illegal, and it doesn't work.[27]

While the precise nature of this ostensible social harm remains unnamed in such announcements, the implications are clear to Israeli listeners: non-Jewish migrant workers are not Israeli, nor can they or will they become Israelis in the future, and therefore they must be sent home to their countries of origin by whatever means necessary. Equally clear is the degree to which employer-citizens are now being taken to task for their complicity with the gray-market employment arrangements that the government had almost completely ignored for a decade. Announcements like these implicitly acknowledged that unauthorized migrant workers had become a substantial presence within the local labor market and publicized the state's intent to bring the practice to a halt.

Other, less-subtle advertisements—one of which included a photograph of migrant workers in jail beneath the headline "Soon They'll Be Going Home"—were deemed racist and xenophobic by local civil rights organizations. One such organization, the Israel Religious Action Center (IRAC), filed a protest petition with the Israeli High Court of Justice, arguing:

> The contents of messages disseminated on the [Immigration Authority's] Internet site and [in] the electronic media encourage xenophobia. The ads and the Internet site contain threatening and racist messages that portray the foreign workers as an element that harms the Israeli economy, social morality and even security.
>
> These messages could cause, even inadvertently, incitement against and persecution of foreign workers. (Izenberg 2003)

Indeed, in December 2003 the high court ruled that some of the first ads broadcast by the Immigration Authority were "hateful and inciting," and ordered the Immigration Authority to revise its procedure for developing the content of their announcements (Izenberg 2003).

Nonetheless, by fomenting anti-immigrant attitudes and anxieties via its unmistakable and insistent presence across a variety of mainstream media venues, the Israeli Immigration Authority succeeded in pushing a relatively unfamiliar population from the fringes of the country's public attention squarely into the center. In so doing, even after toning down its language, this newly created government body sought to whip up the sort of xenophobic sentiment that could then be exploited in the service of the government's agenda: the systematic and highly public criminalization of unauthorized migrants—and, as a "logical" next step, their expulsion. By drawing this population into the public spotlight and attempting to imbue their presence (and, indeed, their very persons) with a laundry list of powerful negative connotations, the state clarified its implicit view of unauthorized migrants as yet another form of detritus humanity who can efficiently, indeed common-sensically, be distinguished from ratified Jewish-Israeli interiorized humanity. Importantly, however, the Immigration Authority appears to have been concerned that simply naming this new enemy would not suffice; as such, xenophobic advertisements were paired with the (infrequently enforced) threat of steep fines against Israelis who continued to employ unauthorized migrants. Put differently, the campaign reformulated their previous condition of inclusion (within the labor market) coupled with exclusion (from the social body and body politic) into a straightforward program of total exclusion via physical expulsion.

Biosocial Profiling and the Threat of Violence

In addition to vilifying transnational migrants in the mainstream media, the Immigration Authority has also employed other techniques in recasting them as criminals who should be forcibly arrested and deported. These include the two modalities of governmental power identified earlier: first, racialized biosocial profiling, and second, the state's newfound readiness to approach unauthorized migrants with batons raised.

With the initiation of the deportation campaign, Immigration Police officers' default stance vis-à-vis individuals suspected of being "illegal" migrants stemmed from the presumption that they are "guilty until proven innocent." Indeed, this paradigm of suspicion has led police officers to make mistakes by arresting "legal" migrant workers, asylum seekers, visiting professionals, and even, in at least one instance, an Israeli citizen.[28] In cases like these—where the logic of presumed guilt is applied in excess—police officers' interpellation of phenotypic others inadvertently reveals two of the Immigration Authority's underlying assumptions: first, that certain forms of phenotypic otherness necessarily index criminality and deportability, and second, that these forms of otherness—like the widely accepted "real" otherness of Palestinians—legitimize verbal abuse, humiliation, and even physical violence. The Immigration Police's tendency toward knee-jerk presumptions of criminalizable otherness is illustrated in the following two ethnographic examples.

Guilty Until Proven Innocent: Dr. Mary Grace Parreño

In an incident that was reported in the Israeli media, Dr. Mary Grace Parreño, a Filipina neurosurgery resident at one of the most prestigious Israeli public hospitals, was arrested on a central Tel Aviv thoroughfare, forcibly pushed into a police van under the serendipitous gaze of a filmmaker's camera, and taken to police headquarters. The arresting officers refused to call her supervisor at the hospital to verify her identity and instead, apparently incapable of believing that a Filipina woman in Tel Aviv could truly be a physician, joked to one another that "there's a doctor here if anyone isn't feeling well" (Meir 2005). Playing on the shock factor of this particular incident, the footage of the arrest was broadcast on the national television news along with a clip of Dr. Parreño, at work and dressed in hospital scrubs, displaying the purple bruises on her body. She later authorized the incident in a detailed letter to two left-wing members of the Israeli Parliament, which she shared with me after a December 2006 interview. Her narrative of bioprofiling, criminalization, and assault is worth quoting at length.

> I was walking with a Filipina friend at 9:00 p.m. . . . outside the shopping mall when a man in uniform asked for our passports. We asked for his identification and my friend who can read Hebrew better than I do, confirmed that he is a policeman. . . . My friend gave him her Israeli identity card while I gave him my hospital ID—a plastic card which has my picture on it and which says that I am a doctor. He insisted that I give him my passport and I told him that the ID was enough.[29] When I asked why, he said that this is the law. At some point in the conversation, he raised his voice and said, "Why are you shouting at me?" [to] which I replied, "I am not shouting at you. This is just the way that I talk." From then on, the conversation started to become more unpleasant as we were yelling at each other. This was the time that he grabbed my arm and motioned me to go to the police car. Then I told him that I am going to

give him my passport. I got it from my bag and handed it to him and he took it. In spite of this, he held my arm very firmly and dragged me towards the vehicle. I fought against him and against the policemen who later on joined him in crushing my arms and legs and pushing me inside the van. I told them, "Why are you arresting me? I already gave you my ID and my passport. This is not fair. Give me a reason why you are arresting me." All I heard from them was, "Get inside!" At this point, several people gathered around us, and I heard them yelling in Hebrew which, in my own understanding, was, "She already gave you her passport and ID. Why do you need to take her? Why can't you examine her outside?" As the policemen were pushing me inside, passers-by were pulling me from the van. I was turned upside down with my head almost hitting the ground. It appeared like I was a rope in their game of tug-of-war. A filmmaker by the name of——caught some of it on tape when I was saying, "I'm Mary Grace Parreño. I'm a doctor from Ichilov [Hospital]. I gave them my ID and my passport and they are treating me like a criminal." I fought so hard to break free while repeating this question several times: "Why are you arresting me?" I never received an answer from any of the policemen. In my mind, something was not right there. It is a dictum that when a human being is arrested by a person in authority, this person in authority should say something like, "You are under arrest. You have the right to remain silent. Anything you say and do can or will be used against you in a court of law. You have the right to an attorney. If you don't have one, one will be provided for you . . . and so on." I never heard any of these words whether they be in English or something like this in Hebrew.

Given the rigid machinery of biosocial profiling in place, this visiting physician—whose skin color and facial features instantly "revealed" her to be a "body out of place" (cf. Puwar 2004; Tormey 2007)—could in the arresting officers' minds only be construed as an "illegal" resident and, as such, a danger to the integrity and security of the state. According to this logic, the police officers' response—to arrest her without clear explanation, verbally abuse her, physically injure her, and turn her "upside down with [her] head almost hitting the ground . . . like . . . a rope in their game of tug-of-war"—was legitimate.

Raphael's Story

I heard a strikingly similar story in an interview with Raphael Malonga,[30] an asylum seeker from Congo. In addition to the waves of unauthorized migration to Israel from dozens of countries across the globe, a handful

of individuals from conflict-ridden countries such as Congo, Sierra Le-
one, Liberia, Ivory Coast, Ethiopia, and most recently Sudan and Eritrea
have entered Israel in recent years and applied for status as asylum seekers through the local office of the United Nations High Commissioner for
Refugees (UNHCR) (Adout 2007; Ben-Dor and Adout 2003; Ben-Dor and
Kagan 2007).[31] Until 2007, many of those petitioning for asylum had lived
and worked alongside unauthorized immigrants in Israel for extended periods of time while waiting for their petitions to be reviewed. Individuals
whose petitions have been approved, as well as those with pending petitions, receive official letters from UNHCR that they are instructed to carry
with them as proof of their Temporary Protected Status (TPS). In theory,
therefore, valid documents should grant immunity to arrest. As in the
case of Mary Parreño, however, the Immigration Police often pay more
attention to asylum seekers' biosocial profile than to the documents they
present—or try to present. In such cases, whether the arresting officers
choose not to read such papers or, alternatively, fail to understand their
professional and legal obligations to release their bearers, they approach
asylum seekers—like others who also "look illegal"—as criminals.

I first met Raphael Malonga, a mild-mannered, mustached Congolese
man in his late twenties, when he came, complaining of shoulder and arm
pain, to the open clinic operated by the local nongovernment organization where I was volunteering at the time. He suffered these injuries, he
explained, when he was arrested—and beaten—by police officers. The arrest, as he explained to me in an interview in February 2002, took place
at one of the numerous long-distance phone and Internet shops that have
sprung up in South Tel Aviv with the influx of transnational migrants to
the area. Such shops offer migrants one of their only opportunities to stay
in touch with relatives and friends abroad, since most do not have home
phones, and international cell phone calls are exorbitantly expensive.
They are also, therefore, an easy target for Immigration Police units trying
to meet their quotas (Willen 2007b).

Raphael explained that he was arrested along with one man from Ivory
Coast and another from either Mongolia or China, he couldn't tell which.
After refusing to examine his UNHCR documents, the arresting officers
took Raphael to the police station along with the other two men. At the
station, he said, "They asked me many questions. They wanted me to sign
a form, but I refused to sign because it was in Hebrew." Assuming the officers were following usual protocols, the document was probably a declaration of "relinquishment of property," which detained migrant workers
are asked to sign upon their arrest. When Raphael refused to sign the

Hebrew document presented to him, he was harassed by the officers in charge.

> They said, "Why? Everyone else signs." I said, "If you bring it to me in French, I'll read it and maybe I'll sign." Then they started hitting me, beating me. I said, "You can kill me, but I won't sign. I was in prison in my own country, and I came this close to being killed."

Educated, articulate, tempered by his previous experiences of political repression and imprisonment in Congo, and aware that he had been arrested unjustly, Raphael refused to capitulate to the officers' demand. In Althusser's terms, and like Mary Parreño, he refused to turn around in response to their hail, thus rejecting the criminal subject position into which these agents of the state were trying to force him.

Not long afterward, Raphael was taken from the police detention center to Ma'asiyahu Prison in the city of Ramleh. Eventually one of the prison officials called UNHCR; the validity of Raphael's identifying documents was confirmed, and he was released. A volunteer from a local human rights organization picked him up from the prison and took him back to his home in Tel Aviv. The director of the organization, who had been involved in obtaining Raphael's release, strongly encouraged him to file a lawsuit and testify against the officers who had violently assaulted him, but he would not. Even after this ordeal involving unwarranted arrest, verbal harassment, physical abuse, and imprisonment, Raphael told me that he did not want to file such a suit, since he did not harbor ill will toward Israel or Israelis. His reasoning was theological: "You must love and bless the people of Israel because it says so in the Bible; bless and you'll be blessed, curse and you'll be cursed." "Even after everything that happened with the police?" I asked. "Yes," he insisted. While I had difficulty believing that Raphael was truly committed to this position, particularly after seeing him come repeatedly to the open clinic seeking medical care for his injured arm and shoulder, his tone and demeanor suggested that the religious message he cited was a guiding principle in his everyday life as an unwelcome—although, in his case, not "illegal"—foreigner in Israel (see Willen 2007a, 175–80).

While it is certainly within the scope of police authority to question the authenticity of documents presented to them, the quick resorts to verbal abuse and physical violence characterizing the arrests of Dr. Mary Grace Parreño, the Filipina doctor, and Raphael Malonga, the Congolese asylum seeker, suggest that police officers view phenotypic otherness as an incontrovertible, racialized marker of radical difference, as an indication of these noncitizens' lesser status in relation to Israelis, and ultimately as legitimate grounds for treating them with humiliation and violence. Moreover, when biosocial profiles and legal realities turn out to be misaligned—as they were in both these cases—law enforcement officials associated with the Israeli deportation regime are sometimes slow to ascertain the distinctions. Automatically cast as criminals, individuals with suspicious biosocial profiles thus become legitimate targets for verbal abuse, threats, and even the deployment of physical violence in the eyes of the Immigration Police.

CONCLUSION

This chapter has explored how Israel's treatment of unauthorized migrant workers shifted from a pattern of systematic neglect associated with their generalized othering and exclusion (in the late 1990s) to an active program of criminalization and expulsion (with the initiation of a mass deportation campaign in 2002). As the other chapters in this volume illustrate, Israel's efforts to expel unauthorized migrant workers—and other recently arrived noncitizens—are not unique but rather parallel the ways that other host states conceive of, discursively construct, and materially respond to such groups' uninvited presence. Following Agamben, these forms of categorical treatment hinge on an originary distinction between those granted "politicized life" and those relegated to "bare life"—between citizen and what Agamben characterizes as homo sacer. Drawing on Agamben's thesis as ethnographic frame, it becomes evident that the distinction between citizen and homo sacer is not singular or uniform but rather maps onto existing local configurations of the biopolitics of inclusion and otherness.

In the Israeli context, the influx of unauthorized and other irregular migrants is relatively recent, yet their biopolitical niche in the Israeli political imaginary has come to resonate—in some but, importantly, not all ways—with the niches inhabited by other groups of already present others including, in particular, Palestinians in Israel and in the Occupied Territories. Clearly substantial differences exist between the ways in which these groups are ideologically and discursively constructed and, no less, between the particular threats they are presumed to pose to the state's security. Yet there are also important similarities, many of which emerged in the context of the mass deportation campaign. Indeed, these newer similarities are central to what I have described as a radical reconfiguration of unauthorized migrants' status in Israel from ignored and excluded others into actively hunted criminals.

Three points of similarity between Israel's treatment of its "real others" and "other others" are particularly noteworthy. First, the deportation campaign's portrayals of unauthorized migrants evoked themes related to those commonly employed in popular portrayals of Palestinians. In particular, unauthorized migrants came to be constructed and characterized in public discourse and in the various communicative media associated with the deportation campaign as a threat to both the state's economic security and, crucially, its ethnonational (read: demographic) security as a Jewish state. Second, in practical terms, techniques of biosocial profiling regularly applied to Palestinians have become integral to the Immigration Police's efforts to round up and expel unauthorized migrants. These forms of racialized biosocial profiling are deployed in accordance with a presumption of guilt until innocence can be proved, as the stories of both Dr. Mary Grace Parreño and Raphael Malonga demonstrate.

Third, and most centrally, the threat of violence has become a key component of state efforts to arrest, detain, and expel unauthorized migrants. As demonstrated by the violence against Palestinian citizens in March 1976 and October 2000 and by the everyday deployment of violence in the Occupied Territories, Palestinians' vulnerability to Israeli violence and, more critically, their ability to be injured or even killed with varying degrees of impunity are both emblematic and constitutive of their position as a lesser form of humanity in contrast to ratified Jewish-Israeli citizens. Since 2002, unauthorized migrants have become similarly vulnerable to the deployment of state violence, albeit in different ways and to a lesser degree. Indeed, the threat of violence against migrant workers, while not explicitly sanctioned by the state or police authorities, has nonetheless been acknowledged by some officers of the Immigration Police as implicitly acceptable (Willen 2007b).[32]

In other words, despite substantial differences between the kind of security threat ostensibly posed by both groups of Palestinians, on the one hand, and transnational migrant workers, on the other, there are a number of striking new similarities in how these groups are portrayed and treated. Not only are they subject to ongoing patterns of both symbolic and psychological violence, but their otherness, which is understood in racialized terms as both immutable and written on their bodies, has come to be regarded by at least some agents of the Israeli state as justification for, and legitimation of, the use of physical violence against them. Framed in Agamben's terms, we might say that the experiences of all three groups bear features of bare life. Rather than analytically reducing all such groups to a monolithic notion of homo sacer, however, anthropological efforts to understand these forms of human experience are better served by detailed, grounded, historically anchored ethnography.

I have sought here to identify some of the ways in which Israel's treatment of Palestinian others—that is, those constructed within mainstream Jewish-Israeli discourse as the country's "real others"—prefigured its recent policies of aggressive criminalization and mass expulsion toward unauthorized migrants. I have made this comparison cautiously, careful to show how these groups are cast into different kinds of position and status within Israel's broader and evolving biopolitics of inclusion and otherness (see Willen 2008, forthcoming). The introductory quotation by Supi, a Ghanaian woman who lives in Tel Aviv with her school-age daughter, poses the same question, albeit from a different angle.

> If this is what the Israelis do in the center, where everyone can see, just think of what they must be doing to the Palestinians in the bush, where no one can see what's happening.

Before the deportation campaign, parallels like this one never arose in my conversations with unauthorized migrant workers. In its wake, however, new forms of subjectivity, and potentially new forms of political consciousness, may be emerging—at least, that is, among those migrants who have been able to avoid deportation and whose enduring deportability remains a distinctly incisive standpoint of critique with regard to the sovereignty of the state.

NOTES

This essay is based on twenty-seven nonconsecutive months of ethnographic research conducted between 2000 and 2007 with support from Fulbright-Hays, the National Science Foundation (no. 0135425), the Social Science Research Council, the Wenner Gren Foundation, the Lady Davis Trust at the Hebrew University of Jerusalem, and the Department of Anthropology and Tam Institute for Jewish Studies at Emory University. Any opinions, findings, conclusions, or recommendations expressed are mine and do not necessarily reflect the views of funding agencies. I am grateful to the book's editors, as well as Peter J. Brown, Don Seeman, Jennifer Hirsch, Robert Desjarlais, Anat Rosenthal, Erin Finley, Rephael Peled, Naor Ben-Yehoyada, Honaida Ghanim, Ghassan Hage, and Arthur Kleinman for their critical feedback on earlier versions.

1. While some scholars reject terms like "illegal" and "illegality" as necessarily implying collusion with hegemonic and oppressive ideological forces within host societies, I join those who contend that we must take the notion of migrant "illegality" as an object of analysis (Coutin 2003; De Genova 2002; Suárez-Navaz 2004; Willen 2007a, 2007d; cf. Heyman and Smart 1999). Only by following these concepts through diverse contexts and conversations will it become possible to understand how legally and phenomenologically specific conditions of migrant "illegality" vary across migration settings.

2. Hotline for Migrant Workers, citing statistics collected by the Israeli Prison Authorities, the Central Bureau of Statistics, and the Immigration Authority (2007). After a multiyear lull, the Israeli government reorganized the Immigration Police and initiated a new deportation campaign that went into operation in July 2009 as this chapter went to press.

3. Despite the much-publicized withdrawal of Israeli settlements and troops from Gaza in 2005, Israel has nonetheless retained multiple forms of control that amount to a continuation of the occupation, albeit in altered form.

4. Israel's self-characterization as democratic has been critiqued widely by, among others, Oren Yiftachel, who has analyzed the "duality in the Israeli state between a democratic facade and a deeper undemocratic regime logic, which facilitates the dispossession, control, and peripheralization of groups that do not belong to the dominant ethno-class" (2000, 728).

5. Israel's local biopolitics of otherness became yet more complicated in 2007 and 2008 when over thirteen thousand asylum seekers—among them men, women, and children fleeing Darfur, the civil war in South Sudan, Eritrea, Somalia, and the Ivory Coast—trekked through the Sinai desert and across the long, porous Egyptian-Israeli border seeking protection and assistance (Willen 2008, forthcoming).

6. In fact, the line of critique developed in these pages arguably is already present between the lines of Kemp's comment. More precisely, her assertion that migrant workers are now the "ultimate *homo sacer*" constitutes an implicit critique of the trend within much social scientific scholarship on Israel to recapitulate popular constructions of Palestinians as Israel's "real" or ultimate others (see, for instance, Rabinowitz 2002) and an effort to grapple with multiple forms of othering within the Israeli state system.

7. Despite this clear implication, which I discuss in detail later, an unexpected turn of events took place in 2006, several years after the peak of the deportation campaign. At that point, after a long struggle by local human rights organizations, the Israeli government approved a one-time arrangement according to which a small proportion of migrant workers' children who met a stringent set of eligibility criteria were granted permanent residency, and members of their immediate families received a form of temporary resident status (Rosenhek 2007). Both forms of status include social rights to health care and social welfare services, among other benefits. Eligible children include those who were born in Israel or arrived in the country before age fourteen, who have been

in Israel for at least six years, and whose parents entered the country "legally" (as opposed to entering with forged documents). When these children turn eighteen, they will be eligible for Israeli citizenship, and their families for permanent resident status. The long-term ramifications of this surprising, if small-scale, development have yet to unfold.

8. This section is adapted from Willen 2007c.

9. See Willen 2007b for more on the Israeli government's failure to explore potential parallels to other countries with existing guest worker regimes.

10. Israel Central Bureau of Statistics, October 2003, cited in Kemp 2004. Migrant workers in Israel hail from a vast panoply of countries and world regions. Those arriving in Israel on a recruited, legal basis have included, most prominently, construction workers from Romania, Bulgaria, and China; agricultural workers from Thailand; and elder-care providers from the Philippines. "Illegal" workers hail from a much wider array of world regions including South America (Columbia, Bolivia, Ecuador), Africa (Ghana, Nigeria, South Africa), eastern Europe (Romania, Moldova, Poland, the former Yugoslavia, Russia), Central Asia and the Caucasus (Mongolia, Georgia, Kyrgystan), and Southeast Asia (India, Sri Lanka, the Philippines). All those defined by the state as "foreign workers" are, by definition, non-Jews, for they would automatically be entitled to Israeli citizenship if they could prove Jewish heritage. Of those migrant workers who are religiously affiliated, the vast majority are Christian.

11. For more extensive consideration of Israel as an ethnonational state, see, for example, Rabinowitz and Abu-Baker 2005; Rouhana 1997; Shafir and Peled 1998; Smooha 1997; Yiftachel 1993.

12. But see note 7.

13. Recruitment of foreign labor has become a powerful, tremendously lucrative, and highly unregulated industry in Israel, generating hundreds of millions of dollars in revenue each year. It is also a powerful industry whose leading entrepreneurs enjoy strong ties both with industry leaders and with well-placed public and political figures. See Kemp 2004.

14. Newspaper articles demonstrating the centrality of this public concern include Benn 2002; Y. Cohen 2002; Evron 2002; Galili 2002; Ilan 2007; Sheleg 2002.

15. Key catalysts in this increasingly open self-identification as Palestinian include the Yawm al-Ard (Land Day) events in March 1976, the outbreak of the first intifada in 1988, and the violent suppression of demonstrations at the outbreak of the second intifada in October 2000, as elaborated later.

16. Indeed, the salience of the distinction between Palestinian citizens and noncitizens has also been questioned by scholars and by Palestinians themselves. As Dan Rabinowitz and Khawla Abu-Baker query in their ethnography of Palestinian citizens of Israel: "Identifying the true meaning of the Green Line is a cardinal question for both Israelis and Palestinians. Are the Palestinian citizens of Israel really a separate group with a distinctive history, a discernible sense of identity, and an independent vision of the future? Or is such a distinction nothing but the reification of an artificial separation that Israel created

within Palestine, a schism the Palestinians can never accept?" (2005, 12). Alongside such weighty and abstract questions of identity, ethnographic perspectives on this question are also instructive, including, for instance, Rhoda Kanaaneh's (2002) portrayal of Palestinian citizens in northern Israel as powerfully influenced by Western (Israeli, American, etc.) patterns of identification, desire, and bodily practice, and Avram Bornstein's (2002) ethnographic comparison of Palestinian weddings in the West Bank and within Israel.

17. For critical analysis of the tensions between Israel's Jewish and democratic claims, see Rabinowitz and Abu-Baker 2005; Rouhana 1997; Shafir and Peled 1998; Smooha 1990; Torstrick 2000; Yiftachel 1993, 1997, 2000.

18. While space constraints preclude detailed elaboration, it is important to note that repeated negative or "injurious interpellations," particularly when sedimented over time, can yield significant detrimental consequences at the level of subjective experience (Butler 1997).

19. See also Karp 2001.

20. See also Adalah 2001; Association for Civil Rights in Israel 2001.

21. Caption from photo exhibit on the MachsomWatch website, http://www.ziv-p.com/MW (accessed February 8, 2007).

22. These military restrictions on geographic mobility, heightened considerably in the wake of the second intifada, which began in fall 2000, have effectively stilled major areas of Palestinian society and communal life. The Palestinian economy is in disarray, since neither goods nor workers can move about freely; schools and universities cannot function effectively, since students' and instructors' access is greatly restricted; and the already beleaguered Palestinian health care system cannot care for its desperately underserved, and largely destitute, patient populations, since patients, providers, and supplies can reach hospitals and clinics only with Israeli permission and, as such, only on an irregular basis and with great difficulty. For detailed and personalized accounts of the impact of the occupation on Palestinians' everyday life, see the regular newspaper columns by the journalists Amira Hass and Gideon Levy in the daily newspaper *Ha'aretz* (Hass 1999), and the websites of MachsomWatch, Physicians for Human Rights–Israel, B'tselem, Yesh Din, Human Rights Watch, and Médecins sans Frontiers, among others.

23. For detailed eyewitness descriptions of activity at checkpoints, see the MachsomWatch website, http://www.machsomwatch.org.il.

24. See, for instance, the testimonials of beatings and abuse by soldiers published on B'tselem's website, http://www.btselem.org.

25. In particular, a series called "The New Tel Avivians" appeared regularly in the late 1990s in the local Tel Aviv weekly paper *Ha'Ir*. The journalist who initiated the column then began writing about migrant workers, in a similar tone, for the national daily newspaper *Ha'aretz*.

26. Recorded on November 5, 2002; original translation.

27. Recorded on November 27, 2002; original translation.

28. Hifsh 2002; Krieger 2004; Leibovitch-Dar 2002; Sinai 2004a, 2004b, 2004c.

29. In initially presenting her hospital ID rather than her passport, Parreño was following the explicit instructions of her administrative supervisor.

30. Pseudonym.

31. As of 2005, there were just over five hundred people with TPS and a total of 87 recognized refugees in Israel (Kritzman 2007). The number of TPS recipients increased substantially following an influx of Sudanese and Eritrean asylum seekers in 2007 and 2008 (see Anteby-Yemini 2008; Willen 2008, forthcoming), but the number of individuals granted refugee status during those years was in the single digits (Tel Aviv University Refugee Rights Clinic, personal communication).

32. Only rarely have victims of police brutality dared to file complaints, and even then, little has come of such efforts. Unauthorized migrants arrested by violent means are almost never able to see their abusers formally sanctioned, and even fewer have been able to sue for punitive damages in Israeli courts. When accused, police officers and supervisors tend to play down the use of violence in the course of arrests, and dozens of complaints filed via Israeli human rights organizations have been ignored or closed. This failure to follow through on complaints is no coincidence, for the police possess a simple strategy for evading investigations: detainees who file complaints are simply deported before investigative proceedings can begin, after which investigations are then closed because of "lack of evidence" or "lack of public interest." Indeed, Mary Parreño filed a complaint with the assistance of a pro bono lawyer that was dismissed on these grounds. According to the Hotline for Migrant Workers, more than half of the migrants who filed complaints of police brutality in 2003 were deported before their cases could be investigated or sent to trial.

—∿—

CHAPTER 10

Radical Deportation

Alien Tales from Lodi

and San Francisco

On June 7, 2005, the Federal Bureau of Investigation arrested two Pakistani American men, twenty-two-year-old Hamid Hayat, and his father, Umer Hayat, an ice cream truck driver, for allegedly funding and organizing a terrorist cell in Lodi, California. The initial federal affidavit released to the media alleged that Hamid Hayat, who was a U.S.-born citizen, had attended a terrorist training camp in northeast Pakistan in 2003 and had returned to the United States two years later intending to attack "hospitals and large food stores" (Holstege, Marcucci, and Drucker 2005). Hamid Hayat had initially been detained in South Korea on his way back to the United States but was ultimately cleared and allowed to reenter.[1]

The arrests and allegations created a national media blitz and panic mongering about terrorist sleeper cells in the Central Valley of California, focusing on the small agricultural town of Lodi, about forty miles south of Sacramento. With a population of approximately sixty thousand and known for little other than winemaking and fruit packing, Lodi was suddenly thrust into the national spotlight. Coincidentally, this sensationalized discovery of Muslim terrorists lurking among vineyards and orchards broke just as President George W. Bush was pushing for the renewal of the USA PATRIOT ACT, amid increasing criticism of the erosion of civil liberties and frustration with the lack of tangible breakthroughs in the War on Terror—including the inability to capture the elusive Osama bin Laden or any of the major al-Qaeda operatives.

In this context, the Lodi case clearly had the potential to ratchet up public fear of terrorism and to provide renewed justification for the government's policies of surveillance, detention, and deportation, particularly those targeting Muslims, Arabs, and South Asians.[2] Yet the government affidavit eventually filed in the federal court in Sacramento contained none of the original allegations about sensational terrorist plots, and the two men were charged only with lying to federal investigators about the son's alleged links to al-Qaeda training camps. Three other men in Lodi, two Muslim imams and the son of one of the imams, were also arrested, but only for suspected immigration violations. The FBI also interrogated numerous members of the Pakistani community in Lodi and raided several homes. As it became apparent that the FBI had no tangible evidence that Hamid Hayat was linked to a terrorist group, government prosecutors began downplaying the seriousness of the threat the men posed, admitting that none of the five men had plans to bomb targets in California or anywhere else. "We did not find these guys in the middle of executing an attack. That did not happen," said McGregor Scott, U.S. attorney for the Eastern District of California (Holstege, Marcucci, and Drucker 2005).

Yet the damage had already been done by the lurid stories that fueled a hysteria over terrorist threats and a general suspicion of Muslim immigrants, particularly Arab and South Asian males. Why did the FBI seize these men in Lodi, and how did Hamid Hayat, a twenty-two-year-old cherry packer, become the object of intense government scrutiny? As the story unfolded over the following weeks and months, it became apparent that the answers were tied to another figure who slowly emerged from the background: a Pakistani man in his late twenties, Nasim Khan. Khan had befriended the Hayats and the imams and had stayed at their homes after moving to Lodi, helping them with computers and spending time with their sons, in particular. Khan vanished just after their arrests, but it was soon revealed that he was an FBI informant who had infiltrated the community and had been spying on Lodi residents and recording their conversations for three years; Khan had been paid $250,000 by the FBI by the time the case came to trial (Cockburn 2006). Fifty tapes of conversations in Urdu and Pashto, recorded by Khan, which included comments by Hamid Hayat about his identification with militant groups, were presented by the government as the basis of charges that the Hayats sought to attack the United States (Hood 2006; D. Thompson 2005). The case thus implied that verbal statements expressing militant dissent against the United States are a potential criminal offense, a crucial point that I will return to later.

The legal case made by the government tried to link these political statements made by Hamid Hayat to conversations in which Khan urged Hamid to attend a terrorist training camp. Khan was recorded telling Hamid that he wanted to attend a "jihadi camp" and suggesting that the young man accompany him to Pakistan (Mojaddidi 2006). When Hamid eventually went to Pakistan to get married, he received repeated phone calls from Khan, who urged him to attend a camp and verbally abused him when Hamid insisted that he had no desire to comply. According to Hamid Hayat's lawyer, Wazhma Mojaddidi, the FBI agents who received the tapes barely spoke Urdu or Pashto and relied on Khan, rather than on a translator, for interpretation. Over time, it was revealed that Khan, a permanent U.S. resident, had been convicted of burglary while living in Oregon and, while being interviewed by the FBI about money laundering, had pointed to the TV screen and declared, "I know that man" (Bulwa 2005; Mojaddidi 2006). That man happened to be Ayman al-Zawahiri, al-Qaeda's second-in-command. Khan blithely announced that while he had been living in Lodi, California, Zawahiri had visited the mosque and walked around town (Cockburn 2006). This alone should have given the FBI agents pause, as terrorism experts later proved this claim false and asserted that there was no evidence that the al-Qaeda leader had visited the United States, let alone strolled around Lodi (Bulwa 2006a). Yet unlike the Hayats, Khan was not accused of lying to the FBI.

Khan was first asked by the FBI to inform on the two imams, who had come to the United States on religious-leader visas and were in Lodi to establish an Islamic school for the town's Muslim population. The FBI interrogated the imams after they were detained, but since they refused to admit to any involvement with terrorism, they were charged only with immigration violations (Mojaddidi 2006), and the focus of the investigation shifted to Hamid Hayat. The imams eventually decided to cut their losses and took voluntary departure, so they were never technically deported by the government. This occurred despite the fact that they were presumably the "masterminds" of the terrorist plot in which Hamid Hayat was involved.

DEPORTATION AND DEPORTABILITY

I argue that deportation, or the threat of deportation as in the case of the Hayats and countless other Arabs, South Asians, and Muslims targeted in the roundups after the events of September 11, 2001, is a strategy used by the U.S. state that is fundamentally linked to neoliberal capitalism and imperial domination.[3] Deportation is a euphemistic term for being kicked out of a country. In the United States, the expulsion of individuals by the state is also called "removal," which is more accurate but equally ambiguous and impersonal.[4] The image of unwanted persons being sent by the government to their home countries assumes the "legality" of the process and the "illegality," or at least undesirability, of the deported persons. As such, deportation conjures up fear in those who potentially *could* be deported and evokes some degree of reassurance or acquiescence in those who believe that the nation is thus rid of persons who do not deserve to reside within its borders. Deportation connotes a moral judgment of worthiness and desirability that differentiates between "good" immigrants who are not deported and "bad" immigrants who are, but this line is not as fixed and self-evident as it appears in mainstream discourse about "illegal" immigrants and "un-American" dissidents, both of whom presumably pose a threat to the nation. However, there is a moral economy deeply embedded in deportation that constructs the virtue of citizenship and helps to continually reinscribe the borders of the nation.

The undeclared but arguably ongoing war on immigrants waged by the state, and intensified in the 1990s, has infused the public imagination with the specter of hordes of dark-skinned immigrants from alien backgrounds invading the nation by crossing its borders "illegally," by land, sea, and air, or living furtively within its borders in "illegal" status while leeching off the state's social services (Inda 2006). The official "War on Terror" has deployed a similar rhetoric to target Muslims, Arabs, and South Asians who are undocumented immigrants, as well as permanent residents and even citizens assumed to be threats to national security—a potential fifth column within the nation. Deportation of these immigrant bodies appears to function as a cleansing of unwanted bodies from the nation so that the national body politic is freed of contaminants (Peutz 2006). Underlying the moral panic about expelling these polluting bodies is a racist regime of governmentality that fuels xenophobic hysteria and paranoia about individuals and groups that are sullying or destroying the nation. Like "deportation," the term "extraordinary rendition" is also a euphemism for expelling individuals who are presumably terrorist threats to their home countries, but in this case to be tortured without U.S. culpability, as in the case of Maher Arar, a Canadian citizen who was deported to Syria by the United States and later cleared of links to terrorist groups by the Canadian government, which issued a formal apology.[5] In such cases, deportation becomes a strategy for outsourcing torture to cleanse the nation from further guilt and to absolve the state from responsibility for its atrocities.

Deportation is generally taken for granted as a remedial device that the state has no choice but to use to maintain its integrity and security in response to unwanted pollutants. However, I argue that deportation is actually a constitutive logic of the imperial state and its drive to consolidate and impose neoliberal economic policies globally. Neoliberal capitalism, which was consolidated in the 1990s as the post–Cold War "Washington Consensus" imposing free trade and structural adjustment globally (Smith 2005, 144), envisions citizens as productive, self-reliant individuals who are free of the dependence created by the welfare state, and as consumers of social services that are increasingly privatized in the neoliberal state (Miller 1993). This privatization of citizenship has diminished the right of citizens to public goods and services, which are instead allocated according to individual "worthiness."[6] The domestic regulation of labor and subjection of immigrants are tied to the U.S. state's policies of global military, political, and economic domination, which have historically relied on both direct and indirect methods of control (Harvey 2003; Mamdani 2004). U.S. imperialism is characterized by nebulous, nonterritorial forms of domination that do not resemble traditional forms of territorial colonialism and blur the boundaries of "formal" and "informal" empire (Ahmad 2004).[7] U.S. imperialism has generally enforced its political projects through client states, with the help of complicit elites and covert or proxy wars (Magdoff 2003; Mamdani 2004), a situation that has changed somewhat after the events of September 11, 2001, with the U.S. war on Afghanistan and the direct occupation of Iraq. But U.S. empire continues to rely on the twin processes of foreign coercion and domestic repression (Smith 2005). Global imperial power and neoliberal capitalism go hand in hand, for "the hidden hand of the market will never work without a hidden fist" (Koshy 2003, 169), and repression is necessary to discipline citizens and crush dissent against imperial policies. U.S. foreign policy is linked to the "policing of domestic racial tensions" and the disciplining of subordinated populations through racial and class hierarchies at home (Pease 1993, 31).

The logic behind deportation is both economic and political, for it supports U.S. policies of neoliberal capitalism as well as of political domination and repression. Deportation, as it is used in the United States, is not an exceptional phenomenon in response to exigencies of infiltration or invasion but actually part of the normative regime of controlling and disciplining bodies (Ong 2006, 6). Deportation is a daily technology of subjection for the regulation of citizens, migrants, and workers by a state in which repression and war, at home or overseas, are not a "state of exception" but the everyday state of emergency in U.S. empire (Agamben 2003/2005, 22; Hardt and Negri 2001, 17). The national consensus for U.S. foreign policies is strengthened through historical processes of scapegoating "outsiders" and conflating internal and external enemies that link the domestic and foreign fronts of U.S. imperialism (Stoler 2006, 12). I argue here that deportation, too, links both the overseas and homeland arenas of imperial control.

DEPORTATION'S NEOLIBERAL LOGIC

Deportation is both an economic and a political strategy of the imperial state. In this chapter, I focus primarily on the political uses of deportation policy, but I want to note that the economic and political logics of deportation are distinct but ultimately overlapping, to ensure a docile workforce and target politically threatening dissent—goals that converge in some instances, as I will discuss later. Aihwa Ong observes that the neoliberal state relies on "a biopolitical mode of governing that centers on the capacity and potential of individuals and the population as living resources that may be harnessed and managed by governing regimes" (2006, 6). Immigration law regulates the flow of labor across national borders through immigrant visas and documents that determine who can enter and for how long, based on work and educational credentials. Deportation policy, which determines who must leave, works in tandem with this management of the entry of immigrant labor. Deportation is one of the "spatial practices that engage market forces" by controlling and recruiting certain pools of workers for the neoliberal state to ensure its competitiveness and productivity in the global economy (6). The threat of expulsion is necessary for regulating economic citizenship, for it disciplines immigrant labor and depresses wages. Deportation laws have historically performed this function since the 1888 deportation statute was promulgated to regulate the flow of "cheap" foreign (mainly Chinese) labor (B. Hing 2004, 209–10).

Furthermore, as Nicholas De Genova points out, it is "deportability, and not deportation per se," that is crucial for neoliberal capitalism: "The category 'illegal alien' is a profoundly useful and profitable one that effectively serves to create and sustain a legally vulnerable—and hence relatively tractable and thus 'cheap'—reserve of labor" (2002, 438–40). Deportation, or specifically the legal production of the *category* of deportability, is an economic strategy of the neoliberal state, which requires the presence of noncitizen and undocumented labor. The heightened fear of deportation produced by the War on Terror ensures that wages will continue to be depressed and immigrant workers will be even more hesitant to organize collectively and more intensely subjected to economic exploitation. Yet the implications of this economic logic of deportation and deportability are rarely made explicit in state policies and legislation, unlike policies that openly target political dissenters for presumably posing a threat to national security. This makes it difficult to enact strategies of resistance that challenge the core of this logic rather than simply asserting that "good immigrants" are hardworking, productive, and deserve to stay. The politics of labor subordination, however, are only the most general feature of deportation as a political strategy, as will become clear through the cases discussed here.

Despite the increasing influence and visibility of transnational movements, the possibility of what some have called "postnational citizenship" (Soysal 1996) or "global citizenship" (Hardt and Negri 2001) remains ambiguous given that individual and collective rights still remain largely tied to territorially bounded nation-states (Shafir 2004). Political movements, too, continue to address their claims for immigrant and civil rights to the nation-state as the guarantor of rights. Immigrant rights organizing in the United States after September 11, 2001, has challenged the climate of xenophobia and repression, particularly with the mass-scale immigrant rights protests in 2006 in response to the proposed "immigration reform" bill, HR 3477. Hundreds of thousands of immigrants, the majority of whom were Latinos, marched in cities across the nation under slogans such as "No human being is illegal" (Allday, Zamora, and Rubenstein 2006). Yet the predominant focus of this movement—at least in its mainstream, U.S.-flag-waving manifestation—demonstrated that undocumented immigrants still appeal to the state for legalization of their status. This is understandable given the material reality of the state, but such demands still tend to reinforce the link between state sovereignty and citizenship. At the same time, as Ong argues, "The neoliberal exception thus pries open the seam of sovereignty and citizenship, generating successive degrees of insecurity for low-skilled citizens and migrants who will have to look beyond the state for the safeguarding of their rights" (2006, 19). Immigrants are forced to grapple with the limitations of rights as granted by the state and to consider other ways of responding to issues of deportation, an issue I will return to later. The question of what strategies immigrants and others can use in forging a political movement to challenge the state's disciplining of immigrant labor is tied to the political function of deportation policy, the second major component of the logic of deportation and the focal point of this chapter.

DEPORTATION AS AN INSTRUMENT OF TERROR

Deportation is a political instrument of the neoliberal "warfare state"—a heavily militarized state that wages perpetual war, overtly or covertly— that can be used to contain dissent and suppress political movements that challenge imperial policies. Especially after the passing of the Patriot Act in 2001, but also at other historical junctures, the threat of deportation, along with policies of surveillance and detention, has served as a device for repression and for intimidating critics of state policies. After the events of September 11, the actual as well as threatened deportation of Muslim, Arab, and South Asian immigrants has been used to instill fear in communities that have been targeted in the domestic War on Terror. Muslim families began experiencing the disappearances of their husbands, brothers, and sons, for none of the detainees were identified publicly, and the locations where they were held remained secret (Chang 2002, 69–87).

As part of the domestic War on Terror, at least 1,200 Muslim, Arab, and South Asian immigrant men were rounded up and detained within seven weeks in the immediate aftermath of September 11, none of them with any criminal charges, and some in high-security prisons (Cainkar and Maira 2006).[8] By May 2003 the Department of Justice had also detained over 1,000 foreign nationals under the Absconder Apprehension Initiative, which prioritized the deportation of 6,000 Muslims and Arabs of the over 300,000 immigrants with outstanding deportation orders (Cole 2003, 25). The targeting of Muslim and Arab males highlights the gendered dimension and underlying anti-Arab racism of the War on Terror, whose public discourse relies on often hyper-Orientalist tropes of violent, fanatical Muslim and Arab men and oppressed, veiled Muslim and Arab women who can be rescued by the United States, through military intervention if necessary (see Sheikh 2003).

An interesting point to note that reveals the underlying political logic of deportation is that Pakistani immigrants were disproportionately targeted for detention and deportation, though there were no Pakistani nationals involved in the September 11 hijackings, and Pakistan has been a key ally to the United States. Nevertheless nearly 40 percent of the post–September

11 detainees were estimated to be Pakistani nationals (Schulhofer 2002, 11). Additionally, there were mass deportations of Pakistani nationals on chartered planes, some leaving in the middle of the night from New York state, that went unreported in the mainstream media (Ryan 2003, 16). Pakistanis in the United States became suspect because the U.S. government claimed it was clamping down on Islamist guerrilla networks linked to both al-Qaeda and the Taliban in northwest Pakistan, along the border with Afghanistan—ironically, the same area that provided the mujahedin whom the CIA armed and trained to fight its proxy war in Afghanistan in the 1980s (see Rashid 2000). The selective detention and deportation of Pakistani immigrants within and from the United States, largely due to immigration violations, was linked to increased pressure on Pakistani president Pervez Musharraf to contain "militants" from "tribal" areas opposed to U.S. policies in the Middle East.[9] This is one of many examples that illustrate how deportation links immigration issues with U.S. foreign policy (Hing 2006b).

Furthermore, the post–September 11 sweeps not only included Arab and Muslim immigrants but targeted other communities as well, particularly low-wage undocumented workers. For example, in November 2001 the government began requiring all airport screeners to be U.S. citizens and conducted a multiagency sweep of airports, named Operation Tarmac, that resulted in the detention and deportation of more than one thousand undocumented airport workers, mostly Latinos and Filipinos (Nguyen 2005, xx, 18). A point that is often overlooked in discussions of the War on Terror is that most of the Muslim and Arab males who were deported were low-wage undocumented workers. So while the targeted detentions and deportations had a chilling effect on political dissent among Muslim and Arab Americans, in particular, whose home countries and regions were being targeted by U.S. military incursions, it also served to make even more vulnerable a class of already exploited immigrant labor. The detention of Muslims and Arabs rounded up after September 11 shows most clearly the intertwining of the political and economic logic of deportation policy. Most of the detainees were deported for immigration violations, and except for one or two high-profile cases, none were found guilty of terrorism-related charges. Their detention and deportation were based on *political profiling* linked to the War on Terror, and though they were targeted for being Arab and Muslim and not specifically because of class, the mass warehousing and intimidation of this pool of low-wage labor had an economic effect. The economic and political work of deportation converges in this regime of discipline and punishment.

Deportation is accompanied by regimes of surveillance and detention that work in tandem as part of the disciplining technologies of the state. Surveillance has been conducted through FBI infiltration of political groups and Muslim communities and the use of "insider" informants, as I will discuss later, but also through FBI interviews of targeted populations, such as Iraqis during the buildup for the war on Iraq, and later Iranians (Cainkar 2004). The state created official policies for openly monitoring and collecting information on suspected populations after September 11. In June 2002 the National Security Entry-Exit Registration System (NSEERS), commonly known as Special Registration, was established, requiring all male nationals over sixteen from twenty-four Muslim-majority countries (including Pakistan and Bangladesh), as well as from North Korea, to submit to photographing, fingerprinting, and interviews at federal immigration facilities.[10] Over 80,000 men complied with Special Registration; many of these men, however, never returned home, as 2,870 men were detained and 13,799 were put into deportation proceedings (Nguyen 2005, xviii). After news broke of mass arrests of nearly a thousand Iranians complying with Special Registration in Southern California in December 2002 (52), some undocumented immigrants and those with pending immigration applications fled to the Canadian border and tried to apply for asylum (Ryan 2003), demonstrating that their fear of detention and deportation was linked to a fear of persecution in the United States based on religion and national origin.

The indirect but arguably intended outcome of the threat of deportation is that it creates terror and stifles dissent among those who consider themselves "deportable" as immigrants or suspect populations. Corey Robin argues that "fear does the work—or enhances the work—of repression," noting that the "effects of 'Fear, American Style,'" have been most evident in immigrant, Middle Eastern, and South Asian communities, as well as in the workplace, where "suppression of dissent" is evident since September 11, 2001, in countless examples of direct and indirect harassment and intimidation of those expressing views considered "unpatriotic" (2003, 48). Robin points out that repression works on two levels to silence dissent: on a state level, through agencies such as the FBI and the Department of Homeland Security, but also on the level of civil society, where individuals internalize repression and censor themselves. This is the larger political problem and painful paradox created by the War on Terror, for the targeted communities that most need to mobilize collectively in response are also the ones who are, understandably, the most afraid of being punished for political speech, let alone political organizing. The broader and ultimately more far-reaching effects of regimes of deportation and deportability on individuals who are not political activists, in the traditional sense, is an issue that has received less scholarly attention, but one that I argue is pressing in the era of the Patriot Act.

DEPORTING "ALIEN" IDEOLOGIES

It must be noted that deportation has long been used for repression and coercion by the imperial state, and so its normative character is rooted in historical precedent in the United States (see Kanstroom 2007). In fact, as Bill Hing points out, "The first deportation and expulsion provision was related to political ideology" (2004, 209). In 1798, anticipating war with France, Congress passed the Alien and Sedition Acts, which "made it a crime to criticize the government" and authorized the deportation of alien males over fourteen (Chang 2002, 22; see also R. Delgado 2003, 68). During World War I, the Espionage Act of 1917, drawing on nativist fears directed at anarchists and socialists, was passed to suppress dissent, as was the 1918 Anarchist Act targeting "subversive aliens" (B. Hing 2004). The infamous Palmer Raids of 1919–20 led to the rounding up of almost 3,000 foreign nationals for deportation, most of them workers and union members. During the Red Scare, Attorney General Mitchell Palmer created a "Radical Division" within the Department of Justice that, with the help of J. Edgar Hoover, employed spies to infiltrate labor unions (B. Hing 2004, 216–20). Conducted in a wartime climate of nativism and hysteria about foreign "subversives," the Palmer Raids are perhaps the historical event that most closely parallels the post–September 11 mass detentions and deportations initiated by Attorney General John Ashcroft, which now targeted Muslim and Arab men.

The anticommunist witch hunts of the 1940s and 1950s and the Smith Act of 1940 are infamous for driving the "second Red Scare" of the Cold War, but the targeting of political dissidents who were noncitizens persisted long after the McCarthy era. For example, the McCarran-Walter Act of 1952, which contained "the most extensive ideological deportation and exclusion provisions" based on association with the Communist Party, was used by the FBI and the INS to arrest seven Palestinians and one Kenyan in Los Angeles in 1987 (Cole 2003, 131). The case of the "L.A. Eight" is important because it demonstrates that the political profiling of Arabs and Muslims did not begin only after the events of September 11, 2001, and those who have protested U.S. policy in the Middle East have been targeted by the government at various moments since the 1967 Arab-Israeli War.[11]

The government charged that the affiliation of the L.A. Eight with the Popular Front for the Liberation of Palestine (PFLP) implied that they advocated "world communism," still a deportable offense at the time (Cole and Dempsey 2002, 35–38). The L.A. Eight successfully challenged the government's targeting of political activism and its use of secret evidence, but though the government eventually dropped the charges of association with communism, it prosecuted the six noncitizens on immigration violations. The INS continued to seek the deportation of Khader Hamide and Michel Shehadeh, who were permanent residents, on grounds of providing "material support" to the PFLP, allegedly a "terrorist organization" (36–37). In this, the INS conducted an ideologically motivated deportation campaign based on government disapproval of the PFLP's political activity. The FBI's goal was admittedly "to identify key PFLP people in Southern California so that law enforcement agencies capable of disrupting the PFLP's activities through legal action can do so" (cited in Cole and Dempsey 2002, 38).

The political irony that must be noted here is that the FBI and INS charged these Palestinian activists with belonging to an organization that was not a threat to the United States but was opposed to the policies of the Israeli government and the occupation of Palestine. In charging the L.A. Eight on behalf of the Israeli government and trying to squash pro-Palestine organizing in the United States, the government was revealing its support for Israeli policies and its willingness to prosecute these activists for opposing a foreign government. The other troubling aspect of the L.A. Eight's fifteen-year battle in the courts to fight their deportation is that it occurred *after* the political persecution of the FBI's COINTELPRO program of the 1960s and 1970s had been brought to light and criticized for its surveillance, infiltration, and disruption of civil rights and antiwar organizing in the United States (Chang 2002, 29–32). David Cole points out that these ideologically motivated deportation campaigns targeting particular political groups and activists relied on immigration law because noncitizens tried in immigration courts have none of the rights afforded to citizens during a criminal trial (2003, 126–27). After September 11, 2001, the government reopened the case of the L.A. Eight under the provisions of the Patriot Act in an attempt to finally deport the remaining two Palestinian activists (Shehadeh 2007).[12] A similarly ideologically motivated campaign directed at activists opposing U.S.-backed regimes involved the government's surveillance of the Committee in Solidarity with the People of El Salvador (CISPES) in the 1980s, a group of mostly U.S. citizens who opposed U.S. military aid to the repressive right-wing regime in El Salvador (Churchill 2006; Cole and Dempsey 2002, 22–23).[13]

There are two significant features of this historical pattern of state surveillance and political repression in the United States, according to Cole (2003, 85): first, "antialien sentiments and tactics" were generally used to target noncitizens, but this political repression eventually extended to citizens as well and broke down the sanctity of the citizen-noncitizen divide. The second point, as illustrated by the CISPES case, is that the end of the Cold War saw the substitution of "terrorism" for "communism" in the U.S. state's cross hairs. The Reagan administration proposed legislation to make "support for terrorism" a crime in 1984,[14] a measure later introduced in the 1996 Antiterrorism and Effective Death Penalty Act (AEDPA) passed by the Clinton administration (Cole and Dempsey 2002, 29). What these two points together suggest is that political deportation in the United States has historically been aimed not just at individual activists or even organizations and activities but also at the suppression of ideologies viewed as threatening to state interests.[15]

Deportation is thus a device not just for removing and repressing "alien" or "radical" bodies and organizations but an instrument for eliminating or preempting the spread of radical ideas—radical because they are opposed to key U.S. policies of neoliberal economic expansion and global political domination. The word "alien" is problematic when applied to immigrant bodies, but it is revealing when applied to the actual target of deportation: the *ideas* that are deemed fundamentally alien to the imperial state. This is what we need to consider in reframing our understanding of the political work of deportation: targeting bodies, organizations, and also ideas.

Suppressing radical or alien ideas involves the targeting not just of radical activists and organizations but also of ordinary individuals who are assumed to be associated with political ideas or organizations that are deemed anti-American or who may at some point act on such ideas or at the behest of such organizations. This is the fundamental logic of the government's War on Terror, yet much more attention has been paid to the state's targeting of individuals or organizations who are publicly political, such as the L.A. Eight or CISPES. While this work is extremely important in exposing the often hidden political logic of detention and deportation (cf. Churchill 2006), little work has examined the wide impact of deportation policies or cases on those who are considered outside formal politics and on whom such policies have a less-publicized but equally important effect in terms of the political culture after September 11, 2001. Examining cases of individuals who are not considered political activists in the traditionally defined sense also forces us to grapple with the broader meaning of politics and the nature of politicization, particularly in light of the state's assumptions about which groups of people are likely to be politicized or have political views that are considered threatening to the national security state's imperial policies in its global War on Terror.

LAW AS A WAR ZONE

It is important to note that the legal groundwork for targeting immigrants for deportation in the War on Terror was laid well before September 11, 2001, and that the Patriot Act actually extended provisions in the AEDPA and the Illegal Immigration Reform and Immigrant Responsibility Act of 1996, introduced under a Democratic administration. Kathleen Moore argues that the national anxiety about political, economic, and cultural threats to the nation from immigrants and aliens after the Cold War is a response to the ongoing and "heightened sense of insecurity required to maintain a restructured, wartime regulatory state after the primary security target disappears" (1999, 95). This manufactured sense of national insecurity that shores up the warfare state, even in peacetime, is reflected in U.S. law and has persisted well beyond the dissolution of the Soviet Union, as the foregoing examples demonstrate. Contrary to the notion that "the fate of justice during war is an aberration," Richard Delgado argues that the recurrent pattern of suspension of civil liberties and use of the law to execute U.S. government policies suggests that these are not "exceptions to an otherwise scrupulously fair system" but, in fact, "the rule, the most obvious, most visible case" (2003, 80). In Delgado's view, the law is embedded in, not outside, the social system and linked to a coercive state apparatus; it is a mechanism for framing the terms of conflict that it is presumably designed to mediate—for example, defining who is an enemy combatant and who deserves habeas corpus. Delgado suggests, like other critical legal theorists, that "all of law is a war zone" (80).

Furthermore, the targeting of noncitizens and citizens who embody "alien" ideologies in the War on Terror connects U.S. foreign policy concerns with domestic issues of immigration, criminalization, and incarceration. Deportation connects overseas wars with racial profiling and domestic assaults on civilian populations, revealing the links between the War on Terror, the unofficial but ongoing war on immigrants, and also the so-called War on Drugs (Nguyen 2005). The blurring of panics about terrorists, immigrants, and young men of color is evident also in the war on gangs, which has used antiterrorist strategies to annually deport up to forty thousand alleged Latino gang members to Mexico and Central America for "aggravated felonies" since 1996.[16] Anxieties about border security and presumed infiltration of terrorists through the U.S.-Mexico border show how "homeland insecurities" about immigration are linked to foreign-policy concerns about war and terrorism.

Detention is a necessary precursor to deportation, since all deportees are detained for varying lengths of time before they are deported. The process of detention connects Arab, Muslim, and South Asian detainees to other criminalized minority and immigrant populations who are overrepresented in the prison system (Cainkar and Maira 2006). Deportation is thus necessarily linked to the expanding U.S. prison-industrial complex, "a vast system of immigration prisons that had been detaining 150,000 people annually since the mid-1990s and now hold more than 200,000 people each year" (Nguyen 2005, 7). The INS, which has been restructured and now functions partly as the Bureau of Immigration and Customs Enforcement (ICE) under the Department of Homeland Security (DHS), warehouses immigrants in local jails as well as privately run prisons. As Tram Nguyen observes, "this almost invisible system of warehousing—and "removal" or deportation—had been operating and growing quietly for years before September 11" (7).[17] In *American Gulag: Inside U.S. Immigration Prisons*, Mark Dow documents the workings of the vast but largely "invisible" prison system run by the INS and its later incarnation as the DHS (2004, 11–12), where immigrant detainees have been abused, even tortured, by prison officials and held in secret detention.

For example, an infamous report of the Department of Justice's Office of Inspector General (OIG) investigated conditions at the Metropolitan Detention Center in Brooklyn and Passaic County Jail in Paterson, New Jersey, where many of the post–September 11 detainees were held.[18] Released in 2003, the OIG's report found three hundred videotapes documenting numerous incidents of cruel, inhumane, and degrading punishment, including prison guards slamming detainees into walls, smashing their faces into a T-shirt with an American flag, beating them and dragging them over floors and stairs, conducting unnecessary strip searches, leaving detainees naked for extended periods of time, and routinely subjecting them to verbal abuse, racist comments, and threats. This report became public before the torture of Iraqi detainees by the U.S. military in Abu Ghraib prison came to light, but it was barely noticed in the mainstream media and disappeared quickly without any of the public outrage provoked by the Abu Ghraib scandal. This instance of domestic torture of detainees exemplifies what Dylan Rodríguez describes as the

> illegal and unconstitutional abuses of state power, unabashed use of strategic and deadly violence, and development of invasive, terrorizing surveillance technologies [that] might be seen as the state's prototyping of the era's broadly revivified (and significantly extrastate) domestic low-intensity warfare techniques against racially pathologized "activist" and "civilian" populations alike. (2006, 23)

This is a crucial point, for Rodríguez elucidates the ways in which distinctions between "activists" and "civilians" are in some ways less meaningful in defining populations selectively targeted by the state through technologies of surveillance, police brutality, incarceration, prison abuse, and legal warfare than are racialized categories of criminalization (see also Cainkar and Maira 2006).[19] Rodríguez argues that "the prison regime has become an indispensable element of American statecraft, simultaneously a cornerstone of its militarized (local and global) ascendancy and spectacle of its extracted (or coerced) authority over targeted publics" (2006, 44).

The closely related processes of detention and deportation are part of everyday regimes of state control that link domestic and foreign policies, the two fronts of imperial domination. As Rodríguez suggests in the case of detainees, deportees too are targeted because of domestic and international politics, so that even if they are not traditionally political prisoners, they are constituted politically in their encounter with the state. Certainly there are cases of detention and deportation that involve political activists who are explicitly targeted because of their organizing activity, as in the case of the L.A. Eight and CISPES, among many others. However, a continuum exists between so-called political prisoners and detainees and deportees who are not traditional activists but are nonetheless subjects of a political process that targets populations selectively in accordance with wider political projects of intimidation and control. In fact, it is as a result of having to deal with detention or deportation at the hands of the government that many Arab, Muslim, and South Asian immigrants have become politicized, ironically, and it is the awareness of the larger scapegoating and profiling of these targeted communities that may, in fact, lead to a radicalization of their responses.

In this light, I offer the story of two South Asian immigrants, Hamid and Umer Hayat, targeted for deportation after September 11, to illustrate the work of deportation as a political, economic, and social technology of U.S. empire. This story also draws on my own experiences working on issues of immigrant and civil rights in South Asian communities after September 11, 2001, in the San Francisco Bay Area and in the Boston area. While I focus on the case in Lodi, California, which received extensive national coverage, I also touch on a local story of deportations in the Bay Area that (like most other stories of immigrant deportations) hardly emerged in the mainstream media at all but suggests possibilities for framing a political response. While not all the South Asian immigrants in these cases were eventually deported, their stories show the range of experiences that South Asian immigrants have in their encounter with the state through the regime of deportation and how this encounter crystallizes the state's definition of the nature and locus of potentially radical politics.

LODI: ON CANNERY WORKERS, TERRORISTS, AND WIGS

The Lodi case involving Hamid and Umer Hayat is an excellent example of how the government's political logic of deportation targeted two South Asian Muslim men, who were by all accounts far removed from any organized political activity, on the assumption that radical political ideologies and anti-American sentiments were lurking among cannery workers in this sleepy little town. In fact, the premise of "sleeper cell" cases is that there are would-be terrorists in our midst who are by definition invisible and unknown, but potentially dangerous. The Lodi case was also based on a broader pattern of preemptive deportation and of framing individuals for political expressions and alleged intentions that has troubling implications for political dissent, as I will discuss later.

After I heard about the arrests of Hamid and Umer Hayat in June 2005, I visited Lodi with Veena Dubal, a law school student and member of the Bay Area–based Alliance for South Asians Taking Action (ASATA), in which I was also involved in doing immigrant and civil rights work. When we arrived in Lodi, we found that FBI agents were swarming all over the town and were continuing to monitor the mosque. Several Pakistani men were standing outside the mosque in the early evening, relaxing on the grass and chatting after work. They told us that the FBI had begun coming to Lodi immediately after September 11 and "making friends" with mosque members (Dubal and Maira 2005). One man, without looking around, described to us exactly where each federal agent's car was parked; we saw the three large SUVs with black-tinted windows, just yards from the mosque, where some young South Asian and Latino boys were playing basketball. One middle-aged Pakistani man said quietly, "Let them come ask us questions. We have nothing to hide." While this resilience was inspiring, it also bespoke a certain resigned acceptance of the surveillance; others we spoke to were understandably concerned about the impact of the surveillance and racist backlash in Lodi on their children and families. One woman reported that her young child had been followed by the FBI while going to get ice cream. Several Pakistani men had been hauled off for questioning by the FBI without access to attorneys; a few had been detained. Others complained that they had been taken from their workplaces for interrogation and could not return because their coworkers became suspicious of them. The most shocking report was of an FBI raid on the home of one of the imams, which had been under close surveillance, when only three women and five children were inside. The agents broke down the front door and put a gun to the head of one of the women. Her eleven-year-old daughter passed out, but the FBI denied entry to medical personnel and refused to let her go to the hospital. This gross violation of human rights outraged even the local emergency care personnel but went unreported in most media coverage.

When meeting with members of the Council on American Islamic Relations (CAIR) and the ACLU who were providing legal support and civil rights information to the local community, we noticed a blue SUV driving around the motel where we had congregated. Undercover agents had been monitoring the legal team in their motel for days, and as we drove by, the man driving the SUV circled our car and took photographs from his window. When we tried to approach him, he fled, only to return later and take more photos. Strangely, the man was wearing a large Afro wig and dark glasses, a rather crude disguise that seemed surreal in the middle of Lodi. This was such a conspicuous cover that it confirmed that the principal purpose of the FBI surveillance was to intimidate the community.

Despite the support provided by civil rights activists from Sacramento and the Bay Area, it became apparent that one of the reasons that Lodi might have provided a convenient location for such intense FBI surveillance, not to mention the staging of the sleeper cell case itself, was the lack of political mobilization in the South Asian community in this rural area. The Pakistani community is a largely working-class population, numbering between 2,000 and 4,000, many of whom work at the local fruit-canning factory close to the mosque (Hua 2005). The community has lived in Lodi since the 1920s (Grudin 2005), and some men we spoke to said their ancestors had come to the United States as early as 1908 to work on the railroads, so it is a much older community than the upwardly mobile South Asian population in the San Francisco Bay Area or other parts of California. Yet South Asians in Lodi are geographically and politically isolated from their compatriots in the major urban and suburban South Asian enclaves, and most do not speak English (Grudin 2005), so they are an easier target for surveillance and intimidation. Compared to the Bay Area, where there is a plethora of civil and immigrant rights organizations, Lodi had no South Asian or Asian American organizations to advocate for or educate the Pakistani community in civil and immigrant rights issues.

Hamid Hayat, like other men in Lodi, had opened his door to the FBI when they arrived at his home, three days after he returned from Pakistan. Without consulting a lawyer, he had agreed to repeated questioning and volunteered to drive to Sacramento to take a polygraph test. When he was told that he had failed the lie detector test, he was never shown the actual report by the FBI. However, given the FBI's intense desire to discover a terrorist plot, civil rights education would probably have been a thin shield. His attorney pointed out that both father and son were pressured into admitting that Hamid had attended a terrorist camp through the repeated interviews to which they were subjected and in a language they did not fully understand (Mojaddidi 2006). The FBI even showed Hamid photos of his own wedding in Pakistan as evidence, claiming that the Pakistani men with guns were terrorists, even though Hamid tried to explain that they were shooting blanks, as is the custom at weddings in Pakistan and the Middle East.

The Hayats were eventually brought to trial separately in spring 2006, and Hamid Hayat was found guilty of making false statements and providing "material support" for terrorism, facing up to thirty-nine years in prison (Bulwa 2006a). His father's trial ended in a hung jury, and Umer Hayat was charged only with lying to Customs upon returning to the United States; his terrorism charges were eventually dismissed, and he was sentenced to the 330 days in prison he had already served (Bulwa 2006a). By the time the jury reached a verdict, even the mainstream media acknowledged that the case basically rested on the use of preventive detention based on fear of an alleged plot rather than on evidence of actual terrorist activity and that the Hayat case was a much-needed victory for the Department of Justice given its lack of success in prosecuting terrorism cases. At the time of my writing this chapter, Hamid Hayat's attorney and the new co-counsel Dennis Riordan had filed a motion for a new trial, hoping to bring in evidence and testimonies that the government had denied them during the trial.

SURVEILLANCE, REPRESSION, AND RESISTANCE

The case also brought to light an important issue that began surfacing in the media: that of paid FBI informants infiltrating mosques and South Asian, Arab, and Muslim immigrant communities across the United States. A pattern emerged of informants framing suspects, usually young Muslim men critical of the War on Terror and angry about the U.S. occupation of Iraq and atrocities related to U.S. interventions in the Middle East, by provoking and recording statements of their desire to attack U.S. targets or, as in Hamid Hayat's case, simply supporting militant dissent against U.S. policies. As Paul Ehrlich observes, "If that was illegal, the jails would be filled. If every person in the Middle East and Asia who's displeased with the U.S.'s performance is a terrorist, then we have millions of them" (cited in Hood 2006). The corollary of what seems to be a strategy of "preemptive denunciation" is that Muslim and Arab Americans have become increasingly reluctant to express dissenting political views, even with others who are from the same communities, since the informants are generally Muslim or Arab themselves. The FBI has used informants to provoke declarations of dissent by Muslim Americans, so in a sense it seeks out and even desires to prosecute the potential for radical ideas or expressions of political dissent, which it then uses as examples of terrorist conspiracies and networks. This is the cruel irony at the heart of deportation's political logic in the current conjuncture: the state needs the existence of radical ideas and movements to justify its assault on civil liberties, and if they don't exist as visibly and tangibly as needed, it must call them into public being to prove the threat to national security. This is a complex issue that is not just about entrapment but about the twisted logic embedded in the War on Terror—a war that by definition *needs* terrorism.

Arab and Muslim American communities around the nation—particularly in places with significant concentrations of Arab and Muslim immigrants such as Brooklyn, New York—have become familiar with the "telltale signs" of informers, who "like to talk politics . . . have plenty of free time," and "live in the neighborhood" (Elliott 2006). The use of insider informants was publicized in the trial of Shawahar Siraj, a Pakistani man, in an alleged plot to blow up a New York subway station in 2004. An Egyptian informant who was spying on the Muslim community around the Brooklyn mosque had shown Siraj pictures of Muslims overseas being mistreated and offered explosives to Siraj, who was then found guilty of the plot in 2006 (Rashbaum 2006). This strategy has prompted public debate and soul-searching within Muslim immigrant communities about whether the role of these informants, including imams and community leaders who enter into dialogues with the FBI, can be considered complicity with the government or benign cooperation with law enforcement. At the least, in many cases it has sown the seeds of distrust and division within communities that are not always politically mobilized and barely have the organizational resources to respond adequately to the post–September 11 crisis of civil rights.

The Lodi case brought attention to government strategies of infiltration and surveillance, but they also predictably heightened the sense of fear and suspicion within South Asian Muslim and Arab American communities. Arab American communities in general already have a collective memory of historical patterns of surveillance and often violent tactics of intimidation directed at Arab or pro-Palestine political organizations in the United States, such as the American Arab Anti-discrimination Committee (ADC).[20] The use of government informants, including religious leaders, has deepened the sense of vulnerability and distrust already permeating these communities after September 11, 2001, for it directed suspicion inward. The mosque and home were no longer safe havens free of state intrusion, since informants could be everywhere, as the Lodi case demonstrated, given that Nasim Khan worked with the imams and sometimes even slept over at their homes (Bulwa 2005). The state's penetration of the intimate corners of domains believed to be private made it apparent that the strategy of surveillance, detention, and deportation was not just about the policing of national borders or the border between citizens and noncitizens but about the dissolution of the boundary between state and community, and state and home, or perhaps the dissolution of a possibly unified community. The public sphere has enlarged to encompass all private spheres for Muslim Americans, even as the possibilities for open political discussion in the public sphere have diminished, if not disappeared for some.

Detentions and deportations after September 11, 2001, thus have a deep social impact and have led to the reconstitution and reorganizing of social relations for Muslim and Arab Americans, demonstrating how the political and economic technologies of subjection have a social logic as well (see Maira 2004). It is also evident that for some subjects, particularly Muslims and Arabs, the distinction between private and public has become meaningless in the realms where it has the most serious consequences. The intimacy of the state is heightened through practices of surveillance, detention, and deportation, so that, ironically, knowledge of the full reach of the state's powers and familiarity with certain aspects of the law are often greatest in the segments of the population that are least protected by the state. This political education inflicted by the War on Terror is involuntary because of the state's regulation and collective punishment of communities that are forced to directly confront its power.

The painful—but perhaps intended—outcome of the fear and distrust sown in Arab, Muslim, and South Asian communities by surveillance and deportation is the suppression of political organizing and the very collective organizing that these communities need to respond to the political crisis. The surveillance and infiltration of activist groups by the FBI affect antiwar and other movements as well, but noncitizens are obviously more vulnerable owing to the threat of deportation. Awareness of government informants and infiltration has also heightened fear of simply sharing information or political views, for all private spaces are experienced as public by Muslim Americans after September 11, 2001. The only statements that Muslim Americans feel secure making in this all-encompassing public space are denunciations of terrorism and insistence on Islam as a peace-loving, nonviolent religion. Steven Salaita calls this the "prerequisite to speaking" for Arabs and Muslims after September 11 and proposes an ethics of refusal of this disclaimer (2006, 51). He rightly observes that the use of the word "terrorism" is embedded in cultural prejudice about Arabs and Muslims and a decontextualized picture of violence that evades discussions of political grievances as well as state-sponsored violence. Invoking terrorism by denying it thus reinscribes this set of cultural and political assumptions about Arab, and Islamist, politics and cultures (Salaita 2006, 50–51; see also Puar and Rai 2002).

Even if Muslim commentators privately oppose U.S. policies in the War on Terror, many of them publicly perform the role of peace-loving "good Muslims" who are willing to be made into loyal citizens of the United States, as opposed to "bad Muslims" who critique the expansionist policies and imperial strategies of the United States under the guise of promoting democracy (Mamdani 2004, 15). There is obviously a concern about self-defense in this performance of good citizenship by Muslim and Arab Americans who feel that their political views are being monitored by the state and are afraid to openly express their dissent, and the "good Muslim" category is commonly invoked in legal cases and in the mainstream political arena as a defensive strategy. However, the deeper implications of this strategy are troubling in the longer term if it is a defense that remains within the terms set by the state in the War on Terror and refuses to acknowledge the root causes of terrorism and opposition to the United States, in the Middle East and elsewhere. Those who are most vulnerable may not be in the position to challenge the dichotomy of "good" and "bad" Muslims and the fundamental premise of the War on Terror, but I would extend Salaita's point and suggest that there also needs to be a collective defense of the right to express dissent, even radical ideas.

The Lodi case also created other kinds of responses within local communities, given that the profiling of Muslims and Arabs was often based on confused identifications of Muslim and Arab. Sikhs, particularly turbaned Sikh men, were disproportionately targeted in the post–September 11 backlash and were among the men murdered immediately after the September 11 hijackings.[21] After the Hayat arrests, CAIR conducted workshops on civil rights in the Lodi area in mosques and also in Sikh *gurudwaras* (temples). The Lodi case prompted racist paranoia about Muslim terrorists lurking in California, and it was also followed by racist graffiti on a gurudwara in Lodi in October 2005 (Ioffee 2005). There have also been racist incidents targeting Latinos and African Americans in the area, but what is interesting is that the Muslim American community in Lodi, sensitized to the issue of racial profiling, made public statements of solidarity with the Sikh community in the Central Valley. Some Lodi residents even became involved in antiracist projects in Lodi to combat hate crimes by fostering intercultural understanding. In my view, these efforts are laudable and necessary, but not sufficient, for they raise other questions about how to respond to racial profiling and what this term really means.

The liberal view that hate crimes can be addressed through cross-cultural understanding and multicultural education continues to evade the role of state-sanctioned racial profiling and political, not just cultural, processes of discrimination. Local responses to the profiling of Lodi's Muslims, as evident in stories in the mainstream media, generally reinscribed the pervasive Orientalist focus on Islam, gender, and youth that is part of the dominant discourse about the War on Terror. For example, media articles about Lodi's Muslim community focused on Pakistani American youth struggling with "the social pull" between "the many freedoms offered to Americans," particularly to young women, and the restrictions of conservative traditions in the Pakistani immigrant community (Giese 2005). These commentaries, and many other narratives about Muslim Americans after September 11, suggest that the conflict at the heart of the War on Terror is rooted in differences of culture and religion, a clash of cultures that pits Islam, if not the Middle East, against Western democracy and modernity. Liberal multicultural narratives about Islam and the Middle East do not always fall into this trap of essentialized or Oriental-ized understandings, but even those that rightly condemn the racism and Islamophobia in the War on Terror do not generally critically consider its political context. Viewing post–September 11 racial profiling simply as a problem of domestic racism fails to acknowledge its link to the global dimensions of the War on Terror and the invasions of Afghanistan and Iraq. This is also true for responses to racial profiling within Muslim and Arab immigrant communities, but in some instances cultural empathy with other minorities has extended to a political solidarity based on a deeper understanding of U.S. racism and imperial power. Alliances have emerged or strengthened after September 11, 2001, in some instances be-tween groups and political movements focused on civil and immigrant rights, incarceration, war, and occupation that link policies within the United States to interventions in the Middle East. These linkages formed in response to the state regime of surveillance, detention, and deportation point to new kinds of affiliations in the shifting racial and religious politics of post–September 11 America.

DEPORTING LA MIGRA

An example of these new alliances in response to deportation and deten-tion, and their implications for political analysis and organizing, is the Deporten a La Migra (Deport the INS, now ICE) coalition in the Bay Area. The coalition includes a variety of Latino, Asian American, antiwar, im-migrant rights, housing rights, and labor groups in San Francisco, such as members of La Raza Centro Legal, St. Peter's Housing Committee, Day Labor Program, Heads Up Collective, SRO Families United, Asian Pacific Islander Legal Outreach, and ASATA. I became involved in the coalition as a member of ASATA after an ICE raid on Hotel Sunrise, a residential hotel in the Mission District of San Francisco. On May 6, 2004, federal agents detained nine immigrant men, deporting seven Mexican immi-grant workers and detaining two men of Indian origin, one of whom was eventually released and another who disappeared into the U.S. detention system. The raid violated the city's INS Raid Free Resolution supporting undocumented immigrants' right to live in San Francisco without fear of abuse and raids by federal immigration officials and also the city's sanctu-ary policy forbidding cooperation between the ICE and local law enforce-ment on deportation cases involving only immigration issues.

A few days after the raid, the coalition organized a press conference outside the Hotel Sunrise. Tenants at the hotel spoke about the impact of the ICE raids in terrorizing the community, and other speakers connected the raids to the broader context of the unofficial war on immigrants and the official War on Terror. One of the hotel tenants interrogated in the raid was involved with a tenants' rights campaign, and members of the coalition feared that the raid would have a chilling effect on this mobilization, but the immigrant activist spoke at the protest anyway. Members of the coalition spoke to the tenants about their legal rights as part of their ongoing educational campaign in immigrant communities. I and others in ASATA tried to track down the South Asian men who had disappeared and make sure they had legal representation. Significantly, the focus of the Deporten a La Migra campaign combined efforts to support the particular immigrants involved in the Sunrise raid with a larger critique of state policies related to the economic and political logics of immigration and deportation policy and the War on Terror.

This is just one of many instances of cross-ethnic alliances uniting immigrant rights, civil rights, labor, and other antiwar movements that emerged in response to post–September 11 deportations and detention. As I and others in the Deporten a La Migra coalition were trying to solve the mystery of the Sunrise raid, local Muslim, Arab, and South Asian American groups were working to monitor the increasingly secretive and unpublicized raids on Muslim immigrant homes and workplaces that are part of what I call the "Secret Registration," which took place outside the media spotlight that had focused on the Special Registration. A Filipino community support group, FOCUS, was engaged in a campaign to stop the deportation of Filipino American families from the Bay Area by organizing airport workers, women, and youth. Others in Cambodian, Vietnamese, Salvadoran, and Mexican immigrant communities across the nation were trying to address the "tidal wave" of deportations after a 1996 law made all noncitizens subject to deportation if they had previously been sentenced to more than a year in prison, regardless of the seriousness of the crime (B. Hing 2004, 230–31; Richard 2003). These campaigns inevitably give rise to debates about whether some immigrants are indeed more deportable than others. There are also many who belong to these communities, including Muslim, South Asian, and Arab Americans, who argue that those who have violated the law *should* be deported, distancing themselves from the "true" criminals or terrorists (Saliba, n.d.). The larger point that is overlooked in this distinction between "good" and "bad" immigrants is that there are certain communities that are inevitably targeted for deportation on both counts, as dangerous criminals or terrorists and as immigrants, and that certain groups are overrepresented in detention and deportation for both these categories. Furthermore, the "good" versus "bad" immigrant dichotomy ignores the fundamental notion that deportability is itself a tool used to regulate immigrant labor and suppress political movements. The few examples discussed here point to the many campaigns that have attempted to resist the political repression and to challenge the religious, ethnic, and racial divisions fostered by the War on Terror.

CONCLUSION

Deportation is a technology used by the state not just to regulate its borders through the removal of individuals but to remove or suppress radical ideologies. As such, the theater of deportation is a site in which the state is itself ideologically constituted as well as contested, as movements and campaigns resisting deportation bring to light the political and economic functions of deportation. The political and economic logic of deportation often works in tandem, as I have shown, particularly in cases that simultaneously terrorize immigrant workers and (potential) critics of U.S. policy—disciplining labor as well as political dissent. Young Muslim and Arab American men who have been detained and deported after September 11, 2001, such as Hamid Hayat, have generally not been political activists in the traditional sense, but the state is aware that they are a source of critique of its policies in the Middle East, the major front in the War on Terror, and that their communities represent historical knowledge of the not so pretty face of U.S. imperial power. If deportees and detainees are constituted politically in their encounter with the state—even if they are not technically political deportees—their experiences of deportability also help construct the image and understanding of the state in the public sphere as coercive or democratic, racist or "tough on crime" and terrorism. As De Genova points out, the state is not a "fixed institutional matrix but rather . . . a site of struggle in itself" (2002, 428). This struggle, as I argue here, is ultimately a battle over the imperial state's desire to expand its military, economic, and political power and to crush dissent against its policies at home and abroad. Moreover, it is a battle over defining the very limits of politics itself.

Although the United States is now the lone global superpower, and its military and political domination is unrivaled, the imperial state is (increasingly) intolerant of the possibility of dissenting views and move-ments within its borders (and even outside), betraying a sense of ideologi-cal insecurity in its repression and expulsion of "alien" ideas during this new cold war—which has replaced the threat of communism with the threat of Islamic terrorism to freedom (of market capitalism), democracy (under occupation), and the American way of life (as the best and only way). Bush's doctrine of preemptive war overseas is paralleled by the pre-emptive detention and deportation policies under the guise of homeland security, based on a similar doctrine of preempting terrorism as a pretext for repressing and regulating immigrants, workers, and dissidents. Other states also engage in these strategies in ways that are racist and xenopho-bic, but owing to the economic and military might of the United States, the lone superpower's waging of perpetual war, as well as its pivotal role in global immigration, makes its regime of deportation and the War on Terror a significant factor in shaping the global geography of removal and repression.[22]

Immigrants and citizens respond to state practices of surveillance, de-tention, and deportation in ways that are not always predictable. Political movements and alliances have emerged that sometimes defy the catego-ries established by the state to distinguish its policing processes focused on various communities. On the one hand, some Muslim immigrants who are afraid of deportation and subjected to surveillance, such as those in Lodi, are likely to assert that they are "good citizens" who believe in U.S. democracy and freedom, even as the limits of that freedom are tested on their own bodies (Saliba n.d.). Some participate in the reinscription of the image of the "Muslim" and "Arab terrorist" and the dichotomy of "good" and "bad" Muslims and Arabs as a prerequisite to acceptance into virtuous citizenship (Mamdani 2004). These are often strategies of self-defense for Arab, Muslim, and South Asian immigrants, for those who are not citizens, in particular, are justifiably concerned about publicly ex-pressing political dissent.

Yet this self-censorship allows the deportation strategy to achieve pre-cisely the effect it intends: inhibiting political dissent and suppressing col-lective mobilization. It is important for members of targeted communi-ties to think strategically of ways to collectively resist this reinscription of the discourse about terrorism while protecting vulnerable individuals or segments of these communities. Some have resisted this performance of good citizenship and have challenged deportations, not just in the courts, where the law generally upholds the warfare state's need for national se-curity, but also in the public sphere, highlighting the connections between the economic disciplining and the political repression conducted through deportation, as was the case with the immigrants who protested the Sunrise raid.

However, collective responses from the targeted communities have also sometimes worked within the parameters outlined by the state in its War on Terror, attempting mainly to shield immigrants from excessive harassment or violations or, in some cases, cooperating with the government in its hunt for the "real terrorists." The issue of complicity with such surveillance is obviously a controversial one and gives rise to difficult debates within the community about the meanings of citizenship, loyalty, and betrayal. Yet other kinds of collective responses have challenged the government's premise in the War on Terror and, in some cases, gone even further, making links between the war(s) on immigrants, minorities, and the underprivileged at home and the war overseas—as was the case with the Deporten a La Migra coalition and groups that exposed the government's tactics in the Lodi case.

In naming the coalition Deporten a La Migra, the organizers were not just trying to use a clever phrase but also suggesting a larger political critique: that resistance needs to be focused not just on specific deportation policies and on preventing or challenging deportations that target specific individuals or groups but also on the agencies of the state itself that regulate and discipline populations and enforce imperial policies of coercion, violence, and intimidation. If deportation is a struggle about eradicating ideologies and not just removing individuals or organizations, then our resistance needs to work to end the imperial state's increasingly globalized regime of terror and repression by exposing the underlying political and economic logic of the War on Terror, refusing to fashion dissent to empire in terms framed by its own ideological conceits, and creating broader alliances among those who are targeted as immigrants, workers, and dissenters.

NOTES

I would like to thank Magid Shihade, Nicholas De Genova, and Nathalie Peutz for their thoughtful comments and helpful feedback, and Veena Dubal and members of Deporten a La Migra for their courage and astute analysis.

1. In an unusual case, Hayat's uncle and U.S.-born cousin were refused reentry to the United States when returning from Pakistan in April 2006, as the trial was in progress, because they were on a no-fly list and were asked to submit to interrogation by the FBI without a lawyer present (Demian Bulwa, "Men OK'd to Return to the U.S. from Pakistan," *San Francisco Chronicle,*

September 13, 2006). The refusal of reentry to the United States, sometimes to citizens, is akin to a reverse deportation; even if only temporary in certain cases, it is part of the same process of regulating bodies in the name of national security.

2. While most of the persons targeted after September 11, 2001, in connection with the War on Terror were Muslim, many were non-Muslim Arabs and non-Muslim South Asians (including, in particular, Sikh American men). The men targeted for detention and deportation, however, were almost all either Muslim or Arab in origin. Yet the intensified racialization, even ethnicization, of the category "Muslim" since 2001 has occurred in the context of a prevailing discourse about a clash of civilizations between Islam and the West that shifts attention away from the ways in which this so-called racial profiling of Muslims by the U.S. state is actually linked to U.S. strategic interests in the Middle East and to historical anti-Arab racism. Thus most commentators and activists addressing post–September 11 state profiling have used some variant of the inclusive, though somewhat cumbersome, category "Muslim, Arab, and South Asian" rather than glossing them as "Muslim."

3. David Harvey has demonstrated how both neoliberalism and imperialism are clearly linked by showing how neoliberal economic principles of free-market enterprise and privatization were accompanied by a political project to "re-establish the conditions for capital accumulation and to restore the power of economic elites," with the help of military intervention if necessary, as evident in the "first experiment with neoliberal state formation," the U.S.-backed coup against the socialist government of Salvador Allende in Chile on September 11, 1973, and continuing with policies of structural adjustment and deregulation crystallized in the Reagan-Thatcher era (Harvey 2005, 19, 7).

4. The U.S. Congress changed the terminology of deportation to "removal" in 1996 (B. Hing 2004, 210).

5. At the time of this writing, the U.S. government still refuses to take Arar off its terrorist watch list and allow him entry into the country. Ian Austen, "Canada Reaches Settlement with Torture Victim," New York Times, January 26, 2007.

6. In reality, neoliberal capitalism shored up the wealth and power of economic elites, countering the threat of socialist policies and communist parties after World War II through a combination of political, military, and economic strategies to promote privatization (Harvey 2005).

7. U.S. imperial power uses different strategies of dominance: "control over international bodies (the United Nations, World Bank, International Monetary Fund, World Trade Organization), covert actions, global surveillance methods, direct military interventions, political machinations, and deadly economic sanctions of the sort used against Iraq" (Boggs 2003, 6).

8. In November 2001, as public criticism began to mount, the Department of Justice stopped releasing the numbers of persons detained in the post–September 11 sweeps, so although the official estimate was 1,182 detentions, a conservative estimate of detentions until May 2003 is at least 5,000 (Cole 2003, 25).

9. "Pakistan Fighting Terror in Its Own Interest, Not USA's," *Pakistan Link*, August 17, 2007, 1, 21; "Tribesmen Observe August 14 as 'Black Day,' " *Pakistan Link*, August 17, 2007, 17.

10. The Department of Homeland Security officially ended the program's re-registration component in December 2003 after protests by immigrant and civil rights groups and grassroots community organizations. Other aspects of the program remained in place, however, and the detentions and deportations continued (see Cainkar 2004).

11. For example, the FBI's extensive monitoring of the General Union of Palestinian Students on college campuses and at events around the country in the 1980s, with no objection from the Justice Department (Cole and Dempsey 2002, 35–48). See also Jordan Green, "Silencing Dissent," *ColorLines* 6, no. 2 (2003): 17–20.

12. In February 2007 an immigration court judge finally dismissed the government's twenty-year-old deportation proceedings against Khader Musa Hamide and Michel Shehadeh, the two remaining L.A. Eight defendants, as "an embarrassment to the rule of law." "A Shameful Prosecution," *New York Times*, February 14, 2007.

13. The FBI's extensive nationwide monitoring of CISPES was based on charges that they were supporting and funding the Salvadoran rebel group the FLMN and plotting terrorist attacks in the United States, although the investigation never found any evidence of this (Cole and Dempsey 2002, 22–23).

14. Legislative Initiatives to Curb Domestic and International Terrorism: Hearings before the Subcomm. on Security and Terrorism of the Senate Comm. on the Judiciary, 98th Congress (1984), note 29; cited in Cole and Dempsey 2002, 207.

15. For example, after years of FBI surveillance, John Lennon of the Beatles was targeted for deportation by the Nixon administration to sabotage his concert tour protesting the Vietnam War (B. Hing 2004, 226–28).

16. For example, Operation Community Shield was jointly undertaken by the FBI and Department of Homeland Security in 2005 to round up suspected Salvadoran gang members (Nguyen 2005, 87).

17. See Welch 2000 and Dow 2004 on the connections between immigration and incarceration in the United States.

18. *The September 11 Detainees: A Review of the Treatment of Aliens Held on Immigration Charges in Connection with the Investigation of the September 11 Attacks*, Report by Office of the Inspector General, Department of Justice, April 2003, http://www.fas.org/irp/agency/doj/oig/detainees.pdf (accessed February 20, 2007). See also Camille T. Taiara, "American Payback," *San Francisco Bay Guardian*, May 26, 2004, 19.

19. For example, Ward Churchill (2006) extensively documents cases of political prisoners who were detained for involvement with revolutionary movements in the United States and who were much more harshly sentenced, often on the basis of questionable evidence, than right-wing activists.

20. Bomb threats were made against Arab American organizations in Detroit in the mid-1980s, and the Anti-Defamation League was found guilty of surveilling ADC members (see Abraham 1994).

21. The first man murdered in a hate crime linked to the events of September 11, 2001, was Balbir Singh Sodhi, who was killed at a gas station he owned in Mesa, Arizona, on September 15, 2001 (Prashad 2003, 66).

22. The notion of "perpetual war" has been used to describe the military policies of preemptive and unilateral strikes advocated by the Bush regime, as documented in the Project for the New American Century's goals for the United States to "fight and decisively win multiple, simultaneous threatre wars" to establish U.S. global domination (cited in Kellner 2003, 241).

PART FOUR —m— *Forced Movement*

CHAPTER 11

Fictions of Law

The Trial of Sulaiman Oladokun, or

Reading Kafka in an Immigration Court

As economic instability and political violence escalate in the United States, the migrant's body becomes the convenient ground for displaying state control to a nervous populace. In recent years, a plethora of legislation has concerned itself with the entry of migrants, their "criminality," the management and control of them within national territory, their removal or deportation, and finally their alleged links to terrorism, effectively collapsing the figure of the migrant with that of the "illegal," the "criminal," and the "terrorist." In 1996 a hard-hitting package of laws dramatically increased the grounds for detaining and deporting migrants and denied them the right to appeal before a federal court.[1] The biggest domestic reaction wrought by the attacks of September 11, 2001, according to Manuel Vargas, director of the Immigrant Defense Project at the New York State Defender's Association, was the overturning of the by then widespread political consensus that the 1996 immigration laws had gone too far in the disciplining of migrants. After September 11, 2001, additional laws and "special" or "emergency" state programs were enacted to step up control of migrants. While differing in their details and language, the successive immigration laws have unreservedly served to extend the reach of state power over migrant bodies. The laws have been so many and so beguiling in their details that vast numbers of unsuspecting migrants have been caught in the labyrinthine immigration bureaucracy, one that metes out—as we shall see—an absurd "justice" in the absence of clear or consistent juridical procedure. Examining the case of one such migrant, Sulaiman Oladokun, I attempt here to show how the state incriminates and adjudicates over individual migrants, effectively producing their guilt while effacing its own history of violence and strategic manipulation in a stunning display of state power.

Paradoxically, though Oladokun's trial was conducted through the courts of the U.S. Immigration and Naturalization Service (INS), or the Department of Homeland Security (DHS), as it was later called,[2] furnishing it with the paraphernalia of juridical procedure, the case against him cannot be explained as a transgression of any law: no law corresponds with his case. Immigration law and its practice have always—even before September 11, 2001—exhibited a "threshold of undecidability" over the juridical rights of migrants (Agamben 2003/2005, 29). In *Rafeedie vs. INS* (1989), the INS had sought to use "secret evidence" on the basis of so-called national security concerns to deport Fouad Rafeedie upon his return from a Palestinian youth conference in Syria (Taylor-Saito 2001, 16). But the D.C. circuit court that tried Rafeedie's case rejected the INS's use of secret evidence as unconstitutional. However, new immigration laws passed in 1996, the Illegal Immigration Reform and Immigrant Responsibility Act (IIRIRA) and the Antiterrorism and Effective Death Penalty Act (AEDPA), codified special "alien terrorist removal procedures," designated a special immigration court, limited judicial review of deportation cases, and allowed provisions for the use of secret evidence (16). The 1996 laws overturned the possibility of verdicts like the D.C. circuit court's ruling against secret evidence in cases like Rafeedie's. Even as the 1996 laws were being applied by the INS to deport large numbers of migrants, a Supreme Court hearing in June 2001 narrowed their interpretation, once again giving migrants the right to juridical appeal. In the emergency state that prevailed after 9/11, the USA PATRIOT ACT finally suspended migrants' rights to juridical appeal. The Patriot Act made real Agamben's state of emergency: "an ambiguous and uncertain zone in which de facto proceedings, which are in themselves extra- or antijuridical, pass over into law," and inversely, "law is suspended and obliterated in fact" (Agamben 2003/2005, 29). Thus the peculiar details of Oladokun's trial, and the trials of countless other migrants, cannot be traced to any particular law as much as to a *suspension* of law that gives the state irreproachable powers to exercise its force in varied ways in individual cases.

Additionally, the language of rights and legal justice—while it may be the only one the defendants have recourse to—does not apply to or help elucidate the framework of power that dictates the application of law in the extrajuridical immigration bureaucracy. In his *State of Exception*, Agamben considers the debate between Carl Schmitt and Walter Benjamin on the relationship between exceptional or emergency states of violence and juridical law or justice. Schmitt characterizes as "fictitious" a state of exception that still claims to be regulated by law and feigns to guarantee some degree of individual rights and justice (Agamben 2003/2005, 59). Schmitt's analysis separates the emergency state from the normal legal state, theorizing them as distinguishable states of political order. Benjamin, however, turns Schmitt's distinction between exceptional and normal conditions around by arguing that the state of exception "absolutely cannot be distinguished from the rule" (59). For Benjamin, there is *always* nothing but a "zone of anomie" or "violence without any juridical form" (59). The state's claim to maintain law while suspending it in the state of exception is really a sham by which it hopes to stake control over the zone of extrajuridical violence or anomie. Elaborating on Schmitt's and Benjamin's analysis, Agamben writes that the zone of extrajuridical violence "coincides with an extreme and spectral figure of the law, in which law splits into a pure being-in-force [*vigenza*] without application (the form of law) and a pure application without being in force" (60). In other words, law and state practice, while still referring to each other, do not actually correspond in the state of exception. Thus appeals to migrants' rights and justice in an immigration courtroom that has dispensed with regular juridical procedure invoke an old law no longer in practice and, in so doing, bring into focus the fundamental deception of the emergency state and therefore must be obliterated with the state's crushing power.

Astonishing as Oladokun's case is, few textual references can be called on to explain it. Because it arises more from a suspension of the law than the specifics of a new law, legal treatises are inadequate. Whereas reports published by civil and immigrant rights groups like the American Civil Liberties Union (ACLU) and Amnesty International repeatedly argue for the "constitutional right" of immigrants to a fair trial, their arguments do not offer an analytic framework for the current practices in which the law itself has been suspended. Revealingly, it is in Franz Kafka's explorations of legal and bureaucratic practice that one finds a narrative that resonates with Oladokun's experience of the law. In *The Trial*, the protagonist, K., opens the "law books" only to discover that they are shams devoid of any explication of the laws as they are being practiced on him (Kafka 1925/1999, 51). His plea for proper legislative procedure against the inexplicable actions of "this alleged court of justice" has no effect on his case (45). Through his experience with the courts and the bureaucracy, K. learns that the state's actions, its power, are the law—there is no higher law, in books or courtrooms, to call on. Law "ceases to be law and blurs at all points with life" (Agamben 2003/2005, 63). Because the state holds the power to determine law *in every instance*, it admits to no mistakes and hears no appeal to its charges—there is no acquittal or defense for the accused, only conviction or a perpetual sidestepping of the conviction—what the painter in *The Trial* characterizes as "ostensible acquittal" or "indefinite postponement" (Kafka 1925/1999, 146). K.'s discovery of an empty law in *The Trial* is much like Oladokun's difficult realization (as well as that of his lawyers and of researchers like myself writing about his case) that there is nothing to appeal or refer to. There is only the narrative of his case, a narrative that shows the shape of unchecked power when it is allowed to masquerade as law and lay claim to justice.

CONFIGURING MIGRANT VULNERABILITY: HISTORICAL USES OF LAW

Before turning to Oladokun's particular case, however, I will briefly review contemporary immigration law and state practice to show that present enforcement is embedded in the history of immigration law and the political and economic objectives of the United States. Pointing to a trend in Western democracies, Agamben posits that the declaration of an emergency state of exception itself has gradually been replaced by a "generalization of the paradigm of security as the normal technique of government" (2003/2005, 14), that is, the state of exception or emergency has become integrated in the normal functioning of the state. Additionally, the creation of migrants as a truncated legal category of personhood has been crucial to the normalization of the security state in the United States. Indeed, the present legal status of migrants is an extension of the historical treatment of migrants. In his history of American nativism from 1860 to 1925, John Higham traces the rise of "nativism," or the idea that "some influence originating from abroad threatened the life of the nation from within," showing how domestic economic and political conflict were channeled in anti-immigrant laws and enforcement (1955/1963, 4). In his work on the illegalization of Mexican migration since the 1900s, Nicholas De Genova demonstrates how the U.S. Border Patrol, historically operated by the Department of Labor, coordinated selective law enforcement based on seasonal demand by U.S. employers, allowing mass deportations to be followed by large importations of Mexican migrant labor (2004, 160–85). Immigration law, De Genova shows, is always "conjunctural," used tactically to "refine the parameters of discipline and coercion" of migrant labor (166).

Whereas prior legislation had focused primarily on "legal" immigration and deportations were conducted en masse through enforcement programs, the 1990s saw the emergence of legislation that individualized legal procedure against migrants. In 1986 the Immigration Reform and Control Act (IRCA), the first act to deal specifically with undocumented migration, provided "amnesty," adjusting the status of some undocumented migrants while imposing federal sanctions on employers who hired undocumented workers. The sanctions against employers, however, were tantamount to negligible financial penalties and were enforced through INS raids that gave employers three days' notice, virtually negating actual penal consequences. The Immigration Act of 1990 (IMMACT 90) expanded grounds for deportation, curtailed due-process rights, and transferred the authority to grant naturalization from courts to the office of the Attorney General. The curtailment of due-process rights and the shift of authority from courts to the Attorney General's office were the first steps toward differentiating the quality of legal procedures available to migrants. Then, in 1996, the IIRIRA, together with the AEDPA, further distinguished the migrant as subject to exceptional kinds of "justice."

The IIRIRA and the AEDPA dramatically increased the numbers and types of "criminal" categories by which undocumented immigrants, together with "legal" residents, could be detained and deported (Dow 2004, 173; Cole 2003). These laws enabled larger numbers of detentions by redefining the category of "aggravated felon" to include conviction for battery, shoplifting, and drunk driving. Mark Dow cites an INS circular that explained the consequences of the law using the following example: as a result of the law, a woman who had been convicted of a nonviolent offense for which she paid a fine at eighteen could now, at forty, despite owning her own business, being married to a U.S. citizen, and having U.S. citizen children, be apprehended at an airport on her way back into the country and deported (Dow 2004, 191). Under the 1996 laws, the immigration judge, having lost her or his judicial discretion, could no longer consider the woman's strong ties to the country or community, among other things, and *must* order her deported. By applying retroactively to undocumented migrants and "legal" residents alike, the law eroded the legitimacy of green cards, reducing all migrants, regardless of their "legality," to a state of disposability. Lawmaking, Benjamin theorizes, "specifically establishes as law not an end unalloyed by violence, but one necessarily and intimately bound to it, under the title of power" (1921/1979, 149). The state's 1996 lawmaking, in creating the figure of the exceptionally punishable migrant, consolidated the use of state violence on the migrant's body and thereby the constant display and reassertion of state power.

At the same time, a burgeoning structural apparatus of bureaucratic courts and prisons became the theaters for the display of state power. By denying judicial discretion, the 1996 laws had condemned migrants, "legal" residents and undocumented alike, to the machinelike operations of a bureaucratic apparatus, squashing migrants' claims for legal subjectivity with the bureaucracy's "'objective' discharge of business . . . according to calculable rules and 'without regard for persons'" (M. Weber 1978, 975). As the number of detainees tripled between 1994 and 2001 from 5,532 to 19,533, they came to be held in INS processing centers, in local jails, in facilities owned and operated by private contracted prison companies, and in Bureau of Prisons facilities (Dow 2004, 9). The migrant's body was rendered not only deportable but also detainable and subject to imprisonment in exceptional conditions. Tracing the rise of large-scale migrant incarceration to the 1980s, Mark Dow points to languishing industrial towns like Oakdale, Louisiana, resuscitated by a bid for a federal migrant detention center or, as Oakdale's mayor touted it, the "recession proof industry" (156–57). The first two privatized immigration detention centers, opened in 1984 and contracted to Wackenhut and Corrections Corporation of America (CCA), paved the way for a multi-billion-dollar industry of "for-profit prisons" (97). While immigration detention centers had begun to sprout up in the 1980s, the 1996 laws resulted in an overall retrenchment of immigrant control as the agency received incremental sums of "special appropriations" ($80 million, bringing its deportation budget to $809 million) to expand its detention beds and staff of enforcement officers. From 1997 on, as the number of deportations rose, the immigration agency set annual targets in numbers of "illegal" and "criminal" aliens it would deport that year, and each year it surpassed its own goals, reflecting the aggrandizing tendency of bureaucratized power (Sachs 1999). A bureaucracy, Max Weber writes, is an instrument of "rationally organizing authority relations" or power and is "among those social structures, which are the hardest to destroy" (1978, 987). Arguably, the corporate capital investment in detention centers across the country, as well as the local economies that have become dependent on them, has entrenched the display of state power over migrant bodies in long-term institutionalized structures. The local bureaucratic structures, continuing their work in an effort to justify their existence and extension, help maintain the national security paradigm of the state.

NATIONALIST INSECURITY AND ANTI-IMMIGRANT PRACTICES AFTER SEPTEMBER 11, 2001

Despite talk of political consensus against the severity of the 1996 laws and the "softening" of public attitudes toward immigration, there was no actual change in the 1996 legislation (Lipton 1998). After the events of September 11, 2001, fears of loss of control over national security soared, and the figure of the migrant was brought back into focus as a convenient vehicle for the display of state control and the ventilation of national security fears. A slew of acts were passed: within weeks of the attacks, Attorney General John Ashcroft issued a preventive detention program, allowing the INS to detain migrants on the basis of suspicion of terrorism, and created a national Joint Terrorism Task Force (JTTF) to enforce the new provisions of detaining, prosecuting, and deporting migrant suspects. Resorting to "pretextual law enforcement," the state picked up migrants on the basis of unsubstantiated suspicion and, upon clearing a detainee of terrorism charges, found an immigration violation to enable continued detention (Cole 2003, 24). Most of the detainees picked up were from Arab and Muslim communities—a total of 1,182 in November 2001, the date after which the Justice Department has refused to publicize the numbers of detainees. In January 2002 the state announced the Absconder Apprehension Initiative, ordering the prioritized deportation of 6,000 Arabs and Muslims with outstanding deportation orders and detaining 1,100 of them (25). In January 2003 a Special Registration program required noncitizen men from twenty-five designated countries, mostly Arab and Muslim, to register with the government. Of those who voluntarily came to register in response to the program, 2,747 were detained. The state's policies and practices after September 2001 clearly served to frame the migrant Arab or Muslim male as a "terrorist."

However, a 2003 report issued by the inspector general of the Justice Department revealed that none of the post-September 11 detainees held up to August 2002 had been charged with any terrorism-related crimes (Cole 2003, 30). Moreover, not one of the men picked up by Homeland Security during Special Registration in 2003 was charged with terrorism. Quite simply, not one of these migrant detentions has led to proof of terrorism-related conduct. That those cleared of terrorism charges are denied "voluntary departure" and detained for longer periods on the pretext of prolonged FBI investigations further shows, as David Cole has written, "that the government's real goal is not to remove but to detain" (33). Moreover, the secrecy surrounding detention proceedings and the refusal to release names and numbers of detainees sustains what Nicholas De Genova has called "the 'terrorism' effect." By forcing ethnically identified noncitizens into prolonged detentions on the basis of unsubstantiated suspicion of "terrorism," the state, in an "enforcement spectacle," makes detainees perform their "punishment," effectively *producing* their image as culprits (2007, 435–36).

The production of migrant culprits intersects at crucial points with the explicatory rhetoric of foreign policy. It has been widely noted that U.S. administrations had made military contingency plans against Iraq and potentially other pan-Arabic movements even before the Gulf War in 1991 (see, *inter alia*, Harvey 2003, 14). A group called the Project for the New American Century, which included Donald Rumsfeld and Paul Wolfowitz, had argued for military regime change in 1997. However, a report in 1999 by the same group recognized that it would take "a catastrophic event, like a new Pearl Harbor," to make a military strike acceptable in international and domestic parlance (15). The attempted use of secret evidence to detain and deport people like Rafeedie in 1989, as well as the subsequent abrogation of juridical rights by the 1996 laws criminalizing migrants of Arab descent, could be read as domestic harbingers of the prejudices of foreign policy.

After the events of September 11, 2001, once Afghanistan had submitted to U.S. power and Osama bin Laden continued to remain out of reach, political fervor was channeled toward the (then already long-planned) war on Iraq and the so-called Axis of Evil. Official plans advocating regime change in Iraq explicitly state U.S. aspirations for regime changes in other parts of the Middle East, in the attempt to realign the region with U.S. state objectives and the desire for the control of Middle Eastern oil (Harvey 2003, 19). Justification of interventionist tactics, however, would hinge on the state's ability to produce the image of the Middle East as "evil." The Special Registration program mandated that all male foreign nationals from twenty-five specified countries—Iran, Iraq, Libya, Syria, Lebanon, Morocco, and Pakistan, to name a few—register at specific immigration offices across the country by specified dates from late 2002 to early 2003, creating the spectacle of long lines of Arab or Muslim men submitting themselves to be checked at INS offices, and often unduly detained without evidence. The registration spectacle worked to enhance their image as exceptional foreigners whose nationality—and, by implication, whose nations—constituted them as somehow essentially prone to "evil," thereby sanctioning exceptional preemptive state disciplining. While programs like Special Registration and the Absconder Apprehension Initiative use ethnic and national qualifiers to target largely Arab or Muslim migrants, they also stir up nationalist sentiments facilitating anti-immigrant legislation that encompasses all migrants. Heightened enforcement of latent aspects of the 1996 laws, as well as the heightened attention to, arguments for, and actual provisions of overall immigration reform in the present day, reflect how vilification based on national origin, ethnicity, and gender is eventually congealed around the broader legal category of the migrant.

The continuing extension of state power over migrant bodies demonstrates the effectiveness of state-bureaucratic imagery in producing migrant guilt. In 2002 Florida became "the first jurisdiction to accept a long-dormant federal plan to deputize local police officers as agents of the Immigration and Naturalization Service," giving police the power to arrest "illegal" migrants (Sachs 2002). Such extension of police power over immigrants had been made possible by the 1996 laws, but widespread opposition had blocked enforcement. To explain the shift in practice, the North Miami chief of police said, "We're in a different situation now. . . . We may have people in the country who might want to hurt or kill us." Since "the immigration agency [has the] power to detain indefinitely, without bringing charges," Sachs notes, "a police officer . . . would not have to meet the criminal justice system's usual standard of probable cause when arresting a foreigner." According to a "senior Justice Department official," a police officer may be asked to arrest "a foreigner who was acting suspiciously." While anti-immigrant lobbies push for heightened police disciplining of migrants by invoking "Islamic terrorists," some journalists recognize that the measures affect all of the country's eight million "illegal" immigrants (Sachs 2002; Swarns 2005).

In effect, the merging of police and immigration agencies places the body of the migrant at the complete discretion of individual police officers. Unchecked by habeas corpus or juridical laws of probable cause—unchecked, in fact, by any legal standards whatsoever—the police officer represents the state in exercising sovereign power over a migrant's detention. "What we have witnessed with our own eyes from the end of World War I onward," Agamben writes, is "a process by which the enemy is first of all excluded from civil humanity and branded as a criminal; only in a second moment does it become possible and licit to eliminate the enemy by a 'police operation'" (1991/2000, 105–6). Agamben posits that the extermination of the Jews in Europe became methodical and comprehensive precisely because it was carried out as a police operation, put into practice after Jews had been criminalized by incrementally harsh laws. Similarly stripped of juridical protection, branded a criminal, and subject to police sovereignty, the undocumented migrant is being rendered ever more disposable, if not exterminable, by the exigencies of nationalist politics.

THE CASE OF SULAIMAN OLADOKUN:
MIGRANT, MUSLIM, MALE

Finally, I turn to the case of Sulaiman Oladokun, a case that demonstrates far better how the emergency state applies to individuals than the letter of the law does. Oladokun's case illustrates what absurd forms of justice are born when juridical procedure is withdrawn and state enforcement becomes contiguous with the "law." Additionally, it shows how the language of justice itself experiences a crisis, one that is suppressed by the state with decisive violence.

The Arrest

> Someone must have been telling lies about Joseph K., for without having done anything wrong he was arrested one fine morning. —Kafka, *The Trial*, 7

Less than two months before his graduation, Sulaiman Oladokun was arrested in the college library, without warrant or explanation, by the Joint Terrorism Task Force (JTTF).[3] In statements made to the press and to the courts in his countless letters, Oladokun, a student of the State University of New York Maritime College, said that in February 2003 he had been embroiled in an argument with the college over the details of his past tuition rates.[4] The college changed its tuition rates for foreign students, and Oladokun found himself in debt to the college and unable to register for classes. His education under siege, Oladokun suggested to Dr. Kimberly Kline, vice-president of Maritime College, that he would take legal counsel to settle the tuition fees with the college. In the course of the argument, Dr. Kline apparently threatened Oladokun, saying that she would call the INS. With a valid F-1 student visa, Oladokun did not think that the INS had anything to do with his tuition rates. At the time, he did not guess that as a migrant, albeit a "legal" one, he existed in a different legal and juridical universe from Kline. He could not have realized that as a migrant, a male Muslim migrant, after September 11, 2001, he had become an exception before the law. Toward the end of the month, the college called the JTTF to report that Oladokun had been exhibiting "suspicious behavior."[5]

Preliminary Investigations

> "But how can I be under arrest? And particularly in such a ridiculous fashion?" "So now you're beginning it all over again?" said the warder. . . . "We don't answer such questions."—Kafka, *The Trial*, 11

On March 6, 2003, one day before Oladokun's arrest by the JTTF, an INS document titled "Form I-831" stated:

> The school contacted the JTTF because of what they believed to be suspicious behavior of the Subject. It was determined during the course of JTTF investigation that the Subject used fraudulent documentation in his application to the Maritime College, which sponsored the Subject for an F-1 visa (report from U.S. consulate enclosed). . . . There is no evidence at this time that the Subject is involved in terrorist activity, and there is no further JTTF interest in the Subject at this time.[6]

Lacking evidence, the form states that the JTTF cleared Oladokun of charges of "suspicious" or "terrorist" activity. Thereafter the JTTF accused Oladokun of giving false certificates to the Maritime College. Visa violations, being civil, not criminal, charges, could not warrant arrest by the JTTF. Yet the report stated:

> Subject was apprehended on 3/7/03 by SA [Special Agent] Eric Wein and SA Alex Antes pursuant to an investigation by Det. Vernon Geberth and SA Gus Xhudo of the NY-JTTF.

Having already cleared him of charges *before* March 7, how could the JTTF sanction Oladokun's arrest?

Fraudulent Charges

> "But on the other hand," K. went on, . . . "on the other hand, it can't be an affair of any great importance either. I argue this from the fact that although I am accused of something, I cannot recall the slightest offense that might be charged against me. But that even is of minor importance, the real question is, who accuses me? What authority is conducting these proceedings? Are you officers of the law?"—Kafka, *The Trial*, 16

Painting over the legitimacy of his arrest by the JTTF, the INS served Oladokun a "Notice to Appear" "in removal proceedings under section 240 of the Immigration and Nationality Act," after his arrest.[7] Giving reasons for removal, the INS alleged the following:

(1) You are not a citizen or national of the United States

(2) You are a native of BURKINA FASO and a citizen of NIGERIA

(7) On or about March 3, 2003, an investigation conducted by the U.S. Diplomatic Security Service at the United States Consulate in Lagos, Nigeria revealed that the documentation you submitted to the Maritime College regarding the Federal College of Fisheries and Marine Technology was fraudulent.

(8) You are a non-immigrant not in possession of a valid non-immigrant visa or border crossing identification card.

Although the first allegation could be read as constitutive of Oladokun's culpability, allegations 7 and 8 had been the basis of his arrest. Charges of fraud were pressed on the basis of an investigation conducted by the U.S. Consulate in Lagos to verify the authenticity of Oladokun's College certificates from the Federal College in Victoria Island, Lagos, submitted to SUNY upon admission.

Cross-Continental Bureaucratic Blunderings: The INS Interprets Africa

The letterhead of the U.S. Consulate in Lagos, bearing a "Diplomatic Security Service, Criminal Investigations Division" seal, presented the contents of its Fraud Prevention Program's "Report of Investigation" to the INS.[8] The report's synopsis summarized, "Preliminary investigation indicates that the documents submitted by Subject are suspect" and cited "sources with good knowledge."

The report was based on "source interviews." The first, dated February 28, 2003, states that Davis Anuta, acting provost of the college, was "questioned if the documents submitted by SUBJECT were actually issued by his school" (capitals in original). Pleading busy with meetings, Anuta asked the investigators to return the following Monday, March 3. Upon being asked to glance over the documents, Anuta said he needed to consult his records and again pleaded with the investigators to return on Monday. However, on March 3, the day of the scheduled interview with Anuta, the investigator returned to the college and was "shocked when he ran into a hostile mob of students who were protesting against what they termed 'bad conditions of living.'" "The Students ordered the Consulate car out of their premises and threatened to smash it," the report reads, "and we obliged."

A second entry on March 3 continues, "While leaving the school, the Investigator saw Mr. Emenike, the Students Affairs officer along with Mr. Onyekwere, a colleague of his." Asked for his opinion on the certificates at the gates of the college, Emenike said that "none appeared to be genuine." The report goes on: "In his contribution, Mr. Onyekwere [whose present relationship to the college is nowhere mentioned] stated that he graduated as Marine Engineer from the same college and therefore discountenanced the certificates submitted by SUBJECT as dubious." Thus, unable to reach Provost Anuta, the report deems the certificates "suspect" on the basis of opinions expressed by an unidentified Mr. Onyekwere, whose authority lies in his claims to have graduated from the college. The final "Records Checks" section reads "None." "Full official response is awaited," the last line of the report's synopsis admits.

The INS, however, did not care to await record checks or official responses. On the basis of the Consulate's patchwork report, grounded partly on amateur detective speculation and partly on representations of a generalizable Nigerian chaos, the INS and the JTTF, in form I-182 quoted earlier, deemed Oladokun's documents "fraudulent." Four days after the Fraud Prevention Program investigator casually conducted interviews outside the Federal College gates in Lagos, Sulaiman Oladokun was arrested in the SUNY college library.

Twists in the Paper Trail

> One did not know in general, or at least did not know with any precision, what charges to meet in the first plea; accordingly it could be only by pure chance that it contained really relevant matter. One could draw up genuinely effective and convincing pleas only later on, when the separate charges and the evidence on which they were based emerged more definitely or could be guessed at from the interrogations. . . . For the Defense was not actually countenanced by the Law, but only tolerated. —Kafka, *The Trial*, 109

Even as Oladokun appeared in Immigration Court on March 18, his attorney was sending faxes to the Federal College of Fisheries and Marine Technology in Lagos for the record checks that the U.S. Consulate and the INS no longer deemed necessary. On an officially stamped college letterhead dated March 18, the administrative officer for the deputy provost and former head of department (marine engineering) wrote "to confirm to you that Mr. Oladokun Sulaiman . . . was admitted into the Marine Engineering Department of this College in 1992 and graduated in 1995 . . . [and] awarded an Ordinary National Diploma (OND) Certificate in Marine Engineering at a Pass Level."[9] In another letter, the administrative officer wrote that the U.S. Embassy had asked to confirm not the regular OND but a Certificate on Sea Survival. He explained, "The Certificate . . . could however not be confirmed as it is a Consult Certificate which was run by an external body whose contract has terminated. We will however need some time to locate the then Director of Consult Mr. Adeola to confirm the Certificate."[10] On March 20, the officer wrote Adeola to confirm Oladokun's certificate, sending him the address of Oladokun's attorney, Kenneth Schoenfeld.[11] On March 21, Adeola wrote Schoenfeld "confirming that the certificate is in order and [should] be accepted as being genuine."[12] Thus Oladokun's certificates were finally officially verified by the Federal College in Lagos on March 21.

Meanwhile Oladokun's hearing on March 18 before immigration judge Daniel Meisner in Newark, New Jersey, had been adjourned to March 26, buying Schoenfeld and Oladokun time to present the new evidence of certification.[13] In Immigration Court on March 26, however, Schoenfeld was presented with an INS document dated on that day.[14] The court transcripts show that Schoenfeld, after wavering over an adjournment, decided to plead without delay to speed up the possibility of a bond hearing for Oladokun. He denied the new charges:

> *Judge DM:* The factual allegation is that on March 26, 2003, the State University of New York Maritime College decided to disenroll you, meaning the respondent, effective immediately. Is that admitted or denied?
>
> *Attorney KS:* It's neither. I have no way of knowing whether they have or have not. This is today's date, obviously, and if they have, they can take actions to have them reconsider this unfortunate decision, if they have taken such.

Disenrolling him on the day of his court hearing, SUNY revoked Oladokun's F-1 status, rendering him removable regardless of the genuineness of his certificates.

A New Attorney

> He considered what he could say to win over the whole audience once and for all. . . . "This question of yours, sir [Herr Examining Magistrate], about my being a house-painter . . . is typical of the whole character of this trial that is

being foisted on me. . . . I do not say that your procedure is contemptible, but I should like to present that epithet to you for your private consideration."
K. stopped.—Kafka, *The Trial*, 41

On the day of the next scheduled hearing, April 9, Oladokun's attorney Kenneth Schoenfeld was absent. Oladokun said he tried Schoenfeld's phone, but no one picked up.[15] "So what do you want to do?" acting judge Daniel Meisner asked. "I think we can go [indiscernible] with the bail hearing," Oladokun replied, eager for a bond to release him from detention. At this turn, the court transcripts go "off the record." When they return, there is no more talk of bail. Meisner adjourns the court to April 15.

A new attorney, Olakayode Babalola, represented Oladokun on April 15, 2003.[16] Judge Meisner gave Babalola an overview of the case. Familiar with the case for some time, Babalola said that he would like to plead against the new charges. Reproduced here in full from court transcripts, Babalola's argument, is—much like Joseph K.'s first interrogation—the dramatic *pièce de résistance* in Oladokun's trial, a call for a legitimate law that seemed to hide behind its sheer force.

> *Attorney Babalola:* The charge SUNY Maritime College tried to disenroll you effective immediately, Your Honor, is denied.
> *Judge Meisner:* Okay. Are you aware that the, I'm not sure if you have all the documents, but the Immigration Service received two letters dated March 26, 2003 . . . both indicating that the respondent had been disenrolled, or I suppose that's another way of saying expelled.
> *OB:* Your Honor, I cannot at this time admit it. I can only deny. I will move to [indiscernible] full merits [indiscernible]. If I see additional information indicating that that was done lawfully or legally, Judge, I might be able to consider pleading, changing my plea, [indiscernible].
> *J:* Do you have copies of those two letters I referred to?
> *OB:* I do not have them.
> *J:* Can I suggest it would be difficult for you to be prepared then to go ahead today?
> *OB:* Your Honor, with regard to what this Court did, Your Honor, I don't think that's going to affect the case. From my understanding of the file that I read so far and the allegation, it's been [falsely] alleged that the document, the certificate submitted by the respondent to obtain his F1 student visa was fraudulent. That's the allegation [indiscernible].
> *J:* Well, I agree with you up to a point. But the other point is that there's a further allegation by the Immigration Service that whatever he did or didn't

do in the past, he's been expelled from school and he's no longer entitled to non-immigrant status.

OB: Your Honor, exactly, that is what I'm saying, Judge. This is a court of law and nothing can stand for nothing. If the act leading to the arrest and placing the respondent in removal proceedings is unlawful in the first place and is based on wrong information, Your Honor, there is no way the college can legally and lawfully disenroll him.

J: Well the problem is that the Immigration Court is not a court of general jurisdiction. It's not an equity court and I don't have general jurisdiction, so I don't have any authority to review the actions of the Maritime Academy. In other words, if I'm satisfied that based on the letters that the Maritime Academy has expelled the respondent, then there's nothing I can do about that and I can't review the underlying reasons for their decision.

OB: Your Honor, that is not my prayer at this time, Your Honor. What I'm asking that should be done was to look at the merits of the allegation in the NTA, which is alleging that respondent submitted fraudulent documents to obtain immigration benefits.

J: Let me go off the record.

By pointing out that the court's proceedings were based on unverified allegations, by saying, "this is a court of law and nothing can stand for nothing," Babalola questioned the legitimacy of the court. By invoking a residual law no longer in force, he compelled the judge to admit the fictitious nature of the court and the limits of its claims to justice. "I agree with you up to a point," Meisner conceded, "the problem is that the Immigration Court is not a court of general jurisdiction." The charade had been exposed. When they come back on record, the proceeding continued. The judge delivered his verdict:

> Based on these documents, I'm satisfied that factual allegation number nine is sustained and that the respondent is removable from the U.S. as charged. The evidence shows that the respondent was expelled or disenrolled from his college and therefore is not in valid student status.

The judge asked if the respondent wished to designate a country for removal. Babalola said no. The judge named Nigeria, the country of citizenship.

J: Is there any application addressed to the Immigration Court?

OB: Yes, Your Honor. We'll be asking at this time, subject to further review, for asylum and an application under the CAT Convention.

Examinations in Detail: Under Bureaucratic Scrutiny

> The thought of his case never left him now. He had often considered whether
> it would not be better to draw up a written defense and hand it to the Court. In
> this defense he would give a short account of his life, and when he came to an
> event of any importance explain for what reasons he had acted as he did, inti-
> mate whether he approved or condemned his way of action in retrospect, and
> adduce grounds for the condemnation or approval.—Kafka, *The Trial*, 107

In the first court hearing on March 18, when asked by Meisner "to designate a country for removal if that becomes necessary," Oladokun, assured
of his innocence over the college's injustice, had named Nigeria.[17] At this
late stage in the trial, however, setting aside the injustice meted out to
him by the college and the court, Oladokun and Babalola understood that
the only right Oladokun could stake a claim to in the United States was
stacked in the Convention against Torture (CAT), against the possibility of
his torture in Nigeria. In an oral decision of June 23 on Oladokun's CAT application, Judge Meisner opened: "The respondent before me is a 27 year-
old unmarried male alien."[18] Thereafter Meisner described Oladokun's entire history of entry into and stay in the United States. "The respondent's
I-589 [CAT protection form] provides meager information and really does
not establish any type of a persecution claim," Meisner claimed.

> Among the information that is not provided in the I-589, in answer to ques-
> tion 1 in part A3, it asks for the respondent's addresses before coming to the
> United States. The respondent provides an address in Nigeria from 1992 to
> 1997 . . . but he does not indicate where he was living for up to two years from
> 1997 to 1999. The respondent is also asked in part A3 to provide information
> concerning his parents and siblings. . . . The respondent says he has seven
> brothers and sisters . . . and yet no additional information was provided
> about the respondent's siblings.

Under CAT, then, the law concerns itself with Oladokun's entire existence,
reproducing his life in stark detail.

In his application for protection under CAT, Babalola had helped
Oladokun make his case in the following terms:

> Having been accused of terrorism and document fraud, I have now been set
> up to any government in the world and especially in Nigeria and Burkina
> Faso as a major risk factor. A person to be arrested, watched, interrogated,
> detained, possibly indefinitely with understandable probable cause.

In making his argument, Oladokun actually implicated U.S. actions in producing his vulnerable position. Meisner dismissed the claim as "not factual" but "argument." In trying to conjure the specter of his violation by the Nigerian government, Oladokun's plea had stated, "There is a decree in Nigeria to the effect that if a Nigerian citizen brings the name of the country to disrepute . . . the government will imprison such an individual." Six months later, in a letter titled "Affidavit in support of motions for emergency stay of deportation, to reopen deportation proceedings," Oladokun would argue in a last-ditch effort that his attorney had induced him to make the statement and had neglected to include a copy of the Nigerian decree as promised.[19] In his private confessional letter asking his former judge Meisner to reconsider the June 23 decision, Oladokun also emphasized his college expenses over three and a half years at SUNY and promise that he was a "harmless and a good student."[20] At the time of his CAT hearing before the immigration bureaucracy, however, proving himself to be a tortured subject and Nigeria a torturing state was Oladokun's only recourse before the Immigration Service's web of indictment. Unconvinced by the chronicle of Oladokun's life history and Babalola's argument, Meisner gave his verdict:

> Specific, detailed, and credible testimony or a combination of detailed testimony and corroborative background evidence is necessary to prove a case for asylum. . . . Under the circumstances the respondent is found removable from the United States. . . . So ordered.

TORTURED SUBJECTS: TORTURE AS RIGHTS, TORTURE AS POLITICAL ECONOMY

The United Nations Convention against Torture and Other Cruel, Inhuman or Degrading Treatment or Punishment (CAT) under which Sulaiman Oladokun made his argument for the right to remain in the United States came into force as a UN treaty in 1989. The United States signed the treaty in 1988 and after congressional ratification became a full party to the treaty in 1994. Article 1 of the convention further defines torture as an act "by which severe pain and suffering, whether physical or mental," are inflicted on an individual by "a person acting in an official capacity."[21] More pertinent to migrants, article 3 states, "No state shall expel, return, or extradite a person to another State where there are substantial grounds for believing that he would be in danger of being subjected to torture." In 1998 the U.S. Senate, in accordance with CAT's article 3, passed the Foreign Affairs Reform and Restructuring Act, prohibiting the "transfer of aliens to countries where they would be tortured."

Around the same time that torture became a legally recognized cause for migration to the United States, two other sets of international treaties and domestic laws were passed. In 1994, the same year CAT was ratified, international treaties like NAFTA and organizations like the WTO came into force to promote capital mobility and free trade with new urgency. In the domestic sphere, two years before the 1998 reforms to prohibit migrant transfer to torturing countries, the 1996 immigration reforms dramatically reduced the rights of migrants. To understand the significance of the antitorture legislation's coincidence with free-trade economic treaties and immigration control, Wendy Brown's analysis of "liberal juridical modalities" and their processes of individualization and regulation that destabilize wider critiques of capitalism and state power may be helpful (1995, 58–66).

In her book *States of Injury*, Brown considers how legislative protection against racism, sexual harassment, and homophobia "casts the law in particular and the state more generally as neutral arbiters of injury rather than as themselves invested with the power to injure." Brown asks whether "the effort to 'outlaw' social injury powerfully legitimizes law and the state as appropriate protectors against injury and casts injured individuals as needing such protection by such protectors" (27). In the international arena, treaties like CAT enshrine the language of protection from torture and human rights in law, implicitly enjoining the task of protection on Western democratic states. By instituting torture violations by foreign states as necessary causes of migration, the state establishes itself as protector, eliding the role of its economic and political actions in producing such migration and its own subsequent violation of migrants.

According to CAT's definition of torture, "severe pain and suffering, whether physical or mental . . . [inflicted by] a person acting in an official capacity," the U.S. immigration bureaucracy can be accused of having mentally tortured Oladokun with unnecessarily prolonged detention and inconsistent juridical procedure. However, in the emergency or security state, freed from juridical review and given the ability to exercise its power as law, the immigration court refuses to recognize its own injustices. By continuously altering its case against Oladokun to justify his apprehension and deportation, the immigration court forces Oladokun to project blame onto foreign states. By finally adjudicating Oladokun's risk of torture in

Nigeria, the court erases its own critical steps in producing Oladokun before it as a tortured subject. Didier Fassin and Estelle D'Halluin (2005) have shown how, owing to the recent effort in France to control immigration and the corresponding decrease in the acceptance rate of asylum seekers, medical certificates attesting to the tortured condition of the asylum seeker's body have become the ultimate evidence for potential migrants. The paradox of contemporary global governance structures is such that global economic treaties foster migration, yet migrants must articulate their economically stimulated desire to migrate as a plea to flee torture. What is remarkable about contemporary state practice in the United States, however, is that it is not only undocumented migrants seeking to obtain legal status but also so-called "legal" migrants who have been illegalized and forced to reconfigure pleas for justice against the right to flee torture from foreign countries.

Needless to say, the threat of torture is a legitimate cause for migration. The question here, however, is how the particular international emphasis on legal inscription and bureaucratic management of migration with respect to torturability in the 1990s may work to "codify, entrench, and mask" disproportionate distributions of social powers rather than to contest or challenge them (Brown 1995, 12). Does CAT liberate migrants from torture and human rights violations, or does it paradoxically reinscribe the migrant as susceptible to states of exception, to emergency laws, to torture? Mark Dow's in-depth research on the INS shows how asylum hearings before the immigration bureaucracy become venues for humiliation as well as detention (2004). The public outcry over the use of torture at Guantanamo, for instance, against years of silence over the exploitation, criminalization, and detention of migrants, suggests how deeply "protection from torture" may be embedded as the only defining right of the migrant. Not only upon entry but (as Oladokun's case demonstrates) even in subsequent legal procedures involving migrants, the clause "protection from torture," cited in CAT as a legitimate cause of migration, seems to make torture—torture being understood as the most crude form of physical torture—the benchmark of a migrant's rights. In Oladokun's trial, the terms of the debate suddenly switch to torture, in this case by the Nigerian state, as the U.S. immigration agency sidesteps the circumstances of Oladokun's case and hides its own culpability. In Kafka's *The Trial*, torture hovers at the edges—in K.'s nightmares and fears, in the hidden underbelly of the bureaucracy—by comparison rendering every other form of manipulation that operates under the guise of legal and bureaucratic procedure normal.

NOTES

1. The laws were widely criticized and eventually reined in by a Supreme Court ruling of June 2001. See http://www.aclu.org/scotus/2000/11769prs20010625 .html (accessed May 19, 2007).

2. The U.S. Immigration and Naturalization Service (INS), which oversaw all aspects of "legal" and "illegal" immigration, was dissolved in March 2003, around the same time as Oladokun's case began. The functions of the INS were transferred to the new Department of Homeland Security (DHS) and distributed among its three agencies, the U.S. Citizenship and Immigration Services (USCIS), U.S. Immigration and Customs Enforcement (ICE), and U.S. Customs and Border Protection (CBP). For reasons of continuity and clarity, I use INS or "immigration agency" to refer to the immigration agencies, first INS and later DHS, that dealt with Oladokun's case.

3. I obtained copies of the court transcripts of Sulaiman Oladokun's case, INS forms, and his letters from a community organization that helped people subjected to antiterror investigations after September 11, 2001, find legal and financial support. I was given access to these documents with Oladokun's consent. Although I was not in direct contact with him when I wrote this paper in 2006, I was subsequently able to correspond with him by e-mail. He is reported to be currently working in Malaysia (for another account of Oladokun's case, see Fernandes 2007, 145–52).

4. http://www.humanrights.net.nz/big-issues/war-on-terrorism/sulaiman-story (accessed May 19, 2007). For further media coverage of Oladokun's case, see Tavernese 2003; D. Hafetz 2006.

5. INS Form I-831, March 6, 2003 (file A078 711 270, case NYC0303000415).

6. Ibid.

7. INS Form I-862, "Notice to Appear," March 7, 2003.

8. U.S. Consulate and Department of State's Fraud Prevention Program report.

9. Letter from Administrative Officer, Federal College, Lagos, "Re: Confirmation: Mr. Oladokun Sulaiman," March 18, 2003.

10. Letter from Administrative Officer to Schoenfeld, Federal College, Lagos, March 19, 2003.

11. Letter from Administrative Officer to Adeola, "Re—Confirmation of Sea Survival Certificate . . . ," March 20, 2003.

12. Letter from Adeola to Schoenfeld, "Re: Confirmation of Sea Survival Certificate . . . ," March 21, 2003.

13. U.S. Department of Justice (DOJ), "Executive Office for Immigration Review," Immigration Court, Transcript of Hearing, March 18, 2003.

14. U.S. DOJ, Immigration Court, Transcript of Hearing, March 26, 2003.

15. U.S. DOJ, Immigration Court, Transcript of Hearing, April 9, 2003.

16. U.S. DOJ, Immigration Court, Transcript of Hearing, April 15, 2003.

17. U.S. DOJ, Immigration Court, Transcript of Hearing, March 18, 2003.

18. U.S. DOJ, Immigration Court, Transcript of Hearing, June 23, 2003.

19. U.S. DOJ, Executive Office of Immigration Review, Affidavit, January 16, 2004.

20. Letter from Oladokun to Meisner, "Re: Custody Review/Re-determination," September 15, 2003.

21. See http://www.unhchr.ch/html/menu3/b/h_cat39.htm (accessed May 19, 2007).

—⚏—

CHAPTER 12

Exiled by Law

Deportation and the Inviability of Life

A Rampart Division CRASH [Community Resources Against Street Hoodlums] officer pursuing a case against a 15-year-old accused of a fatal double shooting attempted to arrange the deportation of a high-profile activist whose testimony could clear the youth of murder charges, the activist says. . . .

Alex Sanchez, who is being held at the federal immigration detention facility in San Pedro, said his Jan. 21 arrest by Rampart Officer Jesus Amezcua came after months of threats and harassment against him and other activists in Homies Unidos, a group working to end gang violence. . . .

Sanchez and others say Jose Rodriguez, the teenager accused of murder, was at a Homies Unidos meeting at the time the shooting took place in August. . . .

The arrest of Sanchez—whose detention has made him something of a cause celebre—is the most recent example of what critics say is Rampart Division officers' use of immigration issues to eliminate troublesome witnesses by having them deported. . . .

In an interview, Sanchez said he and Amezcua were well-acquainted by the time the officer arrested him. Last summer, Amezcua stopped him and photographed him, saying he looked suspicious, Sanchez said.

A few weeks later, on Aug. 6, Amezcua kicked open the door at a birthday party for Sanchez's fiancee, along with another officer who shoved a girl's face against the wall several times and hit Sanchez in the head with a baton, Sanchez said.

He said he next saw Amezcua after the slaying, at a Juvenile Court hearing for Rodriguez. After that, according to Sanchez, Amezcua began to stop him routinely on the street and search him, sometimes punching him in the groin, telling him: "We'll see who wins the court trial—his gang or our gang."

Sanchez and others said Amezcua was one of the officers who regularly harassed many members of Homies Unidos, stopping them on their way to and from the group's Thursday night meetings at Immanuel Presbyterian Church on Wilshire Boulevard.

He said Amezcua was one of several officers who went to the church in September just hours before state Sen. Tom Hayden (D–Los Angeles) was to hold a nighttime hearing on harassment of the group. Sanchez said the officers asked if they could hide in the church during Homies Unidos meetings.

Church custodian Victor Cosme said LAPD officers did show up at the church one day in September, but he could not remember the day or their names.

"They wanted to hide in a room where a meeting was taking place, perhaps in a closet. I said no," he recalled. "They asked where Homies Unidos met. I showed them the room. I never saw them again."

A group of LAPD officers, including Amezcua, appeared that night at the Hayden hearings, where Sanchez testified, according to Rocky Rushing, Hayden's chief of staff.

When Amezcua saw Sanchez on the street later, he said "he was going to see me behind bars, and he gave Homies Unidos six months to live," Sanchez alleged. . . .

Not long before his arrest, Sanchez said, Amezcua searched him and a friend, Ricardo Hernandez, who was arrested on a minor charge and then held because of his own illegal immigration status.

Then at 8 p.m. Jan. 21, Amezcua stopped Sanchez and told him he was wanted by the INS, saying: " 'It's over. You can take Homies Unidos and shove it.' . . [were his] exact words," Sanchez said. . . .

He said Amezcua refused to let him call a lawyer or Hayden's office. He was taken to Men's Central Jail but not booked, then transported to Parker Center, he said.—Anne-Marie O'Connor, "Activist Says Officer Sought His Deportation"

Alex Sanchez's experience of being arrested and placed in deportation proceedings after having spent most of his life in the United States is unusual in that he was the leader of a gang violence prevention program, he had the support of respected public officials such as California state senator Tom Hayden, and his case became part of the controversy over the Rampart scandal, in which officers in the Los Angeles Police Department were convicted of violence and the falsification of evidence against alleged gang members (Zilberg 2002, 2004). At the same time, his experience is not unusual in that deporting aliens with criminal convictions has increasingly been a goal of both immigration and crime control policies in the United States (Coutin 2005). Further, U.S. antigang policies, which assign gang membership based on tattoos, association, and dress style, forbid suspected gang members from congregating in particular areas, and increase penalties for those deemed to be gang members, have been exported to Central American nations and other countries, making life for deported gang members difficult at best (Zilberg 2007c).

In this chapter, I analyze how the transnational conjuncture of immigration and criminal justice policies constitutes "criminal aliens" or émigrés as expendable and indeed exiles them not only from particular legal territories but also from the social domains that make life itself viable. In the United States, removal—the legal term for deportation—has emerged as a seemingly benign technique for extricating seemingly problematic ("illegal," "criminal") noncitizens from U.S. territory. The neutrality of the term hides the violence that removal wreaks on individuals, families, communities, and the law itself. Through removal, individuals are legally stripped of their de facto or de jure (i.e., legal permanent residency) membership in the United States and are constituted as fully alien. They are then sent to countries where they are de jure citizens, but where, as long-term émigrés who were convicted of crimes, many lack social connections or clearly recognized legal rights. In fact, antigang policies in their countries of origin may drive them out—and back to the United States—once more. Such departures are akin to a de facto or unofficial deportation, in that law enforcement policies, lack of economic opportunity, and social stigmatization lead them to leave their "home" countries (Zilberg 2007c). By constituting "criminal aliens" as so-called enemies whose right to exist is in question, nations claim to have bolstered public security (De Genova 2007). In fact, however, such policies may contribute to insecurity by rendering the law itself unstable.[1]

To analyze the ways that criminal justice and immigration policies constitute certain noncitizens as expendable others, I interweave accounts of Alex Sanchez's experiences with analyses of U.S. and Salvadoran government policies. I have chosen to focus on Alex Sanchez both because of the variety of his experiences—he was deported to El Salvador in 1994, he returned to the United States in 1996, and he was placed in removal proceedings again in 2000—and because his immigration case draws attention to the violence and persecution experienced by former gang members. I also draw on fieldwork conducted in El Salvador and Los

Angeles between 2000 and 2004, consisting primarily of interviews with Salvadoran immigrants in the United States, immigrant rights advocates and government officials in the United States and El Salvador, and deportees affiliated with Homies Unidos in El Salvador. This fieldwork suggests that noncitizens who have been convicted of crimes are facing a transnational injunction of sorts, such that they are not permitted to exist anywhere (see also Ngai 2004). Their lives are rendered inviable as they are pushed underground either figuratively, in that they must live as fugitives, or literally, in that they are subjected to violence that can lead to their deaths.

I [Alex Sanchez] was born in San Salvador. It was a little town, on the outskirts of San Salvador going towards Cojutepeque. From San Martin. . . . I remember the scene where I lived. The area, the streets, the railroad tracks and this bridge and the cliff on the back of the house I lived in. So I remember most of that stuff, but in a blur, you know. It was all in a blur. . . .

I mean, the country [of El Salvador] was in conflict, and my dad had family that was involved in the movement. And, well, he had us. He had children. So he wanted something else for us. And then the area right there where we lived was like the spot where they'd throw bodies. You know, so he really wanted to get us out of there. . . .

We flew to, I think, Mexico. From Mexico City, I think, I'm not too sure. I know we went on train from, I guess, Mexico to another place. And then, then there was this other friend. The same people that was taking us, took us across the border in a van. . . . I remember it was real scary. . . .

I started 3rd grade. And I went to the school, Wilshire Crest. And it was really an experience because it was about speaking English and I didn't know anything. But I kind of, I mean there wasn't no ESL classes. And there wasn't, you know, that much help. And there weren't that many people around that were immigrants during that time. You know? It was mostly Chicanos or white. There weren't many blacks around that area. But I hanged around with these Chicanos and started learning English pretty fast. So then I went to 4th grade, I came to Hobart, and by that time I knew a lot of English. . . .

But when I actually really felt it was when I was in 6th grade. When people used to ask me, "Well, where are you from?" And I would say, "El Salvador." And "What place?" And I would say, "San Salvador." "But where in San Salvador?" I would say, "I don't know. I just know that I'm from down there and that's it." I felt kind of frustrated that I didn't know where exactly I was from. But at the same time I felt proud of being a Salvadorean. I had pride in it. I would never deny it. . . .

I didn't know the place [El Salvador]. They talk about los Chorros, they talk about Apulo, they talked about la Costa del Sol, all these places. Las piscinas. And I just didn't know. Los volcanes de San Vicente. And so many things they talked about that I just didn't relate to that. And I even ended up, kind of, losing my slang through years. Salvadorean slang. So you lose a lot of things. But during the time that I came, there weren't that many Salvadoreans here in L.A. So it was, like in ... '85, '86, the schools were filled with Salvadorean kids by then, you know. There were a lot of people from El Salvador. And so I started kind of getting my slang back. And that's when I found out about this neighborhood, this gang that was a Salvadorean gang! You know, I related, I really related to it. And ... I liked being with them because they spoke Spanish, they weren't always speaking English. Because I still had a little bit of trouble with pronunciations? So sometime I'd rather speak Spanish than English. So I felt more comfortable being with these guys and speaking Spanish. It wasn't like they were like the other crowd I was with that only spoke English. In a way it helped me because I learned it faster than anything because, you know, I wasn't speaking Spanish all the time. And I was learning, trying to learn it too so I could have a conversation with them, you know. But that's when I found out about the gang, Mara Salvatrucha, and the relationship with El Salvador. Because I didn't even know what a Salvatrucha was, a mara, you know, I didn't. And I found out and I said, "Wait a minute. This is me. This is the people I belong with." (Interview, May 8, 2001)

The complex belongings that Alex Sanchez described in my interview with him are belied by legal constructs that assign citizenship to a single nation. Noncitizens can be removed from the United States because, even if they are legal permanent residents, they lack incontrovertible membership in the U.S. polity. If they are apprehended by U.S. immigration authorities or if they are convicted of crimes that make them ineligible for legal permanent residency, they can be removed to their site of legal citizenship. In the case of Alex Sanchez, that site was El Salvador, a place that he left at age seven and remembered only as "a blur." During his childhood, Sanchez, like many other immigrants, was situated in multiple places and nowhere at the same time. He "lost" something of El Salvador—his memories, his slang—even as he found the United States somewhat unwelcoming. There were few services for immigrant children in the public schools of Los Angeles, and though he learned English quickly, he "still had a little bit of trouble with pronunciations." As a teenager, he found himself most at home with the Mara Salvatrucha, a gang that was made up of people who, like him, were from El Salvador, spoke both Spanish and English, and were somewhat set apart from Anglo and even Chicano or Mexican American society. Such complex positionings—as outsiders within their country of origin and residency, yet members of youth subgroups belonging in some sense to both places—cannot be acknowledged by laws that elevate a legal origin as citizen over other measures of belonging, and that treat the presence of noncitizens as always, in some sense, probationary (Kanstroom 2000).

Officially, removing a noncitizen—at the time, Sanchez was undocumented—from the United States is not considered to be a punishment but is deemed merely to place individuals who are not "legally" part of the polity outside U.S. territory. Unlike incarceration and other criminal penalties, which ostensibly "correct" (i.e., rehabilitate) while also punishing an individual for his or her wrongdoing, removal is simply the consequence of lacking the right to enter or remain within U.S. territory. Therefore, although the United States does not sentence citizens to exile or deportation, noncitizens can, in essence, be exiled. As Daniel Kanstroom points out, "Federal deportation laws based on post-entry criminal conduct require a theoretical explanation for why banishment is a punishment when applied to citizens, but is not a punishment when applied to lawful resident aliens. This explanation . . . derived from the status of alienage being seen as an increasingly tenuous claim to any rights against deportation" (2000, 1909). As individuals who have tenuous claims, noncitizens are placed in the position of supplicant—they must request the right to be present. Removal is the default position and, though it may have devastating consequences for the individuals involved, does not carry the due process protections (such as the right to a state-appointed attorney) that accompany criminal proceedings (Cole and Dempsey 2002).

In the United States, removal has become increasingly common as criminal justice and immigration policies have converged (Welch 2002). In 1996 the Antiterrorism and Effective Death Penalty Act (AEDPA) and the Illegal Immigration Reform and Immigrant Responsibility Act (IIRIRA) expanded the definition of aggravated felony for immigration purposes, creating a situation that the legal scholar Nancy Morawetz referred to as "Alice-in-Wonderland-like." Morawetz explains, "As the term is defined, a crime need not be either aggravated or a felony. For example, a conviction for simple battery or for shoplifting with a one-year suspended sentence—either of which would be a misdemeanor or a violation in most states—can be deemed an aggravated felony" (2000, 1939).[2] Legal permanent residents who are convicted of such aggravated felonies are stripped of their residency and made deportable. Before 1996, noncitizens with criminal convictions could request waivers by arguing that their equities—relatives, lengthy period of residence, educational history—in the United States weighed against their deportation. The 1996 laws eliminated such challenges, made both detention and removal mandatory, and applied this new policy retroactively to convictions that occurred before 1996 (J. Hafetz 1998).[3] Noncitizens were made a particular target of law enforcement practices, and criminals were made a target of deportation policies. As Kanstroom points out, "Deportation policy . . . has aimed increasingly at permanently 'cleansing' our society of those with undesirable qualities, especially criminal behavior" (2000, 1892).

The convergence between immigration and criminal justice policies extends the logic of mass-incarceration policies to immigrant populations. Correctional practices have recently moved from a rehabilitation model to what Malcolm Feeley and Jonathan Simon (1992) term "risk management." Instead of attempting to reform socially deviant individuals, prisons now attempt to "manage" dangerous persons, who are then "warehoused" as part of ever-growing prison populations. Prisons are conceptualized as a space *outside* society (Schinkel 2002), as evidenced by the increasing use of the term "reentry" to refer to being released from prison (Petersilia 2003). Targeting noncitizens who have been convicted of crimes extends this spatialized logic in that such individuals are physically removed from U.S. society and territory, initially through detention centers and eventually through deportation. Warehousing offenders and deporting noncitizens with criminal convictions also have similar social consequences. In both cases, individuals are removed from communities, family members are subjected to lengthy separations, and populations are excluded from the electoral process (felons are often disenfranchised, and noncitizens cannot vote in the United States). A Bureau of Justice Statistics report attributed 14 percent of the growth in the federal prison population between 1985 and 2000 to increases in the incarceration of immigration offenders (Scalia and Litras 2002). The 1996 laws had an immediate and dramatic effect on the number of noncitizens forcibly removed from the United States, as table 1 shows.

The number of noncitizens forcibly removed increased by a dramatic 37 percent in 1996, when IIRIRA and AEDPA were passed, followed by even larger increases of 64 percent and 53 percent in 1997 and 1998 respectively. Subsequently, removals remained at high levels, with the exception of 2001, which remained stable, and 2002, in which there was a small decrease. Cumulatively, between 1996 and 2007, deportations more than

TABLE 1. Aliens Expelled, 1991–2007

YEAR	FORMAL REMOVALS	PERCENT INCREASE	TO EL SALVADOR	PERCENT INCREASE
1991	33,189		1,496	
1992	43,671	31%	1,937	29%
1993	42,542	−3%	2,117	9%
1994	45,674	7%	1,900	−10%
1995	50,924	11%	1,932	2%
1996	69,680	37%	2,493	29%
1997	114,432	64%	3,900	56%
1998	174,813	53%	5,465	40%
1999	183,114	5%	4,160	−24%
2000	188,467	3%	4,736	14%
2001	189,026	0%	3,928	−17%
2002	165,168	−13%	4,066	4%
2003	211,098	28%	5,561	37%
2004	240,665	14%	7,269	31%
2005	246,431	2%	8,305	14%
2006	280,974	14%	11,050	33%
2007	319,382	14%	20,045	81%

Source: U.S. Department of Homeland Security, *2007 Yearbook of Immigration Statistics*, tables 36 and 37d, and earlier DHS and INS statistical yearbooks.

quadrupled. Strikingly, in the year 2007 alone, deportations to El Salvador increased by 81 percent.

Although criminal justice and immigration policies attempt to resituate noncitizens who are convicted of crimes in a space outside the U.S. territory and polity, such individuals may in fact have myriad ties to the United States, whether or not they are physically present. As Elana Zilberg notes, "Banished though they may be from the U.S., these deported youth and young adults remain linked to that landscape through, among other things, ongoing ties with family. . . . Deportees remain an integral part of the 'structure of feeling' [of] the *barrio*, of its internal relations and the everyday practices of its residents" (2007b, 495; Williams 1992, 128–35; see also Zilberg 2004). The individuals who are subjected to removal may have relatives in the United States; they may have attended U.S. schools, worked in the United States, developed fluent English skills, acclimated to U.S. culture (particularly to youth subcultures), and envisioned futures within this country. In the earlier interview excerpt, Alex Sanchez names the Los Angeles public schools that he attended as a young child. The landscape of Los Angeles pervades his personal history. As Judge Learned Hand wrote about a Polish deportation case in 1926, "Whether the relator came here in arms or at the age of ten, he is as much our product as though his mother had borne him on American soil. He knows no other language, no other people, no other habits, than ours; he will be as much a stranger in Poland as any one born of ancestors who immigrated in the seventeenth century" (quoted in Kanstroom 2000, 1890). Forcible removal requires reconstituting such complexly situated individuals as alien.

> Alan Diamante, Sánchez's attorney, indicated that during his youth his client was involved in a Mara Salvatrucha gang that operated on 8th Street and Normandie Avenue.
>
> He also said that when he was 18 years old, Sánchez already had a criminal record. On his rap sheet there appears a conviction for car theft, accusations of weapons possession and of intimidating witnesses.
>
> "For committing certain crimes and for having a criminal history, they deported him in 1994," stated Diamante.
>
> During his stay in El Salvador, Sánchez received threats, was persecuted and detained, according to his attorney.
>
> Those factors and the fact that a son of his was born, motivated him to abandon gangs and return to the United States, Diamante noted.
>
> "He supposedly entered in an illegal fashion," he noted, adding that his defense only has two legal avenues.
>
> One, the attorney said literally, is to solicit suspension of removal [from the country], as a political case, and the other is to base the case on international law against torture, which states that a person cannot be sent to a country when there is sufficient proof that if he is returned, he will be tortured at the hands of the government or other groups. (Linares 2000)[4]

The process of removal officially transforms de facto community members into aliens with no right to remain in the United States. Noncitizens who are subjected to deportation may find this transformation shocking. A Homies Unidos member who was interviewed for this project after having been deported to El Salvador could not imagine that he could never return "legally" to the United States: "You can't just say, 'You're expelled for life. You're deported for life.' I mean, I hope not!" Of course, deportation is not supposed to *transform* individuals. Rather, it is supposed to be a consequence of already being both alien and unauthorized. Note that in Alex Sanchez's case, his only legal option when faced with deportation was to demonstrate that he could not safely return to El Salvador and therefore had to remain in the United States. Despite having lived in this country for more than two decades and having U.S. citizen relatives (including a wife and son), his criminal convictions, prior deportation, and unauthorized reentry defined him as alien and his presence as illicit. Nonetheless there is a sense in which the process of deportation *produces* the very "alienage" and "illegality" from which it is supposed to flow.

The transformative nature of deportation is demonstrated by the experiences of King (a pseudonym), whom I interviewed in El Salvador in 2001. King came to the United States in the early 1980s at age four or five and became a legal permanent resident in the late 1980s, when he was approximately nine or ten. As a teenager, he began to have trouble with the law and served time in juvenile hall, but he was not concerned about immigration consequences: "Because I had the residency, I figured, oh, shssh, I got it made, you know, a resident." King was incarcerated in 1993, and in 1996 he learned about the passage of AEDPA and IIRIRA: "I *always* watched the news in prison. . . . And then after that Timothy McVeigh blew up that building? They passed a law, . . . instead of, you know, going after the guys that did that, they decided to wash their hands and throw it out from all the [immigrants] and residents, uh-huh. They called 'em, uh, 'a terrorist threat.' To them, we're a terrorist threat. Just because of what Timothy, Timothy McVeigh did." An immigration hold was placed on King, and when he completed his prison sentence, he was transferred to an immigration detention center, where he unsuccessfully fought his deportation case for six months. Although King had projected a future in the United States, he was ordered deported.

Before being deported, King was transferred to a holding cell, where conditions were difficult: "We were there all night, and we were cold." From the holding cell, he and others were bused to Arizona, where, in shackles, they were flown to Houston, Texas. In Texas, they were processed for deportation and then taken to a county jail, which King described as "messed up. . . . They wouldn't let us buy nothing at the store or nothing, so we didn't have no deodorant, no razor, no toothbrush. And they wouldn't, uh, give us any, because they were treating us like lower, you know what I mean? Like, you're getting deported anyways, you don't need none of that." Being treated as "lower" continued as King was placed in another holding cell: "And it was like hot, moisture. Like everything starts sweating, you know, with the body heat. And the water was no good. There was no drinking water. Only a shower to shower. The toilets were messed up, there was no pressure." King was in the holding cell for four or five days. King found these conditions dehumanizing, telling one of the sergeants, "Look, Sergeant, man, what's going on? We don't get rec, yard, nothing. You know? You're treating us like animals, man!" Finally King and other deportees were shackled and placed on one of the oldest planes that King had ever seen: "And we took off. Fshshshshoooooooooo! All shackled up. T-t-t-t. And then, like, they give us, like, a tore-up sandwich and stuff? To eat up there? You know, I wasn't hungry, I didn't eat nothing. That's the least thing I had on my mind was food after leaving, you know, the country you were raised in." King found the shackles particularly debasing: "They think they can treat you like you don't know your rights, you know what I mean? Even if you're deportable, you still got rights, human rights."

King's account of deportation is replete with references to humiliating experiences, to being treated as an animal, as debased, as lacking rights. The shackles—which King reported were removed before landing, after flying out of U.S. airspace—were a particularly vivid marker of criminalized "illegality" and alienage. King experienced deportation not as a *return* but as a *departure*, "leaving, you know, the country you were raised in." Deportation officially transformed King in ways that he experienced bodily (heat, cold, shackles, and deprivation). Officially he was not only a noncitizen of the United States but also a citizen of El Salvador. Unofficially, however, deportees' membership in their countries of origin can also be questioned.

I [Alex Sanchez] just said, "I've always wanted to know how El Salvador looks like." I mean, I could have fought it [deportation] for a while but I still wanted to know where I was from. I wanted to know where exactly in San Salvador I was from. So I signed it [the paperwork] and got deported. . . .

I was anxious to smell the air. I was anxious to go see that curve and the railroad tracks and the bridge that I remembered. I wanted to see the scene from that cliff on the back of where we lived that had the view of the mountains over by San Vincente and el Lago de Apulo en Ilopango. We had that view from up there. And I wanted to, I wanted to go. I mean when I got off there, I was like, riding in the back of a truck. There was nobody waiting for me. Nobody. Nobody knew I was going over there. . . .

I was in the back of this truck going towards this address that I had in this envelope. I was just enjoying the view and everything green and nice and beautiful. You know, you can't ride in a pickup truck standing up in back, here [in the United States]. So I was like, standing up and getting all that air.

And all of a sudden, you know, I was enjoying the view and I seen like this big rock coming up out of the mountain. And it had some writing on it. And it said, "MS-13." It had my gang name on it. And that's what I said, "I can't get away from them." (Interview, May 8, 2001)

Although they are deported as citizens of El Salvador, Salvadoran deportees who have lived in the United States for considerable periods may find themselves alienated within El Salvador. In the interview excerpt, Sanchez hoped that being deported would enable him to reencounter places that he remembered only dimly, and thus to know where he was from. He returned, however, without anyone knowing. No one met him at the airport. He only had the address of a relative, written on the back of an envelope. Such experiences are not unusual. King, whose experiences were described earlier, found that when he first returned to El Salvador, "I was *lost*, man! I was like, if I was busted again, if I was in *jail!* Because I was like, I knew a place that, I knew how it was, and I knew I could be there [in the United States], and I knew I had family, and people I know there. I wouldn't face the facts, you know, reality, that I was here [in El Salvador], you know what I mean?" Although they may have childhood memories, and although their networks may span U.S. and Salvadoran territory (as when Sanchez encountered the name of his gang on a rock), El Salvador is also, for many deported long-term U.S. residents, alien territory.

Such alienation assumes a quasi-legal form. Having been deported from the United States for being undocumented, deportees may also, somewhat surprisingly, find themselves undocumented in El Salvador, their country of legal citizenship. Deportees were issued a provisional Salvadoran passport, which was then taken from them at the airport when they arrived. Those who had been outside El Salvador for many years might lack Salvadoran identity documents. Obtaining such documents could be difficult, as their appearance and language skills might make them appear foreign. One interviewee, who had been adopted by a U.S. family as an infant, then been convicted of crimes and (as his parents failed to apply for his naturalization) subsequently deported, described his difficulties:

Here they wanted ID in order for me to get ID from here. . . . I spent about a *month* trying to get my paperwork. Of running from here to there, waiting in lines, not understanding what they're telling me, buying things that I don't need. I get to the window, "No, this is not what you need. You need to go back and you need to wait in line. And you need to do this again." Every now and then I would find someone who spoke English to help me out a little. But it was a very long process to get your *cédula* [national ID card].

Though his experiences may have been more frustrating than most, problems obtaining Salvadoran identity documents are common among deportees who immigrated to the United States as children. An NGO member who worked with deportees reported, "The authorities don't want to give [them] cédulas. . . . . In some cases, we have been told that they have to conduct an identity trial. Bring witnesses to say, 'He was born here, he left at a certain age.' " Another NGO member characterized deportees as *doblemente mojados*, doubly "illegal," given their undocumented status in the United States and their difficulties obtaining identity documents in El Salvador.

The alienation and stigmatization that makes officials doubt deportees' Salvadoranness can also exclude deportees from other domains of social life. Within El Salvador, deportees are generally suspected of being criminals and possibly gang members (Zilberg 2007c, forthcoming). Those who have tattoos and wear the baggy clothing typical of U.S. youth cultures are especially stigmatized. Employers may be reluctant to hire such individuals, neighbors may reject deportees, and even relatives are not always welcoming. A lack of cultural and social knowledge exacerbates these problems; as an NGO member reported, "It's like a child who doesn't know, they don't have any idea what the country is like, how it works." By the late 1990s, social programs, such as migrant shelters, limited financial assistance (e.g., bus fare), an orientation course, and vocational training, provided some assistance to returnees; however, the scope of such aid was limited (Coutin 2007; Zilberg 2002).[5] The predominant governmental response to deportees, however, has been subsumed within a broader antigang initiative known as Super Mano Dura, or "super heavy hand." Instead of welcoming deportees, Super Mano Dura focuses on incarceration (Zilberg 2007c).

> The Chief of Police of San Salvador, Alfonso Linares, arrives today in Los Angeles to testify about the dangers that activist Alex Sánchez can face in the event that he is deported to El Salvador.
>
> Linares will go before the federal court as of Wednesday, July 26, where he will serve as a witness in relation to the assassinations of three members of Homies Unidos. Those crimes occurred in the last 16 months, after they were deported, said Rocky Rushing, chief administrator in the office of Senator Tom Hayden. . . .
>
> According to documents obtained by *La Opinión* about the testimony of Linares, he will speak about the deaths that have occurred in El Salvador at the hands of death squads.

"It is believed that the assassinations have been the work of ... those groups, which dedicate themselves to social 'cleansing.' This group is similar to those death squads known as La Sombra Negra, an extremist group that has terrorized the country with its extrajudicial killings," stated Linares' written declaration.

Moreover, this establishes that he considers "it certain that Alex could be killed if he returns to El Salvador. I do not think that the law can protect him."

"Alex Sánchez has the profile of a victim. He is an ex-gang member and currently advocates for the rights of other gang members in his organization Homies Unidos. In fact his photograph has appeared in the paper and he has been characterized as a gang-member," stated the declaration that Linares will present to the court next week. (Delgado 2000)

The death squads that San Salvador chief of police Linares referred to in his testimony in Alex Sanchez's deportation case are perhaps the most extreme version of the antigang climate generated by policies adopted in El Salvador beginning in the late 1990s. The Salvadoran government does not condone death squads, but between 1999 and 2005, it criminalized gang membership, increased police presence in areas of high gang activity, mobilized soldiers alongside police in antigang units, rounded up suspected gang members, and increased prison terms for convicted suspects. These policies, known during the presidency of Francisco Flores as "Mano Dura" or "Heavy Hand" and during the presidency of Tony Saca as "Super Mano Dura" or "Super Heavy Hand," responded to a crime wave that struck El Salvador during the postwar years.[6] In 1994 the homicide rate in El Salvador reached 138 per 100,000 residents, as compared to 30 per 100,000 residents in the prewar years (Dalton 2002a, 2002b),[7] and by 1996, according to World Bank statistics, El Salvador was considered the most dangerous country in the Americas (Dalton 2001a). By 2001, an average of fourteen cars were being stolen and six homicides were being committed daily (Dalton 2001b), and a survey conducted in 2002 found that 25 percent of all Salvadorans reported having been the victim of an assault or robbery in the previous four months (El Diario de Hoy 2002). While crime in El Salvador assumed many forms, including "minor urban crime, private and public corruption, white collar financial embezzlement of large fraudulent financiers, organized crime (like the international bands of car thieves and drug smugglers), intrafamily and youth violence, massacres of entire families, the activities of assassins and the aftermath, pseudo-political or not, of kidnappers who cling to the past" (Bejar 1998, 98), publicly gangs were blamed for the crime problem. In 2004, when Super Mano Dura was launched, newspaper advertisements announced, "¡A los pandilleros se les acabó la fiesta! Hoy sí tenemos Súper Mano Dura" (The gang members' party is over! We now have Super Mano Dura).[8]

Government antigang policies have made it difficult for deportees who may be or resemble gang members to survive within El Salvador. These initiatives created a temporary special security regimen to contend with the emergency created by gangs and high crime (see also D. Goldstein 2007). Within this regimen, gangs were defined as "illicit associations," making gang membership—as evidenced by displaying tattoos, throwing hand signs, or obeying gang leaders—a crime. Soldiers joined police in the fight against gangs, resulting in the detention of 19,275 suspected gang members (FESPAD and CEPES 2004). This public effort was accompanied by the securitization or militarization of private space. In El Salvador, it was common for businesses, offices, banks, stores, fast-food restaurants, gas stations, pharmacies, car repair shops, and even homes (in the case of affluent individuals) to hire security guards who prominently displayed their guns (see also Caldeira 2000). Owners of small, street-side shops sometimes sold their products to customers through barred windows (Godoy 2005). Homes were frequently behind walls or, in the case of those who were economically advantaged, behind gates with security systems and armed guards. Public discourse conflated crime with gangs, and gangs with deportation, as one NGO member who worked with deportees noted during an interview: "Here, we (Salvadoran society) blame the deportees for everything bad that happens. For crime, for murders, for drug problems, for gang problems, for everything. There is an extreme stigmatization, which the communication media contribute to as well. There will be an article in the paper—'100 murderers deported,' or '100 gang members deported.' Salvadoran society closes its doors to the reinsertion of deportees."

Such security measures and public discourse made it hard for deportees to pursue everyday activities such as traveling, shopping, working, socializing, or going to school. One deportee interviewed in 2004 explained, "Let's say that you apply for a job and they see that you speak English. Then they won't want to know anything else about the situation here. They'll just say, 'How did you learn English? How long were you there? Oh, you were deported? What for?' and then they think that it's better not to hire you for the job." Another deportee, who worked with Homies Unidos, commented during an interview in 2004 that almost all deportees who stay in El Salvador are in prison. "Or," he said, "they stay in prisons of their own, locking themselves in their houses and remaining hidden. They can only be gang members inside their homes. When they go out, they have to wear elegant clothing, get elegant haircuts." In these circumstances, deportees (particularly those with criminal convictions) had few options. Immigrant advocates who worked with deportees in El Salvador estimated that between 40 and 60 percent of deportees returned without authorization to the United States, where they faced incarceration if apprehended. The near impossibility of living in the United States or in El Salvador placed deportees with criminal convictions outside the bounds of the citizenry of each nation, and indeed almost outside the bounds of humanity.

> I [Alex Sanchez] was like stuck during that time, I was stuck in El Salvador. By this time I had been there for six months and I was stuck. It was like this warfare [between gangs and death squads]. And I was like, "Man, I've got to get out of here." So yeah, so we had a lot of people being killed. And the target was mostly the guy that had been deported. And the thing was, everything that happened in El Salvador that was a crime, it was blamed on gangs. . . . It's kind of sort of [like] here, you know. Because I mean, which politician doesn't use gangs for their campaign? Or immigration? . . .
>
> Not all the gang members have to carry a gun or shoot people. They don't. Out of ten probably one or two are the ones that really evolve into serious violence and like really want to put their name up high because they want to be recognized. Probably one out of ten. The rest are just a bunch of followers that do what this person tells them to. With these [Three Strikes] laws that came in [in the United States], yeah, it scared some of these followers, but they weren't doing anything first of all. The majority were just followers or they were youth at risk and they said, "Oh, my god." But they were not the ones. They probably get arrested for doing drugs, or petty theft or maybe a, stealing a car. Not a carjacking but maybe just stealing a car just for joy ride. All of sudden these guys are scared, of course, they're not seriously involved in violence. But what about the one person or that two persons out of that ten? You know, he's been involved with violence all his life. He's hard, you know. All of a sudden, though, this guy's probably getting out of jail, you know, a two-striker. "You get one more strike, you're through, Mister." This guy gets out, you know, what's out there for him? I mean, "Yeah. They threatened me. I'm a two-striker. What the hell am I going to do? There's no jobs. I try to work someplace. They say I'm a two-striker. Been in prison. They're not going to give me the job!" So they have all

these problems, you know. They get desperate. They get really desperate, you know. . . .

It gets them into a certain situation, a desperate situation, when they go ahead and get desperate and go and do it. And sell drugs to maintain or to do something or get drunk and get in a fight, you know. And all of a sudden, you know, they're carrying a gun and that's a strike. . . . You put them in situations where—bam! if I get busted. You're not thinking about getting busted, but you're thinking about, "Man, if the police get me, then that's it." So all of a sudden you have the police right there, what are you going to do? You're going to try to get away because now all of a sudden you're thinking about the third strike.

I go crazy sometimes just thinking about things like this because I look at 'em in a different way. (Interview, May 8, 2001)

In this interview excerpt, Alex Sanchez details ways that, by making people desperate to avoid additional convictions, harsh criminal justice policies can fuel rather than reduce violence. In the United States, increased penalties for illegal entry, stiffened border enforcement, reductions in the available means of legalizing, expanded definitions of offenses for which one becomes deportable, and the elimination of waivers that would prevent deportation have given rise to an abject class of individuals who could be deported if apprehended. This abject class includes undocumented individuals, as well as former legal permanent residents who have been deported and returned "illegally" to the United States. Similarly, in El Salvador, stiffened antigang policies have made life nearly impossible for deportees who have been convicted of crimes in the United States or resemble gang members. Whether they are located in El Salvador, the United States, or somewhere in between, members of this class have few legal options. Denied work authorization in the United States, subjected to employment discrimination in El Salvador, and made targets of police activity in both countries, such individuals face great difficulties in entering the legal economy. Members of this subgroup must often work under the table or enter the illicit economy. Such policies affect not only unauthorized immigrants but also, as Sanchez notes, anyone who develops a criminal record and for whom an additional strike can mean a lengthy or perhaps perpetual prison sentence. Policies that deny unauthorized migrants and other excluded individuals access to employment, social domains, and even national territories can fuel the very sorts of lawlessness that they are designed to combat, thus doing violence to the law itself. Such policies also have deadly effects on the unauthorized, pushing them into illicit domains, unlawful activities, and dangerous spaces where their lives are in jeopardy, whether from the hazards of migrating "illegally," the lack of access to health care and social services, or violence at the hands of those (not excluding officials) caught up in networks of illegality. In short, deportation can remove people not only from national territory but also from any legal means of supporting themselves and finally even from life itself.

> An immigration judge granted political asylum yesterday to the activist Alex Sánchez, an ex-gang member who now is the director of the program Homies Unidos, who helps young people leave the criminal life.
>
> It is the first time that immigration authorities overlooked or removed the criminal history of an ex-gang member to give him haven in this country, said Alan Diamante, attorney of Sánchez. . . .
>
> Sánchez, Diamante explained, was able to demonstrate to the immigration judge that his life was in danger if he was deported to El Salvador, his country of origin. (Amador 2002)

POSTSCRIPT

On June 24, 2009, Alex Sanchez was rearrested and charged with federal racketeering and conspiracy charges. Authorities allege that he failed to sever his ties with the Mara Salvatrucha and that he conspired to commit a murder in 2006 (Glover and Winton 2009). Supporters contend that he is innocent of these charges and that he was targeted due to his work as a gang interventionist. Prior to his arrest, Alex Sanchez directed the gang violence prevention group Homies Unidos in Los Angeles, where he counseled youths, gang members, and their families, and advocated for the rights of immigrants and of noncitizens convicted of crimes. In the days following his arrest, supporters raised 1.2 million dollars in bond securities and solicited 110 letters attesting to his character. A statement posted on the Homies Unidos website reads:

> The Homies Unidos Board stands united in full support, behind our executive director, Alex Sanchez and his family. For the past 11 years, Alex has been committed to helping bring about change in his community. He is an exemplary leader, respected colleague and dedicated husband and father. Just as we are confident in Alex's innocence, we are confident that Los Angeles and the nation will remember that an indictment is an allegation only. As stated in the FBI press release, "Every defendant is presumed to be innocent until proven guilty in court." (Homies Unidos 2009)

NOTES

I am grateful to Homies Unidos and to the individuals who were interviewed for this project for all their assistance. I am particularly grateful to Alex Sanchez for so generously sharing his experiences. The research on which this paper is based was supported by a grant from the National Science Foundation's Law and Social Science Program (awards SES-0001890 and SES-0296050) and a research and writing grant from the John D. and Catherine T. MacArthur Foundation. I thank Nathalie Peutz and Nick De Genova for inviting me to participate in this volume and for their comments on an earlier draft, and I am grateful to Elana Zilberg for conversations about the issues discussed in this chapter and for her comments on an earlier draft. Ester Hernandez also assisted with interviews for this project.

1. Antigang policies, can, for example, encourage police harassment or even, as occurred in the Rampart scandal, fabrications of evidence by authorities. Such policies can thus bolster insecurity rather than security (see, e.g., González-Portillo 2000).

2. An infraction is punishable by a fine, whereas a misdemeanor can be punished by a fine, jail time for up to one year, or both.

3. In *Immigration and Naturalization Service v. St. Cyr.*, 2001, 533 U.S. 289, the U.S. Supreme Court provided limited relief to aliens who pled guilty before 1996 on the grounds that the immigration consequences of a guilty plea were altered retroactively. In this case, the court reasoned, "Now that prosecutors have received the benefit of plea agreements, agreements that were likely facilitated by the aliens' belief in their continued eligibility for 212(c) relief, it would be contrary to 'familiar considerations of fair notice, reasonable reliance, and settled expectations' to hold that IIRIRA's subsequent restrictions deprives them of any possibility of such relief" (2292). See also *Fernandez-Vargaz v. Gonzales*, No. 04–1376, Supreme Court of the United States, 126 S. Ct. 2422; March 22, 2006, argued, June 22, 2006, for a discussion of the retroactivity of the 1996 laws.

4. Unless otherwise noted, translations of Spanish sources are mine.

5. This assistance was provided as part of a program known as Bienvenidos a Casa, or Welcome Home. Bienvenidos a Casa was conceptualized through the Conferencia Regional de Migración (Regional Migration Conference), a regional governmental effort to coordinate migration and migration policies in North and Central America, and grew out of concern about the effects of deportations on receiving countries and on migrants themselves (see Mahler 2000). The program was initiated in 1999 with institutional support from the Salvadoran government, funding from the U.S. government, and technical assistance from governmental and nongovernmental entities in San Salvador and was administered by Catholic Relief Services, an NGO. In 2002 the Salvadoran government assumed responsibility for this program and in 2005 placed another NGO, Programa La Fundación de Desarrollo Integral (FUNDI), in charge of administering it (see República de El Salvador 2007).

6. For a comparison of Mano Dura and Super Mano Dura policies, see FESPAD and CEPES 2004. Zilberg 2007c also provides a history of these policies.

7. By 2002 the homicide rate had declined to 60 per 100,000 residents (Dalton 2002a).

8. See advertisement published by the Ministerio de Gobernación in *La Prensa Gráfica*, September 8, 2004, 21.

CHAPTER 13

"Criminal Alien"
Deportees in Somaliland

An Ethnography of Removal

Monday, I do the interview with a representative of the FBI. Me and him are joking. He says: Do I go to a mosque? Do I pray? I said: "No, I go to your local clubs, man." He says: "Do you drink alcohol?" I said: "Yeah." He said: "What's your favorite?" I said: "Hennessey." I mean, we're just talking like two regular human beings, but he's writing this down, and at the same time he's cracking up. ("This guy doesn't look like he's your profile of some weirdo that might do something!") He looked at my rap sheet. He said: "You know, you don't even have a criminal record." I said: "Other than for the assault." He said: "Yeah, but for the assault. You don't have nothing else on there," he says. He asked me another few questions about do I know about al-Ittihaad, any representatives in it: do I know any Somalis that belonged to al-Ittihaad? Because they were closing down al-Barakaat in Minneapolis [and in other offices across North America] and he's just [asking] basic questions.[1] I'm like, I don't even know these. I don't even go to no mosques. How am I supposed to know these people? I hang out at clubs on Friday and Saturday nights. What am I supposed to be, hanging around at the mosques, reading the Quran, with a bottle of Hennessey in my hand? I mean, he was cracking up. He finally put his signature on it and said, "Uh, you know this is out of my hands. You seem like, you know, a young man, American as apple pie. I don't know why I'm doing this, but it's my job, so I'll just pass it on to the supervisor." And I guess the supervisor must have put his signature on the paper and said: "Put this guy on the plane."
Tariq, on his deportation to Somalia, July 2002

The word *banish* rhymes with *vanish*. Through banishment or deportation there is the literal threat of invisibility. Not only when the event is concretized, but in the anguish and the uncertainty leading to that. Made invisible. Made meaningless. Superfluous. To others. To ourselves.—Margaret Randall, "Threatened with Deportation"

On February 7, 2002, Tariq was surprised by a home visit from the Immigration and Naturalization Service (INS).[2] Told by his deportation officer that he was wanted for questioning, Tariq was taken to the Oakland city jail, where he spent the weekend waiting for his interview on Monday. During the week he was transferred twice, and on Thursday, February 14, 2002, before his lawyer could challenge the deportation, he and thirty other Somali "nationals" were deported to Mogadishu, Somalia.

The deportation of an individual may take only a few days, but the significance of this episode—replicating and engendering as it does histories of suffering and subjection—will continue to reverberate in the lives of the "deportees" and their kin.[3] As a starting point, it is worth asking whether deportation may be experienced and thus theorized as a kind of reversed refugeeness: instead of being forced to leave one's home, deportees are forcibly "repatriated." This is a question both of subjectification and of categorization. How are deportability and deportation experienced? Does the deportation produce a certain kind of (deportee) subjectivity? And how does the deportee figure in the anthropological literatures on displacement and belonging?

After more than a decade of intensive anthropological scrutiny of transnationalism and globalization, the premillennial enthusiasm for transcendent flows, organizations, and beings has waned as anthropologists are called on to confront the tenacity of the state (even a "failed" one) and the inevitable logic of its exclusionary practices, especially during the global War on Terror (cf. Aretxaga 2003; Trouillot 2001). In the 1990s, in an attempt to determine what was new about globalization at the turn of the century, scholars identified emergent modes of (transnational) personhood and often privilege: "discrepant cosmopolitanisms" (Clifford 1992), "cultural citizenship" (Rosaldo 1994), "creolized cultures" (Hannerz 1996), "ethnoscapes" (Appadurai 1996), and "flexible citizenship" (Ong 1999). This literature's main shortcoming, however, was that the perhaps overused concept of the "transnational" seldom gained the explanatory power it needed to determine who was or was not a transnational subject or "agent" (Ong 1999, 93) and what exactly such disparate groups—refugees, expatriates, migrants, capitalists, aliens, hybrids, travelers, and nomads—

might have in common (a transnational subjectivity?). Although this problem is not solved by my adding another cluster to this list, I here propose "deportee" as a "contrast category" (Ong 1999, 43) that catapults the state and its exclusions directly into the transnational arena and shows how neoliberal globalization generates a disturbing sort of immobility (and opacity) for some individuals in conjunction with the more transparent "flexibilities" forced on others. I suggest, then, that a "trans-statal" (Kearney 1995, 548) category—and therefore subject (Hacking 1999)—is newly coming into focus even as its very formation hinges on the person's being rendered invisible, meaningless, and superfluous to the nation-state. It is not only the deportee who is (symbolically) cast outside the state and into a "state of exception" (Agamben 2003/2005) but also "enemy combatants" and "rendered" aliens (Cole 2003; Mayer 2005): subjects that are made to inhabit a "zone of indistinction" in that their exclusion is the necessary condition of their inclusion (Agamben 1995/1998, 6–7). Although deportation has long been legitimized as a sovereign prerogative, it must be considered as part of a wider array of practices of removal—including extrajudicial renditions—that have become increasingly ingrained in our political and cultural landscapes as states eager to assert their sovereignty in an age of terror team up with private corporations experienced in the industrialization of confinement and exclusion. Accordingly, the study of removals—in contrast to, and in conjunction with, the study of departures, transitions, and arrivals—is both theoretically and ethically critical and should enrich the anthropologies of citizenship and governmentality, transnationalism, globalization, and the state.

What might the anthropology, or even ethnography, of removal—and, specifically, deportation—look like? William Walters has identified a number of studies of expulsion in its more shocking form (e.g., ethnic cleansing, political exile, transportation of criminals) but concludes that "deportation, because it remains embedded within the contemporary administrative practices of Western states, strikes us as less remarkable" (2002a, 266). Indeed, only in the past ten years have scholars of various disciplines begun to critically analyze deportation as a distinct and defining state practice, one that is all the more remarkable for having been cast as routine (for examples of this literature, see Peutz and De Genova, this volume). Nevertheless—and mainly due to their exclusion and subsequent invisibility—not as much progress has been made in examining deportation from the perspectives of deportees, especially after their coerced "return" to their purported country of origin. With a few notable exceptions (cf. Zilberg 2004, 2007a; Coutin 2007, this volume; Talavera, Núñez, and Heyman, this volume), it has been primarily journalists and novelists who have managed to track and narrate the subjective experiences of deportees in adjusting to their enforced, sometimes even new, locations (di Giovanni 2002; Gordimer 2001; Sontag 2003). Yet given the numbers of individuals deported from the United States every year (356,739 in 2008), it is necessary that the multiple and enduring *effects* of deportation—not only as a state practice but also as an individual and individualizing experience—be explored more fully.[4]

Based on the narratives of eleven of the thirty-one individuals deported to Somalia in February 2002, this chapter follows the trajectory of their deportation arranged according to four of the various contexts through which they experienced it: legal, economic, embodied, and spatial. This framework is only a skeletal model of the many ways in which such an analysis can take shape; whereas I focus here on these deportees' reports of their imprisonment, detention, deportation, and return, other sites for ethnographic inquiry should include state agencies charged with apprehension and deportation, such as the U.S. Department of Homeland Security (DHS), the private corporations that benefit from these practices of exclusion (Dow 2004), the transnational organizations or local networks that, in some countries, assist arriving deportees (Sontag 2003; Zilberg 2004, 2007c), and the activist groups, including deportable populations and their communities, that rally the opposition to deportation (Burman 2006; Nyers, this volume).

This specific group of Somalis—thirty men age eighteen to forty-three and a woman in her early twenties—comprised U.S. and Canadian asylum seekers, "legal" migrants, and permanent residents. The majority, however, had lost their previous legal status and were now classified as "criminal aliens" who had served their prison sentences but had not yet been deported because of the continued instability in Somalia. Notably, the deportable are classified according to different criteria by the administration that orders their removal and the government that tolerates their return. Clan and subclan—not country of birth, state of residence, legal status, or criminal record—are what became relevant to these individuals when they learned that they were being deported. Whereas I had originally tried to place these deportees according to their state of residence in the United States or Canada, Tariq offered to "break [it] down" for me by clan: fifteen individuals were from the Hawiyya clan, located primarily in the south and, at the time of their deportation, in control of Mogadishu; five were children of transnational marriages between Somalis and other East African nationalities; and eleven were members of the Isaaq, the clan located primarily in the self-declared independent state of Somaliland.[5] It was largely these genealogical distinctions that guided their subsequent attempts to return to their "home" in Somalia or Somaliland.

I was introduced to Tariq in July 2002 in Hargeysa, Somaliland, by Nuruddin, a journalist who himself had been sentenced to deportation by the government of Oman for his role in organizing the Somali National Movement (SNM), aimed at overthrowing the Barre regime. In Nuruddin's case, a deportation order to Somalia was tantamount to a death sentence, but through diplomatic pressure, the order had been revoked. When I met Tariq, he had been living with his grandfather for four months. He agreed to an interview and spoke at length about his childhood on a U.S. Aramco base in Saudi Arabia before moving with his family to the United States, where they had hoped to achieve "the American dream." After detailing his multiple jobs, Tariq arrived at what he described as his "one mistake." In 1994 he was driving a taxicab when a passenger attempted to mug him, and Tariq, having beaten the passenger before leaving him on the sidewalk, was charged with assault and lost his permanent-resident status. Eight years later, as a direct result of this event, Tariq was "put on the plane."

Writing about deportation raises a number of methodological and ethical concerns. Practically speaking, the deported are difficult to locate—and not only because deportation itself is an exclusionary practice, a removal from, as opposed to a placement in. *Deportee*, like *refugee*, is a "legal or descriptive rubric" that applies to individuals in vastly different circumstances and often for limited periods of time (Malkki 1995, 496). At most, these Somali deportees had formed what Liisa Malkki calls an "accidental community" (1997, 99), but even then their identity as a group was tenuous and fleeting. One-third of the deportees had traveled north to Somaliland, where they were residing alone or with family but ran into each other on occasion. While a few had become friends, chewing *chat* (*Catha edulis*, a mildly narcotic leaf chewed daily in the Horn of Africa and Yemen) together and assisting each other when needed, it was arguably only my interest in their lives that framed them once again as a "community."[6] Other methodological challenges involve the difficulty of gaining access to, and being present at, the various sites of the deportation grid: the DHS offices, hearings (Coutin 2003b), and detention centers (Welch 2002); the airports with their security teams and anti-deportation activists; and the families and communities affected at home and abroad (Burman 2006). The deported themselves are made to vanish, figuratively and sometimes literally (Bach 2001), and even if they can be located may be embarrassed to speak of this stigmatized encounter or fearful of government reprisals "at home" (Peutz 2007). Thus, in many cases, they are effectively silenced as well.

Similarly problematic is the ethical quandary of such an ethnography mimicking and continuing the surveillance of already interrogated individuals and thus reifying the category of the deportee. For example, it soon became clear to me—both by the content of these individuals' testimonies and their manner—that the interview was a familiar act, one to which they had been subjected numerous times before, by immigration officials, police, lawyers, judges, and reporters. Each of the deportees knew that I was interested in hearing about his or her deportation case and experience and thus structured his or her narrative to culminate in this event. A general and even shared teleology emerged from these individual discussions: arrival in the United States, employment and "hard work," a (usually single) "mistake" that resulted in arrest, imprisonment, indefinite detention, new beginnings (for most, some remained in detention until the time of their deportation), a second, unexpected arrest followed by involuntary deportation from the United States, the flight, arrival in Mogadishu, and "return" to Somaliland. Nicholas De Genova cautions against these methodological traps and consequences—the continuation of surveillance and the reification of juridical categories—in his work on migrant "illegality" and deportability: "By constituting undocumented migrants (the people) as an epistemological and ethnographic 'object' of study, social scientists, however unwittingly, become agents in an aspect of the everyday production of those migrants' 'illegality'—in effect, accomplices to the discursive power of immigration law" (2002, 423). He concludes that social scientists ought instead to study "illegality" and deportability as sociopolitical conditions generated by law, citing as a model Susan Bibler Coutin's research on Salvadoran immigrants' legalization struggles, which she structures as "an ethnography of a legal process rather than of a particular group of people" (2000, 23).

De Genova's insightful critique is more than relevant to further work on deportation and the deported. However, it is important to note that deportees are removed physically from the social landscape, thus becoming all too invisible as people or as subjects of study, and that the deportees discussed in this chapter wished to have their stories circulated, mainly in the media but also in legal and academic circles. Already bereft of legal status, they had little to lose, but perhaps something to gain, from a sustained scrutiny of their cases and a public debate on deportation policy. From the perspective of the "host" state, the removal of "illegal aliens," "criminal aliens," or even "enemy combatants" brings a certain closure to their cases, allowing for a general lack of interest in what happens to them as soon as they are outside its borders. A study that repudiates this easy closure by showing the continuing rupture endured by the deported, their families, and their communities would at the least resist the removal of these individuals from discursive spaces, if not from physical ones.

CRIME AND BANISHMENT

The increasing criminalization of unauthorized migrants and asylum seekers in the United States and Europe has been well documented (Morris 1997; Bhabha 1998; Simon 1998; Welch 2002; Cole 2003; Fekete 2005; Kanstroom 2007). Although the detention of entering and deportable noncitizens corresponds to just a fraction of the extensive domestic "corrections" industry, it replicates the performance of what Lorna Rhodes describes as "a kind of social, economic, and political 'magic' by 'disappearing' large numbers of poor and minority people" (2001, 67). The *magic* of domestic prisons lies in their power to repress disorder, create jobs in economically depressed areas, obscure the extent of unemployment, add to census figures where needed, and conceal racism while disenfranchising a large proportion of the African American community. Apprehended "criminal aliens" are disappeared into the same system—often twice, first as criminals and then as civil detainees. Yet it is not enough that noncitizens are housed within this "second country" inside the nation's borders (Rhodes 2001, 68). Instead many are removed from the second country to a third country outside—their purported homeland or a "safe third country" or a camp—in a move that Jacqueline Bhabha calls "double jeopardy": a double punishment that "violates human rights norms of non-discrimination and presumptions of equality of treatment before the law" (1998, 615). But a double punishment requires double the work and cost on behalf of the penalizing state. This raises the question why it is not sufficient that "criminal aliens" (who are often permanent residents) serve their sentences before being released again to their previous situation and status. What role does deportation play for the nation (or rather for the citizens who may be incarcerated but not deported)?

Walters demonstrates that deportation is a governmental practice that is "*constitutive* of citizenship," policing migration on a global scale and disciplining the migrants at home (2002a, 267). Moreover, as a practice aimed today only at noncitizens, modern deportation reinforces the citizen-alien divide. Linda Bosniak observes that the "hardening [of] the distinction between citizen and noncitizen" stemming from the legal impetus for making citizenship "count for something" has resulted in the simultaneous devaluation of the "alien" (1998, 30). Essentially the conception of citizenship as a national project takes as fact this distinction; the presence of aliens is what defines "our" privilege(s) as citizens (Bosniak 2006). This identification of self through the immigrant other is especially relevant to the American myth, argues Bonnie Honig, demonstrating a national reliance in the United States on "the foreigner" as one who, through naturalization, performs the act of consent to the regime. This "good" immigrant, however, is always shadowed by the "bad" immigrant: the "illegal alien" who does not consent to U.S. laws and to whose presence United States citizens do not consent (Honig 1998, 2001). Further, Honig points to the way the "illegal" immigrant "slides from being a person defined by a juridical status that positions him or her as always already in violation of the (immigration) law to being a daily lawbreaker" (1998, 15). When it comes to "criminal aliens," the metaphor of "illegality" ricochets between juridical status and social behavior in such a way that a "criminal alien" is deemed forever dangerous to society. Hence "criminal aliens" make for convenient scapegoats, and through their deportation "the violence within the national community is displaced to an insider-outsider, a familiar stranger forcefully cast out of the polity" (Aretxaga 2003, 397).

The definition of citizen-self through the alien-other and the consequent purging of the "bad," "illegal," and nonconsenting alien within provides a partial answer to the question of the role that deportation plays for the nation-state. Yet there is something more than the cleansing of self and society at stake. Jonathan Simon points out that imprisonment is "a tool of accountability, guaranteeing that a person is on hand and in a certain condition" (1998, 600). Conditions may be horrible, but they are observable (more or less); by placing people under control and rendering their status legible, the imprisonment of aliens "remains a status that tends to be generative of [their] rights" (600). In the following examples, two of the Somali deportees discuss how it was in prison that they "learned the law" and started to regard themselves as rights-bearing subjects. It was also from prison and through his imprisonment that at least one deportee was able to challenge the very "legality" of the judicial system. Through the act of deportation, however, the state relinquishes all accountability, and the deportee is divested of his or her legal rights as well as his or her access to the apparatus of the deporting state and, in the worst cases, of the receiving state, as well.

In 1988, at the outset of Somalia's civil war, Nasser came on a student visa to the United States, where he attended English-language classes and worked various jobs. In 1990 he applied for asylum and received his permanent-resident status. Then, as he put it, he ended up at "the wrong time, the wrong place." He claimed to have been framed in a drug deal involving fifty dollars worth of cocaine. As he had been found guilty twice already for driving under the influence, he was sentenced to three years in prison. He believes that the judge should have informed him that, since he was not a citizen, the conviction would render him deportable. It was not until later, in jail and during his INS detention, he said, that he "learned a little bit about the law, but it's too late, you know."

On the day of his release, Nasser was picked up at the county jail by INS officers, who took him to another Virginia jail, where he was held for nine days to be classified. I asked Nasser on what charge he was held, but Tariq, who was present during this interview, answered for him: "You committed the felony, you did the time; now you're a danger to society, and we can't release you on the street. And there are laws in Washington that support this." Here Tariq was referring to the 1996 immigration legislation that had created new mandatory detention provisions for "criminal aliens" found deportable under its reforms. Noncitizens convicted of certain crimes— aggravated felony, drug trafficking, drug abuse, terrorist activities, multiple crimes of (the vaguely defined) moral turpitude, or one crime of moral turpitude resulting in at least a one-year sentence—are to be detained immediately following their release from incarceration and held until their removal.[7] Legally these individuals are not prisoners but "civil detainees" held under similar legal stipulations and physical conditions as asylum seekers awaiting refugee status, undocumented immigrants awaiting deportation, and other noncitizens who cannot be deported because they are "stateless" or originate from countries whose governments have collapsed. Awaiting deportation to Somalia—a country that had been without government from 1991 until 2000, when a transitional but extremely weak government (of various warlords) was appointed—Nasser became an indefinite detainee who, like other "long-term unremovables," was not awaiting any impending decisions or transfers. He was simply waiting.

Nasser was held in INS detention from February 1995 to May 2001. Originally placed in a Bureau of Prisons facility intended for INS administrative detainees, he was later transferred to local county jails in which the detainees were commingled with the inmate populations. The sheer increase in the number of noncitizens detained as a result of the 1996 legislation impeded the INS from housing all its detainees in federal detention centers, and instead it had to contract out to private corrections companies or rent spaces in local jails, often for twice the amount charged for county inmates (Human Rights Watch 1998). In fact, "In some states, local taxes have been eliminated due to the profit made through housing the INS's detainees" (1). This was not lost on these deportees, many of whom complained about the "prison business" and told me specifically how much the INS had been paying to house them.[8]

Another deportee, Abdullahi, had filed for a writ of habeas corpus to challenge the indefiniteness of his three-year detention and was appointed a federal defender who informed him that he was "one of the first on this [West] coast to challenge unlimited detention." Abdullahi explained how as a teenager he had narrowly escaped being "drafted" for the Ogaden War,[9] moved to the United Arab Emirates, where he finished high school, and then in 1984 traveled to the United States on a student visa to complete his studies. He then attended community college but was having difficulty "dealing with the system" and "kind of drifted along" until he "became an alcoholic." In 1991 he had been granted protective status, but after a slew of arrests (jaywalking, possession of marijuana, public drunkenness, littering), his status was revoked, and in 1994 he became deportable. Because of the current unrest in Somalia, Abdullahi was released under supervision, but a felony charge for possession of cocaine (which he disputes) landed him back in jail. After serving more than one-third of his ninety-day sentence, he had been "released" for good behavior and was transferred immediately to immigration hold—without leaving the county jail. It was during this period that he "learned the law" and filed for a writ of habeas corpus. After a number of intrastate transfers to local jails, he "had [his] day in court" and was granted a conditional release. He moved to a new city, entered a rehabilitation program administered by the Salvation Army, surmounted his addictions, and found a maintenance job at a private yacht club: "Basically, I was there just rebuilding my life, like I said, I wanted to buy a house, build credit, what have you; credit cards, paid my bills on time, taxes. . . . Job's good—great—a lot of work, which I needed. Because I had other plans; I wanted to finish school again."

It is uncertain how long Abdullahi or Nasser—who after his release remained in the area of his last incarceration and got a job in a local plant—would have been able to remain in the United States on the grounds of Somalia's disintegration. Both stressed the satisfaction they received from their jobs (specifically from "hard work") and from finally moving forward. Tariq believed that he would have stayed in America, eventually undergoing naturalization with his family, "if psycho number one over here hadn't bombed the Twin Towers." Whether or not, as Tariq stated, it was "Osama [who] kicked in the door," the post–September 11, 2001, atmosphere of anxiety and racial-religious profiling surely did affect their cases, though the INS spokesperson Russ Bergeron asserted that theirs was just "a rather routine removal process" (Hutchinson 2002). It has been noted that of the 300,000 foreign nationals who have remained in the United States after having been ordered deported, the Justice Department prioritized the deportation of the 6,000 noncitizens from "countries where al-Qaeda support is strong" (Cole 2002, 975). In February 2002, the same month that the foreign media speculated that the U.S. military would target "anarchic" Somalia, Nasser and Abdullahi were picked up by the INS and detained one last time. Like Tariq, Nasser had just returned home from work when immigration officers came to his door. The same day, Abdullahi was picked up at the yacht club where he worked. Although not as quick as Tariq to attribute his unexpected deportation to terrorist plots or responses, Abdullahi did believe that it had something to do with his own role in "kicking in the door" of the business of indefinite detention:

> So, in 2002 they come and pick you up for something I did in 1993, '94, '95. But I guess like I told you I did file that [writ]. When I filed my case, I basically opened the door for a lot of them [for other indefinite detainees to be released]. . . . And each governor and senator has his own district or county jail, and fills it up: *I'm gonna fill it up* [he says mockingly]. Because it was a business. Anyway, it was slavery of a different kind. You just take a person because he is drunk, throw him over there in unlimited detention; he's a risk to the society. . . . Wait a minute, I've been in here with you for how many years now? What did I do? And they got mad because I did open the doors for a lot. And I don't think they forgot that. As a taxpayer I was working; I had the keys for the whole [name] yacht club on me sometimes. Millions and millions and millions of dollars. Wait a minute, what? Terrorist? Huh? Who? Eighteen years here and never left the States.

That is, not until he found himself in Mogadishu, a week later, in his janitorial uniform.

THE BUSINESS OF DEPORTATION

It should not be surprising that the booming U.S. prison industrial complex would provide fertile ground for the growing industry of removals, which not only replicates the containment model but also models new methods of economic rationalization: flexibility, low-cost buildings, less organized labor, and increasing privatization (Simon 1998). Indeed, the deportation process as a whole is perhaps best described as an industry that employs airlines, pilots, and private security companies in addition to DHS officials, deportation officers, and detention center staff (Walters 2002a, 266). Tellingly, anti-deportation activists now target the commercial viability of deportation by creating mock company websites, staging protests at airports, and distributing literature to passenger-consumers on how to disrupt deportations occurring on their flights. The transfer of bodies cannot be executed, however, without the prior determination of where they "belong" (Coutin 2003a). Foreign bodies are thus made legible through a number of techniques requiring expert knowledge. In England, for example, the government has employed linguists to determine the dialect of origin of its asylum seekers; astonishingly, "one company [of Swedish experts] recently reported it could pinpoint the origin of a Somali asylum seeker to a particular suburb of north Mogadishu" (Barnett and Brace 2002). Further studies of the business of deportation may help to illuminate the expanding relationship between government and privatization in today's security state. Walters has pointed to the use of deportation as a "corollary" to labor immigration in the sense that it can "regulate and enforce the return of these temporary hands during times of economic downturn" (2002a, 279; see also De Genova 2005). What other corporations or individuals may profit from the outsourcing (and offshoring) of corrections? Much as overdeveloped countries export their toxic wastes to the global South, the practice of deportation supplies corporations with a lucrative export of bodies while representing for others (southern governments or weaker states) an import of "dangerous" or "polluting" matter. Governments and multinational corporations are in the business of exchanging bodies: workers for the unwanted.

The deportation of these Somalis, administered by the U.S. Justice Prison Alien Transportation System (JPATS), was one of a number of joint U.S.-Canadian operations undertaken after September 11, 2001, to divide deportation costs between the two North American countries (McClintock 2004). Ali, one of the Canadian-based Somalis who had been arrested for "hustling dope," described his surprise at his encounter with the militarism of the U.S. government's security measures:

> They took us to Buffalo to a very private military airport. Next thing is, there was all U.S. marshals over there, guns, everything, very scary! See, in Canada it's different from America, it's like the immigration don't even carry guns.

But in America, it was like, yo' mate, it was a terrorist movement. They did terrorism to us. They kidnapped us. All these guys pointing guns at us; if you do any small mistakes, you could be shot right there.

Stunned by the show of force, Ali was more astounded that he was to be deported by a Dutch charter flight rather than an American airline. Others also took this as evidence that their deportation was "illegal," concealed, and evidence of "a world-planned organization" (Abdullahi).

The trip was not without incident. According to the deportees, the plane had been grounded in Amsterdam's Schiphol airport for a number of hours because of "technical difficulties" (Ibraahim). When the deportees protested, the pilot said, "It's not secure. I'm not going to take this plane, this time, with this group" (Mubarak). The first pilot left, and the deportees waited for hours until "an American pilot came in from Holland. . . . He spoke to us in English, said, 'It'll be a safe trip,' this and that. . . . At least we felt a little bit different [comparing him with] these Dutch, you know. A very open-minded guy" (Ali). The deportees all claimed to have been sedated throughout much of the trip, attributing their stupor to "sleeping pills" (Mahmoud) in their beverages. Some recalled waking up to an argument and seeing two of their fellow passengers being held down and "[shot up] with drugs and stuff" (Omar). After Ali had been escorted to the toilet by the security staff, he refused to return to his seat. The security team pinned him down, along with another deportee, and both were given injections by an Australian "doctor" (Ali).[10]

What is striking in their story—aside from the use of flexi-cuffs, sedatives, and tranquilization—is the welcome presence of the "American" in a situation characterized by an absence of governmental intervention and knowledge. During my interview with Nasser, at the point when he was telling me about the "Australian contractor" who "lives in London," Tariq interjected the comment: "An American pilot wouldn't have lifted that airplane off the ground; they would have been sued!" Nasser then affirmed that an American pilot would never have accepted such a mission, "so they knew they had to use another country or contractor. Contractor gets his money, so his security will do whatever you tell him. He has no country, so you don't know how to get him. A good plan there." What these foreign middlemen represent is a lack of accountability: nonstate actors that are international in origin and thus in ambiguous relation to the jurisdiction of any particular national state authority, if not effectively outside any such Rule of Law altogether. In a sense, they resemble the deportees, unmoored from their place of belonging and difficult to trace. When an

American pilot did eventually agree to fly, the deportees felt reassured. Perhaps the mere involvement of the American signaled to them that their removal might not go unnoticed. Once the plane took off, however, the pilot was no longer accessible, and the Australian contractor and the Dutch crew—corporate mercenaries—took control. According to Tariq, the Dutch government did not know that "there was a plane with people that were forcibly deported," because if it had, it "would have let us out, or sent us back to the United States" (Omar). Although these deportees had already experienced a certain lack of government accountability during their imprisonment and detention, their comments here express a residual attachment to the notion that a government will comply with the Rule of Law. Without government control and regulation, however, the deportees were at the mercy of the even more formidable forces of global capital and exchange, for which deportation is simply business as usual.

The deportees were acutely aware "that private companies make money from this form of suffering" (Walters 2002a, 266). Many claimed to know what their deportation was costing the INS and what it was earning those involved. According to Tariq, "The little Australian guy told us he was getting $15,000 per head, just to transport us." This consciousness of the monetary value of one's deportation is similar to the knowledge the deportees had of the value of their presence to local communities with county jails. Having lost or invalidated their worth as "legal" aliens (presumably lawful and productive workers), detained and deported individuals are revalued as quantifiable and lucrative "beds" or "heads" by and for the citizens and transnational actors who gain from this procedure.

Once in Mogadishu, the deportees split up immediately into separate groups based to some extent on clan, age, and money. "So everything changes now," Ali explained. "No more American mentality, no more Western mentality now. This is Somali now, now everybody's got to go with his own clan." Those from the ruling Hawiyya clan set out to locate family in Mogadishu. The rest made their way to cheap hotels from which they contacted their families back home, arranged for money transfers, and planned their departures for Somaliland, Kenya, or the Arab Gulf States. Perhaps it was in these simple and shared hotel rooms that the reality of their situation finally started to sink in. Venturing outside mainly for meals and cigarettes—still nervous about the profusion of AK-47s and the threat of being kidnapped in an alleyway to be held for ransom—the men shared their meager resources and, in the case of the Isaaqs, waited for the regionally based Daallo Airlines to fly them north to Hargeysa. Some tried to make the best of their situation: chewing chat, flirting with local women, enjoying the general licentiousness of a city then considered to be (slowly) emerging from war. But even if they did drop their "Western mentality," as Ali claimed, their encounter with Mogadishu was, by most accounts, an encounter with their own foreignness.

DEPORTED BODIES AND PHANTOM LIVES

Having been dismembered verbally into "heads" (or its metaphor, "beds"), physically constrained, forcibly relocated, and then dumped into a city (Ali: "This is the dumping place for all these reject outcasts") where their movement was restricted once again because of fear, these deportees experienced their removal in a profoundly corporeal way. Moreover, the deportee body is doubly stigmatized—polluted and polluting—both in the "host" society and at "home." Simply put, *deportable* bodies exude the danger of their transitional state(s); as ex-prisoners having "spent any time 'inside' [they are] put permanently 'outside' the ordinary social system" (Douglas 1966/2002, 121), and as aliens, they are all the more outcasts. Similarly, *deported* bodies are suspected of carrying with them the pollution contracted abroad while also remaining anomalies at home, their forced return subverting the mythologized immigrant success story. Deportable/deported bodies are also racialized and gendered bodies. While I lack the space to discuss the racialization of citizenship and incarceration (Torres, Mirón, and Inda 1999; Pager 2007; Mauer 2006), it is important to note that these Somali deportees spoke repeatedly of having been subjected to systemic discrimination such as racial profiling and uneven sentencing. Further, as their own examples show, deportation's disruptions—of family, (re)production, work—are often gendered ones.

Significantly, all these deportees placed tremendous emphasis on their desire for bodily acceptance. Several recounted acute physical discomfort upon their arrival in Mogadishu, worrying about their conspicuousness not only as "Americans" but also as Somalis. Two of the deportees, I was told, belonged to the same clan as the late Somali president Siyaad Barre; this affiliation alone could be life threatening. Additionally, most arrived wearing their work uniforms, brand-name athletic shoes, or tank tops—apparel that marked them for derision as well as theft. At least two of the younger men wore their long hair in a ponytail, a trait that Ali stated was viewed in Mogadishu as a sign of "wasted culture, a bad culture."

Of this group, the person who expressed the most concern about not fitting in was Deeqa. She had been deported in her "American" clothing—tight-fitting pants, a small T-shirt, and no *hijab*: "I was getting crazy when I was sent to Hamar [Mogadishu] 'cause I didn't know how to deal with people, I forgot my culture, I cannot walk, I cannot wear the clothes I'm supposed to wear, I cannot have a conversation with a person because I'm scared who's gonna kill you. Is this person gonna know you're not from here?" These external adjustments are not superficial. A number of women in Somaliland expressed a similar anxiety about having to learn how to dress when returning to Somaliland from Europe or the United States. A woman in her mid-twenties, who had grown up in Brooklyn, claimed that after living in Hargeysa for more than a year and covering herself completely, people could still tell that she was "not from here" simply by her walk. Seemingly trivial but constant efforts to keep a scarf pinned in place, to adjust one's gait, and to pronounce words or use slang correctly constitute significant attempts at adapting one's habitus to align with local norms. In Deeqa's case, her deported body was not only removed physically from her environment but also made to undergo a physical transformation to exhibit her "belonging."

Consistent with Walters's suggestion that the practice of deportation is invested with historical memory (2002a, 276), Deeqa's deportation replicated a history of loss. On the first day of our acquaintance, Deeqa told me that she had been two months pregnant at the time of her deportation. Recounting in detail her career success and her personal security in terms of marriage, close friends, and financial independence, she explained how her immediate goal of starting a family had been interrupted by her deportation. It is understandable how under these circumstances the fetus would have represented Deeqa's hopes for her (and her family's) future, as well as a physical connection to her husband during a time of imposed separation. However, soon after her arrival in Mogadishu, she miscarried. Deeqa criticized the brutal treatment accorded her by the U.S. immigration officers and the substandard prison conditions during their one-night layover in Djibouti. She also talked about an earlier pregnancy that had resulted in her child being placed for adoption. Her narrative of this missing child developed into a longer, older narrative of the deaths of her father's children and siblings during the Somali civil war. Unable to cope with further loss, her father had moved the family to the United States. Deeqa's return journey to Somalia—a forced removal that reversed the original condition of forced migration—mirrored the loss of children and family and, as a narrative, symbolized the inability under such circumstances to create a future or to preserve a connection to one's past. Nevertheless, within six months of her deportation, Deeqa would pride herself on having learned to dress and behave just like a Somali woman—to the extent that no one would know simply from her appearance that she was "not from here."

Likewise, the deported men were wrenched away from their spouses and children in North America. While Deeqa focused on her loss of family, the men spoke regularly of their ruined careers and their failed productivity. Many of the men expressed their shame at having been returned to Somalia rather than returning of their own volition and with evidence of success. Even if they had amassed significant capital abroad, they were not given the time or the chance to liquidate it before their deportation; instead they arrived in Mogadishu with whatever money had been in their pockets at the time of their arrest. Somaliland's economy is fueled by remittances from migrant workers and family members abroad (Ahmed 2000; see also Little 2003, 147–50). Whereas the deportees had counted previously as potential remitters capable of supporting family in Somaliland, they would now have to depend primarily on remittances for their livelihoods and on relatives in Somaliland for housing, food, and cash. Having failed to live up to their own and their relatives' expectation of a prosperous and promising return, their aberrant journey was a familial as well as personal disappointment—a double disgrace.

Rumors about the deportation preceded their arrival. In addition to their foreign dress and deportment and their lack of financial preparedness or street savvy, the shame associated with their deportation was manifested in speculation regarding the reasons for it. The deportees were met, both in Djibouti and in Mogadishu, with the suspicion of having been expelled from the United States for carrying HIV/AIDS or for being drug addicts. The deported bodies were deemed infected bodies—if not literally contagious, then at least metaphorically they embodied the danger of Western cultural contamination. In other words, they were deemed suspect because of their association with the United States, much as in the United States they had been considered suspect for their connection to Somalia. The suspicion they raised on both continents simply reinforced their growing mistrust of the motives for, and the legality of, their deportation.

Of the three accusations leveled against them—AIDS, drugs, and terrorism—the charge of terrorism was one that they could discount or appropriate. In contrast to drug use (too realistic) and AIDS (too shameful), a wrongful accusation of terrorism could be converted into a comical kind of symbolic capital. Whether or not they had ever been questioned along these lines, all the deported men connected their deportation, to some extent, to the U.S. preoccupation with the alleged Islamist threat after September 11, 2001. From the time of their arrival, many said, they were greeted as notorious celebrities by Djiboutian crowds who had come to the airport "to see al-Qaeda and al-Ittihaad" (Nasser). In this case, government was neither absent nor silent; according to several deportees, it was the Djibouti government that spread the news of their arrival and identified them as al-Qaeda members deported from the United States. Ali recounted his arrival in Djibouti:

> We were brought out like we are part of al-Qaeda. After this, September 11, whatever, we were considered as one of those terrorists. That's how they make it up. Just to get rid of us, eh? Saying these guys are involved, whatever, but it was not written in the paper, it was not televised, it was not in the local news, nothing, secret mission; but in the files maybe we are part of al-Qaeda, in their files. Secretly, you know? So, anyway, when we get in Djibouti, they were singing, the women, "*La-la-la-la, al-Qaeda, al-Qaeda.*" They were making a lot of noise, making fun of us.

Ali's narrative contrasts the secrecy or silence of their U.S. departure with the racket made upon their arrival. Mubarak suggested that it was only through the scrutiny they received in Djibouti that he was able to understand why exactly he had been deported at this particular time: "We spent all the night [in prison]. In the morning, all Djiboutis came watching us, like a zoo: the terrorist guys, the terrorist guys. 'What's going on? Who is a terrorist?' '*You! We came to watch you!*' What?! Now we understand something. Now we get some answers." Yet when I gave an early draft of this chapter to Tariq for review in 2003, he refuted these stories and laughed loudly at the images conjured by Ali. According to Tariq, "military men" in riot gear had been present at the Djibouti airport, but "without any AKs or modern weaponry." Moreover, women had not been singing about al-Qaeda, although it was true that three prostitutes had come to the jail and handed out their phone numbers, welcoming the men to chew chat with them upon their release. "They thought we had money," Tariq explained. Whether taunted or tempted by their female spectators, in essence these accounts reflect the deportees' attempt to portray the objectifying nature of their deportation and return. Whereas corporations and governments may be dealing in bodies, the deportees must bank on their reputations: the chief social currency that these cashless, jobless, and no longer independent return migrants could realize lay in their claim of having been wrongly discriminated against.

In his address to Minnesota's Somali community with regard to the ten men deported from there, U.S. Attorney Tom Heffelfinger portrayed this as but another routine deportation (Black and Leslie 2002). Yet the individuals in this group regarded their circumstances as anything but regular. In fact, a predominant way that these deportees described their shock, fear, and sense of the absurdity of it all was to compare their deportation to "one of those bad movies" (Tariq). During the interviews, the deportees made frequent reference to films to relate their experience: arrests, security forces, airport takeoffs and landings invoking the glorified chase scenes of crime and action films. In many of these narratives, the deportees came to star in their own spectacular deportation.

One film that became particularly central as an example of what they had experienced was Ridley Scott's *Black Hawk Down*, released in the United States on January 18, 2002.[11] Tariq criticized the film for being "just straight Hollywood, you know, they just put a total spin on reality." For others, the main issue was not the film's accuracy but how the fictionalized film or actual incident came to bear on their lives. In recounting a conversation with "immigration guys," Farah claimed to have said, "I don't care about *Black Hawk*, you know, I'm doing good over here working, you know, my family is here. I see myself as a U.S. citizen." He said the officers responded, "We don't care. We're deporting you. They don't like Americans—Somali people." Farah used *Black Hawk Down* as a symbol for what he is not and, at the same time, referred to the movie as an example of the U.S. xenophobia that triggered his deportation. As did Farah, Ali drew on the film to accentuate the horror of the event. Instead of locating this connection in the U.S. treatment of Somalis, however, he placed himself directly at the scene—importing himself, so to speak, into history:

> *Ali:* [The taxi driver] took us to the Olympic Hotel where *Black Hawk*, the movie, was shot down . . . the American plane was shot down. . . . He took us there. That's the hotel at where the Rangers came with their helicopters on top of the hotel. You can see it in the movie, that hotel, right? It was a tourist area for us, you know, we went to a historical place. We went to the roof, feeling nice, you know—oh, that's where the Rangers came! Wow! Where's the helicopter? We looked for the helicopter. I saw the helicopter, itself.
>
> *Nathalie:* Is it still there?
>
> *Ali:* Yeah, two guys are living in it. It's like a nice condominium, you know. [He laughs, slapping his knee.] It's so funny that I said, "Oh, no, I got to go there and chew some green grass [*chat*] in that helicopter." Just to make history, you know? "Oh, I was in that, you know, in that American thing, whatever."

Although Ali corrected himself, noting that it was the American plane and not the movie that was shot (down) in Mogadishu, his slip of the tongue expresses the very connection that he was drawing between his presence in

Mogadishu and the 1993 battle and 2002 film. Not only does the story of Ali's "making history" in Mogadishu turn his deportation into something exceptional, but it underscored his claim on America. He was in (or near) "that American thing"; he had slept "where the Rangers came." For Ali and the others, the ability to imagine themselves in a historic or Hollywood battle scene and their purported association with al-Qaeda gave them a sense, albeit poignantly limited, of empowerment. It projected them onto a larger stage where their deportation carried global meaning.[12]

That the association of the deportation with the events of September 11, 2001, served the deportees' reputations is elucidated by one of the most public of accounts: the human-interest story. On October 30, 2002, nearly nine months after his deportation, Tariq publicized his experience in a one-page interview in the *Republic*, the leading of Somaliland's three daily newspapers. Significantly, his story appeared in a column, written by a former member of the Somali National Movement, titled "What Was Your Worst Experience?" that usually features accounts of his fellow insurgents' most frightening days in the bush and their near loss of life or limb. In this edition, Tariq detailed his arrival in the United States, his early work experiences, the fight that had led to his imprisonment for "failing to go to the police station," where he had been on September 11, 2001, his coworkers' early suspicions of him as a Muslim, and his arrest and deportation in February 2002. In this account, Tariq's crime was neatly erased from the public record. Instead he was portrayed, in the words of his interviewer, as a sacrificial animal, a "deer" unexpectedly struck by the "club" of U.S. suspicion and reactive treatment of Muslims after September 11. Indeed, his own culpability was omitted in favor of an emphasis on the physical ordeal of his deportation. Not only did this retelling mitigate the stigma of his forced return, but it appropriated the very suspicions first raised against him to turn him into the victim of U.S. aggression, the survivor of the War on Terror, and the hero of his (phantom) life.

"RETURN TO CULTURE"

In addition to experiencing at least some degree of corporeal subjection during their removal and upon their return to their purported homeland, many deportees are "returned" to a certain place and time in such a way that it can never be a homecoming for them, only another arrival (cf. Coutin, this volume). Elana Zilberg's work demonstrates how deported Salvadoran immigrant gang youths must negotiate their return to a city remapped not only by the civil war but also by the geography of gang violence back in Los Angeles. While these youths suffer "spatial alienation and fettered mobility" in this new environment (2004, 771), it is their very dislocation that drives in part the urban transformation and transnationalization of San Salvador. Zilberg's study reveals "a structural interdependence and complicity in identity formation between the United States and El Salvador" (774) that in this Somali example exists only to a limited extent. Although these Somali deportees similarly endured the "embodiment of a forced transnationality" (762), their identities seem to have become less *trans-* and more *sub-* (or restricted) through and after their deportation. I have earlier invoked Ian Hacking's work on categories and subjectivities, in which he shows how the creation of new categories of people simultaneously creates new ways for people to be. Who we are, however, is not only how we are categorized but also the extent of our possibilities. With their possibilities now diminished, I argue, these Somali deportees were required to narrow their identity, not broaden it. A few of them mentioned that they had been marked "black" in the United States but had reidentified themselves as "Muslim" (transcending race) while in prison. Upon their arrival in Somalia, however, race and religion no longer worked to differentiate or unite them. Instead, as they described it, they were made to identify with clan and subclan in a geography mapped by genealogy and allegiances. In comparison with the returning diaspora juggling businesses, homes, and family in Somaliland and abroad, these deportees found their "forced transnationality" almost worthless as they were made to work at becoming (subnational) "Somalilanders."

Many of the northerners (now Somalilanders) were able to locate family in Hargeysa or other towns, in many cases bringing about reunions with grandparents, parents, or siblings for the first time since the war. The "East Africans," in contrast—those who were born in Kenya or Tanzania or those who may have falsified their Somali identity in the first place, hoping to achieve asylum in this way—were not always able to track down relatives. Most rented small rooms in strangers' homes; almost all had to learn how to speak Somali and navigate unfamiliar terrain. Ibraahim had been born in Kenya and lived there until his seventh year, when his family emigrated. His deportation to Mogadishu from Canada was his first encounter with Somalia. From Mogadishu he had considered traveling on to Kenya, but his father in Canada had warned him against arriving in Kenya without official documents. Consequently Ibraahim moved to Hargeysa, where he was awaiting the outcome of a lawsuit filed by his father against the Canadian government claiming that his son's deportation was conducted illegally. Not having been accustomed to identifying himself according to clan, Ibraahim struggled with his genealogical place in the social landscape. Here Ibraahim describes a conversation with a police officer:

> He goes: "What's your tribe?" I go: "I don't know." He goes: "What's your tribe?" I go: "Muslim, *bas* [that's all]." He started yelling, he goes: "You Muslim, huh? You"—what did he call me again? The Ethiopian thing, *habashi*—he goes: "You *habashi* [Ethiopian], huh?" I go: "No, I'm not *habashi*. I'm Somali." "What's your tribe? Who's your father? Who's your mother?" I go: "Even if I told you, you wouldn't know them. Why do you want to know?" I call my dad, I go: "What tribe am I?" He goes: "Habar Yunis, something else, something else." I go: "I'm sticking to just Muslim. If they want to shoot me, they can shoot me. I'll die as a Muslim."

Ibraahim's claim to be "just Muslim" serves additionally as a claim against belonging in Somalia or Somaliland. Not only does he refuse to be placed by the Somalilanders, but he rejects the idea of any association between "these" Somalis and himself: "In the Quran it tells you a Muslim is supposed to help a Muslim, no matter what. These people just changed the routine. So that's why I don't really talk to them, because it's not really Islam what they do. It's something else. They believe more in tribes than Muslims."

Ali, who was born and grew up in Tanzania, wished similarly to distinguish himself from his alleged countrymen: "We [East Africans] are the most segregated Somalis in all Somalia, and we are smarter than all of them because we were born outside Somalia, we don't believe what they believe, they call us *sijuis*." *Sijui*—the Swahili term for "I don't know"—is used by Somalis in Somaliland and in Somalia to refer to East African Somalis like Ibraahim who profess ignorance of their clan affiliation (McGowan 1999, 81). Ali explained that the joke, in fact, is on the locals, as the sijui do know their lineage but have made themselves free of it:

> It's like when they come to us, they ask me, "Mahad shegtay?" [How are you?], "Nabad?" [Peace?], "What's your tribe?" I know my tribe but I'll say *sijui*. We go like this [shrugging his shoulders], *sijui*. It means "I don't know." Because I know, but we don't want to be like them. You see, we all live together, we all love each other; we're all more civilized.

Both Ali and Ibraahim, while being "ethnically" Somali, tried to differentiate themselves from the Somali nationals living in Somalia and Somaliland by disavowing any knowledge of clan affiliation and instead (re)situating themselves within a greater geographic and religious community, East African and Muslim.[13] Nevertheless the experience of having grown up between cultures and yet feeling estranged from one's homeland is an experience not limited to the sijui.

When I first met Ibraahim and asked him if he remained in contact with any other deportees, he claimed that he could introduce me to "about twenty other guys" who had been deported from the West by their parents. I thought that he must be exaggerating, and failed to pursue this avenue. Weeks later, in another region of Somaliland, I was approached in the market by two teenage boys, each speaking a distinctive English. The one with a Canadian accent recounted how his parents had taken him to Somaliland to meet his relatives and left him there without his passport or a return ticket. As of August 2002, he had been in Somaliland for five months, living with distant relatives and waiting to return to his Canadian home. The British-sounding teenager told a similar story. Just as I was wondering whether this might be a ruse, Deeqa and her coworker arrived. "Oh, you know them," the coworker said, signaling toward the teenagers. "They were deported." Deeqa explained that youths such as these had been in gangs or had been "hanging out with Rastafarians" at home. Their parents had worried about their losing their Somali culture, if not ending up in jail, and had decided to "deport" them (that is, forcibly remove them) to Somaliland, where they would be surrounded by "traditional values." After I expressed my surprise at this parental response, Deeqa offered her defense, arguing that if these teenagers did end up in jail, they would probably be deported thereafter. Thus, in her view, it was wise for the parents to deport their children preemptively.

In her study of the Somali diaspora, Rima McGowan finds that "the greatest single fear expressed by Somalis in both London and Toronto was a concern that they would be unable to teach Islam, and an Islamic value system, effectively to their children in a Western environment—with its multiplicity of choices and its seemingly endless smorgasbord of competing values" (1999, 101). Somali parents were concerned about "losing their children": losing them to an alien Western culture of individualism while also losing control over them. As McGowan points out, many parents assumed that their teenage children were "lost" simply because they saw them experiment with new styles of dress and comportment (211). In more serious cases, Somali children had become involved in gang-related violence or drug abuse after, according to the parents interviewed, having lost their religion and their self-respect. The author of an editorial printed in the *Somaliland Times* (titled "Lost in America") notes that the Somali children who arrived in the United States at a young age "are almost lost culturally and many are in dire need for cultural restoration, and drug rehabilitation for some" (Gagale 2003). Strikingly, the author argues that it is government interference with respect to parenting and government laxity with respect to the "negative-cultural revolution of violent movies, video games, shootings, sex, and nudity" that contributes to this no-win situation for Somali parents. If parents attempt to control their children through disciplinary measures that include corporal punishment, then the government may take their children away from them; yet if these children are charged for any misdemeanors or felonies, then parents will lose their children to detention centers or government-enforced deportation. The only remedy, according to the editorial, is "cultural restoration."

Cultural restoration is one translation for what the Somalilanders refer to as *dhaqancelin*, "returning to culture." Accordingly, a teenager sent back to Somaliland or "deported" there by his or her parents is labeled a *dhaqancelis*; the story of parents suggesting a vacation in Somaliland and then deliberately leaving their children there is common. By spending time with relatives and attending Quran schools, these teenagers are expected to relearn their culture, improve their Somali-language abilities, and perhaps learn Arabic in the process. Like the East African sijuis who lack knowledge of, or proper reverence for, their genealogical roots, the dhaqancelis are accused of lacking knowledge of their culture, religion, and language. Not only are they lost in America, as the author of the editorial contends, but—as Nuruddin, the journalist, noted of the deported—they are lost in Somaliland, as well.

Similar to those deported by the state, the teenagers removed to Somaliland by their parents are received guardedly by many other Somalis. Although they have been sent back to absorb their cultural and religious heritage, in this transitional state they are considered dangerous to other Somali youths. "Culture here is based on the religion," a Somali-language teacher explained. "Anything which is strange to the culture and the religion we call *dhaqanbi'is* [spoiled culture]." Wearing tight-fitting clothing or holding hands with boys in public (for girls) and having long hair or shaven heads (for boys) are among the first signs that someone may be "spoiling" the culture by spreading Western habits. Moreover, someone who is spoiling the culture is often suspected of drug use and abuse, as one government-deported teenage girl complained: "They think if you're an outsider and you come here, you've all done drugs. Because there's some people here that are brought for that, and once they've seen one, you're all the same." Indeed, whether deported by the state or transported by their families, those who are forcibly returned to Somaliland are considered potential spoilers of the true culture at home. In contrast to the tacit belief that aliens who break the law are implicitly dangerous and do not deserve to remain in the "host" state, the presence of the dhaqancelis teenagers complicates this moral geography by reversing the notion of who pollutes whom: it is not the immigrant who is dangerous but the land of refuge. Deportation, in this context, is not just a disciplinary move governed by the state but also a corrective one directed by self-disciplining individuals.

LEGAL FANTASIES, ILLEGAL STATES

The deportees—northerner, southerner, sijui—have been deprived of almost all access to the legal documentation that regulates movement and mobility. Having been stripped of all their papers (except for their single-journey travel documents), the deportees were left in a country that had no state, with only some having the possibility of relocation to a country where the state was unrecognized. Deeqa found herself in Somaliland waiting to receive copies from the INS/DHS of her "papers": her driver's license, passport, and social security card. To a certain extent, the routine procedure of awaiting documentation that she had experienced while living in the United States had followed her to Somaliland. Others were waiting for tax forms that had presumably been sent to their homes soon after their departure. One continued to receive letters (in the United States) from state institutions—"They [the state government] think I'm still there: ID, driver's license, everything's still in order. Only the federal government knows that I'm deported"—while another received "papers" from the DHS concerning upcoming reviews: "Washington [D.C.] obviously don't know anything about me being deported." In contrast to the undocumented migrants who are physically but not "legally" present in the United States (Coutin 2000), these deportees appear to maintain a lingering administrative presence in the United States even after their bodies have been removed. Even so, the deportees occupy what Coutin calls a "space of non-existence" both in the United States and in Somaliland (2000, 28).

Six months after their deportation, in the summer of 2002, the deportees expressed outrage over their deportation and shock at the situation in which they now found themselves. Some tried to clothe their feelings of vulnerability in bravado or recriminations. Others professed to be resigned to their fate or to more conspiratorial forces; Mubarak believed that Pim Fortuijn, the prominent Dutch anti-immigration politician who was assassinated on May 6, 2002, had something to do with his deportation. Nevertheless, in 2002, I read optimism in the deportees' self-presentation. In a country that was rebuilding itself after a war (Somaliland), there seemed to be space for people to remake themselves as well. The deportees found themselves, in fact, amid returning Somalilanders eager to mine the country—literally and metaphorically—for new prospects.[14]

Some of the younger deportees were enthralled by Somaliland's recent history and excited to be involved in what Tariq called "the real world" as opposed to "that whole techno-industrial world" they had left behind. Tariq often talked enthusiastically about his new camaraderie with his uncle, a former SNM fighter who had "really seen a lot of death." Ibraahim spoke with equal fervor of his new interest in Somaliland's mineral wealth: "I believe that I am here to find something. And I found it." He had met a Somali from Denmark who claimed to be unearthing platinum, uranium, crystals, and antique jewelry, and had found a dinosaur egg. One day, Ibraahim brought this fossilized "egg" to my house with the hope that I might help locate an international team of scientists, an interested museum, or a foreign buyer. Others believed that their proficiency in English would secure them a job with one of the international or local NGOs in town; at this time, however, only Deeqa was working (for a European NGO). Meanwhile the young men continued to depend on their families' monthly remittances from the West while waiting for the fabled opportunity to arrive. A few individuals claimed to have initiated lawsuits against the U.S. or Canadian government for unlawful deportation and hoped that they would earn an earlier return or at least substantial compensation. Farah, a thirty-one-year-old wedding singer with two young U.S.-citizen children still in the United States, was considering buying land and sending for his family. Abdullahi, the only person I met who, within the first six months, had accepted the fact of his permanent resettlement, was in the process of arranging his marriage with a Somalilander. Whenever I ran into him during the summer of 2002, he was busy repairing walls, installing plumbing, or buying furniture for what would be their new home.

A year later, in the fall of 2003, many of these deportees appeared less optimistic about their future in Somaliland. The success stories were not, as had once been imagined, those of discovery but those of departure.[15] Farah, the singer, had been granted entry to Britain, where he was performing with a group of Somali musicians. His wife and children had moved to Canada. Mahmoud had been recruited to play basketball for a club in Qatar and had been gone for more than the three-month initial trial period, which suggested that he had been granted a longer stay. Omar had moved to Kenya to join his mother and was rumored to have traveled onward to London. Ali had spent three months in Djibouti and returned claiming to have worked as a translator for the U.S. Special Forces stationed there. Now he was assisting his friend (deported a few years before him) in transporting raw salt from the Somaliland coast to the capital for sale.

Those who remained had been unable thus far to capitalize on Somaliland's reconstruction venture. While numerous Somalilanders were returning from neighboring Arab states or from Europe and North America to set up businesses or to work for NGOs, the deportees had neither the capital nor the training to take advantage of such opportunities. Even their command of English and basic computer skills were not sufficient to make them competitive in an environment where clan ties prevailed and local connections mattered. Tariq reported despairingly that his attempts to apply for various low-level UN positions had been thwarted by nepotism. Perhaps one of the greatest obstacles, however, was his (and the others') reluctance to work for wages that, by U.S. standards, were negligible (cf. Sontag 2003).

In the eyes of these younger men, the only solution lay abroad. While Ibraahim still hoped that the fossilized egg might hatch a lucrative return someday, his immediate wish was to find work in Kenya. Tariq had toyed with the idea of traveling to Djibouti to seek work with the U.S. Marine Expeditionary Force but then dismissed this wild scheme: "That would be the last thing on my mind—to play Mr. Translator to the same folks that deported me. Seriously!" A more likely prospect had been suggested by his aunt in Saudi Arabia, who could procure him a visa to work as a chauffeur. After the March 2003 bombings of foreign housing complexes in Riyadh, however, this plan no longer appealed to him. By the time I returned to Somaliland in the autumn of 2003, Tariq's job search had been transformed into a quixotic quest for wealth either through poaching rhinoceros horns in Kenya or by reentering the United States, from which he had been barred for at least a decade. Yet Tariq argued:

> If I can make a case out of it that I was illegally deported, I don't think that they [the DHS] would want to go to court over this. That's my two cents on that debate. But, I mean, if a Mexican that's been deported thirty or forty

times can get in, I'm sure someone as intelligent and as agile as I am can get back in there. 'Cause, right now, to be honest with you—unless of course a miracle happens and I get some kind of US$6,000 grant from one of my relatives to go buy a visa in Hargeysa to go to London and become a refugee— there is nowhere else I would want to live. And this thing about the rhino is not just some fantasy in the back of my head, you know.

Indeed, the rhino fantasy, much like Ibraahim's dinosaur egg discovery, was genuine to the extent that becoming wealthy from eggs or horns seemed about as plausible as did an unauthorized reentry. The main difference between the one fantasy and the other was that the means to success, which used to be located in Somaliland itself, now increasingly lay in foreign lands.

The difficulty of outside travel is amplified in a country that cannot issue internationally recognized passports to its citizens. At the time of this writing (2005), Somaliland citizens traveled abroad under other nationalities or were limited to the use of Somali passports, which, purchased on the black market for US$20, were rarely accepted by any state outside the region. Entry visas to Britain could be purchased for US$6,000, however, and it was only after this initial investment that Somali identity itself gained any value. It is not unusual for African or Arab (e.g., Yemeni) migrants to have entered Heathrow by declaring themselves to be Somali refugees, having destroyed their travel documents and personal identification en route. Tariq was hoping to leave Somaliland in this manner; yet at the same time he was surrounded by family members with similar aspirations.[16]

In the first year of their deportation, many had been certain that the "illegality" of this particular incident (e.g., being dropped into a war zone, unable to inform their families before departure, and without access to lawyers) would become their saving grace.[17] But without U.S. representation in Somaliland and with little means to appeal their cases from there, these deportees would have had to resort to unlawful ways of leaving Somaliland and reentering the United States, where—they claimed—they would immediately seek legal assistance. The irony of the situation was clear. When I asked Tariq if he would mind signing the consent form required by the Institutional Review Panel for Human Subjects, he laughed about "that legalistic country" that would "kidnap you right after you come home from work after putting in eight hours for an industrial slave master and, at the same time, not accord you all your due rights [as] guaranteed in the Constitution." But rather than disparage the law, Tariq explained that the current regime had simply "put Lady Justice, with her scales, up-side down." For them, he supposed, "it's a way of safeguarding American national security, but to us," he added, "it's totally railroading the true legal justice system of the U.S." Poignantly, these deportees' belief in "the true legal justice system" rang as being deeply patriotic; once branded as "aliens" and "criminals," however, they have little chance of a future in the United States without an "illegal" reentry.

Only two of the five deportees I met on my second visit had reconciled themselves to the idea of remaining in Somaliland. Nasser, who a year earlier had been distressed by his new surroundings and consumed with financial worry, said that he now felt "adjusted to the city." Although he remained unemployed and relied on the US$50 per month sent by his mother in England, Nasser was proud of his progress: "I help people now. [Last year] I was getting help, now I help people. . . . I realized I had to accept my reality." Every morning, Nasser walked to a local government office to dispute a family land case. In the afternoons, he chewed chat at home—mostly alone, but sometimes with Abdullahi and Ibraahim, who lived nearby. Asked how he regarded his deportation now, Nasser said, "I don't think about America anymore. I'm doing good now. But I just want some answers for my nine years [in prison and detention]. Can you help me with that? Why did they do that to me, those nine years?"

Abdullahi, the only deportee I met who had been determined to stay in Somaliland after his deportation, was the most settled of the depor-tees I reencountered in 2003. Although he remained preoccupied with his financial (in)stability and was anxious about his prospects in the "new" Somaliland, he was also proud of his ability to shape his immediate environment according to his U.S. sensibility. He had been able to use his U.S. credit cards to purchase amenities in the United Arab Emirates as well as to pay for shipments from the United States: a VCR, stereos, his clothing, and a collection of U.S. films (legitimate copies, he pointed out, not the pirated ones that dominate the local markets). It seemed important to him that he demonstrate not only his relative well-being and initiative but also his choice in the matter of his resettlement. While he had not cho-sen to leave the United States, he could at least choose not to return. Al-though he claimed that he could enter the United States through Mexico or move to England using a friend's passport, he had decided against a life of continued migration: "As soon as I landed in Mogadishu, I decided I wasn't going to move anymore. I'd come back to my roots." He still had to work, however, at reclaiming his forced return as a success story. During a tour of his house, he was eager to show me that he had succeeded in his adoption of Western consumer tastes and in his ability to acquire these commodities even from within Somaliland. Entering the bedroom, where his wife was napping with their newborn son, Abdullahi pointed to the bed, closet, dresser, and nightstand, saying, "See, this is just like a bedroom in the States." Next he showed me the dining table in—what few families in Somaliland have—a formal dining room, and the kitchen that he would outfit "like an American kitchen," and the bathroom that would have running water, a washing machine, and a Western-style toilet. Additionally, he was planning to build a garage to house his car. Aware that his Somali wife, who had never emigrated, had been living in Mogadishu at the height of the war, I told Abdullahi that she must be very happy. "Well, we are still getting used to each other," he replied, standing amid the clutter of foreign goods that represented both his achievements and his hope for a future sense of security and belonging.

Still, Abdullahi remained bitter about his deportation from the United States after having lived there for eighteen years. He continued to think that his deportation, ten years after his original sentence, was aimed at punishing him not so much for his earlier misdemeanors as for the fact that "they didn't like a man who was smart," who had challenged his unlimited detention. Abdullahi—with his "American" house in Hargeysa and what we may call his U.S. sense of entitlement—recounted just how good it felt to stand up in front of the judge and before the law. "But you said the U.S. had thrown out all the laws," I reminded him. "Yes, but not if you take them on," he replied.

Common to the deportees' narratives was a strong desire for legal recognition that was paralleled by the desire for state recognition expressed by the populace and by the administration of the country in which they now reside. Although every account began with the "one mistake" that had brought them into initial conflict with the law, it was in the law that they had ultimately placed and continued to place their hopes (Peutz 2007). Describing the INS administration as a bureaucracy that neglected or even feared the law—for example, in denying the deportees access to legal counsel and conducting the deportation under the veil of secrecy (but also in the guise of legality)—the deportees characterized themselves as having mastered the law and therefore continually invoked it as an ally in their struggle. The state too became an object of desire (Aretxaga 2003) when it was the very failure of government—both in the United States and in Somalia—that the deportees lamented. Ironically, this same desire was performed by Somali parents who deported their own children ahead of the state, either in mimicry or in anticipation.

THE GLOBALIZATION SQUEEZE

Like the stronger states it emulates, the unrecognized but de facto state of Somaliland performs its sovereignty—and thus legitimacy—through its exclusions. In October 2003 three European humanitarian workers were murdered in cities near Hargeysa. Immediately the government condemned the murders, and the public staged demonstrations for peace in Hargeysa's main square, directly beneath the mounted warplane that had been commanded by Siyaad Barre to level Hargeysa in 1989. While suspicion was cast equally on local groups, national parties, and foreign governments, the Somaliland government and its detractors agreed on at least one thing: the murders had been aimed directly at the reputation of Somaliland and at the security of its current government. Newspaper headlines warned of a "Satanic alliance between 'al-Itihad' and the forces hostile to the Independence of Somaliland" or announced: "Terrorism Is Here!" Meanwhile the government instituted a twofold response to foreigners. Armed police patrolled and protected the downtown, the areas surrounding the upscale hotels, and the neighborhoods where the internationally run NGO compounds were located. At the same time, the government ordered the removal of up to 77,000 "illegal" foreigners within a forty-five-day period, appealing to the citizens of Somaliland for their assistance (*Republic*, November 1, 2003). Although framed as a response to global terrorism, the actual danger as depicted by the Somali National Intelligence Agency lay in the "bad effect" that these types of foreigners (undocumented Ethiopians, Djiboutians, and southern Somalis) exerted on the social body. Moreover, these "burdensome" foreigners were considered to be infecting the moral community with the same vices as the Somali deportees returning from the United States: HIV/AIDS, drugs, and spoiled culture (in the newspaper article, "black magic"). Thus the government of Somaliland predictably did what any other state might do when faced with a supposed terrorist threat: expel the unwanted.

After receiving a tour of Abdullahi's "American"-style home, I asked him what he thought about the expulsion of 77,000 foreigners from Somaliland. "Well, if they are causing problems, get rid of them, throw them into the sea," he answered, laughing. His answer surprised me. "Isn't that basically what happened to you, though?" I asked.

> *Abdullahi:* No, because the problems we caused were a lot earlier; this [deportation] was later. I was working, paying taxes, putting in my share for the

cost of a MIG or a fighter plane. What're they gonna come and bother me for? There were other people causing problems; deport them. We weren't causing any problems then. They could have also done it differently. They could have approached me and said, "Abdullahi, we know you're no terrorist, you don't have connections to al-Qaeda, why don't you infiltrate for us and you can stay?"

Nathalie: Would you have done that?

Abdullahi: Well, I don't know. If someone threatens the security of my country I am living in, they threaten me.

Although Abdullahi was drawing a distinction between his *productive* presence in the United States and the "illegal" foreigners' *problematic* (and, widely presumed, parasitic) presence in Somaliland, his nonchalant comment regarding this mass expulsion reveals also a certain security of belonging. Ironically, it was perhaps this event (even more than the performative "Americanization" of his house) that allowed Abdullahi to feel that he had returned to his roots. One's *national* home is a place that one cannot be deported from—although the extraordinary detentions and renditions immediately after September 11, 2001, call into question even this conventional distinction.

Given the sensitive nature of today's removals, it is striking that these deportees were willing to share their stories and experiences with me. They all spoke with me, I believe, because in contrast to deportees to many nations, they had little or no fear of any state surveillance upon their arrival. Moreover, through recounting their deportation, they were "being political" (Isin 2002), even as they were speaking about being excluded from the political space of the U.S. or Canadian nation-state. These deportees had been arrested originally for conducting themselves immorally in the public space of the virtuous citizenry: shoplifting, fighting, selling drugs, and being drunk in public. Engin Isin's work on citizenship demonstrates that "when social groups succeed in inculcating their own virtues as dominant, citizenship is constituted as an expression and embodiment of those virtues against others who lack them" (2002, 275). Thus it is likely that when these Somalis were incarcerated or when they had served their sentences but still languished in administrative detention in the beds freed by local inmates, they may have "experience[d] their *power* inferiority as a sign of *human* inferiority" (Elias 1976/1994, xxvi, cited in Isin 2002, 36; italics in original). However, in the moment they recognized themselves as a group—arbitrarily rounded up and placed, handcuffed, on a flight to Mogadishu with an imprisoned layover in Djibouti—these deportees became political in their critique: "Becoming political is that moment when the naturalness of the dominant virtues is called into question and their arbitrariness revealed. . . . Being political is that moment when one constitutes oneself as a being capable of judgment about just and unjust, takes responsibility for that judgment, and associates oneself with or against others in fulfilling that responsibility" (Isin 2002, 275–76). The deportees were therefore the first to draw my attention to the multiply violent paradoxes of being deported to one's nominal place of origin after years or even a lifetime of living abroad, after political and social boundaries have been redrawn, after ethnicity and nationality have come undone,[18] and after the crimes they had committed in North America had been punished—although their causes (e.g., drug addiction and poverty) remained untreated.[19] It was by accident that I met Tariq in Hargeysa in 2002 and therefore was able to speak to the eleven deportees who had made their way north to Somaliland from Mogadishu. However, it was not accidental that thirty-one persons were deported to Somalia in February 2002. If it had not been these particular individuals, it would have been others just like them—other "aliens" deported so that the rest would remain virtuous/ly.

So what can we learn from an ethnography of removal? First, such efforts contribute to the endless but vital interrogation of the "natural"/ "national" order of things (Malkki 1995). With the increasing entrenchment of the (normalized) "state of exception" (Agamben 2003/2005), concealed detentions and expulsions will continue to render individuals invisible. Anthropologists are well placed for locating deportees, witnessing their ordeal, and finally translating their narratives for an audience of citizens who may not view these punishments as arbitrary. This translation, the ethnography, shows not only how removed subjects become caught up in manifold discursive and disciplinary webs within the "host" state but also how they continue to live out their removal abroad. Second, an ethnography of removal—in contrast to the equally valuable studies of citizenship and its exclusions, or transnationalism and its flows—requires a focus not only on the reversal of movements and rights but especially on the *transfer* of peoples by state or corporate, local or global actors. The "re-move" suggests a second move, or a third or a tenth, emphasizing that displacements occur multiply, successively, and in various contexts. The four contexts discussed in this chapter—legal, economic, embodied, and spatial—represent just a few of the areas that require further exploration. How fixed, for example, is the distinction between those who can and cannot be deported? Does deportation disrupt the very citizen-alien divide that it is employed to reify? How do removals shape the political and social communities that remain? To what extent does deportation continue to be gendered and racialized? Does deportation make up new subjectivities? Are they transnational? Cosmopolitan? Abject (see Nyers, this volume)?

I spent much of Ramadan 2003 breaking fast in Hargeysa with Abdullahi's sister, Ayaan, and the rest of the members of her unusual household, all of them deportees. Ayaan was living in Somaliland for the first time; she had joined her husband, who had been deported recently from the United Arab Emirates, where, as cousins, they had both grown up. Since they had an extra room in their house, they had allowed Ibraahim's sister, who had been deported from Canada in the past six months, to live with them, and consequently Ibraahim stayed there as well. Each of the four wanted to leave Hargeysa, Ayaan most of all, and they often spent their evenings together bemoaning their situation in a kitchen mix of English, Arabic, and rudimentary Somali. Contemplating this fragile family of deportees, I thought about the Somali neologism for "globalization": *xeroedegayn.* Coined from the terms used to describe a corral for keeping adult livestock, *xero*, and a corral for keeping their offspring, *edeg*, *xeroedegayn* depicts a world in which the larger herds pour out into the smaller pen and the defenseless are squeezed elsewhere or crushed.[20]

NOTES

This chapter is a slightly modified version of an article first published in *Current Anthropology* 47, no. 2 (April 2006): 217–41, with commentary and reply. It is based on research conducted in Somaliland in the summer of 2002 and in autumn 2003 that was supported by grants from the Social Science Research Council (IPFP Fellowship), the Princeton Council on Regional Studies, and the Princeton Graduate School. I remain most grateful to the article's earlier readers, to the five anonymous reviewers of the journal, and to the seven commentators whose insightful critiques were published alongside the original version. I must express my gratitude, once again, to Nicholas De Genova and Justin Stearns, who have graciously read and commented on this manuscript on more than one occasion. I also remain deeply thankful to my interlocutors in Somaliland, whose names have been changed to preserve their anonymity. (The Somali spellings of proper names have been made familiar for an English-speaking readership, e.g., Cumar has been changed to Omar; Cali to Ali; and Xamar [Mogadishu] to Hamar.)

1. Al-Ittihaad al-Islami (the Islamic Union, or AIAI; also transliterated as al Itihad, among other variants) is a now-dissolved Islamist organization based

in Somalia that had aimed to overthrow the former Somali president Siyaad Barre and establish an Islamic state within the Horn of Africa. Al-Ittihaad was alleged to have ties with al-Qaeda and to carry some responsibility for the U.S. embassy bombings in Kenya and Tanzania in 1998, as well as the killing in 1993 of eighteen U.S. Rangers in Mogadishu (Dagne 2002). On September 23, 2001, al-Ittihaad was designated a terrorist entity by President Bush (Executive Order 13224), and its training camps were dismantled shortly thereafter by Ethiopian forces—although many of its former members played an active role in the Islamic Courts Union that had controlled most of southern Somalia and Mogadishu in 2006. On November 7, 2001, U.S. federal agents raided the Minneapolis office and seven other U.S.-based offices of the Somali telecommunications and informal money transfer company al-Barakaat, which was accused of transferring funds to al-Ittihaad and al-Qaeda. By the end of the month, al-Barakaat was designated by the Bush administration as a terrorist entity, its offices in North America and in several countries around the world were forcibly shut down, and its assets were frozen, temporarily disabling the critical transfer of remittances from the Somali diaspora to their relatives remaining in Somalia. No evidence, however, of al-Barakaat funding either al-Ittihaad or al-Qaeda was found (Roth, Greenburg, and Wille 2004). Although Tariq was living in California in 2001 and at the time of his arrest in 2002, the closing of the Minneapolis office in particular would have caught his attention owing to its negative effects on the sizable Somali community residing in Minnesota.

2. On March 1, 2003, the Immigration and Naturalization Service (INS) was subsumed by the Department of Homeland Security (DHS). The U.S. Immigration and Customs Enforcement (ICE), a component of the DHS, was made responsible for border control and enforcement; the Office of Detention and Removal (DRO), a division of ICE, transports and removes aliens within and from the United States. Since the majority of my interlocutors discuss INS activities previous to its reconfiguration within the DHS, this chapter refers primarily to the now defunct INS. With regard to immigration services or enforcement occurring since March 2003, however, I refer to the DHS as a whole.

3. Although I refer to Tariq and the thirty other individuals deported along with him as "deportees" throughout this chapter, I do not mean to reduce their complex personal and social identities to this singular event. Nevertheless it is predominantly as a deportee that each of these individuals experienced his or her coerced "emplacement" (Malkki 1995) within Somalia or Somaliland. My use of the term "deportees," then, intends to signal the profoundly "transformative" (Coutin, this volume) *and* circumscribing nature of their deportation without, however, essentializing the lives of those who have been deported (for similar terminological concerns, see De Genova 2002; Malkki 1995).

4. According to its annual report, ICE removed 356,739 "illegal aliens" (a figure that includes "more than 100,000" voluntary returns) from the United States in fiscal year 2008. See http://www.ice.gov/doclib/about/ice08ar_final .pdf (accessed July 1, 2009).

5. The Republic of Somaliland, known as the British Somaliland Protectorate until its colonial independence and subsequent unification with Italian Somalia in 1960, declared its independence from Somalia on May 18, 1991, after a decade of fighting against the regime of president Mohamad Siyaad Barre. Since then, the Somaliland state has been pressing for international recognition of its sovereignty. Although the functioning government of Somaliland has conducted a constitutional referendum and has held successful municipal, presidential, and parliamentary elections between 2001 and 2005 (Peutz 2005), the international community—in accord with the African Union, which prohibits its signatories from altering their colonial boundaries—has encouraged primarily the reunification of Somaliland with Somalia. Nonetheless the government of Somaliland remains adamant about the recognition that would invite, among other things, international monetary aid, human rights monitoring (to begin the excavation of mass graves), and international mining companies. As of 2005, the two monuments that graced Hargeysa's central street were, on the one end, one of the warplanes that was commanded by Siyaad Barre to bomb Hargeysa in the late eighties—now mounted on a base painted with images of physical dismemberment—and, on the other end, a small, uneven globe made of papier-mâché.

6. Tariq knew where to locate two of the men with whom he had been deported. Through each of them, I was able to contact another, and this process continued until I had interviewed the eleven deportees who traveled north to Somaliland (now residing in various towns around the country), as well as two of their acquaintances who had been deported separately (from North America) and two who had been deported from neighboring Arab states. Additionally, I interviewed five youths who had been "deported" by their parents (whom I met by chance or through their deported friends). At the same time, I was meeting, interviewing, and spending time with other Somalis who had returned voluntarily to Somaliland from North America or Europe, alone or with their families. All interviews were conducted in English, a language in which each of the interviewees was fluent or at least quite proficient, except for the interviews with the deportees from Arab states, which were conducted in Arabic. I had no research assistants or translators, and except for the one occasion of a joint interview that I indicate later in the chapter, all interviews were conducted in private.

7. In 1996 the U.S. Congress passed two laws—the Antiterrorism and Effective Death Penalty Act (AEDPA) and the Illegal Immigration and Reform Act (IIRIRA)—which, while intended to target illegal migration, also intensified the economic hardships faced by legal migrants who were made ineligible for food stamps or supplementary income (Espenshade, Baraka, and Huber 1997). At the same time, all noncitizens were made increasingly vulnerable to removal from the United States. For a general overview of the 1996 reforms, see Fragoman 1997. For a more detailed review of the 1996 changes in deportation law, see, *inter alia*, Morawetz 1998, 2000; Bhartia, this volume; Coutin, this volume.

8. In 1998, during the midst of Nasser's administrative detention, Human Rights Watch reported that there were then about 1,800 *indefinite* detainees

languishing in U.S. jails without any hope for removal or release. The same year, the INS was housing more than 60 percent of all its detainees (a total of approximately 15,000 individuals, a 70 percent increase from 1996) in local jails throughout the country. In 1997 county jails charged the INS an average of $58 per day per detainee, or approximately $10,000 per detainee in a six-month period. Liberty County Jail, a for-profit run by the Corrections Corporation of America, charged the INS $52.50 per day for each INS detainee but charged only $25 for county inmates (Human Rights Watch 1998). In 2001, the year of Nasser's release from indefinite detention, the INS had in custody approximately 22,000 individuals on an average day (Human Rights Watch 2002, 68). Although the housing of INS detainees in local county jails was highly lucrative for companies and communities, it was exceedingly punitive for the detainees, who, although theoretically detained on "administrative" and not "corrective" grounds, were often treated as inmates or worse. Nasser recounted having his hand broken by a prison guard, being beaten, and participating in hunger strikes to demonstrate against such treatment. Similar incidents were reported by Human Rights Watch, which conducted interviews at the time that Nasser was in detention and with detainees held in at least three of the parish jails in which he had spent time (Human Rights Watch 1998; see also Welch 2002; Dow 2004).

9. The Ogaden War (1977–78) erupted when Somalia invaded and occupied the Ogaden, the Somali-inhabited region of eastern Ethiopia, in an attempt to establish a Greater Somalia (consisting of the region encompassing the former Italian Somaliland [southern Somalia], British Somaliland [today's Somaliland], French Somaliland [Djibouti], eastern Ethiopia [the Ogaden], and northeastern Kenya). Although Somalia had been a Soviet client state embarked on a course of "scientific socialism" under the directive of its president Mohammad Siyaad Barre (1969–91), its (ultimately unsuccessful) invasion of the Ogaden reversed the former Cold War alliances as the Soviet Union shifted its support to Ethiopia and Somalia turned to the United States. It was this war, then, that was the catalyst for direct U.S. involvement and aid in Somalia, which contributed to the destabilization of Somalia and its resulting catastrophic dissolution in 1991, followed by the U.S.-led humanitarian operations in 1992 and its infamous invasion and withdrawal in 1993. For an ethnographic analysis of the U.S. interventions in the 1980s and their effects, see Simons 1995. Abdullahi, who was born in Aden, Yemen, in 1961 and lived there with his (Somali) parents until 1977, was visiting family in Hargeysa (Somaliland) when the Ogaden War began. His expressed fear of being "drafted" refers to the danger of possibly being forced, as a teenager, to join the "freedom fighters" (the Somali forces). His grandmother in Hargeysa arranged for him to be smuggled to Djibouti, where he remained until he received a visa to enter the United Arab Emirates (in 1978). Six years later, Abdullahi moved to the United States and did not return to Somali or Somaliland until his deportation in 2002.

10. For a recent exposé of the use of sedation during deportations from the United States, see Goldstein and Priest 2008.

11. *Black Hawk Down*, a film directed by Ridley Scott, is based on Mark Bowden's book of the same name (1999), which depicts the Battle of Mogadishu in 1993, during which eighteen U.S. soldiers and more than one thousand Somali civilians and militia members were killed.

12. It is not surprising that the deportees were suspicious of the timing, the destination, and the motives behind their deportation. Almost neglected by the foreign media since the disastrous U.S. intervention in 1993, Somalia regained the media spotlight only after the events of September 11, 2001, when it attracted the attention of U.S.-led counterterrorism efforts. In September 2001, U.S. intelligence forces speculated that Osama bin Laden might be headed toward Somalia, and the Bush administration added al-Ittihaad al-Islami, an Islamist organization based in Somalia, to the list of "specially designated global terrorist" entities. In November 2001 the Somali telecommunications company al-Barakaat was shut down, and its assets were frozen. In December 2001, U.S. officials visited Somalia, and in early January 2002 the Pentagon confirmed that the U.S. Navy was conducting regular surveillance missions off the coast of Somalia and Yemen. Both English and Arabic news sources speculated about Somalia's becoming the next target of the War on Terror (see Dagne 2002). It was during the height of this conjecture—and just after the release of the film *Black Hawk Down*—that the thirty-one Somali "nationals" were deported to Mogadishu. Even in May 2005, sightings of U.S. military presence off the coasts of Somali and Somaliland were reported in the Arab press, along with the official U.S. refutations.

13. Ibraahim's and Ali's professed aversion to tribal or clan identifications and affiliations must be understood not only in the context of their sudden "emplacement"—or even "displacement"—within Somalia (after years in North America) but also in relation to their respective upbringings in Kenya and Tanzania, where tribal politics and the politics of detribalization followed a different historical course. Ali's comments may be attributed, in part, to his birth and upbringing in Dar es Salaam, Tanzania (1970–85), at a time when then President Julius Nyerere (in office 1964–85) promoted a distinctly *nationalist* agenda; he thus speaks not only as a sijui "ignorant" of tribe but also as a *Tanzanian* citizen distinctly shaped by Nyerere's detribalization policies. Ibraahim, on the other hand, left Kenya with his family at age seven; consequently, his aversion to tribal affiliation may have been influenced less by Kenya's tribal politics than by his own formative experiences in Canada.

14. In 2002 rumor had it that someone had found a diamond in a dry riverbed and sold it in Dubai for a small fortune. That summer, within just a two-month period, I was approached by seven individuals each of whom anticipated making money from emeralds or diamonds discovered in the ground and asked for my help in finding overseas buyers.

15. Four of the original group of deportees had left the country. I met with five of the eleven individuals who had ended up in Somaliland, but could not locate the other two (one was said by neighbors to have emigrated to Europe, but they were not certain). Deeqa continued to work for a European-based NGO in her parents' town.

16. During my autumn 2003 visit, Tariq's family was trying to send his grand-mother abroad for kidney dialysis. First, his grandmother had received treatment in Qatar, but after this had failed, one of her sons took her to Abu Dhabi and from there tried to put her on a plane to London. She was caught using her deceased friend's passport, however, and was denied boarding. In May 2004 the BBC reported that Kenya and the UAE had stopped issuing visas to Somalis traveling on Somali passports because of the preponderance of fraud. See http://news.bbc.co.uk/1/hi/world/africa/3700525.stm (accessed May 15, 2008). This one example demonstrates how tricky it can be even for those with medical emergencies to travel from Somaliland (Somalia) to the West. Moreover, the deportees were not the only Somalis to have to violate the law to access it.

17. Lawsuits against further deportations of Somali nationals, based on the impermissibility of deporting an alien without a foreign government acceptance (or owing to the absence of a foreign government), were filed in the United States between 2002 and 2004. For a legal analysis of the Eighth and Ninth Circuit Court split over whether the acceptance by—and thus existence of—the foreign government of the receiving state is indeed required (and specifically in the context of Somalia), see E. Hing 2004.

18. Before the dissolution of Somalia, Somali studies scholars claimed that Somalia was a homogeneous nation: one language, one ethnicity, and one race. More recent works have challenged this supposition, demonstrating long-existing tensions based on conflicts of class, ethnic, and racial identities (see, for example, Ahmad 1995; Besteman 1999; Cassanelli 1996). However, what I am referring to here specifically is that the deportation of ethnic Somalis to the territory of former Somalia ignores the more complex positionings of Somalis within East Africa and the Horn of Africa.

19. Nuruddin, the journalist, was critical of the fact that most of the deportees to Somaliland were deported for addictions they had acquired in the West. Then, after having been considered too dangerous to their "host" society, they were "sent back" to Somaliland without regard for the danger they may pose there. While his view of addiction may overemphasize the importance of the environment, it is worth pointing out that individuals with substance dependencies were sent, in the case of Somalia, to a country without adequate treatment facilities and to a region that already suffers from widespread addiction to chat.

20. Tragically, within the year, Ayaan died of first-degree burns sustained during a kitchen fire. When I returned to Somaliland in 2005, their house was occupied by strangers; Ibraahim and his sister had moved to Kenya; Ayaan's husband was rumored to have remarried or to have returned to the United Arab Emirates. I did not meet Abdullahi but heard that he had successfully opened a cafe, but that he and his wife were recently divorced.

PART FIVE ━━ *Freedom*

PETER NYERS

—〰—

CHAPTER 14

Abject Cosmopolitanism

The Politics of Protection in

the Anti-Deportation Movement

To flee is to produce the real, to create life, to find a weapon.—Gilles Deleuze

The topic of refugees and immigration has always been deeply political, as it invariably raises important questions about the changing nature of boundaries, self-other relations, and ethical and political practice. In recent years, Western governments have opted to frame these questions through the prism of security. Their restrictive laws and policies have created an elaborate array of bureaucratic and physical impediments to cross-border travel; a vast armory of technologies of control and exclusion attempt to enforce these barriers. The trend toward securitizing migration has only intensified in the wake of the violent attacks on New York and Washington.[1] In this nervous state of affairs, Didier Bigo (2002) argues that a "governmentality of unease" has transformed global anxieties about migration into a mode of ruling. He warns of the emergence not of a global panopticon (where *everyone* is watched) but of a "ban-opticon" (where profiling technologies determine who is to be placed under surveillance, questioning, detention, or removal and who is to be free of such interventions). Asylum seekers, refugees, nonstatus residents, undocumented workers, so-called overstayers and "illegals"—together they have come to constitute a kind of "abject class" of global migrants (S. Bell 2000). Whatever their designation, these migrants are increasingly cast as the *objects* of securitized fears and anxieties, possessing either an unsavory agency (i.e., they are identity frauds, queue jumpers, people who undermine consent in the polity) or a dangerous agency (i.e., they are criminals, terrorists, agents of insecurity).

FROM DIASPORA TO DEPORTSPORA

While global migrations are rendering internal and external borders less distinct and secure, it is clear that state capacities to enable inclusions and enforce exclusions have not diminished, only taken on new forms. This point is often lost in all the hype about the hybrid identities generated through border transgressions. Western states have, in fact, demonstrated a remarkable flexibility in responding to the dynamism of contemporary migration flows. For example, Sandro Mezzadra sees in "safe-third-country" agreements not simply a bilateral pact but a broader transnational system of exclusion. These agreements act in ways that reverse the flows of established transnational migratory paths, turning them into transnational corridors of expulsion. In the case of the European Union, Mezzadra explains that this involves exporting border control technologies to frontier countries eager to gain entry into the EU.

> Having been identified as a "safe third country," Poland must accept all refugees and migrants expelled from Germany that entered through its territory. But Poland has in turn concluded a series of similar agreements, for example with the Ukraine. As a result, there are now plans to construct detention centres in the Ukraine on the German model, which already exist in Poland. The point is that this path of expulsion—Germany, Poland, Ukraine—follows in reverse the path established by the migrants themselves. (Mezzadra and Neilson 2003, 8)

Since it is the migrants themselves, mostly from Asia and Africa, who have chosen the Ukraine as their preferred point of entry into the frontier zone of the EU, Mezzadra gives them credit for possessing enough agency to relegate "the exclusionary measures to the status of a mere response." Nonetheless, in their desire to manage and control the migration process, these border control policies are creating an abject diaspora—a *deportspora*.

There is a growing interest in critically analyzing how restrictive immigration measures are being contested and countered by global-local political movements of refugees, migrants, and their allies (Burman 2006; McNevin 2006; Nyers 2006c). This chapter seeks to contribute to this literature by approaching the topic through a cosmopolitan frame of analysis. Such a framework is advantageous for developing a strategy for contesting the security fixations of the sovereign state, as well as providing a possible antidote to the anxious subjectivities fostered by recent securitizations. To consider how the political campaigns by abject migrants are potential sites of a critical cosmopolitanism involves identifying and assessing such acts of citizenship for how they contest and reshape the traditional terms of political community, identity, and practice. To contribute to an understanding of this complex politics, this chapter focuses on the contested governance of "protection" in contemporary Canadian asylum and deportation practices.

Whenever a state ponders whether or not to grant asylum to an individual, it is making an intervention into the politics of protection. This is a significant political issue because the capacity to decide upon matters of inclusion and exclusion is a key element of sovereign power. Since Hobbes, the modern state has asserted a monopoly over matters of security, claiming to protect citizens both from each other (through laws and police) and from the external aggression of other states (through the military, border policing, etc.). This monopoly, we know, is a crucial source of legitimacy for sovereign power. In the case of asylum seekers, the decision about who will and will not be provided with protection is not just a humanitarian determination but a moment when the sovereign state (re)founds its claim to monopolize the political. Anti-deportation activism can therefore be read in terms of contemporary disputes over who has the authority to protect, and under what terms and conditions. Such activism can reveal new problematizations as well as new ways of thinking and acting politically. Who is to be protected? Who will do the protecting? Who represents those in need of protection? Can the endangered speak for themselves? What are the possibilities and constraints that (dis)allow political activism by non- or quasi citizens? For their agency to be recognized as legitimate and heard as political, does it require mediation from other citizen groups? Most important, what implications does the activism of abject migrants have for regimes of the political that operate on the assumption that such acts of agency are, in fact, impossible? The struggle over these questions can be revealing in terms of emerging forms of political subjectivity and practice that contest the state's claim to monopolize the subject(s) of protection on its territory (Huysmans, Dobson, and Prokhovnik 2006). To problematize or contest this claim therefore becomes a critical moment of cosmopolitan dissent.

My argument begins by introducing the concept of abjection and its relevance to understanding the theory and practice of a critical cosmopolitanism. Next I consider Bonnie Honig's recent intervention into cosmopolitan theory. Honig argues that the ambiguous narratives regarding the figure of the foreigner can serve as a critical resource for moving beyond state-centric accounts of political agency. Her thinking is thus quite relevant to understanding the significance of the critical citizenship practices of abject migrants. Drawing on the political theory of Jacques Rancière, Honig argues that in these political campaigns is an emerging and democratic *taking subjectivity* that can potentially be aligned with a democratic cosmopolitan politics.

Who are these taking-subjects, these abject cosmopolitans? In the chapter's second half, I consider the activism of a group of Algerian nonstatus refugees living in Montreal, Quebec, who have self-organized as the Comité d'Action des Sans-Statut Algeriens (CASS). These Algerians had their applications for refugee status refused by the Canadian state; however, they could not be returned to Algeria because a moratorium on removals to that country had been in effect since March 1997. Held in immigration limbo, these Algerians continued to live in Canada, mostly in Montreal, but without the formal legal status that would allow them to have secure access to work, education, social services, and so on (hence the designation "nonstatus"). After the Canadian government removed its moratorium in April 2002, the CASS mounted a vigorous and highly visible campaign to end the deportations and to regularize their immigration status in Canada. In doing so, the CASS employed tactics to amplify their political voice and claim political space. Does this make them viable candidates for democratic cosmopolitanism?

ABJECT COSMOPOLITANISM

The idea of cosmopolitanism has made something of a comeback in contemporary political theory and practice. No longer a "dead idea" to be relegated to the footnotes of critical inquiry, cosmopolitanism is the subject of a growing number of academic studies of impressive quality (e.g., Cheah and Robbins 1998). The reasons for this resurgence are complicated, to be sure. However, it is clear that the globalization of late modernity has created a historical context for rethinking the possibilities for cultural engagement, social affiliations, legal authority, and political action beyond the state. But just as globalization represents a diverse, uneven, and unequal set of dynamics and processes, so the range of histories and practices associated with cosmopolitanism is also quite large and marked by its own controversies. This is an age of protean cosmopolitanisms, and the concept needs to be thoroughly pluralized, historicized, and differentiated.

To think of cosmopolitanism in the plural is to upset much of the received knowledge we possess about the subject. Cosmopolitanism, after all, is famously universalistic in its aspirations. It is well known for disregarding the particularistic logic of nationalism, with its imagined spatial communities and territorialized identities. Cosmopolitanism follows its own categorical imperative, taking all humanity, irrespective of place, along for the ride. For all its association with universality, however, the sheer diversity of perspectives and practices of contemporary cosmopolitanism testifies to the deep plurality of modes of cosmopolitan conduct. James Clifford, for one, doubts whether "a coherent cluster of experiences" could ever fall under the banner of cosmopolitanism. He prefers instead to talk of "discrepant" cosmopolitanisms, pluralized "to account for a range of uneven affiliations" (1998, 362, 365). But if Clifford's discrepant cosmopolitanisms "begin and end with historical interconnection and often violent attachment," the cosmopolitan actions I am interested in analyzing and theorizing concern those who have been *de-connected*, subjected to often violent detachment. As the editors of a recent volume on cosmopolitanism point out, "Cosmopolitans today are often the victims of modernity, failed by capitalism's upward mobility, and bereft of these comforts and customs of national belonging" (Pollock et al. 2002, 6). Therefore, while these scholars call for a "situated universalism" to ground cosmopolitan practice, we must ask: what is the "situated" context of these "victims of modernity"? For abject migrants, the cast-offs of world order, their situatedness *is* displacement. Therefore, if cosmopolitanism "catches something of our need to ground our sense of *mutuality* in conditions of *mutability*" (4), we should also add *mobility* to these conditions. I use the concept of *abject cosmopolitanism* to describe the emerging political practices and enduring political problematics associated with refugee and immigrant groups resisting their targeted exclusion.

When the word "abject" is used to describe a dimension of world affairs, it is usually employed to highlight some of the gravest ills of the contemporary age. The global problem of "abject poverty" is a good example. But what does it mean to speak of an abject cosmopolitanism? The conjoining of these two terms invites serious conceptual confusion, as their use and meaning could not, it would seem, be further apart. While the *OED* defines cosmopolitanism as "belonging to all parts of the world," etymologies of abjection point to its Latin root *abjectus*, meaning "throw away" or "cast off." The abject is someone who is cast out, discarded, and rejected. In contrast to the vaunted status of cosmopolitanism, the abject are held in low regard as outcasts. While the cosmopolitan is at home everywhere, the abject has been jettisoned, forced out into a life of displacement. When considered together, therefore, the abject and the cosmopolitan appear as stark contrasts, relating to each other only in highly oppositional terms: high-low, hope-despair, beautiful-ugly, belonging-exclusion, everywhere-nowhere.

Abjection therefore describes a degraded, wretched, and displaced condition. Cosmopolitanism, we are told, is quite a different thing, calling for an inclusive, sophisticated, and worldly demeanor. But abject cosmopolitanism? Is the state of cosmopolitan theory and practice today such that it deserves the same adjective used to describe global patterns of inequality and poverty? Is the problem of universalism too great to be successfully navigated without (re-)creating imperialist prejudices under the guise of, say, a common Europe, a global civil society, or the family of humanity? Are today's cosmopolitans none other than the subjects of Empire? Perhaps. However, there are many who would surely oppose characterizing cosmopolitanism in this abject manner, calling it a disservice to the noble and highly regarded tradition of thinking and acting beyond the state. But what if cosmopolitanism's high value nonetheless relied on a relationship with an abject nonvalue for its condition of possibility? Judith Butler argues that "the exclusionary matrix by which subjects are formed requires the simultaneous production of a domain of abject beings" (1993, 3). Do cosmopolitan subjects constitute themselves similarly? Julia Kristeva calls abjection "a precondition of narcissism" (1982, 13). Does the elevated status of cosmopolitanism—its narcissism, as it were—also rely on the construction of an abject other?

The discordance of abject cosmopolitanism thus exceeds the implied pejorative connotation over the state of cosmopolitan theory today. The "abject" is not just an adjective qualifying the noun "cosmopolitanism." Instead the abject subject has an important constitutive role in encounters and relationships between self and other—including those of the cosmopolitan variety. The "moral cartography" of abjection is, however, riddled with some familiar us-them power relations (Shapiro 1999, 57). All too often it is "us" (Westerners, Europeans, humanitarians, etc.) who are the cosmopolitans, the champions of justice, human rights, and world order, leaving "them" (the Third Worlders, the global poor, the "wretched of the earth") as the abject, the societies and subjects in crisis, the failed states in need of intervention. Consequently, answering the questions about alternative meanings about abject cosmopolitanism requires some critical self-reflection on what Linda McDowell calls the "categorization of the classifiers" (1999, 205). She warns in particular against "those Western theorizers who see themselves as cosmopolitans but define others, the classified, as creoles"—or, in this case, abject human beings.

The tendency to see the relationship between cosmopolitanism and abjection as one of mutual exclusion needs to be problematized. Indeed, relationships of exclusion should always be regarded with some suspicion, especially when they involve sharp binary distinctions. These dualisms tend not to be balanced or symmetrical but are rather deeply hierarchical and disjointed, riddled with unequal power relations. According to Engin Isin, one of the key assumptions of any discourse deploying a "logic of exclusion" is that the characteristics associated with the excluded preexist their expulsion.

> The logic of exclusion presupposes that the excluding and the excluded are conceived as irreconcilable; that the excluded is perceived in purely negative terms, having no property of its own, but merely expressing the absence of the properties of the other; that these properties are essential; that the properties of the excluded are experienced as strange, hidden, frightful, or menacing; that the properties of the excluding are a mere negation of the properties of the other; and that exclusion itself (or confinement or annihilation) is actuated socially. (Isin 2002, 3)

As the embodiment of exclusion, the abject are prime candidates for "hidden, frightful, or menacing" subjectivities to define their condition. Understood politically, they stand in contrast to the purity of citizenship, that is, the authoritative, articulate, visible, and political form of human subjectivity. Instead the abject suffer from a form of purity that demands them to be speechless victims, invisible and apolitical. In a twisted reversal, the impurity of abjection becomes the purity of the abject. Thus there is an easy association with the "cast-offs," the "rejected," with a form of bodily wretchedness, muted political agency, criminality, and moral disrepute (Nyers 2006b; Pratt 2005).

It is important to highlight the arbitrariness of these designations and the violence that goes into the enforcement of prevailing accounts of political speech, agency, visibility, and reputable behavior. After all, the lowly status of the abject is by no means their "natural" condition. "Abjection," as Nikolas Rose declares, "is an act of force" (1999, 253). The historical practices of casting off, of demoting an/other's status to a lower mode of existence, are as varied as they are complicated. However, to see abjection as a practice of force underscores how "being abject" is, in fact, always a matter of "becoming abject." As Rose states:

> Abjection is a matter of the energies, the practices, the works of division that act upon persons and collectivities such that some ways of being, some forms of existence are cast into a zone of shame, disgrace or debasement, rendered beyond the limits of the liveable, denied the warrant of tolerability, accorded purely a negative value. (253)

Does this process of abjection not describe the experience of large numbers of today's global "cast-offs"—the refugee, the asylum seeker, the "illegal" worker? Is their "zone of shame, disgrace or debasement" not the interminable "waiting areas," detention facilities, deportation flights, and lives forced underground? What are the possibilities for political agency in such abject zones today? When confronted by such questions, we should not be entirely pessimistic in our response. Butler, for one, argues that abjection can serve as "a critical resource in the struggle to rearticulate the very terms of symbolic legitimacy and intelligibility" (1993, 3). How are the cast-off today taking up the cosmopolitan call and, with their practices, recasting the possibilities for local-global political life? In answering this question, I seek to emphasize how abject cosmopolitanism describes not a problematic cosmopolitanism for the abject but *a problematizing cosmopolitanism of the abject*.

DEMOCRATIC COSMOPOLITANISM: TAKING ON THE POLITICAL

In Canada, the topic of abject migration brings forth a remarkably messy mix of xenophilic and xenophobic statements and practices. For example, after a census report in January 2003 indicated that the number of immigrants choosing to settle in Canada had risen steadily throughout the 1990s, Minister of Citizenship and Immigration Denis Coderre boasted that Canada is "a place where immigrants will find hope, hospitality and opportunity." Coderre indicated his immense pleasure that so many immigrants deem Canada "choiceworthy" and thus seek membership through citizenship: "So many immigrants choose to become Canadians because they recognize the Canadian values of respect, freedom, peace and belonging."[2] Only a few days later, however, an incident at the Vancouver International Airport revealed another, more troubling, side to Canada's relationship with foreigners. When an Iranian woman whose refugee claim had been rejected by Canadian officials was about to be deported, she made headlines by making a dramatic escape—"running for her life," as her supporters put it (Mickleburgh 2003). The woman and her family had been living and working in Canada for four years, had never been on welfare, had strong ties to the local community, and so on. By all accounts they were a "model" immigrant family, the kind praised by Coderre only a few days earlier. However, instead of praising her determination to stay in a country where "respect, freedom, peace and belonging" supposedly reign, the minister rose in Parliament to reassure the populace that the Iranian woman and her family had been apprehended and deported. He also chose the moment to publicly boast about the number of deportations his ministry successfully carries out per year (about 8,400).

How should we understand this confused state of affairs that surrounds the foreigner? An important book by Bonnie Honig, *Democracy and the Foreigner*, responds to this thorny political problem. Honig argues that the stories told about a recurring figure in Western political culture—that of the "foreign-founder"—are important because they reveal the pivotal role that foreigners play in founding political communities. An important part of this argument is that the moment of founding is not only locatable somewhere in a nation's past. Honig persuasively argues that the distinctiveness of every national culture has to be periodically refurbished; populations have to be reassured, and their affections for the nation reaffirmed. Every political community must, in short, refound itself. Honig explores this process of renewal by considering narratives about foreigners (wanted and unwanted, "legal" and "illegal," celebrated and scorned) and the various ways they are received by political communities. What emerges from her analysis is an appreciation for what might be called a "doubleness" to foreignness: it can operate as both a support *and* a threat to the political community in question. From this perspective, the seemingly contradictory comments made by the Canadian minister of citizenship and immigration take on renewed import; they are part of the ongoing process of utilizing the "foreigner" for the purpose of national (re)founding.

While there is nothing inherent in foreignness to make it correspond to nationalization or denationalization projects, Honig makes it clear that she favors denationalization, albeit in the qualified form of "democratic cosmopolitanism." This critical cosmopolitanism is not an argument in favor of a specified form of transnational governance; it does not have global citizenship or world government as its telos. Honig's cosmopolitanism similarly avoids the entrapments of international law, recognizing that this arena, while significant, is no substitute for the difficult and complex politics that democratic cosmopolitanism calls for. Rather, democratic cosmopolitanism seeks to "widen the resources and energies of an emerging international civil society to contest or support state actions in matters of transnational and local interest such as environmental, economic, military, cultural, and immigration policies." As a form of activism, democratic cosmopolitanism seeks to "denationalize the state" by "scrambling" the oppositions of "instrumental" versus "affective" citizenship. In doing so, it renders visible "already existing sites of sub- and international activisms and memberships that are affective, but not nationalist, rooted but not simply in culture, deep but not particularist, transnational but not simply disloyal." This is a *democratic* form of cosmopolitanism, moreover, because of its commitment to promote at the local, national, and international levels "popular empowerment, effective representation, and the generation of actions in concert across lines of difference." Honig has a vigorous understanding of democratic practice in mind, calling for cosmopolitans to "risk their cosmopolitan (and nationalist) principles by engaging others in their particularities, while *at the same time* defending, (re)discovering and (re)articulating located universalisms such as human rights and the equal dignity of persons." Finally, and perhaps most importantly, democratic cosmopolitanism is about transforming the meaning and practice of citizenship from "a juridical status distributed (or not) by states" to "a *practice* in which denizens, migrants, residents, and their allies hold states accountable for their definitions and distributions of goods, powers, rights, freedoms, privileges, and justice" (Honig 2001, 103, 104–5, 103, 67, 104).

There is much to admire in Honig's cosmo-political thinking. Honig is an exemplary contemporary thinker about the abject zones and subjects, the limit spaces and conditions of the political. In the figure of the foreign founder, she critically examines subjectivities that are simultaneously "inside" (because of their residency) and "outside" (because of their lack of status) the political community. In doing so, Honig's argument has some fairly radical implications for who counts as a political subject and what counts as political agency. Her discussion of the "myth of immigrant America" is a revealing example in this regard. This myth posits that the continuation of democratic political culture of the United States is dependent upon the vitality and enthusiasm of incoming immigrant populations. Here the foreigner serves as an important "supplement to the nation, an agent of national reenchantment that might rescue the regime from corruption and return it to its first principles" (Honig 2001,

74). Such moments of (re)founding by immigrants can readily be seen, for example, in naturalization ceremonies in which immigrants swear their allegiance to the United States. These performances—significantly, the newcomers' first sanctioned act of citizenship—are meant to provide ongoing evidence that the nation remains "choiceworthy," still capable of enchanting newcomers to desire and seek out membership. The consenting immigrant is therefore crucial for holding up—for refounding—the principles of American liberal democracy.

Through some astute analysis and creative thinking, Honig reveals that a deep uncertainty marks the figure of the "good" immigrant. In the first place, the arguments used to promote the good immigrant can quickly be turned around, thereby creating the conditions for anti-immigrant sentiments and conflicts. For example, the same valued energies that immigrants bring to refurbish and reenergize the nation can just as quickly be deemed suspicious and turned against them:

> "Their" admirable hard work and boundless acquisition puts "us" out of jobs. "Their" good, reinvigorative communities also look like fragmentary ethnic enclaves. "Their" traditional family values threaten to overturn our still new and fragile gains in gender equality. "Their" voluntarist embrace of America, effective only to the extent that they come from elsewhere, works to reaffirm but also endangers "our" way of life. (Honig 2001, 76)

The xenophilic myth of immigrant America thus has a nationalist xenophobia as its (re)founding partner. A similar dynamic is at work in arguments that emphasize the "good" immigrant's consenting nature. Praising the achievements of the consenting foreigner creates the conditions for demonizing the efforts of the nonconsenting foreigner (e.g., the "illegal" alien). The "bad" immigrant always shadows the "good" immigrant. One consents; the other undermines consent. Consequently, then, "the iconic good immigrant—the supercitizen—who upholds American liberal democracy is not accidentally or coincidentally partnered with the iconic bad immigrant who threatens to tear it down" (Honig 2001, 97).[3]

The undecidability of foreignness presents dangers as well as opportunities. Honig negotiates both through a productive reading of Derrida's work on the politics of friendship and then by connecting this analysis to Rancière's call to "take on" the political through a radical accounting of human agency. In *Politics of Friendship*, Derrida (1997) invokes Aristotle's distinction between three kinds of friendship: use, pleasure, and virtue. While for Aristotle political relations were the hallmark of "use" friendships, Derrida argues that politics arises from the *mistakes* that are made between the different kinds of friendship. Honig seizes upon this insight to show that the foreigner can be read as a "would-be friend," except sometimes mistakes are made as to what kind of friendship is being embarked upon. The disappointments that arise because of these misunderstandings, Honig argues, are often "expressed by way of the charge that the other is a *taker* who is just using us rather than a *giver* who really wants to be one of us." In Honig's hands, however, this much-maligned figure of the "taking" foreigner acquires a renewed import. Taking is not something to be ashamed about. To the contrary, the "practice of taking rights and privileges rather than waiting for them to be granted by a sovereign power is a quintessentially democratic practice." This positive assessment of the foreigner as a "democratic taker" paves the way for Honig to consider how foreignness works on behalf of a democratic cosmopolitan project (2001, 79, 99, 101).

The idea of a taking-subjectivity is one that Honig borrows from the French political theorist Jacques Rancière. Politics, for Rancière, is an activity that "turns on equality as its principle." Equality, however, "is not a given that politics then presses into service, an essence embodied in the law or a goal politics sets itself the task of attaining." Rather, equality is an "assumption that needs to be discerned within the practices of implementing it." The practices that enact political equality, however, are not necessarily coextensive with the legal status of citizenship. Acts of citizenship are as likely to be enacted by abject subjects as by citizen subjects. For Rancière, the point is that politics is "a specific kind of connection" that "comes about solely through interruption" (Rancière 1999, ix, 33, 12–13). This involves those moments when abject subjects (in Rancière's terms, those who have "no part" in the social order) articulate a grievance as an equal speaking being. For Rancière, this is a radical political moment. It qualifies as a quintessential political moment, what Isin identifies as the "moment when the naturalness of the dominant virtues is called into question and their arbitrariness revealed." Such moments enable the excluded—the abject—"to constitute themselves as political agents under new terms, taking different positions in the social space than those in which they were previously positioned" (Isin 2002, 275–76).

Honig's taking foreigner is in the peculiar position of being an unwanted stranger to the polity and may therefore be classified as ill qualified to possess a legitimate political voice. The first target of taking-subjects is therefore always speech: political speech. Our received traditions of politics tell us that political speech is an attribute belonging to the realm of citizenship. Denied this legal status—and along with it the onto-political status of a speaking being—these foreigners (historically represented by alien suffrage movements in their various forms) have to interrupt the dominant political (speaking) order not just to be heard but to be recognized as a speaking being as such. Not surprisingly, then, Honig applauds Rancière's accounting of "political activity," which he describes as a form of activity that "shifts a body from the place assigned to it or changes a place's destination. It makes visible what had no business being seen, and makes heard a discourse where once there was only place for noise; it makes heard as discourse what was once only heard as noise" (Rancière 1999, 30; quoted in Honig 2001, 101; Nyers 2006c).

THE LIMITS OF DEMOCRATIC COSMOPOLITANISM

Honig admits that her focus on the myth of immigrant America has its limitations. In the first place, it focuses quite narrowly on a particular class of immigrant, that is, the one that consents out of his or her own free will to immigrate to the United States. This account, of course, obscures how almost all states are founded on an unpleasant array of non-consenting practices. Honig recognizes that American liberal democracy is founded

> not only on immigration but also on conquest (Native Americans) and slavery (the forced importation of African slave labor) and, in the postfounding era, on expansion (Hawaii, Alaska, Puerto Rico, etc.), annexation (French settlements in Illinois, St. Louis, and New Orleans as well as a significant Spanish-speaking population in the South-west as a result of a war with Mexico), and more slavery. (Honig 2001, 75)

It would be unreasonable to expect anyone to address *all* these moments of (re)founding, no matter how significant they are. But Honig's noted omissions are nonetheless notable. Her focus seems to be on a contested politics of co-optation and national integration involving foreigners who *come to* America—willingly or forced, "legally" or clandestinely, admirably it doesn't matter to Honig. She problematizes this integration, unsettles it, finds emerging subjectivities and politics there. But for all her emphasis on the foreigner, Honig doesn't consider the *external* dimension to (re)founding moments. Expulsions, deportations, defections, population transfers, forced transportations, and coerced migrations are an important dimension of the constitutive relationship between political communities and foreigners. And yet Honig's focus is unidirectional. She looks at the local-global struggles of foreigners residing within a state. She does not consider the difficult struggles of those on their way out.

Unfortunately this is a significant omission on Honig's behalf, because it forecloses some important theoretical and practical considerations. In particular, by excluding from consideration the abject foreigner (the deportee, the failed asylum applicant, the overstayer, etc.), Honig sidesteps the crucial issue of sovereign power. Her unwillingness to confront the question of sovereignty is a puzzle, especially given that her concluding statement about democratic cosmopolitanism is an expression of hope that it may "stop us from rescripting [the paradoxes of foreignness] into political problematics that usually end up pitting 'us' against 'them'" (122). Given such concerns, it is surprising that Honig does not consider the particular form of us-them relationship of political communities constituted as specifically *sovereign* states. This is an important omission because with sovereignty, as Schmitt and others have observed, the relationship of self and foreigner tends to be resolved as a confrontation between self and enemy. In this context, it seems obvious that to be a foreigner, not least in the United States today, is to be an easy target of the sovereign's exceptional powers, especially in matters of inclusion and exclusion. In fact, in this globalized world, "deportation class" has become one of the fastest and cheapest ways to fly (see Peutz in this volume).

For all the ambiguity that Honig attributes to self-foreigner relationships, the lines between these identities become very sharp indeed once the question of sovereignty is provoked. The violence that is the concomitant partner to sovereignty's self-other resolution makes sovereignty an especially interesting, dangerous, and politically pressing object of critical analysis. What is Honig's assessment of this violence? How would her "democratic cosmopolitanism" resolve the problem of (re)founding in ways different from (and presumably less violent than) that of the sovereignty dynamic? Honig never confronts the issue of sovereignty and therefore has no explicit answer to these questions.

In this respect, our discussion of the changing possibilities for political agency and subjectivity would benefit from taking into account the spatial dimension of (re)founding practices. Isin emphasizes how spatial practices are key factors in the constitution of citizenship. He argues that "space is a condition of being political" and points to the various buildings (Parliament, guildhall), configurations (forum, plaza), and arrangements (assembly) that are spatial expressions of citizenship (Isin 2002, 45). In a similar fashion, we need to discern the spatial practices of abjection and their relationship to political practice (Walters 2002a). What buildings, configurations, and arrangements are the spatial expressions of the foreigner without legal status? At the limit, there is the airport "waiting area," the immigration detention facilities, the deportation flight. These are the *mezzanine spaces of sovereignty*—that is, the spaces that are in between the inside and the outside of the state. A common question arises from sites as diverse as the sanctuaries of the sans-papiers in France, the rioting refugees in the detention camps of Australia, and the nonstatus Algerians organizing against deportations in Montreal: what are the implications that arise from the political becoming of the abject? If these foreigners demonstrate a taking-subjectivity, then their abject cosmopolitanism constitutes a difficult moment for the state. Through an impossible activism—"impossible" because the nonstatus do not possess the "authentic" identity (i.e., citizenship) that would allow them to be political, to be activists—they make visible the violent paradoxes of sovereignty. Consequently the risks taken by the taking abject foreigner—that is, taking the risk to become a speaking agent—are risky for the sovereign account of the political as well. Not surprisingly, representatives of the sovereign order display a striking anxiety whenever the abject foreigner takes on the status of a political activist engaged in acts of self-determination (e.g., stopping their deportation).

TAKING STATUS: MONTREAL'S COMITÉ D'ACTION DES SANS-STATUT ALGERIENS

An emerging global politics is critically engaging with the politics of protection in the form of anti-deportation campaigns and immigrant regularization movements. To be sure, while governments are taking formidable measures to tighten borders and limit the right of asylum, social movements around the world are mounting political campaigns set on retaking these rights. The radical cosmopolitanism of chants such as "no one is illegal," "no borders, no nations, no deportations," and "neither here nor elsewhere" is being heard from the barrens of Australia to the cosmopolitan streets of Montreal to the activist border camps on the outskirts of Fortress Europe. Nandita Sharma (2003) describes these movements—often called "no border" movements—as having "developed an integrated politics calling for an end to displacement worldwide, the free movement of people and committed support for Indigenous struggles for traditional land and self-determination." No-border campaigns appear in various forms and take on a diverse set of tactics to suit their particular contexts and circumstances. Wherever they exist, they have not been stingy in doling out surprising and innovative forms of political action. In Australia, the policy of placing undocumented refugees and migrants under mandatory detention has been met by diverse anti-detention and anti-deportation campaigns. The militancy of some of the detained asylum seekers has inspired some audacious tactics, including the creation of sanctuary zones and mass convergences on the detention centers of Woomera and Baxter. In Europe an extremely well-developed no-borders movement has seen some notable successes. For example, detention centers such as the Via Corelli in Milan and Campsfield House in England have been successfully shut down. A well-developed tactic of targeting private companies that profit from the detention and deportation industries, such as Codex (catering) and Lufthansa (airline), has similarly proved to be quite effective in both raising public awareness and, in some cases, stopping deportations. Finally, not satisfied with a nationally or regionally based campaign, activists have gone global by taking on the International Organization for Migration for its role in the international management of migration (Hayter 2000; Stevens 2001).

A number of questions animate the debates within these campaigns. Should advocates relate to nonstatus immigrants as clients or as allies? Should they speak on behalf of the nonstatus or in conversation with them? Do radical actions help or hinder the cause of refugees and migrants with precarious legal status? More to the point, what place is there for abject migrants in the politics of their own liberation? Are refugees and migrants from the global South simply victims of neoliberal globalizations, or can they be protagonists in shaping the process of contemporary local-global transformations? These are difficult questions, but ones that campaigns for refugee and migrant rights everywhere must ultimately confront. There are, of course, no simple answers to these questions, as considerations of place and context matter. In France, for example, much of the energy in immigrant rights campaigns has come from the undocumented themselves, as demonstrated by the massive intervention the sans-papiers movement has made into public life. In Germany, the caravan movement has made concerted efforts to create enduring links between activist and migrant groups. During the 1998 elections, for example, caravans of refugees, migrants, and their allies traveled to forty-four German cities, organizing meetings and forums to allow noncitizens to express themselves politically. When the city of Köln hosted the EU and G7 summits in June 1999, the Caravan Hunger Strike was organized with the slogan "We are here because you destroy our countries." The massive Refugee Congress held in Jena in April 2000 is widely regarded as an important moment of solidarity politics. In Italy a series of massive rallies held by self-organized migrants ensured that the question of migration would take a central place when the European Social Forum met in Florence in November 2002. Refugees and migrants proved to be effective players at this level of "global civil society," organizing a highly successful Migrants European Assembly.

The situation facing refugee and migrant rights activists in Canada, as elsewhere, is immensely complicated by recent internal and external securitizations of migration and refugees issues. Key developments in this regard include the adoption of a "Smart Border" (smart, so-called) initiative between Canada and the United States, which includes measures such as information sharing, visa policy coordination, the prescreening of refugee claimants by security officials, and enhanced powers to interdict, detain, and deport undocumented arrivals and failed asylum seekers (Salter 2004). Perhaps the most significant component of this initiative is the Safe Third Country Agreement, which was signed by Canada and the United States on December 5, 2002. This agreement stipulates that, with certain exceptions, asylum seekers who seek Canada's protection at the U.S.-Canada border will be denied the right to make a claim in Canada. Instead they will be sent back to pursue a claim in the United States. On both sides of the border, refugee advocates and human rights NGOs criticize this agreement on the grounds that it increases the risks for asylum seekers and provides less protection for refugees. The Canadian Council of Refugees (CCR) has repeatedly pointed to evidence indicating that the United States is not a particularly "safe" country for asylum seekers. For example, asylum seekers returned to the United States will be subjected to that country's system of detaining refugee claimants, often among general prison populations, and expediting their removal and deportation.[4] To be sure, even the Canadian government seems to recognize this: it issued a travel advisory in fall 2002 warning foreign-born residents about the risks of traveling to the United States.

In addition to the statements of concern and the political lobbying by NGOS such as the CCR and Amnesty International, there have also been some more radical social responses. In October 2002 a coalition of faith groups responded to the state's restrictions on protection with a call to revive a sanctuary movement in Canada and create an underground railroad, despite the considerable risks and severe penalties.[5] Similarly, antiracist and antiglobalization activists in major Canadian cities are increasingly involved in local-global campaigns to defend refugee and migrant rights. For example, Montreal, Toronto, and Vancouver each host an activist group named No One Is Illegal. These groups and others have organized campaigns to stop the deportation and detention of nonstatus migrants. Major, nationally coordinated protest marches have been organized, including one in June 2005 that saw hundreds of nonstatus people and their allies make a weeklong march from Montreal to Ottawa to present their demands to Parliament.

The campaign to stop the deportations of the nonstatus Algerians living in Montreal is worth examining in some detail. The activism of Montreal's CASS is interesting as a case for considering the limits and possibilities associated with Honig's conception of democratic cosmopolitanism. The CASS is composed of people who are most directly affected by the exclusionary practices of the Canadian state. As with the sans-papiers in France, the nonstatus refugees have themselves taken the lead in the campaign to stop their deportations and regularize their status in Canada and Quebec. The majority of the nonstatus Algerians arrived in Canada as refugees seeking asylum. All were fleeing the violence and conflict that has pitted armed Islamist groups and a corrupt military regime against one another since elections were suspended and a state of emergency was instated in 1992. The conflict in Algeria has taken a disastrous toll on the population: over 150,000 dead, 12,000 disappeared, a million displaced, and a civilian population harassed by regular kidnappings, summary executions, and violent repression. Of the Algerians who managed to reach Canada, some were granted refugee status; many were not. While the individualistic bias of the Canadian refugee-determination process separates "genuine" and "nongenuine" refugees, the Canadian government nonetheless deemed the situation in Algeria to be so dangerous that on March 3, 1997, a moratorium was instated prohibiting all deportations to that country. Many of the failed asylum seekers—now so-called nonstatus persons—noted the irony of the situation: "It's ironic that you can be refused as refugees but you can't be sent back to your own country because you'll be persecuted" (quoted in Virk 2002).

In February 2002, Amnesty International released a report stating that there had been no substantial change in the political or human rights situation in Algeria since 1999.

> Human rights violations in Algeria have become institutionalized. In the last year alone, more than 80 civilians were unlawfully killed by security forces and dozens more tortured or held for varying periods of time in secret detention. Some 200 people continue to die every month as a result of the continuing decade-long armed conflict. The level of killing has remained largely unchanged since early 1999. Many of those are civilians, including women and children, killed in targeted and indiscriminate attacks by armed groups.[6]

Recognizing the ongoing danger to human life in Algeria, the Department of Foreign Affairs issued a travel advisory stating that "Canadians should defer all tourist travel to Algeria." However, only one day later, on April 5, 2002, the minister of immigration lifted the moratorium on deportations to Algeria. Approximately 1,069 Algerians whose refugee claims had been denied would be sent back to a country deemed too dangerous for Canadian tourists.

The reaction of the nonstatus Algerian community in Montreal has been to fight the government's policy reversal. The CASS, along with allied groups such as No One Is Illegal, mounted a vigorous campaign to raise public awareness about their situation and to organize an effective political and legal response. Their demands to the Canadian and Quebec governments were for (1) an immediate end to all deportations, (2) a return to the moratorium on removals to Algeria, and (3) the regularization of nonstatus Algerian residents in Canada.[7] The CASS employed a wide array of actions and strategies to push this agenda into the public realm, many of which are more in line with the radical tactics of antiglobalization protesters than with the conventional legal avenues taken by human rights NGOs. In addition to the legal approach, the actions organized by the CASS have included regular assemblies to mobilize directly affected Algerians; weekly information pickets outside the offices of Citizenship and Immigration Canada; unannounced delegation visits, large and small, to these offices; regular public demonstrations and marches, at times with over a thousand participants; leafleting against deportations at airports, drawing attention to the private carriers that profit from carrying out state deportations; and creating a solidarity network with a diverse group of supporters and allies in Montreal, across Canada, and around the world.

On one level, these actions have added weight to the demand to stop the deportations and to regularize the status of members of the nonstatus Algerian community. On another level, the significance of these measures exceeds their tactical utility and raises some fundamental questions about the changing possibilities for political subjectivity and agency. Do the nonstatus activists possess a taking-subjectivity, as understood by Honig? To better answer this question, I will briefly examine two particular tactics employed by members of the CASS: (1) delegation visits to immigration offices and (2) sanctuary. These tactics have been proven to be important for how they disrupt the administration, the routines, and, above all, the "normality" of deportations. They are also significant, however, as a form of taking-politics: delegations visits allow the nonstatus, those who have "no part," to assert their political voice; the creation of sanctuary zones similarly allows for a recasting of political space. Understood together, these tactical measures are crucial for the possibilities of an abject cosmopolitan political agency.

Taking Speech

The CASS organized a number of delegation visits to immigration offices beginning in summer 2002. There are a number of advantages to these kinds of visits. An occupation by nonstatus people disrupts the normality of office affairs; they bring their own personal "states of emergency" directly to the state apparatus. Direct-action tactics work best when they organize around existing weaknesses and vulnerabilities in the system. Canadian immigration offices in particular do not tolerate disruption well, as they operate in the context of a massive backlog of casework.[8] Since these offices cannot afford to be upset, a well-coordinated disruption can create considerable pressure for officials to submit to the request of a meeting with management or political officials. These meetings usually include forcing officials to read the individual case files and hear the testimonies of the refugee claimants. This is the other key advantage of delegation visits: they allow for face-to-face encounters with state officials invested with enormous powers of discretion. As one member of CASS complained, "We are treated as file numbers, not as human beings" (quoted in Papadopoulos 2002). Once the compelling individual stories behind these numbers are completed, it is not unusual for immigration staff to be moved to tears (Montgomery 2002a).

But will they be moved enough to change their minds about a deportation order? The dynamics of delegation visits are revealing in this respect, as they demonstrate the ongoing struggle of the nonstatus in being recognized and heard as political actors. In an account of an unannounced visit to the offices of Immigration Canada made by members of the CASS's Women's Committee and their children, Nacera Kellou describes the intense unwillingness of the government officials to speak with the nonstatus Algerians.[9] She also describes the panic these officials showed when they realized that other nonstatus refugees and immigrants in the waiting room of the immigration offices could *see* and *hear* the CASS demonstration.

> They were hard headed. They were telling us, "Give us your letter and we will get back to you." They didn't want to speak to us all at once. They were saying, "This is not the way things are done in Canada. We don't do it this way." . . . The Immigration officials—they wanted us to provide the good respectful

image: that we'd come in, and we'd go upstairs, and we'd sit down, and we'd wait, and we'd talk to them like things are normal. But things aren't normal! This was panic, and we acted in such a way. We occupied all the rooms to show that this was a serious situation. They didn't want the other people [i.e., other nonstatus refugees] in the waiting room to see us because this would dirty up their image. This would take away from their image of their administrative life, of things being done normally. This would ruin that. So that's how we approached it. (Lowry and Nyers 2003, 69–70)

Clearly, Kellou's account demonstrates that immigration officials were interlocutors in "a determined kind of speech situation," one in which they simultaneously understood and did not understand what the other (i.e., the nonstatus Algerian) was saying (Rancière 1999, x). From the outset, the prior expectation of docility and patience on the part of refugees (i.e., they should wait to be called on) was shattered. They were instead faced with a loud, assertive group of nonstatus people who were unwilling to be separated as (speaking) "leaders" and (silent) "followers." The audacity of such tactics threatens to subvert the entire framework of "authoritative citizen" versus "passive refugee." In this context, the significance of immigration officials moving asylum seekers and other nonstatus people out of the ministry's waiting room is revealed: the dominant order of speaking beings cannot tolerate the sight or sounds of noncitizens acting as political agents. Consequently this activism must be hidden from other nonstatus people lest they follow the example of the CASS.

Taking Space

By October 2002 the Canadian government had deported thirty-two Algerians. At the same time, the Stop the Deportations campaign found a rallying point in the case of the Bourouisa family: Mourad, Yakout, and their two-year-old Canadian-born son, Ahmed. This "good" immigrant family captivated the media. The Bourouisa family spoke excellent French, had never been on welfare, and had worked throughout their lengthy stay in Canada. To all appearances, they were the "model" immigrant family employed by nation-states to (re)found their distinctiveness, their "choiceworthiness." And yet the family was facing a type of Catch-22 situation that is so typical of the nonstatus experience. Shortly after Mourad received his Canadian work permit in September 2002—nonstatus refugees and immigrants have to make the $150 application every year—the Bourouisa family received a deportation order. Their hopes were raised, however, when they received word that the Quebec government had scheduled an immigration interview for them in New York City. But this appointment was set for two weeks *after* their scheduled deportation. To add to this absurd situation, the Bourouisa family could not attend their immigration interview because the Canadian government was in possession of their passports, and because the Bourouisas were Algerian nationals, it was unlikely that the U.S. government would issue them travel visas. Faced with a deportation date of October 20, 2002, the family chose to accept the Union United Church's offer of protection instead and began an eleven-day period of sanctuary there.

The taking of sanctuary has a long history and is rooted in the idea of a "sacred space" of protection, free from governmental power (Lippert 2005). In North America, a well-developed sanctuary movement emerged in the 1980s to provide asylum and protection to Central American refugees. Informed by a theology that held to a radical expansion of the definition of "sin" to include social and economic injustices—not just individual transgressions—these faith activists understood the Gospel as one of earthly salvation, as a kind of higher politics. This appeal to a non-territorial and universalistic "higher politics" constitutes an important challenge to an order that already claims to have resolved the relationship between universality and particularity through the principle of territorial state sovereignty (Walker 1993). Indeed, the whole idea of sanctuary as a kind of "sacred space"—or, if one secularizes the concept, a "liberated zone"—presents a challenge to the principle of state sovereignty. In the context of deportations, Walters suggests that the taking of sanctuary guarantees that deportation will no longer be a routine administrative process. Rather, it ensures that the deportation act is revealed as a site where sovereignty is performed: "either the state negotiating with the subjects of deportation (and thereby recognizing them *as* subjects), or the state as armed bodies of men smashing down church doors, seizing, arresting, pacifying, terrifying, removing bodies in full display of the public" (Walters 2002a, 257). In the fall of 2002, after several years of dealing with the sans-papiers' strategy of sanctuary, authorities in France chose the latter option, forcibly evicting over seventy Iraqi and Kurdish asylum seekers from a Catholic church in November 2002. In Canada, the political pressure created by the existence of a sanctuary space in Montreal was still relatively novel. The visible and audible presence of noncitizen political subjects was therefore successful in forcing the Canadian and Quebec governments to make some important concessions, at least in the short term.

SOVEREIGN (RE)TAKINGS

On October 30, 2002, the federal and Quebec immigration ministers responded to what they called "an extraordinary situation"—the appearance of a sanctuary space in Montreal, but more generally the political activism on noncitizens—and announced the Joint Procedures for the Processing of the Applications of Certain Algerian Nationals. "For humanitarian reasons, you no longer have to leave Canada," said the federal minister, conveniently choosing to ignore the political pressure created by the nonstatus activists and their allies. The major government concession was to allow nonstatus Algerians to make in-land applications for permanent residence in Canada. Since the length of the application procedure was three months, in the short term this amounted to a victory: a ninety-day reprieve on deportations would apply to all nonstatus Algerians who made the application.

While taking this as an important achievement, the CASS nonetheless recognized the limitations and indeed the trappings of this concession. In the first place, the Joint Procedures reaffirmed the sovereign's ability to decide upon the exception by excluding a number of categories of nonstatus people of Algerian origin: for example, those who live outside Quebec; those who have a criminal record, however minor; those who have already received deportation orders or have been deported; and those who cannot afford to pay the expensive application fees ($550 per adult, $150 per child). For the 174 nonstatus Algerians who went underground or left Canada—and soon had warrants issued for their arrest—the Joint Procedures were obviously an inadequate response. Indeed, the Joint Procedures actually serve as a self-fulfilling prophecy in this respect. By forcing certain segments of the nonstatus Algerian population to go underground, the Joint Procedures re-create the supposed "problem" of "illegal" migration, false documentation, human smuggling, et cetera, and thereby reaffirm (to politicians and security professionals, at least) the importance of securitizing this sector.

Sovereign power reasserted itself through the Joint Procedures in a number of ways. Most significantly, however, it did so by treating the nonstatus Algerians as potential immigrants, not as refugees. In doing so, the Joint Procedures do more than just ignore the dangers of returning to Algeria. They also reject the way in which the CASS had been formulating its politics as a politics of self-identified refugees. While the members of the CASS forced the government to recognize them as speaking political agents, they failed in being recognized as political agents speaking *as* refugees. Under the Joint Procedures, the nonstatus Algerian becomes an applicant for permanent residency: an "immigrant." A CASS member describes the importance of framing their struggle as a politics of protection, not immigration: "We don't agree with this, because immigration is granted to people based on their job skills, their language skills. Should not speaking French or English mean you have less of a right not to be returned to a situation where you could be tortured and killed?" (Podur 2002). For the sovereign state, however, the category of the refugee remained as it must: speechless and agentless.

The Joint Procedures provide an important lesson for abject cosmopolitans: that radical takings can nonetheless be captured by the logic and practices of state sovereignty. This is what I call "sovereignty's retakings." Indeed, the Joint Procedures represent a dimension of sovereign power that allows itself to appear in places of absence. That abject agents sometimes make an appearance—to take space, to take voice—is, Honig says, a sign of a radical democratic politics at work. However, these radical takings can themselves become implicated in some of the traditional constitutive dualisms of modern politics (included-excluded, vocal-silent, visible-invisible). This is worrying, as sovereign power thrives off the ambiguity and the transgression of dualistic distinctions. As Slavoj Žižek has suggested in his critique of Rancière, to characterize politics in terms of the sudden intrusion of the "part of no part" as a visible, articulate, and equal member of the dominant political order misses how this order itself relies on such subversions for its own condition of being. The dominant order, Žižek says, "is never simply a positive order: to function at all, it has to cheat, to misname, and so on—*in short, to engage in politics*, to do what its subversive opponents are supposed to do" (1999, 234–35).[10] In other words, the visible and articulate defenders of order at times use strategies that obscure and misrepresent. They too have a "diversity of tactics" at their disposal. What makes sovereign power so vexing is its capacity to find presence *in* absence. Consequently any radical politics needs to beware of the subversive elements of sovereign power—its nondemocratic retakings.

INTERNATIONAL (RE)FOUNDINGS

When the immigration minister refers to Canadian border policy as "not based on building walls but on controlling doors," we know that the border is no longer only about the ramparts, fortifications, and barricades that separate an inside from an outside. They also involve the employ-ment of complicated technologies that are designed to absorb, control, and manage flows and movements as much as repel them. Consequently, like all borders, the Canadian one is "polysemic" in the sense that it does not have the same meaning for everyone, and the experience of the bor-der varies quite dramatically according to race, gender, class, and national origin (Balibar 2002). According to Barry Hindess (1998), one of the con-stitutive effects of citizenship is to divide and allocate the global human population into smaller subpopulations of territorial states. It is a normal and acceptable—not to mention quite legal—practice for states to dis-criminate on the basis of noncitizenship. National (re)foundings there-fore do not exist as an abstraction, separate from the overall system of nation-states. Consequently, while Honig emphasizes how foreignness plays an important role in national (re)founding, by ignoring sovereign-ty's retakings, she misses the important role that the deportation of for-eigners plays in *international* (re)foundings. To engage with deportation is to engage not only with practices that are constitutive of citizenship but also with practices that are constitutive of the state-centric world order.

The Canadian government's position with respect to Algeria is an ex-cellent example of how the external dimension of sovereignty is repro-duced through deportations. The lifting of the moratorium qualifies as a (re)founding moment for the international system of states in two re-spects. First, it reconfirms as uncontroversial the idea that every desig-nated national (e.g., Algerian) can be allocated to a designated territory (e.g., Algeria). From an international perspective, as Walters explains, "deportation represents the compulsory allocation of subjects of their proper sovereigns" (2002a, 282). The Canadian immigration minister con-firms this when he says, "The people we deport, there will be no prob-lem for them," adding that the suspension of elections and the declaration of a state of emergency in 1992 saved Algeria from turning into another Afghanistan (E. Thompson 2003). The immigration minister's easy efface-ment of the extremely antidemocratic and violent practices of Algerian statecraft would seem to be a contradictory stance for a representative of a democratic polity committed to the idea of universal human rights, as Canada is. But according to some of the prevailing conceptions of cosmo-politanism, deportation in and of itself does not negate the viability of a world order where, say, constitutional states and universal human rights reign. For example, Hindess notes how Kant's famous vision of cosmo-politanism recognized that a cosmopolitan world order would likely be forced upon states as both an effect of, and a reasonable solution to, the problem of interstate conflict and competition. Hindess reminds us of this dimension of cosmopolitanism to suggest that

> the often brutal and inhumane practices of contemporary democratic states show, not that the Kantian vision itself is misleading, but how far we still have to go before that vision can be realized. On this view, lack of elementary hospitality towards migrants would be seen as a feature of the modern world that will be overcome as poor, weak, or undemocratic states become wealthier, stronger and more democratic—that is, as their own citizens have less reason to flee and other states have more reason to treat these citizens with respect. (Hindess 1998, 62)

Following this logic, as an important condition for Algeria to be recognized as a full partner in the international community of states, deportations of nonstatus Algerians must take place. We can read such rationales in the immigration minister's assessment of Algeria: "There is a future for Algeria. There is an improvement in human rights. There is an improvement with the reforms they want to bring forward." This, surely, is an abject cosmopolitanism of the worst sort.

The return to deporting Algerian nationals back to Algeria counts as a moment of international (re)founding in a second sense. Canadian border policies reference, among other things, a neoliberal economic world order and so count toward the (re)founding of the international political economy. Since 1992 most Western media attention on Algeria has focused on the violence and the human rights abuses resulting from the civil war. However, during that time the country has also adopted a more globalized neoliberal state structure in the course of implementing IMF structural adjustment policies. Algeria is now Canada's primary economic partner in Africa and the Middle East, with an annual commercial trade valued at $2 billion. The privatization of public services in Algeria has resulted in a Canadian company, SNC-Lavallin, being awarded a $141 million water contract in April 2002 (Montgomery 2002b). In January 2003 the company received another water contract in Algeria, this one valued at $96 million. These developments have not been lost on the nonstatus Algerians in Canada: "We are sacrificed for money," says one (quoted in Papadopoulos 2002). The timing of the lifting of the moratorium coincided within days of the Canadian prime minister's trade mission to Algeria, suggesting that when countries successfully enter the international economic order, the deportation of nationals from that country will be part of recognizing and normalizing relations. In short, an important condition for Algeria to be "regularized" as a proper member of the international community of states—or, more to the point in this case, the international economic order—is that Algeria be deemed an appropriate place to which its nonstatus citizens abroad may be deported.

CONCLUSION: COSMOPOLITANISMS NOW

Cosmopolitanism encourages us to look up, toward a future, beyond the horizon of possible existence.[11] But horizons recede as quickly as they are approached, and many refugees and abject migrants have run out of time and patience. Abject cosmopolitanism does not aim for a higher ground so much as burrow into the apparatuses and technologies of exclusion to disrupt the administrative routines, the day-to-day perceptions and constructions of normality. The abject put the question of the speaking subject front and center, into the limelight of critical scrutiny, and as an object of radical retaking. They provoke fundamental questions about politics: Who speaks? Who counts? Who belongs? Who can express themselves politically? In short, who can be political? When speechless victims begin to speak about the politics of protection, they put the political under question. This is what makes "No one is illegal" such a radical proclamation. Our received traditions of the political *require* that some human beings be "illegal." To say that no human is illegal is to call into question the entire architecture of sovereignty, all its borders, locks and doors, and internal hierarchies.

My aim here has been to assess anti-deportation campaigns for how they intervene in the politics of protection. While I have noted the limitations of such actions, the way the nonstatus activists of the CASS took political speech through delegation visits and (re)politicized public space through sanctuary makes them excellent candidates for the status of democratic cosmopolitans. Recalling Honig's criteria, the CASS have "widened the resources and energies" of activism within Montreal and beyond. They have struggled to be democratic. Their politics favor the "denationalization of the state," in the sense of organizing both to stop their own deportations and to regularize the status of all nonstatus persons in Canada. In the public campaign to stop deportations, the CASS has broken through the nervous subjectivities of citizens anxious about supposed correlations between abject migration and insecure polities. The CASS convinced large parts of the population of the city of Montreal, the province of Quebec, and the rest of Canada (and elsewhere) that they were not threats, and that they were refugees who needed protection, despite what immigration officials said. Further, the public acts of citizenship of these abject non-citizens came to represent a troubling anomaly to the sovereign order, one that ultimately forced a response from the Canadian and Quebec governments. The end result was that over 95 percent of the nonstatus Algerians had their status regularized in Canada.

The activism of nonstatus immigrants and refugees is re-creating citizenship in ways that demands recognition and support, not criminalization and securitization. In this regard, the CASS is among a growing population of the displaced that is reinvigorating democratic politics today. But the challenge to do both simultaneously—to be a refugee, to be political—is considerable. The CASS found that while they received recognition by the Canadian and Quebec governments, they were unsuccessful in defining the conditions of this recognition. The radical takings of foreigners are always at risk of being deflected and absorbed by the nondemocratic re-takings of sovereign power for the purposes of national and international (re)foundings.

NOTES

An earlier version of this chapter appeared in *Third World Quarterly* 24, no. 6 (December 2003): 1069–93.

1. It is important to emphasize that the trend toward framing refugee policies within a security framework preexisted the attacks of September 11, 2001. See Whitaker 2002; Huysmans 1995; Wacquant 1999.

2. Office of the Minister of Citizenship and Immigration, "Census Release Confirms Immigration's Important Role in Canada's Future," news release, January 21, 2003.

3. This focus on consent and nonconsent becomes further problematic once we note the ambiguous position the state takes on the issue. As Honig notes: "Illegal migration is not only combated by the state; it is also simultaneously enabled, covertly courted, often managed, and certainly tolerated by it. Established citizens profit from the subsidies that cheap migrant labor provides to their child-care costs and food prices" (97). I discuss Honig's ambivalence regarding the state hereafter.

4. Canadian Council for Refugees, "Refugee Claimants Sent Back to Detention in U.S.," media release, January 31, 2003.

5. Southern Ontario Sanctuary Coalition, "A Declaration: A Civil Initiative to Protect Refugees," mimeo, October 7, 2002. In author's possession.

6. Amnesty International, "Algeria: Ten Years of State of Emergency, Ten Years of Grave Human Rights Abuses," February 8, 2002. This assessment is reconfirmed in a briefing in December 2002 to European decision makers,

published as *Algeria: Asylum-Seekers Fleeing a Continuing Human Rights Crisis* (AI Index: MDE 28/007/2003).

7. Significantly, this last demand was changed in the fall of 2002 to the much more radical call for the regularization of *all* nonstatus residents in Canada.

8. For example, at the end of 2002, the Immigration and Refugee Board had a record 52,761 cases in the pipeline, despite a significant drop in the number of refugee claims.

9. One particular concern within the CASS was the opportunities for women to become actively involved. In September 2000, the Women's Committee of the CASS was organized to address this concern. To date, they have organized some of the most successful demonstrations and delegation visits. Madjiguène Cissé, a prominent activist within the sans-papiers movement in France, speaks of the challenges of sexism within nonstatus movements in a way that resonates powerfully with the situation in Montreal. See Freedman and Tarr 2000.

10. Isin offers an important caveat to Žižek's assessment, indicating that Žižek himself might be contributing to the depoliticization of becoming political: "While Žižek is right to recognize that becoming political is that moment of questioning the part that a being occupies in social space and is not simply an interruption by those beings who have no part, he depoliticizes those acts of becoming political by restricting the political to those 'revolutionary' actions that seek universal restructuring. This restriction of the properly political to acts of a 'revolutionary' character is itself a political strategy" (2002, 277).

11. For a critique of the vertical trajectories of postsovereign politics, see Walker 2002.

References

Abele, Robert. 2005. *A User's Guide to the USA Patriot Act and Beyond.* Lanham, Md.: University Press of America.

Abraham, Nabeel. 1994. "Anti-Arab Racism and Violence in the United States." In *The Development of Arab-American Identity*, ed. Ernest M. Carus, 155–214. Ann Arbor: University of Michigan Press.

Abramsky, Sasha. 2008. "Gimme Shelter." *Nation*, February 25.

Achermann, Christin. 2003. "Krankenversicherung für Sans-Papiers: Die aktuelle Situation in Recht und Praxis." *Asyl: Schweizerische Zeitschrift für Asylrecht und Praxis* 3:8–11.

Acuña, Rodolfo. 1988. *Occupied America: A History of Chicanos.* 3rd ed. New York: Harper and Row.

Adalah. 2001. "Summary of the Report to the Israeli Commission of Inquiry on the October 2000 Events, Shafa 'Amr, 21 January 2001 (Excerpts)." *Journal of Palestine Studies* 30:166–71.

Adout, Rami. 2007. "Trafficked Women and Political Asylum Seekers." In *Transnational Migration to Israel in Global Comparative Context*, ed. Sarah S. Willen, 139–56. Lanham, Md.: Lexington Books.

Agamben, Giorgio. 1991/2000. "Sovereign Police." In *Means without End: Notes on Politics*, trans. Vincenzo Binetti and Cesare Casarino. Minneapolis: University of Minnesota Press.

———. 1993/2000. "Beyond Human Rights." In *Means without End: Notes on Politics*, trans. Vincenzo Binetti and Cesare Casarino, 15–27. Minneapolis: University of Minnesota Press.

———. 1995/1998. *Homo Sacer: Sovereign Power and Bare Life*, trans. Daniel Heller-Roazen. Stanford, Calif.: Stanford University Press.

———. 1996/2000. *Means without End: Notes on Politics*, trans. Vincenzo Binetti and Cesare Casarino. Minneapolis: University of Minnesota Press.

———. 2003/2005. *State of Exception*, trans. Kevin Attell. Chicago: University of Chicago Press.

Agnew, John A. 1994. "The Territorial Trap: The Geographical Assumptions of International Relations Theory." *Review of International Political Economy* 1 (1): 53–80.

Ahmad, Aijaz. 2004. *Iraq, Afghanistan, and the Imperialism of Our Time*. New Delhi: LeftWord Books.

Ahmad, Ali Jimale, ed. 1995. *The Invention of Somalia*. Lawrenceville, N.J.: Red Sea Press.

Ahmed, Ismail I. 2002. "Remittances and Their Economic Impact in Post-war Somaliland." *Disasters* 24 (4): 380–89.

Al-Haj, Majid. 2005. "Whither the Green Line? Trends in the Orientation of the Palestinians in Israel and the Territories." *Israel Affairs* 11:183–206.

Al Muraikhi, Khalil M. 1991. *Glimpses of Bahrain from Its Past*. Manama, Bahrain: Government Press, Ministry of Information.

Alexander, Michael. 2007. "Local Migrant Policies in a Guestworker Regime: The Case of Tel Aviv." In *Transnational Migration to Israel in Global Comparative Context*, ed. Sarah S. Willen, 73–86. Lanham, Md.: Lexington.

Allday, Erin, Jim Zamora, and Steve Rubenstein. 2006. "Immigrants, Labor Walk on Common Ground." *New York Times*, September 5.

Allen, John W. 1926/1967. "Jean Bodin." In *The Social and Political Ideas of Some Great Thinkers of the Sixteenth and Seventeenth Centuries: A Series of Lectures Delivered at King's College, University of London, during the Session 1925–26*, ed. F. J. C. Hearnshaw, 42–62. New York: Barnes and Noble.

Althusser, Louis. 1971. "Ideology and Ideological State Apparatuses (Notes towards an Investigation)." In *Lenin and Philosophy and Other Essays*, by Louis Althusser, 127–86. New York: Monthly Review Press.

Amador, Lucero. 2002. "Otorgan asilo político a activista." *La Opinión*, July 11. http://www.laopinion.com (accessed December 6, 2006).

Amnesty International. 2004. *Libya: Time to Make Human Rights a Reality*. AI index MDE 19/002/2004. http://web.amnesty.org/en/library/info/MDE19/007/2004.

———. 2005. *Italy: Temporary Stay—Permanent Rights: The Treatment of Foreign Nationals Detained in "Temporary Stay and Assistance Centres."* http://web.amnesty.org/en/library/info/EUR30/004/2005.

———. 2006. "Rendition and Secret Detention: A Global System of Human Rights Violations—Questions and Answers." http://web.amnesty.org/en/library/info/POL30/003/2006 (accessed November 6, 2006).

Anderson, Benedict. 1983/1991. *Imagined Communities: Reflections on the Origins and Spread of Nationalism*. Rev. ed. New York: Verso.

———. 1994. "Exodus." *Critical Inquiry* 20:314–27.

Andreas, Peter. 2001. *Border Games: Policing the U.S.-Mexico Divide*. Ithaca, N.Y.: Cornell University Press.

Andreas, Peter, and Timothy Snyder, eds. 2000. *The Wall around the West: State Borders and Immigration Controls in North America and Europe*. Lanham, Md.: Rowman and Littlefield.

Andrijasevic, Rutvica. 2003. "The Difference Borders Make: (Il)legality, Migration, and Trafficking in Italy among 'Eastern' European Women in Prostitution." In *Uprootings/Regroundings: Questions of Home and Migration*, ed.

Sara Ahmed, Claudia Castañeda, Anne-Marie Fortier, and Mimi Sheller, 251–72. New York: Berg.

———. 2004. "I confini fanno la differenza: (Il)legalità migrazione e tratta in Italia dall'Est europeo." *Studi Culturali* 1 (1): 59–82.

———. 2006. *How to Balance Rights and Responsibilities on Asylum at the EU's External Border of Italy and Libya*. Centre on Migration, Policy, and Society, University of Oxford, WP-06–27. http://www.compas.ox.ac.uk/publications/working-papers/wp-06–27.

———. 2007. "Beautiful Dead Bodies: Gender, Migration, and Representation in Anti-trafficking Campaigns." *Feminist Review* 86:24–44.

Anteby-Yemini, Lisa. 2008. "Migrations africaines et nouveaux enjeux de la frontière israélo-égyptienne." *Cultures & Conflits* 72 (winter).

Appadurai, Arjun. 1996. *Modernity at Large: Cultural Dimensions of Globalization*. Minneapolis: University of Minnesota Press.

Arango, Joaquín, and Maia Jachimowicz. 2005. "Regularization and Immigration Policy Reform in Spain." In *Amnesty for Illegal Migrants*, ed. Friedrich Heckmann and Tanja Wunderlich, 79–88. Bamberg: European Forum for Migration Studies.

Arendt, Hannah. 1951/1966. *The Origins of Totalitarianism*. New York: Harcourt, Brace and World.

———. 1954/1968. "What Is Freedom?" In *Between Past and Future: Eight Exercises in Political Thought*, by Hannah Arendt, 143–71. New York: Viking.

———. 1958/1998. *The Human Condition*. 2nd ed. Chicago: University of Chicago Press.

———. 1959/1968. "On Humanity in Dark Times: Thoughts about Lessing." In *Men in Dark Times*, by Hannah Arendt, 3–31. New York: Harcourt, Brace and World.

———. 1994. "We Refugees." In *Altogether Elsewhere: Writers on Exile*, ed. Marc Robinson, 110–19. Boston and London: Faber and Faber.

Aretxaga, Begoña. 2003. "Maddening States." *Annual Review of Anthropology* 32:393–410.

Askola, Heli. 2007. "Violence against Women, Trafficking, and Migration in the EU." *European Law Journal* 13 (2): 204–17.

Association for Civil Rights in Israel, Adalah, and the Arab Association for Human Rights. 2001. "Report on the October 2000 Violence against Arab Citizens of Israel, 7 January 2001." *Journal of Palestine Studies* 30:164–66.

Azhar, Muhammad. 1999. "Indo-Bahrain Economic Relations in the Nineties." In *India, Bahrain, and Qatar: Political, Economic, and Strategic Dimensions*, ed. Aftab Kamal Pasha. Delhi: Gyan Sugar Publications.

Baby, Soman. 2006a. "Kidnap Ordeal Stuns Officials." *Gulf Daily News*, March 2.

———. 2006b. "Sponsorship System to Be Scrapped." *Gulf Daily News*, May 4.

Bach, Amy. 2001. "Deported . . . Disappeared?" *Nation*, December 24.

Bales, Kevin. 2004. *Disposable People: New Slavery in the Global Economy*. Berkeley: University of California Press.

——. 2005. *Understanding Global Slavery: A Reader*. Berkeley: University of California Press.

Balibar, Étienne. 1991a. "*Es Gibt Keinen Staat in Europa*: Racism and Politics in Europe Today." *New Left Review* 186:5–19.

——. 1991b. "Is There a 'Neo-Racism'?" In *Race, Nation, Class: Ambiguous Identities*, by Étienne Balibar and Immanuel Wallerstein, 17–28. New York: Verso.

——. 1991c. "Racism and Nationalism." In *Race, Nation, Class: Ambiguous Identities*, by Étienne Balibar and Immanuel Wallerstein, 37–67. New York: Verso.

——. 1998. "Propositions sur la citoyenneté." In *Citoyenneté et les changements de structures sociale et nationale de la population française*, ed. Catherine Wihtol de Wenden. Nouvelle encyclopédie des sciences et des techniques, 221–34. Paris: Édilig-Fondation Diderot–La Nouvelle Encyclopédie.

——. 2001/2004. *We, the People of Europe? Reflections on Transnational Citizenship*. Princeton, N.J.: Princeton University Press.

——. 2002. *Politics and the Other Scene*. London: Verso.

——. 2003. "Europe, An 'Unimagined' Frontier of Democracy." *Diacritics* 33 (3–4): 36–44.

——. 2004. "Europe as Borderland." Alexander von Humboldt Lecture in Human Geography, University of Nijmegen, Netherlands, November 10, 2004. http://socgeo.ruhusting.nl/colloquium/Europe%20as%20Borderland .pdf.

——. 2007. "Il diritto al territorio." In *Europa di confine: Trasformazioni della cittadinanza nell'Unione allargata*, ed. Enrica Rigo, 7–31. Rome: Meltemi.

Barnett, Anthony, and Matthew Brace. 2002. "Voice Experts to Root Out False Asylum Claims." *Guardian*, May 5.

Barry, Andrew, Thomas Osborne, and Nikolas Rose, eds. 1996. *Foucault and Political Reason: Liberalism, Neo-liberalism, and Rationalities of Government*. London: UCL Press.

Bar-Tal, Daniel, and Yona Teichman. 2005. *Stereotypes and Prejudices in Conflict: Representations of Arabs in Israeli-Jewish Society*. Cambridge: Cambridge University Press.

Bartram, David V. 1998. "Foreign Workers in Israel: History and Theory." *International Migration Review* 32:303–25.

Bauböck, Rainer. 1994a. *From Aliens to Citizens: Redefining the Status of Immigrants in Europe*. Brookfield, Vt.: Avebury.

——. 1994b. *Transnational Citizenship: Membership and Rights in International Migration*. Brookfield, Vt.: E. Elgar.

——. 2003. "Multilevel Citizenship and Territorial Borders in the EU Polity." Working Paper. Vienna: Österreichische Akademie Wissenschaften.

Beccaria, Cesare. 1963. *On Crimes and Punishments*. Indianapolis: Bobbs-Merrill.

Beck, Ulrich, and Edgar Grande. 2004. *Das kosmopolitische Europa*. Frankfurt am Main: Suhrkamp.

Bejar, Rafael Guido. 1998. "El Salvador de posguerra: Formas de violencia en la transición." In *Violencia en una sociedad en transición*, ed. Renos Papadopoulos et al., 96–105. San Salvador: Programa de las Naciones Unidas para el Desarrollo (PNUD).

Bell, Nicholas. 2002. "Der bittere Geschmack von unserem Obst und Gemüse." *Forum Wissenschaft* 4.

Bell, Shannon. 2000. "Abject Class." Paper presented at the conference "The Party's Not Over: Marxism 2000," University of Massachusetts, Amherst, September 21–24.

Bell-Fialkoff, Andrew. 1993. "A Brief History of Ethnic Cleansing." *Foreign Affairs*, summer, 110–21.

Ben-Dor, Anat, and Rami Adout. 2003. *Israel—a Safe Haven? Problems in the Treatment Offered by the State of Israel to Refugees and Asylum Seekers.* Physicians for Human Rights, Israel. http://phr.org.il/phr/files/articlefile_1108318126083.pdf.

Ben-Dor, Anat, and Michael Kagan. 2007. "The Refugee from My Enemy Is My Enemy: The Detention and Exclusion of Sudanese Refugees in Israel." Paper presented at Minerva Center for Human Rights Biannual Conference for Human Rights in Israel.

Benhabib, Seyla. 1999. "Citizens, Residents, and Aliens in a Changing World: Political Membership in the Global Era." *Social Research* 66 (3): 709–44.

Benjamin, Walter. 1921/1979. "Critique of Violence." In *One-Way Street and Other Writings*, 132–54. London: New Left Books.

———. 1940/1968. "Theses on the Philosophy of History." In *Illuminations: Essays and Reflections*, 253–64. New York: Schocken Books.

Benn, Aluf. 2002. "NSC: The National Priority Is a Jewish Majority and a Democracy." *Ha'aretz* (Israel), August 23.

Besteman, Catherine. 1999. *Unraveling Somalia: Race, Violence, and the Legacy of Slavery*. Philadelphia: University of Pennsylvania Press.

Bew, Geoffrey. 2006. "Fury as Worker 'Jailed' by Firm." *Gulf Daily News*, February 23.

Bhabha, Jacqueline. 1998. " 'Get Back to Where You Once Belonged': Identity, Citizenship, and Exclusion in Europe." *Human Rights Quarterly* 20 (3): 592–627.

Bigo, Didier. 2002. "Security and Immigration: Toward a Critique of the Governmentality of Unease." *Alternatives: Global, Local, Political* 27:63–92.

———. 2003. "Criminalization of 'Migrants': The Side Effect of the Will to Control the Frontiers and the Sovereign Illusion." Paper presented at the "Irregular Migration and Human Rights Conference," Centre for European Law and Integration, University of Leicester, June 2003.

———. 2006. "Globalized (In)Security: The Field and the Ban-Opticon." In *Illiberal Practices of Liberal Regimes: The (In)Security Games*, ed. Didier Bigo and Anastassia Tsoukala, 5–49. Paris: L'Harmattan.

Bigo, Didier, and Elspeth Guild. 2003. "Le visa Schengen: Expression d'une stratégie de 'police' à distance." *Cultures et Conflits*, nos. 49–50:19–33.

Bishara, Azmi. 2001. "Reflections on October 2000: A Landmark in Jewish-Arab Relations in Israel." *Journal of Palestine Studies* 30:54–67.

Black, Eric, and Lourdes Medrano Leslie. 2002. "Legality of Deporting Anyone to Somalia Is Questioned." *Minneapolis Star Tribune*, March 8.

Black, Peter R. 2001. "Review of Jan Erik Schulte, *Zwangsarbeit und Vernichtung: Das Wirtschaftsimperium der SS; Oswald Pohl und das SS-Wirtschafts-Verwaltungshauptamt, 1933–1945.*" *Holocaust and Genocide Studies* 15 (3): 487–92.

Bloch, Alice, and Liza Schuster. 2005. "At the Extremes of Exclusion: Deportation, Detention, and Dispersal." *Ethnic and Racial Studies* 28 (3): 491–512.

Bodin, Jean. 1576/1986. *Les six livres de la république*. Ed. Christiane Fremont, Marie-Dominique Couzinet, and Henri Rochet. Paris: Fayard.

Boggs, Carl. 2003. "Introduction: Empire and Globalization." In *Masters of War: Militarism and Blowback in the Era of American Empire*, ed. Carl Boggs, 1–16. New York: Routledge.

Bojadžijev, Manuela. 2008. *Die windige Internazionale: Rassismus und Kämpfe der Migration*. Münster: Westfälischis Dampfboot.

Bojadžijev, Manuela, and Isabelle Saint-Saëns. 2006. "Borders, Citizenship, War, Class: A Discussion with Étienne Balibar and Sandro Mezzadra." *New Formations* 58:10–30.

Bornstein, Avram S. 2002. *Crossing the Green Line between the West Bank and Israel*. Philadelphia: University of Pennsylvania Press.

Bosniak, Linda. 1998. "The Citizenship of Aliens." *Social Text* 56:29–35.

———. 2000. "Citizenship Denationalized." *Indiana Journal of Global Legal Studies* 7:447–509.

———. 2006. *The Citizen and the Alien: Dilemmas of Contemporary Membership*. Princeton, N.J.: Princeton University Press.

———. 2007. "Being Here: Ethical Territoriality and the Rights of Immigrants." *Theoretical Inquiries in Law* 8 (2): 389–410.

Boubakri, Hassen. 2004. "Transit Migration between Tunisia, Libya, and Sub-Saharan Africa: Study Based on Greater Tunis." Paper presented at the regional conference "Migrants in Transit Countries: Sharing Responsibility for Management and Protection," Istanbul, September 30–October 1, 2004, Strasbourg: Council of Europe, MG-RCONF (2004) 6e.

Boutang, Yann Moulier. 2007. "Europa, Autonomie der Migration, Biopolitik." In *Empire und die biopolitische Wende: Die internationale Diskussion im Anschluss an Hardt und Negri*, ed. Marianne Pieper, Thomas Atzert, Serhat Karakayali, and Vassilis Tsianos, 169–78. Frankfurt am Main: Campus Verlag.

Boutang, Yann Moulier, Jean-Pierre Garson, Roxane Silberman, and Georges Tapinos. 1986. *Economie politique des migrations clandestines de main-d'oeuvre: Comparaisons internationales et exemple français*. Paris: Publisud.

Brenner, Neil, Bob Jessop, Martin Jones, and Gordon MacLeod. 2003. "Introduction: State Space in Question." In *State/Space: A Reader*, ed. Neil Brenner,

Bob Jessop, Martin Jones, and Gordon MacLeod, 1–26. Malden, Mass.: Blackwell.

Brochmann, Grete. 1993. *Middle East Avenue: Female Migration from Sri Lanka to the Gulf.* Boulder, Colo.: Westview Press.

Brown, Wendy. 1995. *States of Injury: Power and Freedom in Late Modernity.* Princeton, N.J.: Princeton University Press.

Brubaker, William Rogers. 1989. Introduction to *Immigration and the Politics of Citizenship in Europe and North America,* ed. William Rogers Brubaker, 1–27. Lanham, Md.: University Press of America.

———. 1992. *Citizenship and Nationhood in France and Germany.* Cambridge, Mass.: Harvard University Press.

Buckingham, James Silk. 1829/1971. *Travels in Assyria, Media, and Persia.* Westmead, England: Gregg International.

Bulwa, Demian. 2005. "Muslims in Lodi Believe Mystery Man Who Spoke of Jihad Was a Federal Mole in Investigation." *San Francisco Chronicle,* August 27.

———. 2006a. "Lodi Verdict Foiled Terror Plot, Prosecutors Say." *San Francisco Chronicle,* April 27.

———. 2006b. "Two Lodi Residents Refused Entry Back into U.S." *San Francisco Chronicle,* August 26.

Burchell, Graham, Colin Gordon, and Peter Miller, eds. 1991. *The Foucault Effect: Studies in Governmentality.* Chicago: University of Chicago Press.

Burkens, Marten Cornelis. 1989. *Algemene Leerstukken van Grondrechten naar Nederlands Constitutioneel Recht.* Zwolle: W. E. J. Tjeenk Willink.

Burman, Jenny. 2006. "Absence, 'Removal,' and Everyday Life in the Diasporic City: Antidetention/Antideportation Activism in Montréal." *Space and Culture* 9 (3): 279–93.

Butler, Judith. 1993. *Bodies That Matter: On the Discursive Limits of "Sex."* New York: Routledge.

———. 1997. *The Psychic Life of Power.* Stanford: Stanford University Press.

Butler, Judith, and Gayatri Chakravorty Spivak. 2007. *Who Sings the Nation-State? Language, Politics, and Belonging.* New York: Seagull Books.

Byrne, Rosemary, Gregor Noll, and J. Jens Vedsted-Hansen, eds. 2002. *New Asylum Countries? Migration Control and Refugee Protection in an Enlarged European Union.* The Hague: Kluwer Law International.

Caestecker, Frank. 1998. "The Changing Modalities of Regulation in International Migration within Continental Europe, 1870–1940." In *Regulation of Migration: International Experiences,* ed. Anita Böcker, Kees Groenendijk, Tetty Havinga, and Paul Minderhoud, 73–98. Amsterdam: Het Spinhuis.

———. 2003. "The Transformation of Nineteenth-Century West European Expulsion Policy." In *Migration Control in the North Atlantic World: The Evolution of State Practices in Europe and the United States from the French Revolution to the Inter-war Period,* ed. Andreas Fahrmeir, Olivier Faron, and Patrick Weil, 120–37. New York: Berghahn Books.

Cainkar, Louise. 2004. "Post 9/11 Domestic Policies Affecting U.S. Arabs and Muslims: A Brief Review." *Comparative Studies of South Asia, Africa, and the Middle East* 24 (1): 245–48.

Cainkar, Louise, and Sunaina Maira. 2006. "Targeting Arab/Muslim/South Asian Americans: Criminalization and Cultural Citizenship." *Amerasia Journal* 31 (3): 1–27.

Calavita, Kitty. 1984. *U.S. Immigration Law and the Control of Labor, 1820–1924.* New York: Harcourt Brace Jovanovich.

———. 2003. "A 'Reserve Army of Delinquents': The Criminalization and Economic Punishment of Immigrants in Spain." *Punishment and Society* 5: 399–413.

Caldeira, Teresa P. R. 2000. *City of Walls: Crime, Segregation, and Citizenship in São Paulo.* Berkeley: University of California Press.

Carens, Joseph. 1995. "Aliens and Citizens: The Case for Open Borders." In *Theorizing Citizenship*, ed. Ronald Beiner, 229–54. Albany, N.Y.: SUNY Press.

Cassanelli, Lee. 1996. "Explaining the Somali Crisis." In *The Struggle for the Land in Southern Somalia: The War behind the War*, ed. Catherine Besteman and Lee Cassanelli, 13–26. London: Haan.

Castles, Stephen, and Godula Kosack. 1972. *Immigrant Workers and Class Structure in Western Europe.* London: Oxford University Press.

Castles, Stephen, and Mark J. Miller. 2003. *The Age of Migration: International Population Movement in the Modern World.* New York: Guilford Press.

Central Bureau of Statistics [CBS], Israel. 2002. *Statistical Abstract of Israel, 2001.* Jerusalem: CBS.

Challenge. 2006. "The Long Way to Ceuta and Melilla." *Challenge* 11 (April). http://www.libertysecurity.org/article862.html.

Champion, Daryl. 1999. "The Kingdom of Saudi Arabia: Elements of Instability within Stability." *Meria* 3 (4): 1–23.

Chang, Nancy. 2002. *Silencing Political Dissent: How Post–September 11 Antiterrorism Measures Threaten Our Civil Liberties.* New York: Seven Stories/Open Media.

Chavez, Leo. 1992/1998. *Shadowed Lives: Undocumented Immigrants in American Society.* 2nd ed. Belmont, Calif.: Wadsworth/Thomson Learning.

Cheah, Pheng, and Bruce Robbins, eds. 1998. *Cosmopolitics: Thinking and Feeling beyond the Nation.* Minneapolis: University of Minnesota Press.

Chimienti, Milena, Denise Efionay-Mäder, and Romaine Farquet. 2003. "La repression du travail clandestine à Genève: Application des sanctions et conséquences pour les personnes concernées." Rapport de recherche. Neuchâtel: Forum suisse pour l'étude des migrations et de la population.

Churchill, Ward. 2006. "A Not So Friendly Fascism: Political Prisons and Prisoners in the United States." *CR: The New Centennial Review* 6 (1): 1–54.

Clark, Jane Perry. 1931/1969. *Deportation of Aliens from the United States to Europe.* New York: Columbia University Press.

Clifford, James. 1992. "Traveling Cultures." In *Cultural Studies*, ed. Lawrence Grossberg, Cary Nelson, and Paula Treichler, 96–112. New York: Routledge.

————. 1994. "Diasporas." *Cultural Anthropology* 9 (3): 302–38.

————. 1998. "Mixed Feelings." In *Cosmopolitics: Thinking and Feeling beyond the Nation*, ed. Pheng Cheah and Bruce Robbins, 362–70. Minneapolis: University of Minnesota Press.

Cockburn, Alexander. 2006. "The War on Terror on the Lodi Front." *Counterpunch*. http://www.counterpunch.org (accessed May 9, 2006).

Cohen, Miriam, and Michael Hanagan. 1996. "Politics, Industrialization, and Citizenship: Unemployment Policy in England, France, and the United States, 1890–1950." In *Citizenship, Identity, and Social History*, ed. Charles Tilly, 91–130. Cambridge, Mass.: Cambridge University Press.

Cohen, Robin. 1997. "Shaping the Nation, Excluding the Other: The Deportation of Migrants from Britain." In *Migration, Migration History, History: Old Paradigms and New Perspectives*, ed. Jan Lucassen and Leo Lucassen, 351–73. Bern: Peter Lang AG Europaïshcher Verlag der Wissenschaften.

Cohen, Yinon. 2002. "Sum Thing for Everyone: The Annual Abstract Put Out by the Central Bureau of Statistics Is Much More Than a Collection of Dry Statistics." *Ha'aretz* (Israel), November 29, 2002.

Cohen-Eliya, Moshe. 2004. "Discrimination against Arabs in Israel in Public Accommodations." *New York University Journal of International Law and Politics* 36:717–48.

Cole, David. 2002. "Enemy Aliens." *Stanford Law Review* 54:953–1004.

————. 2003. *Enemy Aliens: Double Standards and Constitutional Freedoms in the War on Terrorism*. New York: New Press.

Cole, David, and James Dempsey. 2002. *Terrorism and the Constitution: Sacrificing Civil Liberties in the Name of National Security*. New York: New Press.

Cornelisse, Galina N. 2004. "Human Rights for Immigration Detainees in Strasbourg: Limited Sovereignty or a Limited Discourse?" *European Journal of Migration and Law* 6 (2): 93–110.

Council of Europe. 2000. "Arrival of Asylum Seekers at European Airports." http://www.refugeelawreader.org/680/Recommendation_1475_2000_on_Arrival_of_Asylum-seekers_at_European_Airports.pdf.

Coutin, Susan Bibler. 1993. *The Culture of Protest: Religious Activism and the U.S. Sanctuary Movement*. Boulder, Colo.: Westview Press.

————. 2000. *Legalizing Moves: Salvadoran Immigrants' Struggle for U.S. Residency*. Ann Arbor: University of Michigan Press.

————. 2003a. "Cultural Logics of Belonging and Movement: Transnationalism, Naturalization, and U.S. Immigration Politics." *American Ethnologist* 30 (4): 508–26.

————. 2003b. "Suspension of Deportation Hearings and Measures of 'Americanness.' " *Journal of Latin American Anthropology* 8 (2): 58–95.

————. 2005. "Contesting Criminality: Illegal Immigration and the Spatialization of Legality." *Theoretical Criminology* 9 (1): 5–33.

————. 2007. *Nations of Emigrants: Shifting Boundaries of Citizenship in El Salvador and the United States*. Ithaca, N.Y.: Cornell University Press.

CPT. *See* European Committee for the Prevention of Torture and Inhuman or Degrading Treatment or Punishment.

Cremona, Marise. 2008. "Circular Migration: A Legal Perspective." CARIM AS 2008/30, Robert Schuman Centre for Advanced Studies, San Domenico di Fiesole (FI), European University Institute.

Cruikshank, Barbara. 1999. *The Will to Empower: Democratic Citizens and Other Subjects*. Ithaca, N.Y.: Cornell University Press.

Cunningham, Hilary, and Josiah McC. Heyman. 2004. "Introduction: Mobilities and Enclosures at Borders." *Identities: Global Studies in Culture and Power* 11:289–302.

Cuttitta, Paolo. 2006. "I confine d'Europa a sud del Mediterraneo: Strumenti e incentivi per l'esternalizzazione dei controlli." In *Migrazioni, Frontiere, Diritti*, ed. Paolo Cuttitta and Fulvio Vassallo Paleologo, 13–40. Napoli: Edizioni Scientifiche Italiane.

Dagne, Theodros. 2002. "Africa and the War on Terrorism: The Case of Somalia." *Mediterranean Quarterly*, fall, 62–73.

Dalton, Juan José. 2001a. "Endurecen condenas por delitos graves en El Salvador." *La Opinión*, July 20. http://www.laopinion.com.

———. 2001b. "Pobreza, violencia y corrupción son una realidad en El Salvador." *La Opinión*, July 8. http://www.laopinion.com.

———. 2002a. "Armas y muerta van de la mano en El Salvador." *La Opinión*, April 25. http://www.laopinion.com (accessed August 5, 2002).

———. 2002b. "Reportaje: La violencia no cede en El Salvador." *La Opinión*, March 11. http://www.laopinion.com (accessed August 9, 2002).

Dauvergne, Catherine. 2007. "Citizenship with a Vengeance." *Theoretical Inquiries in Law* 8 (2): 489–507.

Davies, Carole Boyce. 2001. "Deportable Subjects: U.S. Immigration Laws and the Criminalization of Communism." *South Atlantic Quarterly* 100 (4): 949–66.

Dean, Mitchell. 1991. *The Constitution of Poverty: Toward a Genealogy of Liberal Governance*. New York: Routledge.

———. 1999. *Governmentality: Power and Rule in Modern Society*. London: Sage.

———. 2002. "Liberal Government and Authoritarianism." *Economy and Society* 31 (1): 37–61.

Dean, Mitchell, and Barry Hindess. 1998. "Introduction: Government, Liberalism, Society." In *Governing Australia: Studies in Contemporary Rationalities of Government*, ed. Mitchell Dean and Barry Hindess, 1–19. Cambridge: Cambridge University Press.

De Genova, Nicholas. 1998. "Race, Space, and the Reinvention of Latin America in Mexican Chicago." *Latin American Perspectives* 25 (5): 91–120.

———. 2002. "Migrant 'Illegality' and Deportability in Everyday Life." *Annual Review of Anthropology* 31:419–47.

———. 2004. "The Legal Production of Mexican/Migrant 'Illegality.' " *Latino Studies* 2:160–85.

———. 2005. *Working the Boundaries: Race, Space, and "Illegality" in Mexican Chicago.* Durham, N.C.: Duke University Press.

———. 2006. "Introduction: Latino and Asian Racial Formations at the Frontiers of U.S. Nationalism." In *Racial Transformations: Latinos and Asians Remaking the United States,* ed. Nicholas De Genova, 1–20. Durham, N.C.: Duke University Press.

———. 2007. "The Production of Culprits: From Deportability to Detainability in the Aftermath of 'Homeland Security.'" *Citizenship Studies* 11 (5): 421–48.

de Haas, Hein. 2005. "Morocco: From Emigration Country to Africa's Migration Passage to Europe." *Migration Policy Institute.* http://www.migration information.org/Profiles/display.cfm?ID=339.

Delgado, Hilda Marella. 2000. "Jefe policial salvadoreño testifica en case de deportación." *La Opinión,* July 22. http://www.laopinion.com (accessed December 6, 2006).

Delgado, Richard. 2003. *Justice at War: Civil Liberties and Civil Rights during Times of Crisis.* New York: New York University Press.

Delle Donne, Enrica. 1970. *L'espulsione dei Gesuiti dal Regno di Napoli.* Napoli: Libreria Scientifica Editrice.

Demery, Lionel. 1986. "Asian Labor Migration: An Empirical Assessment." In *Asian Labor Migration: Pipeline to the Middle East,* ed. Fred Arnold and Nasra M. Shah, 17–46. Boulder, Colo.: Westview Press.

DeParle, Jason. 2008. "Spain, like U.S., Grapples with Immigration." *New York Times,* 10 June.

Derrida, Jacques. 1997. *Politics of Friendship.* London: Verso.

de Zayas, Alfred-Maurice. 1985. "Population, Expulsion, and Transfer." In *Encyclopedia of Public International Law,* vol. 8, ed. Rudolf Bernhardt, 438–44. Amsterdam: North Holland.

———. 1988. "A Historical Survey of Twentieth Century Expulsions." In *Refugees in the Age of Total War,* ed. Anna Bramwell, 15–37. London: Unwin Hyman.

———. 1989. *Nemesis at Potsdam: The Expulsion of the Germans from the East.* Lincoln: University of Nebraska Press.

di Giovanni, Janine. 2002. "How American Dream Faded in Downtown Mogadishu." *Times* (London), February 26, overseas news section.

Diken, Bülent, and Carsten Bagge Laustsen. 2003. " 'Camping' as Contemporary Strategy—from Refugee Camps to Gated Communities." Academy for Migration Studies in Denmark Working Paper Series 32.

———. 2006. "The Camp." *Geografiska Annaler,* series B, *Human Geography* 88 (4): 443–52.

Diminescu, Dana. 2000. "Le 'système D' contre les frontières informatiques." *Hommes et migrations* 1230 (March–April): 28–33.

Donati, Donato. 1924. *Stato e territorio.* Rome: Athenaeum.

Donnelly, Jack. 1994. "Human Rights in a New World Order: Implications for a New Europe." In *Human Rights in the New Europe,* ed. David P. Forsythe, 7–32. Lincoln: University of Nebraska Press.

Douglas, Mary. 1966/2002. *Purity and Danger: An Analysis of the Concept of Pollution and Taboo.* New York: Routledge.

Dow, Mark. 2004. *American Gulag: Inside U.S. Immigration Prisons.* Berkeley: University of California Press.

Dower, Nigel. 2003. *An Introduction to Global Citizenship.* Edinburgh: Edinburgh University Press.

Dubal, Veena, and Sunaina Maira. 2005. "The FBI 'Witch-Hunt' in Lodi." *India Currents,* August 2. http://indiacurrents.com/news (accessed March 30, 2006).

Dummet, Ann, and Andrew Nicol. 1990. *Subjects, Citizens, Aliens, and Others: Nationality and Immigration Law.* London: Weidenfeld and Nicolson.

Dunn, Timothy J. 1996. *The Militarization of the U.S.-Mexico Border, 1978–1992: Low-Intensity Conflict Doctrine Comes Home.* Austin: CMAS Books, University of Texas, Austin.

Düvell, Frank. 2004. "Illegal Immigration: What to Do about It." Working Paper. Working Group Migration-Mobility-Minorities-Membership, Florence, EUI/RSCAS.

Eelens, F., Toon Schampers, and Johan Dirk Speckman. 1992. *Labour Migration to the Middle East: From Sri Lanka to the Gulf.* London: Kegan Paul International.

Efionay-Mäder, Denise, Milena Chimienti, Janine Dahinden, and Etienne Piguet. 2001. *Asyldestination Europa: Eine Geographie der Asylbewegungen.* Zürich: Seismo.

El Diario de Hoy. 2002. "El 25% tiene al menos un familiar asaltado." June 24. http://www.elsalvador.com (accessed June 24, 2002).

Elias, Norbert. 1976/1994. "Introduction: A Theoretical Essay on Established and Outsider Relations." In *The Established and the Outsiders: A Sociological Enquiry into Community Problems,* ed. Norbert Elias and John L. Scotson, xv–lii. 2d ed. London: Sage.

Ellermann, Antje. 2006. "Street-Level Democracy: How Immigration Bureaucrats Manage Public Opposition." *West European Politics* 29 (2): 293–309.

Elliott, Andrea. 2006. "As Police Watch for Terrorists, Brooklyn Muslims Feel the Eyes." *New York Times,* May 27.

Engbersen, Godfried. 2001. "The Unanticipated Consequences of Panopticon Europe: Residence Strategies of Illegal Immigrants." In *Controlling a New Migration World,* ed. Virginie Guiraudon and Christian Joppke, 222–46. London: Routledge.

Eschbach, Karl, Jacqueline M. Hagan, and Nestor P. Rodríguez. 2003. "Deaths during Undocumented Migration: Trends and Policy Implications in the New Era of Homeland Security." *Defense of the Alien* 26:37–52.

Espenshade, Thomas J., Jessica L. Baraka, and Gregory A. Huber. 1997. "Implications of the 1996 Welfare and Immigration Reform Acts for U.S. Immigration." *Population and Development Review* 23 (4): 769–801.

European Commission. 2005. European Commission, Technical Mission to

Libya on Illegal Immigration, November 27–December 6, 2004, Report. Brussels.

———. 2006. Press Release. Brussels: 2006 Jul 10 (IP 06/967).

European Committee for the Prevention of Torture and Inhuman or Degrading Treatment or Punishment (CPT). 2007. Rapport au gouvernement de la république française relatif à la visite effectuée en France par le comité européen pour la prévention de la torture et des peines ou traitements inhumains ou dégradants (CPT) du 27 septembre au 9 octobre 2006, December 17, 2007, CPT/Inf (2007) 44.

———. 2008a. Report to the Government of Cyprus on the Visit to Cyprus Carried Out by the European Committee for the Prevention of Torture and Inhuman or Degrading Treatment or Punishment (CPT) from 8 to 17 December 2004, Strasbourg, April 15, 2008, CPT/Inf (2008) 17.

———. 2008b. Report to the authorities of the Kingdom of the Netherlands on the Visits Carried out to the Kingdom in Europe, Aruba, and the Netherlands Antilles by the European Committee for the Prevention of Torture and Inhuman or Degrading Treatment or Punishment (CPT) in June 2007, Strasbourg, February 5, 2008, CPT/Inf (2008) 2.

Evron, Boaz. 2002. "Demography as the Enemy of Democracy." Ha'aretz (Israel), September 11.

Falk, Richard. 1993. "The Making of Global Citizenship." In Global Visions: Beyond the New World Order, ed. J. Brecher, 39–50. Boston: South End Press.

Farmer, Paul. 2003. Pathologies of Power: Health, Human Rights, and the New War on the Poor. Berkeley: University of California Press.

———. 2004. "An Anthropology of Structural Violence." Current Anthropology 45 (3): 305–25.

Fassin, Didier. 2001. "The Biopolitics of Otherness: Undocumented Foreigners and Racial Discrimination in French Public Debate." Anthropology Today 17:3–7.

———. 2005. "Compassion and Repression: The Moral Economy of Immigrant Policies in France." Cultural Anthropology 20 (3): 362–87.

Fassin, Didier, and Estelle D'Halluin. 2005. "The Truth from the Body: Medical Certificates as Ultimate Evidence for Asylum Seekers." American Anthropology 17 (4): 597–608.

Feeley, Malcolm M., and Jonathan Simon. 1992. "The New Penology: Notes on the Emerging Strategy of Corrections and Its Implications." Criminology 30 (4): 449–74.

Fekete, Liz. 1997. "Blackening the Economy: The Path to Convergence." Race and Class 39 (1): 1–17.

———. 2005. "The Deportation Machine: Europe, Asylum, and Human Rights." Special issue, European Race Bulletin, no. 51. London: Institute of Race Relations.

———. 2007a. "Detained: Foreign Children in Europe." Race and Class 49 (1): 93–104.

————. 2007b. "They Are Children Too: A Study of Europe's Deportation Policies." Special Issue, *European Race Bulletin*, nos. 58–59. London: Institute of Race Relations.

Fernandes, Deepa. 2007. *Targeted: Homeland Security and the Business of Immigration*. New York: Seven Stories Press.

Fernandez-Vargas v. Gonzales, no. 04–1376, Supreme Court of the United States, 126 S. Ct. 2422; March 22, 2006, argued, June 22, 2006.

FESPAD (Fundación de Estudios para la Aplicación del Derecho) and CEPES (Centro de Estudios Penales de El Salvador). 2004. *Informe Anual Sobre Justicia Penal Juvenil El Salvador 2004*. San Salvador, El Salvador: FESPAD.

FIDH (International Federation for Human Rights). 2005. "Right of Asylum in Italy: Access to Procedures and Treatment of Asylum-Seekers." *Report of the International Fact-Finding Mission*, no. 419/2. http://www.fidh.org/IMG/pdf/eu_asylum419a.pdf.

Filc, Dani, and Nadav Davidovitch. 2005. "Health Care as a National Right? The Development of Health Care Services for Migrant Workers in Israel." *Social Theory and Health* 15:1–14.

Finotelli, Claudia. 2005. "Regularisations for Illegal Migrants in Italy: Background, Processes, Results." In *Amnesty for Illegal Migrants*, ed. Friedrich Heckmann and Tanja Wunderlich, 69–78. Bamberg: European Forum for Migration Studies.

Fitzpatrick, Joan. 2002. "Sovereignty, Territoriality, and the Rule of Law." *Hastings International and Comparative Law Review* 25 (3): 303–40.

Fitzpatrick, Peter, ed. 1995. *Nationalism, Racism, and the Rule of Law*. Aldershot: Dartmouth Publishing Group.

Fitzsimmons, Michael P. 1993. "The National Assembly and the Invention of Citizenship." In *The French Revolution and the Meaning of Citizenship*, ed. Renaee Waldinger, Philip Dawson, and Isser Woloch, 29–41. Westport, Conn.: Greenwood Press.

Flusser, Vilém. 1984. "Exile and Creativity." In *The Freedom of the Migrant: Objections to Nationalism*, 81–87. Urbana: University of Illinois Press.

————. 1985. "The Challenge of the Migrant." In *The Freedom of the Migrant: Objections to Nationalism*, 1–15. Urbana: University of Illinois Press.

————. 1989. "To Be Unsettled, One First Has to Be Settled." In *The Freedom of the Migrant: Objections to Nationalism*, 25–27. Urbana: University of Illinois Press.

————. 2003. *The Freedom of the Migrant: Objections to Nationalism*. Urbana: University of Illinois Press.

Fonce-Olivas, Tammy. 2006. "Samaniego Will Reinstate Controversial Checkpoints." *El Paso Times*, October 11.

Foucault, Michel. 1967. *Madness and Civilization: A History of Insanity in the Age of Reason*. London: Tavistock.

————. 1973/1994. "La vérité et les formes juridiques." In *Dits et écrits*, vol. 2, 538–646. Paris: Gallimard.

———. 1975/1977. *Discipline and Punish: The Birth of the Prison.* Trans. Alan Sheridan. New York: Pantheon Books.

———. 1976/1978. *The History of Sexuality.* Vol. 1, *An Introduction.* New York: Vintage Books.

———. 1976/2003. *"Society Must Be Defended": Lectures at the Collège de France, 1975–1976.* New York: Picador.

———. 1978/2007. *Security, Territory, Population: Lectures at the Collège de France, 1977–1978.* New York: Picador.

———. 1980. "The Eye of Power." In *Power/Knowledge: Selected Interviews and Other Writings, 1972–1977,* ed. Colin Gordon, 146–65. New York: Pantheon.

———. 1982. "The Subject and Power." *Critical Inquiry* 8:777–95.

———. 1991. "Governmentality." In *The Foucault Effect: Studies in Governmentality,* ed. Graham Burchell, Colin Gordon, and Peter Miller, 87–104. Hemel Hempstead: Harvester Wheatsheaf.

———. 1992. *Genealogia del racismo: De la guerre de las razas al racismo de estado.* Madrid: Las Ediciones de la Piqueta.

Fragoman, Austin T., Jr. 1997. "The Illegal Immigrant Reform and Immigrant Responsibility Act of 1996: An Overview." *International Migration Review* 31 (2): 438–60.

Freedman, Jane, and Carrie Tarr. 2000. "The Sans-Papières: An Interview with Madjiguène Cissé." In *Women, Immigration, and Identities in France,* ed. Jane Freedman and Carrie Tarr, 29–38. Oxford: Berg.

Freeman, Gary P. 1986. "Migration and the Political Economy of the Welfare State." *Annals of the American Academy of Political and Social Science* 485:51–63.

———. 1992. "The Consequence of Immigration Policies for Immigrant Status: A British and French Comparison." In *Ethnic and Racial Minorities in Advanced Industrial Democracies,* ed. Anthony Messina and Luis Fraga, 17–32. New York: Greenwood Press.

Freudenstein, Roland. 2000. "Río Odra, Río Buh: Poland, Germany, and the Borders of Twenty-First-Century." In *The Wall around the West: State Borders and Immigration Controls in North America and Europe,* ed. Peter Andreas and Timothy Snyder, 173–84. Lanham, Md.: Rowman and Littlefield.

Fuglerud, Øivind. 1999. *Life on the Outside: The Tamil Diaspora and Long-Distance Nationalism.* London: Pluto Press.

Gagale, Ibrahim Hassan. 2003. "Lost in America: Somali Children." *Somaliland Times* (Hargeysa, Somaliland), December 28. http://www.somalilandtimes.net/2003/100/10020.shtml (accessed June 5, 2008).

Galili, Lili. 2002. "A Jewish Demographic State." *Ha'aretz* (Israel), June 28, 2002.

Galtung, Johan. 1969. "Violence, Peace, and Peace Research." *Journal of Peace Research* 6:167–91.

Gamburd, Michele Ruth. 2000. *The Kitchen Spoon's Handle: Transnationalism and Sri Lanka's Migrant Housemaids.* Ithaca, N.Y.: Cornell University Press.

Gardner, Andrew. 2006. "The Unwelcome Guest: Episodes from a Year in Bahrain." In *Dispatches from the Field,* ed. Andrew Gardner and David Hoffman, 69–82. Long Grove, Ill.: Waveland Press.

Gehrig, Tina. 2004. "The Afghan Experience of Asylum in Germany: Towards an Anthropology of Legal Categories." *Tsantsa: Journal of the Swiss Ethnological Society* 9:72–80.

Gibney, Matthew J. 2000. *Outside the Protection of the Law: The Situation of Irregular Migrants in Europe.* Oxford: Refugee Studies Centre.

Gibney, Matthew J., and Randall Hansen. 2003. "Deportation and the Liberal State: The Forcible Return of Asylum Seekers and Unlawful Migrants in Canada, Germany, and the United Kingdom." UNHCR New Issues in Refugee Research Working Paper, no. 77, Geneva. http://www.unhcr.org/3e59de764. html.

Giese, Julie. 2005. "Lodi's Young Pakistani Americans Find Themselves Caught between Cultures." *Lodi News-Sentinel.* http://www.lodinews.com/pakistan/ html/youth.shtml (accessed July 18, 2005).

Gilot, Louie. 2007. "D.C. Hears El Pasoan's Ideas about Reforms." *El Paso Times,* January 15.

Gilroy, Paul. 1999. "Race and Culture in Postmodernity." *Economy and Society* 28 (2): 183–97.

Gingrich, Andre, and Gudrun Kroner. 2006. "Response to Nathalie Peutz' 'Embarking on an Anthropology of Removal.' " *Current Anthropology* 47 (2): 234–35.

Glover, Scott, and Richard Winton. 2009. "Activist Accused of Gang Crimes." *Los Angeles Times,* June 25.

Godoy, Angelina Snodgrass. 2005. "Democracy, 'Mano Dura,' and the Criminalization of Politics." In *(Un)Civil societies: Human Rights and Democratic Transitions in Eastern Europe and Latin America,* ed. Rachel May and Andrew Milton, 109–37. Lanham, Md.: Lexington Books.

Goldring, Luin, Carolina Berinstein, and Judith Bernhard. 2007. "Institutionalizing Precarious Immigration Status in Canada." CERIS Working Paper Series 61. http://www.ceris.metropolis.net/Virtual%20Library/EResources/ Goldring_et_a12007.pdf.

Goldstein, Amy, and Dana Priest. 2008. "Some Detainees Are Drugged for Deportation: Immigrants Sedated without Medical Reason." *Washington Post,* May 14.

Goldstein, Daniel M. 2007. "The Violence of Rights: Human Rights as Culprit, Human Rights as Victim." In *The Practice of Human Rights: Tracking Law between the Global and the Local,* ed. Mark Goodale and Sally Engle Merry. Cambridge: Cambridge University Press.

González-Portillo, Patricia A. 2000. "Vecinos de Rampart, ¿Se fían del LAPD?" *La Opinión,* May 28. http://www.laopinion.com (accessed December 6, 2006).

Goodwin-Gill, Guy. 1978. *International Law and the Movement of Persons between States.* Oxford: Clarendon.

Gordimer, Nadine. 2001. *The Pickup*. New York: Farrar, Straus and Giroux.

Gordon, Colin. 1991. "Governmental Rationality: An Introduction." In *The Foucault Effect: Studies in Governmentality*, ed. Graham Burchell, Colin Gordon, and Peter Miller, 1–52. Chicago: University of Chicago Press.

Green, Leslie. 1994. "International Minorities and Their Rights." In *Group Rights*, ed. Judith Baker, 101–17. Toronto: University of Toronto Press.

Green, Linda. 1999. *Fear as a Way of Life: Mayan Widows in Rural Guatemala*. New York: Columbia University Press.

Grudin, Nicholas. 2005. "Pakistani Men Adjust to Life in Lodi." *Lodi News-Sentinel.* http://www.lodinews.com/pakistan/html/men.shtml (accessed July 18, 2005).

Guild, Elspeth. 2005. Memorandum by Professor Elspeth Guild, written evidence. In House of Lords, "The Hague Programme: A Five Year Agenda for EU Justice and Home Affairs," Report with Evidence, HL Paper 84, pp. 27–29. London, March 23.

———. 2007. "Who Is a Neighbour? Examining Immigration and Asylum in the European Neighbourhood Policy (ENP) Instruments." Paper presented at COMPAS seminar series "Migration on the Fringes of Europe: Trends, Patterns, Transformation." Centre on Migration, Policy, and Society (COMPAS), University of Oxford.

Gupta, Akhil. 2006. "Blurred Boundaries: The Discourse of Corruption, the Culture of Politics, and the Imagined State." In *The Anthropology of the State: A Reader*, ed. Aradhana Sharma and Akhil Gupta, 211–43. Malden, Mass.: Blackwell.

Gurr, Ted. 1993. *Minorities at Risk: A Global View of Ethno-political Conflict*. Washington: Institute of Peace Press.

Habermas, Jürgen. 1996. "The European Nation-State: Its Achievements and Its Limits; On the Past and Future of Sovereignty and Citizenship." In *Mapping the Nation*, ed. Gopal Balakrishnan, 281–94. London: Verso.

Hacking, Ian. 1999. "Making Up People." In *The Science Studies Reader*, ed. Mario Biagioli, 160–75. New York: Routledge.

Hafetz, David. 2006. "Terror Lie Suit." *New York Post*, April 9.

Hafetz, Jonathan L. 1998. "The Untold Story of Noncriminal Habeas Corpus and the 1996 Immigration Acts." *Yale Law Journal* 107 (8): 2509–44.

Hall, Stuart, and David Held. 1989. "Citizens and Citizenship." In *New Times: The Changing Face of Politics in the 1990s*, ed. Stuart Hall and Martin Jacques, 173–88. London: Lawrence and Wishart.

Hameed, Kanwal Tariq. 2006a. "Man Held 'for Locking Six in Freezer Truck.' " *Gulf Daily News*, February 26.

———. 2006b. "Steps Needed to Safeguard Expat Workers." *Gulf Daily News*, February 27.

Hamood, Sara. 2006. *African Transit Migration through Libya to Europe: The Human Costs*. Cairo: American University of Cairo, Forced Migration and Refugee Studies.

Hannerz, Ulf. 1996. *Transnational Connections: Culture, People, Places*. New York: Routledge.

Hardt, Michael, and Antonio Negri. 1994. *Labor of Dionysus: A Critique of the State-Form*. Minneapolis: University of Minnesota Press.

———. 2001. *Empire*. Cambridge, Mass.: Harvard University Press.

Harel, Isser. 1989. *Security and Democracy in Israel*. Tel Aviv: Idanim Publishers, Yediot Aharonot.

Harris, Nigel. 2003. "Migration without Borders: The Economic Perspective." http://www.unesco.org/most/migration/paper_n_harris.pdf.

Harvey, David. 2003. *The New Imperialism*. New York: Oxford University Press.

———. 2005. *A Brief History of Neoliberalism*. Oxford: Oxford University Press.

Hass, Amira. 1999. *Drinking the Sea at Gaza: Days and Nights in a Land under Siege*. New York: Metropolitan Books.

Hayter, Teresa. 2000. *Open Borders: The Case against Immigration Controls*. London: Pluto.

Helmut, Dietrich. 2005. "The Desert Front: EU Refugee Camps in North Africa?" *Statewatch*. March. http://www.statewatch.org.

Henckaerts, Jean-Marie. 1995. *Mass Expulsion in Modern International Law and Practice*. The Hague: Martinus Nijhoff.

Henkin, Louis. 1999. "That 'S' Word: Sovereignty, and Globalization, and Human Rights, et Cetera." *Fordham Law Review* 68 (1): 1–14.

Heyman, Josiah McC. 1998. "State Effects on Labor Exploitation: The INS and Undocumented Immigrants at the Mexico–United States Border." *Critique of Anthropology* 18:157–80.

———. 1999. "Why Interdiction? Immigration Law Enforcement at the United States–Mexico Border." *Regional Studies* 33:619–30.

———. 2001. "Class and Classification on the U.S.-Mexico Border." *Human Organization* 60:128–40.

———. 2004. "Ports of Entry as Nodes in the World System." *Identities* 11: 303–27.

Heyman, Josiah McC., and Alan Smart. 1999. "States and Illegal Practices: An Overview." In *States and Illegal Practices*, ed. Josiah McC. Heyman, 1–24. New York: Berg.

Hifsh, Rami. 2002. "Former NBA All Star Detained for Three Hours at Ben Gurion Airport." *Ha'aretz* (Israel), December 29.

Higgins, Lesley, and Marie Christine Leps. 1998. " 'Passport, Please': Legal, Literary, and Critical Functions of Identity." *College Literature* 25 (1): 94–138.

Higham, John. 1955/1963. *Strangers in the Land: Patterns of American Nativism (1860–1925)*. New York: Atheneum.

Hindess, Barry. 1998. "Divide and Rule: The International Character of Modern Citizenship." *European Journal of Social Theory* 1 (1): 57–70.

———. 2000. "Citizenship in the International Management of Populations." *American Behavioral Scientist* 43 (9): 1486–97.

———. 2002. "Neo-liberal Citizenship." *Citizenship Studies* 6 (2): 127–43.

———. 2004. "Citizenship for All." *Citizenship Studies* 8 (3): 305–15.

Hing, Bill Ong. 2004. *Defining America through Immigration Policy*. Philadelphia: Temple University Press.

———. 2006a. *Deporting Our Souls: Values, Morality, and Immigration Policy*. New York: Cambridge University Press.

———. 2006b. "Misusing Immigration Policies in the Name of Homeland Security." *New Centennial Review* 6 (1): 195–224.

Hing, Eric Jeffrey Ong. 2004. "Deportation into Chaos: The Questionable Removal of Somali Refugees." *UC Davis Law Review* 38:309–42.

Holden, David. 1966. *Farewell to Arabia*. New York: Walker.

Holloway, John. 1994. "Global Capital and the National State." *Capital and Class* 52:23–49.

Holmes, Seth. 2007. " 'Oaxacans Like to Work Bent Over': The Naturalization of Social Suffering among Berry Farm Workers." *International Migration* 45 (3): 39–68.

Holstege, Sean, Michele Marcucci, and David Drucker. 2005. "Three More Arrests in Lodi Terrorism Case." *Oakland Tribune*, June 9.

Homies Unidos. 2009. "Homies Unidos." http://www.homiesunidos.org (accessed July 6, 2009).

Honig, Bonnie. 1998. "Immigrant America? How Foreignness 'Solves' Democracy's Problems." *Social Text* 56:1–27.

———. 2001. *Democracy and the Foreigner*. Princeton, N.J.: Princeton University Press.

Hood, Jeff. 2006. "Links to Terrorism Still Vague: Observer Says FBI Needs a 'Perry Mason' Moment." February 25. http://www.recordnet.com (accessed February 26, 2006).

Hopper, Kim, and Norweeta G. Milburn. 1996. "Homelessness among African Americans: A Historical and Contemporary Perspective." In *Homelessness in America*, ed. Jim Baumohl, 123–31. Phoenix, Ariz.: Onyx Press.

Hua, Vanessa. 2005. "Probe Expected to Widen, FBI Says." *San Francisco Chronicle*, June 9.

Hughes, Robert. 1986. *The Fatal Shore: A History of the Transportation of Convicts to Australia, 1787–1868*. London: Collins Harvill.

Human Rights Watch. 1998. "Locked Away: Immigration Detainees in Jails in the United States." *Human Rights Watch* 10 (1): 1–86.

———. 2002. "Presumption of Guilt: Human Rights Abuses of Post–September 11 Detainees." *Human Rights Watch* 14 (4): 1–95.

———. 2007. "Forced Apart: Families Separated and Immigrants Harmed by United States Deportation Policy." *Human Rights Watch* 19 (3): 1–86.

———. 2009. *Forced Apart (by the Numbers): Non-Citizens Deported Mostly for Nonviolent Offenses*. New York: Human Rights Watch.

Hutchinson, Brian. 2002. "Snatched." *Seattle Weekly*, March 21–27. http://www.seattleweekly.com/2002–03–20/news/snatched (accessed June 5, 2008).

Huysmans, Jef. 1995. "Migrants as a Security Problem: Dangers of 'Securitizing' Societal Issues." In *Migration and European Integration: The Dynamics of Inclusion and Exclusion*, ed. R. Miles and D. Thränhardt, 53–72. London: Pinter.

Huysmans, Jef, Andrew Dobson, and Raia Prokhovnik, eds. 2006. *The Politics of Protection: Sites of Insecurity and Political Agency*. London: Routledge.

Ilan, Shahar. 2007. "Entering the Age of Post-Aliyah?" *Ha'aretz* (Israel), February 1.

Immigration and Naturalization Service v. St. Cyr., 2001, 533 U.S. 289.

Inda, Jonathan X. 2006. "Border Prophylaxis: Technology, Illegality, and the Government of Immigration." *Cultural Dynamics* 18 (2): 115–38.

Ioffee, Karina. 2005. "Few Answers in Lodi Graffiti." October 15. http://www .recordnet.com (accessed October 22, 2005).

Isin, Engin F. 2002. *Being Political: Genealogies of Citizenship*. Minneapolis: University of Minnesota Press.

Izenberg, Dan. 2003. "Court: Ads against Illegal Workers Were Hateful." *Jerusalem Post*, December 15.

Jackson Preece, Jennifer. 1998. "Ethnic Cleansing as an Instrument of Nation-State Creation: Changing State Practices and Evolving Legal Norms." *Human Rights Quarterly* 20:817–42.

Jamin, Mathilde. 1998. "Die deutsch-türkische Anwerbevereinbarung von 1961 und 1964." In *Fremde Heimat: Eine Geschichte der Einwanderung aus der Türkei*, ed. Aytaç Eryilmaz and Mathilde Jamin, 69–82. Essen: Klartext.

Jaramillo, Velia. 2001. "Mexico's 'Southern Plan': The Facts; Crackdown Underway on Migration from Central America." Originally published in *Proceso* (Mexico City, June 26, 2001). Published in English translation in *World Press Review* 48 (9). http://www.worldpress.org/0901feature22.htm.

Jellinek, Georg. 1892/1949. *System der subjektiven öffentlichen Rechte*. Darmstadt: Wissenschaftliche Buchgesellschaft. Republished in Italian as *Sistema dei diritti pubblici subiettivi* (Milan: Società Editrice Libraria, 1949).

———. 1900/1949. *Allgemeine Staatslehre*. Berlin: Springer. Republished in Italian as *La dottrina generale del diritto dello stato* (Milan: Giuffrè, 1949).

Kafka, Franz. 1925/1999. *The Trial*. New York: Vintage Classics.

Kahn, Susan Martha. 2000. *Reproducing Jews: A Cultural Account of Assisted Conception in Israel*. Durham, N.C.: Duke University Press.

Kanaaneh, Rhoda. 2002. *Birthing the Nation: Strategies of Palestinian Women in Israel*. Berkeley: University of California.

Kanstroom, Daniel. 2000. "Deportation, Social Control, and Punishment: Some Thoughts about Why Hard Laws Make Bad Cases." *Harvard Law Review* 113 (8): 1890–1935.

———. 2007. *Deportation Nation: Outsiders in American History*. Cambridge, Mass.: Harvard University Press.

Kapiszewski, Andrzej. 2001. *Nationals and Expatriates: Population and Labour in the Gulf Cooperation Council States*. Reading, UK: Ithaca Press.

Kapur, Ratna. 2007. "The Citizen and the Migrant: Postcolonial Anxieties, Law, and the Politics of Exclusion/Inclusion." *Theoretical Inquiries in Law* 8 (2): 537–69.

Karakayali, Serhat. 2008. *Gespenster der Migration: Zur Genealogie illegaler Einwanderung in der Bundesrepublik Deutschland.* Bielefeld: Transcript Verlag.

Karp, Jonathan. 2001. "El Al's Airtight Security Is Now in Demand." *Wall Street Journal,* September 26.

Kasimis, Charalambos, Apostolos Papadopoulos, and Ersi Zacopoulou. 2003. "Migrants in Rural Greece." *Sociologica Ruralis* 43:167–84.

Kearney, Michael. 1995. "The Local and the Global: The Anthropology of Globalization and Transnationalism." *Annual Review of Anthropology* 24: 547–65.

———. 2004. "The Classifying and Value-Filtering Mission of Borders." *Anthropological Theory* 4:131–56.

Kedar, Benjamin. 1996. "Expulsion as an Issue of World History." *Journal of World History* 7 (2): 165–80.

Kellner, Douglas. 2003. "Postmodern Military and Permanent War." In *Masters of War: Militarism and Blowback in the Era of American Empire,* ed. Carl Boggs, 229–44. New York: Routledge.

Kelsen, Hans. 1925. *Allgemeine Staatslehre.* Berlin: Springer. Republished in Italian as *Lineamenti di una teoria generale dello stato e altri scritti* (Rome: Anonima Romana Editoriale, 1932).

———. 1945. *General Theory of Law and State.* Cambridge, Mass.: Harvard University Press. Republished in Italian as *Teoria generale del diritto e dello stato* (Milan: Etaslibri, 1994).

Kemp, Adriana. 2004. "Labour Migration and Racialisation: Labour Market Mechanisms and Labour Migration Control Policies in Israel." *Social Identities* 10:267–92.

Kemp, Adriana, and Rebecca Raijman. 2000. "'Foreigners' in the Jewish State: The New Politics of Labor Migration to Israel." *Sotziologia Yisraelit* 3: 79–110.

———. 2004. " 'Tel Aviv Is Not Foreign to You': Urban Incorporation Policy on Labor Migrants in Israel." *International Migration Review* 38 (1): 26–51.

Kemp, Adriana, Rebecca Raijman, Julia Resnik, and Silvina Schammah Gesser. 2000. "Contesting the Limits of Political Participation: Latinos and Black African Migrant Workers in Israel." *Ethnic and Racial Studies* 23:94–119.

Kerber, Linda. 2007. "The Stateless as the Citizen's Other: A View from the United States (Presidential Address)." *American Historical Review* 112 (1): 1–34.

Khalaf, Sulayman, and Saad Alkobaisi. 1999. "Migrants' Strategies of Coping and Patterns of Accommodation in the Oil-Rich Gulf Societies: Evidence from the UAE." *British Journal of Middle Eastern Studies* 26 (2): 271–98.

Khosravi, Shahram. 2009. "Sweden: Detention and Deportation of Asylum Seekers." *Race and Class* 50 (4): 38–56.

Khuri, Fuad. 1980. *Tribe and State in Bahrain: The Transformation of Social and Political Authority in an Arab State.* Chicago: University of Chicago Press.

Killias, Martin. 2001. *Précis de criminologie.* Bern: Stämpfli.

King, Mike. 1997. "Le controle des differences en Europe: L'inclusion et l'exclusion comme logiques securitaires et economiques." *Cultures et Conflits* 26–27:35–49.

Kingston, Rebecca. 2005. "The Unmaking of Citizens: Banishment and the Modern Citizenship Regime in France." *Citizenship Studies* 9 (1): 23–40.

Kleinman, Arthur, Veena Das, and Margaret Lock. 1997. Introduction to *Social Suffering*, ed. Arthur Kleinman, Veena Das, and Margaret Lock, ix–xxvii. Berkeley: University of California.

Koser, Khalid. 2000. "Return, Readmission, and Reintegration: Changing Agendas, Policy Frameworks, and Operational Programmes." In *Return Migration: Journey of Hope or Despair*, ed. Bimal Ghosh, 57–100. Geneva: International Organization for Migration.

Koshy, Ninan. 2003. *The War on Terror: Reordering the World*. New Delhi: LeftWord Books.

Krieger, Hilary Leila. 2004. "Wrongly Held Asylum Seekers Released." *Jerusalem Post*. July 6.

Kristeva, Julia. 1982. *Powers of Horror: An Essay on Abjection*. New York: Columbia University Press.

———. 1991. *Strangers to Ourselves*. New York: Columbia University Press.

Kritzman, Tally. 2007. "Not in My Backyard: On the Moral Responsibility of Sharing in Refugee Law." *Brook Journal of International Law* 34 (2): 355–93.

Kurien, Prema. 2002. *Kaleidoscopic Ethnicity: International Migration and the Reconstruction of Community Identities in India*. New Brunswick, N.J.: Rutgers University Press.

Lavenex, Sandra. 1999. *Safe Third Countries: Extending the EU Asylum and Immigration Policies to Central and Eastern Europe*. Budapest: Central European University.

Lefebvre, Henri. 1974/1991. *The Production of Space*. Cambridge, Mass.: Blackwell.

Leibovitch-Dar, Sara. 2002. "Entry Denied." *Ha'aretz*, December 13.

Leonard, Karen. 2002. "South Asian Women in the Gulf: Families and Futures Reconfigured." In *Trans-status Subjects: Gender in the Globalization of South and Southeast Asia*, ed. Sonita Sarker and Esha Niyogi De, 213–31. Durham, N.C.: Duke University Press.

———. 2003. "South Asian Workers in the Gulf: Jockeying for Places." In *Globalization under Construction: Governmentality, Law, and Identity*, ed. Richard Perry and William Maurer, 129–70. Minneapolis: University of Minnesota Press.

Linares, Jesse J. 2000. "Pandilleros deportados corren peligro in El Salvador." *La Opinión*, July 24. http://www.laopinion.com (accessed December 6, 2006).

Linklater, Andrew. 1998a. "Cosmopolitan Citizenship." *Citizenship Studies* 2 (1) 23–41.

———. 1998b. *The Transformation of Political Community*. Cambridge: Polity Press.

Lippert, Randy K. 2005. *Sanctuary, Sovereignty, Sacrifice: Canadian Sanctuary Incidents, Power, and Law*. Vancouver: University of British Columbia Press.

Lipton, Eric. 1999. "As More Are Deported, a '96 Law Faces Scrutiny." *New York Times*, December 21.

Little, Peter. 2003. *Somalia: Economy without State*. Bloomington: Indiana University Press.

Lomnitz, Larissa Adler. 1977. *Networks and Marginality: Life in a Mexican Shantytown*. Trans. Cinna Lomnitz. New York: Academic Press.

Longva, Anh. 1997. *Walls Built on Sand: Migration, Exclusion, and Society in Kuwait*. Boulder, Colo.: Westview Press.

———. 1999. "Keeping Migrant Workers in Check: The *Kafala* System in the Gulf." *Middle East Report* 211 (summer): 20–22.

———. 2000. "Citizenship in the Gulf States: Conceptualization and Practice." In *Citizenship and the State in the Middle East: Approaches and Application*, ed. Nils A. Butenschon, Uri Davis, and Manuel Hassassian, 179–97. Syracuse, N.Y.: Syracuse University Press.

———. 2005. "Neither Autocracy nor Democracy but Ethnocracy: Citizens, Expatriates, and the Socio-political Regime in Kuwait." In *Monarchies and Nations: Globalization and Identity in the Arab States of the Gulf*, ed. Paul Dresch and James Piscatori, 114–35. London: I. B. Tauris.

Louër, Laurence. 2005. "The Political Impact of Labor Migration in Bahrain." Paper presented at the conference "Transnational Migration: Foreign Labor and Its Impact in the Gulf," Bellagio, Italy, June 20–25.

Lowry, Michelle, and Peter Nyers. 2003. "Roundtable: 'No One Is Illegal'; The Fight for Refugee and Migrant Rights in Canada." *Refuge: Canada's Periodical on Refugees* 21 (3): 69–70.

Lucassen, Leo. 1997. "Eternal Vagrants? State Formation, Migration, and Travelling Groups in Western Europe, 1350–1914." In *Migration, Migration History, History: Old Paradigms and New Perspectives*, ed. Jan Lucassen and Leo Lucassen, 225–51. Bern: Peter Lang AG Europaïshcher Verlag der Wissenschaften.

Lustick, Ian S. 1999. "Israel as a Non-Arab State: The Political Implications of Mass Immigration of Non-Jews." *Middle East Journal* 53:417–33.

Lynskey, Oria. 2006. "Complementing and Completing the Common European Asylum System: A Legal Analysis of the Emerging Extraterritorial Elements of EU Refugee Protection Policy." *European Law Review* 31 (2): 230–50.

Macklin, Audrey. 2007. "Who Is the Citizen's Other? Considering the Heft of Citizenship." *Theoretical Inquiries in Law* 8 (2): 333–66.

Magdoff, Harry. 2003. *Imperialism without Colonies*. New York: Monthly Review Press.

Mahler, Sarah J. 2000. "Migration and Transnational Issues: Recent Trends and Prospects for 2020." CA 2020: Working Paper 4. Hamburg: Institut für Iberoamericka-Kunde.

Maira, Sunaina. 2004. "Youth Culture Studies, Empire, and Globalization." *Comparative Studies of South Asia, Africa, and the Middle East* 24 (1): 219–31.

Malkki, Liisa H. 1995. "Refugees and Exiles: From 'Refugee Studies' to the National Order of Things." *Annual Review of Anthropology* 24:495–523.

———. 1997. "News and Culture: Transitory Phenomena and the Fieldwork Tradition." In *Anthropological Locations: Boundaries and Grounds of a Field Science*, ed. Akhil Gupta and James Ferguson, 86–101. Berkeley: University of California Press.

Mamdani, Mahmood. 1996. *Citizen and Subject: Contemporary Africa and the Legacy of Late Colonialism*. Princeton, N.J.: Princeton University Press.

———. 2004. *Good Muslim, Bad Muslim: America, the Cold War, and the Roots of Terror*. New York: Pantheon.

Mann, Michael. 1987. "Ruling Class Strategies and Citizenship." *Sociology* 21:339–54.

———. 1993. *The Sources of Social Power*. Vol. 2, *The Rise of Classes and Nation States, 1760–1914*. New York: Cambridge University Press.

Mansbach, Richard W., and Franke Wilmer. 2001. "War, Violence, and the Westphalian State System as a Moral Community." In *Identities, Borders, Orders: Rethinking International Relations Theory*, ed. Mathias Albert, David Jacobson, and Yosef Lapid, 51–71. Minneapolis: University of Minnesota Press.

Marques, José Carlos, and Pedro Góis. 2005. "Legalization Processes of Immigrants in Portugal during the 1990s and at the Beginning of the New Millennium." In *Amnesty for Illegal Migrants*, ed. Friedrich Heckmann and Tanja Wunderlich, 55–67. Bamberg: European Forum for Migration Studies.

Martini, Alexis. 1909. *L'expulsion des etrangers*. Paris: Sirey.

Marx, Karl. 1843/1978. "On the Jewish Question." In *The Marx-Engels Reader*, ed. Robert C. Tucker, 26–52. 2nd ed. New York: W. W. Norton.

———. 1844a/1975. *Economic and Philosophic Manuscripts of 1844*. In *Karl Marx–Friedrich Engels: Collected Works*, vol. 3, 229–346. London: Lawrence and Wishart.

———. 1844b/1975. "Introduction to *A Contribution to the Critique of Hegel's 'Philosophy of Right.'*" In *Karl Marx–Friedrich Engels: Collected Works*, vol. 3, 175–87. London: Lawrence and Wishart.

———. 1858/1973. *Grundrisse: Foundations of the Critique of Political Economy*. New York: Vintage.

———. 1867/1976. *Capital: A Critique of Political Economy*. Vol. 1. Trans. Ben Fowkes. New York: Penguin Books.

Massey, Douglas S., Rafael Alarcon, Jorge Durand, and Humberto González. 1987. *Return to Aztlan: The Social Process of International Migration from Western Mexico*. Berkeley: University of California Press.

Massey, Douglas S., Jorge Durand, and Nolan J. Malone. 2002. *Beyond Smoke and Mirrors: Mexican Immigration in an Era of Economic Integration*. Russell Sage Foundation.

Mattawa, Khaled. 2003. *Zodiac of Echoes*. Keene, N.Y.: Ausable Press.

Mauer, Marc. 2006. *Race to Incarcerate*. Rev. ed. New York: New Press.

Mayer, Jane. 2005. "Outsourcing Torture: The Secret History of America's Extraordinary Rendition Program." *New Yorker*, February 14.

McClintock, Maria. 2004. "Deportation Plan Saves Feds Money." *Calgary Sun*, May 16.

McCorquodale, Robert. 2001. "International Law, Boundaries, and Imagination." In *Boundaries and Justice: Diverse Ethical Perspectives*, ed. David L. Miller and Sohail H. Hashmi, 136–63. Princeton, N.J.: Princeton University Press.

McDowell, Linda. 1999. *Gender, Identity, and Place: Understanding Feminist Geographies*. Minneapolis: University of Minnesota Press.

McGarry, John. 1998. " 'Demographic Engineering': The State-Directed Movement of Ethnic Groups as a Technique of Conflict Regulation." *Ethnic and Racial Studies* 21 (4): 613–38.

McGowan, Rima Berns. 1999. *Muslims in the Diaspora: The Somali Communities of London and Toronto*. Toronto: University of Toronto Press.

McNevin, Anne. 2006. "Political Belonging in a Neoliberal Era: The Struggle of the Sans-Papiers." *Citizenship Studies* 10 (2): 135–51.

Médecins sans Frontières. 2005. "Violence and Immigration: Report on Illegal Sub-Saharan Immigrants (ISSs) in Morocco." September 30.

Meir, Ofer. 2005. " 'You're a Filipina Doctor? No Way, You're a Foreign Worker.' " *Y-net Electronic News Source*, January 16.

Melzer, Arthur. 2000. "Rousseau, Nationalism, and the Politics of Sympathetic Identification." In *Educating the Prince: Essays in Honor of Harvey Mansfield*, ed. Mark Blitz and William Kristol, 11–128. Lanham: Rowman and Littlefield.

Mezzadra, Sandro. 2004. "The Right to Escape." *Ephemera* 4 (3): 267–75. http://www.ephemeraweb.org.

———. 2006. "Citizen and Subject: A Postcolonial Constitution for the European Union?" *Situations: Project of the Radical Imagination* 1 (2): 31–42.

Mezzadra, Sandro, and Brett Neilson. 2003. "Né qui, né altrove—Migration, Detention, Desertion: A Dialogue." *Borderlands e-journal* 2 (1). http://www.borderlands.net.au.

Mezzadra, Sandro, and Federico Rahola. 2006. "The Postcolonial Condition: A Few Notes on the Quality of Historical Time in the Global Present." *Postcolonial Text* 2 (1). http://postcolonial.org/index.php/pct/article/view/393/139.

Mezzadra, Sandro, and Enrica Rigo. 2003. "L'Europa dei migranti." In *Europa: Costituzione e movimenti sociali*, ed. Giuseppe Bronzini, Heidrun Friese, Antonio Negri, and Peter Wagner, 213–30. Rome: Manifestolibri.

Mickleburgh, Rod. 2003. "Woman's Escape an Embarrassment for Immigration." *Globe and Mail*, January 23.

Miller, Toby. 1993. *The Well-Tempered Subject: Citizenship, Culture, and the Postmodern Subject*. Baltimore, Md.: Johns Hopkins University Press.

Mills, Kurt. 1996. "Permeable Borders: Human Migration and Sovereignty." *Global Society* 10 (2): 77–106.

Mirzoeff, Nicholas. 2005. *Watching Babylon: The War in Iraq and Global Visual Culture*. New York: Routledge.

Mojaddidi, Wazhma. 2006. "How Politics Influenced the Case of *U.S. vs. Hamid Hayat*." Talk given for Ruth Chance Lecture, Boalt Law School, University of California, Berkeley, September 5.

Montgomery, Sue. 2002a. "Algerians Stage Talk-In." *Montreal Gazette*, October 12.

———. 2002b. "Tears Linked to Water Deal? Deportation Seems to Make No Sense." *Montreal Gazette*, October 19.

Moore, Kathleen. 1999. "A Closer Look at Anti-terrorism Law: *American Arab Anti-discrimination Committee v. Reno* and the Construction of Aliens' Rights." In *Arabs in America: Building a New Future*, ed. Michael Suleiman, 84–99. Philadelphia: Temple University Press.

Morawetz, Nancy. 1998. "Rethinking Retroactive Deportation Laws and the Due Process Clause." *New York University Law Review* 73 (97): 117–14.

———. 2000. "Understanding the Impact of the 1996 Deportation Laws and the Limited Scope of Proposed Reforms." *Harvard Law Review* 113 (8): 1936–62.

Morgan, Edmund S. 1999. *The Puritan Dilemma: The Story of John Winthrop*. New York: Longman.

Morice, Alain. 1997. "Schöne neue Welt der Marktwirtschaft: Lohndrücker, Fremdenfeinde, und Nomaden des Liberalismus." *Le Monde Diplomatique*, no. 5130 (January 17).

Morris, Helen. 1997. "Zero Tolerance: The Increasing Criminalization of Immigration Law." *Interpreter Releases* 74 (29): 1317–26.

Muller, Benjamin J. 2004. "(Dis)Qualified Bodies: Securitization, Citizenship, and 'Identity Management.' " *Citizenship Studies* 8 (3): 279–94.

Nagy, Sharon. 1998. " 'This Time I Think I'll Try a Filipina': Global and Local Influences on Relations between Foreign Household Workers and Their Employers in Doha, Qatar." *City and Society* 10 (1).

Nair, P. R. Gopinathan. 1999. "Return of Overseas Contract Workers and Their Rehabilitation and Development in Kerala (India): A Critical Account of Policies, Performance, and Prospects." *International Migration* 37 (1): 209–42.

Nakhleh, Emile A. 1976. *Bahrain*. Lexington, Mass.: Lexington Books.

Nambiar, A. C. Kutti Krishnan. 1995. "The Socio-economic Conditions of Gulf Migrants." Report by the Malabar Institute for Development, Research, and Action. New Delhi: Commonwealth Publishers.

Nascimbene, Bruno, ed. 2001. *Expulsion and Detention of Aliens in the European Union Countries*. Milan: Giuffré Editore.

Neilson, Brett. 2004. "*Potenza Nuda*? Sovereignty, Biopolitics, Capitalism." *Contretemps* 5:63–78.

Neilson, Brett, and Angela Mitropoulos. 2007. "Exceptional Times, Nongovernmental Spacings, and Impolitical Movements." In *Nongovernmental Politics*, ed. Michel Feher, 469–81. New York: Zone Books.

Nevins, Joseph. 2002. *Operation Gatekeeper: The Rise of the "Illegal Alien" and the Making of the U.S.-Mexico Boundary*. New York: Routledge.

Ngai, Mae M. 2003. "The Strange Career of the Illegal Alien: Immigration Restriction and Deportation Policy in the United States, 1921–1965." *Law and History Review* 21 (1): 69–107.

———. 2004. *Impossible Subjects: Illegal Aliens and the Making of Modern America*. Princeton, N.J.: Princeton University Press.

———. 2005. "We Need a Deportation Deadline: A Statute of Limitations on Unlawful Entry Would Humanely Address Illegal Immigration." *Washington Post*, June 14.

Nguyen, Tram. 2005. *We Are All Suspects Now: Untold Stories from Immigrant Communities after 9/11*. Boston: Beacon Press.

Nijhawan, Michael. 2005. "Deportability, Medicine, and the Law." *Anthropology and Medicine* 12 (3): 271–85.

Nijman, Janne Elisabeth. 2004. *The Concept of International Legal Personality: An Inquiry into the History and Theory of International Law*. Den Haag: T. M. C. Asser Press.

Noiriel, Gérard. 1988. *Le creuset français: Histoire de l'immigration, XIXe–XXe siècle*. Paris: Seuil.

———. 1996. *The French Melting Pot: Immigration, Citizenship, and National Identity*. Minneapolis: University of Minnesota Press.

Noll, Gregor. 1999. "Rejected Asylum Seekers: The Problem of Return." New Issues in Refugee Research, UNHCR working paper no. 4.

———. 2003. "Visions of the Exceptional: Legal and Theoretical Issues Raised by Transit Processing Centres and Protection Zones." *European Journal of Migration and Law* 5:303–41.

Núñez, Guillermina, and Josiah McC. Heyman. 2007. "Entrapment Processes and Immigrant Communities in a Time of Heightened Border Vigilance." *Human Organization* 66 (4): 354–65.

Nyers, Peter. 2003. "Abject Cosmopolitanism: The Politics of Protection in the Anti-deportation Movement." *Third World Quarterly* 24:1069–93.

———. 2004. "Introduction: What's Left of Citizenship?" *Citizenship Studies* 8 (3): 203–15.

———. 2006a. "The Accidental Citizen: Acts of Sovereignty and (Un)Making Citizenship." *Economy and Society* 35 (1): 22–41.

———. 2006b. *Rethinking Refugees: Beyond States of Emergency*. New York: Routledge.

———. 2006c. "Taking Rights, Mediating Wrongs: Disagreements over the Political Agency of Non-status Refugees." In *The Politics of Protection: Sites of Insecurity and Political Agency*, ed. J. Huysmans, A. Dobson, and R. Prokhovnik, 48–67. London: Routledge.

O'Connor, Anne-Marie. 2000. "Activist Says Officer Sought His Deportation." *Los Angeles Times*, February 17.

Oda, Shigeru. 1968. "The Individual in International Law." In *Manual of Public International Law*, ed. Max Sørensen, 469–530. London: Macmillan.

Olivio, Antonio. 2007. "Immigration Activist Will Leave Church: With D.C. Trip, She Risks Deportation." *Chicago Tribune*, August 16.

Ong, Aihwa. 1999. *Flexible Citizenship: The Cultural Logics of Transnationality.* Durham, N.C.: Duke University Press.

———. 2003. *Buddha Is Hiding: Refugees, Citizenship, the New America.* Berkeley: University of California Press.

———. 2006. *Neoliberalism as Exception: Mutations in Citizenship and Sovereignty.* Durham, N.C.: Duke University Press.

Or, Theodor. 2006. "The Report by the State Commission of Inquiry into the Events of October 2000." *Israel Studies* 11:23–53.

Orrenius, Pia M. 2001. "Illegal Immigration and Enforcement along the U.S.-Mexico Border: An Overview." In *Economic and Financial Review, First Quarter 2001.* Dallas: Federal Reserve Bank of Dallas.

Osella, Filippo, and Caroline Osella. 2000a. "Migration, Money, and Masculinity in Kerala." *Journal of the Royal Anthropological Institute* 6:117–33.

———. 2000b. *Social Mobility in Kerala: Modernity and Identity in Conflict.* London: Pluto Press.

Pager, Devah. 2007. *Marked: Race, Crime, and Finding Work in an Era of Mass Incarceration.* Chicago: University of Chicago Press.

Palgrave, William Gifford. 1865/1982. *Narrative of a Year's Journey through Central and Eastern Arabia (1862–1863).* Amersham, England: Demand Reprints.

Panagiotidis, Efthimia, and Vassilis Tsianos. 2007. "Denaturalizing Camps: Überwachen und Entschleunigen in der Schengener Ägäis-Zone." In *Transit Migration: Turbulente Ränder: Neue Perspektiven auf Migration an den Grenzen Europas,* ed. Transit Migration Forschungsgruppe, 59–88. Bielefeld: Transcript Verlag.

Papadopoulos, Dimitris, Niamh Stephenson, and Vassilis Tsianos. 2008. *Escape Routes: Control and Subversion in the Twenty-first Century.* London: Pluto Press.

Papadopoulos, Dimitris, and Vassilis Tsianos. 2007. "How to Do Sovereignty without People? The Subjectless Condition of Postliberal Power." *Boundary 2: International Journal of Literature and Culture* 34 (1): 135–72.

Papadopoulos, Stavroula. 2002. "When You Can't Go Home: Demonstrators Support Plight of Algerians Faced with Deportation." *Concordian,* October 16.

Papastergiadis, Nikos. 2000. *The Turbulence of Migration: Globalization, Deterritorialization, and Hybridity.* Cambridge: Polity Press.

———. 2006. "The Invasion Complex: The Abject Other and Spaces of Violence." *Geografiska Annaler,* series B, *Human Geography* 88 (4): 429–42.

Paredes, Américo. 1958. *"With His Pistol in His Hand": A Border Ballad and Its Hero.* Austin: University of Texas Press.

Pashukanis, Evgeny B. 1929/1989. *Law and Marxism: A General Theory towards a Critique of the Fundamental Juridical Concepts.* Worcester, UK: Pluto Publishing.

Passel, Jeffrey S. 2005. *Unauthorized Migrants: Numbers and Characteristics*. Washington: Pew Hispanic Center. http://www.pewhispanic.org/files/reports/46.pdf.

Pease, Donald. 1993. "New Perspectives on U.S. Culture and Imperialism." In *Cultures of United States Imperialism*, ed. Amy Kaplan and Donald Pease, 22–37. Durham, N.C.: Duke University Press.

Peled, Yoav. 1992. "Ethnic Democracy and the Legal Construction of Citizenship: Arab Citizens of the Jewish State." *American Political Science Review* 86:432–43.

Pelonpää, Matti. 1984. *Expulsion in International Law: A Study in Aliens Law and Human Rights with Special Reference to Finland*. Helsinki: Academia Scientiarum Fennica.

Perera, Suvendrini. 2002. "What Is a Camp . . . ?" *Borderlands e-journal* 1 (1). http://www.borderlands.net.au.

Pertierra, Raul. 1994. "Lured Abroad: The Case of Ilocano Overseas Workers." *Sojourn: Journel of Social Isssues in Southeast Asia* 9 (1): 54–80.

Petersilia, Joan. 2003. *When Prisoners Come Home: Parole and Prisoner Reentry*. New York: Oxford University Press.

Peutz, Nathalie. 2005. "Signpost in Somaliland's Quest for Sovereignty." *Middle East Report Online*, September 28. http://merip.org/mero/mero092805.html.

———. 2006. "Embarking on an Anthropology of Removal." *Current Anthropology* 47 (2): 217–41.

———. 2007. "Out-laws: Deportees, Desire, and 'The Law.' " In "Exploring 'Illegal' and 'Irregular' Migrants' Lived Experiences of Law and State Power," special issue, *International Migration* 45 (3): 350–59.

Piguet, Etienne, and Stefano Losa. 2001. *Demande de main-d'oeuvre du domaine de l'asile en Suisse et ampleur du travail clandestin*. Zürich: Seismo.

Pinkas, Alon. 1993. "Garrison Democracy: The Impact of the 1967 Occupation of Territories on Institutional Democracy in Israel." In *Democracy, Peace, and the Israeli-Palestinian Conflict*, ed. Edy Kaufman, Shukri B. Abed, and Robert L. Rothstein, 61–83. Boulder, Colo.: Lynne Rienner.

Piore, Michael J. 1980. *Birds of Passage: Migrant Labour in Industrial Societies*. Cambridge: Cambridge University Press.

Plender, Richard. 1972. *International Migration Law*. Leiden: Sijthoff.

Pliez, Olivier. 2005. "La troisième migratoire, les conséquences de la politique européenne de lutte contre les migrations clandestines." Paper written for Asia-Europe Foundation workshop "The Management of Humanitarian Aids and of Transnational Movements of Persons in the Euro-Mediterranean Area and in South-East Asia," University of Genova, August 28–30, Lampedusa.

Podur, Justin. 2002. "Fighting the Deportation: A Rabble Interview with the Action Committee of Non-status Algerians." *rabble.ca*, December 18. http://news.infoshop.org.

Polanyi, Karl. 1957. *The Great Transformation: The Political and Economic Origins of Our Time*. Boston: Beacon Press.

Pollock, Sheldon, Homi K. Bhabha, Carol A. Breckenridge, and Dipesh Chakrabarty. 2002. "Cosmopolitanisms." In *Cosmopolitanism*, ed. Sheldon Pollock, Homi K. Bhabha, Carol A. Breckenridge, and Dipesh Chakrabarty, 1–14. Durham, N.C.: Duke University Press.

Prashad, Vijay. 2003. "The Green Menace: McCarthyism after 9/11." *Subcontinental: A Journal of South Asian American Political Identity* 1 (1): 65–75.

Pratt, Anna. 2005. *Securing Borders: Detention and Deportation in Canada.* Vancouver: University of British Columbia Press.

Preuss, Ulrich. 1998. "Citizenship in the European Union: A Paradigm for Transnational Democracy?" In *Re-imagining Political Community: Studies in Cosmopolitan Democracy*, ed. Daniele Archibugi, David Held, and Martin Köhler, 138–51. Cambridge: Polity.

Preuss, Ulrich, Michelle Everson, Mathias Koenig-Archibugi, and Edwige Lefebvre. 2003. "Tradition of Citizenship in the European Union." *Citizenship Studies* 7 (1): 3–14.

Procacci, Giovanna. 1991. "Social Economy and the Government of Poverty." In *The Foucault Effect: Studies in Governmentality*, ed. Graham Burchell, Colin Gordon, and Peter Miller, 151–68. Hemel Hempstead: Harvester Wheatsheaf.

Puar, Jasbir, and Amit S. Rai. 2002. "Monster, Terrorist, Fag: The War on Terrorism and the Production of Docile Patriots." *Social Text* 72:117–48.

Puwar, Nirmal. 2004. *Space Invaders: Race, Gender, and Bodies Out of Place.* New York: Berg.

Rabinowitz, Dan. 1997. *Overlooking Nazareth: The Ethnography of Exclusion in the Galilee.* Cambridge: Cambridge University Press.

———. 2002. "Oriental Othering and National Identity: A Review of Early Israeli Anthropological Studies of Palestinians." *Identities: Global Studies in Culture and Power* 9:305–24.

Rabinowitz, Dan, and Khawla Abu-Baker. 2005. *Coffins on Our Shoulders: The Experience of the Palestinian Citizens of Israel.* Berkeley: University of California Press.

Ragin, Charles C. 1994. *Constructing Social Research: The Unity and Diversity of Method.* Thousand Oaks, Calif.: Pine Forge Press.

Rahola, Federico. 2007. "La forma campo: Per una genealogia dei luoghi di transito e di internamento del presente." *Conflitti Globali* 4:11–27.

Raijman, Rebecca, and Adriana Kemp. 2007. "Labor Migration, Managing the Ethno-national Conflict, and Client Politics in Israel." In *Transnational Migration to Israel in Global Comparative Context*, ed. Sarah S. Willen, 31–50. Lanham, Md.: Lexington.

Rajaram, Prem Kumar, and Carl Grundy-Warr. 2004. "The Irregular Migrant as Homo Sacer: Migration and Detention in Australia, Malaysia, and Thailand." *International Migration* 42:33–64.

Rancière, Jacques. 1995. *La mesensante: Politique et philosophie.* Paris: Galilee.

———. 1999. *Dis-agreement: Politics and Philosophy.* Minneapolis: University of Minnesota Press.

———. 2004. "Who Is the Subject of the Rights of Man?" *South Atlantic Quarterly* 103 (2–3): 297–310.

Randall, Margaret. 1987. "Threatened with Deportation." *Latin American Perspectives* 14 (4): 465–80.

Rapoport, Tamar, and Edna Lomsky-Feder. 2001. "Reflections on Strangeness in Context: The Case of Russian-Jewish Immigrants in the Kibbutz." *Qualitative Sociology* 24:483–506.

Rashbaum, William. 2006. "Terror Case May Offer Clues into Police Use of Informants." *New York Times*, April 24.

Rashid, Ahmed. 2000. *Taliban: Militant Islam, Oil, and Fundamentalism in Central Asia*. New Haven, Conn.: Yale University Press.

Reiss, Nira. 1991. *The Health Care of the Arabs in Israel*. Westview Special Studies on the Middle East. Boulder, Colo.: Westview Press.

The Republic. 2003. "77,000 Foreigners Ordered to Leave." *Republic* (Hargeysa, Somaliland), November 1.

República de El Salvador. 2007. "Primer informe de El Salvador sobre la aplicación de la Convención Internacional sobre la Protección de los Derechos de Todos los Trabajadores Migratorios y de sus Familiares." San Salvador: El Salvador. http://www.ohchr.org/english/bodies/cmw/docs/CMW.C.SLV.1_sp.pdf (accessed March 22, 2007).

Rhodes, Lorna A. 2001. "Toward an Anthropology of Prisons." *Annual Review of Anthropology* 30:65–83.

Richard, Randall. 2003. "Banned for Life: Jailed at 17, Kim Ho Ma Can Never Live in America." Associated Press, November 21. http://news.asianweek.com/news (accessed November 28, 2003).

Rieber, Alfred J. 2000. "Repressive Population Transfers in Central, Eastern, and South-Eastern Europe: A Historical Overview." *Journal of Communist Studies and Transition Politics* 16 (1–2): 1–27.

Riechmann, Deb. 2006. "Bush Signs Homeland Security Bill." Associated Press, October 4.

Rigo, Enrica. 2003. "Citizens and Foreigners in the Enlarged Europe: Implications of Enlargement for the Rule of Law and Constitutionalism in Postcommunist Legal Orders." Draft paper, European University Institute, Florence, November 28–29.

———. 2005. "Citizenship at Europe's Borders: Some Reflections on the Postcolonial Condition of Europe in the Context of EU Enlargement." *Citizenship Studies* 9 (1): 3–22.

———. 2007. *Europa di confine: Trasformazioni della cittadinanza nell'Unione allargata*. Rome: Meltemi.

———. 2008. "The Right to Territory and the Contemporary Transformation of European Citizenship." In *Citizenship between Past and Future*, ed. Engin F. Isin, Peter Nyers, and Bryan S. Turner, 150–60. New York: Routledge.

Robbins, Bruce. 1998. "Comparative Cosmopolitanisms." In *Cosmopolitics: Thinking and Feeling beyond the Nation*, ed. Pheng Cheah and Bruce Robbins, 246–64. Minneapolis: University of Minnesota Press.

Robin, Corey. 2003. "Fear, American Style: Civil Liberty after 9/11." In *Implicating Empire: Globalization and Resistance in the 21st Century World Order*, ed. Stanley Aronowitz and Heather Gautney, 47–64. New York: Basic Books.

Rodríguez, Dylan. 2006. *Forced Passages: Imprisoned Radical Intellectuals and the U.S. Prison Regime*. Minneapolis: University of Minnesota Press.

Rosaldo, Renato. 1994. "Cultural Citizenship and Education Democracy." *Cultural Anthropology* 9 (3): 402–11.

Rose, Nikolas. 1999. *Powers of Freedom: Reframing Political Thought*. Cambridge: Cambridge University Press.

Rosenhek, Zeev. 1999. "The Politics of Claims-Making by Labour Migrants in Israel." *Journal of Ethnic and Migration Studies* 25:575–95.

———. 2000. "Migration Regimes, Intra-state Conflicts, and the Politics of Exclusion and Inclusion: Migrant Workers in the Israeli Welfare State." *Social Problems* 47:49–67.

———. 2007. "Challenging Exclusionary Migration Regimes: Labor Migration in Israel in Comparative Perspective." In *Transnational Migration to Israel in Global Comparative Perspective*, ed. Sarah S. Willen, 217–32. Lanham, Md.: Lexington Books.

Roth, John, Douglas Greenburg, and Serene Wille. 2004. "Al Barakaat Case Study." In *Monograph on Terrorist Financing*, 67–86. Staff Report to the National Commission on Terrorist Attacks upon the United States. http://govinfo.library.unt.edu/911/staff_statements/911_TerrFin_Ch5.pdf (accessed June 17, 2008).

Rouhana, Nadim. 1997. *Palestinian Citizens in an Ethnic Jewish State: Identities in Conflict*. New Haven, Conn.: Yale University Press.

Rouse, Roger. 1992. "Making Sense of Settlement: Class Transformation, Cultural Struggle, and Transnationalism among Mexican Migrants in the United States." In "Towards a Transnational Perspective on Migration: Race, Class, Ethnicity, and Nationalism Reconsidered," ed. Nina Glick Schiller, Linda Basch, and Cristina Blanc-Szanton, special issue, *Annals of the New York Academy of Sciences* 645:25–52.

Royal Commission on Alien Immigration. 1903. *Report of the Royal Commission on Alien Immigration*. Cmd 1741. London: His Majesty's Stationary Office.

Rusche, George, and Otto Kirchheimer. 1939. *Punishment and Social Structure*. New York: Columbia University Press.

Ryan, Oliver. 2003. "Empty Shops, Empty Promises for Coney Island Pakistanis." *ColorLines* 6 (2): 14–16.

Sabar, Galia. 2007. "The Rise and Fall of African Migrant Churches: Transformations in African Religious Discourse and Practice in Tel Aviv." In *Transnational Migration to Israel in Global Comparative Context*, ed. Sarah S. Willen, 185–202. Lanham, Md.: Lexington.

Sabine, G. H. 1941. *A History of Political Theory*. London: George G. Harrap.

Sachs, Susan. 1999. "More Immigrants Are Deported as Officials' Power Increases." *New York Times*, November 13.

———. 2002. "Long Resistant, Police Start Embracing Immigration Duties." *New York Times*, March 15.

Salaita, Steven. 2006. *Anti-Arab Racism in the USA: Where It Comes From and What It Means for Politics Today*. Ann Arbor, Mich.: Pluto.

Saliba, Therese. n.d. "Virtual Camps: Arab Detentions and Community Activism in the Northwest." Paper presented at Mapping Arab Diasporas Conference, University of Michigan, Dearborn, April 2006.

Salter, Mark B. 2004. "Passports, Mobility, and Security: How Smart Can the Border Be?" *International Studies Perspectives* 5 (1): 71–91.

Sassen, Saskia. 1999. *Guests and Aliens*. New York: New Press.

———. 2002. "The Repositioning of Citizenship: Emergent Subjects and Spaces for Politics." *Berkeley Journal of Sociology* 46:4–26.

———. 2006. *Territory, Authority, Rights: From Medieval to Global Assemblages*. Princeton, N.J.: Princeton University Press.

Scalia, John, and Marika F. X. Litras. 2000. *Immigration Offenders in the Federal Criminal Justice System, 2000: Bureau of Justice Statistics Special Report*. Washington: Office of Justice Programs, U.S. Department of Justice.

Schechtman, Joseph B. 1946. *European Population Transfers, 1939–45*. New York: Russell and Russell.

Scheper-Hughes, Nancy. 2004. "Dangerous and Endangered Youth: Social Structures and Determinants of Violence." *Annals of the New York Academy of Sciences* 1036: 13–46.

Schinkel, Willem. 2002. "The Modernist Myth in Criminology." *Theoretical Criminology* 6 (2): 123–44.

Schmitt, Carl. 1922/1985. *Political Theology: Four Chapters on the Concept of Sovereignty*. Cambridge, Mass.: MIT Press.

———. 1927/1996. *The Concept of the Political*. Chicago: University of Chicago Press.

Schnapper, Dominique. 1994. *La communauté des citoyens: Sur l'idée moderne de nation*. Paris: Gallimard.

———. 1997. "The European Debate on Citizenship." *Daedalus* 126 (3): 199–222.

Schuck, Peter H., and Rogers M. Smith. 1985. *Citizenship without Consent: Illegal Aliens in the American Polity*. New Haven, Conn.: Yale University Press.

Schulhofer, Stephen J. 2002. *The Enemy Within: Intelligence Gathering, Law Enforcement, and Civil Liberties in the Wake of September 11*. New York: Century Foundation Press.

Schuster, Liza. 2005. "A Sledgehammer to Crack a Nut: Deportation, Detention, and Dispersal in Europe." *Social Policy and Administration* 39 (6): 606–21.

———. 2006. "Nuovi paradigmi di asilo: Cosa sta accadendo sul campo?" *Studi emigrazione* 162 (June): 267–87.

Seccombe, Ian, and Richard Lawless. 1986. "The Gulf Labour Market and the Early Oil Industry: Traditional Structures and New Forms of Organisation." In *The Gulf in the Early Twentieth Century: Foreign Institutions and Local*

Responses, ed. Richard Lawless, 94–98. Occasional Papers Series, no. 31. Centre for Middle Eastern and Islamic Studies, University of Durham, England.

Seeman, Don. 1997. " 'One People, One Blood': Religious Conversion, Public Health, and Immigration as Social Experience for Ethiopian Israelis." Ph.D. diss., Harvard University.

Sekhar, T. V. 1996. "Male Emigration and Changes in the Family: Impact on Female Sex Roles." *Indian Journal of Social Work* 57 (2): 27–294.

Shafir, Gershon. 2004. "Citizenship and Human Rights in an Era of Globalization." In *People Out of Place: Globalization, Human Rights, and the Citizenship Gap*, ed. Alison Brysk and Gershon Shafir, 11–28. New York: Routledge.

Shafir, Gershon, and Yoav Peled. 1998. "Citizenship and Stratification in an Ethnic Democracy." *Ethnic and Racial Studies* 21:408–27.

Shahani, Aarti. 2008. "Sanctuary's Human Face." *ColorLines*, no. 42 (January–February). http://www.colorlines.com/article.php?ID=263.

Shamir, Ronan. 2005. "Without Borders? Notes on Globalization as a Mobility Regime." *Sociological Theory* 23:197–217.

Shapiro, Michael J. 1999. "The Ethics of Encounter: Unreading, Unmapping the Imperium." In *Moral Spaces: Rethinking Ethics and World Politics*, ed. David Campbell and Michael J. Shapiro, 57–91. Minneapolis: University of Minnesota Press.

Sharma, Nandita. 2003. "No Borders Movements and the Rejection of Left Nationalism." *Canadian Dimension* 37 (3).

Shehadeh, Michel. 2007. "Free Speech Prevails for the L.A. 8: A Palestinian Immigrant in Legal Limbo for 20 Years Hopes His Deportation Battles Are Finally Over." *Los Angeles Times*, February 6.

Sheikh, Irum. 2003. "The Female Detainee: Reading, Tracing, and Locating Gender in 9/11 Detentions." *Subcontinental: A Journal of South Asian American Political Identity* 1 (3): 71–78.

Sheleg, Yair. 2002. "Come Forth, Marry, and Multiply for a Strong Israel." *Ha'aretz* (Israel), June 24.

Silvey, Rachel. 2004. "Transnational Domestication: State Power and Indonesian Migrant Women in Saudi Arabia." *Political Geography* 23:245–64.

Simmel, Georg. 1908. *Soziologie: Untersuchungen über die Formen der Vergesellschaftung*. Leipzig: Duncker and Humblot.

Simon, Jonathan. 1998. "Refugees in a Carceral Age: The Rebirth of Immigration Prisons in the United States, 1976–1992." *Public Culture* 10 (3): 577–606.

Simoncini, Alessandro. 2000. "Migranti, frontiere, spazi di confine: I lavoratori migranti nell'ordine salariale." *Altreragioni* 10:29–45.

Simons, Anna. 1995. *Networks of Dissolution: Somalia Undone*. Boulder, Colo.: Westview Press.

Simpson, Bob. 2000. "Imagined Genetic Communities: Ethnicity and Essentialism in the Twenty-First Century." *Anthropology Today* 16 (3): 3–6.

Sinai, Ruth. 2004a. "Finished with the Foreigners? At the Immigration Authority They Deal with Israelis Too." *Ha'aretz* (Israel), October 26.

————. 2004b. "Immigration Police Arrest Boxing Champion from Ethiopia." *Ha'aretz* (Israel), May 6.

————. 2004c. "Immigration Police: Investigation or Persecution?" *Ha'aretz* (Israel), February 16.

Slot, Ben J. 1993. "The Dutch East India Company and Bahrain." In *Bahrain through the Ages: The History*, ed. 'Abdullah bin Khalid Al-Khalifa and Michael Rice. London: Kegan Paul International.

Slyomovics, Susan. 1998. *The Object of Memory: Arab and Jew Narrate the Palestinian Village*. Philadelphia: University of Pennsylvania Press.

Smith, Neil. 2005. *The Endgame of Globalization*. New York: Routledge.

Smooha, Sammy. 1990. "Minority Status in an Ethnic Democracy: The Status of the Arab Minority in Israel." *Ethnic and Racial Studies* 13:389–413.

————. 1997. "Ethnic Democracy: Israel as an Archetype." *Israel Studies* 2: 198–241.

Soguk, Nevzat. 1999. "Predicaments of Territorial Democracy and Statecraft in Europe: How European Democracies Regiment Migratory Movements." *Alternatives* 22 (3): 313–52.

Sontag, Deborah. 2003. "In a Homeland Far from Home." *New York Times*, November 16.

Soysal, Yasemin Nuhoglu. 1994. *Limits of Citizenship: Migrants and Postnational Membership in Europe*. Chicago: University of Chicago Press.

————. 1996. "Changing Citizenship in Europe: Remarks on Postnational Membership and the National State." In *Citizenship, Nationality, and Migration in Europe*, ed. David Cesarani and Mary Fulbrook, 17–29. New York: Routledge.

Stasiulis, Daiva. 2004. "Hybrid Citizenship and What's Left." *Citizenship Studies* 8 (3): 295–303.

Stasiulis, Daiva, and Abigail B. Bakan. 1997. "Negotiating Citizenship: The Case of Foreign Domestic Workers in Canada." *Feminist Review* 57:112–39.

Stasiulis, Daiva, and Darryl Ross. 2006. "Security, Flexible Sovereignty, and the Perils of Multiple Citizenship." *Citizenship Studies* 10 (3): 329–48.

Stevens, Jacob. 2001. "Barring the Doors." *New Left Review* 12:152–59.

Stevenson, Robert Louis. 1886/1999. *The Strange Case of Dr. Jekyll and Mr. Hyde, and Other Stories*. Ware. U.K.: Wordsworth.

Stöbbe, Holk. 2000. *Undocumented Migration in the U.S.A. and Germany: An Analysis of the German Case with Cross-References to the U.S. Situation*. La Jolla, Calif.: Center for Comparative Immigration Studies, University of California, San Diego.

Stoler, Ann L. 2006. "Intimidations of Empire: Predicaments of the Tactile and Unseen." In *Haunted by Empire: Geographies of Intimacy in North American History*, ed. Ann L. Stoler, 1–22. Durham, N.C.: Duke University Press.

Strikwerda, Carl. 1997. "Reinterpreting the History of European Integration: Business, Labor, and Social Citizenship in Twentieth-Century Europe." In *European Integration in Social and Historical Perspective: 1850 to the Present*, ed. Jytte Klausen and Louise A. Tilly, 51–70. Lanham, Md.: Rowman and Littlefield.

Suárez-Navaz, Liliana. 2004. *Rebordering the Mediterranean: Boundaries and Citizenship in Southern Europe*. New York: Berghahn Books.

Swarns, Rachel L. 2005. "Crime Database Often Wrong on Immigration, Study Finds." *New York Times*, December 9.

Tamanaha, Brian Z. 2004. *On the Rule of Law*. Cambridge: Cambridge University Press.

Tavernese, Sabrina. 2003. "Muslim SUNY Student's Expulsion Is Protested." *New York Times*, November 22.

Taylor-Saito, Natsu. 2001. "Symbolism under Siege: Japanese American Redress and the 'Racing' of Arab Americans as 'Terrorists.'" *Asian Law Journal* 8 (1).

Terray, Emmanuel. 2002. "Illegale Arbeit ist rentabel." *Archipel* 92 (3).

Terry, Don. 2007. "No Way Out: When the Immigration-Reform Bill Died in Congress, the Door Closed on Elvira Arellano's Hopes of Finding a Path from Her Sanctuary to Legal Status in the U.S." *Chicago Tribune Magazine*, August 5.

Thompson, Don. 2005. "Lodi Pakistani Community Secretly Taped for Three Years." *San Francisco Chronicle*, June 9.

Thompson, Elizabeth. 2003. "Algeria Safe, Coderre Says: Immigration Minister Defends Deportations Despite Travel Advisory, Warnings of Violence." *Montreal Gazette*, January 28.

Thomsen, Rudi. 1972. *The Origin of Ostracism: A Synthesis*. Copenhagen: Gyldenal.

Ticktin, Miriam. 2002. "Between Justice and Compassion: 'Les Sans Papiers' and the Political Economy of Health, Human Rights, and Humanitarianism in France." Ph.D. diss., Stanford University.

———. 2006. "Where Ethics and Politics Meet: The Violence of Humanitarianism in France." *American Ethnologist* 33 (1): 33–49.

Tilly, Charles. 1985. "War Making and State Making as Organized Crime." In *Bringing the State Back In*, ed. Peter B. Evans, Dietrich Rueschemeyer, and Theda Skocpol, 169–91. Cambridge: Cambridge University Press.

———. 1992. *Coercion, Capital, and European States: AD 990–1992*. Oxford: Basil Blackwell.

Tonry, Michael, ed. 1997. *Ethnicity, Crime, and Immigration: Comparative and Cross-National Perspectives*. Chicago: University of Chicago Press.

Tormey, Anwen. 2007. "'Everyone with Eyes Can See the Problem': Moral Citizens and the Space of Irish Nationhood." In "'Illegal' and 'Irregular' Migrants' Lived Experiences of Law and State Power," special issue, *International Migration* 45 (3): 69–100.

Torpey, John. 1999. *The Invention of the Passport: Surveillance, Citizenship, and the State*. Cambridge: Cambridge University Press.

Torres, Rodolfo, Louis Mirón, and Jonathan Xavier Inda, eds. 1999. *Race, Identity, and Citizenship: A Reader*. Malden, Mass.: Blackwell.

Torstrick, Rebecca L. 1993. "Raising and Rupturing Boundaries: The Politics of Identity in Acre, Israel." Ph.D. diss., Washington University, St. Louis.

———. 2000. *The Limits of Coexistence: Identity Politics in Israel.* Ann Arbor: University of Michigan Press.

Transit Migration Forschungsgruppe, ed. 2007. *Turbulente Ränder: Neue Perspektiven auf Migration an den Grenzen Europas.* Bielefeld: Transcript Verlag.

Trouillot, Michel-Rolph. 2001. "The Anthropology of the State in the Age of Globalization: Close Encounters of the Deceptive Kind." *Current Anthropology* 42 (1): 125–38.

Tully, James. 1999. "The Agonic Freedom of Citizens." *Economy and Society* 28 (2): 161–82.

United Nations. 2002. "International Migration Report 2002." New York: United Nations Department of Economic and Social Affairs. http://www.un.org/esa/population/publications/ittmig2002/2002ITTMIGTEXT22–11.pdf.

United Nations High Commissioner for Refugees. 2002a. "Israel Takes Over Review of Local Asylum Claims from UNHCR." UNHCR.

———. 2002b. "Israel: National Refugee Status Granting Body Inaugurated." UNHCR.

U.S. Department of Homeland Security, Bureau of Immigration and Customs Enforcement (USDHS-ICE). 2003. *Endgame: Office of Detention and Removal Strategic Plan, 2003–2012: Detention and Removal Strategy for a Secure Homeland.* http://www.ice.gov/graphics/dro/endgame.pdf.

———. 2005. *2005 Yearbook of Immigration Statistics.* Washington: U.S. Department of Homeland Security, Office of Immigration Statistics.

———. 2007. "ICE Deports High-Profile Criminal Fugitive Alien to Mexico: Woman Who Sought Refuge in Chicago Church Arrested during Weekend Trip to L.A." News Release. http://www.ice.gov/pi/news/newsreleases/articles/0708201a.htm.

van Aken, Mauro. 2007. "Rifugiati, migranti, nomadi: Un laboratorio sulle rive del Giordano." *Conflitti Globali* 4:118–32.

van der Pot, C. W., and A. M. Donner. 1995. *Handboek van het Nederlandse Staatsrecht.* Zwolle: Tjeenk Willink.

Veenkamp, Theo, Tom Bentley, and Allesandra Buonfino. 2003. *People Flow: Migration in a New European Commonwealth.* London.

Vélez-Ibáñez, Carlos G. 1983. *Bonds of Mutual Trust: The Cultural Systems of Rotating Credit Associations among Urban Mexicans and Chicanos.* New Brunswick, N.J.: Rutgers University Press.

Virilio, Paul. 1986. *Speed and Politics: An Essay on Dromology.* New York: Columbia University Press.

Virk, Sobia. 2002. "Algerian Refugees Facing Mass Persecution upon Deportation." *Link* 47.

Virno, Paolo. 2002. "General Intellect, Exodus, Multitude: Interview with Paolo Virno, Published in Spanish in *Archipélago* Number 54." English translation at http://www.generation-online.org/p/fpvirno2.htm.

Wacquant, Loïc. 1999. "Suitable Enemies: Foreigners and Immigrants in the Prisons of Europe." *Punishment and Society* 1 (2): 215–22.

Walker, R. B. J. 1993. *Inside/Outside: International Relations as Political Theory.* Cambridge: Cambridge University Press.

———. 2002. "After the Future: Enclosures, Connections, Politics." In *Reframing the International: Law, Culture, Politics,* ed. Richard Falk, Lester E. J. Ruiz, and R. B. J. Walker, 18–21. New York: Routledge.

Walters, William. 2000. *Unemployment and Government: Genealogies of the Social.* Cambridge: Cambridge University Press.

———. 2002a. "Deportation, Expulsion, and the International Police of Aliens." *Citizenship Studies* 6 (3): 256–92.

———. 2002b. "Mapping Schengenland: Denaturalizing the Border." *Environment and Planning D: Society and Space* 20 (5): 561–80.

———. 2004. "Secure Borders, Safe Haven, Domopolitics." *Citizenship Studies* 8 (3): 237–60.

Walzer, Michael. 1983. *Spheres of Justice: A Defense of Pluralism and Equality.* New York: Basic Books.

Weber, Frank P. 1996. "Expulsion: Genese et pratique d'un contrôle en Allemagne." *Cultures and Conflits* 23. http://www.conflits.org/index627.html.

Weber, Max. 1978. "Bureaucracy." In *Economy and Society: An Outline of Interpretative Sociology,* ed. Guenther Roth and Claus Wittich, vol. 2, 956–1005. Berkeley: University of California Press.

Weiner, Myron. 1986. "Labor Migrations as Incipient Diasporas." In *Modern Diasporas in International Politics,* ed. Gabriel Sheffer, 47–74. New York: St. Martin's Press.

Welch, Michael. 2000. "The Role of the Immigration and Naturalization Service in the Prison-Industrial Complex." In "Critical Resistance to the Prison-Industrial Complex," special issue, *Social Justice* 27 (3): 73–88.

———. 2002. *Detained: Immigration Laws and the Expanding INS Jail Complex.* Philadelphia: Temple University Press.

Whitaker, Reg. 2002. "Refugee Policy after September 11: Not Much New." *Refuge: Canada's Periodical on Refugees* 20 (4): 29–33.

Wicker, Hans-Rudolf. 2002a. "Ethnologische Überlegungen zu einem Strafvollzug im Zeitalter zunehmender transnationaler Mobilität." In *Brennpunkt Strafvollzug: Regards sur la prison,* ed. Andrea Baechtold and Ariane Senn, 223–37. Bern: Stämpfli.

———. 2002b. "Von der 'Fremdenpolizei' zum 'Dienst für Migration': Reaktionen von Staat und Gesellschaft auf zunehmende internationale Mobilität." *Erlanger Forschungen* (Universitätsbibliothek Erlangen-Nürnberg) 98: 43–67.

———. 2004. "Foreigners' Policy, Differentiated Citizenship Rights, and Naturalization." *Tsantsa: Revue de la société Suisse d'ethnologie* 9:6–17.

Willen, Sarah. 2003. "Perspectives on Transnational Labor Migration in Israel." *Revue Européene des Migrations Internationales* 19:243–62.

———. 2005. "Birthing 'Invisible' Children: State Power, NGO Activism, and Reproductive Health among Undocumented Migrant Workers in Tel Aviv, Israel." *Journal of Middle East Women's Studies* 1:55–88.

———. 2006. " 'No Person Is Illegal'? Configurations and Experiences of 'Illegality' among Undocumented West African and Filipino Migrant Workers in Tel Aviv, Israel." Ph.D. diss., Emory University.

———. 2007a. " 'Flesh of Our Flesh'? Terror and Mourning at the Boundaries of the Israeli Body Politic." In *Transnational Migration to Israel in Global Comparative Context*, ed. Sarah S. Willen, 159–84. Lanham, Md.: Lexington.

———. 2007b. " 'Illegality,' Mass Deportation, and the Threat of Violent Arrest: Structural Violence and Social Suffering in the Lives of Undocumented Migrant Workers in Israel." In *Trauma and Memory: Reading, Healing, and Making Law*, ed. Austin Sarat, Michal Alberstein, and Nadav Davidovitch, 168–203. Stanford, Calif.: Stanford University Press.

———. 2007c. Introduction to *Transnational Migration to Israel in Global Comparative Context*, ed. Sarah S. Willen, 1–27. Lanham, Md.: Lexington Books.

———. 2007d. "Toward a Critical Phenomenology of 'Illegality': State Power, Criminalization, and Embodied Experience among Undocumented Migrant Workers in Tel Aviv, Israel." In " 'Illegal' and 'Irregular' Migrants' Lived Experiences of Law and State Power. Special Issue, *Internation Migration* 45 (3): 8–38.

———. 2008. "L'hyperpolitique du 'Plus jamais ça!': demandeurs d'asile soudanais, turbulence gouvernementale et politiques de contrôle des réfugiés en Israël." *Cultures et Conflits: Sociologie Politique de l'International* 71 (3): 93-112.

———. Forthcoming. "Sudanese Asylum Seekers and the Politics of Humanitarian Compassion in Israel: Political Emotions, Symbolic (Mis)Identifications, and Unruly Biopolitical Dramas." In *Anthropology of Medicine: From Medical Anthropology to Biotechnology and the Biomedical Sciences*, ed. Byron Good, Mary-Jo DelVecchio Good, Sarah S. Willen, and Michael M. J. Fischer. Malden, Mass.: Blackwell Publishing.

Williams, Raymond. 1992. *Marxism and Literature*. Oxford: Oxford University Press.

Xenos, Nicholas. 1996. "Refugees: The Modern Political Condition." In *Challenging Boundaries: Global Flows, Territorial Identities*, ed. Michael J. Shapiro and Haywar R. Alker, 233–46. Minneapolis: University of Minneapolis Press.

Yack, Bernard. 2001. "Popular Sovereignty and Nationalism." *Political Theory* 29 (4): 517–36.

Yano, Haseshi. 1998. " 'Wir sind benötigt, aber nicht erwünscht.' " In *Fremde Heimat: Eine Geschichte der Einwanderung*, ed. DoMiT, 39–61. Essen.

Yiftachel, Oren. 1993. "The Concept of 'Ethnic Democracy' and Its Applicability to the Case of Israel." *Ethnic and Racial Studies* 15:125–36.

———. 1995. "The Dark Side of Modernism: Planning as Control of an Ethnic Minority." In *Postmodern Cities and Spaces*, ed. Sophie Watson and Katherine Gibson, 216–42. Cambridge: Basil Blackwell.

———. 1997. "Israeli Society and Jewish-Palestinian Reconciliation: 'Ethnocracy' and Its Territorial Contradictions." *Middle East Journal* 51:505–19.

———. 2000. " 'Ethnocracy' and Its Discontents: Minorities, Protests, and the Israeli Polity." *Critical Inquiry* 26:725–57.

Zahlan, Rosemarie Said. 1989. *The Making of the Modern Gulf States*. London: Unwin Hyman.

Zilberg, Elana Jean. 2002. "From Riots to Rampart: A Spatial Cultural Politics of Salvadoran Migration to and from Los Angeles." Ph.D. diss., University of Texas, Austin.

———. 2004. "Fools Banished from the Kingdom: Remapping Geographies of Gang Violence between the Americas (Los Angeles and San Salvador)." *American Quarterly* 56 (3): 759–79.

———. 2007a. "Gangster in Guerilla Face: A Transnational Mirror of Production between the U.S.A. and El Salvador." *Anthropological Theory* 7:37–57.

———. 2007b. "Inter-American Ethnography: Tracking Salvadoran Transnationality at the Borders of Latino and Latin American Studies." In *Companion to Latina/o Studies*, ed. Juan Flores and Renato Rosaldo, 492–501. Oxford: Blackwell.

———. 2007c. "Refugee Gang Youth: Zero Tolerance and the Security State in Contemporary U.S.-Salvadoran Relations." In *Youth, Globalization, and the Law*, ed. Sudhir Venkatesh and Ronald Kassimir, 61–89. Palo Alto, Calif.: Stanford University Press.

———. Forthcoming. *Transnational Geographies of Violence: An Inter-American Encounter from the Cold War to the War on Terror*. Durham, N.C.: Duke University Press.

Žižek, Slavoj. 1997. "Multiculturalism; or, The Cultural Logic of Multinational Capitalism." *New Left Review* 225:28–51.

———. 1999. *The Ticklish Subject: The Absent Centre of Political Ontology*. New York: Verso.

Zlolniski, Christian. 2006. *Janitors, Street Vendors, and Activists: The Lives of Mexican Immigrants in Silicon Valley*. Berkeley: University of California Press.

Contributors

RUTVICA ANDRIJASEVIC is a lecturer in politics and international studies at the Open University. She is currently completing a book manuscript titled *Sex Trafficking: Migration, Agency and Citizenship* (Palgrave 2010). She has published on the topics of sex trafficking, gendered migration, citizenship, and transnationalism in various journals, including *Feminist Review, International Migration, Environment and Planning D: Society and Space,* and *Subjectivity.* She is one of the founding members of the European feminist network Next-GENDERation and a member of the *Feminist Review* Collective.

AASHTI BHARTIA has been involved in immigrant rights activism with various groups in the New York City metropolitan area and has written on immigrant issues in the United States for *Civil Society,* a magazine published in New Delhi. She now lives in New Delhi where she has written for the *Indian Express,* a national newspaper, and is editor of the India-centered politics and design blog picklepost.com. She holds a bachelor of arts in anthropology and history from Columbia University.

HEIDE CASTAÑEDA is an assistant professor of anthropology at the University of South Florida. Her work has appeared in the journals *Medical Anthropology Quarterly, Social Science and Medicine,* and *Medical Anthropology.* She has contributed to *Gender and Illegal Migration in Global and Historical Perspective* (IMSCOE–Amsterdam University Press, 2008) and *Transnational Migration to Israel in Global Comparative Context* (Lexington Books, 2007). She is completing a book manuscript titled *Without Papers: Illegalized Migration to Germany since Reunification.* Her primary research interests include undocumented migration, health inequalities, health policy, the anthropology of human rights and humanitarianism, and the politics of citizenship.

GALINA CORNELISSE is a lecturer in constitutional law at Utrecht University. She has published in the *European Journal of Migration and Law,* as well as in academic journals in the Netherlands. She is the author of *Immigration Detention and Human Rights: Rethinking Territorial Sovereignty* (Brill, 2010).

SUSAN BIBLER COUTIN is a professor in the Departments of Criminology, Law and Society and Anthropology at the University of California, Irvine, where she also codirects the Center in Law, Society, and Culture. She is the author of *The Culture of Protest: Religious Activism and the U.S. Sanctuary Movement* (Westview Press, 1993), *Legalizing Moves: Salvadoran Immigrants' Struggle for U.S. Residency* (University of Michigan Press, 2000), and *Nations of Emigrants: Shifting Boundaries of Citizenship in El Salvador and the United States* (Cornell University Press, 2007). Her current research examines the legal and immigration experiences of 1.5 generation Salvadoran migrants.

NICHOLAS DE GENOVA has taught anthropology and Latino studies at Columbia University and Stanford University. In 2007-8 he was a Marie Curie international research fellow at the University of Warwick (U.K.) and more recently held the Swiss Chair in Mobility Studies as a visiting professor in the Institut für Sozialanthropologie at the University of Bern. He is the author of *Working the Boundaries: Race, Space, and "Illegality" in Mexican Chicago* (Duke University Press, 2005), coauthor of *Latino Crossings: Mexicans, Puerto Ricans, and the Politics of Race and Citizenship* (Routledge, 2003), and editor of *Racial Transformations: Latinos and Asians Remaking the United States* (Duke University Press, 2006). He is completing a new book titled *The Spectacle of Terror: Immigration, Race, and the Homeland Security State.*

ANDREW M. GARDNER is an assistant professor of anthropology at the University of Puget Sound. He is the coeditor of *Dispatches from the Field: Neophyte Ethnographers in a Changing World* (Waveland, 2006) and the author of several articles concerning the political ecology of Bedouin nomadism in the Kingdom of Saudi Arabia. A companion piece to the chapter presented here is forthcoming in *City and Society*. He is completing a book manuscript that explores transnational movement to the Gulf states.

JOSIAH HEYMAN is a professor of anthropology and chair of the Department of Anthropology and Sociology at the University of Texas, El Paso. He is the author of *Finding a Moral Heart for U.S. Immigration Policy: An Anthropological Perspective* (American Anthropological Association, 1998) and *Life and Labor on the Border: Working People of Northeastern Sonora, Mexico, 1886-1986* (University of Arizona Press, 1991), as well as editor of *States and Illegal Practices* (Berg, 1999). His previous work has addressed border society and culture, migration, the U.S. state, and values in engaged social science. His most recent research examines access and barriers to health care for uninsured immigrants in El Paso.

SERHAT KARAKAYALI is an assistant professor at the Institute for Sociology at the University of Halle (Germany) and also a member of the research network Preclab. He is the author of *Gespenster der Migration: Zur Genealogie der Illegalen Migration in der Bundesrepublik Deutschland* (Transcript Verlag, 2008) and coeditor of four books: *Turbulente Ränder: Neue Perspektiven auf*

Migration an den Grenzen Europas (Transcript Verlag, 2007), *Empire und die biopolitische Wende* (Campus Press, 2007), *Staatstheorie: Zur Aktualität von Nicos Poulantzas* (Nomos, 2008), and *Biopolitik: In der Debatte* (Verlag für Sozialwissenschaften, 2008). He is also an activist with the antiracist network Kanak Attak.

SUNAINA MAIRA is an associate professor of Asian American Studies at the University of California, Davis. She is the author of *Missing: Youth, Citizenship, and Empire after 9/11* (Duke University Press, 2009) and *Desis in the House: Indian American Youth Culture in New York City* (Temple University Press, 2002), as well as coeditor of *Youthscapes: The Popular, the National, the Global* (University of Pennsylvania Press, 2004) and *Contours of the Heart: South Asians Map North America* (Asian American Writers' Workshop, 1997).

GUILLERMINA GINA NÚÑEZ-MCHIRI is an assistant professor of anthropology at the University of Texas, El Paso. She has published (with Josiah Heyman) in *Human Organization*. She is currently completing a book titled *Roots, Transplants, and Transformations: Building Community in the Colonias of New Mexico*, based on three years of ethnographic and applied research in southern New Mexico. She is also coauthoring another book titled *Multiple Identities on the U.S.-Mexico Border* (with Cheryl Howard).

PETER NYERS is an associate professor of the politics of citizenship and intercultural relations in the Department of Political Science at McMaster University (Canada). He is the author of *Rethinking Refugees: Beyond States of Emergency* (Routledge, 2006), coeditor of *Citizenship Between Past and Future* (Routledge, 2008), editor of *Securitizations of Citizenship* (Routledge, 2009), and associate editor of the journal *Citizenship Studies*.

NATHALIE PEUTZ is an assistant professor of anthropology at Wayne State University. She was previously a postgraduate research fellow at the Council on Middle East Studies at Yale University and has also taught anthropology at Middlebury College. She has conducted ethnographic research in Somalia and Yemen and formerly worked as a field administrator for the International Rescue Committee distributing aid to Rwandan refugee camps in Tanzania. Her research has appeared in *Current Anthropology, International Migration, Revue des mondes musulmans et de la Méditerranée*, and *MERIP*. Currently, she is completing a book on environment, citizenship, and the state in Yemen titled *Hosting the State at the Margins of Arabia*.

ENRICA RIGO is a lecturer in the philosophy of law at the University of Rome-III. She was previously a Jean Monnet Fellow at the Robert Schuman Centre for Advanced Studies at the European University Institute in Florence. In addition to numerous scholarly articles on migration, citizenship, and border studies, including one in *Citizenship Studies*, she is the author of *Europa di confine: Trasformazioni della cittadinanza nell'Unione allargata* (Meltemi, 2007). She is actively involved in the Italian and European migrant rights movement.

VICTOR TALAVERA is the project manager for the National Center for Border Security and Immigration. He is an educator and an instructor of the social sciences. He is completing a manuscript that evolved from original research for his master's thesis, which concerns issues of access to medical services among undocumented migrants and the diverse health-related behaviors exhibited in a single immigrant household as a consequence of the respective legal status of each individual.

WILLIAM WALTERS is a professor in the Departments of Political Science and Sociology/Anthropology at Carleton University (Canada). He is the author of *Unemployment and Government: Genealogies of the Social* (Cambridge University Press, 2000), coauthor of *Governing Europe: Discourse, Governmentality and European Integration* (Routledge, 2005), and coeditor of *Global Governmentality* (Routledge, 2004). His current research concerns the geopolitical sociology of state borders, migration, and (non)citizenship in Europe and North America.

HANS-RUDOLF WICKER is a professor of social anthropology at the University of Bern (Switzerland). He is the author of numerous articles and books, including the edited volumes *Rethinking Nationalism and Ethnicity: The Struggle for Meaning and Order in Europa* (1997), *Migration und die Schweiz* (2003), and *Paradoxien im Bürgerrecht* (2004). He has conducted ethnographic fieldwork on St. Lawrence Island (Alaska), in rural Paraguay, and in Switzerland and writes on issues of anthropological theory, medical anthropology, migration, and citizenship.

SARAH S. WILLEN is an assistant professor of anthropology at Southern Methodist University and has been a postdoctoral research fellow in the Department of Global Health and Social Medicine at Harvard Medical School. She is the editor of *Transnational Migration to Israel in Global Comparative Context* (Lexington Books, 2007), coeditor of *Medical Anthropology: Theoretical Trajectories* (Blackwell, 2010), and guest editor of a special issue of *International Migration*, titled "Exploring 'Illegal' and 'Irregular' Migrants' Lived Experiences of Law and State Power" (August 2007). Her work has appeared in *International Migration, the Revue Européene des Migrations Internationales, Cultures et Conflits*, and the *Journal of Middle East Women's Studies*, and she has also published chapters in *Reapproaching Borders: New Perspectives on the Study of Israel/Palestine* (Rowman and Littlefield, 2007) and *Trauma and Memory: Reading, Healing, and Making Law* (Stanford University Press, 2007). She is completing a book titled *Working Hands, Unwanted Bodies: "Illegal" Labor Migration, State Power, and the Embodiment of Otherness in Israel*.

Index

An earlier version of chapter 1 appeared as "Deportation, Expulsion, and the International Police of Aliens," *Citizenship Studies* 6, no. 3 (2002): 256–92. Reprinted with permission of Taylor and Francis.

An earlier version of chapter 13 appeared as "Embarking on an Anthropology of Removal," *Current Anthropology* 47, no. 2 (2006): 217–41. Reprinted with permission of the University of Chicago Press.

An earlier version of chapter 14 appeared as "Abject Cosmopolitanism: The Politics of Protection in the Antideportation Movement," *Third World Quarterly* 24 (2003): 1069–93. Reprinted with permission of Taylor and Francis.

NICHOLAS DE GENOVA has taught anthropology
and Latino studies at Columbia University and Stanford
University. During the fall semester of 2009, he held the
Swiss Chair in mobility studies as a visiting professor at
the University of Bern, and during the spring of 2010, he
was a visiting professor in the Institute for Migration
and Ethnic Studies at the University of Amsterdam.

NATHALIE PEUTZ is an assistant professor of
anthropology at Wayne State University.

Library of Congress Cataloging-in-Publication Data

The deportation regime : sovereignty, space, and the
freedom of movement / Nicholas De Genova and
Nathalie Peutz, editors.
p. cm.
Includes bibliographical references and index.
ISBN 978-0-8223-4561-9 (cloth : alk. paper)
ISBN 978-0-8223-4576-3 (pbk. : alk. paper)
1. Deportation. 2. Exile (Punishment)
I. De Genova, Nicholas. II. Peutz, Nathalie Mae
K3277.D47 2010
342.08'2—dc22 2009043779